stems

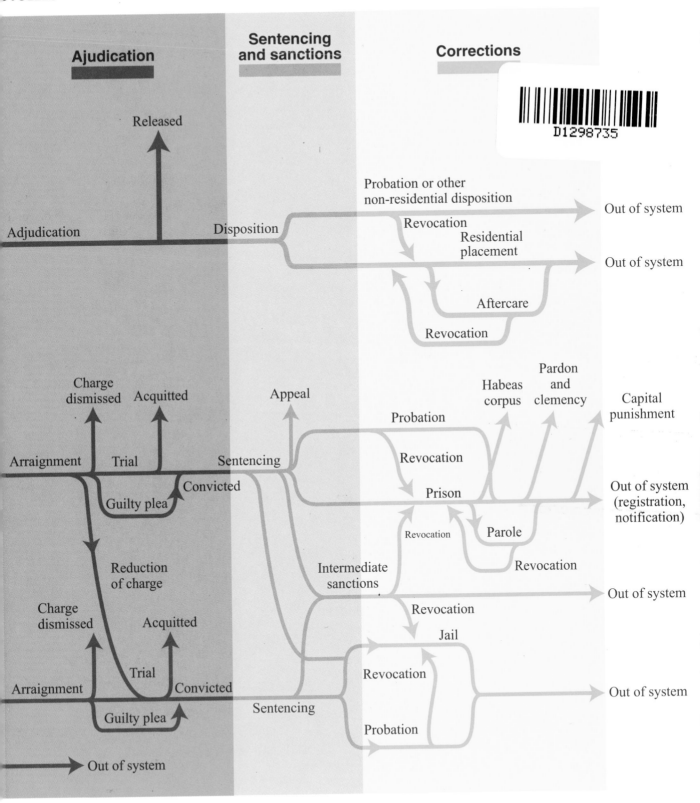

Ajudication

Sentencing and sanctions

Corrections

Released

Adjudication

Disposition

Probation or other non-residential disposition → Out of system

Revocation

Residential placement → Out of system

Aftercare

Revocation

Charge dismissed   Acquitted

Appeal

Habeas corpus

Pardon and clemency

Capital punishment

Probation

Arraignment   Trial

Sentencing

Revocation

Convicted

Guilty plea

Prison

Out of system (registration, notification)

Revocation   Parole

Revocation

Reduction of charge

Intermediate sanctions

Out of system

Charge dismissed

Acquitted

Revocation

Jail

Trial

Arraignment   Guilty plea   Convicted

Sentencing

Revocation

Out of system

Probation

→ Out of system

Adapted from *The challenge of crime in a free society.* President's Commission on Law Enforcement and Administration of Justice, 1967. The revision this art is based on was prepared as a result of the Symposium on the 30th Anniversary of the President's Commission by the Bureau of Justice Statistics in 1997.

www.wadsworth.com

www.wadsworth.com is the World Wide Web site for Thomson Wadsworth and is your direct source to dozens of online resources.

At *www.wadsworth.com* you can find out about supplements, demonstration software, and student resources. You can also send email to many of our authors and preview new publications and exciting new technologies.

www.wadsworth.com
Changing the way the world learns®

Juvenile Justice

THE SYSTEM, PROCESS, AND LAW

Rolando V. del Carmen

Sam Houston State University

Chad R. Trulson

University of North Texas

THOMSON

WADSWORTH

Australia • Brazil • Canada • Mexico • Singapore
Spain • United Kingdom • United States

THOMSON
WADSWORTH

Senior Acquisitions Editor, Criminal Justice:
    Carolyn Henderson Meier

Development Editor: Elise Smith

Assistant Editor: Jana Davis

Editorial Assistant: Rebecca Johnson

Technology Project Manager: Susan DeVanna

Marketing Manager: Terra Schultz

Marketing Assistant: Gregory Hughes

Marketing Communications Manager: Stacey Purviance

Project Manager, Editorial Production: Jennie Redwitz

Art Director: Vernon Boes

Print Buyer: Barbara Britton

Permissions Editor: Sarah Harkrader

Production Service: Melanie Field, Strawberry Field Publishing

Text Designer: Lisa Devenish

Photo Researcher: Stephen Forsling

Copy Editor: Donald Pharr

Illustrator: ATLIS Graphics

Cover Designer: Yvo

Cover Image: From left to right: © Workbookstock;
    © John Neubaur/PhotoEdit; © PictureQuest

Compositor: ATLIS Graphics

Text and Cover Printer: Transcontinental Printing/Louiseville

ExamView® and ExamView Pro® are registered trademarks of FSCreations, Inc. Windows is a registered trademark of the Microsoft Corporation used herein under license. Macintosh and Power Macintosh are registered trademarks of Apple Computer, Inc. Used herein under license.

Library of Congress Control Number: 2005922301

ISBN-13 978-0-534-52158-5

ISBN 0-534-52158-4

Thomson Higher Education
10 Davis Drive
Belmont, CA 94002-3098
USA

For more information about our products, contact us at:
Thomson Learning Academic Resource Center
1-800-423-0563

For permission to use material from this text or product, submit a request online at
http://www.thomsonrights.com.

Any additional questions about permissions can be submitted by email to **thomsonrights@thomson.com.**

This book is dedicated to my wife, Josie, my daughter, Jocelyn, and to my many students over the years from whom I have learned so much and who have made teaching and research such a joy for me.

Rolando V. del Carmen

For my parents, Dick and Pat, for their unyielding support in everything I have done.

Chad R. Trulson

Rolando V. del Carmen is a Distinguished Professor of Criminal Justice (Law) in the College of Criminal Justice, Sam Houston State University. He received a Bachelor of Laws degree (the equivalent of a J.D. degree) from the Philippines, a Master of Comparative Law from Southern Methodist University, a Master of Laws from the University of California–Berkeley, and a Doctor of the Science of Law from the University of Illinois–Urbana. He has authored numerous books and articles in law and criminal justice. He lectures nationally and internationally on various law-related topics. His *Criminal Procedure: Law and Practice* (Wadsworth) has been translated into Japanese, Korean, and Chinese. A recipient of many national and state awards, he has the rare distinction of having received all three major awards given annually by the Academy of Criminal Justice Sciences: the Bruce Smith Award, the Founders Award, and the Academy Fellow Award. He has taught numerous graduate and undergraduate classes and is mentor and friend to many students.

Chad R. Trulson is an Assistant Professor of Criminal Justice at the University of North Texas. He has worked as a juvenile parole officer and juvenile detention officer in Texas and as a juvenile resident counselor in Iowa before receiving his Ph.D. in criminal justice from Sam Houston State University. Dr. Trulson has published articles in such journals as *Law and Society Review, Crime and Delinquency, The Prison Journal, Criminology and Public Policy, Journal of Criminal Justice Education, Criminal Justice Review,* and *Journal for Juvenile Justice and Detention Services.* His current research interests include recidivism of delinquents released from state institutionalization, sexual assault in prisons, and racial segregation and violence in prisons. Dr. Trulson's most recent research (with Dr. James W. Marquart) on racial violence in prisons was used in the U.S. Supreme Court case of *Johnson v. California* (2005).

CHAPTER 1

An Overview of Juvenile Justice   1

CHAPTER 2

Theories and Measurement
of Juvenile Delinquency   31

CHAPTER 3

Juveniles and the Police   70

CHAPTER 4

Intake and Diversion   111

CHAPTER 5

Status Offenders, Dependent and Neglected
Youths, and Juvenile Victimizations   141

CHAPTER 6

Detention and Transfer to Adult Court   177

CHAPTER 7

The National Court System and the
Juvenile Courts   208

CHAPTER 8

Adjudication of Juveniles   243

CHAPTER 9

Disposition and Appeal   269

CHAPTER 10

Juvenile Probation and Parole   301

CHAPTER 11

Juvenile Correctional Institutions   333

CHAPTER 12

The Death Penalty for Juveniles: *Roper v.
Simmons* (2005)   381

CHAPTER 13

Schools, School Crime, and the Rights
of Students   402

CHAPTER 14

Juvenile Justice: Past, Present, and Future   437

APPENDIX A

U.S. Supreme Court Decisions in Juvenile
Justice   459

APPENDIX B

Where State Juvenile Laws Are Found   461

APPENDIX C

Finding and Interpreting Court Cases   464

Glossary   467

Notes   476

Index   497

CONTENTS

Preface / xviii

CHAPTER 1

An Overview of Juvenile Justice / 1

The Background and History of the Juvenile Justice System / 3
    The Concept of Juvenile Responsibility / 3
    Parens Patriae: The State as Parent / 3
    Juvenile Justice History in America / 5

Juvenile Versus Adult Justice Systems / 9
    Differences Between the Two Systems / 9
    Similarities Between the Two Systems / 10

Juveniles, Delinquency, and the Law / 13
    Juvenile Defined / 13
    Delinquency Defined / 15

The Scope of the Juvenile Justice System / 17
    Delinquent Offenders / 17
    Status Offenders / 18
    Dependent and Neglected Children / 18

An Overview of the Juvenile Justice Process / 19
    Initial Contact / 19
    Intake / 21
    Adjudication / 22
    Disposition / 22
    Aftercare / 25

Summary / 27
Review Questions / 27
Key Terms and Definitions / 28
For Further Research / 30

CHAPTER 2

Theories and Measurement of Juvenile Delinquency / 31

Theories of Juvenile Delinquency / 33
    The Emergence of the Classical School / 34
    Biology, Determinism, and the Positive School / 36
    Psychological Explanations of Delinquency / 40

    Sociological Explanations of Delinquency / 41
    Developmental and Life-Course Perspectives / 52
    Delinquency Theories and the Juvenile Justice System, Process, and Law / 55

Measuring Juvenile Crime and Victimizations / 56
    Official Data / 58
    Self-Report Data / 61
    Victimization Data / 63

Summary / 65
Review Questions / 66
Key Terms and Definitions / 67
For Further Research / 68

CHAPTER 3

Juveniles and the Police / 70

Juvenile Conduct Leading to Police Involvement / 72

Taking Juveniles into Custody / 73
    The Arrest Requirement and Probable Cause / 73
    Who Determines Probable Cause? / 73
    Establishing Probable Cause / 74
    Arrests of Juveniles / 74

Police Discretion When Arresting Juveniles / 77
    Factors That Influence Juvenile Arrest Decisions / 77

Juvenile Arrests / 83
    How Arrests Are Counted / 83
    The Number and Trend of Juvenile Arrests / 83

Legal Rights of Juveniles During Stop and Frisk, Arrests, and Searches and Seizures / 85
    Stop and Frisk of Juveniles / 86
    Arrests of Persons / 86
    Searches and Seizures / 88
    School Searches and Police Assistance / 90

Case Brief: New Jersey v. T. L. O. / 91
    General Search Conditions for Juvenile Probationers / 94

Custody and Interrogation of Juveniles / 95
    Miranda Wording and Juveniles / 96
    When Is a Suspect Under "Custodial Interrogation" for *Miranda* Purposes? / 96

A Juvenile May Waive *Miranda* Rights: The Totality
of Circumstances Test / 99
Per Se Rules and Juvenile Waiver / 100
Refusal to Waive *Miranda* Must Be Clear
and Unambiguous / 102

Confidentiality and the Police / 102
Fingerprinting / 103
DNA Samples / 105
Lineups and Photographs / 106
Media, Juveniles, and the Police / 106

Summary / 107
Review Questions / 108
Key Terms and Definitions / 109
For Further Research / 110

CHAPTER 4

Intake and Diversion / 111

The Intake Process / 113
What Is Intake? / 113
Who Handles Intake? / 114
Who Makes a Delinquency Referral
to Intake Officers? / 116
Procedures and Decisions at Intake / 117

The Legal Rights of Juveniles at Intake / 120
Is Intake a "Critical Stage" Requiring Counsel? / 121
Admissibility of Intake Information
at Adjudication Proceedings / 122

Case Brief: In re Wayne H. / 123
General Guidelines on the Admissibility of Intake Information
in Adjudication Proceedings / 124

The Diversion Process / 126
What Is Diversion? / 126
Examples of Diversion Programs / 127
Who Qualifies for Diversion? / 127
What Happens If a Youth Refuses to
Accept Diversion? / 128

The Legal Rights of Juveniles in Diversion / 129
Do Juveniles Have a Constitutional Right
to Diversion? / 129
Is a Hearing Required to Deny Diversion? / 130
Cases Similarly Situated and Diversion Offers / 130
Removing a Youth from Diversion / 131

Diversion and Double Jeopardy / 132
May Prior Diversions Be Used to Increase
Future Sentences? / 133

Extralegal Issues in Diversion / 134
Bias in Selection for Diversion / 134
Does Diversion Promote Further Contact with the Juvenile
Justice System? / 136
Diversion and Net Widening / 137

Summary / 138
Review Questions / 139
Key Terms and Definitions / 139
For Further Research / 140

CHAPTER 5

Status Offenders, Dependent and Neglected Youths, and Juvenile Victimizations / 141

Historical Methods of Dealing with Nondelinquents / 143

The Juvenile Justice and Delinquency Prevention Act (JJDPA) of 1974 / 145
Core Requirements of the JJDPA of 1974 / 146
Amendments to the JJDPA of 1974 / 147

The Juvenile Justice System and Status Offenders / 147
Justification for Juvenile Justice Intervention for Status
Offenders Today / 148
The Juvenile Court Process for Status Offenders / 148
The Rights of Status Offenders in
Adjudication Proceedings / 149
Dispositions for Status Offenders / 149

Status Offense Case Processing in the Juvenile Justice System / 151
Initial Contact / 152
Intake / 154
Adjudication / 154
Disposition / 154

Dependency, Neglect, and the Juvenile Justice System / 155
Reasons for Juvenile Court Intervention for Dependent
and Neglected Youths / 155
Forms of Dependency and Neglect / 158
Agencies Dealing with Dependency and Neglect / 159
The Extent of Dependency and Neglect / 163

Juvenile Court Processing for Dependency and Neglect / 166
    Court Petition or Complaint / 167
    Mediation / 168
    Court Hearing / 168
    Disposition / 169
Juvenile Victimizations / 170

Summary / 173

Review Questions / 174

Key Terms and Definitions / 174

For Further Research / 176

CHAPTER 6

Detention and Transfer to Adult Court / 177

Pre-adjudication Detention of Juveniles / 179
    The Purpose of Juvenile Detention / 179
    Detention Trends / 180

Detention Procedures and the Rights of Detained Juveniles / 181
    Detention Intake / 181
    The Required Detention Hearing / 182
    The Rights of Juveniles at Detention Hearings / 185
    Do Juveniles Have a Constitutional Right to Bail If Detained? / 185
    May a Juvenile Be Detained in an Adult Jail? / 186

Juvenile Transfer to Adult Court / 187
    The Purpose of Juvenile Transfer / 187
    Factors Influencing Transfer / 189

Types of Juvenile Transfer and Procedures / 189
    Judicial Waiver / 191

Case Brief: Kent v. United States / 192
    Prosecutorial Waiver / 196
    Legislative Waiver / 197

Choosing the Transfer Method / 199

The Impact of Juvenile Transfer / 202
    Removing Serious Offenders / 203
    Longer Sentences and Harsher Penalties? / 203

Summary / 204

Review Questions / 205

Key Terms and Definitions / 206

For Further Research / 207

CHAPTER 7

The National Court System and the Juvenile Courts / 208

The Court System and Its Process / 210
    The Federal Court System / 210
    The State Court System / 211
    The Appeals Process / 213
    The Geographical Boundaries of Court Decisions / 214
    Judicial Precedent (*Stare Decisis*) / 214
    Federal Versus State Jurisdiction / 216
    Juveniles in Federal Court / 217
    A Cautionary Note / 219

The Origin and Formation of the First Juvenile Court / 219
    What Led Up to Juvenile Courts / 219
    The First Juvenile Court / 221

The Juvenile Court Structure / 224
    The Organization of Juvenile Courts / 224
    Do Juvenile Courts Have Jurisdiction in All Matters Involving Juveniles? / 224
    Should There Be a Unified or Coordinated Juvenile Court? / 225
    The Administration of Juvenile Courts / 226
    Specialized Juvenile Courts / 229
    Juvenile Court Personnel / 233

Is a Separate Juvenile Court Needed? / 237

Summary / 239

Review Questions / 240

Key Terms and Definitions / 241

For Further Research / 242

CHAPTER 8

Adjudication of Juveniles / 243

The Past and the Present / 245
    Adjudication of Juveniles in the Past / 245
    Adjudication of Juveniles Today / 246

Juvenile Adjudication Compared with Adult Criminal Trial / 246
    Similarities to the Adult Trial / 246
    Differences with the Adult Trial / 247

Procedures During Adjudication / 247

   The Arraignment / 247

   The Plea / 248

   The Selection of Jurors (in Cases Tried
Before a Jury) / 249

   The Presentation of the Case for the Prosecution / 250

   The Presentation of the Case for the Defense / 250

   The Closing Arguments / 250

   The Judge's Instructions to the Jury / 251

   Jury Deliberation / 251

   The Verdict / 251

The Rights of Juveniles During Trial / 252

   In re Gault (1967): The Leading Case
in Juvenile Adjudication / 252

   The Right to a Lawyer / 253

   The Privilege Against Self-Incrimination / 256

   The Right to Notice of the Charges / 257

   The Right Against Double Jeopardy:
Breed v. Jones (1975) / 258

   The Right to Due Process / 258

   The Right to Proof of Guilt Beyond
a Reasonable Doubt / 259

Case Brief: **In re Winship / 260**

   Waiver of Constitutional Rights / 261

Constitutional Rights During Trial Not Given to Juveniles / 262

   No Right to a Trial by Jury / 262

   No Right to a Public Trial / 264

The Exclusionary Rule and Juvenile Adjudication / 265

Summary / 266

Review Questions / 267

Key Terms and Definitions / 267

For Further Research / 268

CHAPTER 9

Disposition and Appeal / 269

Disposition / 271

   The Goals of Disposition: Ideals Versus Reality / 272

   Discretion in Dispositions / 276

   When Disposition Takes Place / 276

   The Disposition Plan / 278

   Roles During Dispositions / 278

Kinds of Dispositions / 279

   Placement in an Institution / 280

   Probation / 281

   Other Sanctions That Leave the Juvenile
in the Community / 282

   The Death Penalty / 285

Blended Sentencing / 286

Legal and Constitutional Issues in Dispositions / 289

   The Rights of Juveniles During Dispositions / 289

   The Use of Illegally Obtained Evidence
in Dispositions / 289

Case Brief: **Haley v. Ohio / 290**

   Juveniles and "Three Strikes and You're Out"
Sentences / 292

   Juveniles Confined Longer Than Adults
for Similar Offenses / 293

   The Use of Juvenile Records If Later Sentenced
as an Adult / 293

   Punishing Parents for What Their Children Do / 294

Juveniles and the Right to Appeal / 296

   Juveniles May Appeal a Conviction and Disposition / 296

   Juveniles May Be Released While an Appeal
Is Pending / 296

   Appeal Distinguished from Habeas Corpus / 297

Towards a More Progressive Approach to
Juvenile Disposition / 297

Summary / 298

Review Questions / 299

Key Terms and Definitions / 299

For Further Research / 300

CHAPTER 10

Juvenile Probation and Parole / 301

Probation and Parole / 303

   Similarities / 303

   Differences / 303

The Origin and History of Juvenile Probation / 304

The Organization and Administration of Probation
and Parole / 305

Conditions of Probation and Parole / 306

   General Conditions / 306

   Kinds of Conditions / 308

   Modification of Conditions / 309

Supervision / 309
Standards and Goals / 309
The Juvenile Probation Officer / 310
Fare v. Michael C. (1979): An Important Case
in Juvenile Supervision / 312

Other Community-Based Programs / 314
Intensive Supervision Probation (ISP) / 315
Shock Probation / 315
School-Based Probation / 316
Family Counseling / 317
Juvenile Boot Camps / 318

Legal Issues in Probation and Parole Practices / 319
Searches and Seizures of Probationers
and Parolees / 319
Miranda Warnings and Interrogation by
Probation Officers / 320
Problems in Partnerships Between Probation Officers
and Police Officers / 321
Testing Juveniles for Drugs / 323
Curfews / 324
The Probation Records of Juveniles / 325

Revocation of Probation / 326
The Initiation of Revocation / 327
The Lack of Legal Standards for Revocation / 327
Juveniles' Rights Prior to Revocation / 327
The Results of Revocation / 328

Case Brief: **Gagnon v. Scarpelli / 329**

Summary / 330
Review Questions / 331
Key Terms and Definitions / 331
For Further Research / 332

CHAPTER 11

Juvenile Correctional Institutions / 333

The Development and Evolution of Juvenile Institutions / 335
The Early Seeds of Juvenile Institutions: Almshouses
and Orphanages (1600s–1820s) / 335
The First Juvenile Institutions: Houses of Refuge
(1825–1850s) / 337
Reformatories, Training Schools, and the Cottage System
(1846–1980s) / 338
The Juvenile Correctional Facility (1980s–Present) / 341

Types of Juvenile Placements / 342
Pre-adjudication Placements for Delinquents / 342
Post-adjudication Placements for Delinquents / 347
Placements for Nondelinquents / 362

**Conditions of Confinement and the Rights
of Institutionalized Juveniles / 364**
Conditions of Confinement in Juvenile Institutions / 364
The Rights of Institutionalized Juveniles / 367

Case Brief: **Morales v. Turman / 370**

Summary / 377
Review Questions / 378
Key Terms and Definitions / 378
For Further Research / 379

CHAPTER 12

The Death Penalty for Juveniles: *Roper v. Simmons* (2005) / 381

The Death Penalty in General / 383
Background / 383
U.S. Supreme Court Cases / 384

The Death Penalty for Juveniles Before *Simmons* / 386
Background / 386
The Laws and Practices Before *Simmons* / 386
U.S. Supreme Court Cases Before *Simmons* / 388
"Evolving Standards of Decency" as a Test
for Constitutionality / 390

Developments Before *Simmons* / 392
Infrequent Executions / 392
The International Scene / 392
Atkins v. Virginia (2002): A Judicial Precedent
for *Simmons* / 392

***Roper v. Simmons* (2005): The Death Penalty for Juveniles
Is Unconstitutional / 393**
The Holding and the Issue / 393
The Facts / 393
Unusual Circumstances / 394
The Majority Opinion by Five Justices / 395
The Dissenting Opinions by Four Justices / 396

What Happens After *Roper v. Simmons?* / 398

Summary / 399
Review Questions / 400
Key Terms and Definitions / 400
For Further Research / 401

CHAPTER 13

Schools, School Crime, and the Rights of Students / 402

Juveniles, the Law, and Schools / 404
    The Legal Basis of School Authority / 404
    Legal Issues in Regulating Student Behavior / 405

Case Brief: Pottawatomie County v. Earls / 414

The Extent of School Crime / 417
    Measuring School Crime / 418
    School Crime in the 1990s / 418
    The Bottom Line on School Crime / 424

Making Schools Safe—Can It Be Done? / 425
    Zero Tolerance Policies / 425
    Security Measures in Schools—Are They Effective? / 429
    School Partnerships with the Criminal and Juvenile Justice Systems / 431

Summary / 434
Review Questions / 435
Key Terms and Definitions / 435
For Further Research / 436

CHAPTER 14

Juvenile Justice: Past, Present, and Future / 437

Reliving the Past / 439
    The Discovery of Childhood / 439
    A Separate Legal System for Youths / 440
    Juvenile Justice Reform and the Erosion of *Parens Patriae* / 440
    Recognizing Nondelinquents and Diversity in Juvenile Courts / 441
    A Juvenile Crime Wave? / 441
    The Dual Path of Juvenile Justice / 442

A Look at the Present / 442
    The Current State of the Juvenile Court and the Juvenile Justice System / 442
    Some Current Issues and Trends / 443
    Public Opinion and Pendulum Shifts / 449

A Glimpse of the Future / 450
    Females and Juvenile Justice / 450
    Reinventing Juvenile Probation / 451
    Five Themes and Trends in State Laws Targeting Serious Crimes Committed by Juveniles / 453
    A Juvenile Justice System for This Century / 454

Summary / 455
Review Questions / 456
Key Terms and Definitions / 457
For Further Research / 458

APPENDIX A

U.S. Supreme Court Decisions in Juvenile Justice / 459

APPENDIX B

Where State Juvenile Laws Are Found / 461

APPENDIX C

Finding and Interpreting Court Cases / 464

Glossary / 467
Notes / 476
Index / 497

LIST OF BOXES

Controversial Issue: Which Side Do You Favor?

At what minimum age should juveniles be held accountable?   15

How far does a child's right to privacy extend?   90

Should incriminating evidence obtained at intake be used in an adjudication proceeding (trial)?   125

Are juvenile curfews best imposed by parents or by the government?   153

Do parents have the right to deny medical care for their child and contribute to a situation of dependency and neglect based on their religious beliefs?   160

Should teens be responsible for sanctioning other teens?   231

Should juvenile defense lawyers act as social workers or as client-advocates?   236

Should juveniles have the constitutional right to trial by jury?   263

Should parents be held legally liable for what their children do?   295

Should juvenile probation and parole officers act as social workers or police officers?   324

Should juvenile institutions serve double duty as mental hospitals?   350

Should juveniles receive special treatment in adult prisons or simply be incapacitated?   361

Should police officers be in schools?   434

You Are a(n) . . .

Police Officer   88

Intake Officer   121

Child Protective Services Specialist   164

Detention Intake Officer   183

Prosecutor   199

State Juvenile Justice Legislator   238

State Legislator   265

Juvenile Court Judge   273

Juvenile Probation Officer   312

Juvenile Correctional Officer   343

School Disciplinary Officer   426

Juvenile Justice Policy Maker   455

Abernathy v. United States, F.2d 288 (5th Cir. 1969)

Alabama v. White, 496 U.S. 325 (1990)

Alexander v. Boyd, 876 F. Supp. 773 (D.S.C. 1995)

Alexander v. South Carolina Department of Juvenile Justice, 876 F. Supp. 773 (D.S.C. 1995)

Alfredo A. v. Superior Court of Los Angeles County, 865 P.2d 1253 (Cal. 1994)

Alvarado v. Hickman, 316 F.3d 841 (9th Cir. 2002)

Anthony, Mark G., 739 S.W.2d 37 (SCNY 1987)

Atkins v. Virginia, 536 U.S. 304 (2002)

B. C. v. Plumas Unified School District, 192 F.3d 1260 (9th Cir. 1999)

Bellnier v. Lund, 438 F. Supp. 47 (N.D.N.Y. 1977)

Blackledge v. Perry, 417 U.S. 21 (1974)

Board of School Trustees v. Barnell, 678 N.E.2d 799 (Ind. App. 1997)

Bordenkircher v. Hayes, 434 U.S. 357 (1978)

Breed v. Jones, 421 U.S. 517 (1975)

Brennan v. State, 754 So.2d 1 (Fla. 1999)

Bringar v. United States, 338 U.S. 160 (1949)

Board of Education of Independent School District v. Earls, 536 U.S. 822 (2003)

Brown v. Ashton, 611 A.2d 599 (Md. App. 1992)

Bykosky v. Borough of Middleton, 410 F. Supp. 1242 (M.D. Pa. 1975)

Cason v. Cook, 810 F.2d 188 (8th Cir. 1987)

Chimel v. California, 395 U.S. 752 (1969)

City of Maquoketa v. Russell, 484 N.W.2d 179 (Iowa 1992)

Clinton Municipal Separate School District v. Byrd, 477 So.2d 237 (Miss. 1985)

Colvin v. Lowndes County School District, 114 F. Supp. 504 (ND Miss. 1999)

Commonwealth v. Martin, 626 A.2d 556 (Pa. 1993)

Commonwealth v. Rames, 573 A.2d 1027 (Ariz. Super. 1990)

Commonwealth v. Williams, 475 A.2d 1283 (S.Ct. Pa. 1984)

Cornfield v. Consolidated High School District No. 230, 991 F.2d 1316 (7th Cir. 1993)

Davis v. Alaska, 415 U.S. 308 (1974)

Davis v. United States, 512 U.S. 452 (1994)

D. H. v. State of Indiana, 688 N.E.2d 221 (Ind. Ct. App. 1997)

Dixon v. Alabama State Board of Education, 294 F.2d 150 (5th Cir. 1961)

Doe v. Renfrow, 631 F.2d 91 (7th Cir. 1980)

Dunaway v. New York, 442 U.S. 200 (1979)

Eddings v. Oklahoma, 455 U.S. 104 (1982)

Ewing v. California, 71 U.S.L.W. 4167 (2003)

Ewing v. Lockyers, 71 U.S.L.W. 4161 (2003)

Ex parte Crouse, 4 Whart. 9 (Pa. 1838)

Fare v. Michael C., 441 U.S. 707 (1979)

Furman v. Georgia. 408 U.S. 238 (1972)

Gagnon v. Scarpelli, 411 U.S. 778 (1973)

Gary H. v. Hegstrom, 831 F.2d 1430 (9th Cir. 1987)

Germany v. Vance, 868 F.2d 9 (1st Cir. 1989)

Gerstein v. Pugh, 420 U.S. 103 (1975)

Givens v. Poe, 346 F. Supp. 202 (1972)

Goss v. Lopez, 419 U.S. 565 (1975)

Gregg v. Georgia, 428 U.S. 153 (1976)

Griffin v. California, 380 U.S. 609 (1965)

Griffin v. Wisconsin, 483 U.S. 868

Guidry v. Rapides Parish School Board, 560 So.2d 125 (La. Ct. App. 1990)

Hamilton v. Alabama, 368 U.S. 52 (1961)

H. C. v. Hewett by Jarrard, 786 F.2d 1080 (11th Cir. 1986)

Horton v. Goose Creek Independent School District, 690 F.2d 470 (5th Cir. 1982)

In re D. S. S., 506 N.W.2d 650 (Mn. Ct. Ap. 1993)

In re Dumas, 515 A.2d 984 (Pa. Super. 1986)

In re F. B., 658 A.2d 1378 (Pa. Super. 1995)

In re Frank H., 337 N.Y.S.2d 118 (1972)

In re Frank V., 233 Cal.App.3d 1232 (Cal. Ct. App. 1991)

In re Gardini, 243 Pa.Super. 338 (1976)

In re Gault, 387 U.S. 1 (1967)

In re Jason W., 94 Md.App. 731 (1993)

In re Jermaine, 582 A.2d 1058 (Pa. Sup. 1990)

In re John G., 191 Ariz. 205 (Ariz. Ct. App. 1998)

In re Marcellus L., 278 Cal. Rptr. 901 (Cal. App. 1991)

In re McCall, 438 N.E. 2d 1269 (1982)

In re Robert H., 144 Cal. Rptr. 565 (Cal. Ct. App. [1978])

In re Robert M., 576 A.2d 549 (Conn. App. 1990)

In re Salyer, 358 N.E.2d 1333 (Ill. App. Ct. 1977)

In re Scott K., P.2d 105 (Supreme Court Ca. 1979)

In re Terrence G., 109 A.D.2d 440 (N.Y.A.D. 1985)

In re Interest of Torrey B., 6 Neb.App. 658 (Neb. Ct. App.1998)

In re Tyrell J., 876 P.2d 519 (Cal. 1994)

In re Wayne H., 596 P.2d 1 (Cal. 1979)

In re Winship, 397 U.S. 358 (1970)

In the Interest of Isiah B., 176 Wis.2d 639 (1993)

In the Interest of J. E. S, 817 P.2d 508 (Colo. 1991)

In the Interest of Johnnie F., 313 S.C. 5331 (1994)

In the Interest of M. W., Supreme Court of Pennsylvania, 1999 W.L. 111370 (1999)

In the Interests of J. L., A Child, 623 So.2d 860 (Fla. App. 1993)

In the Matter of Edwin L., 671 N.E.2d 1247 (1996)

In the Matter of Appeal in Maricopa County, Juvenile Action No. JV–508801, 183 Ariz. 175 (Ariz. App. 1995)

In the Matter of Peter B., 84 Cal.App.3d 583 (1978)

Inmates of the Boys' Training School v. Affleck, 346 F. Supp. 1354 (D.R.I. 1972)

Ingraham v. Wright, 430 U.S. 651 (1977)

Jenkins v. Talladega City Board of Education, 115 F.3d 821 (11th Cir. 1997)

John L. v. Adams, 969 F.2d 228 (6th Cir. 1992)

Johnson v. City of Apelousas, 658 F.2d 1065 (5th Cir. 1981)

J. R. W. v. State, 879 S.W.2d 254 (Tex. App. 1994)

Kent v. United States, 383 U.S. 541 (1966)

Kirby v. Illinois, 406 U.S. 682 (1972)

Konop v. Northwestern School District, 26 F. Supp. 2d 1189 (D.S.D. 1998)

Lanes v. State, 7678 S.W.3d 789 (Tex. Crim. App. 1989)

Lewis v. State, 288 N.E.2d 138 (Ind. 1972)

Lillis v. New York State Department of Social Services, 322 F. Supp. 473 (S.D.N.Y. 1970)

L. O. W. v. The District Court, 623 P.2d 1253 (Colo. 1981)

Lyons v. Penn Hills School District, 723 A.2d 1073 (Pa. Commonwealth 1999)

Mapp v. Ohio, 367 U.S. 643 (1961)

Massiah v. United States, 377 U.S. 201 (1964)

Mathews v. State, 677 S.W.2d 809 (1984)

McKeiver v. Pennsylvania, 403 U.S. 528 (1971)

Michael G. v. Superior Court, 243 Cal. Rptr. 224 (Cal. 1988)

Minnesota v. Dickerson, 113 S.Ct. 2130 (1993)

Minnesota v. Murphy, 465 U.S. 420 (1984)

Miranda v. Arizona, 384 U.S. 436 (1966)

M. M. v. Anker, 607 F.2d 588 (2nd Cir. 1979)

Moore v. United States, 345 F.2d 97 DC Cir. (1965)

Morales v. Turman, 364 F. Supp 166 (E.D. Texas 1973)

Morales v. Turman, 383 F. Supp 53 (E.D. Tex. 1974)

Morgan v. Sproat, 423 F. Supp. 1130 (S.D. Miss. 1977)

Morrissey v. Brewer, 408 U.S. 471 (1972)

Neil v. Biggers, 409 U.S. 188 (1973)

Nelson v. Heyne, 491 F.2d 352 (7th Cir. 1974)

New Jersey v. T. L. O., 469 U.S. 325 (1985)

O'Connell v. Turner, 55 Ill. 280 (1870)

Oklahoma Publishing Company v. District Court, 480 U.S. 308 (1977)

Oliver v. McClung, 919 F. Supp. 1206 (N.D. Ind. 1995)

Parham v. J. R., 442 U.S. 584 (1979)

Pena v. New York State Division for Youth, 419 F. Supp. 203 (S.D.N.Y. 1976)

Pennsylvania Board of Probation and Parole v. Scott, 524 U.S. 357 (1988)

People in Interest of J. M., 768 P.2d 219 (Colo. 1989)

People v. Dilworth, 661 N.E.2d 310 (Ill. 1996)

People v. Dukes, 580 N.Y.S.2d 850 (1992)

People v. J. D., 989 P.2d 762 (Colo. 1999)

People v. Lampitok, III, No. 93699 (9/18/03)

People v. Lee, 4 Cal. Rptr. 3d 642 (2003)

People v. Lilientha, 22 Cal.3d 89 (1978)

People v. Parker, 672 N.E.2d 813 (Ill. App. 1996)

People v. Pruitt, 662 N.E.2d 540, 544–546 (Ill. App. 1996)

People v. Smith, Slip copy, Cal. App. 3rd Dist. (2003)

Pottawatomie County v. Earls, 122 S.Ct. 2559 (2002)

Quib v. Strauss, 11 F.3d 488 (5th Cir. 1993)

Ralston v. Robinson, 454 U.S. 201 (1981)

Roper v. Simmons (case number SC84454 [2003])

Roper v. Simmons, SC 03-633 (2005)

Santana v. Collazo, 714 F.2d 1172 (1st Cir. 1983)

Santosky v. Kramer, 455 U.S. 745 (1982)

Schall v. Martin, 104 S.Ct. 2403 (1984)

Schneckloth v. Bustamonte, 412 U.S. 218 (1973)

Smith v. Daily Mail Publishing Company, 443 U.S. 97 (1979)

Stanford v. Kentucky, 492 U.S. 361 (1989)

State of West Virginia v. Werner, 242 S.E.2d 907 (W.Va. 1978)

State v. Chatham, 624 P.2d 1180 (Wash. Ct. App. 1981)

State Ex Rel. D. D. H. v. Dostert (165 W.Va. 1980)

State v. Farmbrough, 66 Wash.App.223 (Wa. Ct. App. 1992)

State v. Furman, 122 Wash.2d 440 (1993)

State v. Kristopher G., 201 W.Va. 703 (1997)

State v. Lowry, 230 A.2d 907 (1967)

State v. McDowell, 685 P.2d 595 (Wash. 1984)

State v. Nicholas S., 444 A.2d 373 (Me. 1982)

State v. Quiroz, 733 P.2d 963 (Wash. 1987)

State v. Slattery, 791 P.2d 534 (1990)

State v. Tracy M., 720 P.2d 841 (Wash Ct. App. 1986)

State v. Wade, 388 U.S. 97 (1979)

State v. Werner, 242 S.E.2d 907 (W.Va. 1978)

State v. W. S., 700 P.2d 1192 (Wash. Ct. App. 1985)

Terry v. Ohio, 392 U.S. 1 (1968)

Thompson v. Carthage School District, 87 F.3d 979 (8th Cir. 1996)

Thompson v. Oklahoma, 487 U.S. 815 (1988)

United States v. Ash, 413 U.S. 300 (1973)

United States v. David, 932 F.2d 752 (9th Cir. 1991)

United States v. Giannetta, 909 F.2d 571 (1st Cir. 1990)

United States v. Knights, 534 U.S. 112 (2001)

United States v. Matlock, 415 U.S. 164 (1974)

United States v. Robinson, 414 U.S. 218 (1973)

United States v. Wade, 388 U.S. 218 (1967)

United States v. Watson, 423 U.S. 411 (1976)

Vasquez v. State, 739 S.W.2d 37 (Tex. Crim. App. 1987)

Vernonia School District v. Acton, 115 S.Ct. 2386 (1995)

Vernonia School District 47J v. Action, 515 U.S. 646 (1995)

Washington v. Chatham, 624 P.2d 1180 (Wash. App. 1981)

White v. Maryland, 373 U.S. 59 (1964)

White v. Reid, 125 F. Supp. 647 (D.C. D.C. 1954)

Wilkins v. Missouri, 109 S.Ct. 2969 (1989)

Williams v. Ellington, 936 F.2d 881 (6th Cir. 1991)

Yarborough v. Alvarado, 124 S.Ct. 2140 (2004)

Zamora v. Pomeroy, 639 F.2d 662 (10th Cir. 1981)

Teaching a course on the juvenile justice system in the United States can be daunting. This is mainly because juvenile justice in the United States is far from monolithic; it is made up of fifty different state systems and that of the federal government. No two systems are completely alike, and significant variations abound from one jurisdiction to another even within a state. What may be true in California may not be true in Iowa; practices in Michigan may be different from those in Mississippi; treatment programs in Oregon may be completely different from those in Texas. It is often difficult to simplify diverse juvenile procedures and practices without running the risk of gross inaccuracy or misleading oversimplification.

Why This Book?

Anyone who teaches undergraduate juvenile justice with some legal orientation finds the market devoid of a usable textbook. Most juvenile justice books focus on delinquency theories, with a few chapters or sections devoted to the juvenile justice system and process. In many cases, juvenile law is an afterthought and an almost unwelcome add-on that is usually squeezed into one chapter, which makes student comprehension difficult. Thus, the legal dimension of juvenile justice is often marginalized. Adding to the problem is the absence of materials that blend social science and the legal approaches to juvenile justice. Social science research is crucial to juvenile justice, but so are law and the courts, because they set the framework and operational environment for juvenile justice. The gap between the two must be bridged if the whole juvenile justice system and process is to be better understood.

This book is written to fill a need for a textbook that:

- Integrates system, process, and law in clear and lucid language

- Is comprehensive and bridges the gap between theory and practice in juvenile justice

- Discusses juvenile justice substance but does not neglect formal or informal procedure

- Focuses on juvenile justice as a system and as a process based on social science research, statutory law, and court decisions

- Identifies the latest social science research and court cases on an array of juvenile justice topics

- Contains logical and proper sequencing of the juvenile justice process to make it easier to understand and remember

- Focuses on important information and data about juvenile justice and is not cluttered with details that apply only to a few jurisdictions

The Book's Content

The book has fourteen chapters, arranged in procedural sequence. Here is a preview of each chapter:

Chapter 1, An Overview of Juvenile Justice   This chapter presents the background and history of the juvenile justice system, compares juvenile and adult systems, and gives an overview of the juvenile justice process. It is an introductory chapter that presents a foundation for the remainder of the book, including definitions of important juvenile justice terms and ideas that are repeated throughout the text.

Chapter 2, Theories and Measurement of Juvenile Offending   Theories of juvenile offending are identified and discussed. This is the juvenile delinquency dimension of the book, and explanations of delinquency are tied to the characteristics of the juvenile justice system and process. This part is followed by a discussion of the ways whereby juvenile offending in the United States is measured and the advantages and disadvantages associated with each approach.

Chapter 3, Juveniles and the Police   The chapter starts with identifying juvenile conduct that leads to police involvement, followed by how juveniles are taken into custody. A section looks at police discretion when arresting juveniles and then presents the legal rights of juveniles during stop and frisks, arrests, and searches and seizures in a variety of juvenile-specific contexts. It ends with a discussion of the rights of juveniles during custody and interrogation, and juvenile rights to confidentiality. This chapter has a legal orientation not found in many other books.

Chapter 4, Intake and Diversion   This chapter examines the procedure during the intake process, including the many options at the disposal of intake officers. This discussion is followed by an examination of the legal rights of juveniles during intake and during the diversion process. The chapter concludes by discussing nonlegal issues in diversion such as whether diversion has the unintended consequence of actually promoting further contact with the juvenile justice system.

Chapter 5, Status Offenders, Dependent and Neglected Youths, and Juvenile Victimizations   After identifying the historical methods of dealing with nondelinquents, the chapter discusses the Juvenile Justice and Delinquency Prevention Act of 1974 and its impact on juvenile justice. The main focus of this chapter is on juveniles considered nondelinquents, namely status offenders and dependent and neglected youths, and how they are processed in the juvenile justice system. This chapter also includes a section on juvenile victimizations beyond dependency and neglect cases, a topic in juvenile justice mentioned in many books but not covered extensively.

Chapter 6, Detention and Transfer to Adult Court   The overwhelming number of juveniles who come into contact with the juvenile justice system are not detained until their adjudication hearing, and even fewer are transferred to the adult system for trial. An extended discussion of the small minority of juveniles detained and/or transferred is warranted because these offenders often present a disproportionate number of challenges to the system. This chapter identifies the procedures involved and the rights of juveniles during these proceedings. It ends with a discussion of the many types of juvenile transfers and their impact. This chapter discusses in detail transfer procedures that have become more important in juvenile justice because of the narrowing gap between the juvenile justice and adult justice systems.

Chapter 7, The National Court System and the Juvenile Courts This chapter presents an overview of the federal and state court systems and process. The chapter then goes into the origin and formation of the first juvenile courts, followed by a discussion of the juvenile court structure today. It ends by examining both sides of the debate on whether there is a need for a separate juvenile court.

Chapter 8, Adjudication of Juveniles This chapter starts by comparing the juvenile adjudication hearing to an adult trial. It goes through the various stages of juvenile adjudication and ends with a discussion of the constitutional rights of juveniles during trial. This chapter addresses a topic that is often given perfunctory treatment in other books.

Chapter 9, Disposition and Appeal This chapter features the kinds of dispositions used in juvenile proceedings, the recent practice of blended sentencing, and the legal and constitutional issues in dispositions, including "Three Strikes and You're Out" sentences for juveniles and punishing parents for what their children do. This is another chapter in the book that deals with two topics that are barely mentioned in other books but are nonetheless important.

Chapter 10, Juvenile Probation and Parole This chapter discusses the origin and history of juvenile probation and parole, their organization and administration, and conditions of supervision. It explores the legal issues involved in community-based juvenile supervision in general and considers specific legal issues in probation and parole. The chapter deals with the type of disposition that is the most often used in juvenile justice.

Chapter 11, Juvenile Correctional Institutions This chapter explores the development and evolution of juvenile institutions in the United States, followed by a discussion of the many different types of juvenile placements, from youth shelters to boot camps to adult prisons. The chapter ends with a discussion of the conditions of juvenile confinement and the rights of institutionalized juveniles.

Chapter 12, The Death Penalty for Juveniles: *Roper v. Simmons* (2005) This chapter analyzes the current and highly emotional issue of executing juveniles. It discusses U.S. Supreme Court cases on the execution of juveniles and the latest developments on the issue of death penalty for the young, ending with a discussion of *Roper v. Simmons* (2005), which proclaimed the juvenile death penalty unconstitutional.

Chapter 13, Schools, School Crime, and the Rights of Students The legal basis of school authority is discussed in this chapter, followed by legal issues in regulating student behavior. Important legal issues involving searches and seizures in schools are presented both from a legal and extralegal perspective. The chapter ends by probing into the extent of school crime and the responses to it. The last section also examines controversial school–juvenile justice system partnerships. It is an important topic that other books do not cover in such detail.

Chapter 14, Juvenile Justice: Past, Present, and Future This final chapter relives the past, takes a look at the present, and provides a glimpse of what the future holds for juvenile justice.

The Target Market

The main market for the book is undergraduate students in two- and four-year colleges. Despite its legal orientation, it may be used in courses where students do not have a background in juvenile justice or law. The book fits any juvenile justice course except those that focus solely on theories of delinquency, although there is an extended chapter on delinquency theories that are tied to juvenile justice practice. The book is also useful for juvenile justice field professionals who are knowledgeable in a specific area of juvenile justice work (such as intake, detention, probation, or aftercare) but may be less conversant with the bigger juvenile justice picture either nationally or within their own state. It should be informative for other personnel in juvenile justice (police officers, prosecutors, defense lawyers, and judges) who want to get a comprehensive view of the field and the latest issues that face juvenile justice professionals.

Features of the Book

This book has the following features:

- **"In this chapter you will learn,"** which presents the main themes in summary format at the beginning of each chapter

- **Summaries** of the main points in each chapter, broken down into concise bulleted lists

- **Review Questions**

- **Key Terms and Definitions**

- **Case Briefs** of the leading juvenile cases decided by the U.S. Supreme Court. Some of the important cases briefed include:
  In re Gault (1976)
  Haley v. Ohio (1948)
  Kent v. United States (1966)
  Gagnon v. Scarpelli (1973)
  New Jersey v. T. L. O. (1985)
  Thompson v. Oklahoma (1988)
  Roper v. Simmons (2005)

- **For Further Research,** which lists further sources of information available on the web

Topics of interest in the book that are not usually discussed at length in other books include the following:

- Police discretion when arresting juveniles
- The national court system and juvenile courts
- Laws on arrests and stop and frisks of juveniles
- Laws on police custody and interrogation of juveniles
- Confidentiality provisions in the juvenile justice system
- Transfer of jurisdiction to adult court
- The exclusionary rule and juveniles
- Status offense case processing in the juvenile justice system
- Dependency and neglect case processing in the juvenile justice system
- A juvenile's right to a lawyer
- Legal and constitutional issues in disposition
- Legal issues in probation and parole practices
- Conditions of confinement and the rights of institutionalized juveniles
- The death penalty for juveniles
- Schools, school crime, the rights of students, and school–juvenile justice system collaboration

Pedagogical Aids and High-Interest Features

All chapters in this book have one or more features that should attract student interest, including the following:

Controversial Issue: Which Side Do You Favor?   Controversial issue features are focused examinations of a particular topic in juvenile justice. These features give both sides of an argument and allow students to think critically about the issue and to make an informed judgment about which side they favor. Controversial issue features are particularly useful for in-class discussions of similar events in the news. Here are some examples of controversial issues in this book:

- At what minimum age should juveniles be held accountable for their delinquent acts?
- Should juvenile defense lawyers act as social workers or client-advocates?
- Should parents be liable for what their children do?
- Should schools depend on criminal justice and juvenile justice system personnel to maintain order?

You are a(n) . . .   This feature describes scenarios that juvenile justice practitioners and personnel face when they deal with juvenile offenders. Each feature uses probing questions that allow students to think and respond to how they might act in the various roles among a variety of situations. Many of these features are taken from real or similar headline events, which make them more salient as students can actually follow a scenario and see how it was finally dealt with in the juvenile justice system. Here are some examples:

- You Are an Intake Officer
- You Are a Child Protective Services Specialist
- You Are a Juvenile Court Judge
- You Are a Juvenile Correctional Officer

Exhibits   A number of chapters have exhibits that provide a deeper look into a particular topic or extend information discussed in the text. Some of these include the following:

- Delinquency as Probabilistic
- Applying Theories of Delinquency
- A Juvenile Court by Any Other Name
- Mandatory Reporters Have Immunity
- The Training of Juvenile Court Judges
- A Recommendation About Juvenile Court Judges
- Juvenile Probation Officers Need to Know the Law
- Ten Survival Strategies for Juvenile Probation Officers
- Schools Represent a "Special Need" Situation

Ancillaries and Technology for This Text

Available to qualified adopters. Please consult your local Thomson Wadsworth representative for details.

- **Instructor's Resource Manual and Test Bank**   This helpful manual provides chapter outlines, chapter summaries, reviews of key terms, classroom activities, discussion questions, and a test bank featuring multiple choice, true or false, fill-in-the-blank, and essay questions with a full answer key.

- **ExamView® on Windows and Macintosh**   Create, deliver, and customize tests and study guides (both print and online) in minutes with this easy-to-use assessment and tutorial system. ExamView offers both a Quick Test Wizard and an Online Test Wizard that guide instructors step by step through the process of creating tests, while its "what you see is what you get" interface allows instructors to view the test they are creating on the screen exactly as it will print or display online. Instructors can build tests of up to 250 questions using up to 12 question types. Using the complete word processing capabilities contained in ExamView, instructors can enter an unlimited number of new questions or edit existing questions.

- **Book Companion Website (http://cj.wadsworth.com/ del_carmen_trulson_jj)**   This Website provides students and instructors with an array of online exercises and resources such as Chapter Outlines, Chapter Review and Summaries, Internet Activities, Web Links, a Glossary, and related games like flashcards, concentration, and crossword puzzles. See the site for the complete text of the ground-breaking juvenile justice case *In re Gault* as well. The site gives you direct access to the **Wadsworth Criminal Justice Resource Center** at **http://cj.wadsworth.com** which has exciting, hot-topic daily news feeds, research modules, and more!

Acknowledgments

Every book is the product of a team effort; this book is no exception. The authors acknowledge their debt of gratitude to the following reviewers, who provided valuable suggestions and insights that the authors appreciatively adopted. We certainly benefited immensely from their careful review of the book and suggestions:

Barry Anderson, Western Illinois University

Lori Elis, Florida Atlantic University

John Gehm, University of South Dakota

Camille Gibson, Prairie View A&M University

J. Scott Harr, Concordia University, St. Paul

O. Elmer Polk, University of Texas at Arlington

Frances Reddington, Central Missouri State University

Kim Tobin, Westfield State College

All books are the product of a publishing team that works diligently behind the scene but whose contributions are immeasurable. The collective expertise of the publishing team has made the work of the authors easier and a lot better. They ferret out mistakes and in general make writers look good and feel good. We are lucky to have had a seasoned publishing team working with us on this book and are deeply grateful to them. They are Sabra Horne, Elise Smith, Eve Howard, Carolyn Henderson Meier, Jennie Redwitz, Jana Davis, Terra Schultz, Susan DeVanna, Donald Pharr, and Melanie Field.

No undertaking of this magnitude can be successful without relying on the substantial amount of extant literature in the field for guidance and reference. We relied on numerous documents published by entities including the Bureau of Justice Statistics, the National Institute of Justice, the Office of Juvenile Justice and Delinquency Prevention, the National Center for Education Statistics, the National Center for Juvenile Justice, and the Urban Institute. The documents produced and made readily available by these and other agencies benefited us tremendously and provided a national view of the juvenile justice system, process, and law that we could not otherwise have obtained. We also benefited from the excellent work of numerous other criminal and juvenile justice scholars who have been cited in this book: Jeffrey Butts, Robert Dawson,

Barry Feld, Patrick Griffin, Adele Harrell, Richard Lawrence, Ojmarrh Mitchell, Mary Parker, David Rothman, H. Ted Rubin, Melissa Sickmund, Howard Snyder, Linda Szymanski, and Patricia Torbet. This list is not exhaustive, for the work of many others also benefited this book. A substantial portion of what is good in this book is due to the important work of the agencies and individuals mentioned.

Rolando V. del Carmen extends thanks to the staff at the College of Criminal Justice, Sam Houston State University, who helped in the legal research and provided secretarial support for the manuscript: Kelly Cheeseman, Jillian Harris, Mckensey McAdams, and Connie Alvarez. Dean Richard Ward and Associate Dean Wesley Johnson of the College of Criminal Justice have been highly supportive of this book. To them I owe a debt of gratitude. Lastly, but most importantly, I express heartfelt thanks to my wife, Josie, and my daughter, Jocelyn, who provided full moral support and encouragement in the writing of this book. My share of the effort in the writing of this book is dedicated to them.

Chad R. Trulson would like to thank the faculty of the Department of Criminal Justice, University of North Texas, for support and encouragement in the writing of this text. Robert W. Taylor afforded me the necessary time, support, and encouragement to accomplish such a task. A special note of gratitude goes to Tory Caeti and Eric Fritsch, who were always ready and willing to provide guidance, encouragement, and support. I received much benefit from their knowledge of juvenile justice. Thanks also goes to Angela French who assisted in various aspects of this book. I would also like to recognize a number of individuals who have substantially influenced my academic career over the years: Clemens Bartollas, Keith Crew, Margaret Farnworth, Charles Friel, Robert Hunter, W. Wesley Johnson, Michael Leiber, Tina Mawhorr, Janet Mullings, Arlo Stoltenberg, Ruth Triplett, and Richard Ward. Special thanks go to James Marquart, Sam Houston State University, who has helped me in numerous ways. Most importantly, I thank my beautiful wife, Lori, who has endured more than her share of the long hours put into this book without complaint.

Rolando V. del Carmen
College of Criminal Justice
Sam Houston State University

Chad R. Trulson
Department of Criminal Justice
University of North Texas

An Overview of Juvenile Justice

CHAPTER ONE OUTLINE

The Background and History of the Juvenile Justice System / 3

The Concept of Juvenile Responsibility / 3
Parens Patriae: The State as Parent / 3
Juvenile Justice History in America / 5

The Pre-Juvenile Court Era (1600–1898) / 5
The Juvenile Court Era (1899–1966) / 6
The Juvenile Rights Era (1967–1979) / 7
The Crime Control Era (1980–Present) / 8

Juvenile Versus Adult Justice Systems / 9

Differences Between the Two Systems / 9
Similarities Between the Two Systems / 10

Juveniles, Delinquency, and the Law / 13

Juvenile Defined / 13
Delinquency Defined / 15

The Scope of the Juvenile Justice System / 17

Delinquent Offenders / 17
Status Offenders / 18
Dependent and Neglected Children / 18

An Overview of the Juvenile Justice Process / 19

Initial Contact / 19

Informal Options / 20
Formal Options / 21

Intake / 21
Adjudication / 22
Disposition / 22

Probation / 24
Institutionalization / 25

Aftercare / 25

Revocation / 26
Discharge / 26

IN THIS CHAPTER YOU WILL LEARN

- The concept of juvenile responsibility and the historical foundation of the juvenile justice system.

- About the development and evolution of juvenile justice in the United States.

- About the jurisdiction of the juvenile court.

- Who is considered a juvenile and what is delinquency.

- The distinction between a delinquent and a status offender.

- The difference between the criminal and juvenile justice systems.

- The stages in the formal juvenile justice process.

INTRODUCTION

The rates of most forms of juvenile crime, including serious and violent juvenile crime, have been decreasing for almost a decade. Yet despite these decreases, crime incidents perpetrated by juveniles tend to invite much sensationalism. Not surprisingly, media attention to sporadic school shootings, family violence by juveniles, juvenile rape, and talk of juvenile "superpredators" has fueled the perception that juveniles are a "crime bomb" waiting to happen.[1] This perception has led to much debate on the best way to deal with juvenile lawbreakers.

Finding solutions to juvenile offending is not easy. On the one hand, policy makers believe that the juvenile justice system should rehabilitate juveniles. Proponents of this philosophy focus on the circumstances that lead to delinquency, such as poverty, drugs, and criminal parents. They conclude that juveniles are not entirely responsible for their actions because of these circumstances. On the other hand, advocates of a "get what you deserve" philosophy propose harsher penalties to deal with juvenile offenders, especially serious and violent juveniles. Advocates of this philosophy focus on the act committed rather than the individual circumstances of the offender. They conclude that juveniles, particularly older ones, are rational and know what they are doing when they commit a crime. Thus, they should be held responsible and punished accordingly.

This chapter serves as a snapshot orientation to critical aspects of juvenile justice and provides a basic foundation for the remainder of the book. This chapter discusses the history of the juvenile justice system and how dealing with juvenile offending has changed over time. It also examines the distinction between the juvenile and adult justice systems, the legal definition of a *juvenile* and of *delinquency,* the scope of the juvenile justice system, and an overview of the juvenile justice process.

The Background and History of the Juvenile Justice System
The Concept of Juvenile Responsibility

Responsibility for delinquent behavior is based on the concept of **mens rea,** which is a Latin term meaning "a guilty mind."[2] A guilty mind means that the individual had the intent to commit the act. Without intent, an act is not usually considered criminal under our penal codes. In some states, children below a certain age are determined by law to be incapable of forming *mens rea* and are presumed to be unaware of the full consequences for what they do. In other states, a child at any age may be presumed capable of forming *mens rea.* Such determinations are made by state law.

There is much controversy about the age when children should be considered capable of intent and held responsible for their actions. Historically, children younger than age seven were deemed incapable of *mens rea* and were exempt from criminal responsibility. English common law considered age seven as the age of responsibility for young offenders; this age was later adopted by the U.S. justice system as a general guideline.[3]

Although age seven is a general benchmark, states vary today on when a child crosses the line from a juvenile with no responsibility to a juvenile who knows what he or she is doing. As Table 1.1 shows, North Carolina sets the age of responsibility as low as six, and states such as Arkansas use age ten. This means that a juvenile cannot be held criminally responsible for offenses committed below that age. In states without a specified **minimum age of responsibility,** a juvenile can technically be held responsible at any age.

Parens Patriae: The State as Parent

Until the early nineteenth century, children were generally treated as adults by the justice system. Youths lived like miniature adults and were viewed as little people in big people's clothing.[4] Over the years, however, the outlook that

TABLE 1.1

Minimum Age of Responsibility by State

Age	State
6	North Carolina
7	Maryland, Massachusetts, New York
8	Arizona
10	Arkansas, Colorado, Kansas, Louisiana, Minnesota, Mississippi, Pennsylvania, South Dakota, Texas, Vermont, Wisconsin
No minimum age specified	Alabama, Alaska, California, Connecticut, Delaware, District of Columbia, Florida, Georgia, Hawaii, Idaho, Illinois, Indiana, Iowa, Kentucky, Maine, Michigan, Missouri, Montana, Nebraska, Nevada, New Hampshire, New Jersey, New Mexico, North Dakota, Ohio, Oklahoma, Oregon, Puerto Rico, Rhode Island, South Carolina, Tennessee, Utah, Virginia, Washington, West Virginia, Wyoming

Source: Adapted from Howard N. Snyder and Melissa Sickmund, *Juvenile Offenders and Victims: 1999 National Report* (Washington, DC: Office of Juvenile Justice and Delinquency Prevention, 1999), 93.

children were smaller versions of adults has changed. Much of this change came to an apex with the development of a separate juvenile court in Cook County, Illinois, in 1899. The philosophy of this separate juvenile court was heavily influenced by **parens patriae** (literally meaning "parent of a country"). *Parens patriae* is a Latin term for the doctrine that the state functions as the ultimate parent and guardian in the best interests of children who cannot care for themselves.[5]

The juvenile court recognized that juveniles were different from adults, and this perception was reflected in the court's practice. Unlike the adult system, the juvenile court's mission was to be flexible, informal, and focused on individualized attention.[6] This was the upside. The downside was that, acting in the place of "wise parents," the juvenile court provided few procedural protections (such as the right to a lawyer) that were afforded adults in the criminal justice system. Theoretically, young people had no need for procedural rights to protect them from the juvenile court because the judge acted in their best interests. However, the reality in some cases was far from this ideal, and what was supposed to be rehabilitation more often resembled punishment.

Today, the foundation of *parens patriae* has been eroded. Instead of the absence of legal protections, juveniles now receive many of the same safeguards that adults enjoy. However, it took more than sixty years after the formation of the first juvenile court in 1899 for the constitutionalization of the juvenile justice process. This chapter next examines in brief the history of the juvenile justice system and the evolution of the treatment of juveniles.

Juvenile Justice History in America

Juvenile justice is a process that has unfolded over many years. A general understanding of the evolution of the juvenile justice process at this point in the book provides an important foundation for studying the juvenile justice system and process of today. The evolution of juvenile justice may be divided into four eras: the **pre-juvenile court era,** the **juvenile court era,** the **juvenile rights era,** and the **crime control era.***

The Pre-Juvenile Court Era (1600–1898)

Prior to the development of a separate juvenile justice system, youthful lawbreakers were dealt with by the family, which was the primary source of child control. In early America, youths did not face intervention by an organized criminal or juvenile justice system—police, human service workers, or probation officers—because no such services were available until the mid- to late nineteenth century. The family served as the police, prosecutor, judge, and—sometimes—executioner. However, "family" was not limited to the immediate family. It included neighbors, townspeople, and members of other social institutions, especially the church.

The church played an integral role in the control of wayward children in early America. Misbehavior could result in severe punishments, often meted out by the church in conjunction with the family. There simply was no pretense about rehabilitating the wayward, meaning that punishments for juveniles were swift and severe by today's standards, with whippings, beatings, and shame-generating events common. More serious and persistent juvenile offenders faced banishment and even capital punishment.[7] These harsh punishments were sometimes justified on the belief that youths should be held responsible for their acts and that their tender age was not an excuse. Punishments for children also attached to the behaviors of their parents. When parents raised their child to a life of idleness, indulgence, and vagrancy, the child would be removed from the home to be sent to work for and be cared for by more puritanical families (a practice called "placing out" or "binding out"). Rarely did juvenile misbehavior go unnoticed or unpunished by the ever-watchful townspeople of close-knit colonial America.

Over time, those concerned with juvenile offending saw shortcomings in the ability of the family and community to handle juvenile offenders. As the population of America grew because of increasing immigration, rising birthrates, and lower infant mortality, so did vice and other ills that served to break up communities.[8] In need of a way to protect children from morally corrupt parents who succumbed to the evils of deteriorating social conditions,

---

*The eras of juvenile justice evolution are approximations offering a broad analysis. This section's divisions align closely with an excellent article by Barry Krisberg, Ira M. Schwartz, Paul Litsky, and James Austin, "The Watershed of Juvenile Justice Reform." *Crime and Delinquency* 32 (1986): 5–38. Also see U.S. Department of Justice, *A Preliminary National Assessment of Status Offenders and the Juvenile Justice System* (Washington, DC: U.S. Government Printing Office, 1980). For another excellent review with similar divisions, see Clemens Bartollas, *Juvenile Delinquency,* 6th ed. (Boston: Allyn and Bacon, 2003), 15–22. Finally, see David J. Rothman, *Conscience and Convenience: The Asylum and Its Alternatives in Progressive America* (Boston: Little, Brown, 1980).

reformers searched for an environment that could insulate children from the problems of society. At the same time, social reformers sought to provide children all the amenities of the ideal puritanical family. To simulate this ideal society, delinquent children, including the orphaned and abandoned, were placed in **houses of refuge** in the early 1800s. Houses of refuge are considered the first juvenile institutions in America. They operated on the belief that children could be "saved" through hard work, education, and religion. Houses of refuge protected young people from society's problems and instilled them with proper habits so that when they were released, they might resist the delinquent temptations of society. An important turning point in juvenile justice history occurred with the houses of refuge—an acknowledgment that the family, the church, and the community could not prevent delinquency single-handedly.[9]

Houses of refuge seemed like the perfect solution. They would provide the ideal life, with all the advantages and none of the disadvantages of a deteriorating society. As time went on, however, these institutions became places of rampant abuse and began to reflect the environments from which youths were to be protected in the first place. Although these institutions continued to survive, albeit with different names, the abuse of children, combined with filthy and dangerous conditions, led to changes in how youths were handled by the state.[10] These changes included the development of a separate legal forum for delinquent and wayward juveniles. Driven by *parens patriae*, this approach shunned punishments, preferring rehabilitation instead.

The Juvenile Court Era (1899–1966)

The first juvenile court in the United States was created by the Juvenile Court Act, which was passed by the Illinois Legislature in Cook County, Illinois, in 1899.[11] Several states followed the lead of Illinois. By 1910, thirty-two states had passed similar legislation; by 1925, all but two states had established separate juvenile courts; and by 1950, every state had a separate juvenile court.[12] The juvenile court's mission was to provide individualized care to all youths who needed it. In the place of parents, the state would play the role of "superparent," exercising guardianship rights for juveniles in ways that could identify, treat, and cure conditions contributing to their misdeeds.

Important to the formation of the juvenile court was the concept that youths were not entirely responsible for their behavior, a far cry from the thinking in early colonial America. Proponents of the juvenile court viewed youthful offenders as victims of society's problems: poverty, alcohol, broken families, and deteriorating neighborhoods. Young people were not seen as entirely rational beings; instead, they were considered victims of circumstances. Therefore, reformers rejected the idea of dealing with juveniles through the adult justice system, which was based on punishment. It would be unfair to punish a child for something that was not entirely his or her fault. Punishment was for adults, not for juveniles—according to the juvenile court.

Treatment for youths who came under the supervision of the juvenile court included a wide range of dispositions: from warnings to probation to institutionalization. One unique feature during the juvenile court era was the introduction of the **indeterminate sentence.**[13] Receiving an indeterminate sentence meant that a child would remain under the watchful eye of the juvenile court and its agencies until he or she was "cured" or until reaching adulthood. Indeterminacy was considered to be in the best interests of the child in that the juvenile court supervised the youth only as long as it took to accomplish the goal of rehabilitation. However, the indeterminate approach was controversial; its erosion became inevitable. Indeterminate sentencing led to a number of cases where juveniles—some of them lawbreakers but many who were not—would be held for long periods of time (in reformatories and/or state schools) because they had not been "cured." These and other problems led some to question the philosophy underlying the juvenile justice system and the power of the juvenile court.

The Juvenile Rights Era (1967–1979)

Reformers did not object so much to the goal of the juvenile court as they did to the way the court went about accomplishing it. Critics of the juvenile court said that sentences for juveniles were unfair, biased, and disproportionately long compared to the nature of the offense and that the indeterminate confinement of juveniles was too harsh for many types of youths, especially status offenders and other noncriminals such as the dependent and neglected.[14] These criticisms led to reforms in the juvenile court and called for the development of a set of procedural rights that would protect juveniles from the system that was formed to protect them in the first place.

The advent of the juvenile rights era followed the leading case of *In re Gault* (1967).[15] Fifteen-year-old Gerald Gault and a friend were taken into police custody following a complaint that they made lewd phone calls to a woman. Gault's parents were not informed he was in custody, they never saw the complaint against their son, the complainant did not appear at any hearing, and there was no written record made of the proceeding. Gault was eventually adjudicated in juvenile court and committed to six years in the state industrial school in Arizona. The same punishment for an adult found guilty of the same offense would have been a fine of five to fifty dollars, and imprisonment for a maximum of two months.

The U.S. Supreme Court held in *Gault* that juveniles must be given certain procedural due process rights in adjudication proceedings that could result in confinement in a juvenile institution in which their freedom would be curtailed.[16] These rights would ensure that the procedures for depriving juveniles of their freedom were "fundamentally fair" (the definition of due process). These constitutional protections included a notice of the charges against the juvenile, the right to a lawyer, the right to confront and cross-examine witnesses, the right to remain silent, and the privilege against self-incrimination. Prior to 1967, many young people were institutionalized without the benefit of these protections.

The *Gault* case is important for juvenile justice because the U.S. Supreme Court recognized that juvenile courts were not necessarily operated in the best interests of the child. A year earlier, the Court had expressed strong reservations about the juvenile justice process: "There is evidence . . . that the child receives the worst of both worlds; that he gets neither the protections accorded to adults nor the solicitous care and regenerative treatment postulated for children."[17] Minors were receiving the same sentences as adults (or worse) for similar or lesser offenses, without the legal protections that adults enjoyed. The *Gault* case spurred efforts to ensure that juveniles received due process protections in delinquency proceedings to make them fundamentally fair.

Gault was limited in scope because it applied only to proceedings in which a juvenile could be placed in an institution. Other juveniles, including status offenders and dependent and neglected youths, made up a significant portion of all juveniles involved in various stages of the juvenile justice system at the time of *Gault*. They lost their freedom in many ways, but because their dispositions did not involve secure institutionalization, the procedural protections did not apply to them. Protections for these youths came later in the juvenile rights era in the form of the federal Juvenile Justice and Delinquency Prevention Act of 1974 (JJDPA). The main purpose of the JJDPA was to remove status offenders and other noncriminal juveniles from juvenile institutions meant for delinquents. It also mandated the "sight and sound" separation of juveniles from adults when they were held in the same institution—a common practice during that time.[18]

Gault signaled an era that accelerated the erosion of *parens patriae* in juvenile justice. Instead of leaving all juvenile justice decisions to state juvenile authorities, the U.S. Supreme Court adopted a "hands-on" approach during the juvenile rights era. In this mode, the Court decided several significant cases that resulted in the expansion of due process rights for juveniles to ensure they were treated with fundamental fairness in the juvenile justice system. This momentum extended into the early 1970s, with the JJDPA and its concern with nondelinquents. But, at about the same time that the mandates of the juvenile rights era were being implemented, a new era arose and again signaled changes in how juvenile offenders were viewed and processed by the juvenile justice system. With the focus on providing procedural rights for delinquents and removing nondelinquents from secure institutions, the justice system failed to pay equal attention to serious juvenile offending. The public wanted more controls. The crime control era that began in the 1980s and continued into the twenty-first century represented another shift in the pendulum concerning the treatment of juveniles.

The Crime Control Era (1980–Present)

The focus on less serious juveniles in the juvenile rights era led to criticisms that the juvenile justice system was soft on delinquents. More than anything else, an increase in certain forms of juvenile crime fueled public sentiments about juvenile offenders and literally transformed the juvenile justice process into a get-tough mode.

Much of the concern with juvenile offenders in the 1980s, and consequent toughening of the juvenile justice process, appears to have resulted from a few serious offenses. In general, serious juvenile crime did not increase substantially until 1988–1989. The only offenses that increased substantially prior to 1988 were murder and forcible rape. In 1986, for example, the arrest rate for murder began to climb sharply, starting at 6 per 100,000 juveniles age 10–17 and peaking in 1994 at nearly 15 per 100,000. The arrest rate for forcible rape climbed from 18 per 100,000 in 1983 to 23 per 100,000 in 1991. However, the rise in juvenile arrests for most serious crimes did not commence until the very late 1980s. For example, burglary is one serious offense that has consistently declined from the 1980s.[19] Thus, murder and forcible rape appeared to be the only offenses that pushed the system into a get-tough mode during the 1980s, when the system was changing. Despite these two offenses, which are relatively infrequent when compared to other types of delinquency, the perception of juvenile rapists and murderers was enough to usher in a new era that viewed *all* delinquents as rational predators who needed to be stopped and punished.

The perception of the juvenile as a "superpredator" led to an emphasis on imposing harsher and longer penalties for serious and violent juvenile offenders. This shift was evident in federally supported crime control policies. Federal efforts focused on three areas in particular during the crime control era: the increased transfer of violent juveniles into the adult justice system, determinate or mandatory sentencing for violent juvenile offenders, and the increased use of institutionalization for serious and persistent juveniles.[20] States soon adopted these federal initiatives and transformed the juvenile justice process into a miniature version of the adult justice system while further eroding *parens patriae.*

The 1990s and the turn of the twenty-first century saw many of the same policies in place. However, instead of having a one-sided focus on persistent and violent juveniles, the agenda for juvenile crime in the 1990s focused on identifying, treating, and preventing delinquency for at-risk youth, protecting and supervising status offenders and other noncriminal youths, and at the same time remaining tough on serious, violent, and chronic juvenile offenders. Two modes of operation in the juvenile justice system emerged. One mode was based on protection, prevention, and rehabilitation, the other on deterrence and punishment. The first was used for nonserious delinquents, status offenders, and dependent and neglected youths; the latter focused on serious, violent, and chronic delinquents.

Juvenile Versus Adult Justice Systems
Differences Between the Two Systems

Despite the erosion of the foundation of the juvenile court, two separate justice systems, juvenile and criminal, still remain in U.S. society. A key difference between the juvenile and adult system today is the way responsibility is viewed. Most juvenile offenders are considered victims of circumstances out of their control, not as guilty perpetrators of their own free will. Adult offenders are seen as rational actors deserving blame for their criminal acts. Despite this difference in the perception of responsibility, the procedures in the juvenile and adult systems are similar. However, the terminologies of the two systems, despite their procedural similarity, do differ. The discussion below highlights these terminological differences.

A juvenile who is detained by police is said to have been *taken into custody*, whereas an adult has been *arrested*. The prosecutor in a juvenile case will *petition the court*, whereas the prosecutor in an adult case will *charge an adult with a crime*. The act that the prosecutor brings to the court will come under a *violation of juvenile/family code* for juveniles; adults will be charged with a crime under the *penal code*.

Juveniles face an *adjudication hearing*, whereas adults will go to *trial*. **Adjudication hearings** for juveniles are generally *private, informal, and non-criminal (or civil)* in nature. Trials for adults are usually *formal, public, and follow rules of criminal court procedure*. The judge in a juvenile adjudication hearing is a *fact finder and acts as a wise parent*, whereas the judge in an adult trial is *neutral and intervenes only to keep order in the court* among adversarial prosecutors and defense attorneys. The end of the trial features a determination of blameworthiness for both adults and juveniles. Juveniles can be found to have *engaged in delinquent conduct and adjudicated*, whereas adults can be *found guilty*. Once this determination has been made, the next stage is *disposition* for juveniles, also called *sentencing* for adults.

Following disposition, juveniles may be *committed to a state facility for juveniles*, and adults may be *sent to jail or prison*. The juvenile court judge determines the *minimum length of stay* for juveniles, with final release decisions generally left up to institutional authorities. However, adults are subject to a *length of incarceration* by the judge or jury. Generally, disposition lengths for juveniles are *indeterminate*, and offenders must usually be released upon reaching the age of majority (unless released sooner on parole by institutional authorities). Adults generally serve a sentence for a *definite/determinate term*, subject to state parole laws.

Similarities Between the Two Systems

As noted above, the differences between the juvenile and adult justice processes are largely symbolic and terminological. For example, being taken into custody (for juveniles) and being arrested (for adults) both result in the offender being deprived of liberty. There is little difference in a prosecutor petitioning the court for a juvenile or the prosecutor filing charges against an adult offender—both processes lead to hearings that can result in a loss of freedom. Moreover, both juvenile and adult offenders are subject to sanction, including institutionalization. Despite these actual similarities in procedure, the juvenile justice system avoids the use of adult criminal terms for juveniles, perhaps guided by the dual beliefs that juveniles are less responsible than adults in general and that rehabilitation is better served by not labeling them as criminals. Table 1.2 outlines the assumptions of the juvenile and adult systems and the common ground between the two. As shown, there is a great degree of similarity between the two systems despite the different populations served and the two systems' differing philosophies.

Although there are many similarities between both systems, maybe the most important difference between the juvenile and adult justice systems is the programs available in juvenile justice that are not available in adult justice. Juvenile courts have at their disposal a variety of intervention, prevention, and youth-specific programs that are not found in the adult justice system. Thus,

TABLE 1.2

Comparison of Juvenile and Adult Justice Systems

Although the juvenile and criminal justice systems are more alike in some jurisdictions than in
tions can be made about the distinctions between the two systems and about their common grou

Juvenile Justice System	Common Ground	Criminal Justice System
Operating Assumptions		
■ Youth behavior is malleable. ■ Rehabilitation is usually a viable goal. ■ Youth are in families and not independent.	■ Community protection is a primary goal. ■ Law violators must be held accountable. ■ Constitutional rights apply.	■ Sanctions should be proportional to the offense. ■ General deterrence works. ■ Rehabilitation is not a primary goal.
Prevention		
■ Many specific delinquency prevention activities (e.g., school, church, recreation) are used. ■ Prevention is intended to change individual behavior and is often focused on reducing risk factors and increasing protective factors in the individual, family, and community.	■ Educational approaches are taken to specific behaviors (drunk driving, drug use).	■ Prevention activities are generalized and are aimed at deterrence (e.g., Crime Watch).
Law Enforcement		
■ Specialized "juvenile" units are used. ■ Some additional behaviors are prohibited (truancy, running away, curfew violations). ■ Some limitations are placed on public access to information. ■ A significant number of youth are diverted away from the juvenile justice system, often into alternative programs.	■ Jurisdiction involves the full range of criminal behavior. ■ Constitutional and procedural safeguards exist. ■ Both reactive and proactive approaches (targeted at offense types, neighborhoods, etc.) are used. ■ Community policing strategies are employed.	■ Open public access to all information is required. ■ Law enforcement exercises discretion to divert offenders out of the criminal justice system.
Intake—Prosecution		
■ In many instances, juvenile court intake, not the prosecutor, decides what cases to file. ■ The decision to file a petition for court action is based on both social and legal factors. ■ A significant portion of cases are diverted from formal case processing. ■ Intake or the prosecutor diverts cases from formal processing to services operated by the juvenile court, prosecutor's office, or outside agencies.	■ Probable cause must be established. ■ The prosecutor acts on behalf of the State.	■ Plea bargaining is common. ■ The prosecution decision is based largely on legal facts. ■ Prosecution is valuable in building history for subsequent offenses. ■ Prosecution exercises discretion to withhold charges or divert offenders out of the criminal justice system.

(continued)

mparison of Juvenile and Adult Justice Systems (continued)

Juvenile Justice System	Common Ground	Criminal Justice System
Detention—Jail/lockup		
■ Juveniles may be detained for their own protection or the community's protection. ■ Juveniles may not be confined with adults unless there is "sight and sound separation."	■ Accused offenders may be held in custody to ensure their appearance in court. ■ Detention alternatives of home or electronic detention are used.	■ Accused individuals have the right to apply for bond/bail release.
Adjudication—Conviction		
■ Juvenile court proceedings are "quasi-civil" (not criminal) and may be confidential. ■ If guilt is established, the youth is adjudicated delinquent regardless of offense. ■ Right to jury trial is not afforded in all States.	■ Standard of "proof beyond a reasonable doubt" is required. ■ Rights to be represented by an attorney, to confront witnesses, and to remain silent are afforded. ■ Appeals to a higher court are allowed. ■ Experimentation with specialized courts (i.e., drug courts, gun courts) is under way.	■ Defendants have a constitutional right to a jury trial. ■ Guilt must be established on individual offenses charged for conviction. ■ All proceedings are open.
Disposition—Sentencing		
■ Disposition decisions are based on individual and social factors, offense severity, and youth's offense history. ■ Dispositional philosophy includes a significant rehabilitation component. ■ Many dispositional alternatives are operated by the juvenile court. ■ Dispositions cover a wide range of community-based and residential services. ■ Disposition orders may be directed to people other than the offender (e.g., parents). ■ Disposition may be indeterminate, based on progress demonstrated by the youth.	■ Decisions are influenced by current offense, offending history, and social factors. ■ Decisions hold offenders accountable. ■ Decisions may give consideration to victims (e.g., restitution and "no contact" orders). ■ Decisions may not be cruel or unusual.	■ Sentencing decisions are bound primarily by the severity of the current offense and by the offender's criminal history. ■ Sentencing philosophy is based largely on proportionality and punishment. ■ Sentence is often determinate, based on offense.
Aftercare—Parole		
■ Function combines surveillance and reintegration activities (e.g., family, school, work).	■ The behavior of individuals released from correctional settings is monitored. ■ Violation of conditions can result in reincarceration.	■ Function is primarily surveillance and reporting to monitor illicit behavior.

Source: Howard N. Snyder and Melissa Sickmund, *Juvenile Offenders and Victims: 1999 National Report* (Washington, DC: Office of Juvenile Justice and Delinquency Prevention, 1999), 94, 95, 96.

despite similarities in overall process, in many ways juvenile justice is still very different from adult justice.

Juveniles, Delinquency, and the Law
Juvenile Defined

Who is a juvenile? Most people would say that a juvenile is someone under eighteen years of age. That answer may or may not be correct—depending upon state law. The definition of a *juvenile* as "someone under eighteen" is simplistic because each state or jurisdiction determines, usually by law, at what age a person is considered a juvenile. This is the **upper age of jurisdiction.** The upper age of jurisdiction is the oldest age at which the juvenile court has authority over a youth charged with committing a crime.[21] Persons who commit an offense and are above the upper age of juvenile court jurisdiction are processed in adult criminal court because they are considered adults. Persons below the upper age are considered juveniles and must usually be processed in juvenile court.[22]

As shown in Table 1.3, the upper age of original jurisdiction is seventeen in the majority of states (thirty-seven states and the District of Columbia). Anyone eighteen and older in these states is considered an adult and will be processed in the adult court. In ten states, the upper age of jurisdiction is sixteen (meaning that a person is considered an adult at age seventeen), and in three states the upper age is fifteen (meaning that a person is considered an adult at age sixteen). There is no national consensus on the minimum age at which an individual should be legally considered an adult; each state determines what these age limits are and consequently who and what is considered a juvenile.

TABLE 1.3

Upper Age of Juvenile Court Jurisdiction by State

Age	State
15	Connecticut, New York, North Carolina
16	Georgia, Illinois, Louisiana, Massachusetts, Michigan, Missouri, New Hampshire, South Carolina, Texas, Wisconsin
17	Alabama, Alaska, Arizona, Arkansas, California, Colorado, Delaware, District of Columbia, Florida, Hawaii, Idaho, Indiana, Iowa, Kansas, Kentucky, Maine, Maryland, Minnesota, Mississippi, Montana, Nebraska, Nevada, New Jersey, New Mexico, North Dakota, Ohio, Oklahoma, Oregon, Pennsylvania, Rhode Island, South Dakota, Tennessee, Utah, Vermont, Virginia, Washington, West Virginia, Wyoming

Source: Adapted from Howard N. Snyder and Melissa Sickmund, *Juvenile Offenders and Victims: 1999 National Report* (Washington, DC: Office of Juvenile Justice and Delinquency Prevention, 1999), 93.

As mentioned, persons below the upper age of jurisdiction must usually be handled in juvenile court because they are considered juveniles, and persons above the upper age must usually be handled in adult court because they are considered adults. In many states, however, the juvenile court may have **original jurisdiction** over legal adults who committed offenses as juveniles. This practice is extremely rare and usually involves situations where new evidence is discovered in an unsolved or "cold" case or, more typically, where an individual reaches the upper age of juvenile court jurisdiction before his or her adjudication hearing. (An example is the 2002 case against forty-one-year-old Michael Skakel, who fought to have his juvenile murder case tried in juvenile court but was unsuccessful.)

Alternatively, a juvenile can be "waived" or "transferred" to adult court for trial even though he or she is considered a juvenile based on the state's upper age of jurisdiction.[23] Thus, although the individual is technically considered a juvenile by state law, circumstances may allow him or her to be treated as an adult for prosecution purposes. Such circumstances usually entail serious, violent, or chronic offending on the part of the juvenile. There are several forms of transfer, and this subject is discussed more completely in Chapter 6. It is important to know at this point that a juvenile can be tried in adult court even though state law considers him or her a juvenile by age. However, this practice does not occur often.[24]

Sometimes a juvenile is so young that he or she cannot be prosecuted by either the juvenile or the adult court, regardless of offense. Although each state has an upper age of jurisdiction, not all states define the minimum age at which juveniles can be held accountable for their actions (see Table 1.1). This situation creates a **controversy of culpability.** The controversy revolves around the belief that young people below a certain age should not be held responsible for their acts because they do not understand the consequences of what they do. States are not uniform in their views of when children should become responsible for their acts. Thus, a controversy arises when a juvenile who is below the minimum age of jurisdiction/responsibility commits a crime, and particularly when a minimum age of responsibility has not been established by state law. (See "Controversial Issue: Which Side Do You Favor?")

Currently, the minimum age of jurisdiction is age ten in eleven states, age eight in one state, age seven in three states, and age six in one state.[25] For example, the minimum age of jurisdiction for delinquency cases in Louisiana is ten; thus, a youth who is under age ten and commits an offense cannot be processed by the juvenile or adult court or be held legally responsible for his or her actions. In states that have not established a minimum age of jurisdiction, prosecutors must determine on a case-by-case basis which juveniles will be prosecuted for which crimes and at what age.

Suppose that a juvenile commits a delinquent offense and he or she is below the age of responsibility. Does this youth then go free without consequences? The answer is no, not really. Although youths below the minimum age of responsibility may avoid punitive legal sanctions from the juvenile justice system, such as secure institutionalization in a state school, they may be subject to nonpunitive options such as counseling or mental health institutionalization. Where minimum age is not established by state law, a youth can theoretically be held legally responsible at any age. These cases differ in practice,

CONTROVERSIAL ISSUE: WHICH SIDE DO YOU FAVOR?

At what minimum age should juveniles be held accountable?

There is no nationally agreed-upon minimum age at which juveniles should be held responsible for delinquent acts. Even when states have defined a minimum age, there is much variation. For example, some states set the age of responsibility as low as age six. Other states set the age of responsibility at ten. A few states fall between these limits. Some states do not set an age of responsibility. In these states, a juvenile may technically be held responsible at any age.

This raises a question: *Should states set at what age juveniles should be held responsible for delinquent acts?*

States with a minimum age of responsibility have determined that there is a definite age when juveniles know the difference between right and wrong and therefore should be held responsible for their delinquent acts. Responsibility in these states is usually tied to the juvenile's chronological age rather than his or her mental age. States that have established a minimum age of responsibility believe that all juveniles mature the same and that a day makes a difference in the life of a juvenile. States are essentially saying that today the juvenile is not responsible for any act, but that by tomorrow, he or she may be; therefore, this is the only way to deal with delinquency by young children. It allows a uniform standard to be applied to all youths.

States that have not adopted a minimum age of responsibility argue that maturity among juveniles varies and that chronological age is not the same as mental age. A juvenile who is ten years old may have a mental age of six, or a juvenile who is six years old may have a mental age of ten. These states prefer the idea that offenses committed by young children must be handled on a case-by-case basis. Each youth is different and thus must be judged by an individualized standard concerning responsibility. In sum, one age does not fit all. Which side do you favor?

and in states without a minimum age specified, prosecution decisions usually proceed on a case-by-case basis.

In sum, for juvenile justice purposes, a juvenile is considered:

- Anyone under eighteen in thirty-seven states and the District of Columbia but over the minimum age of jurisdiction if one has been established by state law.

- Anyone under seventeen in ten states but over the minimum age of jurisdiction if one has been established by state law.

- Anyone under sixteen in three states but over the minimum age of jurisdiction if one has been established by state law.

Delinquency Defined

The definition of *delinquency* varies from state to state. Delinquency in one state may not be delinquency in another.[26] Generally, however, **delinquency** is defined as "acts committed by a juvenile that, if committed by an adult, would be a criminal act."[27] Although there are variations among states and jurisdictions, there is general agreement about the core offenses that constitute delinquency. These acts are classified into four types: crimes against persons, crimes against property, drug law violations, and offenses against public order. Table 1.4 lists certain crimes under the four categories mentioned.

Delinquency may include another category, depending upon state law. This category covers acts called **status offenses.** Status offenses are acts that are illegal only because the person committing them is not an adult. An adult cannot be charged with a status offense. For example, an adult cannot be arrested for smoking, being truant from school, or breaking a juvenile curfew law. There are four major types of status offenses: running away, truancy, ungovernability (failure to obey parents), and liquor law violations.[28] Note that

TABLE 1.4

Delinquent and Status Offenses

Delinquent Offenses	Status Offenses
Crimes Against Persons	
Criminal homicide	Runaway
Forcible rape	Truancy
Robbery	
Assault	
Aggravated assault	
Simple assault	
Kidnapping	
Violent sex acts (other than rape)	
Custody interference	
Unlawful restraint	
False imprisonment	
Harassment	
Reckless endangerment	
Attempts to commit above acts	
Crimes Against Property	**Ungovernability**
Burglary	Beyond control of parents/guardians
Larceny	Disobedient
Motor vehicle theft	Unruly, unmanageable, incorrigible
Arson	
Vandalism	
Stolen property	
Trespassing	
Forgery	
Counterfeiting	

(continued)

TABLE 1.4   *(continued)*

Delinquent Offenses	Status Offenses
Drug Law Violations	*Status Liquor Law Violations*
Unlawful sale, purchase, distribution, manufacture, cultivation, transport, possession, or use of a controlled substance	Possession, purchase, or consumption of liquor by minors*
Sniffing glue, paint, gasoline, and other inhalants	
Offenses Against Public Order	*Miscellaneous Status Offenses*
Weapons offenses	Curfew violation
Sex offenses (indecent exposure)	Tobacco violation
Liquor law violations*	
Disorderly conduct	
Obstruction of justice	

*Some states/jurisdictions view liquor law violations as status offenses; others view them as delinquent offenses.

Source: Adapted from Charles Puzzanchera, Anne L. Stahl, Terrence A. Finnegan, Howard N. Snyder, Rowen S. Poole, and Nancy Tierney, *Juvenile Court Statistics 1997* (Pittsburgh: National Center for Juvenile Justice, 2000).

a status offense in one state is sometimes considered a delinquency violation in another. Because of this possible overlap, status offenses are discussed under the definition of *delinquency*.

The Scope of the Juvenile Justice System
Delinquent Offenders

First and foremost, the juvenile justice system has jurisdiction over delinquent offenders. Delinquent offenders are defined as juveniles who commit acts that if committed by an adult would be considered a crime. Of the types of youths served by the juvenile justice system, the delinquent offender occupies the most attention. Rarely do we associate juvenile delinquency with cigarette smoking or skipping school; rather, we think of juvenile murder, robbery, gang participation, theft, and assault.

A clear understanding of the crimes that juveniles typically commit serves as an important foundation of what is to be learned throughout this text. There is a need to distinguish typical delinquents from nontypical delinquents because not all delinquency is the same in its degree of seriousness. The public's perception of juvenile offending has been influenced by the attention paid to extreme incidents of juvenile crime, such as school shootings and predatory murders. However, these acts are not common, as indicated by arrest statistics (see Chapter 2 for a discussion of the Uniform Crime Reports [UCR] and juvenile arrest statistics).

Typical delinquents are nonviolent property or "other" crime offenders. Of the arrests of persons under eighteen in the year 2002 (roughly 17 percent of all arrests, adult and juvenile), almost one-half of arrests were for larceny-theft, vandalism, drug abuse violations, liquor law violations, disorderly conduct, curfew violations, and loitering.[29] Based on the same data, another 40 percent of arrests were for such offenses as gambling, driving under the influence, simple assault, running away, and weapons possession. Thus, almost 90 percent of all delinquency offenses were relatively nonserious, and mainly misdemeanors.

Nontypical delinquents constitute a smaller proportion; their offenses are more frequent and serious than those of other delinquents. Official arrest statistics for the year 2002 revealed that 10 percent of arrests of persons under eighteen were for murder, forcible rape, robbery, aggravated assault, burglary, and arson. Just over 4 percent of these juvenile arrests were for person-related crimes (murder, forcible rape, robbery, and aggravated assault), with the remaining 6 percent considered serious property crimes (burglary).[30] In sum, the vast majority of juvenile offending is relatively nonserious, but some juveniles do commit serious "adult-like" offenses.[31]

Status Offenders

The juvenile justice system also has jurisdiction over status offenders. Status offenders differ from delinquent offenders in the types of acts they commit and in the way the juvenile justice system views them. Delinquent offenders are to be rehabilitated or punished; status offenders are considered in need of supervision or assistance.

Status offenders have been given many labels over the years, including such terms as *incorrigible, wayward, pre-delinquent,* and *malcontent.* These terms generally reflect status offenders' noncriminal but problematic behavior. Terms today for status offenders vary among the states. Current terms for status offenders include but are not limited to minors in need of supervision (MINS), children in need of assistance (CINA), children in need of supervision **(CINS),** and persons in need of supervision (PINS). Although the labels may vary, the underlying characteristic is that status offenders have committed acts that are prohibited only because they are committed by juveniles. These acts, such as smoking or skipping school, are prohibited because the status of the offenders (being young) implies that they are unable to handle certain responsibilities or are not mature enough to make certain decisions about their own lives. Thus, the state intervenes and regulates such noncriminal behavior.

Dependent and Neglected Children

The juvenile justice system also has jurisdiction over *dependent* and *neglected* children. Often overlooked, dependent and neglected children are involved with agencies of the juvenile justice system not because of what they did, but because of what others failed to do for them.

Dependency and neglect cases come to the attention of the juvenile justice system because parents or guardians have failed to provide for their children in some way. **Dependency** usually involves the absence of parents or guardians, generally through death or disability. **Neglect** cases are based on the lack of physical, emotional, or financial support from parents, and in the most severe cases, neglect includes outright abandonment and/or abuse. In sum, dependent children are those whose parents cannot (usually through death or disability) take care of them, and neglected children are those whose parents could take care of them but choose not to. Some agencies in the juvenile system deal specifically with delinquent offenders; others are human-service-type agencies providing support for youths in need of assistance. The second type of agency deals with dependent and neglected youths.

It is a common misperception that the juvenile court handles only lawbreakers. In reality, the juvenile court has jurisdiction over juveniles—be they delinquent, status offenders, or dependent and neglected. The juvenile court also has jurisdiction over a number of other noncriminal matters involving juveniles and their families. The court's jurisdiction may extend to divorce decrees concerning child visitation, custody and support, estate arrangements, termination of parental rights, emancipation of youths, and civil commitment procedures of youths who are judged mentally ill, mentally challenged, or in need of special support, such as a severe need for substance abuse counseling. Therefore, the juvenile court is the separate legal forum that deals with matters involving all juveniles. It is sometimes called the family court, domestic relations court, or probate court to reflect the broad jurisdiction it has over matters involving juveniles.

An Overview of the Juvenile Justice Process

Because of the many types of youths served by the juvenile justice system (delinquents, status offenders, dependent and neglected), a concise description of the process for all types would invite confusion. Therefore, this section examines the process for delinquent offenders. The process for status offenders and dependent and neglected youths is covered in Chapter 5.

The five major stages in the juvenile justice system for youths involved in delinquent behavior are initial contact, intake, adjudication, disposition, and aftercare. Exhibit 1.1 shows the stages of the juvenile justice system from initial contact to aftercare.

Initial Contact

At the forefront of the juvenile justice system are the police and other law enforcement agencies. As "gatekeepers" to the juvenile justice system, police and other law enforcement agencies often have first contact with juvenile offenders. Law enforcement officers account for approximately 85 percent of delinquency referrals to the juvenile justice system. The remaining 15 percent of referrals are made by parents, victims, schools, and probation officers.[32]

EXHIBIT 1.1

Stages of Delinquency Processing in Juvenile Justice

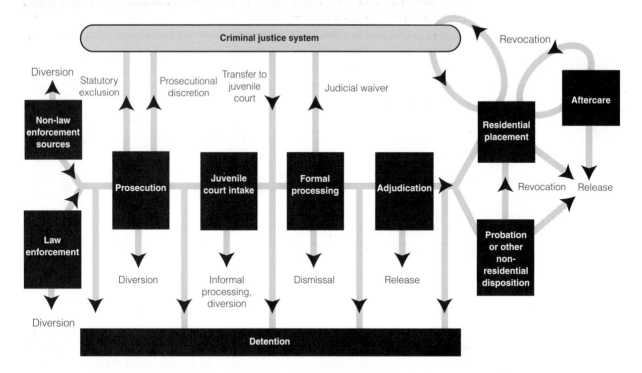

Note: This chart gives a simplified view of case flow through the juvenile justice system. Procedures vary among jurisdictions.

Source: Howard N. Snyder and Melissa Sickmund, *Juvenile Offenders and Victims: 1999 National Report* (Washington, DC: Office of Juvenile Justice and Delinquency Prevention, 1999), 98.

Juveniles can come into contact with law enforcement in three ways. First, law enforcement officers may observe a law violation and respond. Second, officers may receive a report of delinquency (from a citizen, victim, school, church, or family member) and investigate it. Third, youthful offenders might turn themselves in, accepting responsibility for a delinquent act. Law enforcement officers have a variety of options to handle juveniles when they come into contact with them. These options can be grouped into informal options and formal options.

Informal Options

The more serious the delinquent act, the less discretion that law enforcement officers have to informally resolve the matter (in other words, not arrest the juvenile). Informal resolution is an important aspect of police work because police officers cannot enforce all the rules all the time. Law enforcement officers have four *informal options* when dealing with juvenile offenders: (1) ignore the behavior, (2) give the youth a warning and call his or her parents, (3) make a referral to a social service agency, or (4) take the youth to the police department to give an official statement and receive an official warning. This last option is sometimes called a "station adjustment."

The use of informal options is the least restrictive means when dealing with juveniles. The officer chooses to give the youth a second chance. However, the use of informal options usually depends on the seriousness of the crime and other considerations, such as departmental policy, victim complaint, demeanor of the juvenile, prior contacts with the police, and community pressure/ opinion. These factors are detailed in Chapter 3.

Formal Options

Formal options are an official response to juvenile lawbreaking by law enforcement personnel that results in the juvenile being taken into custody. The use of formal measures signals entry into the juvenile justice system. Two formal options available to law enforcement officers are (1) issue a citation and allow the juvenile to go home with his or her parents or guardian, or (2) issue a formal citation to the juvenile, take him or her into custody, and transport him or her to a juvenile **detention facility.** In each formal option, the juvenile and his or her parents or guardian will have to appear before a juvenile court officer at a later date. This occurs in a process called intake.

Intake

Intake officers, who are usually probation officers or prosecutors, decide at intake whether the juvenile will face an adjudication hearing or be diverted from the formal juvenile system.[33] Like law enforcement officers, intake officers have much discretion: They can resolve the case formally through an adjudication hearing or informally by diverting or adjusting it. For example, an intake officer could divert a juvenile by offering him or her a chance at community service in lieu of a petition for an adjudication hearing and possible adjudication.

Intake officers decide whether to dismiss the case altogether, process the youth informally (diversion), or **petition** the youth for an adjudication hearing in front of the juvenile court.[34] These decisions are based on a number of factors, including the amount and quality of evidence, prior arrests, probation status, and the seriousness of the current offense. Intake officers may also decide whether or not the case deserves to be handled in adult court and can petition to waive the case or transfer it to adult court.

In the petition process, the court intake officer makes a formal application to the juvenile court detailing the youth's conduct and requesting a hearing. The petitioned youth will face an adjudication hearing. **Nonpetitioned** youths will be subject to the various informal options available to intake officers. For example, nonpetitioned youths may be placed on **deferred prosecution** or **deferred/informal probation** (generally called diversion or adjustment), where they must complete a period of time, usually six months or less, without further law violation. In instances of deferred prosecution, deferred/informal probation, or other diversionary alternatives (such as Teen Court), youths who successfully complete the requirements will be discharged from agency supervision, often without an official court record.

Adjudication

Once the decision is made to petition the youth to the juvenile court, and provided that the youth is not diverted, the next stage in the juvenile justice process is the juvenile trial or the adjudication hearing. At the adjudication stage, the juvenile develops an official record in the court.

The adjudication hearing parallels the trial in the adult justice system. Adjudication hearings are typically less formal than trials in the adult justice system and are closed to the public, except if state law provides otherwise. Juvenile adjudication hearings are usually decided by a judge, but some states grant juveniles the right to have a jury hear their case. The general process in a juvenile adjudication hearing is exploratory instead of adversarial. Therefore, it resembles an inquiry rather than a legal fight and thus is characterized as civil as opposed to criminal in nature. In some jurisdictions, however, adjudication hearings are not much different from adult trials, especially when the juvenile faces serious charges.

In many cases, juvenile adjudication hearings are mere formalities. First, many juveniles do not contest or fight the charges against them, meaning that the petition to the juvenile court has gone **uncontested,** and the youth has admitted to the behavior. Many uncontested petitions may be a result of plea bargaining, wherein the accused youth does not contest a charge and instead enters a plea of guilty in exchange for an alternative option, such as a reduced charge, agreement to participate in a particular program, or the withdrawal of waiver to adult criminal court. Although no national data are available on the extent of plea agreements in the juvenile justice system, one scholar's study of a Philadelphia juvenile court system revealed that almost 20 percent of cases were plea bargained.[35]

Those who do not plead guilty or plea bargain will face the full adjudication hearing. A finding of guilt by a juvenile court judge or jury must be based on a standard of proof like that used in adult trials: guilt beyond a reasonable doubt. Reasonable doubt is "the belief that there is a real possibility that a defendant is not guilty."[36] If guilt is established, the youth is officially labeled a delinquent and must then be sentenced.

Disposition

If allegations of delinquent conduct are found true by the juvenile court judge or jury, the next stage in the juvenile justice system is **disposition,** which is the equivalent of sentencing in the adult criminal process. The justification for this **bifurcated** (two-step) hearing process is that it gives the juvenile court judge time to carefully consider the facts of the case and to design the most beneficial disposition for the juvenile. In some jurisdictions, pre-sentence or **pre-disposition reports** help the juvenile court judge in determining a proper sentence. Pre-disposition reports are typically completed by a probation officer and include both legal and extralegal evidence, such as the child's family life, abuse, psychiatric or psychological evaluations, and other relevant information, such as prior involvement with the juvenile justice system. The disposition hearing also has more relaxed procedures concerning evidence, allowing hearsay and other forms of testimony and evidence not allowed during the adjudication hearing. The reasoning is that the juvenile court judge should be fully informed about all issues relevant to the juvenile's case before choosing a disposition once guilt has been established.

Juvenile court judges have several dispositions available. Table 1.5 details some of these. Dispositions vary based on a number of considerations, such as state sentencing guidelines or the availability of programs in the jurisdiction. The most influential factors may be the seriousness of the crime, the frequency of crimes, or whether the youth had previously been in the system. Other factors include but are not limited to a history of substance abuse, gang involvement, or prior institutionalization.

Of the many dispositions available to juvenile court judges, the two most common are probation and institutionalization.

TABLE 1.5

Common Juvenile Dispositions

Disposition	Explanation
Dismiss the case	A juvenile court judge may dismiss a case against a juvenile despite the fact that the youth has been adjudicated delinquent. This is rare but does occur.
Restitution	Restitution usually involves paying back the victim for the value of property lost or destroyed because of the crime. Restitution is most often "worked off" through forms of community service.
Fines	Today, many juveniles are being fined for participating in delinquent acts. Fines are also becoming commonplace for acts that occur within schools—for example, fighting or truancy.
Various forms of counseling	A juvenile court judge may sentence a juvenile delinquent to a variety of forms of counseling based on the youth's judged need—for example, sex offender counseling, substance abuse counseling, mental health treatment, or violent and serious offender counseling. These forms of counseling can be accomplished both in and out of juvenile facilities.
Institutionalization in a mental hospital	Severely mentally ill youths may be committed to a mental hospital to stabilize their illness before any further juvenile justice intervention, such as serving a probation sentence or being sent to a juvenile justice institution. Youths with less severe emotional disorders may be required to complete outpatient treatment in conjunction with their sentence.
House arrest	A form of community monitoring in which the youth is forbidden to leave his or her home except under approved circumstances. House arrest can be a condition of probation and may be combined with electronic monitoring.
Electronic monitoring	A form of monitoring whereby the juvenile is monitored by phone (checking in) or by an ankle monitor, commonly called a "lowjack." Lowjacks can be monitored via satellite or can transmit a signal to probation officers when the youth enters or leaves a specified area.

(continued)

TABLE 1.5   *Common Juvenile Dispositions (continued)*

Disposition	Explanation
Probation	Probation can be used both before adjudication (probation as a diversion) and after adjudication (probation as a disposition). This sanction is very versatile and, as a result, is the most often used disposition nationally. Probation allows the youth to remain at home under the direct supervision of his or her parents but also requires the youth to be supervised by the juvenile probation department. Requirements commonly include phone reporting, face-to-face meetings with a probation officer, curfew restrictions, and community service.
Day treatment	A disposition whereby youths are directly supervised during the day in a group facility but are allowed to go home at the end of the day.
Intensive supervision probation (ISP)	Similar to traditional or regular probation, but ISP is reserved for more serious juvenile delinquents who would have otherwise been committed to a juvenile institution. ISP is also more intense, meaning more contact with a juvenile probation officer, sometimes called a field officer, who conducts random visits to the youth's home. The first-tier goals of ISP are community protection and risk management.
Commitment to state school or other secure juvenile placement	Usually, this is the last option for juvenile court judges and is used only for the most serious, violent, or chronic delinquents. State schools or training schools are common secure placements, but other secure dispositions may include boot camps, forestry camps, ranches, and detention centers.
Adult prisons	In rare cases, juveniles are sent to an adult prison. To be sent to an adult prison, the juvenile must usually have been waived and tried in adult court. However, some state sentencing schemes allow a juvenile to be placed in an adult institution once he or she has reached a certain age after committing crimes as a juvenile.

Probation

Probation can be used both before adjudication (sometimes called deferred or informal probation, in which probation is used as a diversion) and after adjudication (probation as a disposition). This section focuses on probation after adjudication. Probation after adjudication is a type of disposition in which the delinquent youth is released back home to his or her parents or other legal guardian.[37] He or she is required to abide by the law and other rules and regulations set by the juvenile court and probation department. Nationally, over one-half of adjudicated youth will receive probation as a disposition.[38]

Probation may be referred to as an umbrella designation because many dispositions are sometimes combined with it. For example, a youth on probation may be required to wear an electronic monitoring bracelet, be subject to house arrest, and go to counseling. Used in this way, probation is one of the most popular dispositions in the juvenile justice system because it is versatile and can be specifically tailored to the youth and his or her individual issues.

Failure to abide by the rules of probation can lead to commitment in a state facility. A youth who fails probation can face the juvenile court again and will either be given a second chance on probation, get more intense supervision/requirements, or get placed in a state juvenile facility. In reality, while complete compliance with probation regulations is the goal, it rarely occurs. However, seldom will **probation revocation** result from the breaking of a few rules or even from new crimes committed by a juvenile probationer, and it is even less likely that revocation will result in secure institutionalization. Commitments to state juvenile facilities are usually reserved for the most serious and violent juvenile offenders, or for those who are overtly chronic offenders. Most revoked probationers do not fit into these categories.

Institutionalization

Institutionalization in a state-operated juvenile facility is the most severe penalty for delinquent youths and is equivalent to being sent to prison. Most delinquents who are institutionalized will serve a period of time ranging from nine months to twelve months. The most serious, violent, and persistent juveniles will be sentenced for extended periods of time.[39]

Institutions for juveniles resemble adult prisons and in some cases are actually converted adult prisons. These institutions are referred to as reform schools, industrial schools, state training schools, or state juvenile correctional facilities. Although there are considerable differences between institutions, each usually has the same features. Most juvenile institutions will offer an educational and vocational component. Many offer general counseling services, such as anger management, peer counseling, and employment counseling. Some juvenile institutions also offer specialized counseling services such as sex offender treatment, gang renunciation, mental health treatment, and capital offender programs.

Institutionalization is not limited to prison-type facilities. Some departments have boot camps, ranches, forestry camps, and other "residential placements" for youths deemed in need of a secure environment. Although not a true institution in the sense of bars and walls, forestry camps and other similar placements essentially remove the delinquent from the public and are thus considered a form of institutionalization. These placements are sometimes labeled "noninstitutional institutions."

Around 28 percent of all juvenile adjudications nationwide result in institutionalization.[40] It is sparingly used when dealing with juvenile offenders, and it is usually reserved for the most serious, violent, or chronic juvenile offenders in the state.

Aftercare

After serving a period of time in a juvenile institution, most juvenile offenders are supervised by an officer of the juvenile justice system in the community. Called parole for adults, **aftercare** is parole for juveniles; they are released for a period of supervision in the community before outright **discharge.** The justification for aftercare is that juveniles need a period of adjustment in the community before they are released without supervision. Aftercare also enables juvenile parole officers to provide support for youths when they reenter society in hopes of making a more successful transition. This support may include drug and alcohol counseling or career and job placement. Public safety is a primary goal, but support for juveniles in the form of counseling is also an important aspect of the aftercare process.

There are two types of conditions for youths released to aftercare: standard and special. **Standard conditions** (sometimes called general conditions) are those that all paroled youths will be required to complete, such as abiding by all laws, having regular face-to-face meetings with a juvenile parole officer, avoiding certain individuals and establishments, performing community service, obtaining a GED or high school diploma, and obeying a curfew. **Special conditions** are specific to only some offenders and may include submitting to drug tests, sex offender counseling, anger management, restitution, substance abuse counseling, and house arrest. Not every offender needs such specialized services. For example, not every offender has a substance abuse problem or requires sex offender treatment.

Revocation

Revocation means "taking something away." Because parole or aftercare is considered a "conditional release" and is dependent upon the youth following the laws of the state and rules set by the parole agency, it can be taken away. Revocation of aftercare happens in various ways. First, a juvenile can be found to have engaged in further delinquent conduct while on parole. If the parole officer decides that the delinquent conduct warrants revocation, he or she will arrange a hearing to present the facts to a hearings officer for a decision. Second, a youth's parole status can be revoked for nondelinquent behavior such as failing to meet with his or her parole officer (a technical violation). One or two violations are generally not sufficient to revoke a youth's parole, but persistent technical violations can result in revocation. Third, revocation can result from a combination of delinquent conduct and technical violations.

If a youth's parole is revoked, he or she will generally be sent back to a state juvenile institution. Depending on the state and its facilities, most youths will be sent to a shorter-term, state-operated juvenile detention facility instead of a state training school. Revocation for violations of technical conditions generally causes a return for a shorter period of time than for new delinquent conduct, but this depends on the seriousness and frequency of technical violations; thus, state practices vary tremendously. Although revocation sentences are typically shorter in duration than the original commitment to a state juvenile facility, revoked youths typically face the same institutional requirements as a new commitment.

Discharge

If a youth abides by all the conditions of aftercare throughout the entire time mandated, he or she will be discharged from parole and state supervision. Following discharge, only a new delinquency petition and adjudication will send the youth back to the juvenile justice system. However, further delinquent conduct, combined with past behavior, may make reentry back into the juvenile justice system quicker and the penalties more severe.

SUMMARY

- ❏ *Parens patriae* literally means the "parent of a country." It means that the state exercises guardianship rights over children when parents cannot or do not.

- ❏ Who and what is a juvenile is determined by state law. Most states have determined that anyone under eighteen is a juvenile.

- ❏ The first juvenile court was established in 1899 in Cook County, Illinois. By 1950, all states had established a juvenile court.

- ❏ The upper age of jurisdiction is the oldest age at which the juvenile court has authority over a youth charged with committing a crime.

- ❏ The minimum age of responsibility is the lowest age at which juveniles can be held legally responsible for their actions. Several states have not established a minimum age, and juveniles can be theoretically held responsible at any age in these states.

- ❏ Delinquency is any act committed by a juvenile that if committed by an adult would be considered a criminal act.

- ❏ Status offenses are acts prohibited only for juveniles; these include smoking, truancy, and curfew violation. An adult cannot be arrested for a status offense.

- ❏ Juvenile courts have authority over juveniles in many situations, some that have nothing to do with lawbreaking behavior.

- ❏ The typical delinquent is not a serious offender.

- ❏ The difference between the juvenile justice system and the adult justice system is more terminological and symbolic than real.

- ❏ The juvenile justice system for delinquent offenders is composed of five stages: initial contact, intake, adjudication, disposition, and aftercare.

- ❏ Most juvenile delinquents do not get institutionalized; most receive probation when adjudicated.

REVIEW QUESTIONS

1. Who is a juvenile? Discuss all the considerations involved in answering this question.
2. What is juvenile delinquency?
3. Distinguish between delinquents and status offenders.
4. Define *parens patriae*. Why is this concept important to understanding juvenile justice?

5. What is the most frequent "upper age of jurisdiction" in the United States? What does this term mean?

6. Who is subject to the scope and jurisdiction of the juvenile justice system?

7. In your opinion, why do most adjudicated delinquents receive probation instead of institutionalization?

8. List the five major stages in the juvenile justice process. Write a paragraph describing the general process in each stage.

9. In your own words, what is the "controversy of culpability"?

10. What is the difference between dependency and neglect, as discussed in this chapter?

KEY TERMS AND DEFINITIONS

adjudication hearing: The equivalent of an adult trial.

aftercare (sometimes called **juvenile parole**): A period of supervised time after release from a state juvenile facility.

bifurcated: Refers to the two-part juvenile court process for petitioned juvenile offenders. The adjudication hearing is the first part, and disposition or sentencing is the second part.

CINS: An acronym for children in need of supervision that is typically given to status offenders. Other popular acronyms include PINS (persons in need of supervision) or MINS (minors in need of supervision).

controversy of culpability: Refers to the controversy concerning the age at which a child can be held responsible for his or her actions because of the ability to possess *mens rea,* or a guilty mind. The controversy centers on different ideas about the age of responsibility, as evidenced by the differing minimum ages of jurisdiction in states.

crime control era: Generally, the point in time starting in the 1980s that was known for a concern about the rise in drug use, gun possession, and drug sales (particularly crack cocaine) among juveniles. Public scrutiny of the rise in these types of juvenile crime caused a get-tough policy for juvenile offenders.

deferred/informal probation: An agreement with the court intake officer (either a probation officer or a prosecutor) whereby a juvenile is not petitioned to the juvenile court in lieu of the successful completion of a period of time without further delinquency offenses. The period of time is typically six months.

deferred prosecution: Similar to deferred probation and is an agreement not to prosecute or petition the youth as long as he or she completes a period of time without further delinquent involvement.

delinquency: Any act committed by a juvenile that would be considered a criminal offense if committed by an adult.

dependency: A situation in which parents are not able to adequately take care of their children, typically because of death or disability.

detention facility: A short-term locked facility that holds juveniles at three points in time: after arrest, before the adjudication hearing, and after disposition while the youth awaits transfer to a state-operated juvenile justice facility. Detention facilities also hold probation and parole violators.

discharge: The release from aftercare and state supervision.

disposition: The sentencing stage of the juvenile justice process. Disposition in the juvenile justice system is the equivalent to sentencing in the criminal justice system.

houses of refuge: An institution of the early 1800s for delinquent and other wayward children. Houses of refuge are considered the first juvenile institutions.

indeterminate sentence: A sentence without a fixed amount of time. The juvenile will be held until rehabilitated.

institutionalization: Being placed in a state-operated juvenile justice facility.

juvenile court era: The period of time from 1899, when the first separate juvenile court was established in Cook County, Illinois, until 1966.

juvenile rights era: The period of time from 1967 until 1979—it saw the juvenile justice system become more like the adult system in the processing of juvenile delinquents.

mens rea: A guilty mind.

minimum age of responsibility: The earliest age at which juveniles can be held responsible for their acts.

neglect: A situation in which parents do not take care of their children but have the ability to do so. Abandonment and abuse generally fall under neglect.

nonpetitioned: Youths who will not face a juvenile court hearing but have been diverted in another way or had their cases dismissed.

nontypical delinquent: Serious and violent juveniles. Most delinquents are not serious offenders.

original jurisdiction: The court that will hear a delinquency case originally or for the first time.

parens patriae: "Parent of a country": the doctrine that the state has the authority to intervene in the life of a child.

petition: A formal complaint to the juvenile court by an intake officer requesting an adjudication hearing.

pre-disposition report: A report conducted by a juvenile probation officer that details a juvenile's history, such as substance abuse, home life, abuse, prior juvenile record, and/or evidence of psychological evaluations. This report is used by the juvenile court judge prior to making a ruling on the juvenile's disposition.

pre-juvenile court era: The time period from 1600 to 1898, characterized by juveniles being dealt with the same way as adults. There was no separate juvenile court during this era.

probation: A sentence whereby a youth is released to the custody of his or her parents but is subject to conditions of behavior stipulated by the juvenile court.

probation revocation: The process of taking away a youth's probation status because of noncompliance with the law or with the stipulations of probation. A youth who has had his or her probation revoked can face institutionalization in a state-operated juvenile justice facility.

special conditions: Conditions of probation/aftercare to which only some offenders will be subjected. For example, sex offenders may be subject to a special condition of sex offender counseling.

standard conditions (sometimes called **general conditions**): Conditions of probation or parole that every youth will face. Common examples include reporting and community service.

status offense: An act prohibited only for juveniles.

typical delinquent: A juvenile guilty of nonserious offenses.

uncontested: A situation in which a juvenile does not contest, or dispute, the petition or charges against him or her. An uncontested plea is often the result of a plea bargain between the prosecution and the juvenile.

upper age of jurisdiction: The maximum age in which the juvenile court has decision-making power over a youth. The most common upper age of jurisdiction is seventeen in the United States. In states that use this standard, youths who have reached the age of eighteen are considered adults and must usually be tried in adult court.

FOR FURTHER RESEARCH

- ❏ **The National Center for Juvenile Justice**
  http://ncjj.servehttp.com/NCJJWebsite/main.htm

- ❏ **When a Young Person Commits a Crime: A Look at What Happens in Juvenile Court**
  http://criminal.findlaw.com/articles/1386.html

- ❏ **National Institute of Justice 2002 Annual Report**
  http://www.ncjrs.org/txtfiles1/nij/200338.txt

- ❏ **How Families and Communities Influence Youth Victimization**
  http://www.ncjrs.org/html/ojjdp/201629/contents.html

- ❏ **Juvenile Arrests 2001**
  http://www.ncjrs.org/html/ojjdp/201370/contents.html

For an up-to-date list of web links, go to the Juvenile Justice Companion Website at **http://cj.wadsworth.com/del_carmen_trulson_jj**

CHAPTER 2

Theories and Measurement of Juvenile Delinquency

Theories of Juvenile Delinquency / 33

    The Emergence of the Classical School / 34

        The Devil and Delinquency / 34

        Beccaria and Free Will / 35

    Biology, Determinism, and the Positive School / 36

        Lombroso and the Atavist / 36

        Phrenology and Craniology / 37

        Body-Type Theories / 38

        Genetic Influences / 38

        Other Biological Perspectives / 40

    Psychological Explanations of Delinquency / 40

    Sociological Explanations of Delinquency / 41

        Social Disorganization Theory / 41

        Strain Theory / 42

        Differential Association and Social Learning Theory / 47

        Social Bonding/Control Theory / 49

        Labeling Theory / 50

        Conflict Theory / 51

    Developmental and Life-Course Perspectives / 52

        Gottfredson and Hirschi's General Theory of Crime / 52

        Moffitt's Dual Taxonomy / 52

        Sampson and Laub's Crime and the Life Course / 54

    Delinquency Theories and the Juvenile Justice System, Process, and Law / 55

Measuring Juvenile Crime and Victimizations / 56

    Official Data / 58

        Uniform Crime Reports (UCR) / 58

        National Incident-Based Reporting System (NIBRS) / 60

    Self-Report Data / 61

    Victimization Data / 63

IN THIS CHAPTER YOU WILL LEARN

■ About the various theories of juvenile delinquency, which help to explain "why" juveniles offend.

■ That theories of juvenile delinquency were important to the formation of the first juvenile court and continue to be important to the juvenile justice system, process, and law today.

■ That theories of juvenile delinquency come from various fields, including but not limited to biology, psychology, and sociology. Each field attributes delinquency to different causes or explanations. Some theories bridge several perspectives.

■ That no one single theory is sufficient to provide a concrete reason why juveniles become involved in delinquency.

■ That theories of delinquency generally focus on factors that are thought to make delinquency "more or less likely" but not "always."

■ About the methods used to measure national levels of juvenile offending and victimization in the United States.

■ That juvenile offending and victimization can be measured through official data and self-reports.

■ That the various ways to measure juvenile offending and victimization have both strengths and weaknesses.

■ That using both official records and self-reports gives a more complete picture of juvenile offending and victimization.

INTRODUCTION

Chapter 1 provides a general overview of the juvenile justice system—its formation, history, evolution, and differences from the adult system, including the different types of youths it serves and a step-by-step look at how the system operates. Although this text is system oriented and procedure oriented, it is also important to examine two additional perspectives before delving into the specific stages and issues in the juvenile justice system, process, and law. The first is an explanation of "why" juveniles become involved in delinquency, and the second is on measuring the extent of juvenile delinquency in the United States.

The first section of this chapter examines the various theories of "why" juveniles become involved in delinquency. Theories of delinquency are much older than a separate juvenile court and justice system and include a rich history. Understanding the history and evolution of theories of delinquency is important for many reasons, but primarily because explanations of why juveniles offend were central to the formation of a separate juvenile justice system and have influenced the structure and operation of the juvenile justice system ever since.

This chapter then examines the different methods used to measure national levels of juvenile delinquency and juvenile victimizations in the United States. Although specific levels of offending and victimization are detailed in chapters that address these issues directly (for example, Chapter 3, on juveniles and the police, examines juvenile arrests), it is important at the outset to examine how these statistics are collected. Statistics are only as good as the methods used to collect them. As such, this section places special emphasis on the procedures, advantages, and disadvantages of the various measures of delinquency.

Theories of Juvenile Delinquency

This section provides an overview of theories and perspectives of juvenile delinquency. Delinquency theories are important because they provide some perspective on "why" juveniles break the law.* Whereas the question of "what to do with and what happens to juveniles when they offend" is the central purpose of this book, a look at different perspectives on why juveniles offend is useful because changes to the juvenile justice system, process, and law have been influenced over time by changing theoretical perspectives on the causes of delinquency. These perspectives were central to the formation of the first juvenile court in Cook County, Illinois, in 1899 and remain important today as the juvenile justice system, process, and law adapt to the diverse population of juveniles facing the system. (See Exhibit 2.1.)

---

*We regard "delinquency theory" as a generic reference due to the subject of this text.

EXHIBIT 2.1

Explaining Delinquency Is Probabilistic

Social scientists explain crime and delinquency in probabilistic terms: Delinquency is "more likely" or "less likely" depending on certain conditions. For example, a juvenile who grows up in poverty, is surrounded by drugs, and has delinquent siblings may be more likely to become delinquent. However, growing up in these types of conditions does not mean that this juvenile will automatically become a delinquent. It is simply saying that when these conditions are present, delinquency is more likely or more probable. This approach is different from the "hard" or "physical" sciences such as chemistry, physics, or biology. For example, mixing gasoline and fire will "always" result in a predictable outcome.

Source: Frank Hagan, *Essentials of Research Methods in Criminal Justice and Criminology* (Boston: Pearson, 2003), 8.

The Emergence of the Classical School

The Devil and Delinquency

The earliest systematic efforts to study and understand crime and delinquency (and deviance in general) emerged in the late 1700s. Prior to this time, the dominant view found the roots of crime in the devil (demonology) or in other spiritual/theological explanations. According to the demonological perspective, those who engaged in "criminal behavior" did so because of "temptation" or as a result of being "possessed": During this time, crime and delinquency were generally equated with being a sinner.[1] Because crime meant sin, delinquents were thought to be too weak to resist the devil or to have had little faith in God.

The belief in a demonological explanation of crime is best illustrated by the treatment of "criminals" during those times. The trial and punishment process was characterized by creative and sometimes brutal acts, including torture, exorcisms, and "trial by ordeal" designed to test whether the individual was under the influence of the devil. Surviving these "ordeals" uninjured was proof that God was protecting the alleged sinner, for it was assumed that God would not protect the guilty. As an example, a trial by ordeal might include forcing a criminal to hold his or her hand over a flame. If the flame did not burn the individual, this was taken as evidence that he or she was not possessed or otherwise influenced by the devil.[2] Not surprisingly, few survived the trials without injury.[3]

The belief that the devil or other spiritual/theological factors caused individuals to commit crime was simplistic. Sometimes, what was considered a "possession" was in fact a mental illness or other problem. Explaining crime as the result of "demons" or other theological/supernatural causes was also a problem because one cannot actually "observe" the devil.[4] This view is widely rejected today, but it was a common explanation for crime and delinquency prior to the 1700s for both children and adults.*

---

*Note that the concept of "delinquency" was not generally recognized until the 1899 formation of the world's first juvenile court. Before this time, children were simply considered little criminals and sinners in big people's clothing.

Beccaria and Free Will

A significant turning point in the study of the causes of crime and delinquency came as a result of the theories of several individuals during the late eighteenth century. Cesare Beccaria was one of the most influential theorists. He believed that human beings were essentially rational beings who weigh or calculate costs and benefits (pain versus pleasure) before they act. This thinking was the essence of the **classical school** of thought. Criminals were not possessed by the devil but were individuals with free will who received some benefit or pleasure from criminal behavior. In other words, when the perceived benefits of crime outweighed the potential costs, people with free will would engage in crime. To prevent crime, according to classical school theorists, a system of punishments based on severity was needed to make the pain of crime outweigh the pleasure of a criminal act. The classical school of thought is perhaps best explained by Beccaria's influential work *On Crimes and Punishments,* which was first published in 1764 in Italian and translated into English in 1768.[5]

Beccaria's treatise was not meant to be a theory of crime; instead, Beccaria "simply wanted to delineate the parameters of a just system of dealing with criminals."[6] Beccaria suggested that the purpose of punishment is to prevent crime. To do this, he said that punishments must be swift, certain, and severe—most importantly, certain. He believed that a certain punishment would be much more effective in preventing crime than a severe or swift punishment: A punishment that was certain would guarantee that the offender would experience some consequence as a result of crime. Beccaria also noted that criminal punishments should be graded based on severity. This meant that punishments that were swift, certain, and severe must also be proportionate to the crime committed. If the punishment did not fit the crime, meaning it was too harsh for the act, a certain punishment could actually escalate crime. For example, to punish someone with life imprisonment or death for stealing a loaf of bread might encourage the criminal to kill to avoid being caught.

The classical school's notion of rationality and free will failed to recognize the host of factors that could push someone into delinquency other than free will and choice (for example, mental illness or youthfulness). It also failed to consider whether individuals knew about laws and punishment, and it did not recognize that "rationality" depends on the individual. The classical school assumed that all people were equally rational; thus, punishments were not based on "why" the offender engaged in crime but rather on the nature of the act that he or she committed.[7] All similar acts were treated with the same punishment, regardless of the individual circumstances of the offender. Although this rigid approach lost favor, it was later revived by the neoclassical school, which recognized that in some cases free will is influenced by an individual's circumstances—such as age and mental condition.[8]

The classical school was being challenged in the mid-1800s. However, even now there is still support for the idea that many delinquents become involved in crime because they choose to do so and because they can receive some benefit. Thus, rational choice explanations are still popular today in some circles (called the modern classical school). Classical school assumptions persist among advocates of a juvenile justice system that would punish and incapacitate rather than treat and rehabilitate juveniles for their delinquency. These advocates subscribe to the belief that juveniles are rational actors who know what they are doing and who deserve punishment for their acts.

Biology, Determinism, and the Positive School

Determinism assigns the causes of delinquency to predetermined individual or environmental factors. Crime is not the result of choice. This is how determinism generally differs from free-will–based theories. The earliest perspectives of determinism explained crime as a result of biological anomalies that showed up as physical defects, such as the presence of big ears, an abnormal contour or shape of the skull, or other physical indicators such as body structure.[9] These physical symptoms can be "measured," and **positivism** refers to a perspective that believes causes of behavior can be measured and observed. Early positivists believed that crime could be explained by these observable factors; thus, the **positive school** advocated the application of scientific principles to the study of crime.[10] Physical characteristics that were thought to distinguish criminals from noncriminals were the early focus of the positive school theorists. These ascertainable characteristics stood in contrast to the demonological perspective and the classical school, in which the "devil" and the concepts of "rational choice" or "free will" were difficult to measure and observe.

Lombroso and the Atavist

The major shift in thinking on the causes of crime and delinquency associated with positivism was heavily influenced by the work of Cesare Lombroso in the late 1800s. Lombroso did not accept the classical school proposition that individuals are driven by free will and rationally calculate costs and benefits before they act. Instead, Lombroso believed that delinquents and criminals were "biological throwbacks" to an earlier stage of evolution.[11] In essence, Lombroso believed that criminals were somehow different than noncriminals and that these differences were evident in physical characteristics.

Lombroso's perspective was first introduced in 1876 with the publication of his book *The Criminal Man.* This publication came after several years that Lombroso spent as a physician in the Italian army and in various mental hospitals throughout Italy, where he had the opportunity to observe and study several thousand soldiers and mental patients. As a result of his observations and tests (for example, measuring skull size and head slope), Lombroso maintained that there was something biologically inferior or different about criminals.[12] Lombroso used the term *atavism* (borrowing from Charles Darwin's evolutionary study *On the Origin of Species*) to describe those individuals who had not fully evolved and hence could be considered "throwbacks" to earlier stages of evolution.[13] **Atavists,** or "born criminals" according to Lombroso, could be recognized by certain "stigmata," including "outstanding ears, abundant hair, a sparse beard, enormous frontal sinuses and jaws, a square and projecting chin, [and] broad cheekbones."[14]

Today, Lombroso's work has been discredited. One of the main criticisms of his work is that he never compared his subjects to individuals from the general population (in which he would have found similar characteristics).

Moreover, his early works categorized certain stigmata as those things that were clearly not biological, such as tattoos and scars. Despite criticisms, the importance of Lombroso's work was a recognition that criminal behavior might well be the product of forces out of the control of the individual—whether the forces be biologically based or environmentally based. This is the essence of the positive school, which put a focus on the criminal or delinquent instead of on his or her act. Exhibit 2.2 contains an exercise that allows you to explore the idea that physical characteristics may be an indicator of delinquency.

Phrenology and Craniology

One of the earliest perspectives in the biological tradition is phrenology, the study of the shape and contours of the skull in an effort to classify who would be more likely—or not—to become criminal or delinquent. Whereas phrenologists examined bumps and contours as explanations of behavior, a closely aligned group called "craniologists" developed elaborate maps of the skull with corresponding numbers and explanations for certain behaviors (see "For Further Research" at the end of this chapter for a phrenology website that includes "skull maps"). For example, the portion of the skull just above the forehead is section 34. According to some phrenologists, section 34 is "the faculty which induces men to argue from analogy."[15] A related perspective was physiognomy, the study of facial features in an effort to judge a person's character.[16] Again, the idea was that behavior could be predicted by physical characteristics.

EXHIBIT 2.2

Predicting Delinquency from Physical Features

Cesare Lombroso believed that delinquents and criminals possessed certain physical characteristics that he called *stigmata*. According to Lombroso, these stigmata could be used to differentiate delinquents from nondelinquents because they were indicators that the people in question had not fully evolved and were, in essence, born criminals. For example, Lombroso believed that the "face of the criminal, like those of most animals, is of disproportionate size." Other indicators that could separate delinquents from nondelinquents might also include outstanding ears and large frontal sinuses and jaws. Lombroso believed that these characteristics would not be found or were less prevalent among nondelinquents.

1. Search for an old class photo that was taken during your early elementary school years—for example, from kindergarten to sixth grade.

2. Share the class photo with a group of your peers, and ask them to predict, simply by looking at physical features, which juveniles became involved in delinquency or other problem behaviors throughout elementary, junior, and high school.

3. Assuming that you know about the delinquent or problematic behavior of your early schoolmates, inform the group what percentage of the time they were correct or incorrect about their predictions of delinquency based on physical characteristics.

4. If, in fact, some predictions were correct, does this lend support to the idea that physical features are a good way to distinguish delinquents from nondelinquents? Explain.

Source: Gina Lombroso-Ferrero, *Lombroso's Criminal Man* (Montclair, NJ: Patterson Smith, 1972), 12.

Body-Type Theories

Body-type theories are another section of biological determinism related to physical characteristics. According to body-type theorists, certain body structures are more likely to be associated with crime and delinquency. One of the best known of the body-type theorists was William Sheldon. In 1949, Sheldon and his colleagues examined the body types of some 200 delinquent offenders who had been incarcerated in a Boston juvenile institution and compared them to subjects from an earlier study on male college students. Sheldon concluded that mesomorphs (muscular persons, with big bones and strong bodies) were more likely to be delinquent than endomorphs (soft and round body types) or ectomorphs (tall and thin body types).[17]

Sheldon and Eleanor Glueck conducted a similar study on 500 delinquents incarcerated at the Lyman School for Boys in Westboro, Massachusetts, and compared them to 500 nondelinquents during the same time period. The Gluecks found that almost two times the number of delinquent boys were mesomorphs compared to their sample of nondelinquents. They concluded that body type was one of several factors contributing to delinquency, reasoning that mesomorphs are perhaps more delinquent because they are more likely to possess the characteristics and traits associated with the ability to successfully commit crime (strength, speed, aggressiveness).[18]

Genetic Influences

Perhaps one of the most interesting of the biological explanations of crime comes from family-type theories and genetic explanations. Family-type theories received attention in the late 1800s and suggested that the roots of crime are found in mentally and socially "bankrupt" or "degenerate" families. It is from these degenerate "family trees" that crime is transmitted or inherited through bad genes; therefore, crime is not the product of free will, physical stigmata, or the environment.[19]

Two of the most well-known family-type studies were conducted by Richard Dugdale, who studied the "Jukes" family, and Henry Goddard, who studied the Kallikaks (the Jukes family name was fictitious). The procedure used in both studies was to trace the ancestry of a particular individual or individuals to explain crime or other "immoral" behavior as a result of defective genes produced by "bad breeding."[20] One instance of bad breeding (for example, a child from a "feebleminded" woman), according to family-type theorists, could result in a chain reaction of bad genes being passed to successive generations.

Any theory attempting to link heredity and genes to criminality has to deal with environmental influences, and later studies attempted to isolate the influence of heredity from the environment. Perhaps the most precise way to study the influence of heredity on delinquency—while still considering environmental influences—is to examine twin behavior and the behavior of children adopted at birth. Twin and adoption studies enjoyed prominence in the 1970s, with researchers trying to determine whether nature (genes/heredity) or nurture (environment) has the most influence on a person's behavior—including delinquency.

In twin studies, researchers evaluate the heredity hypothesis by examining the similarity (or concordance) in behavior among identical twins or by comparing the concordance in behavior among identical and fraternal twins. In the second example, if heredity dictates behavior, identical twins should have a higher concordance rate than fraternal twins because identical twins are genetically identical. But if the behavior of identical twins is significantly different, or if identical twin concordance is low or similar to that of fraternal twins, it might be concluded that the environment has more influence than heredity does. This line of thought is problematic. For example, if identical twins act the same, it is not necessarily evidence of nature over nurture because identical twins raised in the same environment may act the same as a result of being reared the same—not necessarily because of the influence of exact genes. Moreover, even if identical twins act more alike than fraternal twins, this could also be explained by environmental differences. For example, identical twins may act alike because they are treated equally by their parents whereas fraternal twins may act much differently because they may be treated differently by their parents. In this same line of reasoning, identical twins can act much differently from each other by being treated differently by their parents whereas fraternal twins can act alike by being treated the same by their parents. As can be seen, each perspective may be correct depending on how one views it.

A more precise way to isolate environment from heredity is to compare identical twins who are not raised in the same environment—in other words, those separated from each other immediately after birth. This kind of study is difficult because it is usually hard to find a large number of identical twins separated at birth or at any point in early life. However, researchers have conducted these studies, and they have generally found that despite being raised apart, identical twins show similarity in antisocial and other behavior. This conclusion offers some evidence for heredity as an explanation of behavior.[21] Again, however, isolating the impact of the environment is difficult even when identical twins are raised apart and demonstrate similar behaviors.[22] They may have been raised in two similar but separate environments, with those environments influencing twin behavior, not genes.

Adoption studies try to determine whether adopted children (who should have had little to no contact with their biological parents) act more like their adoptive parents or their biological parents in terms of criminality or other measurable behaviors. If heredity influences behavior, the assumption is that children separated from their biological parents at birth will act more like their biological parents (heredity) than their adoptive parents (environment). There is some support for the heredity link in studies that have examined the delinquency (or other behaviors) of adopted children compared to the criminality of their biological versus adoptive parents. In short, some studies have found that adopted children act more like their biological parents than their adoptive parents. However, the bottom line in both twin and adoption studies is that researchers usually have a difficult time determining if the behavior is actually the product of heredity or whether the immediate environment is most influential. For example, an adopted child may become criminal like his or her biological parents, but this finding might be a result of the influence of adoptive parents who may be criminal as well.

It is difficult to determine whether defective genes and related hereditary factors are more important than the influence of the environment in which an individual is raised or lives, leading some to conclude that crime (or any behavior) is not necessarily the sole result of bad genes or strictly the environment, but rather that a person's biological makeup may dictate how he or she *responds* to a particular social situation. According to Diana Fishbein, a person's heredity may provide a predisposition to act a certain way in a certain situation.[23] Thus, a combination of biology and the social environment (sociobiology or biosocial criminology) probably determines individual behavior, including delinquency.

Other Biological Perspectives

Different biological explanations of delinquency have been proposed. Some explanations point to the presence of an extra Y chromosome (male chromosome) thought to produce a person more predisposed to crime and delinquency (a "supermale"). This view enjoyed a degree of popularity in the 1950s and 1960s. Contemporary versions of this theoretical line claim that higher levels of testosterone or other chemical imbalances may be responsible for delinquency. An example is that persons with low arousal become hyperactive to a point where they must stimulate their system, leading to delinquency. Other perspectives focus on problems associated with the central nervous system, neurotransmitters, and other biologically based factors.[24]

The significance of the early positive school explanations of behavior and the more contemporary versions lies in the importance given to factors outside of rational choice. Positivists found the root causes of crime and delinquency as a product of individual problems or environmental forces that are out of the control of the individual. The early positivist movement spurred intellectual debate about the causes of crime and, as a result, laid the foundation for a juvenile court that would draw a distinction between children and adults. The juvenile court was based on the premise that children were different from adults and less responsible for their actions. Their delinquency was a product mainly of factors outside of their control. They could be trained, treated, and rehabilitated, but they should not be punished like rational adults. Because their delinquency was a symptom of another underlying problem, it was the duty of the juvenile court, like a physician for a patient, to identify, treat, and cure the problem or problems that led to delinquency.[25]

Psychological Explanations of Delinquency

Psychological theories explain delinquency as the result of the psychological attributes of a person instead of his or her biological makeup. One of the most influential individuals in the psychological tradition was psychiatrist Sigmund Freud, the creator of psychoanalytic theory.

Freud believed that a person possesses three components of personality: the *id* (desire for things, primitive instincts), the *ego* (the part of personality that organizes and decides between choices and alternatives), and the *superego* (a person's conscience, which suppresses impulses). According to Freud, personality is set by the age of five. Whether or not the id, ego, and superego properly develop depends on parental rearing in these early years.[26] Improper formation of the id, ego, and superego can result in delinquency because all three parts will not work together properly. For example, someone with a defective superego may not be able to suppress the gratification desires of the id: Instead of working, that person may steal. The superego in this case would be considered underdeveloped. On the other hand, an overdeveloped superego might result in intense feelings of guilt and shame, causing someone to be involved in crime because he or she desires punishment to alleviate intense feelings of guilt.[27]

As an explanation of crime and delinquency, psychoanalytic theory is problematic. Perhaps the greatest criticism is that the id, ego, and superego are not measurable. Although Freud's theory is appealing as an explanation of delinquency and other behaviors, the inability to measure these concepts leads some to question whether anyone has ever seen an id, ego, or superego. Despite these problems, however, Freud invited awareness to the idea that the delinquent and his or her circumstances, not his or her act, should be the focus of the study of behavior. In sum, the cause of delinquency is not a "choice" but rather a consequence or "symptom" of faulty psychological makeup.[28] If delinquency is not a choice, then it does not make sense to punish a juvenile for an act that is not necessarily his or her fault. Such thinking was embraced by sociologists in the first quarter of the 1900s. It led to the development of explanations of delinquency that found the causes of crime in the juvenile's community and environment instead of in rational choice, physical traits, bad genes, or other faulty biological or psychological development.

Sociological Explanations of Delinquency

Social Disorganization Theory

In social disorganization theory, Clifford Shaw and Henry McKay theorized that something about the characteristics of certain "places or locations" contributes to delinquency. To Shaw and McKay, the roots of delinquency are not found within biological abnormalities or psychological problems but in the characteristics of urban areas. They believed there was something about certain neighborhoods where children lived that produced delinquency.

Shaw and McKay collected data from the Cook County Juvenile Court (the first juvenile court in the world) and plotted the rates of delinquency on a map of Chicago. They found that the highest rates of delinquency could be found in inner urban areas (such as near the business district, railroads, and red-light districts) as opposed to the suburbs. Shaw and McKay concluded that higher rates of delinquency were found here, as opposed to suburbs, not because of the people in them but because the areas were "socially disorganized."

Some evidence for this theory was found when Shaw and McKay discovered that delinquency rates remained high in certain central-city areas *despite an almost complete turnover of the area's population.* This finding was documented for more than four decades in Chicago, from 1900 to the 1940s. Specifically, researchers found that when groups from high delinquency areas moved to the suburbs, the delinquency rate did not follow them. According to Shaw and

McKay, delinquency cannot be a result of the people in central-city areas. If it was the people, their delinquency rate should increase as these groups moved to the suburbs. Because this did not happen, Shaw and McKay focused on the characteristics of the inner-city areas and neighborhoods.[29] They believed that "the explanation for delinquency . . . lies in the kind of community life that deteriorated neighborhoods *produce,* not in the kinds of people who live in them" (italics added).[30]

To understand social disorganization theory, one must understand Chicago in the early to mid-1900s. Chicago was characterized by a massive influx of immigrants from different ethnic cultures. The first wave of immigrants consisted of Germans, Irish, and English. These groups were followed by others, such as the Italians and the Poles. These groups were tightly bound by ethnicity and tended to live together and move together. As immigration continued in Chicago, "the newest immigrants were the poorest and so helped to push the earlier inhabitants into more stable working-class areas."[31] For example, the Irish would move to the suburbs once the Italians arrived. Because the Italians had just arrived in America, they became the inhabitants of inner-city areas because they were the poorest. This constant influx of the poorest populations to the inner-city areas of Chicago contributed to slum conditions, high population density, poverty, and severe social deterioration. Shaw and McKay suggested that these massive migration patterns from urban to suburban areas prevented community identity and a sense of cohesion among inner-city members because residents left the inner city as soon as possible. This situation led to other breakdowns, such as in schools and families, and inner-city neighborhoods eventually became "socially disorganized" and were characterized by the inability to use informal social control to regulate their members.[32] In essence, there was no sense of community because individuals had no allegiance to the inner-city neighborhood—from which they would leave at the earliest opportunity. This absence of community led to deteriorated neighborhoods, a breakdown of social institutions such as the family and schools, and ultimately what Shaw and McKay labeled "social disorganization." Socially disorganized neighborhoods could not produce informal social control to suppress delinquency.

Shaw and McKay did not advocate "environmental determinism," suggesting instead that the conditions in urban areas made delinquency a "normal" as opposed to an "abnormal" choice.[33] Once people moved from socially disorganized areas, delinquency became an abnormal choice because when conditions improved, people would establish longer-term residence, and social institutions such as schools and families would become stronger and be able to attain a degree of informal social control. Social disorganization theory places the root causes of delinquency in the environment rather than attributing delinquency to individual defects or anomalies. This idea led to further research that focused on environmental forces as the causes of delinquency.

Strain Theory

Merton's Social Structure and Anomie   In the late 1930s, Robert Merton theorized that crime and delinquency were a response to the social structure in American society. Whereas Shaw and McKay explained delinquency as a product of "socially disorganized" neighborhoods, Merton believed that delinquency could be explained by the immense pressure that society puts on individuals to behave in a certain way. He argued that the culture of American society places a disproportionate emphasis on monetary success (popularly known as the American Dream) but that the social structure in American society does not provide everyone equal access to socially approved "means" to obtain this success (for example, equal access to education). This gap between the goals of society and socially approved means to achieve those goals results in "strain," or "anomie." According to Merton, individuals may engage in crime and delinquency to deal with this social strain.[34]

Merton developed a typology describing how individuals may "adapt" to the gap between the goals and the means in society. Individuals who accept the cultural goals of society and have access to the means to obtain these goals are viewed as "conformists." These individuals conform to the law because they believe in the goals of society and—more importantly—because they have access to sufficient means to reach societal goals. Merton's second adaptation is "innovation." Innovators subscribe to the American Dream but are not able to attain it because they do not have access to socially approved means (a good job, education, or access to a good education). Therefore, innovators turn to crime and delinquency as ways to obtain the American Dream. For example, if one aspect of the American Dream is to have a new pair of expensive and trendy shoes (a sign of wealth), the innovator will steal the new shoes as opposed to working and saving enough money to pay for them. Merton also believed that some individuals may simply reject the goals of society but still maintain allegiance to socially approved means. Merton called them "ritualists" and the adaptation as "ritualism." Ritualists are not necessarily criminals or delinquents but instead are characterized as those who "go through the motions" but have no real ability or desire to reach the American Dream. A fourth adaptation is "retreatism." Retreatists reject the goals and the socially approved means of society and essentially drop out as a result of their strain. Persons such as drug addicts or "hobos" might be characterized as retreatists— they simply quit trying to attain the American Dream and become social outcasts.* Finally, Merton explained that a last adaptation—"rebellion"—is characterized by the complete rejection of the goals and means of mainstream society. People who rebel are different from retreatists in that these individuals construct or substitute their own goals and means.[35] An example might be David Koresh and the Branch Davidians in Waco, Texas, who created their own goals and means that were dramatically separate from the approved goals and means of the larger society.

Merton's theory is popular because it highlights some obvious structural differences in access to legitimate opportunities in American society and how such differences could lead someone to turn to crime and delinquency. Although his theory primarily applied to adult crime, the central ideas of his theory can and have been applied to juvenile delinquency. One application specific to juveniles was made by Albert Cohen in the 1950s.

*See www.hobo.com for information on hobos and the National Hobo Convention, held in Britt, Iowa, every August.

Cohen's Status and Acceptance   Albert Cohen built on Merton's concept of strain and argued that children, especially lower-class children, do not have equal ability and resources to compete and gain status in conventional society and that this situation produces strain.[36] Thus, whereas Merton believed strain comes from a gap between goals and means, Cohen viewed strain as the "inability to gain status and acceptance in conventional society."[37] Cohen believed that strain from the inability to gain status and acceptance could lead to delinquency.

Cohen said that status and acceptance in society are based on the values and standards espoused by the middle class. For children, status and acceptance are primarily attained from teachers and peers in schools—a place where children spend most of their day and a place with a heavy emphasis on middle-class values, such as how to talk, walk, work, defer to authority, dress, and behave in general. Although status and acceptance are attained in schools based on middle-class values, Cohen believed that there were differences among social classes in society with respect to these values and behaviors. One difference was found in parenting styles, discipline, and general socialization between lower-class and middle-class parents. In comparing both groups, Cohen concluded that parents from the middle class were more strict and demanding than parents from the lower class, whom he characterized as "relatively easy-going."[38] This lax lower-class parenting style would then transfer to the behavior of lower-class children. For example, lax parenting may mean that lower-class children have difficulty following rules established by authority figures. Yet, when lower-class children enter the school grounds, they find themselves subject to a number of rules based on middle-class standards that may not mesh with the life that they lead. Despite the differences in values, at school lower-class children are nonetheless judged by the **middle-class measuring rod.**

Youths from the lower class enter an arena where they may gain status and recognition by peers and teachers only by measuring up to standards different from their own—middle-class standards.[39] When lower-class children find that they cannot compete under this middle-class standard, they experience "status frustration." Cohen believed that lower-class children become frustrated because they want middle-class status despite being from the lower class. When they fail to measure up, the status frustration can lead to a complete denial of middle-class values and everything for which the middle class stands. The result for some is a "reaction formation" whereby lower-class children turn to a delinquent subculture.[40] The delinquent subculture provides them status and acceptance that they could not otherwise obtain when judged by the middle-class measuring rod.[41] For example, whereas the middle-class standard abhors fighting, disorder, and disrespect, the delinquent culture can embrace such behavior as a way for the most violent, disorderly, and disrespectful to gain the most status. See Exhibit 2.3, which discusses status and acceptance in schools in relation to middle-class values.

Cohen believed that subscribing to a delinquent subculture was one of only three paths for lower-class youths. Similar to Merton's adaptations, Cohen said that lower-class youths could adapt in two additional ways outside of being delinquent and subscribing to a delinquent subculture. The first is to become a "corner boy." Corner boys "may have a few minor scrapes with the law, but in

EXHIBIT 2.3

Status and Acceptance in School and Their Relation to Delinquency

School is a place where children will spend most of their day, may be away from their parents for the first time, and may be exposed to children from different cultures, races, and backgrounds. It is also the place where children may experience their first failures in the presence of someone other than parents or other family members.

It is not surprising that children seek acceptance and status among their peers—those who become a support system away from home. Children also may seek status and acceptance in the eyes of their teachers. Yet not all children will attain the same level of status and acceptance.

Schools generally operate under a model that emphasizes principles of standardization, routine, order, and predictability. For good reason, this may be the only way to teach a large batch of diverse children in such a way that they may learn effectively. According to Albert Cohen in 1955, values of standardization, routine, order, and predictability in schools align most closely with values of the middle class. This is not to say that those in the lower class or the upper class do not also value standardization and order but rather that standardization and order in the lower class and upper class may be different from standardization and order in the middle class. Because schools rely heavily on middle-class values, those who do not act accordingly may be blocked from gaining status and acceptance. Thus, although everyone in school is judged by the same standard for status and acceptance, it is possible that not all children are able to meet this standard. Cohen says that this situation may lead to status frustration and delinquency among lower-class children who have not measured up to the middle-class measuring rod.

1. What are your thoughts about status and acceptance in schools as these factors relate to juvenile delinquency?

2. Do you believe that the values of the lower class and the values of the middle class differ substantially when it comes to school-related behaviors such as respect for authority, dress, talk, and general behavior? What about the upper class versus the middle class?

3. Albert Cohen was writing in the 1950s. Do you believe that his perspective has relevance today? Explain.

---

the main, they will acquire a limited education, a blue-collar job, and a family, and will eventually become stable members of working class society."[42] Cohen believed that the corner-boy response was the most common path for lower-class boys. The second response, other than being a delinquent or a corner boy, was the "college boy." College boys were those who were able to "escape" the lower class and become "the few lower-class boys who go on to college and play the game of life according to middle-class rules."[43]

Merton's strain theory focused on crime and delinquency as a response to the inability to obtain the accepted goals of society because of a lack of access to legitimate means, and Cohen's version of strain viewed delinquency as the inability to gain status and acceptance in the middle class, focusing primarily on lower-class boys. More recent perspectives of strain theory are at the social-psychological level and see delinquency resulting from several sources of strain and occurring in all social classes.[44]

Agnew's General Strain Theory   In 1992, Robert Agnew proposed that there are three major types of strain. The first type is characterized as the failure to achieve positively valued goals (closely related to Merton's theory).[45] Within this first category of strain are three subdivisions: (1) strain as the gap between what someone "aspires" to achieve and what he or she actually achieves, (2) strain from a gap between what someone "expects" to achieve and what he or she actually achieves, and (3) strain from a gap between what one considers a just or fair outcome to the actual outcome. For example, a student may exert tremendous effort toward getting good grades and expect to earn an *A*. If that student actually receives a *B*, he or she might experience strain because the expectation to achieve (see #2 above) does not mesh with what he or she actually received.

The second major type of strain results when something that is positively valued by an individual is removed. For example, the removal of positive stimuli for a juvenile might be the loss of a girlfriend or boyfriend, moving to a new school district, or a divorce in the family.[46]

A third major type of strain is the presentation of negative stimuli. These stimuli could be such strains as bullying from another peer or negative relations with parents or teachers.

The appeal of Agnew's version of strain theory is that it helps to answer a basic question: Why don't all individuals who experience strain engage in crime and delinquency to be relieved of it? To answer this, Agnew says that whether or not someone who is strained engages in crime and delinquency depends on a number of factors, such as the amount of strain (how much discomfort it brings), how recent the strain is, how long the strain lasts, and if multiple events of strain are occurring at the same time. Logically, strain is more influential the greater it is, the more recent it is, if it is longer in duration, and if several events of strain occur at once. Thus, not all forms of strain are alike; some strains are "worse" than others.

Agnew also says that only some strained individuals will turn to delinquency and that this outcome depends on the presence or absence of coping mechanisms. Some coping mechanisms are cognitive, such as the ability for juveniles to ignore or minimize the strain, maximize the positives of strain, or accept responsibility for the strain. For example, a juvenile may minimize the strain of a loss of a boyfriend by claiming that he was really not that important or may simply accept responsibility for the strain by believing that "I did not deserve him anyway." In this way, the cognitive coping mechanism would be to simply lower the standard by which the individual previously operated (the boyfriend was not that important, handsome, or smart, or he was out of my league anyway). Other coping mechanisms are behavioral, such as maximizing the positive and minimizing the negative through some form of action. For example, a student is bullied and experiences strain. This student may transfer to another school to avoid getting bullied, thus minimizing the negative stimuli. Another behavioral coping mechanism is to seek revenge. For example, the student getting bullied may seek revenge in a number of ways, such as spreading rumors about the bully or, at the extreme, confronting the bully with a weapon. Finally, Agnew proposes that people can deal with strain by engaging in emotional coping mechanisms to escape it, such as drug use, physical exercise, or meditation.[47]

How someone adapts to strain depends on the ability of the individual to use enough coping mechanisms to deal with the strain constructively. When coping mechanisms are not sufficient or not available, an individual may engage in crime and delinquency out of anger or frustration. Agnew's general strain theory is appealing because it draws from both the sociological and psychological literature and presents a commonsense explanation of why someone becomes involved in crime and delinquency. It also extends Merton's and Cohen's versions of strain because it can explain crime and delinquency for the middle and upper classes. Because of its appeal, it has been the subject of much research in the last several years.

Differential Association and Social Learning Theory

Sutherland's Differential Association Theory   Whereas Shaw and McKay attribute delinquency to social disorganization, and Merton, Cohen, and Agnew explain delinquency as a response to strain, Edwin Sutherland attributes delinquency to learning. His theory of differential association was first published in 1934, appeared in full form in 1939, and since 1947 has remained unchanged.[48] Here are the nine statements of Sutherland's differential association theory:

1. Criminal [delinquent] behavior is learned.
2. Criminal behavior is learned in interaction with other persons in a process of communication.
3. The principal part of learning of criminal behavior occurs within intimate personal groups.
4. When criminal behavior is learned, the learning includes (a) techniques of committing the crime, which are sometimes very complicated, sometimes very simple; (b) the specific direction of motives, drives, rationalizations, and attitudes.
5. The specific direction of motives and drives is learned from definitions of the legal codes as favorable or unfavorable.
6. A person becomes delinquent because of an excess of definitions favorable to violation of law over definitions unfavorable to violation of law.
7. Differential associations may vary in frequency, duration, priority, and intensity.
8. The process of learning criminal behavior by association with criminal and anti-criminal patterns involves all of the mechanisms that are involved in any other learning.
9. While criminal behavior is an expression of general needs and values, it is not explained by those general needs and values since non-criminal behavior is an expression of the same needs and values.[49]

The key components of differential association theory are that delinquent behavior is learned behavior in a process of communication with primary influences, such as friends. According to Sutherland, a person becomes delinquent because he or she has been exposed to more "definitions favorable to violation of law" than definitions that are "unfavorable to violation of law."[50] In this context, *definitions* means "rationalizations and attitudes for or against criminal behavior." Sutherland was essentially saying that "the distinction between lawbreakers and the law-abiding lies not in their personal fiber but in the content of what they have learned."[51]

Differential association theory is commonly misinterpreted to mean that people who associate with delinquent peers will become delinquent. According to the theory, people can learn criminal and noncriminal definitions from *anyone*. So the theory is not necessarily about associations *per se*, but instead the definitions learned from those associations. For example, it might be possible to learn noncriminal definitions from a criminal (for example, as in the Scared Straight program), whereas one may also be able to learn criminal definitions from a noncriminal. However, note that associations can be important in learning: Those who associate with delinquents may be more likely to receive definitions favorable to law violation than those who associate with nondelinquents. Although associations are important, to Sutherland the key is in the definitions learned from associations, regardless of whether the associates are criminal or noncriminal.

Moreover, not all associations and definitions are equal, and Sutherland noted that there are certain factors that may make the source of definitions more important than others. He explained, somewhat vaguely, that differential associations may vary based on frequency, duration, priority, and intensity. In other words, associations (and definitions from associations) are more influential if they are more frequent (frequency), go on for longer periods of time (duration), occur earlier in a person's life or come from those to whom the individual was exposed first (priority), and are more intense—meaning that definitions from "prestigious sources" (such as close friends or parents) are more important than from occasional acquaintances (intensity).[52] This perspective may explain, for example, why most correctional officers do not become criminals. Although they are exposed to criminal influence, these relationships are not usually important (intensity), nor do such criminal definitions usually come early in an officer's life (priority). The previous example reinforces the idea that differential association theory is much more than a theory about bad companions.

Akers's Social Learning Theory   Differential association theory remains one of the most influential theories of delinquency. Like all theoretical perspectives, however, it has shortcomings. For example, Sutherland never explained the specific mechanisms of learning, and some concepts, such as "definitions favorable to law violation," are unclear and sometimes difficult to define. Thus, it is hard to ascertain whether someone who became delinquent actually had a balance of definitions more favorable to law violation than not.[53]

Because of these and other problems, in 1966 Robert Burgess and Ronald Akers reformulated Sutherland's differential association theory to include concepts from behavioral learning theory such as operant conditioning.[54] They retained certain of Sutherland's concepts and ideas, such as "definitions favorable to law violation," and they reformulated the theory to clarify the learning process. Social learning theory explains that delinquent behavior results when individuals associate with others who commit criminal behavior and espouse definitions favorable to it, are relatively more exposed . . . to salient criminal/deviant models, define it as desirable or justified in a situation . . . and have received in the past and anticipate in the current or future situation relatively greater reward than punishment for the behavior.[55]

Burgess and Akers suggest that for delinquency to occur, learning definitions favorable to law violation is necessary, but it is not sufficient to explain why someone chooses a delinquent path. As indicated above, learning definitions favorable to law violation will result in delinquency only when rewards received in the past, or that the individual may expect to receive in the future, are greater than past or current punishments for delinquent behavior. Thus, whether individuals become delinquent "depends on past, present, and anticipated future rewards and punishments for their actions."[56] This statement has its roots in the behavioral learning tradition, which suggests that when actual or anticipated rewards are greater than actual or anticipated punishment, a behavior will be increased or continued because it is reinforced with positive outcomes.

Social Bonding/Control Theory

Social bonding theory explains that delinquency results from the absence of controls by or bonds to society. (This theory is sometimes referred to as social control theory but is actually only one type of control theory.) In contrast to other sociological theories that attempt to explain why people commit crime, social bonding attempts to answer the question "Why doesn't everyone commit crime?" The answer is that people are bonded to society. Only when these bonds are weakened or broken do individuals engage in delinquency.*

Travis Hirschi developed social bonding theory in 1969 in his book *Causes of Delinquency*.[57] He explained that four elements constitute an individual's bond to society: attachment, commitment, involvement, and belief. *Attachment* to "conventional others" (such as parents, schools, and peers) means that individuals are less likely to engage in delinquency the more they are "attached" to others whom they respect or admire. Individuals attached to conventional others avoid delinquency because they do not want to disappoint these persons. *Commitment* is the degree to which individuals are invested in things they value. It is often referred to as having a "stake in conformity": a reason not to become involved in delinquency. Individuals with more to lose, in other words, are less likely to engage in delinquency. According to Hirschi, an individual "must consider . . . the risk he runs of losing the investment he has made in conventional behavior."[58] *Involvement* means that the more involved one is in conventional activities, such as sports, family, and school, the less likely the individual is to become delinquent. This element of the bond is interpreted to mean that individuals who have many things going on do not have time to become delinquent. The final element of Hirschi's theory is *belief*, or the

---

*Not all control theorists begin with the assumption that everyone is ready and willing to become involved in crime and delinquency in the absence of broken or weakened bonds. See, for example, Ronald Akers, *Criminological Theories*, 3rd ed. (Los Angeles: Roxbury, 2000), 99–100.

extent to which individuals subscribe to general laws and rules, and understand that these should be followed.[59]

Hirschi assumed that individuals are more or less naturally motivated to break the law. Thus, when an individual's bond to society is weakened or broken, the assumption is that he or she would engage in crime because there is no longer a bond holding him or her back from the natural motivation to break the law. However, one weak or broken element of the bond may not necessarily make a person delinquent. For example, a weak belief system may not result in delinquency because of strong attachment and commitment. However, Hirschi acknowledged that one weak or broken bond is likely an indication that other bonds are weakened or broken because all the bonds are related.[60] Therefore, juveniles who have little attachment to conventional others such as parents, teachers, and peers are likely to be less committed to conventional activities, be less involved in conventional activities, and have less belief in conventional society's rules and laws. Hence, they are also more likely to become delinquent.

Labeling Theory

Labeling theory finds the causes of delinquency in a process of interaction with others. Labeling theory comes under the general title of "symbolic interactionism" or "societal reaction" because it is concerned with how social reactions to behaviors may influence future behaviors—including crime and delinquency. In sum, the theory holds that individuals may receive negative reactions and treatment as the result of their illegal, immoral, or unethical behavior. They may then be labeled. This labeling process can cause individuals to accept or internalize the label and ultimately become the label they have been given. Thus, it amounts to a self-fulfilling prophecy.

A major premise of labeling theory is that people can actually have "identity transformations" based on how others perceive and react to them. Edwin Lemert explains this as a process that involves primary and secondary deviance.[61] Primary deviance refers to a number of immoral, unethical, or illegal acts that do not affect an individual's self-concept.[62] The "primary deviant" does not consider himself or herself a deviant as a "master status" despite the potential of negative social reactions.[63] For example, a juvenile who is involved in a fight in school might be considered a rule violator but does not identify with the label of a "bully" or "troublemaker." Although fighting may receive a negative social reaction from teachers and peers, the negative social reaction to primary deviance is not something that would cause the person to accept or internalize a deviant label. However, if acts of primary deviance continue, the individual may receive more intense negative reactions, such as stereotyping, labeling, and name-calling.[64] Moreover, the stigma of the label may result in being treated in a way consistent with the label. For example, the fighting juvenile may be labeled a bully and, more importantly, get treated as a bully. The bully might be forced to go to an alternative school, be called names by his or her peers, or get treated with caution by teachers.

Negative social reactions to repeated primary deviance, such as those described above, could result in an individual believing that he or she actually is a bully and accept that as a master status.[65] This identity transformation can result in secondary deviance, which is deviance resulting from an internalized label. Thus, secondary deviance is that which results in response to continued negative reactions and treatment from others; it "becomes a means of defense, attack, or adaptation to the . . . problems created by the societal reaction to primary deviation."[66] Viewed in this way, the cause of delinquency is found in the reactions of others to the person who is labeled. As Akers comments, "persons take on deviant identities and play deviant roles because they are strongly influenced, if not overtly coerced, into doing so by the application of stigmatizing labels to them."[67] In short, if you label someone a delinquent and treat the person accordingly, he or she may begin to believe this label and react by fulfilling this role, acting in a self-fulfilling prophecy.

The labeling perspective is important to the juvenile justice system, process, and law because one of the foundations of the separate juvenile court was that it be structured to protect juveniles from stigmatizing labels and actions by the juvenile system, based on the belief that negative labels produce stigma and may contribute to further delinquency (or secondary deviance). Although confidentiality restrictions have today been eroded for some juvenile offenders (mainly for serious and violent juveniles), there is still a strong emphasis on protecting the confidentiality of most juveniles because doing so is believed to promote rehabilitation. There also still exists a major emphasis on limiting escalation into the formal juvenile system for most juvenile offenders by using diversion and other informal programs to avoid such stigmatizing official labels as "delinquent." Most juvenile offending is of the sort that Lemert referred to as primary deviance—actions that many people engage in at one point or another in their lives but that do not justify an internalized label. Labeling theory sees that the further the juvenile goes into the justice system, the more likely that he or she will adopt or internalize the identity of a "deviant," "delinquent," or "bad kid" and begin to fill the role which that label describes. Although labeling theory and the societal reaction perspective have flaws, these theoretical perspectives have tremendously influenced the way the juvenile justice system works.

Conflict Theory

Conflict theory holds that crime and delinquency are a result of conflict between competing interests in society, usually between those who have power and those who do not. Akers notes that conflict theory explains crime as an expression of conflict that "results when persons acting according to the norms and values of their own group violate those of another group that have been enacted into law."[68] Vold and colleagues explain that criminal behavior is identified with the "behavior of minority power groups."[69] The struggle of these "minority power groups" amounts to a conflict that violates the rules and laws of the powerful.

Conflict theory as applied to delinquency focuses on the roles that powerful entities (such as the government) play in the criminal behavior of certain populations in society. For example, conflict theory is used to explain the disproportionate representation of minority juveniles in all stages of the juvenile justice system, particularly in secure detention and other juvenile lockups. But conflict theory also addresses power differentials in society and how those with power effectively define what is and is not criminal, to whom or what the law should be enforced, and to what extent the powerful create conditions that contribute to crime among those without power.[70] This theory is sometimes difficult to relate to delinquency because unlike most other sociological theories, it suggests that crime and delinquency are the result of larger structural realities in society, implying that delinquency may actually be a desired outcome for certain segments of society.

Developmental and Life-Course Perspectives

In the last several years a number of perspectives have appeared called "developmental" or "life-course" theories, and they borrow from existing biological, psychological, and sociological theories in an attempt to explain delinquent and similar antisocial behaviors throughout a person's life. This section reviews a few of the more popular perspectives in this tradition: Michael Gottfredson and Travis Hirschi's perspective on low self-control, Terrie Moffitt's developmental taxonomy, and Robert Sampson and John Laub's perspective on delinquency and change over the life course.

Gottfredson and Hirschi's General Theory of Crime

In their book *A General Theory of Crime,* Michael Gottfredson and Travis Hirschi say that crime and delinquency result from "low self-control."[71] They explain that low self-control occurs when parents fail to properly raise their children. Low self-control develops in the "absence of nurturance, discipline, or training."[72] When parents fail to *monitor* their child's behavior, fail to *recognize* problem behavior when it occurs, and fail to *punish* such behavior properly, their child will be less capable of delaying gratification, less interested in other people's feelings, and more likely to use force or violence to get something rather than being willing to compromise and talk.[73]

For people with low self-control, crime is a logical outcome because it is "easy" to commit, it requires few special skills, and opportunities for it are abundant. Gottfredson and Hirschi maintain that individuals with low self-control will constantly be involved in delinquency and other problem behaviors because these provide such shortsighted individuals with immediate gratification. In other words, individuals with low self-control will "endlessly succumb to life's temporary temptations . . . will constantly engage in crime and other forms of deviance."[74] To Gottfredson and Hirschi, a delinquent or antisocial path is locked in for those who have not developed self-control at a young age, and any prospect for change from this path is unlikely. Low self-control becomes a constant in life, and its presence can be demonstrated by delinquent or antisocial behaviors throughout that person's existence.

Moffitt's Dual Taxonomy

In 1993, Terrie Moffitt proposed that there are two distinct types of delinquents: life-course-persistent and adolescence-limited:

> There are marked individual differences in the stability of antisocial behavior. Many people behave antisocially, but their antisocial behavior is *temporary*

and situational. In contrast, the antisocial behavior of some people is very *stable and persistent.*[75] (italics added)

Drawing from neuropsychology, developmental psychology, and tenets of sociological theory, Moffitt explains that certain adolescents have deficits in intellectual, motor, executive, and social skills that manifest in characteristics such as impulsivity, hyperactivity, difficulty in reading and problem solving, poor memory, and low verbal IQ. These characteristics supposedly lead to persistent problematic behavior throughout the life course, hence the label "life-course-persistent." Life-course-persistent youths differ from other youths (called adolescence-limited) because their delinquency and other antisocial behaviors are not viewed as a temporary response to certain situations, but rather as the result of problems that begin early and continue throughout life. According to Moffitt, life-course-persistent youths

> exhibit changing manifestations of antisocial behavior: biting and hitting at age 4, shoplifting and truancy at age 10, selling drugs and stealing cars at age 16, robbery and rape at age 22, and fraud and child abuse at age 30; the underlying disposition remains the same, but its expression changes form as new social opportunities arise at different points in development.[76]

Life-course-persistent behavior is prompted by early neuropsychological deficits and remains persistent throughout life as a result of a chain reaction consisting of the interplay among early neuropsychological deficits, failed parental interactions resulting from deficits, and a process of accumulating social consequences for these youths as they age (called cumulative consequences).[77] Moffitt explains that children with neuropsychological deficits are more likely to have parents who are not equipped to deal with them effectively (and who may even have the same neuropsychological problems). She then suggests that even the best parents (those who are patient, loving, and with adequate resources) would have difficulty dealing with children with such deficits. The inability of parents to deal with their child results in a chain of failed parental–child reactions that serves to exacerbate instead of alleviate problems.

Moffitt adds that as children with such deficits enter the social world (for example, day care, preschool, and elementary, junior, and high school), their antisocial and delinquent behavior will result in negative and compounding social consequences. She refers to this as a process of cumulative consequences. This is a term which implies that problematic behavior starting early in a child's life will begin to snowball and grow as the child enters social situations such that the accumulating consequences of this behavior will offer little opportunity for the life-course-persistent child to change his or her path. For example, an adolescent who is constantly viewed as a discipline problem student from elementary to high school will likely miss out on educational opportunities as a result of grade failure, being held back from the age-appropriate grade, suspension, and perhaps expulsion. The outcome may be a limited education, which may result in the failure to obtain job opportunities. This situation might then lead to other negative outcomes, such as drug use, delinquency, crime, and interactions with delinquent or criminal influences. Taken together, these consequences may "keep the person behind" to the point where he or she becomes a member of a smaller group of people who become heavily involved in antisocial, delinquent, and criminal behavior throughout their lives.[78]

At the other end of Moffitt's classification are adolescence-limited youths—a group thought to represent a much larger but less delinquent group of youths than life-course persisters. Moffitt says that adolescence-limited delinquent behavior occurs as a result of the gap between biological maturity and social maturity.[79] As opposed to life-course-persisters, adolescence-limited youths engage in delinquency and other antisocial behaviors as a sort of a rebellion against rules and restrictions. Delinquency for these youths is a temporary and situational effort to gain independence from parents or other authority figures; it becomes "an effective means of knifing-off childhood apron strings."[80] For these youths, delinquency is not a result of neuropsychological problems, early failed parental interactions, or cumulative consequences, but rather a response to a temporary situation. For example, a sixteen-year-old adolescence-limited youth might witness a sixteen-year-old life-course-persistent youth smoking, having a sexual relationship, staying out late at night, and drinking beer. This freedom is tempting to the adolescence-limited offender, who is struggling with feelings of independence but is still bound by parental rules. The adolescence-limited youth may engage in delinquency and other antisocial behaviors to be free from the "apron strings," but this delinquency is situational and temporary. Once these temporary situations are removed, adolescence-limited youths will grow out of delinquency because

> adolescence-limited offenders had ample years to develop an accomplished repertoire of prosocial behaviors and basic academic skills. These social skills and academic achievements make them eligible for postsecondary education, good marriages, and desirable jobs.[81]

Sampson and Laub's Crime and the Life Course

The final perspective in the developmental or life-course tradition reviewed in this section is that by Robert Sampson and John Laub. In their 1993 book, *Crime in the Making: Pathways and Turning Points Through Life,* Sampson and Laub contend that individuals are not necessarily locked into a specific path through life to the degree that Gottfredson and Hirschi's low-self-control or Moffitt's life-course-persistent characterization suggests. Sampson and Laub believe instead that individuals at various points in their life can gain **social capital,** or a reason to avoid crime and change the direction of their life.[82]

Sampson and Laub's theory is interesting because it resulted from the resurrection of Sheldon and Eleanor Glueck's study of delinquent boys in the 1930s and 1940s. As discussed earlier in this chapter, the Gluecks examined 500 delinquents who were committed to the Lyman School for Boys in Westboro, Massachusetts, and compared them to 500 nondelinquents in the Boston area. In the mid-1980s, Sampson and Laub found the Gluecks' records in the basement of the Harvard Law School Library. Through painstaking reconstruction, Sampson and Laub contacted many of the surviving Lyman School boys and were able to construct their life histories up to the present day, which is approximately age 70 for the survivors.

Sampson and Laub wanted to see if and how delinquents could emerge from a delinquent path. One of the key findings of their research on the Lyman boys is that not all of them continued to be delinquent/criminal as they aged. Although Sampson and Laub noted that one of the best indicators of criminality in adulthood is whether someone was delinquent as a child, most antisocial and delinquent children do not actually become antisocial or criminal adults.[83] This basic but important finding led Sampson and Laub to conclude that change is possible for many and that a delinquent's former life circumstances do not "lock" him or her into a path of criminality as he or she ages into adulthood. They suggest that this change can be explained by bonds that can be formed at different periods in life. They emphasize that such bonds can be reaffirmed or renewed and that this strengthening of bonds results from certain events called transitions that may occur over the life course.

Sampson and Laub propose that individuals may gain "social capital" at various points in their life and that this social capital can result in turning away from crime and antisocial behavior as juveniles become adults. They maintain that individuals have a long-term trajectory called their "line of development." Individual trajectories may change as a result of shorter-term transitions. Transitions are described as life events embedded in long-term trajectories, including events such as getting married, joining the military, getting a good job, or having a child.[84] Sampson and Laub believe that the interplay between long-term trajectories and shorter-term transitions can result in a turning point where the individual might be redirected onto a different path. In short, transitions such as school, a good job, the military, marriage, and becoming a parent can lead to a different trajectory in life[85] because these transitions may build social capital. For example, someone who becomes married and has a child has more of an investment in avoiding criminal behavior.

The essence of Sampson and Laub's perspective is that certain life events may occur that change the trajectory of someone who is on a path to criminality. Again, Sampson and Laub's theory is not specific to delinquents but rather on how former delinquents can and do change their paths in adulthood. The importance of this theory lies in the recognition that someone who is delinquent today can change and become a productive citizen as an adult: Important transitions, such as getting married or becoming a parent, can result in social capital. Exhibit 2.4 allows you to evaluate the theories discussed in this section.

Delinquency Theories and the Juvenile Justice System, Process, and Law

This section has provided a general look at theories of "why" juveniles engage in delinquency. There have been many theoretical perspectives on this issue over the past two centuries. The main point to be remembered is that someone can become involved in delinquency for a number of reasons. All of the theories addressed above have something to contribute to explaining delinquency, but no single theory can fully explain it. Moreover, most theories explain delinquency in terms that are not concrete. For example, although being raised in a socially disorganized area or not being attached to conventional

EXHIBIT 2.4

Applying Theories of Delinquency

Some of the more typical forms of juvenile offending include acts such as simple assault, larceny-theft, drug abuse, vandalism, and disorderly conduct. Significantly less frequent acts committed by juveniles are murder, robbery, and burglary.

1. Which theory offers the best explanation for typical forms of juvenile offending? Explain.

2. Which theory offers the best explanation for less frequent but more serious forms of delinquency such as murder, robbery, and burglary? Explain.

3. Pick your favorite theory. Develop a list of the problems with this theory in explaining delinquency. Develop a second list of the advantages with this theory in explaining delinquency. In developing your lists, be sure to comment on whether your theory can explain all forms of crime (such as serious, nonserious, person, and property) for both male and female juveniles, and for youths from different socioeconomic statuses.

---

others may make someone "more likely" to become involved in delinquent behavior, it does not mean that everyone raised in a socially disorganized area will automatically become delinquent: There will always be exceptions. Thus, the best answer to "What causes juvenile delinquency?" may be "It just depends." Delinquency theories acquaint us with the many factors that may make delinquency more likely than not. One of the values of the various theories discussed above is that they indicate not only causes but also some avenues for dealing with these causes.

A look at delinquency theories is useful for the study of the juvenile justice system and its process. The juvenile justice system is built on assumptions about "why" juveniles become involved in delinquency. Knowledge about why juveniles offend is crucial because it provides the system a perspective on the best way to deal with the causes of delinquency. A system that deals only with symptoms is less effective than a system that also understands and responds to causes. See Table 2.1, which contains a general summary of the delinquency theories discussed in this chapter.

Measuring Juvenile Crime and Victimizations

This text contains many references to different findings on the extent of juvenile offending and victimizations; therefore, this section examines the major ways that juvenile crime and victimizations are counted in the United States. It also examines the advantages and disadvantages associated with these measures. As mentioned, specific attention to actual levels and trends in juvenile offending and victimization will be provided in chapters that concentrate on these subjects.

Juvenile offending and victimizations can be measured in several ways. The first way is through official data, which consists of two different types: the **Uniform Crime Reports (UCR)** and the **National Incident-Based**

TABLE 2.1

A General Summary of Theories of Juvenile Offending

Theoretical Perspective	Explanation of Delinquency
Demonological	Delinquency results from being possessed by the devil or falling to the temptations of the devil. Crime is equated with sin.
Classical school	Delinquency is a product of free will and rational choice that results when the perceived benefits of delinquency outweigh the consequences.
Positive school	Delinquency is attributed to physical characteristics, biological differences, or other factors that differentiate the delinquent from the nondelinquent.
Psychological	Delinquency is attributed to improper formation of the id, ego, and superego. Delinquency is considered a symptom of improper parenting that resulted in an underdeveloped or overdeveloped superego.
Social disorganization	Delinquency is the result of social disorganization caused by rapid immigration and migration patterns, poverty, urban decay, and the inability of community members to control their members through informal means.
Strain	*Merton:* Delinquency results from the gap between the socially approved goals of society and young people's access to legitimate means to obtain these goals. *Cohen:* Delinquency results from the inability of lower-class boys to "measure up" or gain status and acceptance based on middle-class values in schools. *Agnew:* Delinquency results from three sources of strain. Not all strained individuals will become delinquent; rather, a delinquent response to strain depends on the strain and its intensity and whether individuals have access to cognitive, behavioral, and emotional coping mechanisms.
Differential association	Delinquency is learned in intimate groups through a process of communication. Delinquency results when one is exposed to a greater balance of definitions favorable to law violation than unfavorable to law violation.
Social learning theory	Delinquency results when individuals associate with others who espouse definitions favorable to law violation, when important role models define delinquency as desirable, and when a person believes that the actual or anticipated rewards of delinquency are greater than the actual or anticipated punishment.
Social bonding/control theory	Delinquency results when someone's "bond" to society is weakened or broken. Four elements of the bond to society are attachment, commitment, involvement, and belief.
Labeling theory	Delinquency results from societal reactions to behaviors. When individuals are labeled, they may internalize the label, accept it as their new identity, and start to act in accordance with the label they have been given.
Conflict theory	Delinquency results from conflict between the powerful and the powerless. In general, conflict theory focuses on how the powerful define what is delinquent and not delinquent, to whom or what the law should be enforced, and the process whereby the powerful create conditions that contribute to delinquency.
Developmental and life-course perspectives	**Gottfredson and Hirschi:** Delinquency is a product of low self-control. Low self-control is formed by an early age when parents fail to monitor, recognize, and punish problematic behavior. **Moffitt:** There are two explanations for delinquency. One focuses on delinquency as a result of the interaction among neuropsychological deficits, failed parental interactions, and cumulative consequences. These youths are "life-course-persistent." The second focuses on "adolescence-limited" youths, who engage in delinquency as a way to gain independence from parental rules and restrictions in the mid-teen years. **Sampson and Laub:** Crime and delinquency result when one's bond to society is weakened or broken. Bonds can be reaffirmed. Long-term trajectories of a person can be altered through significant life events called transitions. Transitions can include marriage, a good job, a child, or joining the military. Transitions can build social capital or a reason to avoid crime. Transitions that build social capital can become turning points at which onetime delinquents modify their long-term trajectories toward a noncriminal path.

Reporting System (NIBRS). The UCR is a count of crimes reported and arrests made in the United States each year (the UCR can be examined at www.fbi.gov). It is considered an "official record" of crime because it is derived from official arrest records collected by law enforcement agencies. Since the UCR has a category indicating the age of persons arrested, it is a useful measure of juvenile crime. The second official record of crime is NIBRS, which acts as a supplement to the UCR and is currently not considered a stand-alone measure of crime. It was devised in the late 1980s as a response to certain criticisms of the UCR and includes much more detailed information about both offenders and victims.

A second way to measure juvenile crime is through **self-report surveys.** The logic here is that if you want to know about juvenile offending, ask juveniles. Numerous types of self-report studies are conducted each year. Unlike the UCR or NIBRS, self-report surveys are usually done on a much smaller scale, meaning they do not examine national levels of offending. Many times, although not always, self-report surveys are given to youths who are known delinquents—such as those in juvenile institutions. But self-report surveys are routinely given to juveniles who may or may not have incurred an official record—for example, children in school. Self-report surveys might also be administered to juvenile victims, asking them to report any victimization they have experienced. Used in this way, self-report surveys can be considered as a measure of offending and victimizations.

Another way to measure juvenile crime is to examine it through victimizations. The **National Crime Victimization Survey (NCVS)** is the best-known national survey that tracks victimizations among juveniles and adults in the United States. It is an annual survey of households and their occupants that asks about any victimizations they have experienced. Although it measures victimizations, the flip side is that information on offending can also be gleaned from these surveys.

When taken together, these measures give the best picture on juvenile crime and victimization in the United States.

Official Data

Official data are considered official because they are collected by agencies connected to cities, counties, states, and the federal government. This section focuses on two forms of official data: the UCR and NIBRS. The UCR and NIBRS are arguably the most comprehensive official U.S. data sources because they cover levels of crime across the nation.

Uniform Crime Reports (UCR)

Begun in 1930, the UCR is a national count of the number of crimes reported to law enforcement agencies and the number of arrests by law enforcement agencies each year. Information on crimes reported and arrests made is originally collected by 17,000 law enforcement agencies in the United States. These agencies cover approximately 95 percent of the entire U.S. population. Once these agencies have a count of crimes reported and arrests, they send reports to the Federal Bureau of Investigation (FBI) on a monthly basis. The FBI publishes these national figures annually in a report titled *Crime in the United States.*[86]

The UCR is a compilation of two sources of information: crimes reported and arrests made. A clear understanding of what these sources of information include will help prevent a misinterpretation of UCR information. The first source of information is the number of crimes reported to law enforcement each year. Crimes are committed each year, but the perpetrators are not always caught and arrested. Therefore, the UCR counts the number of crimes reported to law enforcement agencies even if an arrest does not occur. For example, a citizen calls the police and reports that someone has just burglarized his or her home. This crime is reported, but it does not necessarily mean that an arrest has been made. The second source of information in the UCR includes the number of arrests each year in the United States. To interpret UCR statistics, it is important to realize that arrest statistics are counts of the number of arrests each year—not the number of persons arrested or the number of crimes committed. For example, one person could incur ten arrests in a particular year (counting as ten arrests, not ten people arrested). Moreover, although that same person was arrested ten times, he or she may have committed forty crimes that were not reported or otherwise known to the police.[87] Thus, examining both crimes reported and arrests made gives a better indication than one indicator alone.

The UCR groups crimes reported and arrests made into two categories. The first category is called **Part I offenses,** which are sometimes referred to as "index offenses." Part I offenses are the most serious person and property offenses and are most likely to be reported to law enforcement. There are eight Part I offenses: murder and nonnegligent manslaughter (person), forcible rape (person), robbery (person), aggravated assault (person), burglary (property), larceny-theft (property), motor vehicle theft (property), and arson (property). When counting Part I offenses, the FBI maintains statistics for both reported crimes and arrests made. The UCR also lists **Part II offenses.** These offenses, which are recorded only when an arrest is made, include most other offenses in the United States, with the exception of traffic violations.[88]

Like most ways of measuring crimes, the UCR has limitations, but despite these, the UCR is one of the best sources of offense statistics in the United States for both juveniles and adults. However, a good understanding of the limitations of the UCR is important to understanding its value for counting the extent of juvenile offending. The most important limitations of the UCR in relation to juvenile offending include the following:

- Arrest data include only juveniles who are actually arrested by law enforcement. Each year, a substantial number of juveniles who could be legally arrested are informally dealt with by law enforcement, and these informal resolutions are not reflected in arrest statistics.

- Arrest data provide a count of the number of arrests involving juveniles but do not provide a count of the number of juveniles arrested or the number of crimes committed by juveniles but not resulting in arrest.

- The UCR underestimates status offending. Even if status offenders are taken into custody by law enforcement officers, most status offenses are not technically counted as arrests in the various states, and most status offenses are excluded from the UCR (with the exception of some states that collect curfew, loitering, and runaway violations).

- With crimes reported to the police, but not resulting in arrest, it is difficult to discern whether a juvenile was involved. Many victims are unable to determine whether the perpetrator was a juvenile when and if they report a crime to the police. In many cases, the perpetrator may never have had contact with the victim (a burglary, for example).

- The UCR uses what is called the **hierarchy rule** when multiple crimes occur during one incident. For example, during a robbery, a youth punches the victim several times, steals a TV, kicks the door down, and chokes the family dog, leaving it with an injury. This one incident includes multiple crimes; however, the UCR will count only the most serious crime (robbery).

- The UCR does not distinguish between group and individual crime. Juveniles are more likely than adults to offend in groups. Thus, if in a group of ten juveniles only one youth commits a crime, all ten may be arrested, and this will be counted as ten arrests. Conversely, possibly only one youth may be arrested, and the others may be let go without consequence. In this way, juvenile crime can be both overestimated and underestimated, depending on the practice of local law enforcement involving group delinquency.

There are other general limitations to the UCR. For example, arrest counts and crimes reported are dependent upon the accuracy of the reports made by law enforcement agencies. There is evidence that some law enforcement agencies exaggerate the type and/or underestimate the frequency of arrests and crimes reported. For example, an unsolved murder case where a body has been recovered may be categorized as "other" instead of a "murder," and this would reflect in UCR statistics. Jurisdictions have many reasons to want to misinterpret crime statistics—for example, high crime rates reflect negatively on the police department and the city and may influence tourist business. Moreover, the UCR may underestimate certain crimes because juveniles are less likely to report crimes to the police—especially when they are victimized by other juveniles, acquaintances, or family members (such as a juvenile's brother, sister, or cousin). Because a large number of juvenile victimizations are at the hands of other juveniles, the level of juvenile offending as measured by crimes reported to the police may be underestimated. This situation may also influence arrests made: If police do not know a crime occurred because of a failure to report, they will be unable to investigate and possibly arrest the perpetrator. The nonreporting of crimes is an inherent problem with the UCR for both juveniles and adults, and it means that the UCR underestimates crime for both groups.

National Incident-Based Reporting System (NIBRS)

NIBRS is best categorized as a supplement to the UCR, but it is intended to be a major revision of the UCR and may someday replace it. NIBRS was developed in the 1980s in response to criticisms of the UCR (some of which are mentioned above). In 1989, NIBRS became available to select law enforcement agencies. By 2002, twenty states had been certified to operate NIBRS, and several other states are currently in the process. However, not all law enforcement agencies within those states are certified to use NIBRS, and the overwhelming majority of U.S. cities in NIBRS-certified states do not use this revised crime counting method at the present.

Despite the slow adoption of NIBRS nationwide, it is viewed as an improvement over the UCR in terms of the types of information recorded. One of the most important differences between the UCR and NIBRS is in the number of offenses tracked. The UCR counts crimes reported and arrests made for the eight Part I offenses and provides arrest counts for Part II offenses. In contrast, NIBRS counts crimes reported and arrests made for forty-six categories of crime and their subdivisions. (For example, the UCR records assault, but NIBRS includes subdivisions of assault, such as aggravated assault, simple assault, and intimidation.) NIBRS collects information on all other offenses that are covered in the UCR. Moreover, NIBRS does away with many limitations of the UCR such as the hierarchy rule so that it can account for multiple crimes in the event they occur during one criminal incident.

Probably the major difference between NIBRS and the UCR is the greater specificity of data. Unlike the UCR, NIBRS tracks fifty-three specific pieces of information about each criminal incident, including the victim(s), the offender(s), and other factors of the crime, such as location, weapon type, property loss, and property value. The UCR does collect some of these types of information, but NIBRS is substantially more detailed. As a result, NIBRS offers a promising avenue for examining crime statistics with much more detail than the UCR.[89]

Today, NIBRS is not yet operated nationally, and it has emerged as a supplement to the UCR, not a replacement for it. Although NIBRS holds much promise for the future, in reality, the cost for all law enforcement agencies to establish and maintain such a detailed information storage and retrieval system may mean that most jurisdictions will keep the UCR and that NIBRS will supplement these statistics—especially for serious crimes and in larger cities.

Self-Report Data

Self-report data or self-report surveys are a second measure of juvenile offending. As the name suggests, information about juvenile offending is gathered from juvenile admissions about their behavior. Self-report surveys can be conducted in person, through the mail, or over the telephone through interviews or questionnaires. These surveys may also be conducted in a number of different locations, such as in juvenile institutions or schools.

The procedures for self-report surveys differ substantially from those of the UCR or NIBRS. Self-report surveys are not considered national in scope, are usually done on a much smaller scale, and rely on the juvenile to provide information about offending—not crime reports and official arrest records from law enforcement agencies. Self-report surveys are often given to youths who are currently involved in the juvenile justice system—for example, those who are being detained in juvenile facilities such as detention centers and state schools. Several important answers can be obtained from surveying captive audiences, one of the most important being how many crimes a youth committed but was not arrested for prior to incarceration. However, self-report surveys routinely query youths on a number of important issues beyond delinquency offenses, including but not limited to their family life, drug use history, gang involvement, victimizations, and history of abuse.

As mentioned, self-report surveys are not limited to youths who are officially involved in the juvenile justice system. For example, high school students are often the targets of self-report surveys. One of the most recognized surveys of noninstitutionalized youths is the Monitoring of the Future (MTF) study. Conducted by the Institute for Social Research at the University of Michigan, MTF is an annual survey of approximately 50,000 eighth-, tenth-, and twelfth-grade students. MTF researchers administer to a sample of students during normal class times anonymous questionnaires that ask about a variety of topics, such as alcohol and drug use, tobacco use, and the frequency and type of delinquent behavior, including students' attitudes about drug testing in schools and about the police.[90]

One advantage of self-report surveys is that they are versatile—they can be conducted in a number of ways and can focus on specific problem behaviors. For example, one project is aimed at examining and understanding serious delinquency. This project, officially named the Causes and Correlates of Delinquency Program, is currently being conducted in Denver, Pittsburgh, and Rochester, New York. These three cities are the sites for important self-report surveys of youths in neighborhoods and schools concerning a variety of topics, from serious delinquency to drug use patterns.[91] The goal of the project is to come to a better understanding of the factors that may contribute to serious juvenile delinquency. Self-report surveys may be the only plausible way to answer such specific questions.

Like the UCR and NIBRS, self-report surveys have limitations. Because self-report surveys rely on youths' "self-reports" of their behavior, there is always the possibility that youths may lie, forget, or exaggerate their responses. For example, youths may lie because they feel that they might get into trouble for being honest about their offending despite the anonymous or confidential nature of the surveys. Alternatively, because self-report surveys are often done anonymously or confidentially and no adverse consequences can come from participating—regardless of exaggerated or inaccurate responses—juveniles have no incentive to be accurate in self-reports. Moreover, youths may also misinterpret questions, or questions may be biased. For example, some youths may believe that certain behaviors do not violate the law (such as toilet papering a residential home or breaking windows out of an abandoned dwelling), and if not asked specifically about the behavior, they may not report it or may underreport such behaviors in general. Finally, self-report surveys are often conducted in schools. Some critics argue that a misleading picture of juvenile offending is obtained from self-reports of students, for the most frequent offenders are likely truant from school or may be locked up in a juvenile facility during the survey. Thus, self-report surveys in schools are flawed because the most serious and frequent offenders may well be missed. In sum, the limitations of self-report surveys include the following:

- Youths may lie, forget, or exaggerate their responses.
- Youths may believe they will be punished for being truthful.
- Youths have no incentive to be truthful.

- Youths may interpret questions incorrectly, or questions may be biased in some way.

- Youths may not report a certain behavior if not specifically asked about it because of their belief that it is not a crime.

- Self-report surveys in schools may overlook the most serious or chronic offenders, who might be truant, locked up, or absent in another way.

Despite the limitations inherent whenever persons are asked to report on their behavior, self-report surveys are an important way to measure juvenile offending. Additionally, the potential disadvantages discussed above should not be taken to mean that self-report measures are useless for accurate measuring of levels of offending and other behaviors. In fact, several excellent research studies have found that asking juveniles to self-report about their offending does result in truthful answers and that juveniles do not always lie, exaggerate, or forget about delinquent activity.[92] Moreover, not only do such surveys provide a measure of offending, but they also provide a deeper look into the causes of such offending and the multitude of behaviors involving juveniles that cannot be uncovered by official sources of data such as the UCR and NIBRS.

Victimization Data

Victimization data are collected through surveys of individuals about victimizations they have experienced (thus, these are essentially self-report surveys). An advantage is that information about offending can be gleaned from victimization surveys if the victim is able to report whether a juvenile or adult committed the crime. One of the most popular victimization surveys in the United States is the National Crime Victimization Survey (NCVS), which began in 1973. Twice per year, personnel from the U.S. Bureau of the Census interview (in person or over the phone) anyone at least twelve years of age in a nationally representative sample of households. NCVS personnel conduct approximately 160,000 interviews a year, covering almost 49,000 households. Each household and its members are interviewed every six months and are asked to report about victimizations that occurred during the previous six months. Each household stays in the interview sample for three years, during which time new households continually rotate in and out.[93]

The NCVS collects information about crimes committed against individuals (sexual assault, rape, aggravated and simple assault, personal robbery) and households (household burglary, larceny, vehicle theft). Unlike the UCR, the NCVS measures both crimes reported to the police and those not reported. It also estimates the proportion of each crime type reported to law enforcement and gives a summary finding of the reasons that victims give for not reporting crimes.[94]

Compared to the UCR, NIBRS, and self-report surveys of offending, the NCVS may be the weakest indicator of juvenile offending and juvenile victimizations. First, the NCVS does not count victimizations for persons under twelve years of age unless someone in the household is aware of and reports such victimizations. Because juveniles may not (and often do not) reveal victimizations to their parents or other family members, such victimizations may go unreported in the NCVS. As a measure of juvenile offending, NCVS victims may not be able to adequately distinguish whether the perpetrator was a juvenile or not, provided they had contact with the perpetrator at all. In sum, the major limitations of the NCVS for measuring juvenile victimizations include the following:

- The NCVS does not survey individuals under twelve years of age and may underestimate their victimizations.

- Juveniles may not report their victimizations to parents or other family members; thus, victimizations are underrepresented, especially if the youth's parent or other family member is the perpetrator.

- Victims, provided they had contact with the perpetrator, are often unable to state whether the perpetrator was a juvenile or not.

The NCVS is not the only measure of juvenile victimizations, but it is the most comprehensive national count. Like self-report surveys, however, victimization surveys are administered to juveniles each year in a variety of locations. For example, the Bureau of Justice Statistics (BJS) and the National Center for Education Statistics (NCES) collect information on crime trends within schools, and a substantial part of this report includes self-reports from students about victimizations they have experienced or witnessed (see Chapter 13). Thus, like self-report surveys of offending, victimization surveys can be very versatile and are used in a number of ways beyond the national scope of the NCVS.

The bottom line is that numerous approaches to measuring juvenile offending and victimization in the United States are being used. This section has examined a few of the largest and most well-known measurement methods. However, there are many smaller but still important derivatives of these larger national projects. Ultimately, the value of any one of these methods rests in its ability to measure the extent of juvenile crime and victimizations. Each method has limitations, but taken together, they give a picture of what is known and what is not known about juvenile offending and victimizations. Table 2.2 is a general summary of the methods of measuring delinquency.

Although this section has focused on measures of juvenile offending and victimization, additional types of data go beyond offending and victimization measures in the juvenile justice system. These types of data cover a variety of areas. For example, data in the form of juvenile court statistics and juvenile correctional statistics are used to examine juvenile case processing and what happens to youths as they pass through the juvenile justice system. Data from the National Child Abuse and Neglect Data System (NCANDS) are counts of official reports of cases of dependency and neglect reported to state child protective agencies each year (thus an official form of victimization data). These and other forms of juvenile-specific data will be used throughout the remainder of this book. Like the methods of measuring juvenile crime and victimizations, additional methods examining the juvenile experience have limitations but provide the best look into a variety of areas, including juvenile offending, juvenile victimizations, juvenile processing, and outcomes in the juvenile justice system.

TABLE 2.2

A Summary of Measuring Juvenile Offending

Delinquency Measure	What It Measures
Uniform Crime Reports (UCR)	A count of crimes reported to law enforcement and arrests made/cleared by law enforcement. Monthly reports from law enforcement agencies are compiled by the Federal Bureau of Investigation (FBI) and published annually in *Crime in the United States*.
National Incident Based Reporting System (NIBRS)	Like the UCR, NIBRS is a count of crimes reported to law enforcement and arrests made by law enforcement. However, it is more detailed than the UCR in that it collects more specific information about the criminal incident, any victims and their characteristics, characteristics of any known offenders, and other factors, such as time of crime, relation of victim to offender, location of crime, weapons used, property lost, and the property's value. Viewed as a supplement to the UCR because only 20 states and select cities are currently certified to use NIBRS.
Self-report data	A method of measuring juvenile offending by asking juveniles to report crimes they have committed. Usually conducted with anonymous or confidential surveys or interviews. Those surveyed/interviewed may be in juvenile institutions, schools, or other locations. Can be administered to known delinquents or juveniles not known to be delinquents.
National Crime Victimization Survey (NCVS)	A national survey of selected households and occupants who are more than 12 years of age that asks about victimizations experienced in the last 6 months. Persons are asked about crimes against them and their households, and whether the crimes were reported to the police.

SUMMARY

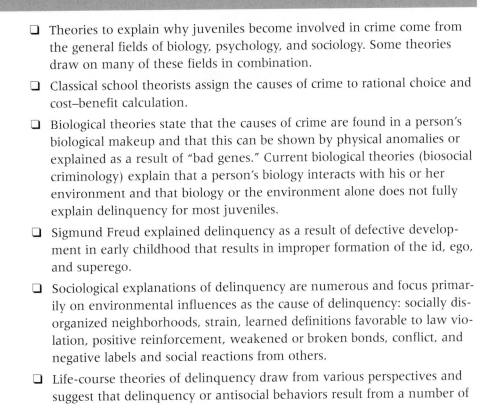

- ❑ Theories to explain why juveniles become involved in crime come from the general fields of biology, psychology, and sociology. Some theories draw on many of these fields in combination.

- ❑ Classical school theorists assign the causes of crime to rational choice and cost–benefit calculation.

- ❑ Biological theories state that the causes of crime are found in a person's biological makeup and that this can be shown by physical anomalies or explained as a result of "bad genes." Current biological theories (biosocial criminology) explain that a person's biology interacts with his or her environment and that biology or the environment alone does not fully explain delinquency for most juveniles.

- ❑ Sigmund Freud explained delinquency as a result of defective development in early childhood that results in improper formation of the id, ego, and superego.

- ❑ Sociological explanations of delinquency are numerous and focus primarily on environmental influences as the cause of delinquency: socially disorganized neighborhoods, strain, learned definitions favorable to law violation, positive reinforcement, weakened or broken bonds, conflict, and negative labels and social reactions from others.

- ❑ Life-course theories of delinquency draw from various perspectives and suggest that delinquency or antisocial behaviors result from a number of issues: failed parental interactions, neuropsychological deficits, and weak or broken bonds. Theorists in this tradition disagree about the possibility of change over the life course. Some life-course or developmental theorists suggest that a person is unlikely to change because of problems early in life whereas others believe change is always possible depending on certain life events.

❑ No one theory is adequate to explain delinquency. However, the various theories do shed much light on the factors, situations, and conditions that may make delinquency a "more or less likely" outcome.

❑ The two types of official data on national levels of juvenile offending are the Uniform Crime Reports (UCR) and the National Incident Based Reporting System (NIBRS).

❑ Self-report measures try to gauge juvenile offending by asking juveniles how many crimes they have committed. Self-report measures can be used to study a variety of behaviors that are not criminal or delinquent.

❑ The National Crime Victimization Survey (NCVS) is the most comprehensive victimization survey measuring national levels of victimization. Information on victimizations provides another indicator of crimes committed in the United States.

❑ All types of methods for measuring juvenile offending and victimizations have limitations. Perhaps the weakest measure of juvenile offending and victimization is the NCVS because it does not track victimizations for children under twelve years old.

❑ The best way to get a gauge on the extent of crime in the United States is to use all three types of measurement: official records, self-reports, and victimization data.

REVIEW QUESTIONS

1. According to the classical school, what is the cause of delinquency? List and discuss several potential problems with this explanation of delinquency.

2. What is the major way in which the classical school differs from the positive school?

3. In your own words, define *determinism*. What is the difference between biological determinism and environmental determinism?

4. How is Robert Agnew's general strain theory an improvement over Robert Merton's theory?

5. Evaluate Albert Cohen's strain theory on status and acceptance. Is it a logical explanation of delinquency? Does this theory do a good job of explaining delinquency committed by juveniles from the middle and upper classes?

6. How has the labeling perspective been important to the operation of the juvenile justice system?

7. What would be some traits of someone with "low self-control"? Do you believe that low self-control is adequate as an explanation of delinquency?

Do you know anyone who exhibits some indicators or traits of low self-control but is not a delinquent or criminal?

8. Make a list of the benefits and drawbacks of official data and self-report data for measuring the extent of juvenile offending. Which measure do you feel is the best for measuring juvenile offending? Explain.

9. What is the major weakness of the NCVS for measuring juvenile offending and/or victimizations perpetrated by juveniles?

10. Although a good predictor of a juvenile becoming a criminal is whether he or she was a delinquent, is it always going to be the case that delinquents grow up to be criminals? Explain. Do you agree with Robert Sampson and John Laub that people can change the path they are on as a result of transitions that give them "social capital"? What are some things that juveniles might value as "social capital"?

KEY TERMS AND DEFINITIONS

atavist: A term used by Cesare Lombroso to describe people he thought were born criminals because they were throwbacks to earlier stages of evolution. Atavists, or born criminals, could be distinguished by physical features or stigmata that only criminals were thought to possess.

classical school: A school of thought, most heavily influenced by Cesare Beccaria, that suggested people are rational beings who engage in acts (such as crime and delinquency) after they calculate the pleasure or benefits versus the costs or pain expected. According to Beccaria, to prevent crime a punishment must be swift, severe, proportionate to the act, and, most importantly, certain.

determinism: A theory which suggests that the causes of crime are predetermined or out of the control of the individual. For example, biological determinism refers to the cause of crime as something inherent or inborn in a person's biological makeup that may manifest in his or her physical features.

hierarchy rule: The UCR procedure in which only the most serious crime is recorded in the event that multiple crimes occur in one incident.

middle-class measuring rod: Proposed by Albert Cohen in 1955, a concept which refers to the idea that lower-class children gain status and acceptance based on the values of the middle class. That is the standard or "measuring rod" with which they must compete in schools.

National Crime Victimization Survey (NCVS): An annual survey that asks household participants age twelve and older about any victimizations they have experienced in the past six months.

National Incident-Based Reporting System (NIBRS): A reporting system developed in the late 1980s as a supplement to the UCR. It provides much more detailed information about criminal incidents, including information about perpetrators, victims, and the location of the crime. Currently, it is not operated nationally, and only twenty states are authorized to use NIBRS when reporting crimes to the FBI.

Part I offenses: The eight most serious person or property offenses that are most likely to be reported to the police: murder and nonnegligent manslaughter, forcible rape, robbery, aggravated assault, burglary, larceny-theft, motor vehicle theft, and arson. UCR counts of these crimes include both crimes reported and arrests made.

Part II offenses: A category that includes all offenses in the United States, with the exception of traffic violations, that are not Part I offenses. UCR counts include only arrests made for these crimes.

positive school: A school of thought that attributed the causes of crime to factors not necessarily in the control of the individual. This school focused on the individual and not the act committed, and it explained delinquency as the result of factors such as the environment. Early positive school theorists, such as Cesare Lombroso, attributed delinquency to a lack of biological development or evolution, which could be demonstrated by physical "stigmata."

positivism: A term that refers to the ability to measure and study a certain phenomenon that is presumed to cause something. For example, positivists would reject demonological explanations of crime (the devil made me do it) because the devil cannot be measured or observed. Thus, positivism is the application of scientific principles, specifically the ability to measure a phenomenon as in the study of crime and delinquency.

self-report surveys: Surveys that inquire about behavior. Regarding juvenile delinquency, self-report surveys are usually anonymous or confidential, conducted over the phone or in person, and attempt to measure how much delinquency a juvenile is involved in and whether the juvenile was caught. Self-report surveys are routinely done on incarcerated juveniles but may be used on schoolchildren and others. The bottom line of self-report surveys is if you want to know something, just ask.

social capital: A concept discussed by Robert Sampson and John Laub that refers to the product of certain events or transitions in life that provide a reason for someone to get off of a delinquent path. For example, getting married and having a child can result in "social capital" whereby the individual has a reason not to continue to be delinquent. In simpler terms, social capital is gaining something valuable that can be lost.

Uniform Crime Reports (UCR): A national program begun in 1930 by the International Association of Chiefs of Police to provide a statistical count of crime, specifically arrests and crimes known to and reported to the police. The UCR is published annually by the FBI in a report titled *Crime in the United States.*

 FOR FURTHER RESEARCH

❑ **The Federal Bureau of Investigation for UCR Statistics**
http://www.fbi.gov

❑ **Phrenology**
http://pages.britishlibrary.net/phrenology

❏ **Criminological Theory**
http://www.crimetheory.com

❏ **Theoretical Perspectives**
http://www.acs.appstate.edu/dept/ps-cj/cj-sour.html

❏ **General Crime Statistics and Criminology**
http://sun.soci.niu.edu/~critcrim/crime/crime.html

For an up-to-date list of web links, go to the Juvenile Justice Companion Website at **http://cj.wadsworth.com/del_carmen_trulson_jj**

Juveniles
and the Police

CHAPTER THREE OUTLINE

Juvenile Conduct Leading to Police Involvement / 72

Taking Juveniles into Custody / 73

    The Arrest Requirement and Probable Cause / 73
    Who Determines Probable Cause? / 73
    Establishing Probable Cause / 74
    Arrests of Juveniles / 74
        Warrantless Arrests of Juveniles for Delinquent Conduct / 74
        Custody for Noncriminal Violations / 75

Police Discretion When Arresting Juveniles / 77

    Factors That Influence Juvenile Arrest Decisions / 77
        Legal Factors Influencing Juvenile Arrests / 77
        Extralegal Factors Influencing Juvenile Arrests / 78
        Other Factors Influencing Juvenile Arrests / 81

Juvenile Arrests / 83

    How Arrests Are Counted / 83
    The Number and Trend of Juvenile Arrests / 83

Legal Rights of Juveniles During Stop and Frisk, Arrests, and Searches and Seizures / 85

    Stop and Frisk of Juveniles / 86
    Arrests of Persons / 86
    Searches and Seizures / 88
        Can a Juvenile Consent to a Search? / 88
        Police Search and Seizure with Parental Consent / 89

    School Searches and Police Assistance / 90
    General Search Conditions for Juvenile Probationers / 94

Custody and Interrogation of Juveniles / 95

    Miranda Wording and Juveniles / 96
    When Is a Suspect Under "Custodial Interrogation" for *Miranda* Purposes? / 96
        The Latest Issue in *Miranda* and Juvenile Custody and Interrogation: *Yarborough v. Alvarado* / 97
        Yarborough v. Alvarado and Its Implications for Juveniles / 98
    A Juvenile May Waive *Miranda* Rights: The Totality of Circumstances Test / 99
    Per Se Rules and Juvenile Waiver / 100
        Parent or Interested Adult Presence May Be Required Before Waiver / 100
        Lawyer Presence May Be Required Before Waiver/ 101
    Refusal to Waive *Miranda* Must Be Clear and Unambiguous / 102

Confidentiality and the Police / 102

    Fingerprinting / 103
    DNA Samples / 105
    Lineups and Photographs / 106
    Media, Juveniles, and the Police / 106

Case Brief: *New Jersey v. T. L. O.* / 91

IN THIS CHAPTER YOU WILL LEARN

- That the police have authority over many juvenile behaviors, including those that are noncriminal.

- That most juvenile arrests are made without a warrant.

- That the police need probable cause to take a juvenile lawbreaker into custody but in some cases may need only "reasonable suspicion" for custody when the youth is deemed in need of supervision.

- About the factors that influence custody of juveniles.

- About the number of juveniles arrested each year.

- About the search and seizure of juveniles in schools.

- About juvenile interrogation and waiver of rights.

- About confidentiality issues concerning juveniles and the police.

INTRODUCTION

Chapter 1 notes that adults are arrested but that juveniles are taken into custody. Although the outcome is similar, procedures for taking juveniles into custody sometimes differ from the procedures for arresting adults. For example, a juvenile might be taken into custody without a warrant, whereas one might be required for an adult arrest. Juveniles may be taken into custody without probable cause in some circumstances, whereas probable cause is always required to arrest an adult. Some state laws require that a juvenile taken into police custody be afforded more safeguards than an adult, even for the same crime.[1] For example, some states prohibit the police from questioning a juvenile unless a lawyer or parent is present. Moreover, a juvenile can be taken into custody for a multitude of behaviors that would never justify an adult arrest. For example, juveniles may be taken into custody for smoking cigarettes, violating curfew, or running away (status offenses). Because of their status (being young), juveniles are given more protection in the juvenile justice system and may be held accountable for a broader range of behaviors than adults.

Dealing with juvenile offenders presents special problems not faced by the police when they deal with adult offenders. This fact sometimes conflicts with their primary mission. Although the main goal of policing is law enforcement, many believe that law officers should act as social workers when dealing with juveniles. Whether police officers are viewed as law enforcers or social workers, however, monitoring juvenile behavior is disproportionately their responsibility. In many cases, their responsibility ends with juveniles being taken into custody.

This chapter examines the custody of juveniles for criminal and noncriminal behavior. It examines the factors that may influence whether police will arrest a juvenile. It also discusses the legal rights of juveniles in various police encounters. The chapter ends with a discussion of confidentiality issues for juveniles in the justice system and a specific look at police–juvenile encounters.

Juvenile Conduct Leading to Police Involvement

Three forms of juvenile conduct come under police scrutiny: delinquent behavior, status offending, and dependency and neglect. Delinquent behavior is any act that if committed by an adult would be considered a crime. Status offending is conduct that is prohibited only for minors. Delinquent conduct and status offending are discussed in this chapter as the major forms of juvenile conduct that can result in police custody. Dependency and neglect involve the conduct (or lack of conduct) of a youth's parents, rather than the youth himself or herself. Dependent and neglected youths are never taken into custody for punitive reasons.

Taking Juveniles into Custody

State law governs the types of conduct that can cause juveniles to be taken into custody and the procedures for such an action. Generally, constitutional protections afforded to adults at arrest are also given to juveniles. However, juveniles may receive greater procedural protections than adults even when they are arrested for the same types of crimes. For example, in many states a juvenile's parents must be notified immediately after the arrest. This is never a requirement in adult arrests.

The Arrest Requirement and Probable Cause

A police officer must have **probable cause** to make a legal arrest, whether for juveniles or adults. *Probable cause* was defined by the U.S. Supreme Court in *Bringar v. United States* (1949) as more than bare suspicion; it exists when "the facts and circumstances within the officers' knowledge and of which they had reasonably trustworthy information are sufficient in themselves to warrant a man of reasonable caution in the belief that an offense has been or is being committed."[2] A more practical definition of probable cause may be stated in mathematical terms. If a police officer is more than 50-percent certain that the suspect has or is committing a crime, probable cause exists and the officer can make a valid arrest.* The validity of the arrest is determined by a court of law.

Although the juvenile justice system avoids the term *arrest* for juveniles, using instead the term *custody*, custody and arrest involve the same procedures.[3] And to avoid confusion, *arrest* and *custody* are used synonymously throughout this chapter.

Who Determines Probable Cause?

There are two ways an arrest can be made: with a **warrant** and without a warrant. A warrant is a written order from a court, based on probable cause, allowing an officer to arrest a person. With a warrant, probable cause is established by a neutral magistrate (a judge who does not have an interest or bias in the case) who reviews alleged facts and determines whether there is enough evidence for probable cause and an arrest. Although all arrests require probable cause, not all arrests require a warrant. In fact, more than 95 percent of arrests are made without a warrant.[4] In warrantless arrests, probable cause is determined by a police officer. However, such a determination is typically reviewed by a magistrate or judge.

Since probable cause is the key to a valid arrest, what probable cause means and who determines it are important. Probable cause is, to an extent, subjective, and if it is challenged in court, it must be established by the police officers who have made a warrantless arrest. The arresting officers must be prepared to articulate the facts and circumstances that existed at the time the arrest was made, and these must amount to probable cause.

*Rolando V. del Carmen, *Criminal Procedure: Law and Practice*, 5th ed. (Belmont, CA: Wadsworth, 2001). This is a general mathematical term for ease of understanding; it is not meant as a rule.

Establishing Probable Cause

Probable cause is a high standard that requires proof. As a general rule, officers may use any "trustworthy" information to establish probable cause. This information may include hearsay, informant information, anonymous tips, victim reports, firsthand observation, years of experience, or a combination of these sources.[5] For example, a police officer with thirty years of experience on a drug task force may use his or her experience to determine whether someone is "high" by detecting a strong odor of marijuana coming from that person's clothes and other physical indicators, such as a dazed look. The officer's experience and observation (ability to recognize the odor of marijuana and a marijuana-induced dazed look) may be enough to establish probable cause for arrest. Police officers should be able to articulate all facts that led them to a determination of probable cause because these determine the admissibility of evidence and the validity of the arrest. As one author notes, "in case of doubt, it is better to include too much rather than too little information, provided such information is true."[6]

Arrests of Juveniles

Law enforcement officers have more control over juvenile behavior than adult behavior, meaning that juveniles can be taken into custody for behaviors that would never justify an adult arrest. The Uniform Juvenile Court Act illustrates the broad scope of authority that police officers have over juvenile conduct. For example, Section 13 (which outlines recommended practices for taking a juvenile into custody) states that a child may be taken into custody pursuant to an order of the court and in accordance with the laws of arrest. A law enforcement officer may also take a juvenile into custody if the officer reasonably believes the child is suffering from an illness or injury, or if the child is in immediate danger. A child may also be taken into custody if there is "reasonable grounds" to believe the youth has run away from his or her parents or guardian.[7] Most states' laws closely follow the general text of the Uniform Juvenile Court Act pertaining to the arrest and custody of juveniles. Exhibit 3.1 examines the Uniform Juvenile Court Act and demonstrates that adults are not subject to the same rules as juveniles.

Just as the juvenile justice system avoids the use of the term *arrest* for juveniles, states also typically note that the taking of a juvenile into custody is not an arrest except for determining the validity of taking him or her into custody. Despite the changed wording in various state juvenile justice codes, arrest and custody imply the same procedures.

Warrantless Arrests of Juveniles for Delinquent Conduct

Unless required by state law, police officers do not need a warrant to take a juvenile into custody. In *United States v. Watson* (1976), the U.S. Supreme Court held that a warrantless arrest is valid as long as there is probable cause, even if there is time to obtain a warrant before the arrest.[8] This same ruling also applies to juveniles. Due to the "protective" nature of the juvenile justice system, however, individual states may require that officers obtain an arrest warrant or

EXHIBIT 3.1

Uniform Juvenile Court Act, Section 13: Taking a Youth into Custody

a. A child may be taken into custody:

1. pursuant to an order of the court under this Act;

2. pursuant to the laws of arrests;

3. by a law enforcement officer (or duly authorized officer of the court) if there are reasonable grounds to believe that the child is suffering from illness or injury or is in immediate danger from his surroundings, and that his removal is necessary; or

4. by a law enforcement officer (or duly authorized officer of the court) if there are reasonable grounds to believe that the child has run away from his parents, guardian, or other custodian.

b. The taking of a child into custody is not an arrest, except for the purposes of determining its validity under the constitution of this State or of the United States.

Source: National Conference of Commissioners on Uniform State Laws, *Uniform Juvenile Court Act* (Chicago: National Conference on Uniform State Laws, 1968), Sect. 13.

custody directive prior to arresting a juvenile, but this is not the case in most states. For example, the Texas Court of Criminal Appeals held in *Vasquez v. State* (1987) that police officers may take a juvenile into custody without a warrant as long as probable cause exists.[9] Although requiring a warrant before arresting a juvenile is rare, the notification of parents or the use of other protective mechanisms is a common practice *after* police take a juvenile offender into custody. These safeguards are not required for adult arrests. For example, law enforcement officers are usually never required to call an adult's spouse or parents once he or she has been arrested, but state law may, and often does, require them to do so after they arrest a juvenile.

Custody for Noncriminal Violations

In most instances when a juvenile is taken into custody, it is for a delinquent offense.[10] However, juveniles, unlike adults, may be subject to police custody for behaviors that are noncriminal but are prohibited because of the offender's age. Noncriminal violations that can result in police custody include situations in which the youth is alleged to be in need of supervision or assistance (such as in instances of status offending) or cases of dependency or neglect. This type of custody is special and deserves attention. Two situations arise for police officers when taking a juvenile into custody for noncriminal behavior: (1) whether they may do so and (2) whether they need probable cause.

The Supreme Court of New York decided *In the Matter of Mark Anthony G.* (1987) that an officer may stop and take custody of a youth even if the officer does not suspect him of criminal wrongdoing.[11] In this case, the officer observed Mark Anthony G. at a bus terminal at 12:30 A.M. The officer approached Mark

Anthony G., suspecting he was a runaway based on his youthful appearance, due to the late hour, and because the youth was alone. Upon further investigation, the officer concluded that Mark Anthony G. was a runaway and informed him that he would be transported to Youth Services, where his parents would be called. Before transport, the police officer searched Mark Anthony G. for weapons. The officer did not find any weapons but did find a clip from a nine-millimeter handgun in the bottom of a bag Mark Anthony G. had in his possession.* This evidence was used in a delinquency proceeding.

During the adjudication hearing, the family court judge concluded that the officer did not have sufficient evidence to reasonably believe Mark Anthony G. was a runaway and thus did not have probable cause for his detention or to seize evidence. On appeal, the appellate court reversed, finding that the officer did have probable cause and that the initial detention of Mark Anthony G., for the noncriminal offense of being a runaway, was appropriate and in accordance with New York state law. This case demonstrates that police may take a juvenile into custody for behavior that is noncriminal. Most state laws allow this. Such custody is usually based on the belief that it is in the best interests of the child and for his or her protection. However, the standards by which officers are able to take a juvenile into custody differ among the various states. In some states, officers must have probable cause, but in most states, officers need only reasonable suspicion/grounds.**

In *Matthews v. State* (1984), a Texas appellate court addressed the issue of whether a police officer may take custody of a youth without probable cause if the officer has "reasonable suspicion" that the child has engaged in conduct in need of supervision (meaning a status offense).[12] "Reasonable suspicion" is a lower standard than probable cause.[13] Mathematically, if probable cause means that the officer is more than 50-percent certain, reasonable suspicion represents a degree of certainty around 30 percent that a crime (in this case, conduct in need of supervision) has been or will be committed. Matthews was detained for truancy by a Fort Worth police officer who observed him out of school at 9:30 A.M. Matthews was later found to be on probation, and upon further questioning by police officers he confessed to participation in two murders. On appeal, Matthews claimed that his truancy detention was not based on probable cause; thus, his murder confession resulting from that detention should be suppressed in court. The court concluded that the detention of Matthews was justified because he engaged in conduct in need of supervision, meaning that he was truant from school and was in public during school hours. This type of custody was authorized under Texas law under a standard of reasonable suspicion instead of probable cause.

These cases illustrate that police officers do not need a warrant to take a juvenile lawbreaker into custody for noncriminal behavior unless otherwise required by state law. Police officers are also authorized, in accordance with state law, to take juveniles into custody without probable cause if there is

*The evidence seized in the search of Mark Anthony G. was a fully loaded nine-millimeter clip. Further investigation revealed another individual who had possession of the weapon, in the bus terminal. This evidence was ruled admissible by the Supreme Court of New York and was used to adjudicate Mark Anthony G.

**"Reasonable suspicion" and "reasonable grounds" are used interchangeably when discussing cases.

"reasonable suspicion" to believe that the youth has engaged in conduct indicating a need for supervision (such as a curfew violation or truancy). This type of custody is common in most states and recommended in the Uniform Juvenile Court Act, but it would never justify the arrest of an adult.

Police Discretion When Arresting Juveniles

Law enforcement officers have much **discretion** when deciding to arrest or to not arrest a juvenile. In making arrest decisions, police officers consider **legal, extralegal,** and "other" factors. Legal factors include but are not limited to the seriousness of the offense, the juvenile's frequency of offending, and the juvenile's prior record—factors that are legally based and are valid in arrest decisions. Extralegal factors are generally not valid in determining arrest decisions. These include the juvenile's race, gender, or socioeconomic status. In theory, extralegal factors should never be a basis for an arrest; however, actual practice may be different. Police officers also use "other" factors in determining arrest, such as a person's demeanor or whether or not the victim demands arrest. These "other" factors are not necessarily legal factors, nor are they necessarily extralegal factors. They are in a gray area.

Police officers have a number of options available after initial contact with a juvenile offender, and these are discussed in Chapter 1. At the least formal levels, police officers can ignore the behavior or give the youth a warning. At the most formal level, police officers can cite the youth with a violation, transport the youth to a detention center, and refer him or her to juvenile court intake. In cases of juvenile lawbreaking, various factors can influence the type of intervention that police officers choose.

Factors That Influence Juvenile Arrest Decisions

Police officers do not take into custody every juvenile who breaks the law. For various reasons, police officers cannot enforce all the rules all the time. Officers have **discretion** when handling a situation. However, some factors may make juvenile arrest more likely.

Legal Factors Influencing Juvenile Arrests

Three legal factors are arguably most influential in determining juvenile arrest: seriousness of offense, frequency of offense, and prior or current involvement with the juvenile justice system. The most important factor is the seriousness of the offense. A general rule is that as the seriousness of the crime increases, police discretion decreases and arrest becomes more likely. For example, police have no discretion to ignore a murder, a drive-by shooting, or an aggravated assault. Failure to take custody of a juvenile accused of a serious crime would constitute a breach of duty on the part of the officer.

Frequency of offending is also important in police–juvenile encounters. If police officers observe a juvenile several times under suspicious circumstances, or if the juvenile is known to be a frequent offender, police are generally more likely to arrest. The more frequent the offending, the more likely an arrest will occur if the behavior is discovered.

A third legal consideration is whether the juvenile has been or is currently involved with the juvenile justice system. For example, a youth may be (or have been) on probation, on parole, or recently released from institutionalization. Juveniles who have previously been involved with the juvenile justice system are more likely to be formally processed by police.

Extralegal Factors Influencing Juvenile Arrests

Extralegal factors are those considered outside of the law and thus should have nothing to do with whether a juvenile is arrested. However, research suggests that extralegal factors may be important in police decision making about juveniles.[14] The most controversial extralegal factors are race, gender, and socioeconomic status.

Race Research studies differ on the impact that race has in determining whether a juvenile will be arrested.[15] Some indirect evidence for a racial bias in arrest shows that black youths constitute approximately 16 percent of the juvenile population ages ten to seventeen, but are overrepresented in all arrests (25 percent).[16] Statistically speaking, however, black youths are more involved (based on arrest statistics) in serious crime than their white counterparts, and with these crimes discretion becomes less important. Black youths account for 41 percent of arrests for all violent crimes, which is disproportionate to their proportion of the population.[17] Moreover, black youths are most overrepresented in robbery offenses (58 percent) and murder offenses (48 percent), well above their proportion in the total U.S. population.[18] Race may play a role in arrests for less serious crimes, but the racial effect tends to disappear if one considers the seriousness of the offense—referring to offenses for which there is less discretion available for police officers, such as robbery and murder.

The connections among race, involvement in delinquency, and arrest are not as clear as the above discussion would suggest. More data are needed to explain the significant number of factors that may influence arrest probability beyond race, such as seriousness, frequency, and prior involvement with the juvenile justice system. Police neighborhood patrol practices may be another influential factor. For example, if there are more police officers in traditionally minority residential areas, one might expect that the number of minority arrests will be disproportionate, not necessarily that minorities commit a disproportionate number of crimes. Or the police may be biased in their arrest policies, such as arresting minority offenders while merely warning offenders of other races.[19] In a recent study, Pope and Snyder found no evidence supporting the claim that police are more likely to arrest minority offenders than white offenders once other attributes were taken into consideration, such as the seriousness of offense or whether multiple victims were unvolved.[20] However, Pope and Snyder did find a connection between victim race and arrest. Those who victimized a white person were more likely to be arrested than those who victimized a nonwhite person. Although most crimes in society are intraracial (same race on same race), the apparent bias for white victims may mean an indirect bias against minority perpetrators with white victims when all other factors are equal, such as crime seriousness, offender age, and whether or not the victim was injured. Although the issue has not been resolved, race should never be a factor in arrests. Exhibit 3.2 presents Pope and Snyder's findings on race and arrest.

Gender   Gender does appear to matter in juvenile arrests. Traditionally, females have been arrested fewer times than males for most forms of illegal behavior. Approximately 28 percent of all juvenile arrests involve females, although girls ages ten to seventeen represent nearly one-half of all juveniles.[21]

Males are arrested much more often than juvenile females overall, but Meda Chesney-Lind suggests that female juveniles are held to a stricter behavioral standard for certain offenses. She contends that females are more often arrested for behaviors that tend to be "sexualized" or morality based—that female adolescents are more likely to be arrested for these offenses than when males demonstrate the same behavior.[22] Some evidence for this claim comes from national arrest statistics which show that the most frequent arrests for female juveniles included running away from home (59 percent of all juvenile arrests for running away) and prostitution (69 percent of all juvenile arrests for prostitution).[23]

EXHIBIT 3.2

Study Finds No Evidence of Racism in Juvenile Arrests

Carl Pope and Howard Snyder examined NIBRS data from seventeen states to examine the impact of race and arrest for juvenile offenders accused of violent crimes. Pope and Snyder examined 102,905 crimes and all arrests resulting from these reported crimes where "victims reported" the offender's characteristics, such as whether the perpetrator was younger than age eighteen and whether the offender was white or nonwhite.

Using these data, Pope and Snyder took into account factors of the criminal incidents, including but not limited to whether there were multiple victims, whether the victim was injured, whether the victim was a family member, victim race, and whether a weapon was involved. After including these additional factors, the researchers found "no difference in the likelihood of arrest for white and nonwhite juvenile offenders." However, further analysis did show that the race of the *victim* had an effect on the likelihood of arrest. If the victim was white, and the perpetrator was nonwhite, the odds of arrest increased. Since 34 percent of the nonwhite juvenile offenders' victims were white, Pope and Snyder said that the victim's race as a factor in arrest might result in an indirect bias towards nonwhite offenders, all other factors being equal.

Overall, Pope and Snyder found that "NIBRS data offer no evidence to support the hypothesis that police are more likely to arrest nonwhite juvenile offenders than white juvenile offenders, once other incident attributes are taken into consideration."

Source: Based on Carl E. Pope and Howard N. Snyder, *Race as a Factor in Juvenile Arrests* (Washington, DC: Office of Juvenile Justice and Delinquency Prevention, 2003), 1–7.

The disproportionate number of arrests of female adolescents for "morality" offenses might be attributed to the **protective factor.** The protective factor suggests that police officers may be more likely to arrest female adolescents for certain offenses to protect them from behavior that may make them more vulnerable to pregnancy, prostitution, drug use, and general victimization. This explains why female adolescents are arrested more for certain offenses, but the **chivalry factor** helps to explain why females are less represented in arrest statistics overall. Otto Pollak suggests that female juveniles are more crime prone than arrest statistics show because police actually "let girls make it" for the same acts that would get a male juvenile arrested. Thus, female juveniles are arrested more frequently than males for morality-based offenses but are treated with chivalry by police officers for other offenses.[24]

Female adolescents are less involved than males in delinquency, but the extent to which they are less involved is arguable. Despite "protection" and "chivalry," evidence shows that the nature and extent of female juvenile crime may be changing—that female arrest patterns are starting to resemble traditional male patterns in seriousness and frequency. Some evidence suggests that chivalry by officers, if in fact it does occur, might be giving way to a more punitive and gender-blind focus in the juvenile justice system.[25] For example, although females under age eighteen account for approximately 28 percent of all juvenile arrests, female juveniles age thirteen to fifteen make up approximately 32 percent of all juvenile arrests in that same age group.[26] Moreover, when females are arrested, adjudicated, and subsequently placed on probation or parole, evidence shows they are more likely than males to be charged with a probation or parole violation.[27] Thus, females are starting to be arrested more often for crimes similar to those of males and may be treated more punitively once they are involved in the formal juvenile system.[28] Despite the changes in female arrest patterns, however, gender should never be a factor in determining whether a juvenile is arrested versus warned.

Socioeconomic Status **Socioeconomic status** is a category based on characteristics such as a person's education, occupation, and earnings. It is used in a society to determine classes, or strata, resulting in lower-, middle-, and upper-class distinctions. For juveniles, socioeconomic status (SES) refers to their family situation.

In juvenile arrests, SES has been examined under the assumption that the lower one's SES, the more likely that he or she will be arrested. The argument is that, for the same offense, lower-class juveniles get arrested whereas upper- and middle-class juveniles do not (they may receive a warning). Research has shown that as the SES of a particular neighborhood or community increases, the likelihood of arrest decreases.[29] Thus, police–juvenile encounters in low-SES neighborhoods (typically involving low-SES youths) are probably more likely to result in arrest.

Explaining the relationship between class and the arrest of juveniles is difficult. For example, it may simply be that upper-class or high-SES youths are warned by police whereas low-SES youths are not. This may be a straightforward bias or, more likely, may occur under the assumption that middle- or upper-class families may be better suited to monitor and discipline their children or get treatment for them than are lower-class families, where supervision or resources may be lacking. It may also be that police patrol activities are more focused on low-SES neighborhoods, where more "undesirable" and visible forms of crime are concentrated; thus, more officers in one particular area equals more arrests of low-SES youths. However, evidence does suggest that lower-class juveniles have higher rates of participation in more serious offenses, offenses in which officer discretion becomes less important and arrest becomes more likely.[30] But such bias cannot be rationalized for less serious offenses. However, a juvenile's SES should never be used as a factor when an officer is considering an arrest.

Other Factors Influencing Juvenile Arrests

Other factors can influence arrest: a juvenile's family situation, a juvenile's peer group associations, his or her demeanor, a citizen complaint, departmental policy, and the community's relationship with the police.

- *Demeanor.* Juveniles who are disrespectful, challenging, and do not show deference to police officer authority are more likely to be arrested.[31] However, demeanor probably makes little difference when considered in light of the frequency and seriousness of the offense. More serious or frequent offenders will likely be arrested whether they show deference to the police or not. But demeanor weighs heavily on an individual officer if the offense is not serious, and the overwhelming majority of juvenile offending is not serious. A typical delinquent is not a murderer or rapist. Instead, a typical delinquent vandalizes and shoplifts. In these cases, police officers have a great deal of discretion to selectively enforce the law. A poor attitude may tip the balance in favor of arrest.

- *Family situation.* Irrespective of social class (SES), whether parents are home, can pick up the youth, or are available to provide adequate supervision and discipline may influence whether the youth is arrested. For example, if officers know that they can call the parents and that the parents will discipline their child, arrest may become less likely. This is particularly the case when the crime is minor.

- *Victim or citizen complaint.* A complaint by a citizen or victim, even after a minor offense, can be an important factor in police–juvenile encounters. Much of police decision making is invisible to the public. The police make many decisions each day, only a few of which face public scrutiny or second-guessing. However, if a victim or witness is present to observe police decision making, and especially if he or she demands that an arrest be made, the juvenile is more likely to be arrested.[32] Police officers are aware that their actions make an important impression on the community. Failure by officers to arrest lawbreakers, especially in the plain view of witnesses or victims, can damage the officers' relations with the community and ultimately affect the public's degree of cooperation.

■ *Departmental style/policy.* In 1968, James Q. Wilson conceptualized a typology of operational styles of policing. After studying eight police departments, Wilson noted that three styles prevailed. The first is the **legalistic style,** characterized by an emphasis on following the law by the book. The second is the **watchman style,** characterized by the informal resolution of conflicts and using arrest as a last resort. Third, the **service style** was prevalent in departments with an emphasis on referral and diversion as the main goal rather than arrest.[33] Police–juvenile encounters involving officers from legalistically oriented departments (by the book) are more likely to end in arrest than under the watchman or service styles.[34]

Departmental policy extends beyond the operational or philosophical styles of police departments. Combined with state law, departmental policy may make arrest more likely for certain offenses. For example, some departments have mandatory arrest policies for domestic violence calls, including domestic violence caused by juvenile boys and girls. If a juvenile in a fit of rage throws a fan against the wall near one of his or her parents, police may categorize this as domestic violence and arrest the juvenile. Departmental policy of this type has resulted in many arrests of youths, especially female juveniles, who are charged with serious offenses (such as aggravated assault or making terroristic threats) after these incidents.

■ *Peer associations.* Arrest decisions may also be influenced by a youth's peer group or peer associations. If a juvenile associates with known gang members or other troublemakers, he or she is more likely to be arrested.

■ *Individual characteristics.* Individual factors may also influence arrest decisions: the juvenile's age, appearance, and maturity level. Theoretically, the older and more mature the juvenile, the more likely arrest will occur because "they should know better."

■ *Juvenile system characteristics.* Juvenile justice system factors are also influential, such as the availability of space in the local juvenile detention center or community referral programs. If juvenile detention space is limited, it is less likely that a youth will be arrested, particularly if the offense is minor. On the other hand, police may be more likely to arrest when community referral programs are not available.

In summary, police officers have a great deal of discretion in dealing with juvenile lawbreaking. Whether the officer opts to arrest a juvenile, as opposed to giving a warning or ignoring the behavior, is perhaps most influenced by the seriousness and frequency of the offense. However, citizen complaints, departmental style, race, gender, SES, demeanor, and community and juvenile justice system resources may also influence arrest decisions. Arguably, when arrest is the option, police officers should do what is best for the juvenile. This may not always be the case: Many officers feel that dealing with juveniles, especially when the majority of the contacts are for minor crimes, is a waste of time and resources that could be better spent catching "hard-core" adult criminals.[35]

Juvenile Arrests

How Arrests Are Counted

As the population of the United States grew in the early twentieth century, so did the incidence of crime. Without a uniform way to measure crime, little was known about its extent. In 1920 the International Association of Chiefs of Police (IACP) formed the Committee on Uniform Crime Records in an effort to develop a system of uniform arrest statistics so that trends in crime could be examined. In 1930 the *Uniform Crime Reports (UCR)* began, and today the UCR is regarded as one of the best indicators of crime in the United States. The Federal Bureau of Investigation (FBI) currently publishes the UCR on an annual basis. This publication, *Crime in the United States,* tracks arrests.

As discussed in Chapter 2, the UCR is divided into two parts, based on the seriousness of offenses. *Part I offenses* are considered the most serious person and property offenses: murder and non-negligent manslaughter, forcible rape, robbery, aggravated assault, burglary, larceny-theft, motor vehicle theft, and arson. *Part II offenses* include a number of offenses, mainly misdemeanors, such as vandalism, drug abuse violations, disorderly conduct, and vagrancy. Part II offenses also include behaviors prohibited only for juveniles, such as running away, curfew violations, and truancy.

As of 2003, the UCR included all arrests in the United States as reported by 17,000 city, county, and state law enforcement agencies. These 17,000 law enforcement agencies cover approximately 95 percent of the U.S. population. The UCR separates arrests by age; thus, it tracks juvenile as well as adult arrests.[36]

The Number and Trend of Juvenile Arrests

In 2001, juveniles accounted for approximately 17 percent of *all* arrests (both juvenile and adult) in the United States, an estimated 2.3 million juvenile arrests. Table 3.1 presents 2001 statistics on the estimated number of juvenile arrests by crime type. The vast majority of juvenile crime is nonviolent and nonperson offenses (approximately 96 percent). The most frequent arrests of juveniles included larceny-theft, drug abuse violations, simple assault, vandalism, liquor law violations, and disorderly conduct. Juveniles were also taken into custody nearly 300,000 times for runaway and curfew violations.[37] Although juveniles commit a relatively small percentage of crime when compared to adults, there are important trends in their offending over time.

Serious juvenile crime (meaning Part I offenses) has been on the decline in recent years. The juvenile arrest rate for violent crime continues to decline, falling 41 percent from its peak in 1994. Between 1993 and 2000, the number of juveniles arrested for murder or non-negligent manslaughter fell from 3,800 to 1,200, a 68-percent decline (murder and non-negligent manslaughter did increase from 1,200 to 1,400 from 2000 to 2001). Juvenile arrest rates for burglary have declined 63 percent between 1980 and 2000. In fact, most forms of juvenile crime have declined considerably in the last ten years since a peak in 1994.[38]

TABLE 3.1

Juvenile Arrests in 2001

The number of juvenile arrests in 2001—2.3 million—was 4% below the 2000 level and 20% below the 1997 level.

Most Serious Offense	2001 Estimated Number of Juvenile Arrests	Percent of Total Juvenile Arrests		Percent Change		
		Female	Under Age 15	1992–2001	1997–2001	2000–2001
Total	**2,273,500**	**28%**	**32%**	**−3%**	**−20%**	**−4%**
Crime Index total	587,900	29	37	−31	−28	−5
Violent Crime Index	96,500	18	33	−21	−21	−2
Murder and nonnegligent manslaughter	1,400	10	12	−62	−47	−2
Forcible rape	4,600	1	38	−24	−14	−1
Robbery	25,600	9	24	−32	−35	−4
Aggravated assault	64,900	23	37	−14	−13	−1
Property Crime Index	491,400	31	38	−32	−29	−6
Burglary	90,300	12	38	−40	−30	−6
Larceny-theft	343,600	39	39	−27	−30	−6
Motor vehicle theft	48,200	17	25	−51	−26	−2
Arson	9,300	12	64	−7	−9	8
Nonindex						
Other assaults	239,000	32	43	30	−2	2
Forgery and counterfeiting	5,800	36	11	−27	−26	−8
Fraud	8,900	33	16	−5	−18	−9
Embezzlement	1,800	44	7	152	24	−10
Stolen property (buying, receiving, possessing)	26,800	17	27	−45	−37	−6
Vandalism	105,300	13	44	−29	−22	−7
Weapons (carrying, possessing, etc.)	37,500	11	34	−35	−26	0
Prostitution and commercialized vice	1,400	69	15	−8	−5	15
Sex offense (except forcible rape and prostitution)	18,000	8	54	−10	6	1
Drug abuse violations	202,500	15	17	121	−7	0
Gambling	1,400	3	13	−53	−47	−17
Offenses against the family and children	9,600	37	37	109	−11	6
Driving under the influence	20,300	18	5	35	5	−3
Liquor law violations	138,100	32	10	21	−9	−11
Drunkenness	20,400	21	13	4	−21	−10
Disorderly conduct	171,700	30	40	34	−21	1
Vagrancy	2,300	19	25	−37	−24	−10
All other offenses (except traffic)	397,200	26	28	27	−13	−3
Suspicion	1,300	36	33	−53	−42	9
Curfew and loitering	142,900	31	28	34	−29	−13
Runaways	133,300	59	38	−25	−30	−6

(continued)

TABLE 3.1

(continued)

- In 2001, there were an estimated 1,400 juvenile arrests for murder. Between 1997 and 2001, juvenile arrests for murder fell 47%.
- Females accounted for 23% of juvenile arrests for aggravated assault and 32% of juvenile arrests for other assaults (i.e., simple assaults and intimidations) in 2001. Females were involved in 59% of all arrests for running away from home and 31% of arrests for curfew and loitering law violations.
- Between 1992 and 2001, there were substantial declines in juvenile arrests for murder (62%), motor vehicle theft (51%), and burglary (40%) and major increases in juvenile arrests for drug abuse violations (121%).

Note: Detail may not add to totals because of rounding.

Source: Howard N. Snyder, "Juvenile Arrests 2001." *Juvenile Justice Bulletin* (December 2003): 3.

The overall picture concerning juvenile arrests is promising. When examined more closely, however, there is still concern. Female juvenile crime is one concern. Juvenile females account for just 28 percent of all juvenile arrests, but between 1991 and 2000, arrests of female juveniles increased at a greater rate than male arrests. Although robbery, burglary, theft, and motor vehicle theft declined for female juveniles over this period, aggravated assault, simple assault, and drug abuse violations increased substantially.[39] Aggravated assault arrests increased 44 percent from 1991 to 2000, simple assault increased 78 percent, and drug abuse violations increased 220 percent. Moreover, young juvenile females are making an impact as well: Arrest statistics show that juvenile females ages thirteen to fifteen accounted for 32 percent of all arrests in that age group.[40] Thus, females are grabbing a large share of the arrests at a young age (see Table 3.1).

Although trends in female juvenile crime suggest increases in certain forms of serious crime at younger ages, note that juvenile females are still much less involved in these types of crimes than juvenile males overall (28 percent of all juvenile arrests are attributed to female juveniles versus 72 percent to male juveniles). Thus, percentage increases tend to inflate perceptions about the extent of female juvenile crime despite actual arrest increases that still remain low compared to males. Nonetheless, such trends are cause for some concern and do indicate that female juvenile crime is on the rise in certain areas.

Legal Rights of Juveniles During Stop and Frisk, Arrests, and Searches and Seizures

The Fourth Amendment to the U.S. Constitution states that "the right of people to be secure in their persons, houses, papers, and effects, against unreasonable searches and seizures, shall not be violated . . . but upon probable cause."[41] This section examines stop and frisk, arrest, and other searches and seizures that are covered by the Fourth Amendment.

Stop and Frisk of Juveniles

Stop and frisk is a form of seizure under the Fourth Amendment, but it does not constitute an arrest and is therefore governed by a different standard than is used for an arrest. The leading case in stop and frisk is *Terry v. Ohio* (1968).[42] In *Terry*, the U.S. Supreme Court held that police officers may stop an individual for a brief investigatory period provided that they have a *reasonable suspicion* that criminal activity may be afoot. **Reasonable suspicion** is defined as a "degree of proof that is less than probable cause, but more than suspicion . . . it represents a degree of certainty (around 30 percent) that a crime has been or will be committed and that the suspect is involved in it."[43]

Because a stop and frisk is less intrusive than an arrest, it is justified under the lower standard of reasonable suspicion rather than probable cause (which is required for an arrest). Once an officer *stops* an individual, the officer may conduct a protective *frisk* of the person for weapons if the officer reasonably suspects that he or she is in danger. However, police officers in stop and frisk cases may conduct only a protective pat-down search, not a full-scale search, according to the U.S. Supreme Court in *Minnesota v. Dickerson* (1993).[44] For example, officers may feel the outside of a coat pocket in a stop and frisk, but they may not jam their hand in the person's pocket and feel, squeeze, or manipulate objects in the pocket. That would constitute elements of a full search not authorized by *Terry* under a reasonable suspicion standard and would require probable cause.

The above discussion demonstrates that law enforcement officers cannot stop and frisk individuals without cause—there must be at least reasonable suspicion. Reasonable suspicion is sometimes difficult to establish, however, depending on the circumstances. For example, in the case of *In the Interests of J. L., A Child* (1993), police officers observed J. L. walking toward an area where a burglary had recently occurred.[45] J. L. was wearing a large coat, which the police officer thought was odd because it was a warm night. J. L. was approached by the officer and was asked a variety of questions, which J. L. answered truthfully and provided a reasonable explanation for being in the area. Despite his answers, J. L. was frisked. The protective frisk revealed a pistol. The Florida appellate court in this case concluded that officers did not have reasonable suspicion to stop and frisk J. L. because being in a particular area does not, in itself, justify such a stop and frisk. This case also demonstrates the principle that an officer's gut feeling about criminal activity may be correct but that a gut feeling must be supported with a degree of proof before an individual is stopped, even for only a brief investigatory period.

Reasonable suspicion during a stop and frisk often turns into probable cause. Therefore, what starts off as reasonable suspicion can escalate into probable cause and then lead to a valid arrest and a full search after the arrest.

Arrests of Persons

A stop and frisk is different from an arrest. An *arrest* is defined as the taking of a person into custody against his or her will for the purpose of criminal prosecution or interrogation.[46] Stop and frisk is not an arrest: It involves a brief investigatory detention, and the person is not stopped for the purpose of later criminal prosecution and interrogation. In sum, stop and frisk is much less intrusive than arrest. However, police officers need probable cause to arrest a juvenile. As previously defined, *probable cause* for arrest is "more than bare suspicion; it exists when the facts and circumstances within the officers' knowledge . . . are sufficient in themselves to warrant a person of reasonable caution in the belief that an offense has been or is being committed."[47]

As mentioned, a stop and frisk situation might turn into probable cause for an arrest. For example, if during a protective frisk officers feel what appears to be a weapon in the coat pocket of the suspect, the officers would have cause to seize the object; if it turns out to be a weapon, the officer could arrest the suspect. After an arrest based upon probable cause, officers are allowed to conduct a full search of the person[48] and of the area in the immediate control of the suspect.[49] These same rules apply to juveniles. However, juveniles may be subject to a full search following "custody" for noncriminal conduct such as curfew and truancy violations, even if such custody is based on reasonable suspicion instead of probable cause as determined by state law.[50] Table 3.2 illustrates the level of proof and degree of certainty and where probable cause and reasonable suspicion fall in relation to other levels of proof. The "You Are a . . . Police Officer" box (p. 88) includes an exercise to determine whether in three scenarios officers have probable cause, reasonable suspicion, or insufficient information.

TABLE 3.2

Levels of Proof and Degree of Certainty

Level of Proof	Degree of Certainty	Type of Proceeding
Absolute certainty	100%	Not required in any legal proceeding
Guilt beyond a reasonable doubt	95%	Convict an accused; prove every element of a criminal act
Clear and convincing evidence	80%	Denial of bail in some states and insanity defense in some states
Probable cause*	More than 50%	Issuance of warrant, search, seizure, and arrest without warrant, filing of an indictment
Preponderance of the evidence*	More than 50%	Winning a civil case; affirmative criminal defense
Reasonable suspicion	30%	Stop and frisk by police
Suspicion	10%	Start a police or grand jury investigation
Reasonable doubt	5%	Acquit an accused
Hunch	0%	Not sufficient in any legal proceeding
No information	0%	Not sufficient in any legal proceeding

*Probable cause and preponderance of the evidence have the same level of certainty—more than 50%. This means that anything above 50% will suffice. The difference is that "probable cause" is used in criminal proceedings, whereas "preponderance of the evidence" is usually used in civil proceedings, although aspects of a criminal proceeding use this term as well.

Source: Rolando V. del Carmen, *Criminal Procedure: Law and Practice,* 5th ed. (Belmont, CA: Wadsworth, 2001), 72.

Police Officer

Scenario 1: A juvenile is walking near a sports warehouse building where several burglaries have occurred in the past six months. Officer A and Officer B notice that the juvenile is wearing a heavy and expensive sports coat. The officers also notice that the juvenile has new sneakers on.

Scenario 2: A group of female juveniles are in a park known to the police for drug transactions. It is 10 P.M. Officer C and Officer D drive by in their patrol car, and one of the juveniles, upon noticing the officers, walks away from the park at a "brisk pace" and appears to throw something in the bushes.

Scenario 3: Officer X and Officer Y pass a car with four male juveniles inside. It is 9 P.M. One of the juveniles, according to Officer Y, "looked at me crazy."

1. In each situation, determine whether officers have probable cause, reasonable suspicion, or not enough information to stop the individual.

2. Are probable cause and/or reasonable suspicion subjective in these cases?

3. What other factors might be helpful for these police officers in deciding whether there is probable cause or reasonable suspicion?

4. Would you stop, and possibly arrest, the juveniles in any of these three situations? Explain.

Searches and Seizures

The general rule is that searches and seizures can be made only with a warrant. In reality, however, there are multiple exceptions to this general rule; therefore, most searches and seizures are made without a warrant. For example, one exception is that a search and seizure without a warrant may be conducted following a lawful arrest as discussed above (search incident to an arrest based on probable cause). Another exception is when a person gives an officer his or her consent to search but officers do not have probable cause or a warrant for the search. The consent exception says that if the person gives proper consent, the consent is valid, and anything illegal found and confiscated during the search may be introduced as evidence in court. The two issues involved with the "consent exception" involving juveniles are whether a juvenile can validly consent to a search, and whether parents can approve of a police search of their child's belongings.

Can a Juvenile Consent to a Search?

Consent is one way that police officers may search and seize person or property without a warrant or probable cause. Because of a juvenile's young age and immaturity, there is a question of whether juveniles can legally consent to a search.

Courts are generally reluctant to hold that juveniles, because of their age and immaturity alone, are incapable of consenting to a search.[51] The standard by which courts determine whether a juvenile is capable of consent is whether such consent was *voluntary, based on the totality of the circumstances.* The totality of the circumstances test says that a juvenile may validly consent to a search of his or her person or property if such consent was given voluntarily (meaning not the result of coercion or deprivation) when evaluated in the context of several factors, such as the juvenile's age, maturity level, and experience in the juvenile justice system.[52] For example, a juvenile may voluntarily consent to a search, but a court may later find such consent invalid when evaluated under the totality of circumstances surrounding it—for example, the juvenile was seven years old, mentally challenged, and had never before been arrested. In this instance, the juvenile's ability to consent is called into question and possibly invalidated, even if it was voluntarily given. When this happens, all evidence obtained from the search is generally inadmissible in court. A juvenile's ability to consent and under what conditions may be determined by state law. Some states hold that juveniles cannot validly consent to a search, even when voluntary, when they are not in the presence of parents or a lawyer. State law prevails in these cases.*

Police Search and Seizure with Parental Consent

Another situation involving juveniles is search and seizure involving parental consent and the juvenile's right to privacy. One issue is whether a warrantless but parent-approved police search of a juvenile's property is valid. In 1974 the U.S. Supreme Court held in *United States v. Matlock* (1974) that a third party (such as a parent) can consent to a warrantless search of a premise where there is common authority.[53] This case did not involve a parent-approved search of a juvenile's belongings, but there is reason to believe it would apply to such a search. Parents are generally authorized to consent to a search of their child's room and personal belongings because it is the parents' right and duty to control their child and because parents are recognized as the authority of the household.[54] Under these justifications, parent-approved, warrantless searches have generally been upheld by lower courts.** However, not all courts have agreed that a parent-approved, warrantless search is valid in every instance. For example, although parents may generally give consent to search the rooms of their minor children, they may not give consent if the child is paying room and board to the parents.†

Parents are increasingly being held accountable for their children's actions, but some states do not allow parents to consent to a search of their child's room and possessions. (However, this is not the case in most states.) When states prohibit parents from consenting to a search of their child's belongings, or when they limit consent, this may become a double-edged sword for parents—on the one hand, they may not consent to a search, but on the other hand, they may be held responsible for their child's illegal actions. The mood today is for allowing parent-approved searches, particularly when the child is

---

*For an excellent review of consent, including examples of state and federal case law and statutes, see Barry Feld, *Juvenile Justice Administration in a Nutshell* (St. Paul, MN: West, 2003), 69–74. This section of the chapter is informed by Feld's review.

**See, for example, *In re Salyer*, 358 N.E.2d 1333 (Ill. App. Ct. [1977]), which holds that a parent's permission to search the locked room of son is valid.

†See also *In re Scott K.*, P.2d 105 (Supreme Court Ca. [1979]), in which parents did not have a "protectible interest" in their child's locked toolbox.

suspected to be in the possession of a weapon or other dangerous contraband. The situation may be different for other forms of alleged delinquent conduct, and state law prevails in these circumstances. (See the "Controversial Issue" box.)

School Searches and Police Assistance

Another exception to the search and seizure with a warrant requirement is called the "special needs beyond law enforcement" exception.[55] Such searches are not purely police searches but instead involve searches conducted by other public officials who perform tasks related to law enforcement. One "special need" situation involves the role of public school officials in dealing with juveniles. In an important case, *New Jersey v. T. L. O.* (1985), the U.S. Supreme

CONTROVERSIAL ISSUE: WHICH SIDE DO YOU FAVOR?

How far does a child's right to privacy extend?

Children are considered persons under the Constitution in that they have rights like adults. Due to their young age, however, some of the rights of juveniles are diminished because it is believed that they are too young to handle certain life responsibilities without guidance. The responsibility to guide juveniles in situations where they may be too young or immature to exercise their rights properly is usually left to a child's parents. When the child's parents turn to law enforcement for assistance, controversial situations sometimes arise.

This raises a question: *Should parents be allowed to consent to a police search of their child's belongings?*

Those who argue that parents should be allowed to consent to a police search of their child's belongings note that parents have authority in their household. Children have diminished rights when they live under their parents' roof. Because parents are being increasingly held accountable for the actions of their children, states should allow parents complete authority to authorize police officers to search their child's belongings. Juveniles are different from adults and are not mature enough to fully regulate their own lives. It is the parents' job to do so, including consenting to police searches of their child's belongings if they believe the child is breaking the law.

Those who argue that parents should not be allowed to consent to a search of their child's belongings note that children are persons under the Constitution irrespective of the fact that they live under their parents' roof. That some states hold parents accountable for their child's actions is no reason to stomp on the privacy rights of youths. Good parents must trust that their children are doing the right thing. Children need privacy like adults, and allowing parents to supersede their child's privacy by consenting to a police search does not contribute to their development as responsible persons. All it does is disturb the relationship between parents and their children by showing that children cannot be trusted—when, in fact, most children can be.

Court decided whether high school officials need probable cause or a warrant (the standard by which police must operate) in order to search a juvenile and his or her belongings.[56]

The facts of the case are as follows: T. L. O. was discovered smoking a cigarette in the school rest room, which was in violation of school policy (see the "Case Brief" box). She was taken to the principal's office by a teacher, and her

Case Brief ## Leading Case on School Searches

New Jersey v. T. L. O., 469 U.S. 325 (1985)

Facts: A fourteen-year-old girl was discovered smoking cigarettes in a school rest room in violation of school rules. She was taken to the principal's office by a high school teacher. When the student denied that she had been smoking, the assistant vice principal demanded to see her purse. Inside the purse the vice principal found numerous contraband items, most notably marijuana, a pipe, a substantial amount of money, and names of students who owed her money. The state brought delinquency charges against the student in juvenile court. She moved to have the evidence found in her purse suppressed, alleging that the search was conducted without probable cause or a warrant by school officials and, hence, violated her rights under the Fourth Amendment.

Issue: Do public high school officials need probable cause or a warrant in order to search juveniles?

Supreme Court Decision: Public school officials do not need a warrant or probable cause before conducting a search. For a search to be valid, all school officials need are "reasonable grounds" to suspect that the search will produce evidence that the student has violated or is violating school rules or the law. Requiring a warrant or probable cause would interfere with swift and informal disciplinary procedures needed in schools to maintain safety and an educational environment for all students.

Case Significance: This case clarifies the issue of whether public school officials must obtain a warrant and have probable cause before searching a public school student. Although public school officials are representatives of the state and are bound by the Fourth Amendment guarantee against unreasonable search and seizure, the Court recognized that in order to maintain an environment suited for learning, some restrictions placed on public school authorities by the Fourth Amendment had to be eased. In other words, schools represent a special-need situation. In this case, public school authorities may search students under a lower standard than most other public authorities. This standard is reasonable grounds, not probable cause.

Excerpts from the Decision: "Today's public school officials do not merely exercise authority voluntarily conferred on them by individual parents; rather, they act in furtherance of publicly mandated educational and disciplinary policies.

(continued)

Case Brief *Leading Case on School Searches (continued)*

"It is evident that the school setting requires some easing of the restrictions to which searches by public authorities are ordinarily subject. The warrant requirement, in particular, is unsuited to the school environment: requiring a teacher to obtain a warrant before searching a child suspected of an infraction of school rules (or of the criminal law) would unduly interfere with the maintenance of the swift and informal disciplinary procedures needed in schools.

"The school setting also requires some modification of the level of suspicion of illicit activity needed to justify a search. . . . Under ordinary circumstances, a search of a student by a teacher or other school official will be 'justified at its inception' when there are reasonable grounds for suspecting that the search will turn up evidence that the student has violated or is violating either a law or the rules of the school. Such a search will be permissible in its scope when the measures adopted are reasonably related to the objectives of the search and not excessively intrusive in light of the age and sex of the student and the nature of the infraction."

Source: This brief originally appeared in Rolando V. del Carmen, Mary Parker, and Frances P. Reddington, *Briefs of Leading Cases in Juvenile Justice* (Cincinnati: Anderson, 1998).

person and property were searched. Inside her purse, the vice principal found several contraband items: a pack of cigarettes, a package of rolling papers, marijuana, a pipe, plastic bags, a substantial amount of money, a list of names of students who owed her money, and two letters that implicated her in marijuana dealing. She was petitioned to the juvenile court and subsequently adjudicated based on this evidence. On appeal, T. L. O. moved to suppress the evidence found in her purse on the grounds that the search was illegal because it was not based upon probable cause or supported by a warrant. The U.S. Supreme Court concluded that public school officials do not need a warrant or probable cause to search a student and his or her possessions. For the search to be valid, the Court noted that all school officials need is "reasonable grounds" to suspect that the search will produce evidence that the student has violated or is about to violate the law or school rules.[57]

The Court's decision in *T. L. O.* was based on the belief that although students are protected from unreasonable search and seizure under the Fourth Amendment, which normally requires probable cause or a warrant, school officials also have a duty to uphold the rules and regulations of the school for the protection of all students and to maintain a learning environment. In short, students do not have the same reasonable expectation of privacy in schools as they do outside of schools. Their individual rights are diminished in the interests of the entire student body.[58]

New Jersey v. T. L. O. is important because it set the standard for public high school officials in the search and seizure of students, but *T. L. O.* did not answer important questions concerning the scope of police officer authority in schools (see Chapter 13, on juveniles in schools, for other issues). Today, many school districts have opted to institute a formal police presence on school grounds, and police officers may frequently come into contact with students at school during potential search and seizure situations. However, *T. L. O.* does not generally allow police officers, who are bound by probable cause, to conduct a search of a student and his or her belongings. The only exceptions might be when officers are employed by the school district (such as a separate school district police officer), when their job description includes substantial school participation (such as a school liaison/resource officer who works in schools), or when police officers are approached by school officials who ask them to assist in a student search and seizure situation. The last two issues were addressed in *Cason v. Cook* (1987).[59]

In *Cason v. Cook*, the Eighth Circuit Court of Appeals examined whether the "reasonable grounds" standard for search and seizure by public school officials applies when such searches are conducted with the help of police officers. In this case, a student's locker was broken into, and several items were stolen. After receiving a report of this incident, the vice principal initiated an investigation and identified four female students whose presence in the area of the theft looked suspicious. One of the four students, Shy Cason, was taken to the principal's office and questioned in the presence of a police officer who was part of a liaison project with the city's police department. Cason's purse was searched, and a coin purse was found that matched the description of an item reported stolen.

The Eighth Circuit Court of Appeals held that the search initiated by school officials, which was based on reasonable suspicion and with the "assistance" of a school liaison officer, was appropriate. The court ruled that assistance from a police officer who was in support of school efforts did not make the search and seizure invalid given that it was not based on probable cause. Thus, the rule from *Cason* is that reasonable grounds instead of probable cause are the standard used in searches made by public school officials, even if the search is conducted with the assistance of a police officer.

However, the key to understanding *Cason* is that the officer was based in the school as a liaison officer and *assisted* school officials. Whether this same holding applies to police officers not acting in a school-related role has not been decided by the U.S. Supreme Court. Also not decided by the Court is whether non-school-related police officers (such as city police officers) who act in an active rather than assisting role are bound by probable cause or reasonable grounds. For example, what is the rule if police officers *request* that school officials search a particular student? Lower courts have addressed these issues. The general rule is that police officers are prohibited from this type of "active" role and need probable cause. The same rule applies when police officers are not employed by the school district or are not in a role with school assistance as their primary duty. Chapter 13 covers the various issues with police and the probable cause debate in schools. For the purposes of this chapter, a juvenile in school may generally be searched without a warrant or probable cause as long as school officials have reasonable grounds. This standard is lower than probable cause and is justified because schools represent a special-need situation in which protection of the entire student body outweighs an individual student's expectation of privacy in some circumstances.

General Search Conditions for Juvenile Probationers

Another unique search and seizure situation involves juveniles on probation. In general, probation is viewed as a privilege in lieu of incarceration; as a result, a juvenile's privacy may be diminished in exchange for allowing him or her to remain in the community. The issue in police–juvenile probationer encounters is to what extent a juvenile has a reasonable expectation of privacy when on probation. A related issue concerns a controversial probation search condition (referred to as a general search condition of probation) that says a juvenile may be searched by any law enforcement officer at any time, without a warrant, probable cause, or, in some cases, reasonable grounds or suspicion.

The U.S. Supreme Court held in *Griffin v. Wisconsin* (1987) that an adult probationer's home could be searched by probation officers without a warrant or probable cause as long as there was a general search condition of probation in place and as long as probation officers had reasonable suspicion to search.[60] In this case, the Court held that an agency rule or state law permitting such searches is a reasonable response to the "special needs" of the probation system and is therefore constitutional. Additionally, the Court held in *United States v. Knights* (2001) that probation officers need only reasonable suspicion to justify a home search of an adult probationer who was subject to a warrantless search condition of probation.[61]

These cases were specific to adult probationers, but there is reason to believe that such cases involving adult probation officers are generally applicable to juvenile probation officers conducting searches of juvenile probationers. A few lower court cases have specifically examined the reasonable expectation of privacy for juvenile probationers. However, these cases answer whether the same search and seizure rules for probation officers apply to *police officers* when they deal with juvenile probationers. Court cases reveal that police officers are generally able to search a juvenile probationer without a warrant or probable cause when juveniles are subject to a general search condition as a part of their probation agreement and if officers have at least reasonable grounds to search.[62] Without a general search condition as part of a probation agreement, law enforcement officers must usually have probable cause or a warrant.[63]

According to Barry Feld, juveniles may have a reduced expectation of privacy on probation because the "rehabilitative goals of juvenile courts are stronger than and require broader authority to deter probation violations than is the case for adults,"[64] meaning that law enforcement officers may need less reason to search a juvenile probationer. For example, a California appellate court held that evidence obtained from an otherwise illegal search may be used in juvenile court because the juvenile probationer was subject to a general search condition of probation.[65] Thus, police officers did not even have reasonable suspicion to search the juvenile, but the court still allowed the evidence.

In a similar case, *In re Tyrell J.* (1994), Tyrell J. agreed to a condition of probation that he submit to a search of his person and property, with or without a warrant, by any law enforcement officer, probation officer, or school official.[66] In this case, police officers noticed Tyrell J. and two friends acting suspiciously at a high school football game, with one of the juveniles wearing a heavy jacket on a warm night. Upon further investigation, one of the officers recognized Tyrell J. and his friends as members of a gang that had caused trouble at a football game a week earlier. The officers proceeded to search the juveniles and found a large hunting knife. Further searching revealed a bag of marijuana on Tyrell J. Although the basis of the search was questionable (and perhaps illegal), the court ruled that the evidence from the search was admissible because Tyrell J. was subject to a search condition as part of his probation agreement. That the police officers did not know about the search condition or that the search was based on questionable grounds and without a warrant, probable cause, or reasonable suspicion did not matter. According to the court, Tyrell J. did not have a reasonable expectation of privacy because of his probation stipulation. This case illustrates that police officers may have more authority over juveniles on probation than over adults and may search juveniles without a warrant or probable cause if a general search condition of probation is in place and as long as officers have reasonable grounds. Note that some courts have held that law enforcement officers do not need to be aware of the general search condition and that any resulting evidence from the search may be used in court—even if the search was based on questionable or illegal grounds or in the absence of reasonable suspicion.

The rehabilitative aims of the juvenile justice system may mean that police officers have more power to intervene and deter potential probation violations for juveniles than for adults. Juveniles on probation may be viewed as being in a greater special-need situation.* As shown, there is much variation among the states, and because the U.S. Supreme Court has not specifically addressed the issue, state law and/or state and lower federal court decisions prevail.

Custody and Interrogation of Juveniles

Interrogation occurs when police officers ask questions that can incriminate.[67] Any incriminating statements obtained from the interrogation can then be used at trial. Before 1966, arrested individuals were not subjected to clear rules on interrogation. In 1966, the U.S. Supreme Court changed the rules on interrogation with its decision in *Miranda v. Arizona* (1966).[68] The *Miranda* ruling holds that suspects under "custodial interrogation" must be informed by the police that

- They have the right to remain silent.
- Any statements they make can be used against them.
- They have the right to counsel.
- If they cannot afford counsel, they will receive a court-appointed lawyer.

---

*See, however, two federal circuit court cases which have said that reasonable suspicion is needed to search a probationer's home regardless of a general search condition of his or her probation: *United States v. Giannetta*, 909 F.2d 571 (1st Cir. 1990), and *United States v. David*, 932 F. 2d 752 (9th Cir. 1991).

Miranda Wording and Juveniles

Some observers wonder whether *Miranda* should be modified in cases where juveniles are arrested and questioned.[69] The question is whether juveniles should be held to the same standard as adults concerning *Miranda* because even adults tend to have difficulty understanding the implications of this ruling. In a landmark study, Thomas Grisso examined the *Miranda* warnings and juveniles. Grisso found that juveniles had less comprehension of the *Miranda* warnings than adults did. Of the juveniles he examined, 55 percent had an inadequate understanding of the warnings compared to 23 percent of adults. Grisso also found that juveniles had difficulty with the words used in *Miranda,* with 63 percent of juveniles misunderstanding at least one crucial word, compared to only 37 percent of adults. Moreover, Grisso revealed that many juveniles did not understand the meaning of the right to remain silent. He found that 62 percent of juveniles believed that they would be penalized by a judge for remaining silent.[70]

Despite Grisso's findings, research has shown that a "simpler" *Miranda* warning would not have a great impact on whether juveniles understood it or not.[71] However, the fact that juveniles appear to have a diminished capacity to understand *Miranda* has led some to suggest that juveniles should be afforded greater protections during interrogation. For example, some courts have suggested that a "fifth *Miranda* warning" be given to ensure that a juvenile adequately understands his or her rights ("you have the right to stop answering questions at any time") or that *Miranda* warnings be given multiple times to juveniles.[72]

When Is a Suspect Under "Custodial Interrogation" for *Miranda* Purposes?

A person is not entitled to *Miranda* warnings unless that person is under "custodial interrogation," meaning that the suspect is (1) in custody and (2) under interrogation. This stipulation implies that being in custody and under interrogation are two different things and that both are necessary for *Miranda* warnings to be required. For example, when a suspect is "in custody," but no interrogating (or incriminating) questions are being asked, *Miranda* warnings are not required. Conversely, if an individual is "under interrogation" but he or she is not "in custody," there is no need to give *Miranda* warnings.[73] Whether a suspect is in custody or not is where most controversy occurs.

A person is "in custody" when he or she is (1) under arrest or (2) deprived of freedom in a significant way. Being under arrest is generally clear, but being deprived of freedom requires explanation because it speaks to the perception of the suspect—especially if police do not inform the suspect that he or she is free to leave or is under arrest. Being deprived of freedom in a significant way generally means that the person's freedom of movement has been limited by law enforcement and that the person is not free to leave *after* police questioning—for all intents and purposes, the person is under arrest. If one or both of the above custody requirements are present (under arrest or deprived of freedom in a significant way), and the person is being asked incriminating questions, *Miranda* warnings are required. When is a person under interrogation? A person is under interrogation when the police are asking questions that tend to incriminate. Both "in custody" and "under interrogation" are required for *Miranda* warnings, and this is the same for adults and juveniles. However, "in custody" determinations were debated for juveniles in a recently decided U.S. Supreme Court case, *Yarborough v. Alvarado* (2004).[74]

The Latest Issue in Miranda *and Juvenile Custody and Interrogation:* Yarborough v. Alvarado

In March 2004, the U.S. Supreme Court heard arguments in the case of *Yarborough v. Alvarado*.[75] In this case, the Court decided whether a juvenile's age and experience must be consulted in determining custody for *Miranda* purposes. As mentioned above, *Miranda* warnings are required only when the person is being interrogated and is under arrest or is deprived of freedom in a significant way (in custody). This case examined whether juveniles are mature enough to know whether they are "deprived of freedom in a significant way" and essentially whether *Miranda* warnings must be given in all cases when juveniles are being asked incriminating questions.

In this case, Michael Alvarado was a suspect in a carjacking that resulted in the death of the victim. After a month-long investigation by the Los Angeles County Sheriff's office, a detective called the Alvarado house and left a message requesting that Michael and his parents come to the sheriff's station to be interviewed about the crime. Michael's parents transported him to the sheriff's station and gave law enforcement officers permission to interview their son.

At the time of the interrogation, Alvarado was seventeen and one-half years old, and his parents were barred from the interview room. Detective Comstock questioned Alvarado and never indicated that he was under arrest and, therefore, never gave Alvarado *Miranda* warnings. During the interview, Alvarado initially denied the crime, but upon further questioning over a two-hour period, he eventually incriminated himself. After the interview, Alvarado went home with his parents. Two months later, he was charged with murder and attempted robbery.

Prior to trial, Alvarado moved to exclude from evidence his statements to Detective Comstock. He argued that he was "in custody" at the time of the interrogation and that his parents were barred from the interrogation; therefore, he should have been given *Miranda* warnings. The prosecution in the case opposed the motion to exclude the statements, arguing that he was not "in custody" during the interview by offering evidence that he was never told he was under arrest, was transported to the police station by his parents, and was allowed to go home *after* the interview. The trial court denied Alvarado's motion to exclude his incriminating statements. Eventually, Michael Alvarado was convicted of murder and attempted robbery and sentenced to prison for fifteen years to life.

Alvarado appealed his conviction. The California Court of Appeals affirmed the conviction by stating "that a reasonable person under the [totality of] circumstances in which Alvarado was questioned would have felt free to leave." Therefore, the California Court of Appeals said he was not in custody and did not need *Miranda* warnings. Alvarado's case was eventually heard by the Ninth Circuit Court of Appeals. The Ninth Circuit held that Alvarado's "juvenile status" should be taken into account to determine whether he was "in custody" or not and reversed the California Court of Appeals. It held that Michael Alvarado was "in custody" and should have been given *Miranda* warnings because he had no prior arrest history, he had limited experience with law enforcement officers, his parents took him to the police station, and his parents were never present in the interrogation. In sum, because of these factors, the Ninth Circuit questioned whether Michael Alvarado would have known he was not under arrest, free to leave, and hence not in custody.[76] The U.S. Supreme Court granted certiorari to review this case in September 2003 on the issue of whether a court must consider "in custody" determinations based on age and experience if the suspect is a juvenile. The case was decided on June 1, 2004.

Yarborough v. Alvarado *and Its Implications for Juveniles*

The case hinged on whether Michael Alvarado was deprived of freedom in a significant way to such an extent that he believed he was not free to leave the interview. The issue before the Court was whether a juvenile's age and experience should be considered in making this "free to leave" custody determination. Los Angeles County Sheriff's detectives argued that they did not have to give Alvarado *Miranda* warnings because he was not in custody and was free to leave the station at any time.

During arguments, several Supreme Court justices questioned whether a teen who had no prior contact with law enforcement would have known he was free to go. In a 5–4 decision, however, the U.S. Supreme Court ruled that an evaluation of a juvenile's age and experience by police officers is not required to determine custody. The Court remarked that police officers should not have the burden of determining whether an individual subjectively feels free to leave for a custody determination. Thus, police officers should not be asked to consider these "contingent psychological" factors when deciding if a person is in custody and should be advised of his or her *Miranda* rights. In short, juveniles receive no special treatment in custody determinations and thus no special treatment for the application of *Miranda*. In dissent to the majority opinion, however, was Justice Stephen Breyer:

> What reasonable person in the circumstances—brought to a police station by his parents at police request, put in a small interrogation room, questioned for a solid two hours, and confronted with claims that there is strong evidence that he participated in a serious crime, could have thought to himself, "Well, anytime I want to leave I can just get up and walk out?" The law in this case asks judges to apply, not arcane or complex legal directives, but ordinary common sense. A court must answer this question in light of "all the circumstances surrounding the interrogation." And the obvious answer is "no."[77]

If the *Yarborough* case had been upheld by the U.S. Supreme Court, law enforcement officers would have had two custody standards governing the *Miranda* warning: one for adults and one for juveniles. In that case, law enforcement officers would have had to give *Miranda* warnings to all juveniles and all persons whom law enforcement officers suspected were juveniles before they asked incriminating questions regardless of whether the suspects were determined to be in custody or not. The Court ruled otherwise. As a result, custody and *Miranda* will stand as they do now, with juveniles not receiving special treatment in custody determinations for *Miranda* purposes. However, individual states could still require that a juvenile's age and experience be evaluated in determining custody despite the ruling of the U.S. Supreme Court.[78]

A Juvenile May Waive *Miranda* Rights: The Totality of Circumstances Test

Once given *Miranda* under the requirements above, a suspect may waive his or her right to a lawyer and the right to remain silent. This situation is the same for both adults and juveniles. A **waiver** is "an intentional relinquishment of a known right or remedy."[79] To be valid, however, a waiver of *Miranda* rights must be intelligent and voluntary. An **intelligent waiver** means that a suspect knows what he or she is doing and is competent to waive legal rights. A **voluntary waiver** is one that is not the result of a threat, empty promise, or force but is made of the suspect's free will.[80] However, whether the waiver is intelligent and voluntary for juveniles is usually determined under the **totality of circumstances test.** As the U.S. Supreme Court noted in the case of *Fare v. Michael C.* (1979):

> This totality of the circumstances approach is adequate to determine whether there has been a waiver even where interrogation of juveniles is involved. The totality approach permits—indeed, it mandates—inquiry into all the circumstances surrounding interrogation. *This includes evaluation of the juvenile's age, experience, education, background, and intelligence, and into whether he has the capacity to understand the warnings given to him, the nature of his Fifth Amendment rights, and the consequences of waiving those rights.*[81] (italics added)

Under the totality of circumstances test, a court determines whether a waiver is valid (and hence any evidence obtained after the waiver such as a confession), based on consideration of a number of factors, such as age, education, experience, background, and intelligence. These are common factors, but some states add additional criteria. For example, some states include in the totality of circumstances a juvenile's prior criminal experience, any physical deprivations during interrogation (such as being held incommunicado), the presence or absence of parents, the length of detention, and the nature of the interrogation.[82]

At the end of 2001, thirty-nine states used the totality of circumstances test in determining the validity of a juvenile waiver to counsel and the privilege against self-incrimination.* In those states that do not use the totality of circumstances test, other protections for juveniles are offered in waiver of rights situations. These tests are usually referred to as *per se* rules.[83] Eleven states use these tests, which examine waivers in light of whether the juvenile was able to confer with an adult either before or during an interrogation. These tests are examined below.

Per Se Rules and Juvenile Waiver

Parent or Interested Adult Presence May Be Required Before Waiver

A few states require that a juvenile consult with parents or another interested adult either before or during interrogation for a waiver to be valid (called a *per se* requirement, interested adult test, friendly adult test, or concerned adult test).[84] In these states, any waiver of rights in the absence of a parent, guardian, or other interested adult and any evidence obtained as a result of the waiver may not be admissible in court.[85] States that require parental or interested adult presence before or during interrogation believe that juveniles are less mature than adults and may not understand the nature and full extent of the proceedings against them. These states compensate for a juvenile's vulnerability and inexperience by making sure that a parent or an adult is present to protect the juvenile.[86] Under these procedures, the validity of a juvenile waiver is determined by a court, which considers among other factors (for example, the juvenile's experience with interrogation) whether the juvenile had the opportunity to consult with a parent or other interested adult before or during interrogation. If the juvenile did not have this opportunity, any evidence obtained may be inadmissible in court according to state law.

States with *per se* laws vary on the extent of parental (or interested adult) participation. For example, some states mandate the following: requiring the *Miranda* warning to be read to both the parents and the juvenile, allowing the juvenile time to privately consult with his or her parents outside of police presence, and requiring that both parent and child sign and consent before any waiver of rights.[87] Some states require the presence of parents during the actual interrogation,[88] whereas others exclude parents during interrogation as long as they have been included in some other way such as during the *Miranda* warnings.[89] States also have *per se* variations based on the juvenile's age. It is generally accepted that younger juveniles need more protection than older juveniles; thus, some states limit or extend parental or interested adult rules based on the child's age. In these states, parental or interested adult presence

---

*Linda Szymanski, *Juvenile Waiver of Miranda Rights: Totality of Circumstances Test* (Pittsburgh: National Center for Juvenile Justice, *NCJJ Snapshot* 7[1], 2002). Note, however, that in circumstances where a juvenile is not "in custody" and no *Miranda* warnings are given, then any voluntary statement may generally be used against the juvenile. This is why "in custody" determinations are important. There is no need to waive *Miranda* rights when none have been given and/or are required. This was the issue at hand in the case of *Yarborough v. Alvarado*, where Alvarado could have theoretically left the interrogation.

is generally required for juveniles under fourteen years of age, whereas older juveniles (over fourteen) are deemed able to make a voluntary and intelligent waiver on their own.[90] These protections are not required by the U.S. Supreme Court, but states may provide these extra safeguards.

Although states vary as to parental or interested adult participation, the general rule is if the juvenile is young (below fourteen), under the influence of alcohol, mentally impaired, or lacks prior experience with the juvenile justice system, states are best served by providing further safeguards to ensure that a juvenile waiver is both intelligent and voluntary.[91] Without such safeguards, a confession resulting from the waiver might not be valid and might be excluded from evidence. Another safeguard for juveniles is to require the presence of a lawyer.

Lawyer Presence May Be Required Before Waiver

Like adults, juveniles have a right to counsel during custodial interrogation.[92] Custodial interrogation is considered a "critical stage" of the juvenile and adult criminal processes; therefore, the right to counsel applies. Unless restricted by state law, juveniles may waive their *Miranda* rights during custodial interrogation, including the right to have counsel present before answering any questions.

Some states require that juveniles have a mandatory consultation with a lawyer before they may waive their *Miranda* rights—including their right to a lawyer.[93] Requiring the presence of a lawyer before a juvenile can intelligently and voluntarily waive his or her rights helps ensure that juveniles are treated in a manner consistent with their age and maturity level. However, these requirements are not widespread in the United States. As a practical matter, law enforcement officers are generally opposed to such laws because they say that lawyer presence prevents many voluntary confessions that could have otherwise been obtained. In the absence of *per se* lawyer laws, alternatives have been used to protect juveniles and safeguard their *Miranda* rights in addition to those already discussed—at the same time not preventing police from questioning juveniles. Videotaped interrogations are one example and are viewed as the middle ground between the strict *per se* requirements and discretionary totality of circumstances determinations.[94] Videotaping has the advantage of protecting juveniles (providing a record and visual context of the interrogation that may be shown in court) while at the same time alleviating the burden of contacting and requiring parents and lawyers every time that a juvenile is taken into custody and/or interrogated.

Whatever method is used, state legislatures are best served by approaching juvenile interrogation with caution and providing safeguards to ensure that a waiver is intelligent and voluntary: A juvenile waiver is likely to be carefully scrutinized at a later time by a court, especially for younger juveniles and those accused of serious offenses. Moreover, as the benevolent function of the juvenile court has given way to an approach that is more punitive and adultlike, extra precaution afforded to juveniles is probably advisable, because despite this punitive shift, there is still belief that most juveniles are less mature than adults and should receive extra protection.[95]

Refusal to Waive *Miranda* Must Be Clear and Unambiguous

Juveniles, as well as adults, must clearly and unambiguously invoke their *Miranda* rights in custodial interrogation and, hence, refuse to waive their rights. This is perhaps most important for juveniles in states that do not have strict *per se* requirements of parent, interested adult, or lawyer presence or where such requirements are not applicable because of the age of the juvenile (over fourteen, generally) in custodial interrogation situations. A silent refusal to answer questions does not suffice, nor does an unclear desire to have a lawyer present ("I think I want to talk to a lawyer"). The burden is on the juvenile to clearly state his or her desire not to participate in a custodial interrogation.[96] If the juvenile does not express a clear desire to invoke *Miranda*, hence the right to counsel and protection from self-incrimination, police officers may continue to question the juvenile and use any resulting evidence.

Confidentiality and the Police

The juvenile justice system is structured so that juvenile matters are kept strictly confidential and anonymous because the stigmatizing label of being delinquent is viewed as a roadblock to rehabilitation. States have prohibited open juvenile court proceedings, used fake or abbreviated names in court cases, avoided the release of information to the media, sealed and destroyed juvenile records, and placed restrictions on the photographing and fingerprinting of juveniles.

Confidentiality and anonymity restrictions in the juvenile justice system have been eroded, however. Several states now allow juvenile proceedings to be open to the public, particularly when the crime is serious. For example, several states open delinquency hearings to the public as long as certain age/offense requirements are met. Only fifteen states close delinquency hearings to the public in all circumstances.[97] States have also relaxed rules concerning the confidentiality of juvenile records, and many states no longer allow juvenile records to be sealed, expunged, or destroyed. For example, nine states allow the public release of juvenile court records with no qualifying restrictions, fifteen states open juvenile court records to the public after a specified offense, and fourteen additional states open records to the public when an age/offense criterion has been met.[98] Additionally, twenty-four states have provisions that certain juvenile records can never be sealed, expunged, or destroyed, and several other states have allowed previously sealed records to be unsealed.[99] Furthermore, a major trend is to provide notice to schools about the delinquent conduct of their students. By the end of 2001, forty-three states had cleared the way for schools to receive some form of notice when a child within that school has been involved with law enforcement or the juvenile court for delinquency.[100] Some states have also authorized juvenile records to be used as evidence of past offending when the juvenile offends as an adult, and several states have enacted laws requiring the registration of juvenile sex offenders with local and/or state law enforcement agencies.[101]

Confidentiality in juvenile justice has eroded considerably, especially when law enforcement officers deal with juveniles. Changes have occurred in the areas of fingerprinting, DNA sampling, lineups, photographs, and the release of information to the media. Such changes are particularly notable for juveniles involved in serious or violent crime. Table 3.3 examines certain state law provisions concerning confidentiality in a number of areas for serious and violent juvenile offenders. (Note that provisions for nonserious or nonviolent juvenile offenders in these states may differ.)

Fingerprinting

The changing philosophy of the juvenile justice system regarding confidentiality is reflected in the rules governing juvenile fingerprinting. Historically, police officers were generally prevented from fingerprinting all juvenile lawbreakers, especially for minor offenses. In the limited circumstances in which law enforcement officers were allowed to fingerprint juveniles, fingerprint cards had to be kept strictly confidential. Today, however, fingerprinting is becoming more common in the juvenile justice system.[102]

Originally, the Juvenile Justice and Delinquency Prevention Act of 1974 recommended that juvenile fingerprints be taken only under strict guidelines.[103] Many states followed these guidelines. For example, state laws required that fingerprints be taken only with the consent of a judge, or restricted fingerprinting to those juveniles who had been arrested for a felony. Many states also required that fingerprint evidence be destroyed after a period of time or in the event that the juvenile was not adjudicated for the offense for which he or she was arrested.

These protections for juveniles have been eroded considerably. Currently, forty-six states and the District of Columbia authorize the police to fingerprint juveniles.* However, such fingerprinting is still subject to certain restrictions, which usually center on the types of offenders who may be fingerprinted and the use and storage of fingerprint evidence. For example, of the forty-seven jurisdictions that permit fingerprinting of juveniles, sixteen states prohibit fingerprinting juveniles who are below fourteen years of age and twenty-two states allow fingerprinting for only those juveniles who have committed a felony.[104] However, some states do allow juveniles to be fingerprinted for misdemeanors. Under Florida law, a juvenile arrested for a variety of misdemeanors, including assault, battery, petty theft, cruelty to animals, or indecent exposure, may be fingerprinted. Moreover, these fingerprints must be submitted to the Florida Department of Law Enforcement for central state storage.[105] The available evidence indicates that forty-four states mandate that fingerprint evidence be a part of a separate juvenile or adult criminal history repository. Other states require the destruction of fingerprint evidence once its purpose has been fulfilled or require that such evidence be kept localized (instead of being stored in state or nationwide databases) and in confidential storage places.[106]

*Patricia Torbet and Linda Szymanski, *State Legislative Responses to Serious and Violent Juvenile Crime: 1996–1997 Update* (Washington, DC: Office of Juvenile Justice and Delinquency Prevention, 1998). Note that four states do not mention fingerprinting in their state statutes or court rules.

TABLE 3.3

Confidentiality Provisions for Serious and Violent Juvenile Offenders

State	Open Hearing	Release of Name	Release of Court Record[1]	Statewide Repository[2]	Fingerprinting	Photo-graphing	Offender Registration	Seal/ Expunge Records Prohibited
Totals:	30	42	48	44	47	46	39	25
Alabama			■	■	■	■	■	
Alaska	■	■	■	■	■	■	■	■
Arizona	■	■	■	■	■	■	■	
Arkansas		■	■	■	■	■	■	
California	■	■	■	■	■	■		■
Colorado	■	■	■	■	■	■		
Connecticut			■		■	■		
Delaware	■	■	■	■	■	■	■	■
Dist. of Columbia			■		■	■		
Florida	■	■	■	■	■	■	■	■
Georgia	■	■	■	■	■	■	■	■
Hawaii	■	■	■	■	■	■	■	
Idaho	■	■	■	■	■	■	■	
Illinois		■	■	■	■	■	■	
Indiana	■	■	■	■	■	■	■	
Iowa	■	■	■	■	■	■		■
Kansas	■	■	■	■	■	■		
Kentucky		■	■	■	■	■		■
Louisiana	■	■	■	■	■	■	■	■
Maine	■	■	■	■			■	
Maryland	■		■			■		
Massachusetts	■	■	■	■	■	■	■	
Michigan	■	■	■	■	■	■		■
Minnesota	■	■	■	■	■	■		■
Mississippi		■	■					
Missouri	■	■	■		■	■		
Montana	■	■	■	■	■	■	■	■
Nebraska		■	■	■	■			
Nevada	■	■	■	■	■	■		■
New Hampshire		■	■			■	■	
New Jersey		■	■	■	■	■	■	
New Mexico	■			■	■	■	■	
New York			■	■	■	■		
North Carolina			■		■	■	■	■
North Dakota		■	■	■	■	■		
Ohio				■	■	■	■	

(continued)

TABLE 3.3

(continued)

State	Open Hearing	Release of Name	Release of Court Record¹	Statewide Repository²	Fingerprinting	Photo-graphing	Offender Registration	Seal/ Expunge Records Prohibited
Oklahoma	■	■	■	■	■	■		■
Oregon		■	■	■	■	■	■	■
Pennsylvania	■	■	■	■	■	■	■	■
Rhode Island		■	■	■			■	■
South Carolina		■	■	■	■	■	■	■
South Dakota	■	■	■	■	■	■		■
Tennessee		■	■		■	■		
Texas	■	■	■	■	■	■	■	■
Utah	■	■	■	■	■	■	■	■
Vermont					■			
Virginia	■	■	■	■	■	■	■	■
Washington	■	■	■	■	■	■	■	■
West Virginia		■	■		■			■
Wisconsin	■	■	■	■			■	
Wyoming		■	■	■	■	■	■	■

Legend: ■ indicates the provision(s) allowed by each State as of the end of the 1997 legislative session.

¹In this category, ■ indicates a provision for juvenile court records to be specifically released to at least one of the following parties: the public, the victims(s), the school(s), the prosecutor, law enforcement, or social agency; however, all States allow records to be released to any party who can show a legitimate interest, typically by court order. ²In this category, ■ indicates a provision for fingerprints to be part of a separate juvenile or adult criminal history repository.

Source: Patricia Torbet and Linda Szymanski, *State Legislative Responses to Serious and Violent Juvenile Crime: 1996–1997 Update* (Washington, DC: Office of Juvenile Justice and Delinquency Prevention, 1998), 10.

DNA Samples

A recent trend that relates to confidentiality involving juveniles and the police is the collection of DNA samples from juvenile arrestees. In 1992 the FBI began collecting DNA samples of adults convicted of state and federal crimes for inclusion in a national DNA database called CODIS (Combined DNA Index System). This DNA database is then used to match the person's DNA to DNA taken from unsolved or future crimes across the nation. Currently, some states have proposed that DNA samples be taken from individuals at arrest and kept even if the suspects are acquitted in court—even for certain juvenile offenders. Advocates of DNA collection programs suggest that collecting DNA is no different than taking a person's fingerprints, which are routinely collected and kept following an arrest regardless of court outcome. Opponents say that taking DNA samples from juveniles amounts to a permanent genetic criminal record that will follow them for life. They contend that such programs further erode the confidential foundation of the juvenile justice system.[107]

As of 2003, thirty states collected DNA samples for in-state use from select juvenile offenders ages thirteen to seventeen.[108] However, these states use different criteria for the collection of DNA samples from juveniles. For example, most states that collect DNA from juveniles restrict such collection to violent felony offenders and/or sex offenders. For example, Texas passed a law in 2003 requiring the collection of DNA samples from juveniles convicted of capital murder. Moreover, some states authorize juvenile DNA samples to be used only until juveniles reach the age of majority, but in other states, such as Arizona and Oregon, DNA samples from juveniles are kept even after a juvenile reaches adulthood. Despite the different practices among the states that take DNA samples from juveniles, federal law currently prevents these samples from being included in the FBI's national database. This exclusion may be changing; laws are being proposed that would authorize expanded DNA testing for both juveniles and adults and authorize such samples to be included in a national database.[109]

Lineups and Photographs

Photographing (taking mug shots) of juveniles brought into custody is as prevalent as fingerprinting. Most states allow this practice.[110] Lineups are also used in many states. This practice is usually done through photograph lineups (called photo packs) instead of in-person lineups involving juveniles.

The U.S. Supreme Court has not ruled specifically on the constitutionality of lineups (either photo or person) involving juveniles. In an adult case, the Court held in *Kirby v. Illinois* (1972) that a suspect has no right to counsel during a police lineup if he or she has not been formally charged with a crime.[111] In *United States v. Wade* (1967), however, the Court held that a suspect has a constitutional right to have a lawyer present during the police lineup once formally charged.[112] However, a suspect does not have a constitutional right to have a lawyer present when a witness reviews only a photo lineup.[113] These rules apply both to juveniles and adults.

For an in-person lineup, juveniles generally do not have greater procedural protections than adults. Thus, unless state law says otherwise, juveniles may be subject to a police lineup provided the lineup meets the standards articulated by the U.S. Supreme Court for adults. For example, the lineup must include at least five people, persons must be of the same sex and race, persons must be dressed in the same type of clothing, and the selection of persons must be random. If these standards are not met, identification from the lineup will not be admissible in court.[114]

Media, Juveniles, and the Police

Two U.S. Supreme Court cases address the media use of confidential juvenile information. In *Oklahoma Publishing Company v. District Court in and for Oklahoma City* (1977), the U.S. Supreme Court ruled that a court order prohibiting the press from reporting the name and photograph of a youth involved in a juvenile proceeding was unconstitutional.[115] The Court held that because the information was obtained legally, and from a source outside the court, a court order that prevented the paper from publishing the information constituted an infringement of the First Amendment protection of freedom of the press. Similarly, in *Smith v. Daily Mail Publishing Company* (1979), the Court ruled that a state law prohibiting the publication of a juvenile's name was unconstitutional because information about the juvenile was obtained lawfully by the media.[116] In this case, the Court noted that the First Amendment interest in a free press takes precedence over preserving the anonymity of juvenile defendants.

Since 1992, several states have revised their laws on the release and publication of a juvenile's name. Release of this information is most prevalent in cases involving serious or violent crimes. Evidence indicates that forty-two states permit the release of a juvenile's name to the media under certain conditions and that forty-six states allow juveniles to be photographed.[117] For example, the Mississippi Legislature has stipulated that the names and addresses of juveniles twice adjudicated for a felony or the unlawful possession of a firearm may be released to the media.[118]

As with fingerprinting and photographs, restrictions on the release of a juvenile's name after committing a crime are being eroded and now resemble the rules that pertain to adults. This is especially the case for serious and violent juvenile offenders.

SUMMARY

- ❑ Most constitutional protections afforded to adults are also given to juveniles.
- ❑ A law enforcement officer must have probable cause to arrest a juvenile for delinquent behavior.
- ❑ Some states allow a juvenile to be taken into custody for behavior that is not criminal or delinquent as long as officers have reasonable suspicion that the youth is in need of supervision. Reasonable suspicion is a lower standard than probable cause.
- ❑ Juveniles may be taken into custody for behaviors that would never justify the arrest of an adult.
- ❑ Police have a great deal of discretion when deciding whether to arrest a juvenile. The seriousness of the crime is arguably the most important factor in determining whether a juvenile will be arrested versus warned by the police.
- ❑ The typical delinquent is not a serious offender, according to official arrest statistics.
- ❑ Police officers may "stop" a juvenile if they have a "reasonable suspicion" that a crime has occurred or is about to occur, and they may "frisk" a juvenile if they believe the juvenile might have a weapon. However, police officers may not conduct a full search unless they have probable cause.
- ❑ Police officers may search a juvenile without probable cause or a warrant if they receive voluntary consent from the juvenile. Some states have restrictions on juvenile consent.
- ❑ In many cases, reasonable suspicion for a stop and frisk may turn into probable cause for an arrest.

❏ Public school officials need only "reasonable grounds," not probable cause, to search a student and his or her property in school.

❏ Unless employed by the school district or having substantial school duty, police officers may not search a student unless they have probable cause.

❏ Juvenile probationers may be subject to general search conditions as a part of their probation agreement. Under these conditions, they may be searched without a warrant or probable cause by law enforcement officers, according to some court decisions.

❏ *Miranda* warnings are required only when the person is both in custody and being interrogated.

❏ Whether a juvenile waiver of rights is valid is usually determined under the "totality of circumstances" test. This test evaluates the age, experience, education, intelligence, and background of the juvenile and whether he or she has the capacity to waive these rights. Such a waiver must be voluntary and intelligent under the totality of circumstances.

❏ In the absence of the totality of circumstances test, some states provide that a parent, guardian, or other interested adult be present before a juvenile can legally waive his or her rights.

❏ Confidentiality protections for juveniles have been eroded. Most states allow juveniles to be fingerprinted and photographed, and several states are now allowing DNA samples to be collected from certain juvenile offenders.

❏ Most states allow a juvenile's name to be released to the media if the juvenile is charged with certain serious offenses.

REVIEW QUESTIONS

1. What is one form of juvenile conduct under police scrutiny that is usually never under scrutiny for adults?

2. What U.S. Supreme Court case governs the stop and frisk of persons? What level of proof must a police officer have to stop and frisk an individual?

3. What are three legal factors that influence the decision to take a juvenile into custody?

4. What are three factors that should never constitute the basis of whether a juvenile is arrested or not?

5. Discretion _____ as crime seriousness increases.

6. What standard must public schools officials have to search a student?

7. *Miranda* warnings must be given when a person is under custodial interrogation. Explain in detail what "custodial interrogation" entails.

8. What are some factors that a court should consider under the totality of circumstances test to determine if a juvenile waiver was intelligent and voluntary?

9. Describe a situation in which a stop and frisk based on reasonable suspicion turns into probable cause for an arrest.

10. Cite and explain three reasons why requiring the presence of a parent might be a good idea before a juvenile can intelligently and voluntarily waive his or her *Miranda* rights.

KEY TERMS AND DEFINITIONS

chivalry factor: The idea that female adolescents are treated more leniently by police officers when they commit crimes that male adolescents typically commit.

discretion: The choice between two or more options that involves personal decision making.

extralegal factors concerning arrest: A factor or factors that are not theoretically relevant to whether a suspect should get arrested versus warned. Examples are race, gender, and SES.

intelligent waiver: A waiver of rights by a suspect who knows what he or she is doing and is competent to waive those rights.

legal factors concerning arrest: A factor or factors that are based on current or past legal criteria and are considered legitimate in arrest decisions. For example, prior record and seriousness of the crime are legal factors.

legalistic style: A police department operational style that is characterized by approaching all situations "by the book," with little to no officer discretion.

probable cause: More than bare suspicion. It exists when an officer has a reasonable belief that an offense took place and that the suspect is the individual who committed or was in the process of committing the offense.

protective factor: The idea that female adolescents are taken into custody more frequently for offenses that are morality based or sexualized than are their male counterparts.

reasonable suspicion: A degree of proof that is less than probable cause but more than suspicion. It represents a degree of certainty (around 30 percent) that a crime has been or will be committed and that the suspect is involved in it.

service style: A police department operational style that is characterized by the use of referral and diversionary alternatives to arrest.

socioeconomic status: A rank based on an individual's education, occupation, and income. Socioeconomic status (SES) is used to determine classes within society, such as lower, middle, and upper class. A juvenile's SES is determined by his or her parents' SES. SES is usually viewed in the aggregate based on residential areas.

stop and frisk: A police practice that allows an officer to make a brief investigatory stop to ask questions if the officer has reason to believe that the individual has or is about to commit a crime and to conduct a protective frisk of the individual for weapons if the officer has a reasonable concern for his or her personal safety.

totality of circumstances test: The test that determines whether a juvenile has made a valid waiver of his or her rights or has given consent to search. The test involves evaluating the juvenile's age, experience, education, background, and intelligence and whether the juvenile has the capacity to sufficiently understand his or her rights and the consequences of waiving those rights or of giving consent to search.

voluntary waiver: A waiver that is not the result of threat, force, or coercion and is of free will.

waiver: An intentional relinquishment of a known right or remedy. A waiver of rights is valid only if it is intelligent and voluntary.

warrant: A written order from a court based on a determination of probable cause that authorizes a law enforcement officer to conduct a search or to arrest a person.

watchman style: A police department operational style that is characterized by the informal resolution of incidents, with arrest as a last resort. Watchman-style departments operate with high discretion.

 ## FOR FURTHER RESEARCH

❑ **State Legislative Responses to Violent Juvenile Crime**
http://www.ncjrs.org/pdffiles/172835.pdf

❑ **Child Development–Community Policing: Partnership in a Climate of Violence**
http://www.ncjrs.org/txtfiles/164380.txt

❑ **Guide for Implementing the Balanced and Restorative Justice Model**
http://www.ojjdp.ncjrs.org/pubs/implementing/index.html

❑ **Youth-Oriented Community Policing**
http://ojjdp.ncjrs.org/search/SearchResults.asp

❑ **Curfew: An Answer to Juvenile Delinquency and Victimization?**
http://www.ncjrs.org/txtfiles/curfew.txt

For an up-to-date list of web links, go to the Juvenile Justice Companion Website at **http://cj.wadsworth.com/del_carmen_trulson_jj**

Intake and Diversion

The Intake Process / 113

What Is Intake? / 113

Who Handles Intake? / 114

Who Makes a Delinquency Referral to Intake Officers? / 116

Procedures and Decisions at Intake / 117

Dismissal of the Case / 117

Informal Adjustment / 118

Formal Processing in Juvenile Court / 119

Adult Court Waiver / 120

The Legal Rights of Juveniles at Intake / 120

Is Intake a "Critical Stage" Requiring Counsel? / 121

Admissibility of Intake Information at Adjudication Proceedings / 122

General Guidelines on the Admissibility of Intake Information in Adjudication Proceedings / 124

The Diversion Process / 126

What Is Diversion? / 126

Examples of Diversion Programs / 127

Who Qualifies for Diversion? / 127

What Happens If a Youth Refuses to Accept Diversion? / 128

Prosecutorial Retaliation for Refusing Diversion / 128

The Legal Rights of Juveniles in Diversion / 129

Do Juveniles Have a Constitutional Right to Diversion? / 129

Is a Hearing Required to Deny Diversion? / 130

Cases Similarly Situated and Diversion Offers / 130

Removing a Youth from Diversion / 131

Diversion and Double Jeopardy / 132

May Prior Diversions Be Used to Increase Future Sentences? / 133

Extralegal Issues in Diversion / 134

Bias in Selection for Diversion / 134

Does Diversion Promote Further Contact with the Juvenile Justice System? / 136

Diversion and Net Widening / 137

Case Brief: *In re Wayne H.* / 123

IN THIS CHAPTER YOU WILL LEARN

- About the purpose of intake and who are considered intake officers.

- About the intake process and the decisions that intake officers make.

- About the legal rights of juveniles at intake.

- That many cases are informally "adjusted" or "diverted" from the juvenile court.

- About the types of juveniles typically selected for diversion.

- That diversion is typically voluntary and that youths may refuse to participate in diversion and request an adjudication hearing so that the facts can be determined by a juvenile court judge.

- That juveniles do not have a constitutional right to diversion and may be removed from it.

- That critics of diversion suggest it may circumvent due process, that diversion selection is biased, that diversion enables further penetration into the formal juvenile system, and that it widens the net of control over youths.

INTRODUCTION

Police officers make initial decisions on whether to divert delinquents from the juvenile justice system or to move them further in the process. Officers typically make this decision after consulting with the victim, the juvenile, and the juvenile's parents. The police also review the juvenile's prior contacts with the juvenile justice system and the seriousness of the crime. Nearly one-quarter of all juveniles arrested by the police are released without further initiation into the juvenile justice system. These juveniles are given a second chance. However, this means that approximately 75 percent of arrested juveniles are referred to juvenile court agencies.[1]

One of the most important stages in the juvenile justice process is the time after a juvenile's arrest. Depending on the seriousness of the alleged law violation and other criteria, the juvenile may be removed informally or processed formally into the system during a stage called *intake*. Intake procedures determine which cases will be handled in juvenile court with an adjudication hearing and which cases will be resolved informally. Cases that are handled in juvenile court are said to be *petitioned*. Cases that are resolved informally are handled in a process called *diversion* (also called *adjustment*) and are *nonpetitioned*. Diverted youths will typically not face an adjudication hearing if they abide by certain requirements determined by intake officers. These requirements may include community service, restitution, counseling, curfew, and a whole host of "other" diversionary programs.

This chapter addresses intake and diversion. Its topics include who is responsible for intake, the types of decisions made at intake, and the legal rights of juveniles during intake. Next, this chapter examines the diversion process and who typically qualifies for it. The chapter ends with a discussion of the legal rights of diverted juveniles and other important issues concerning diversion.

The Intake Process
What Is Intake?

Intake is the process of screening cases referred to the juvenile justice system. Procedures at intake determine which cases will be handled by the juvenile court with an adjudication hearing (trial) and which cases will be resolved without official juvenile court intervention. Intake may best be described as a "weeding-out" process.

Some delinquency cases require more attention by the juvenile justice system and need to be handled with an adjudication hearing. These cases usually involve serious or frequent delinquency, or occur when a juvenile has exhausted other informal options available to the juvenile court. Less serious cases, usually involving first-time offenders arrested for minor crimes, often deserve a different and less formalized outcome. In these cases, diversion is desirable for a number of reasons: The court workload is reserved for serious cases, a formal juvenile record is diverted, the youth is not stigmatized as a "delinquent," and juvenile probation caseloads are kept to a minimum. Intake is the process of categorizing these cases and making informed decisions on how to resolve them.

Who Handles Intake?

Intake officers handle intake responsibility. They may be juvenile probation officers, local or state prosecutors, judges, police officers, or any person designated by the juvenile court in accordance with the laws of the state. Although many people may be considered intake officers, intake responsibilities are typically the duties of juvenile probation officers or prosecutors. These individuals decide whether to divert the case or move it formally into the juvenile court with a delinquency petition. There are four ways that intake decisions are usually made:

- A probation officer (acting as an intake officer) makes the *final* decision to petition or divert the case.

- The prosecutor makes the *final* decision to petition or divert the case.

- A probation officer (acting as an intake officer) makes the *initial* decision to petition or divert the case, but the prosecutor has *final* decision-making and review power over all cases.

- A probation officer (acting as an intake officer) handles minor cases (misdemeanors), which are usually diverted, and the prosecutor handles major or serious cases (felonies), which are usually petitioned.

Table 4.1 examines final decision makers at the intake stage in the fifty states and the District of Columbia. Very few states give complete authority to probation officers to decide how to dispose of a case at intake. These states include Connecticut, Georgia, Maryland, and Mississippi. Nine states leave final intake decisions solely to the prosecutor. In four states (Hawaii, Iowa, Kansas, and Ohio), probation officers and prosecutors work in conjunction, with both having the authority to determine how to handle the case (denoted by an *X* in both of the first two columns of Table 4.1). In the majority of states, the prosecutor makes the final decision whether to petition or divert the case. In some cases, this happens after a decision is initially made by a probation officer or other intake officer. A few states divide responsibility by the type of crime alleged, meaning that probation officers handle misdemeanors and prosecutors handle felonies. Some states have more than one method of resolving matters at intake. Table 4.1 serves as a general guideline.

As Table 4.1 shows, prosecutors are becoming more involved in the intake process today—almost every state gives them final decision powers at intake. In the past, however, probation officers were typically the sole designees of intake decisions. At that time, the juvenile justice system placed less emphasis on legal responsibility and instead emphasized conditions contributing to delinquency. Delinquents were not viewed as persons with complete responsibility for their acts, and extralegal factors such as the juvenile's home life carried more weight in intake decisions. Probation officers were considered better suited to evaluate the social and individual needs of youths and to make the final decision on the best course of action.

This practice has changed.[2] The role and responsibility of probation officers during intake today will usually be found at the early stages of intake (such as interviewing victims, parents, the juvenile), whereas prosecutors will handle most final decisions on how to proceed with the case. One reason for this

TABLE 4.1

Intake Decision Makers by State

State	Probation or Intake Officer Decision	Prosecutor Decision	Probation or Intake Officer Decision with Prosecution Final Review	Probation for Misdemeanors Prosecution for Felonies
Alabama			■	
Alaska				■
Arizona			■	■
Arkansas			■	
California			■	
Colorado		■		
Connecticut	■			
Delaware		■		
District of Columbia			■	
Florida			■	
Georgia	■			
Hawaii	■	■		
Idaho			■	
Illinois			■	
Indiana			■	
Iowa	■	■		
Kansas	■	■		
Kentucky			■	
Louisiana			■	
Maine			■	
Maryland	■			
Massachusetts	■			
Michigan			■	
Minnesota		■		
Mississippi	■			
Missouri	■			
Montana			■	
Nebraska		■		
Nevada			■	
New Hampshire		■		
New Jersey			■	
New Mexico			■	■
New York	■			
North Carolina	■		■	
North Dakota	■			
Ohio	■	■		
Oklahoma			■	
Oregon	■		■	

(continued)

TABLE 4.1

Intake Decision Makers by State (continued)

State	Probation or Intake Officer Decision	Prosecutor Decision	Probation or Intake Officer Decision with Prosecution Final Review	Probation for Misdemeanors Prosecution for Felonies
Pennsylvania	■		■	
Rhode Island	■			
South Carolina			■	
South Dakota		■		
Tennessee	■		■	
Texas	■		■	■
Utah	■		■	■
Vermont		■		
Virginia	■			
Washington		■		
Wisconsin			■	
Wyoming		■		

Note: Some states have multiple methods depending on jurisdiction or may otherwise deviate from this general guideline. Prosecutors usually have the final say in all cases or cases involving serious felonies. Go to http://www.ncjj.org/stateprofiles for specific state information.

Source: Adapted from information found at http://www.ncjj.org/stateprofiles.

change is that the juvenile justice system has become more "adultified." A consequence is that intake decisions today focus more on such legal issues as the amount and quality of evidence, the legal requirements needed for formal processing, and the jurisdictional authority of the court. Thus, the focus is on the offense rather than the characteristics and situation of the offender. Lawyers are usually better qualified to make such determinations than probation officers, who are usually not trained in the law. Although the trend is toward having lawyers make final intake decisions, states' practices vary widely. For example, jurisdictions in Texas are allowed to establish a program for first-offender juveniles whereby law enforcement officers serve as the primary decision makers at intake.[3]

Who Makes a Delinquency Referral to Intake Officers?

Contrary to popular assumptions, police are not the only individuals who can make a **delinquency referral** to intake officers upon discovery of delinquent behavior. Although the police are usually the referral source (approximately 85 percent of the time), in some states parents, victims, school officials, probation officers, and ordinary citizens may refer a youth *directly* to an intake officer for processing. These individuals constitute the remaining 15 percent of intake referrals.

There is a difference between a school official (or a parent, victim, or citizen) who calls a police officer, who then makes a delinquency referral, and a school official (or a parent, victim, or citizen) who can make a delinquency referral on his or her own. State law dictates who may or may not *directly* refer juveniles to intake. For example, in Nebraska, "any person who has credible information" may file a delinquency complaint with an intake officer. In that state, a school official or parent may *directly* file a delinquency complaint. Similarly, in Arizona, intake workers may receive delinquency referrals from law enforcement officers, parents, school officials, probation officers, or "other agencies or individuals in contact with the youth." Referrals that come from individuals other than the police are sometimes called "walk-in" referrals. Other states, such as Connecticut, require that a youth first be arrested by law enforcement officers for delinquent conduct before he or she is referred to intake.* This is the most common method in the United States and explains why police officers make almost 85 percent of all delinquency referrals to intake. It also demonstrates the important "gatekeeping" function that law enforcement officers have in the juvenile justice process.

Procedures and Decisions at Intake

Once a delinquency referral has been made, intake officers schedule an **intake conference** at a later date with a juvenile and his or her parents. In the time between the delinquency referral and the intake conference, the juvenile will either be released to the custody of his or her parents or be placed in a juvenile detention center (see Chapter 6, on detention). Intake conferences are informal gatherings, usually held at a local juvenile probation office, where the juvenile is encouraged to be honest and forthcoming with information concerning the alleged delinquency.[4] Here, officers evaluate a number of criteria to determine the best method to resolve the case. These criteria may include the following:

- The amount and quality of evidence.
- The alleged current offense.
- The prior juvenile record or previous contacts with the juvenile justice system.
- Any problems at home or in school.
- The age, maturity, and attitude of the juvenile.
- Parental ability to control their child.
- Input from the victim.

Intake officers may deal with this information in four ways: dismissal of the case, informal adjustment (diversion), formal processing in juvenile court (delinquency petition), or adult court waiver (waiver petition).

Dismissal of the Case

In 1999 approximately 17 percent (279,100) of all referred cases were dismissed by intake officers. Intake officers will dismiss a case when there is not sufficient evidence to support the allegations against the juvenile.[5]

---

*For particular state guidelines, see http://www.ncjj.org/stateprofiles/profiles and click on the state.

As mentioned previously, the responsibility for intake has shifted in recent years from probation officers to prosecutors. Prosecutors are more involved in the intake process because intake requires a review of facts in light of the law. Using probation officers to make legal determinations at intake is sometimes criticized as resulting in cases not being dismissed even when the evidence does not support formal charges. Probation officers may be more likely to evaluate the youth's need for intervention based on extralegal factors such as deficits in family and home life while placing less emphasis on the legal merits of the case. They may be more likely to suggest intervention to "help" the child, even if the facts and evidence do not support a delinquency petition and an adjudication hearing.

Informal Adjustment

In cases involving less serious delinquency, but with enough evidence to proceed with an adjudication proceeding, intake officers may "adjust" or "divert" the delinquency referral. **Adjustment** means that the case is handled informally, with the juvenile voluntarily agreeing to a disposition without facing an adjudication hearing. In 1999 intake officers adjusted 26 percent (432,000) of referred cases. Dispositions in the adjustment process may include community service, restitution, curfew, and attendance in a counseling program. The adjustment process typically includes a written agreement signed by the juvenile and his or her parents. This agreement is called a "consent decree." A consent decree outlines the juvenile's (and sometimes the parents') responsibility and the consequences if stipulations are not followed.[6]

In most states, a juvenile must admit to allegations of wrongdoing before he or she is offered an informal adjustment. This gives the supervising agency (usually a probation department) authority over the youth even though the youth has not been adjudicated in juvenile court. Typically, informal adjustments are limited to six months, with youths minimally supervised by probation officers to ensure compliance with any stipulations. If the juvenile successfully completes this time without further violation, the case is dismissed. However, if the juvenile fails to meet the conditions of the consent decree, he or she may be referred back to intake, where an intake officer or a prosecutor can file a delinquency petition with the court, causing the youth to face an adjudication hearing.

In reality, before a case is dealt with formally, a juvenile may be given multiple "second chances" and the case may be adjusted several times. This situation depends on state law and several factors. For example, state law may require that certain acts and behaviors always be dealt with informally by intake officers, regardless of their frequency (such as persistent curfew violations or smoking).* Alternatively, juveniles may be petitioned to the juvenile court if they commit a new delinquent offense during the informal adjustment period. State law might require that this juvenile be petitioned even if the offense is nonserious. State law prevails in informal adjustments.

---

*See, for example, the State of Texas Progressive Sanctioning Guidelines for steps 1–7. Step 2 indicates that the recommended sanction for low-level offenses will be deferred prosecution for 3–6 months. In Texas, any deviation from the recommended sanction is required by law to be reported to state authorities.

Formal Processing in Juvenile Court

Intake officers may decide that the case against the juvenile is beyond informal resolution and warrants further involvement in the juvenile justice system. These cases usually include those where the crime is serious (serious misdemeanors and all felonies) and where enough evidence indicates that the juvenile committed the crime.

A delinquency petition is needed to formally process a youth in juvenile court. A **delinquency petition** is a formal request (usually from a prosecutor) asking the juvenile court to adjudicate (or judge) the youth a delinquent. More than one-half of all cases facing the juvenile court in 1999 (about 1 million cases out of a rough total of 1.7 million) involved a delinquency petition.[7] Exhibit 4.1 shows the number of petitioned versus nonpetitioned delinquency cases from 1990 to 1999. It shows that in the last several years, petitioned cases outnumbered nonpetitioned cases.

Once the juvenile court receives a delinquency petition, an adjudication hearing date is scheduled. The adjudication hearing, which is the equivalent to a trial in the adult justice system, is covered in more detail in Chapter 8. As with delinquency referrals and the intake conference, in the time between the delinquency petition and the adjudication hearing, the juvenile will be

EXHIBIT 4.1   *Petitioned and Nonpetitioned Delinquency Cases 1990–1999*

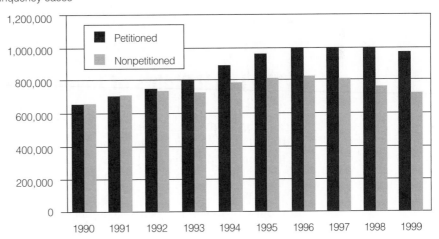

Delinquency cases

Note: Between 1990 and 1999, the number of nonpetitioned cases increased 8%, and the overall delinquency caseload increased 27%. Since 1992, petitioned cases have outnumbered nonpetitioned cases. In 1999, there were 35% more petitioned than nonpetitioned delinquency cases.

Source: Charles Puzzanchera, Anne L. Stahl, Terrence A. Finnegan, Nancy Tierney, and Howard N. Snyder, *Juvenile Court Statistics 1999* (Pittsburgh: National Center for Juvenile Justice, 2003), 26.

placed in juvenile detention or, more typically, released to the custody of his or her parents.

Adult Court Waiver

Intake officers also make initial determinations on whether the case will be handled in juvenile court or potentially be waived to adult criminal court once a decision for formal processing has been made. For a juvenile to be waived to criminal court, intake officers must usually file a **waiver petition,** which is a request by an intake officer or prosecutor who believes that the case can best be handled in criminal court. After a waiver petition is filed, in most cases a juvenile court judge reviews the facts of the case and has the final say on where the case will be tried. The final judgment is determined in a waiver hearing (also called a transfer hearing). However, not all forms of waiver are under the authority of a juvenile court judge and require a hearing. Additional ways in which a juvenile may be waived or transferred to adult court are detailed in Chapter 6.

Very few waiver petitions are made each year, and even fewer are accepted. In 1999 just over 7,000 delinquency cases (less than 1 percent of all cases formally processed by the juvenile courts) were waived to adult criminal courts. Typically, only in cases of serious offending do intake officers recommend that a juvenile be waived or transferred to adult court. In deciding whether to waive a youth, factors such as the seriousness of the offense, the juvenile's prior record, and whether the youth may benefit from treatment in the juvenile justice system are perhaps most influential. In the event that a waiver petition is denied, an adjudication hearing is scheduled. The "You Are an . . . Intake Officer" box includes an exercise in which you determine the appropriate course of action.

The Legal Rights of Juveniles at Intake

As mentioned, a juvenile must meet with an intake officer before a final decision can be made about how to proceed with the case. This meeting occurs at the intake conference, where the intake officer may ask questions that tend to incriminate the juvenile. He or she may ask the juvenile about the alleged crime, whether the juvenile is responsible, and other incriminating questions such as prior offending of the same nature, the location of missing property, the use of weapons, or any accomplices to the act.[8] Moreover, to be offered an informal disposition, a juvenile typically has to admit responsibility for the alleged delinquent behavior. Such procedures raise the question of whether juveniles have a right to procedural protections, such as a lawyer and the right to remain silent, during the intake process.

The U.S. Supreme Court has determined that certain proceedings before trial are considered so critical that due process protections apply, specifically the right to a lawyer and protection from self-incrimination. Such proceedings are considered "critical stages" and include pre-indictment custodial interrogations (*Miranda v. Arizona* [1966]),[9] preliminary hearings (*White v. Maryland*

YOU ARE AN... ▶ ## Intake Officer

Scenario 1: J. J., a sixteen-year-old juvenile, and several of his friends were hanging around outside a local bar during his hometown's annual Bar-B-Q Festival. At approximately 10 P.M., an intoxicated man left the bar in his car and hit one of J. J.'s friends, causing serious injuries, including a broken leg, a broken arm, and a collapsed lung. J. J. chased the man down an alley, where the man, because of his intoxication, hit a light pole. J. J. pulled the man from the car and proceeded to hit him several times with a metal pipe that J. J. found in the alleyway. J. J., who admitted to the act, said he was trying to stop the man from hitting any more people and did what any good citizen would do. The beating by J. J. resulted in a broken jaw and several head contusions. The man made a complete recovery.

Scenario 2: K. H., a fifteen-year-old juvenile, is accused of breaking into several homes and, in two cases, beating the occupants, leaving them with serious injuries. Although never previously adjudicated in juvenile court, K. H. is also believed to be the same person who burned down a local convenience store. Police do not have much evidence against K. H., but they found his fingerprint at one of the victim's homes. However, this is the same home where K. H. does household chores for the owner during weekends.

1. With the information presented in each scenario, decide how you would handle the case if you were the intake officer—dismissal, diversion, delinquency petition, or waiver petition to adult court.

2. Other than the facts presented in the scenarios, what information would assist you in making your decision?

3. What are the three most important factors you would consider in making your decision on how to handle the case?

[1963]),[10] lineups after charges have been filed (*United States v. Wade* [1967]),[11] interrogations after indictment (*Massiah v. United States* [1964]),[12] and the arraignment process (*Hamilton v. Alabama* [1961]).[13] Such stages are considered critical because these are proceedings in which incriminating evidence may be obtained and used against the defendant at trial. Intake is a pretrial proceeding in which potentially incriminating evidence is uncovered. Courts have considered whether juvenile intake is a **critical stage** and whether juveniles have a right to a lawyer and protection from self-incrimination. Courts have also considered whether intake evidence may be introduced in an adjudication hearing.

Is Intake a "Critical Stage" Requiring Counsel?

In the case of *In re Frank H.* (1972), a New York court held that juveniles do not have a constitutional right to counsel at intake because it is not a "critical stage."[14] In this case, Frank H. was taken into custody by the police for auto theft. A delinquency petition was filed, and the juvenile court appointed a lawyer for Frank H. The lawyer moved to vacate the delinquency petition on the grounds that Frank H. had not been provided a lawyer at the intake stage. The court concluded that the intake process was not a critical stage, basing its decision on two factors: (1) that New York law prohibited the use of information gathered at intake to be used in a guilt-finding proceeding (an adjudication hearing) and (2) that the purpose of intake is to gather relevant information to better "help" the juvenile.

In re Frank H. is one of the very few cases that address the rights of juveniles at intake. The court found that intake was not a critical stage requiring due process protection because the information at intake could not be used against the juvenile in an adjudication proceeding. However, the U.S. Supreme Court has not decided this issue, and state law may provide otherwise by allowing juveniles counsel at intake. Note that in the absence of state law that provides for a paid attorney at intake, juveniles may hire a private attorney and have him or her present during intake.

Admissibility of Intake Information at Adjudication Proceedings

A major reason for the holding in the case of *In re Frank H.* was that New York law prohibited in an adjudication hearing the use of information obtained at intake. Thus, intake was not considered a critical stage by the court because no statement made by the juvenile during the intake conference could have been used as evidence against him or her in an adjudication proceeding. Theoretically, no harm could come to the juvenile who did not have a lawyer.

Does this ruling mean that if a juvenile makes a confession to an intake officer ("I robbed the liquor store"), the statement must be excluded from evidence in an adjudication hearing? The court in the case of *In re Wayne H.* (1979) answered this question affirmatively and held that information or statements gathered during an intake conference with a probation officer (or other intake officer) cannot be used in any guilt-finding process (see the "Case Brief").[15] The court held that information acquired during the intake process is "tainted" because of the nature of intake conferences, which encourage juveniles to be truthful and cooperative (see also *In re Frank H.*).[16] The decision noted that the primary purpose of the intake conference is to assemble information relevant to an informed disposition of the case, not to elicit incriminating statements to be later used in an adjudication proceeding or adult trial. This is a controversial finding, however.

The U.S. Supreme Court has not decided whether statements made to juvenile intake officers must be excluded in an adjudication hearing, so most states handle the issue differently—some allow such statements; others do not. The U.S. Supreme Court case that most closely relates to this issue is *Minnesota v. Murphy* (1984), in which the Court held that statements made by a probationer to his probation officer during a meeting *are* admissible in a subsequent criminal trial.[17] In this case, which involved an adult probationer, Murphy's incriminating statements to his probation officer were allowed at trial because the probation conference was not considered "inherently coercive" (much like the case in an intake conference). In situations that are considered inherently coercive, such as in a custodial police interrogation, *Miranda* warnings are normally required, and evidence may be used in court only if the suspect makes a voluntary and intelligent waiver of his or her *Miranda* rights. In this case, Murphy was never given the *Miranda* warning, but the evidence was still used against him at trial.

Case Brief   *Leading Case on the Admissibility of Intake Information at an Adjudication Hearing in Juvenile Justice*

In re Wayne H., 596 P.2d 1 (Cal. 1979)

Facts: Wayne H., a sixteen-year-old male, was the passenger in a vehicle observed by police speeding away from the scene of a gas station robbery. During a pursuit with police, Wayne H. threw a pistol out the car window. Upon arrest, Wayne H. was wearing clothes similar to those worn by the robber and had a dark skin-cap as identified by witnesses. As well, the police found $54 in twenties, fives, and ones on the passenger-side floorboard of the car—exactly the amount stolen from the gas station and in the exact denominations. Wayne H. was taken to Juvenile Hall and was interviewed by a probation officer to determine whether he should be detained and whether transfer proceedings were warranted. Wayne H. was given his *Miranda* rights but denied any involvement in the robbery. At the end of the intake conference, upon hearing that the probation officer intended to recommend detention and a transfer hearing to adult court, Wayne H. said, "I did this one." At the transfer hearing, the probation officer testified about Wayne H.'s admission. Wayne H. objected but was adjudicated delinquent anyway. He then appealed the ruling.

Issue: Is information acquired by a probation officer at intake admissible in a subsequent adjudication or criminal trial?

Court Decision: The purpose of an intake interview between a minor suspect and his or her probation officer is not to gather evidence of guilt, but to assemble all available information relevant to an informed disposition of the case and to assist in evaluating the need for detention and the minor's fitness for treatment as a juvenile. Therefore, it was an error to admit as evidence an incriminating statement that the minor made to the probation officer.

Case Significance: This case dealt with the issue of whether information acquired by an intake officer during an intake conference is admissible in any guilt-finding phase of a judicial processing (such as an adjudication hearing). The court found that the potential use of information acquired during intake would undermine the intent and purpose of intake, which is to assemble all information relevant to an informed disposition of a case so that the juvenile justice system can individualize a juvenile's treatment, based on the particular facts and circumstances surrounding his or her case.

The court saw the use of information acquired at intake as tainted because of the nature of intake interviews, which encourage juveniles to be truthful and cooperative. Although the court said that intake information could be used in determining juvenile detention decisions and in waiver hearings, it clearly distinguished those processes as preliminary to guilt-finding phases and with few long-term ramifications for the juvenile.

The significance of this case rests in its protection of the juvenile during intake by prohibiting the admission of incriminating information obtained by

(continued)

Leading Case on the Admissibility of Intake Information at an Adjudication Hearing in Juvenile Justice (continued)

intake officers at an adjudication proceeding or criminal trial in the event that the youth is waived. However, note that this decision was based primarily on state law. The U.S. Supreme Court has not ruled on the issue of whether exclusion of such evidence is required by the Constitution.

Excerpts from the Decision:

"Admissions by a juvenile to a probation officer for use in the preparation of the social study, and to the juvenile court itself in the course of a . . . jurisdictional hearing, have both been excluded from subsequent adult criminal proceedings.

"The minor who is subject to the possibility of a transfer order should not be put to the unfair choice of being considered uncooperative by the juvenile probation officer and juvenile court because of his refusal to discuss his case with the probation officer, or having his statements to that officer used against him in subsequent criminal proceedings. . . . Such a result would frustrate the rehabilitative purpose of the Juvenile Court Law.

"We conclude that the subsequent use of statements made by a juvenile to a probation officer in an [initial interview] would frustrate important purposes of that statute, and of the Juvenile Court Law generally. We therefore hold that such statements are not admissible as substantive evidence, or for impeachment, in any subsequent proceeding to determine criminal guilt, whether juvenile or adult. Such statements may, of course, be admitted and considered in hearings on the issues of detention and fitness for juvenile treatment."

Source: This brief originally appeared in Rolando V. del Carmen, Mary Parker, and Frances P. Reddington, *Briefs of Leading Cases in Juvenile Justice* (Cincinnati: Anderson, 1998).

The *Murphy* ruling raises the question of whether juvenile intake conferences are comparable to adult probationer–officer conferences. If so, may statements during intake be used as evidence in an adjudication proceeding? One author notes that juvenile intake conferences are even *less* coercive than the probation conference in *Murphy* because of their informal nature and the fact that parents often accompany their child to such conferences.[18] Intake conferences, when viewed in this way, may not be considered inherently coercive, although this conclusion is debatable. Some now argue that information collected at intake should be allowed as evidence in an adjudication proceeding. The "Controversial Issue" box presents arguments on both sides of this subject.

General Guidelines on the Admissibility of Intake Information in Adjudication Proceedings

In the absence of a clear rule on the admissibility of intake evidence in an adjudication hearing, there are general guidelines instead. Generally, if state law permits that incriminating information gathered at juvenile intake may be

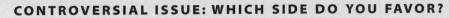

CONTROVERSIAL ISSUE: WHICH SIDE DO YOU FAVOR?

Should incriminating evidence obtained at intake be used in an adjudication proceeding (trial)?

Intake conferences were originally intended to be informal meetings between an intake officer and a juvenile. These conferences were supposed to encourage honesty and openness. This nonthreatening environment ensured that intake officers could obtain the information necessary to make an informed decision about how to handle the case. At the same time, no adverse consequences could come to the juvenile. In practice, this situation has changed. Juvenile intake conferences today, in some jurisdictions, resemble mini-interrogations whereby the intake officer's job is to elicit incriminating evidence to be later used in an adjudication hearing.

This raises a question: *Should juveniles have the right to an attorney and the privilege against self-incrimination at an intake conference?*

Those who argue that juveniles should receive the right to an attorney and the privilege against self-incrimination maintain that the purpose of the intake conference has changed. They say that intake conferences today are a far cry from their original formulation and, in many jurisdictions, are simply custodial interrogations whereby juveniles are coerced into answering incriminating questions. States should provide juveniles the right to an attorney and the privilege against self-incrimination, and should ensure that juveniles fully understand these rights whether or not the information will be used at the adjudication proceeding. Juveniles are immature and may not fully understand the proceedings against them. Without these protections, juveniles will be taken advantage of by intake officers. In some cases, the absence of these protections may mean that innocent juveniles might admit to wrongdoing simply because of pressure by intake officers.

Those who say that juveniles should not receive the right to an attorney and privilege against self-incrimination at intake argue that such requirements would handcuff juvenile officers. Intake is a stage at which intake officers must be able to obtain any and all types of information from the juvenile without fear that the juvenile will "lawyer up" and not talk. Intake officers need this information to be able to handle the case appropriately. Intake is not an interrogation simply because intake officers ask questions that may incriminate the juvenile. The fact that juveniles may give up incriminating information does not necessarily mean that it will be used in an adjudication hearing, even if state law allows it to be used. Often, intake officers are testing juveniles to see if they are honest. If a juvenile is honest, intake officers may divert the case because the juvenile is willing to accept responsibility for his or her act. Giving juveniles the right to a lawyer and the privilege against self-incrimination at intake prevents the collection of this type of information, aggravates the situation, and makes the outcome worse for the juvenile. If juveniles do not provide this information at intake, authorities will get it at another time. It is in the juvenile's best interests to provide it to intake officers because they control what happens to the juvenile's case.

TABLE 4.2

*The Admissibility of Intake Information
in an Adjudication Proceeding*

Use of Evidence Obtained at Intake	Miranda Warning Required?
For intake decision only (petition or divert)	No
For intake and adjudication hearing	Yes

used in an adjudication hearing, it becomes a critical stage and intake officers should advise the youth of his or her *Miranda* warnings, including the right to an attorney and the privilege against self-incrimination. If incriminating information obtained at the intake conference is used only to help make intake decisions, such as to divert the youth or file a delinquent petition and not as evidence during the adjudication hearing, *Miranda* warnings are probably not needed. Although the U.S. Supreme Court never required *Miranda* warnings for adult probationers during a probation conference, it is likely that courts would require such safeguards for juveniles at intake if such information could be used against them in court—whether or not such conferences are considered inherently coercive. In fact, a number of states now have laws providing juveniles a right to a lawyer and the privilege against self-incrimination in all delinquency proceedings where evidence could be used against them, including during intake. Table 4.2 presents the general guidelines.

The Diversion Process

What Is Diversion?

Diversion (also called *informal adjustment* or *informal processing*) occurs when intake officers handle delinquency referrals without formal court intervention or a delinquency petition; therefore, diversion is a pre-adjudicatory procedure. There are two ways diversion can be accomplished: informally and formally. **Informal diversion** refers to the process whereby intake officers require only that a youth remain violation free for a nominal period of time, usually six months or less. Juveniles who are informally diverted are not required to comply with other requirements (such as community service or counseling) and are released without record if they remain violation free. **Formal diversion** refers to the process whereby juveniles are required to comply with other requirements. For example, in addition to remaining violation free, the juvenile may be required to provide restitution to the victim, perform community service, attend counseling, or enroll in an after-school program.

Diversion enables juvenile justice authorities to remove relatively nonserious offenders from the juvenile justice system while at the same time ensuring that juvenile offenders do not get off without consequences for their behavior. The justification is that for many offenders, doing less is actually doing more. Diversion allows the juvenile to avoid the stigma of being labeled a delinquent. It also allows the juvenile justice system to save space for more serious delinquents.

Examples of Diversion Programs

In cases of formal diversion, the diverted juvenile may be subject to a wide variety of diversion programs. Diversion programs vary substantially at the state and local level and are operated or sponsored by police agencies, probation departments, juvenile courts, correctional agencies, and even private entities. Some of the most common and recognizable formal diversion programs include community service, restitution, scared-straight–type programs, teen courts, and various forms of counseling. Numerous programs fall under the general label of counseling. They include family intervention programs to encourage parental participation in the child's rehabilitation and group counseling programs whereby similar offenders are brought together in a counseling format to discuss a broad range of issues, from peer pressure to bullying to conflict resolution. In addition, a prominent trend in diversionary alternatives for juveniles comes under the general label of restorative justice. Restorative-justice–based diversion programs include a host of programs such as victim–offender mediation, in which the juvenile, his or her parents, and the victim meet so that the victim can express his or her feelings about the crime and its effects. The victim and offender may also devise an appropriate remedy to the harm caused to the victim as the result of the crime—for example, monetary restitution to pay for any financial losses. The philosophy of victim–offender mediation programs and other diversion programs based on restorative justice is that bringing the victim and juvenile offender together will promote healing on the part of the victim and also give the juvenile an opportunity to become more aware of the effect that his or her actions had on a real person and the community at large.

The bottom line with diversion programs is that they are numerous and are operated by a number of different agencies. One of the main goals of diversion programs is that they may address problematic behavior early and without formal juvenile court intervention, thus curbing a juvenile's delinquent ways before he or she escalates into more serious offenses that would require a more formalized response by the juvenile justice system.

Who Qualifies for Diversion?

Generally, first-time nonserious juveniles are the types of offenders who qualify for diversion. This determination is usually based on state law. For example, first-time juvenile offenders in Alaska or those who have committed minor offenses are eligible. This is the case in most states.* Serious or chronic juvenile offenders are typically ineligible for diversion unless a special program exists for them. Diversion is intended to intervene in relatively nonserious behavior before it escalates into more serious delinquency. Juveniles who are

*For particular state guidelines, see http://www.ncjj.org/stateprofiles/profiles and click on the state.

already serious or overly chronic in offending require a more formalized response than diversion was intended to provide.

What Happens If a Youth Refuses to Accept Diversion?

State law usually provides that diversion is voluntary: The youth is agreeing to admit to the charges against him or her in lieu of intake officers filing a delinquency petition with the juvenile court. If a youth refuses to accept a diversion offer, however, what happens? Generally, if a youth does not accept diversion, intake officers may file a delinquency petition, and an adjudication hearing will be scheduled. Intake officers providing for diversion are simply giving the youth a chance to avoid adjudication and a possible record with the court. Most youths take advantage of this second chance.

In practice, however, diversion refusals may not be so clear-cut. An offer of diversion does not necessarily mean that the amount and quality of evidence will support guilt in an adjudication hearing. To file a delinquency petition, probable cause may only be required, whereas adjudication for charges must be proved beyond a reasonable doubt (a much higher standard). Moreover, not all states even require probable cause to file a delinquency petition and may allow a lower standard of proof.

The aforementioned facts about the diversion process have led to the perspective that diversion can circumvent due process. As mentioned above, diversion is usually offered only to qualified juveniles who admit to committing the alleged offense. Critics suggest that diversion is sometimes used to force juveniles to admit their guilt out of fear that they might get adjudicated on formal charges despite the fact that prosecutors may have little actual evidence of the juvenile's guilt and adjudication beyond a reasonable doubt would be unlikely. In this way, critics contend that many juveniles may admit guilt to acts they did not actually commit or may admit guilt to an act based on little evidence simply to avoid the possibility of a harsher sentence if adjudicated in juvenile court. This fact also presents a potential dilemma for intake officers. For example, what if the amount and quality of evidence in the case are low and adjudication is unlikely in court but the youth refuses to accept a diversion offer from an intake officer? Should the intake officer try to persuade the youth to accept diversion when the evidence would not likely result in adjudication by a standard of beyond a reasonable doubt? There is no clear-cut answer to this question. If a juvenile refuses a diversion offer and the amount and quality of evidence are unlikely to result in adjudication, prosecutors generally have two options: They can decide to dismiss the case or proceed with the adjudication hearing and hope that the delinquency allegations are proved beyond a reasonable doubt.

Prosecutorial Retaliation for Refusing Diversion

May prosecutors charge a juvenile with a more serious offense if he or she declines a diversion offer? This issue was addressed in the case of *State v. McDowell* (1984).[19] McDowell claimed that he was being punished for exercising his right to a court hearing when he refused a diversion offer, stating that the prosecutor increased the charge after he refused.

It is unconstitutional to punish someone for exercising his or her right to a trial, such as increasing the charges simply because a juvenile fails to accept a diversion offer. However, it is not unconstitutional for a prosecutor to increase the charge if the evidence in the case warrants such a charge *and* the prosecutor's decision was not out of retaliation or vindictiveness.[20] This stipulation applies even when a prosecutor threatens to bring more serious charges if the defendant does not plead guilty (or fails to accept diversion).[21] As long as the decision is not *vindictive* and as long as the charges are consistent with the law and evidence in the case, prosecutors may use their discretion and increase charges.*

It is difficult for a juvenile to *prove* that a prosecutor's motives for increasing charges were made in retaliation or were vindictive. Prosecutors are given substantial discretion to charge as long as the evidence in the case supports their decision. Sometimes, these charges differ substantially from those during the initial arrest or earlier charges. The discovery of new evidence can be a common reason for a prosecutor to increase the charge. For example, a juvenile is arrested for assault on another juvenile. If it is later found out by prosecutors that the juvenile had a gun and pistol-whipped the victim, the prosecutor might seek a higher charge of aggravated assault with a weapon. The general rule is that prosecutors may increase charges as long as the evidence supports such charges and as long as the decision is not out of retaliation or vindictiveness.

The Legal Rights of Juveniles in Diversion
Do Juveniles Have a Constitutional Right to Diversion?

A Washington appellate court considered whether juveniles have a constitutional right to diversion in the case of *Washington v. Chatham* (1981).[22] Chatham was in a group of juveniles who were involved in an altercation with several adult golfers at a golf club. During the altercation, Chatham struck one of the adult golfers and caused serious and permanent eye injuries. According to state law, Chatham was eligible for diversion because he was a first-time offender. The prosecutor contacted the administrator of the local diversionary agency and relayed the facts of the case. Based on that conversation, the chairperson refused to accept Chatham into a diversionary program despite the assault being his first offense. The chairperson denied Chatham's acceptance because of the seriousness of the offense, which did not fall within the acceptable list of offenses for inclusion in the diversion program. Chatham appealed.

The court held that although a juvenile has a right to be *considered* for diversion, he or she does not have a constitutional right to be *guaranteed* admission into the diversion program. The court reasoned that a juvenile's statutory right (a right given by state law) to have his case referred to a diversion agency

*See Barry C. Feld, *Juvenile Justice Administration in a Nutshell* (St. Paul, MN: Thomson/West, 2003), and *Cases and Materials of Juvenile Justice Administration* (St. Paul, MN: West Group, 2000), for additional legal situations surrounding diversion. These excellent sources contain specific legal information about diversion and other juvenile justice processes involving the law.

does not guarantee that the agency must accept the youth. Rather, the court noted that diversion is not always a proper disposition, even in first-offender juvenile cases.[23] Thus, juveniles have a right to be considered for diversion but do not have a right to be placed in a diversion program if they do not meet program criteria. Such decisions are left to the discretion of diversion authorities.

The *Chatham* case dealt with a state law that required all first-time offenders not charged with a felony to be *considered* for diversion. This case demonstrates the principle that states may make laws that give juveniles a right to be considered for diversion for a variety of offenses in a variety of situations (such as being a first offender). However, states do not typically provide an absolute right to diversion.* Even in cases where a juvenile may be a "good" candidate for diversion, states may retain the right to petition for an adjudication hearing.

Is a Hearing Required to Deny Diversion?

What if a juvenile is "appropriate" for diversion according to state law, but prosecutors choose to file a delinquency petition anyway? Does the juvenile have a right to a hearing when he or she is denied diversion? In *State v. Tracy M.* (1986), a Washington appellate court held that a due process hearing is not required when a juvenile is denied diversion.[24] Diversion is a discretionary practice involving decisions (typically by prosecutors) on how to dispose of a case. Diversion is equivalent to making charging decisions that do not require a due process hearing.

Although the Constitution does not require a hearing on decisions to divert or petition a youth, states may provide juveniles a right to a hearing when they are not offered diversion; the U.S. Supreme Court has not decided this issue. Moreover, some states may require diversionary authorities or prosecutors to justify in some way the reasons why a "qualified" juvenile was not offered diversion (such as putting the reasons in writing). This step helps ensure that diversion decisions are fair.[25]

Cases Similarly Situated and Diversion Offers

The Fourteenth Amendment to the U.S. Constitution requires that people be treated equally in the enforcement of the law (this is called the "Equal Protection Clause"). Does this statement mean that juveniles in similar circumstances must be treated the same in decisions to divert or to petition the case? For example, twin sisters are arrested for shoplifting high-powered BB guns. Both juveniles are first offenders and are similarly situated (meaning they are similar or equal in terms of factors that may influence intake decisions, such as age, maturity, family life, prior record, school experience, and crime alleged). Is it a violation of the Equal Protection Clause if one sister is offered diversion and the other is not?

Unless state law provides otherwise, prosecutors are not obligated to treat like offenders the same in diversion decisions.[26] Prosecutors have much discretion

---

*Feld, *Juvenile Justice Administration in a Nutshell*. For diversion guidelines by state, see http://www.ncjj.org/stateprofiles/profiles and click on the state.

and may decide two similarly situated cases in two different ways. This is not an equal protection violation *unless* the prosecutor's decision was arbitrary, which means that the decision was done intentionally with the purpose of discriminating against a certain juvenile or class of juvenile offenders—for example, if one sister was offered diversion and the other was not simply because of her hair color. It would also be a violation of rights if prosecutors decided to never offer diversion to a certain class of offenders even when the crimes they commit are viewed as appropriate for diversion. For example, a prosecutor has a great love of animals, and he systematically denies diversion to all youths referred for animal abuse. Although not all animal abusers must be offered diversion, excluding entire classes of offenders summarily because of their acts while disregarding the individual's circumstances in each case is arbitrary and may amount to illegal discrimination.[27] In reality, the idea of two cases being exactly similar on all relevant characteristics is unlikely, and this is why two cases that are similar in appearance may actually receive different actions in decisions to divert or petition juveniles.

Removing a Youth from Diversion

Diversion is a privilege, not a right, so it may be taken away in certain situations. Intake officers, depending on state law, can remove a juvenile from diversion in two general ways. First, an intake officer can terminate the informal adjustment process early and *dismiss* the juvenile. This outcome may occur for a variety of reasons, such as the juvenile has received maximum benefit from the diversion process and has been in substantial compliance. Second and more typically, an intake officer can terminate the diversion process and file a delinquency or waiver petition with the court. This step may occur when the juvenile does not meet the stipulations of the diversion agreement or consent decree, commits a new delinquent offense, or both.

State procedures for removing youths from a diversion agreement differ. In Alabama, for example, state law permits an intake officer to terminate the informal adjustment process if at any time:

- It appears that the child and his parents or custodian have received the maximum benefit from the informal adjustment process.
- The child or his parents or custodian declines to participate further in the informal adjustment process.
- The child or his parents or custodian denies the jurisdiction of the court (leaves town/country).
- The child or his parents or custodian expresses a desire that the facts be determined by the court.
- The child fails to attend scheduled conferences without reasonable excuse.
- The child appears unable or unwilling to benefit from the informal adjustment process.
- The intake officer becomes apprised of new or additional information which makes it appear that further efforts at informal adjustment would not be in the best interests of the juvenile or of society.

■ Other sufficient reasons exist for terminating the informal adjustment process.[28]

States retain the ultimate right to control the diversion process, and intake officers are generally authorized to determine that the interests of the case are best served by dismissing the juvenile early or by proceeding with a delinquency and/or waiver petition. Thus, juveniles do not have a constitutional right to diversion, nor do they have a right to remain in diversion if they do not adhere to its requirements.

This point raises a question: Do juveniles have a right to a due process hearing if intake officers seek to remove them from diversion and file a delinquency petition? It has already been established that juveniles do not have a constitutional right to a due process hearing when they are not offered diversion, unless state law provides for such a hearing. The case is similar in decisions to revoke diversion. The discussion below examines why.

In *Gagnon v. Scarpelli* (1973)[29] and *Morrissey v. Brewer* (1972),[30] the U.S. Supreme Court held that adult probationers and parolees are entitled to a due process hearing before their probation or parole is revoked. These cases involved revocation procedures against adults, but there is reason to believe that they apply as well to juveniles in probation and parole revocations. Applied to diversion, however, the main question is whether diversion is similar enough to probation and parole to require a due process hearing when it is terminated. In the case of *In the Matter of Edwin L.* (1996), the New York court of appeals addressed such an issue and held that "revoking" a diversion contract is not like revoking probation or parole.[31] The court said that the consequences of probation and parole revocation differ significantly from the consequences resulting from a termination of a diversion contract. Therefore, juveniles who are removed from diversion do not have the same right to due process protections that are afforded probationers or parolees in revocation proceedings because they suffer fewer adverse consequences.[32]

The U.S. Supreme Court has not decided whether juveniles on diversion are entitled to a due process hearing prior to diversion revocation.[33] States may give juveniles this right to a hearing, but it is not required by the Constitution.

Diversion and Double Jeopardy

E. K., a fifteen-year-old Iowa juvenile, was offered formal diversion for breaking into a car and stealing several compact discs (CDs). Four months into his diversion contract, E. K. failed to complete his community service and missed several meetings with the probation officer supervising his case. E. K. was removed from diversion, and the prosecutor filed a delinquency petition with the juvenile court. An adjudication hearing took place, and E. K. was adjudicated on the original offense of breaking into the car and theft. He was sentenced to three years of probation. E. K. was essentially punished twice for the same offense. First, he was punished when he got diversion, and later he was adjudicated and given three years on probation because he failed at diversion. Does this situation constitute double jeopardy?

The U.S. Supreme Court applied the constitutional right against double jeopardy to juveniles in *Breed v. Jones* (1975).[34] *Double jeopardy* is defined as the successive prosecution of a defendant for the same offense by the same jurisdiction. There are three requirements for double jeopardy to occur:

- *Successive prosecution.* This means two adjudication/criminal proceedings. In the juvenile justice system, if a juvenile has an adjudication hearing and the allegations of delinquent conduct are not proven (acquittal), there cannot be another adjudication proceeding in juvenile court.

- *Same offense.* The two cases must be for the same delinquent/criminal offense. If the elements of the two prosecutions are different, there is no double jeopardy. Thus, if a juvenile has an adjudication hearing and the allegations are not proved beyond a reasonable doubt, prosecutors could hold another adjudication hearing for another offense if there is one present. Prosecutors could not hold another adjudication hearing for the same offense.

- *Same jurisdiction.* There can be two prosecutions for the same offense if they take place in different jurisdictions. The case of Lee Boyd Malvo (the juvenile sniper in the Maryland/Washington, D.C., shootings) provides a good example. Malvo could be tried for murder both in Maryland and in the federal court system. This would not be double jeopardy because the federal system and the state systems are considered two separate jurisdictions, or sovereigns. However, Malvo could not be tried for the same offense in juvenile and adult court in Maryland—these are not considered separate sovereigns.[35]

In E. K.'s case, double jeopardy does not apply because all three elements of double jeopardy are not met. Although E. K. was in the same jurisdiction (Iowa) for the same offense (breaking into a car and theft), there was not a successive prosecution—meaning two criminal or adjudication proceedings. Diversion is not considered a prosecution or a conviction. Thus, there is no double jeopardy when diversion is "revoked" and when such revocation results in adjudication and an additional punishment for the original offense.

May Prior Diversions Be Used to Increase Future Sentences?

Diversion is not considered a prosecution, and successfully meeting diversion usually means the juvenile will not have an official record with the court. Despite the fact that juveniles must usually admit to the alleged behavior to be offered diversion, it is not considered a conviction. Since diversion is not a prosecution, or technically a conviction, can evidence of past diversions be used in a later adjudication hearing or a future diversion agreement to enhance a juvenile's sentence by making it longer or harsher? For example, could evidence of a past diversion mean that a second diversion offered to the juvenile is longer and has more requirements? Similarly, could evidence of a past diversion mean that a disposition as a result of an adjudication hearing be longer or harsher than if the juvenile did not have a prior diversion?

In the case of *State v. Quiroz* (1987), the Washington Supreme Court held that evidence of past diversions could be used as evidence of a juvenile's past criminal record and to enhance future sentences.[36] The court said that the procedures given to youths during intake in that state clearly outlined that a diversion agreement could be used to enhance the penalty for a future crime. Because of this potential future use and associated consequences, juveniles in Washington are advised of their right to have an attorney to assist them in making the decision to accept diversion or exercise their right to an adjudication proceeding. Alternatively, in the case of *In re D. S. S.* (1993), the Minnesota Court of Appeals prohibited a juvenile court judge from using evidence of a juvenile's prior diversions in the disposition stage when sentencing the youth.[37] This court held that prior diversions could not be used to enhance a sentence, because at intake, juveniles were not afforded a lawyer in making the decision to accept diversion or to proceed with an adjudication hearing.

This issue has not been decided by the U.S. Supreme Court, and state law prevails. Generally, if it is clear that prior diversions can be used to enhance future sentences, judges may consider this evidence. However, juveniles might need to be informed of a right to an attorney and be able to consult with an attorney before making their decision to "voluntarily" participate in diversion—the consequences of choosing diversion may be used against them as a "prior record" in the future to enhance future sentences.

Extralegal Issues in Diversion
Bias in Selection for Diversion

Intake officers consider legal and extralegal factors when making diversion decisions. Legal factors, such as a juvenile's prior record, the amount and quality of evidence, and the current offense, are legitimate considerations in making diversion decisions. Extralegal factors are controversial, however. Factors such as a juvenile's gender, race, and age may influence diversion decisions and make the process appear biased in favor of some juveniles over others:

- *Gender.* Females are more likely to be diverted than are males, and there are many explanations for this practice. Female adolescents may be treated more leniently (offered diversion versus petitioned for delinquency) because intake officers may tend to be more paternalistic with females than with males. Some intake officers are thought to be more sympathetic to female adolescents by placing more emphasis on their background characteristics than on the legal merits of the alleged crime. In reality, however, female juveniles tend to receive diversion at a greater rate than males because their crimes are less serious—one of the most important determinants of diversion versus a delinquency petition.[38] However, when female juveniles encounter intake officers on more than one occasion, they tend to be treated more harshly than males.[39]

- *Race.* Delinquency cases involving black juveniles are more likely to be petitioned (versus nonpetitioned) than are cases involving youths of other races.[40] Intake decisions should never be influenced by race, but researchers have found evidence that race, after accounting for factors such as crime seriousness, age, and gender, may have some influence on intake decisions. For example, Bishop and Frazier (1996) found that nonwhite juveniles were significantly more likely to be referred for prosecution than white juveniles—after taking into account the aforementioned factors. Although crime seriousness was by far the most influential factor in intake decisions, Bishop and Frazier did find that race had an impact as well.[41]

■ *Age.* There is little research on the influence of age in intake decisions. Available evidence generally shows that older juveniles (ages sixteen and seventeen) are more likely to be petitioned to juvenile court than to be offered diversion. The most recent statistics show that 61 percent of the cases involving youths older than age sixteen were petitioned versus 55 percent for youths fifteen and younger.[42] Although age alone should never influence intake decisions, age often interacts with offense seriousness and prior record, and thus can be considered both a legal and an extralegal factor in intake decisions—age tends to both mitigate and aggravate intake decisions. For example, after committing the same crime, a young offender (under age fourteen) may be treated more leniently (offered diversion) than an older offender might be treated (be petitioned). Intake officers may conclude that older offenders "should know better" and that younger juveniles are less responsible and deserve a second chance. Older offenders are also more likely to have a prior record than younger offenders, and even when they have allegedly committed the same crime, they may be more likely to get petitioned.

As in decisions to arrest (see Chapter 3), several other factors can affect diversion decisions. Socioeconomic status is a good example of an extralegal factor that may influence intake decisions. Youths considered as "low" in socioeconomic status are more likely to be petitioned, just as they are more likely to be arrested. Research covered in Chapter 3 showed that youths from low socioeconomic backgrounds tend to commit more serious crimes, explaining why they are more often arrested versus warned and released for these crimes. This same reasoning may explain why they are more likely to get petitioned versus diverted. Furthermore, low-socioeconomic-status youths (and their families) may be less likely to be able to afford to hire counsel at intake, and if counsel is not provided at intake by state law, this situation may make a delinquency petition more likely. Thus, diversion (and dismissal) might be more likely for youths in the upper socioeconomic statuses simply because they may be more likely to be represented by an attorney who will advocate for diversion versus a petition and adjudication hearing. Therefore, any bias may be in the ability to obtain a lawyer, not necessarily against the youths themselves and their socioeconomic status.

The finding of unequal numbers in intake decisions does not necessarily mean that intake is biased—for example, finding that more females get diverted than males. Intake involves many discretionary decisions on the part of intake officers, who are charged with the responsibility of predicting which factors may or may not lead to a successful diversion. More data need to be collected and analyzed to come to a concrete explanation on intake decision making and whether bias exists when concerning extralegal factors. Ultimately, however, research suggests that bias may disappear when considered in light of legal factors such as the seriousness of the alleged current offense and prior contacts with the system. Note that there is much variation around the country, so this finding may be truer in some places than in others. More controversial is socioeconomic status, however, wherein youths and their families may be at a disadvantage solely because they are unable to afford their own attorney in states that do not provide an attorney at the intake stage.

Does Diversion Promote Further Contact with the Juvenile Justice System?

Arguably, diversion has many positive aspects for juveniles and the juvenile justice system. It allows youths to avoid a delinquency petition and possible adjudication as delinquent, it allows positive intervention in a youth's life, it serves to keep formal probation caseloads lower, and it offers an informal solution when formal processing may not be appropriate. However, some question whether diversion may do more harm than good by promoting further contact with the juvenile justice system. In other words, diversion may be a gateway to the formal juvenile justice system. Evidence suggests that youths who receive diversion have a higher rate of subsequent offending (as measured by re-arrest) than youths who were filtered out of the system at intake.[43] There are various possible reasons for this claim.

Diverted youths may face a higher rate of offending than youths filtered out of the system at intake because of diversion's potential for detection. Diverted youths may well be known to the police and other juvenile justice authorities, and these authorities might pay more attention to them. In this way, diverted youths are given a label that places them under heightened scrutiny for their behaviors.[44] Many behaviors that are not considered illegal could mean a violation if they are listed in a consent decree created through diversion. For example, failing to meet with a probation officer, not obeying parents fully, and failing to attend to a community service contract are not illegal, but they may result in a delinquency petition because they are violations under a diversion consent decree.

In another way, diversion may serve to "pile responsibility" on youths who have a demonstrated record of irresponsible behavior. Giving more responsibility to youths who cannot handle the responsibility they have may set them up for failure, especially for multiple-problem youths who come from multiple-problem homes. For example, youths placed on diversion could be required complete a host of activities, including community service, restitution, reporting to an officer, and attending school. Moreover, youths on diversion often depend on their parents for many things, such as transportation to meet with a probation officer or to attend counseling or to do community service. If parents fail to comply, their children may suffer the consequences. In these ways and likely others, diversion may promote further contact with the juvenile justice system.

A comprehensive evaluation of the success of diversion programs did not provide evidence that diversion has either a positive or negative effect on youths in terms of future involvement with the juvenile justice system.[45] In other words, diversion did not necessarily hurt, but it did not help either.

Other studies have found conflicting results: Diversion is an effective way of "deflecting" youths from further penetration into the juvenile system, or diversion is a gateway that makes further penetration into the system easier.[46] The last point suggests that diversion has "widened the net" of social control rather than served its intended function of deflecting youths from the system.

Diversion and Net Widening

Diversion has always made it possible to deal with youths less formally than in an adjudication proceeding in juvenile court. Since the due process changes in the juvenile court in the 1960s, and calls by the federal government to divert youths to the community when possible, diversion use has increased. Qualified offenders, meaning less serious offenders who might otherwise have been petitioned for an adjudication hearing, were the primary targets of diversion programs. Diverting these youths was supported by the belief that doing less is more for many offenders—that the potentially harmful effects of being labeled an official delinquent could be circumvented while at the same time youths would not go unpunished for their misdeeds. If diversion is focused on offenders who would have been petitioned prior to the greater use of diversion, an argument can be made that its goals of deflecting youths from formal sanctions are being accomplished (at least in the short term).

Today, however, some suggest that diversion is an additional tool that allows intake officers and prosecutors to have legal authority over youths who never would have been petitioned in the first place and who should have their cases dismissed. They contend that the "build it and they will come" phenomenon is at work. The result is a juvenile process that has expanded, or "widened." For example, the number of youths facing the formal juvenile court has remained the same or has increased (youths are not getting deflected into informal diversion) while diversion has created "more room" to capture more offenders who would have had their cases dismissed altogether, a phenomenon called **net widening.**[47] Exhibit 4.2 is a simplified illustration of this process.

EXHIBIT 4.2

Diversion as Net Widening

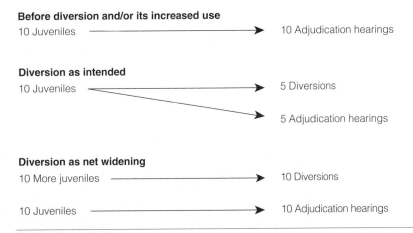

Before diversion and/or its increased use

10 Juveniles ⟶ 10 Adjudication hearings

Diversion as intended

10 Juveniles ⟶ 5 Diversions

⟶ 5 Adjudication hearings

Diversion as net widening

10 More juveniles ⟶ 10 Diversions

10 Juveniles ⟶ 10 Adjudication hearings

The bottom line with diversion and net widening is that diversion serves as an additional space for intake officers and prosecutors to place offenders who may have otherwise had their cases dismissed. Net widening is not a problem when the diverted youths are those who formerly would have faced an adjudication hearing. Determining the impact of net widening in the juvenile justice system involving diversion is difficult because it necessitates looking back and assuming what would have happened to cases in the absence of diversion or before its increased use. Despite this problem, it is possible that diversion is used as a supplement rather than an alternative to the formal juvenile justice system and has indeed widened the net of government control over young people.[48]

SUMMARY

❑ Intake is the process of screening cases after a juvenile has been arrested and referred to intake officers. It is a weeding-out process for determining which cases will be diverted and which will be petitioned to the juvenile court.

❑ Intake officers are typically probation officers or prosecutors.

❑ The practice in most states requires that final intake decisions be made or reviewed by a prosecutor.

❑ At intake, more than 40 percent of all cases are either dismissed or informally adjusted.

❑ More than one-half of all cases referred to intake officers involve a delinquency petition.

❑ Intake is not considered a "critical stage"; therefore, juveniles do not have a constitutional right to a lawyer. However, several states give juveniles a right to a lawyer during intake.

❑ Information at intake is not generally admissible in an adjudication proceeding unless juveniles are given *Miranda* warnings, including the right to a lawyer and the right to remain silent.

❑ A juvenile may refuse a diversion offer from intake officers. In these situations, intake officers will typically file a delinquency petition and schedule an adjudication proceeding.

❑ No hearing is required when intake officers refuse to offer diversion to a juvenile. Juveniles do not have a constitutional right to diversion.

❑ In some states, prior diversions may be viewed as a prior record and be used to enhance future sentences.

❑ The U.S. Supreme Court has not decided a case on juvenile intake and diversion. Thus, states vary in how they handle intake and the rights of juveniles. The best practice is to look to state law for determining intake procedures among the various states.

❑ Diversion may contribute to net widening, which occurs when youths who would have never been petitioned or may have had their cases dismissed are placed in diversion simply because such programs are available.

REVIEW QUESTIONS

1. What types of information do intake officers gather when deciding to dismiss, divert, or file a delinquency petition?

2. Why do prosecutors play a larger role during intake today than in the past?

3. What is a critical stage? Why have some courts decided that intake is not a critical stage?

4. What is the significance of the *Minnesota v. Murphy* decision concerning the admissibility of intake information during adjudication proceedings? Should this case apply to juvenile intake conferences? Why or why not?

5. What is the general rule concerning the admissibility of intake information during adjudication hearings?

6. What is diversion? What are some positive benefits for juveniles and the juvenile court of using diversion?

7. Are juvenile justice authorities required to enter into a diversion agreement with a "qualified" juvenile? Why or why not?

8. Why is it not considered double jeopardy when a juvenile fails at diversion, is removed, and is subsequently adjudicated in juvenile court?

9. Do you agree with the argument that diversion can promote further contact with the juvenile justice system? Can you think of any other ways that diversion can promote further contact with the system?

10. Discuss the goals of diversion. How might diversion contribute to net widening?

KEY TERMS AND DEFINITIONS

adjustment (sometimes called **informal adjustment**): The process of dealing with a delinquency referral informally. The case is "adjusted," which means that the youth is offered diversion in lieu of facing an adjudication hearing.

critical stage: A stage in which incriminating evidence may be obtained from a suspect. Defendants have a right to a lawyer and are protected from self-incrimination at all critical stages.

delinquency petition: A formal complaint or request, typically from a prosecutor, asking the juvenile court judge to adjudicate a youth delinquent. A delinquency petition may contain information about the alleged crime and other information, such as the juvenile's prior record.

delinquency referral: A notice to an intake officer that a juvenile has engaged in delinquent conduct. Delinquency referrals typically come from law enforcement officers, but some states allow school officials, parents, and general citizens to make referrals directly to an intake officer.

diversion: Another name for informal adjustment or informal processing. Diversion refers to the process of "diverting" youths from the formal juvenile justice system by offering them an informal way to resolve their delinquency referral.

formal diversion: A type of diversion in which youths are required to do more than remain violation free during a specified adjustment period. Formal diversion typically includes community service, restitution, and/or attendance in a counseling program.

informal diversion: A type of diversion in which youths are required only to remain violation free during a specified period of time. Youths are not required to attend to other stipulations, such as community service, as they are with formal diversion.

intake: The screening process of all delinquency referrals after arrest. Procedures at intake determine which cases will be informally adjusted and which cases will be petitioned to the juvenile court.

intake conference: An informal meeting, typically including intake officers, the juvenile, and his or her parents. Intake conferences are intended to be informal, information-gathering sessions so that the intake officer can make an informed decision on whether to adjust the youth's case or file a delinquency petition. Intake conferences around the country vary in style, and some of them resemble mini-interrogations with the goal of eliciting incriminating information.

intake officer: Usually a probation officer or prosecutor, who screens all delinquency referrals for their legal merit. Intake officers make decisions on which cases will be dealt with informally and which cases will be petitioned to the juvenile court.

net widening: Occurs when juveniles who would not have been petitioned to juvenile court are placed on diversion. The increasing use of diversion programs brings more youths under the eyes of police and other monitors, making it more likely that juveniles will have further contacts with the juvenile justice system.

waiver petition: A petition or request by an intake officer or prosecutor asking the juvenile court judge to consider that the case be heard in adult court, not juvenile court. Juvenile court judges typically make final decisions on petitions to waive a juvenile. Waiver petitions are usually based on the seriousness of the offense.

 ## FOR FURTHER RESEARCH

❏ **Juvenile Assessment Centers: Strengths, Weaknesses, and Potential**
   http://md2.csa.com/htbin/ids64/procskel.cgi

❏ **The Role of Restorative Justice in Teen Courts: A Preliminary Look**
   http://www.youthcourt.net/publications/justice.htm

❏ **Community Assessment Center Concept**
   http://www.ncjrs.org/html/ojjdp/jjbul2000_03_6/contents.html

❏ **Detention Diversion Advocacy: An Evaluation**
   http://www.ncjrs.org/html/ojjdp/9909-3/contents.html

❏ **Assessing Alcohol, Drug, and Mental Disorders in Juvenile Detainees**
   http://www.ncjrs.org/txtfiles1/ojjdp/fs200102.txt

For an up-to-date list of web links, go to the Juvenile Justice Companion Website at **http://cj.wadsworth.com/del_carmen_trulson_jj**

CHAPTER 5

Status Offenders, Dependent and Neglected Youths, and Juvenile Victimizations

Historical Methods of Dealing with Nondelinquents / 143

The Juvenile Justice and Delinquency Prevention Act (JJDPA) of 1974 / 145

    Core Requirements of the JJDPA of 1974 / 146
    Amendments to the JJDPA of 1974 / 147

The Juvenile Justice System and Status Offenders / 147

    Justification for Juvenile Justice Intervention for Status Offenders Today / 148
    The Juvenile Court Process for Status Offenders / 148
    The Rights of Status Offenders in Adjudication Proceedings / 149
    Dispositions for Status Offenders / 149
        Bootstrapping / 150
        Hidden Delinquency / 151

Status Offense Case Processing in the Juvenile Justice System / 151

    Initial Contact / 152

Intake / 154
Adjudication / 154
Disposition / 154

Dependency, Neglect, and the Juvenile Justice System / 155

    Reasons for Juvenile Court Intervention for Dependent and Neglected Youths / 155
    Forms of Dependency and Neglect / 158
    Agencies Dealing with Dependency and Neglect / 159
    The Extent of Dependency and Neglect / 163
        Collection Methods / 164
        Cases of Dependency and Neglect / 165

Juvenile Court Processing for Dependency and Neglect / 166

    Court Petition or Complaint / 167
    Mediation / 168
    Court Hearing / 168
    Disposition / 169

Juvenile Victimizations / 170

IN THIS CHAPTER YOU WILL LEARN

■ That until the 1970s, status offenders and dependent and neglected youths were treated in much the same way as delinquents in the juvenile justice system.

■ About the Juvenile Justice and Delinquency Prevention Act of 1974 and in what ways it led to change in the treatment of all juveniles, including nondelinquents, in the juvenile justice system.

■ About the juvenile court process for status offenders and the rights of status offenders in juvenile court.

■ That status offenders may receive many of the same dispositions as delinquents, with the exception of placement in a secure facility such as a detention center or juvenile state school.

■ Why the juvenile court intervenes in juveniles' dependency and neglect cases even though these juveniles have not violated the law.

■ About the juvenile justice process for dependent and neglected youths.

■ About the extent of dependency and neglect cases in the United States and the principle of the supremacy of parental rights.

■ That most dependency and neglect cases are resolved without formal juvenile court intervention, with child protection agencies working in conjunction with families.

■ About juvenile victimizations beyond dependency and neglect.

INTRODUCTION

The main focus of this text is the treatment of delinquent youths in the juvenile justice system. However, nondelinquents, such as status offenders and dependent and neglected youths, also come under the jurisdiction of the juvenile court and justice system. Status offenders come in contact with the system because of acts that are prohibited only if done by juveniles. These acts, such as running away or skipping school, are regulated by law because the status of juveniles (being young) indicates that they are too immature to regulate these behaviors on their own. Dependent and neglected youths come to the attention of the juvenile justice system as a result of parental circumstances or conduct. Dependent youths are those whose parents want to take care of them but cannot. Dependency usually occurs in cases of the death of parents or their severe physical or mental disability. Neglected youths are those whose parents are able to take care of them but choose not to. Neglect comes in many forms, from failing to provide proper supervision to extreme physical, sexual, and emotional abuse. Broadly, status offenders and dependent and neglected youths are referred to as nondelinquents.

In the justice system, nondelinquents are viewed and treated differently from delinquents. Whereas delinquents are to be "held accountable and punished," nondelinquents are deemed as children in need of "assistance or supervision." Although the reasons for juvenile justice system intervention differ, nondelinquents are subject to many of the same procedures and dispositions that delinquents face in the juvenile justice system. Nondelinquents, especially status offenders, cannot usually be held in a detention center or institutionalized in a state school, but they may be subject to court referral, diversion, an adjudication hearing (status offenders) or special court hearing (dependent and neglected youths), and a number of other dispositions, including placement in an institution.

This chapter begins by examining the history of nondelinquents in the juvenile justice system. Then the chapter covers one of the most significant events in the treatment of nondelinquents in juvenile justice—the federal Juvenile Justice and Delinquency Prevention Act (JJDPA) of 1974. It then discusses the juvenile court process for status offenders, including a profile of status offense cases formally handled in juvenile court. It continues by examining the forms of dependency and neglect, the extent of these cases in juvenile justice, and the juvenile court process for these types of youths. It ends with a discussion of the victimizations that juveniles experience beyond dependency and neglect.

Historical Methods of Dealing with Nondelinquents

Until the 1970s, there was no legal distinction between a juvenile who committed an act considered criminal if committed by an adult, a juvenile who committed an act considered "wayward" or "predelinquent," and a youth who came from a home with ill, unwitting, destitute, or deceased parents. Under *parens patriae*, the juvenile court believed that it had the duty to intervene if doing so was in the child's best interests. The court could address any behavior or circumstance causing concern, whether the behavior was delinquent or not. The juvenile court was not concerned with precise definitions and categories of conduct that might fall under its jurisdiction because the assumption was that contact with the juvenile court was always good.

The broad jurisdiction of juvenile courts could be found in many state codes prior to the 1970s. For example, here is a provision from the Illinois revised statutes in 1949:

> A delinquent child is any male . . . or any female child who . . . violates any law of this state; or is incorrigible, or knowingly associates with thieves, vicious or immoral persons; or . . . absents itself from its home . . . or is growing up in idleness or crime; or knowingly frequents a house of ill repute; . . . or wanders about the street in the night time . . . ; or habitually wanders any railroad yards or tracks or jumps or attempts to jump onto any moving train; . . . or uses vile, obscene, vulgar, or indecent language; . . . or is guilty of indecent or lascivious conduct.[1]

The above broad definitions ("indecent conduct," "incorrigible," and "idleness") include acts that today are considered status offenses or the product of dependency and neglect. Prior to the 1970s, however, these acts were considered one and the same in juvenile court. Indeed, juvenile court caseloads in many jurisdictions consisted mainly of nondelinquents. Because all youths coming to the juvenile court were considered to have demonstrated a behavior or circumstance indicating the need for juvenile court intervention, it followed that the juvenile court process did not differ much for the hardened delinquent and the vagrant youth. The unrecognized distinction between delinquent and nondelinquent youths remained through the disposition stage in juvenile court. The outcome was that many nondelinquent youths were institutionalized with delinquents prior to the 1970s.[2]

The practice of incarcerating nondelinquents with delinquents led to problems. First, the indeterminate sentencing structure in juvenile courts meant that juveniles would remain incarcerated until they were "fixed" or "cured" of their behavior. This indeterminate scheme created problems for nondelinquents because they were often incarcerated for something their parents failed to do. In some cases, nondelinquents were incarcerated much longer than delinquents. For example, one writer noted that in New York in 1965, children institutionalized for nondelinquent behavior stayed an average of twelve months longer than youths committed for delinquency.[3] Such practice was common throughout the nation until the late 1960s and was especially harmful to dependent and neglected children. With home placement no longer possible because of their parents' conduct, and little hope for foster care or adoption, dependent and neglected youths would simply remain institutionalized until they reached adulthood because there was no place to release them. Nondelinquents were also exposed to hardened delinquents and became victims of these more sophisticated youths. Those institutionalized for "crimes" such as being "incorrigible" or "abandoned" were exposed to criminogenic influences throughout their stay, resulting in many youths learning such techniques as how to steal a car, burglarize a house, and mug someone without being detected.[4] In sum, institutionalization for some nondelinquents consisted of little more than an education in crime and a lesson in victimization.

No wonder that critics and reformers focused on the institutionalization of nondelinquents and the effect that being locked up with hardened delinquents had on them. Critics concluded that juvenile court intervention was not always "in the best interests of the child," and in many cases, juvenile court intervention led to cruel and degrading treatment that promoted a future life of ruin. Change ensued after nearly seventy-five years of juvenile courts treating youths as though they were all alike.

The change process began by making a legal distinction between youths who committed acts considered criminal if committed by an adult and youths who committed acts not considered criminal if committed by an adult—that is, acts prohibited only for juveniles, or status offenses. This second group of juvenile offenders came to be known as **status offenders.** Youths coming under this definition were labeled as CINS (children in need of supervision), MINS (minors in need of supervision), CINA (children in need of assistance), or PINS (persons in need of supervision). Youths who were in court as a result of their parents' failures were called dependent and neglected, and were referred to as nondelinquents. These legal and terminological distinctions signified changes in how these youths would be handled in the juvenile court. Youths considered nondelinquents were not to be treated like criminals. Rather, they were to be helped, supervised, and assisted. This philosophy was reinforced and formalized by one of the most significant pieces of federal legislation involving juveniles: the Juvenile Justice and Delinquency Prevention Act of 1974.

The Juvenile Justice and Delinquency Prevention Act (JJDPA) of 1974

In the 1960s, several changes were occurring in the juvenile justice process. A series of U.S. Supreme Court decisions "constitutionalized" the process, first by requiring formal hearings in transfer or waiver situations (*Kent v. United States* [1966]). The Court also mandated that juveniles who faced possible incarceration be given certain due process rights, such as a right to a lawyer, a right to confront and cross-examine witnesses, and the privilege against self-incrimination (*In re Gault* [1967]). The Court further held that delinquents were to be tried in court using the standard of beyond a reasonable doubt instead of the lesser standard of preponderance of the evidence (*In re Winship* [1970]).[5]

Despite the constitutionalization of the juvenile justice process, nondelinquents were not provided due process protection by the Court unless they faced secure incarceration. However, federal legislation had an effect on their treatment. In 1974 Congress passed the **Juvenile Justice and Delinquency Prevention Act (JJDPA).** This sweeping piece of federal legislation required the removal of nondelinquents from secure institutions such as detention centers and state schools, and prohibited the practice of confining juveniles with adults.

Core Requirements of the JJDPA of 1974

The JJDPA of 1974 has two original core requirements: (1) the deinstitutionalization of status offenders and (2) the sight and sound separation of juveniles (including status offenders and dependent and neglected youths) from adults. These requirements are discussed below:

- *Deinstitutionalization.* The requirement to deinstitutionalize status offenders and other nondelinquent youths specifies that juveniles not charged with acts that would be considered crimes if committed by an adult will not be placed in secure detention facilities or secure correctional facilities. In other words, nondelinquents cannot be placed in a secure facility because such facilities are reserved for delinquents. Status offenders and dependent and neglected youths are not considered delinquents and should not be treated as such.

- *Sight and sound separation.* Juveniles, both delinquent and nondelinquent, will not be detained or confined in any institution in which they have contact with adult incarcerated persons. Juvenile and adults inmates cannot see one another, and no conversation between them is possible.[6]

The passage of the JJDPA by Congress in 1974 did not mean that the states instantly complied with the deinstitutionalization and sight and sound separation requirements. First, states were not even required to comply. Instead, compliance with the JJDPA was a condition that states had to meet to be eligible for federal grant funds. Second, the JJDPA was a vision for change. Congress realized that the historical practice of institutionalizing nondelinquents and placing juveniles in adult jails could not be remedied overnight. For example, ending the practice of placing nondelinquents in detention centers and other secure facilities meant that states and their jurisdictions had to find alternative placements in the community, such as unlocked youth shelters or community diversion programs. This reality necessitated a two-year compliance window in 1974 and several time extensions in the following years. After thirty years, however, in 2003 the Office of Juvenile Justice and Delinquency Prevention (OJJDP) reported that almost every state and territory was in compliance with the mandates of the JJDPA.*

The original requirements of the JJDPA of 1974 brought about important changes in the treatment of nondelinquent youths. However, the JJDPA did not end the practice of processing nondelinquents in the juvenile court, nor did it provide nondelinquents with the due process rights already given to delinquents. Instead, the JJDPA focused primarily on juvenile justice practices

*J. Robert Flores, *OJJDP Annual Report, 2001* (Washington, DC: Office of Juvenile Justice and Delinquency Prevention, 2003), 24–28. Compliance with separation and adult jail removal of juvenile offenders was also examined in the five U.S. territories (American Samoa, Guam, Northern Mariana Islands, Puerto Rico, and the Virgin Islands). These territories were in full compliance with both separation and adult jail removal. South Dakota and Wyoming were the only two states that did not participate in this study.

at the disposition stage by prohibiting the incarceration of status offenders and dependent and neglected youths. Although the JJDPA did not deal with youth processing, its requirements brought changes in these areas for nondelinquents. For example, instead of sending most nondelinquents to the juvenile court for adjudication, several states diverted nondelinquent youths to community-based programs. These changes became the trend in the 1970s and have continued to this day. Since 1974, the JJDPA has been amended several times to address additional issues relating to delinquents and nondelinquents. Thus, it remains one of the most powerful pieces of federal legislation in juvenile justice.

Amendments to the JJDPA of 1974

Two additional amendments to the JJDPA are important to juvenile justice today. These amendments are the 1980 adult jail and lockup removal and the 1992 requirement that states examine disproportionate minority confinement. Although these requirements are more central to delinquents than to nondelinquents, these amendments signify that efforts continue not only to distinguish juveniles from adults, but to distinguish delinquents from nondelinquents as well. The amendments are further elaborated below:

- *Jail and Lockup Removal (1980).* This amendment states that juveniles will not be detained or confined in adult jails or lockups unless the juvenile is being tried as an adult for a felony or has been convicted as a criminal felon. An exception allows juveniles to be held in adult jails and lockups for six hours in urban areas and up to twenty-four hours in rural areas if no alternative arrangements can be made and secure detention is required.

- *Disproportionate Minority Confinement (1992).* This amendment specifies that states must determine the existence and extent of the problem in their state and try to reduce the disproportionate confinement of minorities when it occurs. States that hold a disproportionate number of minority youths in relation to their proportion of the population must determine the extent of the disparity, determine why it exists, and try to reduce it without employing quotas.[7]

The success of the JJDPA in making significant changes in juvenile justice practice was tied to its optional nature. States could choose to participate or not. However, states that did not participate would risk losing federal funds used to repair roads and subsidize other state programs. In essence, the JJDPA of 1974 constituted "mandatory voluntariness" that forced states to change the way they dealt with all juveniles in the system, including nondelinquents.

The Juvenile Justice System and Status Offenders

In most states, the processing of status offenders differs from the processing of dependent and neglected youths. Thus, this section examines the juvenile justice process for status offenders only and includes a discussion on how this process is similar to and different from the processing of delinquents.

Justification for Juvenile Justice Intervention for Status Offenders Today

Juvenile court intervention for status offenders was first justified by the idea that a child who was "vagrant," "wayward," "incorrigible," or "insolent" had to be removed from negative influences in the community. Because such a child's acts were usually the product of improper supervision, it was the duty of the juvenile court to intervene.[8] For the early juvenile courts, this was a way to protect the child. That the juvenile was not yet delinquent did not matter—the behavior implied that the path the child was following would lead to future problems. It was the juvenile court's job to change that direction and ensure a better future for the juvenile.

The reason for juvenile justice intervention for status offenders has not changed much today. Many still believe that status offending is a **slippery slope** toward delinquency and adult criminality. This idea is subject to substantial debate, with researchers examining whether status offenders continue their path and move on to more serious delinquency or **desist** at the level of a status offender. Some studies have found that a substantial number of status offenders escalate to delinquency;[9] others have found that most status offenders do not.[10] Outcomes are mixed, but more representative studies have found that most status offenders do not end up being juvenile delinquents.[11] Proponents of juvenile court intervention for status offenders believe that the reason status offenders do not become delinquents is early juvenile court intervention. Without such intervention, they say, status offenders would be likely to continue into delinquency and adult criminality.

Despite mixed evidence of status offending being a slippery slope, juvenile court intervention is nonetheless justified by the belief that it is better to catch problematic behavior before it escalates into something more serious. As a result, the juvenile justice process for status offenders is generally similar to that for delinquents.

The Juvenile Court Process for Status Offenders

Status offenders are not labeled "delinquent" by our penal codes. This terminological distinction is based on the belief that status offenders are different from delinquents and therefore should not be given that label. Despite terminological differences, status offenders in most states are still subject to the same procedures as delinquents in the juvenile justice system.[12]

Just like delinquents, status offenders may be subject to police custody and be detained at a police station. The only difference is that in many states, status offenders may be detained under the lower standard of reasonable suspicion, instead of probable cause, because custody is for their own protection. If referred by the police, status offenders are also subject to the intake process, which is essentially the same as that for delinquents. Intake officers decide whether the status offense case warrants dismissal or diversion/adjustment. Status offenders may also be petitioned to the juvenile court at intake for an adjudication hearing in much the same way that delinquent cases are petitioned, but status offense cases are never considered appropriate for transfer to adult court. It is a common misperception that status offenders cannot be petitioned to the juvenile court. Although most status offenders are informally diverted, they can face an adjudication hearing in the same way that delinquents do. However, this process for status offenders generally differs from that for delinquents.

The Rights of Status Offenders in Adjudication Proceedings

In 1967 the U.S. Supreme Court held in *In re Gault* (1967) that juveniles must be given four basic due process rights in any adjudication proceeding that can result in confinement in an institution: a reasonable notice of the charges, the right to counsel, the right to confront and cross-examine witnesses, and the privilege against self-incrimination, including the right to remain silent.[13] However, the rights given in *Gault* do not apply to proceedings in which incarceration will not result, and this is usually the case with status offenses. Although states may grant these due process rights to status offenders, they are not required to do so under the Constitution.

Note that status offenders do not have to face an adjudication proceeding without the benefit of counsel or the opportunity to confront evidence and witnesses against them. In reality, states usually allow that status offenders be assisted in court by a lawyer, a guardian ad litem, or a court-appointed special advocate (CASA). Moreover, some states require that in adjudication proceedings status offenders receive the same due process rights as delinquents.

An important difference between the procedure for delinquents and for status offenders lies in the standard of proof required. The U.S. Supreme Court held in the case of *In re Winship* (1970) that proof beyond a reasonable doubt, instead of **preponderance of the evidence,** is required *only* in juvenile adjudication hearings in which the act would have been a crime if it were committed by an adult.[14] This is not the same standard that juvenile courts must use in adjudication hearings for status offenders, who may be adjudicated based on a preponderance of the evidence instead of the higher standard of guilt beyond a reasonable doubt. The exception occurs when state law raises this standard.

Dispositions for Status Offenders

Before the 1970s, juvenile courts sentenced status offenders to the same dispositions as delinquent offenders, including incarceration. Today, however, perhaps the biggest difference between the juvenile court process for delinquents and nondelinquents is at the disposition stage. Although status offenders may still be sentenced to many of the same dispositions as delinquents, status offenders may not normally be held in secure facilities such as juvenile detention centers and juvenile state schools/correctional institutions. On the other hand, they may be held in certain unlocked institutions, such as youth shelters, group homes, halfway houses, or, in some cases, mental institutions and substance abuse treatment facilities. In most cases, however, status offenders are sentenced to probation and other community-based sanctions, including various forms of counseling.

The JJDPA of 1974 specifically prohibited the secure incarceration of status offenders. As a result, almost all states today prohibit placing nondelinquents in secure facilities such as detention centers and state schools. However, some contend that the deinstitutionalization of status offenders has led to unintended consequences, that status offenders have been transformed from "institution kids" to "agency kids" and are now essentially incarcerated in the community.[15] Critics also argue that some status offenders are "bootstrapped" into delinquent status so that they may be incarcerated in secure facilities or so that judges have more punitive disposition options. Still others point out that status offenders are still being incarcerated, with the only difference being that their incarceration is in a mental hospital or other treatment facility for long periods of time. Barry Feld has referred to youths in these situations as "hidden delinquents" captured in a "hidden system."[16]

Bootstrapping

One unintended consequence of deinstitutionalization is the practice of **bootstrapping** status offenders, which is the process whereby a juvenile court elevates (or bootstraps) a status offender to delinquent status as a result of repeated violations of the same status offense that brought the youth to the juvenile court in the first place.[17] According to Harry J. Rothgerber, bootstrapping may occur in two general ways: contempt of court and escape petition.

Contempt of court bootstrapping can be illustrated as follows: A juvenile is adjudicated for the status offense of being truant in school, and the court orders that the youth should not miss school. But the youth continues to be truant and is brought before the court a second time. The youth is then found to be in contempt of court for engaging in the same behavior. The juvenile court then elevates the contempt of court violation to a delinquency offense (as a result of violating a valid court order); therefore, the youth can now be held in a secure setting such as a detention center. Bootstrapping also opens the door for the juvenile to face an adjudication hearing, but this time it will be for delinquent conduct, whereby the juvenile may face possible institutionalization or a host of sanctions reserved for only delinquents. In short, the juvenile is elevated to delinquent status for the same status offense that brought him or her to the court in the first place.

Bootstrapping can also occur as a result of an escape petition. For example, a juvenile court judge sends an adjudicated status offender to a group home for a period of six months for being a runaway. At the unlocked group home, the youth runs away. The youth is now elevated to delinquent status by the juvenile court. Although the youth's behavior did not change (runaway), the fact that he or she ran away from a group home elevated the status offender to that of a delinquent because of a violation of a valid court order.[18]

The JJDPA of 1974 prohibits the confinement of status offenders in secure facilities; however, a 1980 exception provides that a status offender may be confined in a secure juvenile facility if he or she has violated a valid court order (VCO), as is the case in forms of bootstrapping.[19] Even though federal law and some states' laws prohibit bootstrapping and the placement of bootstrapped status offenders in secure detention, many courts disregard these laws. These courts hold that laws which diminish the courts' contempt power to sanction status offenders represent an unconstitutional infringement of judicial power. As a result, most courts have held that status offenders can be elevated to delinquent status for violating court orders, even if the elevation to delinquent status is for the same status offense. These same courts have generally agreed that bootstrapped status offenders may be held in secure detention facilities, and if the offenders are adjudicated for violating a valid court order, they can theoretically be sentenced to a juvenile state school.*

Hidden Delinquency

Another unintended consequence of deinstitutionalization for nondelinquents is the use of alternative institutionalizations, usually mental hospitals or substance abuse treatment facilities. Institutionalization in a mental hospital or substance treatment facility does not violate the mandates of the JJDPA for nondelinquents because such institutions are considered treatment oriented.

Youths sent to these institutions are sometimes labeled "hidden delinquents" and are said to have been captured in a "hidden system."[20] Youths committed to mental hospitals and other treatment-oriented institutions are usually afforded less due process than delinquents receive in juvenile court despite being subject to a form of institutionalization in which their freedom is taken away. For example, in the case of *Parham v. J.R* (1979), the U.S. Supreme Court held that parents may commit their child to a mental hospital (this usually includes substance abuse facilities) as long as a neutral fact finder finds "evidence" of a mental illness.[21] The child may be held indefinitely until either the parents request that their child be released or when there is evidence that the child no longer suffers from a mental illness.

This practice has generated controversy. Some say that mental institutions and other placements have become an alternative way to incarcerate status offenders, with their offending behavior being used to show "evidence of mental illness" or a need for treatment. The hidden system is not limited to substance abuse facilities or mental hospitals, however. As long as a status offender is not placed in a secure detention facility or state school, juvenile courts may have a variety of residential or out-of-home placements at their disposal. These places provide an alternative to institutional dispositions to detention centers and state schools, and are not subject to JJDPA deinstitutionalization guidelines. This whole procedure constitutes the essence of the hidden system.

Status Offense Case Processing in the Juvenile Justice System

For several reasons, no one knows the total number of status offenders who come to the attention of the juvenile justice system. First, status offenders in some states cannot technically be arrested and thus are not reflected in arrest

---

*See *In the Interest of J.E.S,* 817 P.2d 508 (Colo. 1991), in which the Colorado Supreme Court held that when bootstrapping is the result of elevated delinquency, the youth could be held in a secure detention facility. Compare this case to *Michael G. v. Superior Court,* 243 Cal. Rptr. 224 (Cal. 1988), in which this California court permitted bootstrapping but disapproved allowing the juvenile court to place bootstrapped status offenders in secure confinement such as a detention center.

statistics even when they are taken into custody. In other states, status offenders are not included in official counts because they are considered in need of assistance (rather than law violators) and are dealt with by social service agencies instead of the juvenile court. Moreover, some status offense cases are not counted unless a petition is filed in the case and the juvenile goes to court for an adjudication hearing.[22] Therefore, when relying on official data sources such as the UCR or juvenile court statistics to track status offending, the extent of this behavior is almost certainly underestimated.

A major reason that status offense estimates are a problem is that the term *status offense* is an umbrella designation covering numerous behaviors prohibited only for juveniles. Some of these may include being "incorrigible" or "stubborn." These categories are usually not included in official statistics because of their broad nature. For example, running away and truancy are uniform in different states, but being "stubborn" is subject to much interpretation. Tracking all status offense cases that are dealt with by the juvenile justice system is very difficult; therefore, caution must be exercised when dealing with the available statistics.

Despite problems in tracking status offenders, official statistics are able to record certain categories of status offenses with some consistency. For example, the UCR tracks status offenses such as running away, curfew and loitering violations, and liquor law violations. Juvenile court statistics provide data on status offense processing and trends in running away, truancy, ungovernability (not following parental rules), and liquor law violations. These offenses are well recorded compared to other status offenses because they have uniform definitions among the states and arguably represent the most problematic behaviors of status offenders. For example, being truant from school implies missing out on valuable educational opportunities, and violating curfew may mean that youths are putting themselves at an increased risk of victimization. These status offenses are considered more serious than smoking or being stubborn because they are considered more self-destructive. Despite omissions, the UCR and juvenile court statistics provide the best picture available on the extent of status offending and the outcomes for youths if they go to court. The "Controversial Issue" box examines the legal issues surrounding the violation of curfew ordinances, one of the most controversial status offenses today.

Initial Contact

Juveniles were arrested for an estimated 2.3 million offenses in 2001, roughly 400,000 of which were status offenses. Of the 400,000 status offenses recorded by the UCR, 133,300 were for running away, 142,900 were for curfew and loitering, and 138,100 were liquor law violations. Between 1990 and 1999, liquor law violations were the offenses most likely to be referred by law enforcement officers to the juvenile court for formal resolution, perhaps because these acts are among the most self-destructive of all status offenses. In this time period, approximately 90 percent of liquor law violations were referred. Truancy and ungovernability were least likely to result in a formal referral by law enforcement (approximately 10 percent), whereas law enforcement agencies referred 40 percent of runaway cases.[23]

CONTROVERSIAL ISSUE: WHICH SIDE DO YOU FAVOR?

Are juvenile curfews best imposed by parents or by the government?

Curfew ordinances came to the public's attention in the mid-1990s after numerous cities enacted these ordinances as a way to prevent juvenile victimization, to prevent juvenile delinquency, and to promote the development of healthy behavior among juveniles. Although there are many issues with curfew ordinances, the most controversial one is whether a child's parents or the government should handle the matter. Some say that parents should be able to determine their child's curfew and that cities should not act as a child's parents. When a city sets a curfew ordinance, these critics contend that it may violate juveniles' rights. Others say that it is the duty and privilege of local governments to create ordinances promoting the safety and well-being of juveniles. Because juveniles' status (being young) indicates that they lack the maturity and experience to regulate some behaviors on their own, proponents say that juveniles' constitutional rights, and hence their freedom, are diminished in some circumstances.[1]

The U.S. Supreme Court has never decided a curfew case, but the lower federal courts have decided several cases that have addressed whether curfew laws are constitutional and, if so, in what form. Generally, courts have held that curfew ordinances established by local governments are constitutional.[2] In order to be constitutional, however, curfew ordinances generally have to pass what is called the "strict scrutiny test." This test says that jurisdictions must demonstrate that there is a "compelling interest" to have a curfew and that it must be "narrowly tailored." For example, a compelling need or interest for a curfew law might be demonstrated if city officials show evidence that juvenile victimization and crime increase at night. A narrowly tailored curfew ordinance might be one that occurs from 9 P.M. until 6 A.M., but would allow a juvenile to be exempt if he or she was accompanied by an adult, traveling to and from work, or attending a school-sponsored activity such as a sporting event.

1. What are the benefits and drawbacks of curfew laws? Which side of the issue do you favor? Explain.

2. If you were a city administrator responsible for devising a curfew ordinance, what would it look like? Would your ordinance pass both prongs of the "strict scrutiny" test if someone challenged the ordinance in court as a violation of constitutional rights?

3. Find an example of a local curfew ordinance in your state, or search the Internet for examples of curfew ordinances. In your opinion, would this ordinance be considered constitutional under the strict scrutiny test? Explain.

4. Go to http://ojjdp.ncjrs.org (the Office of Juvenile Justice and Delinquency Prevention) and find a publication which examines the time and place that juvenile victimizations typically occur. Based on this information, would a curfew ordinance help to prevent such victimizations?

[1] *Curfew: An Answer to Juvenile Delinquency and Victimization* (Washington, DC: Office of Juvenile Justice and Delinquency Prevention, 1996).
[2] *Qutb v. Strauss*, 11 F.3d 488 (5th Cir. 1993).

Intake

Once status offenders come to the attention of law enforcement officers, they may be referred to juvenile court intake. Intake officers may dismiss the case, divert the case, or petition the court for an adjudication proceeding.

Most status offense cases are diverted from the juvenile justice system at intake, complying with the mandate of the JJDPA that status offenders and other noncriminal youths be diverted from the formal system whenever possible. In some cases, status offenders may be placed on informal or formal diversion, which requires that they cease their status offending behavior, pay fines or restitution, perform community service, attend counseling, or comply with other conditions imposed. If they meet these requirements, they are dismissed from further oversight and avoid further sanctions.[24]

Status offenders who are not diverted may be petitioned for an adjudication hearing. Juvenile courts may adjudicate status offenders and sentence them to a variety of dispositions, such as probation, counseling, or residential placement in youth shelters and group homes. Those who are petitioned may also be held in secure detention while their cases are processed, although states that do so risk losing funds as a result of the requirements of the JJDPA. However, this practice is rare. In 1999, fewer than 8 percent of all petitioned status offenders were placed in juvenile detention until their adjudication hearing.[25]

Adjudication

When status offenders are petitioned to juvenile court, they are usually adjudicated. However, this probability varies based on the type of status offense. From 1990 to 1999, 46 percent of runaways, 61 percent of truancy violators, 62 percent of ungovernable youths, and 59 percent of liquor law violators were adjudicated.

Some other trends with status offenders at adjudication include the following:

- Younger juveniles (at or below age fifteen) were more likely to be adjudicated than were older juveniles.

- Males and females were adjudicated at about the same rate for all status offenses except for liquor law violations, wherein adjudication was more likely for males.

- White youths were more likely to be adjudicated for running away than black youths, but for all other status offenses, adjudication rates were comparable.[26]

Disposition

Of all dispositions available to juvenile court judges in status offense cases, probation was the most common in 1990–1999. It was the disposition in 57 percent of adjudicated runaway cases, 78 percent of truancy cases, 65 percent of ungovernability cases, and 58 percent of liquor law violation cases. Out-of-home placement (such as in a group home) was used 26 percent of the time in runaway cases, 11 percent of the time in truancy cases, 24 percent of the time in ungovernability cases, and 7 percent of the time in liquor law violation cases. Thus, community placement is the preferred disposition for most status offenders. Out-of-home placement, fines, and release back home were other common dispositions.[27]

Exhibit 5.1 provides a look at the typical case processing and dispositions of status offenders who are petitioned for an adjudication hearing in juvenile court. Overall, the exhibit shows that for each status offense listed, about half of the cases are adjudicated. Of the cases not adjudicated, most are dismissed altogether. Again, most adjudicated status offenders are sentenced to probation if adjudicated.

Dependency, Neglect, and the Juvenile Justice System

Most people do not think of the juvenile justice system in situations of dependency and neglect. As mentioned in Chapter 1, a common misperception is that the juvenile court and agencies of the juvenile justice system handle only delinquent youths. Although delinquent youths and status offenders are the primary focus of the juvenile court and its agencies, the court also has jurisdiction over youths in cases where they are the victims of their parents, guardians, or other caretakers. These youths are considered dependent and neglected. For these youths, the juvenile court intervenes to provide protection and assistance, not to hold the youths personally accountable.*

Reasons for Juvenile Court Intervention for Dependent and Neglected Youths

In 1873, residents of a New York City tenement house reported hearing cries for help from a girl in one of the apartments. A local nurse and church worker named Etta Wheeler went to the residence of Francis and Mary Connolly to investigate. After finding out that they had a foster girl named Mary Ellen Wilson, Mrs. Wheeler walked into the Connolly home and was horrified by what she saw. She observed Mary Ellen chained to a bedpost, covered in bruises, and withered from a diet of bread and water. Mrs. Wheeler demanded that the girl be turned over to her, but Francis and Mary slammed the door in her face and told her that it was none of her business. Despite repeated attempts to retrieve the child over the next several weeks, Mrs. Wheeler received the same response.

Mrs. Wheeler eventually turned for help to the only place she could—a local agency that was vested with police power. Mrs. Wheeler contacted the head

---

*As mentioned in Chapter 6, however, a dependent and/or neglected youth may also be involved in delinquency or status offending. Such cases are particularly problematic because they indicate multiple problems, both with the youth and his or her family. In this section, the focus is on treating dependency and neglect alone, but this is not to suggest that these cases do not happen. In cases where there are both issues, the youth may be dealt with both as a dependent and/or neglected child and a delinquent.

EXHIBIT 5.1   *Status Offense Case Processing*

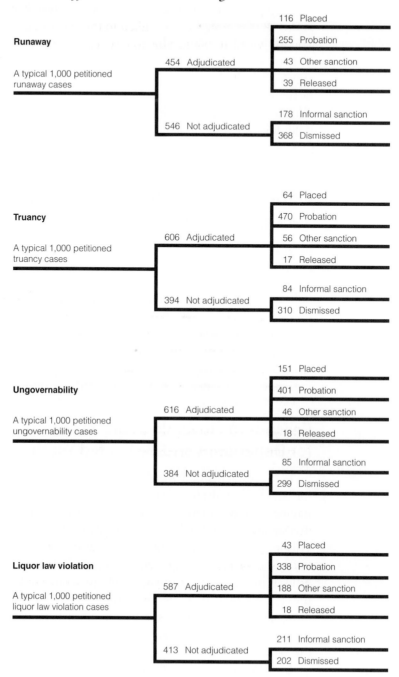

Note: Cases are categorized by their most severe or restrictive sanction. Detail may not add to totals because of rounding.

Source: Charles Puzzanchera, Anne L. Stahl, Terrence A. Finnegan, Nancy Tierney, and Howard N. Snyder, *Juvenile Court Statistics 1999* (Pittsburgh: National Center for Juvenile Justice, 2003), 58.

of this agency, Henry Bergh. After hearing Mrs. Wheeler's story, Mr. Bergh legally removed Mary and took her into protective custody. This occurred in 1874, nearly one year after Mrs. Wheeler had confronted Francis and Mary Connolly.

Mr. Bergh brought Mary Ellen to the courtroom on a stretcher because she was too weak to walk. She was covered with bruises and wounds over her body, and court onlookers and the judge could hardly stand the sight. The judge promptly ordered that Mary Ellen be placed in another home to receive the proper care and attention she deserved.

What is amazing about Mary Ellen's story is that to help her, Mr. Bergh used the only laws available at the time—animal protection laws. In order to legally remove Mary Ellen, Mr. Bergh took an oath in court that Mary Ellen was an "animal." Mr. Bergh was not a police officer; instead, he was the founder and president of the American Society for the Prevention of Cruelty to Animals (ASPCA). Mary Ellen was saved by a law meant for abused animals.*

Society had no laws protecting the rights of children in 1870s, even those who suffered victimization at the hands of parents or guardians. Children were viewed as subservient to their parents and having no need for a separate legal status of their own. As state laws began to recognize child rights at the turn of the twentieth century, however, juvenile courts across the nation were charged with seeing that such laws were enforced and that dependent and neglected children received proper protection and care. Juvenile courts were given this responsibility because it was their duty to look after the best interests of the child. This duty was not limited to delinquents; it included any child in any situation that might lead to delinquency. As one writer noted:

> [T]he juvenile court was created to serve a different and a much broader set of functions than the criminal court. It was devised to raise the standards of child raising for society as a whole; act as a monitor over other societal institutions to ensure that the young are not exploited . . . and even prevent crime by serving as a catch basin for the children of poor, uncaring, or licentious parents.[28]

The justification for juvenile court intervention for dependent and neglected children is not much different today than it was in the early 1900s. Tradition dictates that matters of dependency and neglect remain with the juvenile court. Many still believe strongly that the juvenile court can best deal with dependency and neglect because youths affected by these conditions are more likely to become involved in delinquent behavior in the future than are other youths.[29] Although serious questions have been raised about whether the juvenile court should handle youths who have not violated the law, this court remains one of the major agencies that deal with dependent and neglected youths.

In many states, the court that handles juvenile dependency and neglect cases is not technically referred to as the "juvenile court," although this is the generic term used in this text. Exhibit 5.2 reveals that courts with juvenile

---

*Eric Shelman and Stephen Lazoritz, *Out of the Darkness: The Story of Mary Ellen Wilson* (Baltimore: Dolphin Moon, 1999). For an excellent description of the history of Mary Ellen Connolly and this incident, visit http://www.holdenpd.com/childabuse.html and read "First Case of Child Abuse," by Anjie Coates. See also http://users.fairfieldi.com/~cybertech/abuse.

EXHIBIT 5.2

A Juvenile Court by Any Other Name

All states have at least one court with jurisdiction over juvenile matters, but in most states it is not actually called the "juvenile court." Courts with juvenile jurisdiction are called different things depending on the state—district, county, probate, family, or domestic relations courts. Some courts with juvenile jurisdiction are vested with general jurisdiction and can hear all matters of delinquency, status offending, and dependency and neglect. In other cases, courts with juvenile jurisdiction may have limited or specialized jurisdiction, with one court handling delinquency cases, another handling status offense cases, and another handling dependency and neglect and other juvenile matters. Regardless of how they are named, courts with jurisdiction over juvenile matters are generically referred to as juvenile courts.

Source: Adapted from Howard N. Snyder and Melissa Sickmund, *Juvenile Offenders and Victims: 1999 National Report* (Washington, DC: Office of Juvenile Justice and Delinquency Prevention, 1999), 99.

jurisdiction may have different labels, especially when they deal with dependency and neglect cases. Regardless of what they are called, their central mission is to deal with cases of dependency and neglect.

Forms of Dependency and Neglect

In this text, the term **dependency and neglect** is used to refer to a range of situations in which parents are unable to care for their child (dependency) or when they are able but unwilling to do so (neglect). Despite this convenient labeling, there are numerous forms of dependency and neglect, and other common terms include "child abuse," "child endangerment," and "child maltreatment."[30] The following is a description of the various forms of dependency and neglect:

- *Physical abuse* includes physical acts that caused or could have caused physical injury to the child.
- *Sexual abuse* is involvement of the child in sexual activity to provide sexual gratification or financial benefit to the perpetrator, including contacts for sexual purposes, prostitution, pornography, or other sexually exploitive activities.
- *Emotional abuse* includes acts or omissions that caused or could have caused conduct, cognitive, affective, or other mental disorders.
- *Physical neglect* includes abandonment, expulsion from the home, failure to seek health care or delay in seeking care, inadequate supervision, disregard for hazards in the home, or inadequate food, clothing, or shelter.
- *Emotional neglect* includes inadequate nurturance or affection, permitting maladaptive behavior, and other inattention to emotional/developmental needs.
- *Educational neglect* includes permitting chronic truancy or other inattention to educational needs.[31]

This list shows the wide range of acts that may be considered abusive. Dependency and neglect also range in severity, from mild physical abuse resulting in bruises to severe physical abuse requiring hospitalization. It would be almost impossible to discuss every conceivable form and degree of dependency and neglect, but this discussion indicates the level of responsibility that the juvenile court and agencies dealing with dependency and neglect have. One form of neglect that has led to controversy is one that results from parental exercise of religious beliefs. This situation usually involves physical/medical neglect, but it can also be caused by other practices. The "Controversial Issue" box examines this issue.

Agencies Dealing with Dependency and Neglect

The juvenile court is ultimately responsible for dependency and neglect cases. However, most dependency and neglect cases are handled by child welfare agencies without ever reaching the juvenile court.[32] Common names for these agencies include Department of Human Services (DHS), Department of Protection and Welfare (DPW), and Department of Protective and Regulatory Services (DPRS). The specific division that handles dependency and neglect cases within these agencies is usually called **Child Protective Services (CPS).**

State-level child protective service agencies were created by using funds provided by the federal government in the 1970s after Congress passed the **Child Abuse Prevention and Treatment Act (CAPTA)** of 1974. Like the JJDPA of 1974, this act made states eligible for federal grant monies if they made progress in areas of child protection such as creating protective service agencies, passing mandatory reporting laws, and appointing dependent and neglected youth child advocates in court proceedings. Other federal and state laws since the 1970s have provided additional benefits for dependent and neglected youths. For example, the Child Abuse Prevention and Enforcement Act of 2000 made available more funds for the prevention of dependency and neglect. These federal and state laws have strengthened the effectiveness of child protection agencies in additional ways by mandating continued training for workers and providing funding for essential services (such as providing funds for nonprofit treatment agencies).[33]

The term *child protective services* generally refers to "services provided by an agency authorized to act on behalf of a child when parents are unable or unwilling to do so."[34] As a result of federal legislation, all states today have a child protective services agency that is authorized by law to conduct investigations into reports of child dependency and neglect. Since the majority of dependency and neglect cases are handled by these agencies without juvenile court intervention, the roles and responsibilities of child protective services are diverse. However, when cases of dependency and neglect deserve the court's formal attention, child protective services agencies are the main link to the juvenile court.

The Office of Juvenile Justice and Delinquency Prevention recently summarized the roles and activities of child protective services:

- *Identification.* Identification of a dependency and neglect situation is usually first discovered by those in a position to observe families and children.

Do parents have the right to deny medical care for their child and contribute to a situation of dependency and neglect based on their religious beliefs?

The First Amendment to the U.S. Constitution states that Congress shall make no law respecting an establishment of religion. This generally means that persons have the freedom to choose and practice religion. But how far does this freedom go when parents' religious beliefs lead to the denial of medical care for their children or other situations of dependency and neglect? Each year, many children die or become severely ill because of their parents' religious beliefs. For example, in medical neglect cases, dependency and neglect may arise because parents do not believe or adhere to modern medicine and choose to "heal" their child through prayer or through "spiritual healing." They are sometimes assisted by a religious practitioner.

In many situations, children are clearly dependent or neglected because of their parents' religious beliefs, but several states have statutes providing that a child is not to be considered dependent or neglected merely because he or she is receiving "spiritual treatment" as opposed to medical treatment. These statutes are called "religious exemption clauses." These clauses also severely limit a state's ability to prosecute parents civilly or criminally for dependency and neglect arising from their religious beliefs.

This raises a question: *What is the proper role of the government when a parent's religious beliefs lead to the denial of medical care and a situation of dependency and neglect?*

Those who argue that the government should not interfere with how parents choose to take care of their child say that the Constitution must respect religious freedom at all costs. They say that religious freedom must be respected even if it leads to a situation of dependency and neglect, and even in cases where children die. If a child fails to respond to spiritual healing and becomes severely ill, becomes disabled, or dies, it is the will of the religion's higher power. Just because some religions adhere to principles that may differ from the mainstream does not give the government the right to step in and legislate morality to these parents. Moreover, not only should children be shielded from governmental intervention as a result of their parents' religious beliefs, but parents should be as well. If a parent's religious beliefs lead to what mainstream society labels a situation of "dependency and neglect," parents should not be held criminally responsible. It is their religious choice and must be respected. They should receive religious exemptions from child dependency and neglect laws.

Those who argue that the government should be able to intervene in a situation of dependency and neglect say that religious freedom is not absolute. They cite the U.S. Supreme Court case *Prince v. Massachusetts:* "the family itself is not beyond regulation in the public interest, as against a claim of religious liberty. And neither rights of religion nor rights of parenthood are beyond limitation . . . the

(continued)

(continued)

state as parens patriae may restrict the parent's control . . . its authority is not nullified merely because the parent grounds his claim to control the child's conduct on religion or conscience. . . . The right to practice religion freely does not include liberty to expose the community or the child to communicable disease or the latter to ill health or death. . . . Parents may be free to become martyrs themselves. But it does not follow they are free . . . to make martyrs of their children."[1] When parents expose their child to a situation of dependency and neglect, they should not be free to hide behind a religious curtain authorizing behavior that the rest of society has deemed illegal. In these situations, the child should be removed, at the least. The parents should be held criminally responsible as well. The evolving standards of society have mandated that children are no longer completely subservient to the will of their parents. When parents do not care for their children, the government must do so in spite of religious objections.

[1]*Prince v. Massachusetts,* 321 U.S. 158, 166–167 (1944).

These individuals include teachers, clergy, friends, neighbors, and law enforcement officers. Because a victim of dependency and neglect is unlikely and in some cases unable to report his or her situation, these individuals play an important role in discovering abusive situations. They are usually the first to report a dependency and neglect situation to child protection agencies.

- *Reporting.* Most states have required that certain persons are considered "mandatory reporters" when they hear, observe, or suspect situations of dependency and neglect. Mandatory reporters are usually professionals in the community such as law enforcement officers, teachers, probation officers, clergy, and child-care workers. Some states require any person, such as a regular citizen, to report suspicions of dependency and neglect. If a dependency and neglect situation is identified, these individuals must contact a local law enforcement agency or the state's child protection division to make a report. Once a report is made, law enforcement officers, in conjunction with child protective services workers, may investigate the claim. See Exhibit 5.3 for information about immunity from prosecution for persons who report a dependency and neglect situation.

- *Intake and investigation.* Once a report is made about suspected dependency or neglect, child protective services workers investigate the truthfulness of the claim. They determine whether a response is warranted and, if so, how urgent a response is needed. Many reports do not warrant any further attention because the behavior reported does not rise to the legal definition of dependency and neglect. These cases are said to have been "screened out." Cases that warrant attention are usually handled in two to three days unless it is determined that the child is in immediate danger. If the child is

EXHIBIT 5.3   *Mandatory Reporters Have Immunity*

Most states have determined that certain professionals, such as educators, law enforcement officers, clergy, probation officers, and judges, are considered "mandatory reporters." If they suspect or know a child is being abused in some way, they are mandated by law to report the incident to child protection agencies for review and possible investigation.

As a result of these laws, the federal Child Abuse Prevention and Treatment Act (CAPTA) of 1974 has made it a requirement that any state that applies for federal grant money must provide immunity from prosecution under state and local laws and regulations for individuals who make a "good faith" report of suspected or known instances of dependency and neglect.

Every U.S. state and territory provides some from of immunity from prosecution for persons who in good faith report situations of dependency and neglect under mandatory reporting laws. This protection guarantees that mandatory reporters are protected from civil or criminal liability. Mandatory reporters are provided immunity for the initial report and usually protected in any judicial proceedings arising from it.

Source: Adapted from *Reporting Laws: Immunity for Reporters* (http://nccanch.acf.hhs.gov/general/legal/statutes/readyref/immunity.cfm).

deemed in immediate danger, a child may be "taken into possession" for protective purposes according to state law. Possession may or may not require a court order, depending on state law, but any removal must usually be accompanied by a protective custody court hearing if the child is to remain in custody for a period of time exceeding 24–72 hours. Exhibit 5.4 is a general depiction of the flow of cases after they have been reported and have reached the investigation stage.

- *Assessment.* Assessment is a diagnosis of the situation that contributed to dependency and neglect. Child protective services workers try to get a grasp of the situation so that they may effectively develop a plan of action.

- *Case planning.* A case plan is the map that families will follow to resolve the conditions contributing to dependency and neglect. Case plans include short- and long-term goals that are focused on changing the conditions that resulted in dependency and neglect.

- *Treatment.* Treatment is the specific activities that child protective services and other treatment providers prescribe to the family to remedy the situation.

- *Evaluation of family progress.* After the family has begun treatment, child protective services and other treatment providers evaluate whether or not the family is progressing toward the short- and long-term goals set out in the case plan. If not, the treatment plan may be modified.

- *Case closure.* Cases are closed when the risk level of the situation has decreased or when the family has addressed the situation. Cases may also be

EXHIBIT 5.4   *General Flowchart of a Reported Case of Dependency and Neglect*

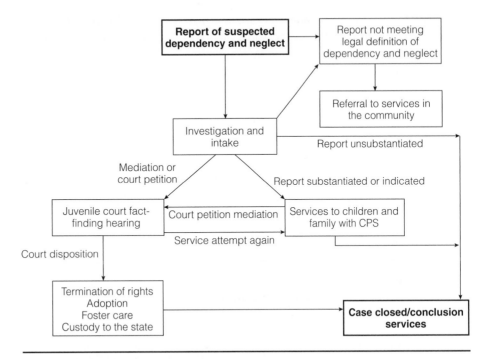

closed when it appears that the family is unable or unwilling to change the dependency and neglect conditions. In these cases, the child may be placed in a foster home or other protective custody while child protective services petitions the juvenile court to terminate parental rights or move for another action.[35]

The reality is that most cases are handled by the family and by child protective services, without the need for formal court involvement. If the family is willing to participate in services and make progress, child protective services will often consider the case resolved, for the conditions contributing to dependency and neglect have been remedied. In other cases, family members may become uncooperative and fail to address the conditions that contributed to dependency and neglect. Child protective services must then petition the juvenile court for resolution.[36] The "You Are a . . . Child Protective Services Specialist" box allows you to make a decision on the appropriate course of action in a neglect case.

The Extent of Dependency and Neglect

Understanding the extent of dependency and neglect cases each year is important. We first examine how dependency and neglect cases are officially counted. We then examine the number of cases of dependency and neglect that are reported and substantiated.

YOU ARE A... **Child Protective Services Specialist**

D. W. was two months old in 1995 when the first case of abuse and neglect against his mother was reported. After child protective specialists spent the next several months working with D. W.'s mother, the case was closed because the abusive situation had been remedied. A few months later, another report of abuse was made against the mother. This time, child protective specialists could not confirm an allegation of emotional abuse, and the case was closed.

Approximately three years later, child protective specialists visited D. W.'s home. During this visit, child protection specialists found evidence of extreme abuse, including bruises on his back from an extension cord and other physical abuse indicators. Protection specialists also noted that at one point in the visit D. W. proclaimed he was hungry. In full view of investigators, D. W. was given a plate of food on the floor. According to one specialist, "He sat in front of the food, mesmerized and did not eat." Although no criminal charges were filed against D. W.'s mother ("there was not enough to make criminal charges stick"), there was enough evidence to remove D. W. and his other siblings from the home and place them in foster care. After D. W.'s mother completed nearly a year of counseling and parenting classes, D. W. was placed back in her care. Only three months later, however, another report was made to state investigators after D. W. was abandoned at school. D. W.'s mother attributed this to a mistake, and D. W. went back home. A few months later, state investigators received another report of abuse. Child protection specialists then began another round of visits to the home, but after a few visits, the family had disappeared and the investigation was closed. Approximately one year later, another report was made to state investigators about D. W.'s mother. This was the sixth visit. Child protection specialists were able to locate the family, but after a few visits, the family again disappeared. This was in 2002.

A final call was received in 2004. This would be the seventh and final investigation into D. W.'s family. D. W. was found dead, at age nine, weighing only thirty-five pounds.

1. If you were a child protective services specialist, how would you have approached this case? Looking back, is there anything that child protective services specialists could have done differently to prevent this outcome? Would such measures have been realistic?

2. As a child protective services specialist, what could be done to ensure that families who move or disappear while being investigated do not get "lost in the system"? Would a system that "flags" those who move while under investigation help in cases such as D. W.'s? Explain.

3. Who is to blame for this situation? What would you say to those who would blame the child protection agency? What would you say to those who suggest that blame should fall solely on D. W.'s mother?

4. In your opinion, do parents have too many rights when it comes to dependency and neglect cases involving their children?

Source: Adapted from Terri Langford, "CPS Officials Had Lost Track of Family." *Dallas Morning News* (28 July 2004), 1A–2A.

Collection Methods

Because of limitations in national data collection and variance in state practices, it is difficult to get a grasp on the extent of dependency and neglect cases handled in the United States. For example, the Uniform Crime Reports (UCR) is limited because it does not distinguish between dependency and neglect situations in arrests. For example, a parent is arrested for sexual assault. The UCR does not distinguish whether the act was perpetrated against that parent's child, someone else's child, or another adult. This crime may simply be recorded as a sexual assault. Moreover, many dependency and neglect situations are not discovered or reported to the police—and sometimes do not even result in arrest when they are reported—so using UCR statistics provides a gross underestimate of dependency and neglect cases.

The National Crime Victimization Survey (NCVS) also has problems with tracking dependency and neglect cases. As mentioned in Chapter 2, the NCVS tracks victimizations for persons age twelve and older, resulting in an underestimate of the dependency and neglect of younger children, who are not covered by the survey. Also, the NCVS relies on self-reports, and it is unlikely that very many children over the age of twelve would report a dependency and/or neglect situation. It is even more unlikely that parents will report such situations: They may often be the perpetrators. These same problems are inherent in most self-report survey methods that rely on the victim and/or the perpetrator for a self-report. For example, the National Survey of Adolescents (NSA) examines juvenile victimizations and their link to mental health problems, substance use, and delinquency, but it is limited in the same general ways as the NCVS; therefore, abuse of these juveniles is likely underestimated.

The most promising method for examining dependency and neglect situations comes from the National Incident Based Reporting System (NIBRS). NIBRS is making progress toward being a more reliable system for counting dependency and neglect situations because of its specific incident-based reporting. For example, if a parent was arrested for sexual assault, NIBRS indicates whether the victim was related to the offender and in what way (son, daughter, wife, nephew, niece, etc.). However, this method of collection is limited because it has been implemented in only a few jurisdictions in the United States.[37] Additionally, NIBRS data are viewed as a supplement to UCR arrest statistics and therefore have some of the same problems that plague the UCR in dealing with dependency and neglect cases (such as needing a report or an arrest). Although NIBRS data are becoming useful for a measure of juvenile victimizations in general, they are less useful for determining the true extent of dependency and neglect situations.

Today, the best measure of U.S. dependency and neglect cases comes from the National Child Abuse and Neglect Data System (NCANDS). This official method of data collection relies on states to report the incidence of dependency and neglect cases that come to the attention of their child protective services agencies each year. Since these data cover only dependency and neglect, this method is seen as superior to other methods despite the fact that it relies on official reports to child protective services.[38] The most recent NCANDS data on dependency and neglect are reviewed below.

Cases of Dependency and Neglect

In 2001, approximately three million referrals involving more than five million children were officially reported to child protective services agencies in the United States. Professionals such as teachers and law enforcement officers submitted more than one-half of all reports, and other sources, such as family members or citizens, submitted the remainder. Of the types of dependency and neglect reported, approximately 80 percent consisted of a form of neglect (57 percent) or physical abuse (19 percent). In the majority of cases, children were reported to be abused by a parent (80 percent), as opposed to being abused by another caretaker or guardian.[39]

As noted previously, not all cases of dependency and neglect are investigated. Moreover, even in cases that are investigated, many do not meet the legal qualifications for dependency and neglect. For example, of the three million cases of dependency and neglect reported in 2001, two-thirds were investigated (about 1.8 million cases), but one-third (approximately 870,000) were not investigated. Of the 1.8 million cases investigated, approximately 30 percent were **substantiated** (meaning that there was enough evidence to support a claim of dependency or neglect), and around 5 percent were **indicated** (meaning that there was reason to believe dependency and neglect occurred but not enough evidence to support a claim)—in other words, a total of just over 600,000 cases were substantiated or indicated. The majority of cases investigated by child protective services agencies were **unsubstantiated** (meaning that there was not enough evidence to support a claim of dependency or neglect), a total of approximately 1.2 million.[40]

What can child protective services agencies do if evidence of dependency or neglect is not found or it does not amount to the legal definition? In general, even if evidence of dependency and neglect is not found, child protective services workers may still refer families to services in the community such as family counseling, drug and alcohol treatment, and parenting classes, and even to agencies offering financial assistance for shelter and medical care. However, without substantiated evidence of dependency or neglect, child protective services have little legal authority to force families to participate in these programs.

Although recent national data suggest that the majority of officially reported dependency and neglect cases are not substantiated, approximately one million children suffered abuse by a parent or other caretaker in the 600,000 substantiated/indicated cases in 2001. Most cases are dealt with by child protective services, with informal court oversight, in conjunction with the family. When this approach does not work, the juvenile court may become formally involved. Comprehensive data on the juvenile court role in dependency and neglect cases are not available, but reports from thirty-seven states show that around 18 percent of substantiated cases eventually go to the juvenile court for formal disposition or other action.[41]

Juvenile Court Processing for Dependency and Neglect

Most dependency and neglect situations are dealt with by child protective services working with the child's family. Although the juvenile court has oversight in these cases, they are generally resolved without the court getting formally involved; most states hold that families have the right to resolve the conditions that contributed to dependency and neglect and, ultimately, reunite their family before formal court disposition. This belief illustrates the principle of the **supremacy of parental rights,** the concept that parents who are "able and willing" to care for their child should retain custody of him or her. Sometimes, families receive multiple "second chances" to show they are "able and willing." In other cases, however, parents become noncompliant, and the system fails to work. These cases may require formal court involvement.

Dependency and neglect cases are driven by the primary goal of protecting the child from harm while keeping the family intact, if at all possible. Intervention by the court is seen as a last resort. Keep this goal in mind as we examine the juvenile court process for dependency and neglect cases.

Court Petition or Complaint

The first stage in the formal juvenile court process for dependency and neglect is the court petition or complaint, which is a written request asking the court to hear the case. Among other areas, the content of the court petition includes a statement about the facts in the case, information about the perpetrator, and the types and frequency of illegal conduct alleged.

The court petition or complaint is completed by child protective services in two general situations:

- When other less restrictive or informal options have failed, such as when parents have become noncompliant with treatment plans and the child is in danger at home or would be in danger if placed back home because conditions contributing to dependency and neglect have not been sufficiently alleviated.

- When the initial complaint is supported by "special considerations" and must be dealt with by the juvenile court without any attempt at informal resolution.

The most common reason for a petition to the juvenile court is that the family has failed at the informal resolution process by not correcting the conditions contributing to dependency and neglect. In other cases, child protective services may petition the court without attempting informal resolution of the case. However, this step is rare, and it usually occurs when a family has been involved with child protection agencies in the past. In some states, only when a family's rights have been terminated in the past can agencies move to a juvenile court hearing without attempting an informal resolution of the situation, an example of a case in which a petition without informal intervention is supported by a special consideration. For example, a family had their parental rights terminated five years ago because of a dependency or neglect situation involving their lone child. If this family has another child, state law may authorize the child protective services agency to file a petition with the juvenile court to terminate the parental rights for the newborn child without attempting informal resolution.

Whichever reason warrants court action, child protective services workers usually file the petition with the court, but final decisions rest with the prosecutor, who must determine whether the case has sufficient legal merit. If the prosecutor determines that the case has merit and if informal options have been tried, the case may go to a court hearing or trial.

Mediation

In reality, even if a case is petitioned to the juvenile court, an agreement can be reached outside of court. This type of agreement occurs during a process called **mediation.**

During mediation, attorneys are present for the accused and the child protection agency. The child's attorney can also be present, along with a guardian ad litem or CASA worker, to advocate for the child. These parties determine if a mutual agreement can be reached that satisfies both parties and ultimately protects the child.

Mediation may or may not be another attempt to informally resolve the dependency and neglect situation. The purpose of mediation varies by state and jurisdiction. Generally, however, once a petition has been filed with the court, family reunification is not the goal because parents have already failed at trying to resolve the dependency and neglect conditions. Mediation usually involves a legal agreement by which parents may waive their right to trial and agree to forfeit or diminish their parental rights in exchange for a certain outcome. Common outcomes in mediation include the following:

- Lowering of any criminal charges by the prosecutor in exchange for a "no contest" to the actions proposed by the child protection agency and the court.

- Permanent custody by the state (the child may be placed in foster care or adopted), wherein the parents may have visits with the child but are not considered legal guardians.

- "Relinquishment" of parental rights, with parents perhaps given the opportunity to have future visits with their child but not legal custody. Relinquishment of parental rights means that parents may keep any future children they might produce.

- "Termination" of parental rights in exchange for dismissal of criminal charges. In some states, termination of parental rights means that any future children the parents have may be taken away from them.

Mediation can have a great effect on cases of dependency and neglect that have been petitioned to the juvenile court. It saves valuable court time, but the greatest benefit of mediation is that child protection is achieved. The practice of mediation varies considerably by state and even by county. Some jurisdictions may use mediation sparingly, whereas other jurisdictions may use mediation often. However, mediation has no guarantees. When the process fails, the case must go for decision to the juvenile court.

Court Hearing

The court hearing for dependency and neglect cases is considered a civil proceeding whose purpose is to determine the facts and devise a suitable resolution of the problem—it does not determine guilt. If there are criminal charges in the case, these will be dealt with by an adult criminal court at a separate time. The court process in dependency and neglect situations is best described as a fact-finding hearing as opposed to an adversarial hearing.

The standard of proof in dependency and neglect hearings is usually either preponderance of the evidence or **clear and convincing evidence.** The standard used depends on the probable outcome of the case. In cases where the outcome sought is the termination of parental rights, the U.S. Supreme Court indicated in *Santosky v. Kramer* (1982) that states must support their allegations by at least clear and convincing evidence, a higher standard than preponderance of the evidence but lower than beyond a reasonable doubt.[42] States may require that dependency and neglect cases be judged by the standard of beyond a reasonable doubt, but this is not required by the Court. In cases where termination of parental rights is not sought, courts may decide dependency and neglect cases by preponderance of the evidence. These minimum standards may be raised by state law, so there is much variation around the country. Dependency and neglect cases that reach the juvenile court are decided by either a judge or a jury, depending on state law. Even in states that allow jury trials, however, the juvenile court judge usually has the final say in determining how to resolve or dispose of the case if allegations against parents have been found true at the trial stage.

Usually, a dependency and neglect case goes to court when the allegations are true and preponderance of the evidence or clear and convincing evidence exists. What happens if the allegations are not proved by either standard? Does the state lose authority to intervene? Must the child be placed back in the home? No—despite the state's failure to prove the allegations, the judge may continue to intervene if such intervention is determined to be in the child's best interests. For example, the judge may order that although the facts and evidence do not support the allegations by the state, there is still a need for continued intervention by child protective services. In these cases, the juvenile court judge may order that the youth should be placed in or remain in protective custody, such as a foster home. A judge may order that the family go through a family reunification process, which is similar to another chance at an informal resolution with child protective service agencies. In some cases, the prosecutor may even bring another separate charge to the court.

Disposition

If the court finds the allegations of dependency and neglect to be true, disposition follows. Several dispositions are available to juvenile court judges. Here are some typical ones:

- Treatment and services provided by child protective services.
- Transfer of legal custody to a relative.
- Permanent custody granted to the state child protective services agency without parental termination of rights.
- Termination of parental rights.[43]

The type of disposition that a juvenile court judge chooses depends on many factors; generally, however, the most important ones are the seriousness of the proven allegation and whether parents have tried or are able to remedy the conditions that led to dependency and neglect. For example, the court may offer the family another chance at treatment and services. In many cases, though, this may not be a suitable option because parents have already demonstrated that treatment and services have not put a stop to abusive conditions.

Although most cases never go to trial, when they do, the more common dispositions include the termination of parental rights and awarding permanent custody of the child to the state child protective services agency. When parental rights are terminated, the child may be placed in foster care or put up for adoption. However, this option diminishes with older children; for example, a fifteen-year-old is unlikely to be adopted. Therefore, the child may remain in foster care until he or she reaches adulthood. The same outcome occurs when the state is awarded permanent custody, but in these cases parental rights have not been terminated, so parents may be allowed to visit their child while he or she remains in foster care. It is important to note that in many states, a child who reaches the age of majority (usually eighteen) is not automatically dumped out of the system to fend for himself or herself. Many states have special programs in place to continue to help victims of dependency or neglect situations even when they have reached adulthood.

Dispositions vary even in similar situations. For example, a case that goes to a court in one jurisdiction may get treatment and services, whereas a case with similar facts and circumstances in another jurisdiction may result in the termination of parental rights: Various judges have different perceptions and philosophies. However, the central expectation is that the juvenile court will act in the best interests of the child.

Juvenile Victimizations

In addition to juveniles who are the victims of their parents, guardians, or other caretakers, juveniles are also the victims of various other forms of crimes that are perpetrated by both juveniles and adults. Exhibit 5.5 is a comparison of juvenile and adult victimizations for select Part I and Part II offenses. (This information is based on NIBRS data from twelve states, so it cannot be generalized to the nation as a whole.) Although not yet national in coverage, NIBRS does collect specific information about a victim's age, specific crimes, and perpetrators, so this twelve-state analysis bridges some of the gaps in knowledge about juvenile victimizations that other national measures cannot.[44] For example, the UCR does not collect information on the age of the victim in reported crimes (with the exception of homicide), and the NCVS does so only for individuals age twelve and older, provided they were interviewed. For these and other reasons, the UCR and NCVS underestimate juvenile victimizations and provide less insight than NIBRS when they do document such victimizations. Despite its limitations, NIBRS may be the best measure of victimizations of juveniles of all ages—when such victimizations are reported to law enforcement. Exhibit 5.5 shows the extent of juvenile victimization as compared to that of adults.

Although juveniles constitute approximately 26 percent of the U.S. population, Exhibit 5.5 shows that they constitute approximately 12 percent of crime victims. Overall, the exhibit shows that juveniles are far less victimized than adults for most forms of crime, based on this twelve-state analysis.[45]

EXHIBIT 5.5   *Juvenile Versus Adult Victimization*

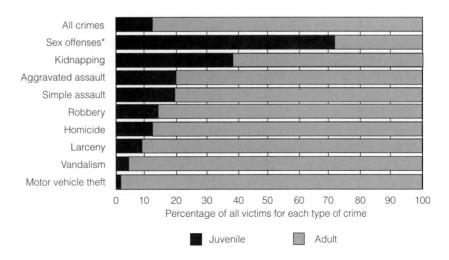

Note: Sex offenses against juveniles include forcible (64 percent) and nonforcible (7 percent) offenses.

Source: David Finkelhor and Richard Ormrod, *Characteristics of Crimes Against Juveniles* (Washington, DC: Office of Juvenile Justice and Delinquency Prevention, 2000), 2.

Many reasons explain this fact, but perhaps first and foremost is that adults far outnumber juveniles. However, adults do not predominate as victims in every form of crime. Juveniles constituted 71 percent of all victims of sex offenses (including forcible and nonforcible sex offenses) and approached adult levels as victims of kidnapping. Thus, although adults are the most victimized overall, juveniles are disproportionately the victims of sex offenses in the United States. Moreover, adults are also most likely to be the perpetrator of juvenile victimizations (55 percent of the time).[46] Some scholars note that this finding might be inflated because adult-perpetrated crimes against juveniles may be more likely to get reported than crimes perpetrated against juveniles by juveniles.[47] Despite this recognition, the finding suggests that juveniles do constitute a large percentage of perpetrators in reported juvenile victimizations. An examination of juvenile-specific victimizations (as opposed to Exhibit 5.5, which examines all victimizations, juvenile and adult) might explain why. Exhibit 5.6 examines juvenile victimizations by type of crime.

Exhibit 5.6 reveals that the most common juvenile victimization is simple assault. Of all juvenile victimizations, 41 percent are for simple assault, approximately 22 percent for larceny (theft), and approximately 12 percent for sex offenses. This breakdown sheds some light on why a large percentage of juvenile victimizations are found to come at the hands of other juveniles: Most are simple assault and theft, the typical things that juveniles do when they offend and thus the most typical juvenile victimizations. The roughly 25 percent of other juvenile victimizations in the study were dispersed among aggravated assault, vandalism, robbery, kidnapping, motor vehicle theft, homicide, and "other" (mostly aggravated assault and vandalism). Overall, then, Exhibit 5.6 shows that

EXHIBIT 5.6   *Juvenile Victimizations*

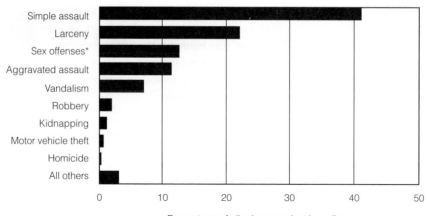

Percentage of all crimes against juveniles

Note: Sex offenses against juveniles include forcible (11 percent) and nonforcible (1 percent) offenses.

Source: David Finkelhor and Richard Ormrod, *Characteristics of Crimes Against Juveniles* (Washington, DC: Office of Juvenile Justice and Delinquency Prevention, 2000), 2.

nearly 75 percent of juvenile victimizations were for simple assault, larceny (theft), vandalism, and "other" victimizations. Serious victimizations, such as sex offenses, homicide, kidnapping, and robbery, are relatively rare among juveniles.

Gender, age, and race do appear to matter in juvenile victimizations. Boys predominate as victims in all of the categories except sex offenses and kidnapping. Moreover, with the exception of kidnapping, juveniles ages twelve to seventeen were the predominant victims as opposed to juveniles who were under six years old or were six to eleven at the time of victimization. Compared to white juveniles, minority juveniles were disproportionately victimized for violent crimes such as aggravated assault and robbery but were underrepresented as victims of property crimes such as larceny, vandalism, and motor vehicle theft.[48] Finally, regardless of whether the victim's perpetrator was a juvenile or adult, most victimizations (for kidnapping, sex offenses, simple assault, aggravated assault, and robbery) were perpetrated by a family member or an acquaintance, with the exception of robbery, which was most frequently committed by a stranger to the victim.[49]

The preceding discussion suggests that in the twelve-state study, juveniles are less victimized than adults for all offenses measured, with the exception of sex offenses. Among juvenile victimizations, however, juveniles were most victimized for simple assault and larceny, and victimization was most likely to occur among older juveniles on the whole than younger juveniles, and among male juveniles as opposed to female juveniles. Violent crime victimizations were experienced disproportionately among minority juveniles as opposed to white juveniles. Victimizations came from adult perpetrators in over one-half of all juvenile victimizations, although much juvenile victimization was actually at the hands of other juveniles. Finally, most juvenile victimization was perpetrated by family members or acquaintances, not random strangers.[50] Thus, most juvenile victims know their attackers.

In addition to providing evidence on dependency and neglect, this section helps to create a picture of juvenile victimizations. However, it does not specifically examine the various other forms of victimizations that juveniles may experience or those forms that may not be reflected in national statistics—for example, victimizations such as those that occur in juvenile facilities or other institutional placements at the hands of staff or other juveniles. These types of victimizations are covered in Chapter 11. Additionally, Internet victimization is an emerging trend. Countless juveniles access the Internet every day, giving child predators many new opportunities. Recent evidence suggests that this type of victimization is becoming more frequent among juveniles, who face direct or indirect sexual solicitation, unsolicited pornography, or other indecent and illegal activities.[51] The Internet's darker possibilities need to be considered in any discussion of juvenile victimization.

SUMMARY

- ❏ The juvenile court deals with status offenders because of the belief that status offending may lead to delinquency.

- ❏ Status offenders do not receive all the due process rights given to delinquents in adjudication proceedings despite the fact that the procedures and outcomes may be similar. Intervention by the juvenile court is viewed as a service rather than interference.

- ❏ Federal law prohibits placing status offenders and other nondelinquents in secure institutions such as detention centers and state schools.

- ❏ Most status offenders are diverted from the formal juvenile justice system at intake. When status offenders are petitioned, however, they are usually adjudicated and receive probation.

- ❏ Child protective services is the agency that handles cases of dependency and neglect. It is the link between the child and the juvenile court.

- ❏ There are approximately three million reported cases of dependency and neglect in the United States each year involving five million children. The majority of these cases are unsubstantiated.

- ❏ Most substantiated cases of dependency and neglect are dealt with by child protective services rather than formally by the juvenile court, but the court has oversight over child protection activities.

- ❏ States usually allow parents to resolve conditions of dependency and neglect before formal court action is taken. Parents have the supreme right to maintain custody of their child if they are "able and willing" to provide care.

- ❏ Many dispositions are available to juvenile court judges in dependency and neglect cases, the most severe being the termination of parental rights.

- ❏ Juveniles are much less victimized than adults in the United States overall. Most juvenile victimizations consist of simple assault and larceny-theft.

1. What was the justification for subjecting nondelinquents to the same procedures and outcomes as delinquents in juvenile court prior to the 1970s? What were some consequences of this practice?

2. What were the two original core components of the JJDPA of 1974? How does the federal government encourage states to comply with the JJDPA?

3. At what stage of the juvenile justice process does the JJDPA have the greatest effect on status offenders and other nondelinquents?

4. In adjudication proceedings, why does the U.S. Supreme Court grant due process rights to delinquents but not to status offenders?

5. What is bootstrapping?

6. In your opinion, why are most reported cases of dependency and neglect unsubstantiated?

7. Discuss the concept of the supremacy of parental rights. Should parents be allowed an opportunity to fix an abusive situation and retain custody of their child? Should this situation depend on the type and severity of abuse alleged? Explain.

8. What might be the effect on the child welfare system if juvenile courts terminated parents' rights without first offering parents an opportunity to solve the problem?

9. List and describe several possible benefits of and drawbacks to mediation in dependency and neglect cases.

10. List and discuss four insights about juvenile victimization based on the NIBRS study of twelve states.

KEY TERMS AND DEFINITIONS

bootstrapping: The practice of elevating a status offender to a delinquent offender for the same status offense that brought the youth to juvenile court the first time. The status offense becomes a delinquent offense because the youth violated a valid court order.

Child Abuse Prevention and Treatment Act (CAPTA): A 1974 federal act that made states eligible for federal grant money if they created child protection agencies, passed mandatory reporting laws, and appointed youth child advocates in court proceedings. The act covered many other areas, including funding for states to establish data-collection procedures to track the incidence and prevalence of dependency and neglect situations.

Child Protective Services (CPS): The state agency responsible for investigating and resolving cases of dependency and neglect. Child protective services are services provided by an agency authorized to act on behalf of the child when the parents are unable or unwilling to do so.

clear and convincing evidence: The burden of proof in dependency and neglect cases when termination of parental rights is sought. It represents a degree of certainty around 80 percent that the allegations are true. States may raise this standard.

dependency and neglect: A broad category that refers to situations in which parents are unable (dependency) or unwilling (neglect) to care for their child, resulting in some form of abuse. Other common terms include *child abuse, child neglect,* and *child maltreatment.*

desist: The stopping of an activity, such as status offending.

indicated: A term used by child protective agencies that means there is reason to believe a situation of dependency and neglect is occurring but there is not enough evidence to support a claim.

Juvenile Justice and Delinquency Prevention Act (JJDPA): A 1974 act that required states to deinstitutionalize status offenders and other non-delinquents from secure facilities and to provide for the sight and sound separation of juveniles from adults in any facility if the states were to receive federal money. Amendments to this act included the adult jail and lockup removal clause of 1980 and the disproportionate minority confinement amendment of 1992.

mediation: A pretrial proceeding in dependency and neglect cases in which the perpetrator, the child protective services agency, the victim, and lawyers consult to determine if the case can be settled out of court.

preponderance of the evidence: The burden of proof in dependency and neglect cases when a disposition other than the termination of parental rights is sought. It represents a degree of certainty around 51 percent that the allegations are true. States may raise this standard.

slippery slope phenomenon: The belief that status offending behavior is a gateway or "slippery slope" to delinquent behavior.

status offenders (CINS, PINS, MINS, CINA): A label given to youths who violate laws prohibiting behavior only for juveniles. Status offenders are commonly referred to as children in need of supervision (CINS), persons in need of supervision (PINS), minors in need of supervision (MINS), or children in need of assistance (CINA).

substantiated: A term used by child protective agencies meaning that according to state law, there is enough evidence to support a claim of dependency and neglect.

supremacy of parental rights: The principle which maintains that parents who are "able and willing" to care for their child have the ultimate custody rights to him or her. In practice, parents should have the opportunity to resolve conditions of dependency and neglect before they must go to court and/or face losing custody of their child.

unsubstantiated: A term used by child protective agencies which means that according to state law, there is not enough evidence to support a claim of dependency and neglect.

FOR FURTHER RESEARCH

❏ **Truancy: First Step to a Lifetime of Problems**
http://www.ncjrs.org/txtfiles/truancy.txt

❏ **Recognizing When a Child's Injury or Illness Is Caused by Abuse**
http://www.ncjrs.org/html/ojjdp/portable_guides/abuse

❏ **Runaway/Thrownaway Children: National Estimates and Characteristics**
http://www.ncjrs.org/html/ojjdp/nismart/04/index.html

❏ **Juvenile Detention to Protect Children from Neglect**
http://campus.westlaw.com/Welcome/WestlawCampus/default.wl?RS=imp1.0&VR=2.0&SP=samhous-2000&FN=_top&MT=Westlaw&SV=Full

❏ **Status Offenders: Our Children's Constitutional Rights Versus What's Right for Them**
http://campus.westlaw.com/Welcome/WestlawCampus/default.wl?RS=imp1.0&VR=2.0&SP=samhous-2000&FN=_top&MT=Westlaw&SV=Full

For an up-to-date list of web links, go to the Juvenile Justice Companion Website at **http://cj.wadsworth.com/del_carmen_trulson_jj**

Detention and Transfer to Adult Court

Pre-adjudication Detention of Juveniles / 179

The Purpose of Juvenile Detention / 179

Detention Trends / 180

Detention Procedures and the Rights of Detained Juveniles / 181

Detention Intake / 181

The Required Detention Hearing / 182

Probable Cause and "Need" for Detention / 183

Evidence in Detention Hearings / 184

Failure to Hold the Detention Hearing Within the Time Set by Law / 184

The Rights of Juveniles at Detention Hearings / 185

Do Juveniles Have a Constitutional Right to Bail If Detained? / 185

May a Juvenile Be Detained in an Adult Jail? / 186

Juvenile Transfer to Adult Court / 187

The Purpose of Juvenile Transfer / 187

Factors Influencing Transfer / 189

Types of Juvenile Transfer and Procedures / 189

Judicial Waiver / 191

Discretionary Waiver / 191

Mandatory Waiver / 194

Presumptive Waiver / 195

Prosecutorial Waiver / 196

Legislative Waiver / 197

Statutory Exclusion / 197

Reverse Waiver / 198

"Once an Adult, Always an Adult" / 198

Choosing the Transfer Method / 199

The Impact of Juvenile Transfer / 202

Removing Serious Offenders / 203

Longer Sentences and Harsher Penalties? / 203

Case Brief: *Kent v. United States* / 192

IN THIS CHAPTER YOU WILL LEARN

- That detention and waiver are two proceedings before adjudication or trial.

- That juveniles are entitled to a hearing before they are detained in a detention center.

- That juveniles do not have a constitutional right to bail if detained in juvenile detention.

- That most juveniles are not detained from referral until the final disposition of their case.

- That juveniles may not normally be held in an adult jail prior to their adjudication hearing.

- About the many ways a juvenile may be transferred to adult court for trial.

- That very few delinquency cases are transferred to adult court.

INTRODUCTION

Chapter 4 examines the procedures for dealing with juveniles referred to intake officers for delinquent conduct. There are generally two options for intake officers upon receiving a delinquency referral: informal adjustment of the case (diversion) and a delinquency petition to the juvenile court for an adjudication hearing. If the case is not diverted and the juvenile must face an adjudication hearing, two additional determinations are made before the trial process begins. The first is whether to hold the juvenile in a detention center until the adjudication hearing and disposition of the case. A juvenile may be confined prior to an adjudication hearing on the belief that if released, he or she might commit pretrial crime, harm himself or herself, or not show up for court. The second determination is whether the adjudication hearing will be in juvenile court or whether the youth will be transferred to adult court for trial. Juvenile transfers or waivers are used because some offenders may be too serious, violent, and/or chronic to be dealt with by the juvenile court; are not amenable to rehabilitation; and deserve adult punishment.

This chapter examines juvenile detention and adult court transfer—two important pre-adjudication procedures in the juvenile justice system. It begins with a discussion of the purpose of juvenile detention and who is most likely to get detained prior to trial. Next, it examines the detention procedure and the legal rights of detained juveniles. This chapter then looks at juvenile transfer to the adult system and ends with a discussion of the impact of juvenile transfer.

Pre-adjudication Detention of Juveniles
The Purpose of Juvenile Detention

Juveniles detention centers are the equivalent of jails in the adult justice system. Detention centers function as holding centers and are often called "bus stops" to reflect their short-term nature (the national average length of stay in detention is fifteen days).* Detention centers hold juveniles at many points in the juvenile justice process and in different situations. However, they are typically used immediately after arrest and before the adjudication hearing. Historically, detention centers were used to ensure a youth's court appearance, or in cases where the juvenile did not have parents or guardians to care for him or her until the adjudication hearing. Over time, the purpose for juvenile detention has changed somewhat. Although ensuring appearance in court and ensuring supervision at home are still important justifications, detention centers today are also used to prevent potential pretrial crime and to ensure the safety of a juvenile who may pose a threat to himself or herself.**

Parens patriae holds that the juvenile justice process should be least stigmatizing whenever possible. In the past, therefore, juvenile detention centers were used as a last resort even for relatively serious offenders because of their potential for branding the delinquent and stigmatizing him or her as a "criminal." Today, *parens patriae* has faded somewhat, affecting the use of detention centers for juveniles. This erosion is best demonstrated by an important U.S. Supreme Court case which held that preventive detention of juveniles is constitutional, thus implying that juvenile detention could be used not just to

---

*Melissa Sickmund, *Census of Juveniles in Residential Placement 1997* (Pittsburgh: National Center for Juvenile Justice, 2000). For national lengths of stay in detention, see also Melissa Sickmund, Howard Snyder, and Eileen Poe-Yamagata, *Juvenile Offenders and Victims: 1997 Update on Violence* (Washington, DC: Office of Juvenile Justice and Delinquency Prevention, 1997).

**See the National Juvenile Detention Association (http://www.njda.com/learn-guiding-ps2.html) for more information on these perspectives and the purposes of juvenile detention today. Detention centers are also becoming popular as separate dispositions or punishments. For example, detention may be used as a disposition in lieu of probation or in combination with probation. The latter example might be referred to as shock probation in some jurisdictions.

protect juveniles but also to protect society (*Schall v. Martin* [1984]).[1] In Schall, the Court recognized the potentially harmful and stigmatizing effects of pretrial detention but held that in some cases the potential harm to society as a result of pretrial crime outweighed the liberty interests of juveniles.

Detention Trends

Most arrested juveniles are not held in a detention center from delinquency referral to the final disposition of their case. Of the approximately 1.7 million cases handled by the juvenile courts in 1999, only 20 percent (336,200) of cases resulted in detention until final disposition. In sum, detention is relatively infrequent when compared to the entire number of cases handled by the juvenile justice system.

Although most juveniles are not detained, detention caseloads have increased during the last several years. Since 1990, the number of youths held in detention has increased approximately 11 percent, with almost 34,000 more delinquency cases resulting in detention in 1999 than in 1990. This trend has persisted despite the fact that serious juvenile crime has decreased since 1994 and the number of cases referred to the juvenile court has declined steadily in recent years.[2] What are some factors that might help explain why the use of detention has increased in the last several years while serious juvenile crime (involving those youths most likely to get detained) and the number of cases facing the juvenile court have decreased?

Detention trends from 1990 to 1999 can be summarized as follows:

- The percentage of delinquency cases detained from referral to disposition declined from 23 percent in 1990 to 20 percent in 1999. The lowest percentage of delinquency cases detained occurred in 1995–1996 at approximately 17 percent. Exhibit 6.1 shows the percentage of cases detained from 1990 to 1999. Note how some crimes are more likely to result in detention than others. Can this be one factor explaining why in recent years detention caseloads have increased while serious crimes overall and the number of cases facing the juvenile court have decreased?

- Although the *percentage* of all delinquency cases detained from 1990 to 1999 declined, the *number* of juveniles detained increased.

- Property offense cases were least likely to involve detention in all years from 1990 to 1999.

- Approximately 70 percent of all juveniles detained are age fifteen or older. This trend has remained stable from 1990 to 1999.

- The number of cases resulting in detention increased 4 percent among males and 50 percent among females from 1990 to 1999. However, in 1999, males still accounted for 80 percent of cases detained.

- Black juveniles accounted for a smaller share of delinquency cases being detained in 1999 compared to 1990. However, black youths were still overrepresented in detention caseloads. For example, black juveniles made up 28 percent of delinquency cases processed in 1999 but accounted for 36 percent of detained cases.[3]

EXHIBIT 6.1

Detention Use in Delinquency Cases, 1990–1999

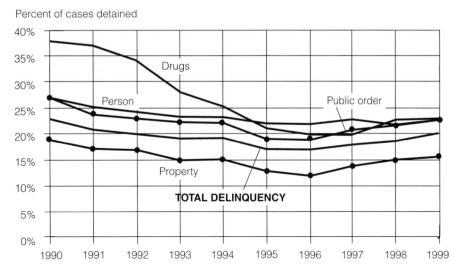

Percent of cases detained

Note: For all four general offense categories, the probability of detention was lower in 1999 than in 1990. This pattern was most pronounced for drug cases. Property offense cases were least likely to involve detention.

Source: Charles Puzzanchera, Anne L. Stahl, Terrence A. Finnegan, Nancy Tierney, and Howard N. Snyder, *Juvenile Court Statistics 1999* (Pittsburgh: National Center for Juvenile Justice, 2003), 22.

Detention Procedures and the Rights of Detained Juveniles

Detention Intake

Once juveniles are arrested, they may be taken to a detention center by police officers and processed in a procedure called **detention intake.** Detention intake should not be confused with the intake process covered in Chapter 4. Detention intake comes immediately after arrest, and decisions are then made on which juveniles will be detained and which will be released prior to the intake conference. Detention intake comes before an intake conference with probation officers and/or prosecutors, who will decide how to proceed with the case.*

Detention intake involves several procedures and is normally handled by juvenile detention officers. Detention officers are not usually probation officers

---

*An instance in which detention intake comes after an intake conference could occur when a juvenile was not taken to detention by police but was issued a citation and referred to an intake officer at a later date. At the intake conference, the intake officer may decide to file a delinquency or waiver petition and detain the juvenile until the case is decided.

but instead are considered county-level correctional officers who have the duty to make an initial determination about which juveniles should be held in detention and which juveniles should be released to a parent or guardian until an intake officer (probation officer or prosecutor) has an opportunity to review the case. Once the juvenile is arrested and arrives at the detention center, a detention officer usually searches the juvenile for weapons and other contraband. Following this search, the officer typically reviews the police or arrest report to determine whether law enforcement officers had probable cause to arrest the youth. If detention officers do not find probable cause, they may be required by state law to release the juvenile.

Once probable cause is established by a detention officer, the juvenile is usually fingerprinted and photographed. Detention officers also question the juvenile for information including but not limited to his or her age, parental or guardian contact information, and any immediate medical needs (such as if the youth takes prescribed medication and if it is needed immediately). Once these steps are completed, detention officers make the initial decision to detain or release the juvenile. This decision is based on many factors, usually including the seriousness of the crime, the juvenile's status in the system (is he or she on probation?), the availability of parents to pick up the youth, the presence of warrants for custody, and facility space. In reality, crime seriousness is likely the most important factor for detention. If probable cause exists, detention officers have little discretion to release a youth arrested for a murder, a family assault, or a drive-by shooting. However, if the crime is not serious and the youth is not wanted for another violation, the availability of parents to pick up their child and facility space may dictate the outcome of many detention decisions.

In most cases, juveniles will be released to the custody of their parents or guardians if they are available. Both detained and released youths will be required to meet with a court intake officer (probation officer or prosecutor) during an intake conference at a later date. The "You Are a . . . Detention Intake Officer" box contains an exercise where as a detention intake officer you must determine whether to release or detain a youth.

The Required Detention Hearing

The U.S. Supreme Court has held that whenever anyone is detained for an extended period of time (usually 24–72 hours), there must be a determination of probable cause by a judicial officer for continued detention.[4] This ruling applies to juveniles as well as adults. Whether probable cause exists to hold the youth longer than the 24–72-hour time frame is determined in a **detention hearing.** These hearings are not full-blown adversarial proceedings to determine guilt or innocence; instead, they are hearings to determine whether probable cause exists that the youth committed the crime and whether the youth needs to be kept in detention until the case against him or her is decided.

Juvenile court judges typically preside over detention hearings. However, these hearings may also be conducted by juvenile court referees, masters, or other individuals designated by the court.[5] "Detention hearing officers" are trained in the law and must make important legal determinations, such as whether probable cause exists and whether the case fits the legal requirements for continued detention according to state law.

Detention Intake Officer

Local law enforcement officers arrive at the juvenile detention center at 8 P.M. on a Friday night and have in their custody a fifteen-year-old girl. Based on the report submitted by the officers, the female juvenile had been involved in an altercation with her stepmother about her curfew. Allegedly, the female juvenile became enraged about an early curfew set by her stepmother (10 P.M.), and after several minutes of verbal abuse and threats, she picked up a candle and slammed it through a wall. The girl's father called the police after his daughter would not calm down. The police have tentatively charged the girl with assault and making a terroristic threat. She does not have a juvenile record, to your knowledge. You place the girl in a temporary holding room until you can investigate further and make an informed decision about her detention or release. During your investigation, you call the girl's stepmother and father.

They describe the whole situation and explain that it was just a misunderstanding and that they would be willing to come pick the girl up from detention if she could be released.

1. As a detention intake officer, what are some factors that might influence your decision to detain or release this juvenile? Are there additional factors not mentioned that would be important to your decision?

2. Of the factors you listed in question one, how would you rank those factors from most important to least important in a decision to detain or release this juvenile?

3. Would you detain or release this girl? Why or why not?

4. If detained, should this juvenile be detained until the intake conference? Explain.

Probable Cause and "Need" for Detention

Two determinations must be made by a juvenile court judge in a detention hearing: probable cause and the suitability for detention need. A probable cause determination is initially made by police officers upon arrest. This decision is later reviewed by a detention officer if police choose to take the juvenile to a detention center. States usually require that probable cause must again be determined by a judge or court officer to justify continued detention of the juvenile. If a judge fails to find probable cause that the juvenile committed the crime, then in most cases he or she must be released from detention.

Juvenile court judges must also evaluate whether there is a "need" for detention, as specified by state law. Therefore, the rule is that probable cause is necessary to detain a youth, but it is not always sufficient to keep a youth detained. For example, probable cause may exist that a juvenile shoplifted a pair of shoes, but this may not warrant that the youth be held in secure detention until a course of action for the case is decided. Factors that determine whether a youth will be detained, even if there is probable cause, include whether the youth was arrested for a serious crime (serious misdemeanor or felony), is an escapee from an institution, has a history of failing to show up to court, has sufficient guardianship at home, and is wanted by another jurisdiction.[6] This list is not exhaustive, and states may depend on additional factors to help determine if detention is justified. Generally, however, states usually specify by law which types of cases should and should not result in detention even if probable cause exists.

Some states permit that a juvenile be kept in detention without probable cause when there is a substantial need for detention. For example, a court may be unable to make an immediate finding on the existence of probable cause for a number of reasons (such as the need to speak with the arresting officers or witnesses), but a need for detention is present (for example, the child has a record of not showing up for court). In these cases, a youth may be held in detention for a period of time without probable cause, but this must not usually exceed 24 hours beyond the time limits already in place by state law (usually 24–72 hours). If probable cause is not determined with this extension, the juvenile must usually be released even if there is a demonstrated need for detention. State laws on detention procedure prevail in these situations.

Evidence in Detention Hearings

The detention hearing is not a guilt-finding process. Therefore, many types of evidence and information may be used by the juvenile court judge in determining whether there is a need for detention and probable cause to hold the youth. However, these forms of evidence may not typically be used in an adjudication hearing. For example, hearsay and opinion evidence, which are almost always excluded from an adjudication hearing, may be used by a juvenile court judge in determining whether the youth will be detained. States differ on their rules of evidence in detention hearings, and state law prevails. Generally, however, evidence that would not be allowed in adjudication proceedings is allowed in a detention hearing so that the court can make an informed decision when determining detention or release.

Not all forms of evidence are admissible in detention hearings. This category usually includes privileged communication—for example, attorney–client discussions or conversations between the juvenile and a psychiatrist. Moreover, the decision to detain or release the youth can never be considered in light of the juvenile's race, color, gender, sexual orientation, religion, national origin, socioeconomic status, or other extralegal factors.

Failure to Hold the Detention Hearing Within the Time Set by Law

What happens when a detention hearing is not held within the time set by law? For example, assume that state law requires that a detention hearing be held no later than forty-eight hours after the youth has been initially detained but a detention hearing is not conducted until the sixtieth hour. What happens? Must the youth be released? Generally, the appropriate remedy in these cases is to release the juvenile to his or her parents or guardians. In some cases, however, releasing a juvenile to his or her parents or guardian would not be in the best interests of either the child or society. For instance, the juvenile is accused of murder. However, holding a juvenile without a judicial probable cause finding is a violation of his or her due process rights. When time limits are not met, state law usually requires that the juvenile is entitled to be released.[7] Dismissal of the charges is not appropriate unless there was an actual effort or prejudice to stall the proceedings.[8]

The Rights of Juveniles at Detention Hearings

States routinely give juveniles certain rights in detention hearings, but there are few court cases that have addressed the issue. Juveniles are generally afforded a notice of the charges for which they were taken into custody, advised of the right to remain silent, informed of the right to have their parents present or a reasonable opportunity to contact and consult with them, and given a statement of the reasons for continued detention if they are detained.[9] States also routinely provide juveniles the right to a lawyer.

The law on the rights of juveniles in detention hearings has not been heavily litigated, and the U.S. Supreme Court has not ruled on whether such rights are needed. This is perhaps because most states today, by law, give juveniles certain due process rights in "all delinquency proceedings," including detention hearings. Most states have provided due process rights to juveniles, so the issue of constitutional rights in detention hearings rarely arises.

Do Juveniles Have a Constitutional Right to Bail If Detained?

Since detention centers may be viewed as the equivalent to adult jail confinement, there is a question of whether juveniles have the right to bail if they are detained in the same way as adults. The Eighth Amendment to the U.S. Constitution provides in part that excessive bail shall not be required. For adults, this means that for most crimes they will be offered bail and that it will not be excessive. For juveniles, the rule is applied differently by the courts.[10]

Unlike adults, juveniles do not have a constitutional right to bail (or right prohibiting excessive bail); however, state law may provide this right to juveniles. There are three ways in which states have dealt with the issue of bail for juveniles: (1) allow bail in the same way as adults, (2) leave bail to the discretion of the juvenile court judge, and (3) allow no bail for juveniles. In Georgia, Oklahoma, and a few other states, for example, juveniles are given the same right to bail as adults. Other states, such as Nebraska and Minnesota, allow bail but leave the final decision to the discretion of the juvenile court judge. Most states simply do not grant juveniles a right to bail, and courts in these states have chosen not to hear the issue.[11]

The primary function of bail for adults is to ensure court appearance. In lieu of jail time before trial, adults are required to ensure their appearance, typically by cash deposit (bail) or by paying a certain nonrefundable percentage of the bail amount to a bail bond agency (usually 10 percent of the original bail set by the judge). Adults do not have an absolute right to bail, and courts may deny bail when public safety is at issue and when the judge does not want the defendant released (such as in capital murder cases). This rationale is sometimes used to deny bail to *serious* juvenile offenders.[12] For juveniles who are not serious offenders, bail can be denied because doing so has been determined to be in their best interest—for example, to protect them from hurting themselves or when appropriate guardianship is not available at home. Therefore, bail denial seeks to protect, not punish, the juvenile. Ensuring court appearance has also been used to justify denying juveniles the right to bail. If the only reason for detention is to ensure court appearance and not to prevent pretrial crime or to protect the juvenile, however, some courts have held that juveniles may have a constitutional right to bail.[13] In reality, bail for juveniles is not much of an issue because only about 20 percent of all juveniles are detained. If youths are not a danger to themselves or others, they are routinely released back to their home with no need to post bail.

The bail issue for juveniles presents many complicated questions when bail is allowed by state law. For example, if juveniles are allowed bail, who may post it? Does the posting of bail have to be by a juvenile's parent or guardian, or can it be posted by a friend of the juvenile, a teacher, a girlfriend/boyfriend, or another friend's parents? Furthermore, what if the parents do not want their child released from detention (for whatever reason), but bail gets posted? Other questions involve the potential use of bail bond agencies: Who is responsible if the juvenile does not show up for the court hearing—the parents, the juvenile, or both? In states that provide a right to bail for juveniles, these problems are usually answered by requiring that only the juvenile's parents or guardians will be allowed to post bail.[14]

May a Juvenile Be Detained in an Adult Jail?

Placing juveniles with adults in adult jails was a common and legal practice before the 1970s. The Juvenile Justice and Delinquency Prevention Act of 1974 (JJDPA) and its amendments required states that received federal money to remove juveniles from adult jails or to separate them by sight and sound if they were in the same facility.

One exception to the JJDPA requirements was and still is that juveniles may be held in an adult jail as long as they are separated by "sight and sound" from adults. (It is also recommended that adult jail staff not have contact with juvenile offenders when this situation occurs.) Another exception is that juveniles may be held in adult jails if a juvenile detention center placement cannot be immediately made but detention is necessary. This situation usually occurs in rural areas that do not have a juvenile detention center, and it usually lasts for only a limited number of hours. Rural areas may have only a few juvenile detention centers, and it is sometimes necessary that a juvenile be held in an adult jail until a "bed" in a juvenile detention center can be found. Generally, rural juveniles may be held in an adult jail for no more than twenty-four hours. Juveniles from urban areas may be held in an adult jail for no more than six hours.[15] Whenever juveniles are in an adult jail, however, they must always be separated from adults by sight and sound.

Thirty years have passed since the JJDPA mandate of removing and/or separating juveniles from adults in jails and lockups, and states have made substantial efforts to conform to this practice. However, compliance with the JJDPA mandate did not happen overnight, and juveniles were routinely held in adult jails well into the 1980s and even the 1990s in some states. This practice has changed since then. In 2003 the Office of Juvenile Justice and Delinquency Prevention (OJJDP) reported that seven states and the District of Columbia had completely removed juveniles from adult jails, forty states were in full compliance with only a few exceptions, and only one state (Ohio) was not in compliance with removing juveniles from adult jails but did separate them by sight and sound.* In sum, very few juveniles are being held in adult jails today, and those few who are have been separated from adults.

Juvenile Transfer to Adult Court

Another pre-adjudicatory procedure in juvenile justice is the decision to transfer or waive juveniles to adult court for trial. **Transfer of jurisdiction** is defined as the process by which a juvenile's case is sent to trial in the adult justice system. In some states, this transfer is called certification, waiver of jurisdiction, bind-over, or remand. There are several ways whereby states can transfer a juvenile's case to adult court. These differ in important ways, but the purpose of each type of transfer is generally the same—to send the juvenile to adult court.

The Purpose of Juvenile Transfer

The nature and extent of juvenile crime in the late 1980s and early 1990s caused much concern about what to do with serious, violent, and chronic juvenile offenders. As a response, the majority of states across the country restructured existing laws or enacted new laws to enable them to deal with juvenile offenders in the adult system. Ever since a separate juvenile system was formed, juveniles in the United States have been eligible for transfer to the adult system. Prior to the 1990s, however, such transfer was usually limited to certain serious crimes and specialized circumstances. Changes in the 1990s made the transfer process more efficient and simplified. Transfer criteria were also expanded to include some offenses previously ineligible for adult system transfer.

The justifications for expanding and simplifying transfer mechanisms were threefold:

- Transfer allows greater flexibility in dealing with serious and violent juveniles by imposing longer and harsher sentences than could be imposed by the juvenile courts.

- Transfer allows another option to deal with chronic offenders who have exhausted all other alternatives in the juvenile justice system.

- Transfer allows prosecutors and judges to purge the juvenile system of juveniles who would not benefit from the rehabilitative activities of the system.[16]

---

*J. Robert Flores, *OJJDP Annual Report, 2001* (Washington, DC: Office of Juvenile Justice and Delinquency Prevention, 2003), 24–28. Compliance with separation and adult jail removal of juvenile offenders was also examined in the five U.S. territories (American Samoa, Guam, Northern Mariana Islands, Puerto Rico, and the Virgin Islands). These territories were in full compliance with both separation and adult jail removal. South Dakota and Wyoming were the only two states that did not participate in this study.

One reason that new transfer provisions were adopted was to help ensure that serious, violent, and chronic juveniles would receive adequate sentences based on their crimes. Those sentences might not be available in the juvenile justice system. For example, prior to expanded and simplified transfer laws, juveniles who committed a serious crime might have to serve only a relatively short sentence before being released because all states require release from a juvenile institution at a certain age (usually, but not always, twenty-one). Table 6.1 shows the age at which juveniles must be released from juvenile court jurisdiction and hence from juvenile institutions. By contrast, if the same juvenile is tried and convicted in an adult court, he or she could be sentenced to serve a prison term that can last as long as life. Using Table 6.1, assume that a thirteen-year-old juvenile was adjudicated in juvenile court for murder in Florida. At what age would this juvenile have to be released from the juvenile correctional system? Would this be an appropriate sentence for a sixteen-year-old who has committed murder?

Transfer laws also allow judges and prosecutors another option to deal with chronic juveniles. Chronic juveniles are not necessarily serious offenders, but they represent a problem because of their multiple crimes. Juvenile court judges often have a difficult time finding appropriate sanctions for chronic offenders because they have been in the juvenile justice system many times before. Transfers allow judges and prosecutors an additional option to deal with those juveniles who continue to offend and have used up all the alternatives in the juvenile system. They are simply turned over to the adult courts to be treated like adult defendants.

TABLE 6.1   *Age at Which Juveniles Must Be Released from Juvenile Court Jurisdiction*

Age	State
18	Arizona, North Carolina
19	Alaska, Iowa, Kentucky, Nebraska, Oklahoma, Tennessee
20	Mississippi, North Dakota
21	Alabama, Arkansas, Connecticut, Delaware, District of Columbia, Florida, Georgia, Idaho, Illinois, Indiana, Louisiana, Maine, Maryland, Massachusetts, Michigan, Minnesota, Missouri, Nevada, New Hampshire, New Mexico, New York, Ohio, Pennsylvania, Rhode Island, South Carolina, South Dakota, Texas, Utah, Vermont, Virginia, Washington, West Virginia, Wyoming
23	Kansas
25	California, Montana, Oregon, Wisconsin
*	Colorado, Hawaii, New Jersey

*Until the full term of the disposition order.

Source: Adapted from Howard N. Snyder and Melissa Sickmund, *Juvenile Offenders and Victims: 1999 National Report* (Washington, DC: Office of Juvenile Justice and Delinquency Prevention, 1999), 93.

Transfer also enables juvenile courts to remove certain juveniles from the juvenile justice system because they cannot benefit from the rehabilitation that underlies juvenile justice. If a juvenile is deemed not amenable to treatment, prosecutors and judges may deal with him or her in the adult justice system, which is based more on punishment. They may do so under the belief that the space in the juvenile system is best reserved for juveniles who might benefit from it.

Factors Influencing Transfer

Transfer decisions are based on a number of factors. Generally, decisions to initiate transfer proceedings against a youth are determined from offense-based or offense-history-based indicators rather than from personal circumstances. For example, transfer depends heavily on the seriousness of the offense, the juvenile's prior record, and subjective determinations on the youth's amenability to treatment and prospect for rehabilitation.[17] Theoretically, the more serious the offense, the longer the prior record, and the less amenable the juvenile is to treatment, the more likely that he or she will be transferred. Realistically, in their decisions to transfer juveniles, judges and prosecutors may consider several other factors, such as the following:

- Whether protection of the community requires transfer.
- The amount and quality of evidence and if the evidence would support a grand jury indictment and adult conviction.
- The maturity of the juvenile.
- If the alleged crime was particularly violent, heinous, or premeditated.
- Victim input and desire for transfer.

Depending on the type of transfer sought, however, some factors may play a more important role than others, a concept that will become evident in the next section, which discusses the various types of transfer and their peculiarities. For example, some types of transfer focus solely on the type of offense and the age of the juvenile without needing to consider the juvenile's prior record, amenability to treatment, or maturity.

Types of Juvenile Transfer and Procedures

There are three ways to transfer or waive a juvenile to the adult justice system to stand trial: judicial waiver, prosecutorial waiver, and legislative waiver. Each type, in turn, has different subdivisions. For example, there are three types of **judicial waiver** (discretionary, mandatory, and presumptive), one type of prosecutorial waiver (direct file), and three types of legislative waiver (statutory exclusion, reverse waiver, "once an adult, always an adult"). Juvenile court judges make waiver decisions in a judicial waiver, prosecutors make transfer decisions in a prosecutorial waiver, and the legislature determines the criteria for transfer in a legislative waiver. All states have at least one method whereby they can transfer a juvenile to adult court, and several states have multiple ways. Table 6.2 shows the availability of the different types of waiver by state.

TABLE 6.2

Summary of Transfer Provisions, 1997

State	Judicial Waiver			Direct File	Statutory Exclusive	Reverse Waiver	Once an Adult, Always an Adult
	Discretionary	Mandatory	Presumptive				
Total States:	46	14	15	15	28	23	31
Alabama	■				■		■
Alaska	■		■		■		
Arizona	■		■*	■	■	■	■
Arkansas	■			■		■	
California	■		■				■
Colorado	■		■	■		■	
Connecticut		■				■	
Delaware	■	■			■	■	■
Dist. of Columbia	■		■	■			■
Florida	■			■	■		■
Georgia	■	■		■	■	■	
Hawaii	■						■
Idaho	■				■		■
Illinois	■	■	■		■		
Indiana	■	■			■		■
Iowa	■				■	■	■
Kansas	■		■				■
Kentucky	■	■				■	
Louisiana	■	■		■	■		
Maine	■						■
Maryland	■				■	■	
Massachusetts				■	■		
Michigan	■			■			■
Minnesota	■		■		■		
Mississippi	■				■	■	■
Missouri	■						■
Montana	■			■	■		
Nebraska				■		■	
Nevada	■		■		■	■	■
New Hampshire	■		■				■
New Jersey	■		■				
New Mexico					■		
New York					■	■	
North Carolina	■	■					
North Dakota	■	■	■				■
Ohio	■	■					■
Oklahoma	■			■	■	■	■
Oregon	■				■	■	■
Pennsylvania	■		■		■	■	■

(continued)

TABLE 6.2

(continued)

State	Judicial Waiver Discretionary	Judicial Waiver Mandatory	Judicial Waiver Presumptive	Direct File	Statutory Exclusive	Reverse Waiver	Once an Adult, Always an Adult
Total States:	**46**	**14**	**15**	**15**	**28**	**23**	**31**
Rhode Island	■	■	■				■
South Carolina	■	■			■	■	■
South Dakota	■				■	■	■
Tennessee	■					■	■
Texas	■						■
Utah	■		■		■		■
Vermont	■			■	■	■	
Virginia	■	■		■		■	■
Washington	■				■		■
West Virginia	■	■					
Wisconsin	■				■	■	■
Wyoming	■			■		■	

Source: Patrick Griffin, Patricia Torbet, and Linda Szymanski, *Trying Juveniles as Adults in Criminal Court: An Analysis of State Transfer Provisions* (Washington, DC: Office of Juvenile Justice and Delinquency Prevention, 1998), 2.

Judicial Waiver

Discretionary Waiver

Judicial **discretionary waivers** are the oldest and most common types of waiver in the United States. They are called a variety of names depending on the state. Some states refer to discretionary waiver as "certification," "remand," "bind-over," or "transfer."[18]

Regardless of terminology, the procedure for judicial discretionary waivers usually involves the prosecutor filing a waiver petition with the juvenile court judge. When the judge receives the waiver petition, a waiver hearing must be held. Such a hearing was mandated by the U.S. Supreme Court in *Kent v. United States* (1966) (see the "Case Brief").[19] In addition to a waiver hearing, the Court held in *Kent* that juveniles are entitled to certain due process rights when facing possible transfer to adult court: (1) the right to be represented by counsel, (2) the right to access records considered by the juvenile court in determining waiver, and (3) the right to hear a statement of the reasons in support of the waiver.

In making a waiver decision, the juvenile court judge considers several factors, according to the *Kent* guidelines:

1. The seriousness of the offense and whether the protection of the community requires a waiver.

2. Whether the alleged offense was committed in an aggressive, violent, premeditated, or willful manner.

Case Brief *Leading Case on "Juvenile Waiver"*

Kent v. United States, 383 U.S. 541 (1966)

Facts: Morris Kent was a sixteen-year-old arrested and charged with housebreaking, robbery, and rape. Because of his age, he came under the jurisdiction of the juvenile court; however, that court waived jurisdiction after a "full investigation" and transferred him to the U.S. district court for an adult criminal trial. Kent's attorney filed motions to have a hearing on the waiver. He also recommended that Kent be hospitalized for psychiatric observations and that he (the attorney) be allowed access to the file that the juvenile court had on his client. The juvenile court did not rule on these motions. Instead, the judge ordered that jurisdiction be transferred to the adult criminal court and stated that this finding was made after the required "full investigation." The judge held no hearing before his ruling and gave no reason for the waiver. Kent was convicted in criminal court on six counts of housebreaking and robbery, and was acquitted on two rape counts by reason of insanity.

Issue: Do juveniles have any due process rights in cases where jurisdiction over a juvenile is transferred from a juvenile court to an adult court?

Supreme Court Decision: A transfer of jurisdiction in a juvenile hearing is a "critically important" stage in the juvenile process. Therefore, the juvenile is entitled to the following due process rights: (1) a hearing, (2) to be represented by counsel at such hearing, (3) to be given access to records considered by the juvenile court, and (4) a statement of the reasons in support of the waiver order.

Case Significance: Although not as significant as *In re Gault,* this case is important because it marked the first time that basic due process rights were extended to juveniles, thus bringing forth the demise of the *parens patriae* approach. The justification for this departure was stated by the Court:

> There is much evidence that some juvenile courts . . . lack the personnel, facilities and techniques to perform adequately as representatives of the State in a *parens patriae* capacity, at least with respect to children charged with law violation. There is evidence, in fact, that there may be grounds for concern that the child receives the worst of both worlds: that he gets neither the protections accorded to adults nor the solicitous care and regenerative treatment postulated for children.

The Supreme Court based its decision in *Kent* on the "critically important" nature of the waiver proceeding. The Court stated that waiver carries several consequences for juveniles; thus, due process protections were required. For example, instead of being kept in a juvenile institution and automatically released upon reaching the age of adulthood, a juvenile tried in an adult criminal court is treated just like any other criminal and can be subjected to incarceration of a period of punishment that extends beyond the age of majority.

(continued)

Case Brief *(continued)*

The consequences of adult proceedings are also vastly different from the effects of a juvenile adjudication. In sum, the Court saw serious consequences to the juvenile after such a transfer and provided for due process rights before the transfer of jurisdiction could take place.

Excerpts from the Decision: "Because the State is supposed to proceed in respect of the child as *parens patriae* and not as adversary, courts have relied on the premise that the proceedings are 'civil' in nature and not criminal, and have asserted that the child cannot complain of the deprivation of important rights available in criminal cases. It has been asserted that he can claim only the fundamental due process right to fair treatment. . . .

"It is clear beyond dispute that the waiver of jurisdiction is a 'critically important' action determining vitally important statutory rights of the juvenile. . . . The statutory scheme makes this plain. The Juvenile Court is vested with 'original and exclusive jurisdiction' of the child. This jurisdiction confers special rights and immunities. He is, as specified by the statute, shielded from publicity. He may be confined, but with rare exceptions he may not be jailed along with adults. He may be detained, but only until he is 21 years of age. The court is admonished by the statute to give preference to retaining the child in custody of the parents 'unless his welfare and the safety and protection of the public can not be adequately safeguarded without . . . removal.' The child is protected against consequences of adult conviction such as the loss of civil rights, the use of the adjudication against him in subsequent proceedings, and disqualification for public employment."

Source: This brief originally appeared in Rolando V. del Carmen, Mary Parker, and Frances P. Reddington, *Briefs of Leading Cases in Juvenile Justice* (Cincinnati: Anderson, 1998).

3. Whether the offense was against person or property, with greater weight being given to person offenses.

4. The degree and quality of evidence and whether a grand jury may be expected to return an indictment.

5. The desirability of trial and disposition of the entire offense in one court when the juvenile's associates in the alleged offense are adults who will be charged with a crime in criminal court.

6. The sophistication and maturity of the juvenile.

7. The current record and previous history of the juvenile, including previous experience in the system such as prior probation or institutionalization.

8. The prospects for adequate rehabilitation and whether the juvenile would benefit from the procedures and services available to the juvenile court.[20]

The number of factors that must be established for a waiver varies by state law. Some states require that only one factor be proven for a judge to be able to waive a juvenile, whereas others require that all factors must be met. States may also add to the list suggested in *Kent*. For example, Arizona adds victim input and juvenile gang membership. Some states mandate that certain factors be given greater weight than others. For example, the seriousness of crime and the juvenile's prior record may hold greater weight in waiver decisions than the maturity of the juvenile or whether the juvenile is a good prospect for rehabilitation. It all depends on state law. In discretionary waivers, the burden of proving these factors rests with the prosecutor, who must prove one or more factors by a "preponderance of the evidence" or, in some states, "clear and convincing evidence" before a waiver may be ordered by the court.[21]

In 1999, 7,500 juveniles were waived to the adult criminal court by juvenile court judges, a figure representing less than 1 percent of all formally processed cases in juvenile courts. The number of discretionary waivers in 1999 was 9 percent less than the number of waivers in 1990, 7 percent less than in 1998, and 38 percent less than the peak year of waivers in 1994 (12,100). Of the 7,500 youths waived in 1999, most were accused of a property offense (40 percent, or 3,000) or a person offense (34 percent, or 2,500), and the remainder were accused of a drug law violation (16 percent, or 1,200) or a public order offense (11 percent, or 800) as the most serious charge. Most youths waived to adult court in 1999 were males (94 percent), most were at least sixteen years of age or older (87 percent), and most were white (54 percent versus 44 percent black and 2 percent other). Waiver decisions were most heavily influenced by the seriousness of the offense, the juvenile's prior record, and whether the youth was deemed amenable to treatment.[22] In sum, the most recent data on discretionary waivers suggest that the majority of youths waived were older and committed serious property or person offenses. Exhibit 6.2 details the number of cases judicially waived to criminal court from 1990 to 1999.

The data in Exhibit 6.2 show that discretionary waivers have declined steadily since 1994. One factor that explains this trend is that violent and serious crime by youths has decreased since 1994 and thus has led to fewer waiver petitions. The second factor, which is probably most important, is that juveniles may now receive long sentences without being transferred to the adult court through a process called blended sentencing (discussed in Chapter 9).[23] Third, discretionary waivers have decreased in recent years because states have enacted several additional types of waiver beyond judicial discretionary waivers. Some of these waivers require less extensive procedures than the due process hearings required for discretionary waivers, and they are sometimes preferable if state law authorizes them. States can have as many types of waiver as they want, and the choice of one over the other does not violate the constitutional rights of the juvenile.

Mandatory Waiver

Mandatory waiver is much different from a discretionary judicial waiver. In mandatory waiver, a juvenile is automatically sent to adult court for trial when certain age, offense, or other requirements (such as prior record) are met according to state law. For example, states may designate mandatory waiver for youths who are at least fourteen years of age and have committed any number

EXHIBIT 6.2

Juvenile Cases Waived to Criminal Court, 1990–1999

Cases judicially waived to adult criminal court

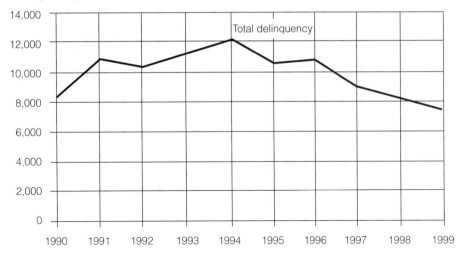

Note: The number of delinquency cases judicially waived to criminal court in 1994 was 45% greater than the number waived in 1990. This increase was followed by a 38% decline between 1994 and 1999. As a result, the number of cases waived in 1999 was 9% below the number waived in 1990.

Source: Charles Puzzanchera, Anne L. Stahl, Terrence A. Finnegan, Nancy Tierney, and Howard N. Snyder, *Juvenile Court Statistics 1999* (Pittsburgh: National Center for Juvenile Justice, 2003), 28.

of serious crimes (such as murder) or when the juvenile has a prior record of serious crimes (for example, two prior felony adjudications). If a case meets the criteria, it is automatically sent to adult court for trial. Fourteen states provide for mandatory waiver.

As well, the procedure for mandatory waiver differs from that of a discretionary waiver. In a mandatory waiver, there is no need for a waiver petition by the prosecutor or a lengthy hearing according to *Kent v. United States* (1966) criteria. The juvenile court judge must determine only whether there is probable cause to believe that the youth is of the minimum age for waiver and committed the offense(s) covered by the mandatory waiver law. This is the extent of the hearing process. If probable cause is established, the youth is automatically waived to adult court. In contrast to discretionary judicial waivers, mandatory waiver laws cause juvenile court judges to have minimal involvement and little discretion.

Presumptive Waiver

To review, in a discretionary waiver, prosecutors must prove by a preponderance of the evidence or by clear and convincing evidence that the juvenile has met the requirements for waiver. This process occurs in a waiver hearing, where final decisions are left to the juvenile court judge. In mandatory waiver, the juvenile court judge need only find probable cause that a youth has met minimum age and offense requirements for waiver. No hearing is required. **Presumptive waiver** combines certain elements of a discretionary waiver (the hearing portion) and mandatory waiver (age and offense requirements).

A presumptive waiver is triggered when a juvenile first meets certain age and offense requirements according to state law. For example, a state may require that any juvenile older than fourteen who commits murder is *eligible* for a presumptive waiver. Once age and offense criteria are met, prosecutors must then demonstrate that there is probable cause to believe the juvenile committed the offense for which he or she is charged. If all criteria are met (age/offense and probable cause), the juvenile must show why he or she should *not* be waived instead of a prosecutor proving why he or she should be. In presumptive waiver situations, the juvenile must usually prove by a standard of clear and convincing evidence that he or she is amenable to treatment in the juvenile justice system and therefore should not be waived to adult court. If the juvenile fails to meet this standard, the judge must send the case to adult court for trial.[24] Fifteen states have presumptive waiver laws.

The essence of the three types of judicial waivers may be stated as follows:

- *Discretionary waiver.* After a waiver petition has been filed by the prosecutor, the juvenile court judge may waive a juvenile's case to adult court only after a due process hearing. The juvenile court judge will consider several factors in the due process hearing to support or reject a waiver petition according to the U.S. Supreme Court in *Kent v. United States.* States may also add additional criteria for judges to consider.

- *Mandatory waiver.* A juvenile court judge *must* send a juvenile's case to adult court if there is probable cause that the juvenile committed the alleged offense and has met certain criteria for waiver by law. The criteria usually include the juvenile's age, current offense, and prior record. No due process hearing is required.

- *Presumptive waiver.* The prosecutor must show that probable cause exists that the juvenile committed the alleged offense, and the youth must meet the age and offense minimums for waiver according to state law. The juvenile, not the prosecutor, has the burden of proving why he or she should not be waived. If the juvenile fails to do so, the judge *must* waive the case to adult court.

Prosecutorial Waiver

There is only one type of **prosecutorial waiver,** and it is called **direct file.** In the fifteen states with direct file laws, prosecutors (not the juvenile court judge) have the authority to choose between filing the case in juvenile court or in adult court. If the prosecutor chooses to file the case in adult court, the youth is essentially waived and must stand trial in the adult system. Direct file is sometimes referred to as "concurrent jurisdiction" because both the juvenile court and the adult court have authority over the case: Where the case is tried is left up to the prosecutor.

States vary on which cases are eligible for direct file. Normally, cases that qualify for direct file are those that meet certain offense, age, or prior record requirements. These requirements are set by state legislatures. Once the requirements are met, prosecutors have the sole discretion on where to proceed with the case. Compared with other forms of waiver, direct file waivers tend to include less serious offenses. For example, some states allow misdemeanors to be transferred to adult court through direct file if the juvenile is older (at least sixteen) and has a serious prior record (for example, two prior felonies).[25] This is not normally the case with other forms of waiver.

Unlike judicial waivers (discretionary, mandatory, or presumptive), direct file need not be supported by a waiver or probable cause hearing, nor are such hearings required to meet the due process requirements of *Kent v. United States* (1966).[26] In fact, direct file waivers may bypass the juvenile court altogether.

Legislative Waiver

Legislative waivers come in three forms: statutory exclusion, reverse waiver, and "once an adult, always an adult."

Statutory Exclusion

Statutory exclusion is a form of transfer to adult court through which state legislatures remove certain categories of offenders or offenses from juvenile court jurisdiction altogether. Legislatures play an important role in most of the previously discussed forms of waiver, usually dictating to prosecutors and judges the categories of offenses or offenders that may be "eligible" for waiver. Only after eligibility has been established do judges and prosecutors have discretion about what to do with the case (they may or may not choose to transfer the case to adult court). In statutory exclusion, once a juvenile is *charged* with an "excluded" crime by a prosecutor, the case is "automatically" transferred to adult court (contrast this type with mandatory judicial waiver, in which a judge must make at least a determination of probable cause on the charged offense). Currently, twenty-eight states have statutory exclusion laws.

Statutory exclusion operates in three general ways: age exclusion, offense exclusion, and age/offense/prior record exclusion. *Age exclusion* is a blanket waiver that occurs when legislatures lower the maximum age for juvenile court jurisdiction. For example, if the Texas Legislature lowered the maximum age of juvenile court jurisdiction from sixteen to fifteen (youths legally become adults at sixteen instead of seventeen), an entire cohort of sixteen-year-olds could be handled in adult court for their crimes. *Offense exclusion* occurs when legislatures determine that certain offenses are not suitable to be dealt with by the juvenile court. The legislatures are effectively saying that "such offenses go beyond what juvenile courts are intended to handle" and thus must be dealt with in adult court regardless of other criteria. *Age/offense/prior record* excludes youths from juvenile court jurisdiction based on some combination of age, offense, and prior record. For example, Mississippi excludes from juvenile court jurisdiction all felonies committed by juveniles at least seventeen years old (this is an example of age and offense combination exclusion). Arizona's exclusion scheme uses all combinations of age/offense/prior record by excluding any felony (offense) committed by a juvenile fifteen years of age or older (age) who has two or more previous adjudications for felonies (prior record).[27]

Unlike judicial waivers, statutory exclusion does not require a hearing. Once the prosecutor has determined the offense to be charged, the case must be transferred to adult court, provided that the offense is excluded from juvenile court jurisdiction by legislation.

Reverse Waiver

Reverse waiver is a process whereby a juvenile who is being prosecuted as an adult may petition to have his or her case "waived back" to the juvenile court for an adjudication hearing or disposition decision.[28] Reverse waiver is authorized in twenty-three states. Cases that qualify for reverse waiver usually get to the adult court in the first place by direct file, statutory exclusion, and sometimes judicial waiver.

Why allow a case to be transferred back to juvenile court after it has been waived? The answer is that reverse waivers allow the courts to deal with certain cases on an individual basis even though such cases meet the general blanket requirements for waiver. For example, a juvenile's age and offense might result in him or her being statutorily excluded from the juvenile court based on state law. However, upon going over the facts and evidence in the case, the adult court judge may deem that the youth's case is better dealt with in juvenile court. Reverse waiver is generally appropriate when the adult court decides that a juvenile court hearing would better serve the interests of both the youth and the public.[29] In sum, it allows adult courts to "recheck" waiver decisions at other levels (such as a prosecution decision in a direct file waiver or a legislative exclusion) and send the youth back to juvenile court. This step is seen as preferable in some states because not all juvenile cases are the same, even though they may involve similar crimes. Therefore, limited or zero-discretion transfer approaches such as statutory exclusion and mandatory waiver may result in cases being waived; at that point, a deeper look at the individual circumstances of the case and at the juvenile calls for another form of action and, hence, a reverse waiver.

"Once an Adult, Always an Adult"

Thirty-one states have a transfer provision labeled **once an adult, always an adult.** "Once an adult" waivers focus on future offenses, not necessarily current ones. These waivers mandate that juveniles who have already been waived to adult court once must face adult court for all subsequent offenses they are accused of as a juvenile.

Most states with this form of waiver require that juveniles be convicted of the offense for which they were first waived. For example, if a juvenile is waived to adult court for trial but is acquitted, most states would not include this youth under "once an adult always an adult" waivers for any subsequent offenses. However, state laws vary on this point. Some states do not require a conviction, other states require subsequent adult prosecution only for certain offenses (such as felonies) even if convicted, and some states limit the applicability of this form of waiver to certain age groups (such as requiring that only for youths at or above age sixteen do "once an adult" waivers apply).[30]

Prosecutor

In 2001, thirteen-year-old Lionel Tate was convicted in adult court in Florida of the first-degree murder of a six-year-old daughter of a family friend. Lionel was given a life sentence for the murder, which occurred when he was practicing his "pro-wrestling moves" on the young girl. The victim, who weighed forty-eight pounds, suffered a fractured skull, lacerated liver, and multiple cuts and bruises after being punched, stomped, kicked, and slammed in Lionel's home. One medical expert testified that her injuries were so severe that they were comparable to a fall from a three-story building. Lionel was the youngest person ever sentenced under a Florida law requiring a life sentence for first-degree murder, regardless of the age of the offender.

On December 10, 2003, Florida's Fourth District Court of Appeals ordered a new trial for Lionel, ruling that Lionel should have had his mental capacity evaluated before trial. The appeals court also noted that Lionel had significant mental issues and had a below-average IQ. On January 4, 2004, prosecutors in Florida offered Lionel a plea bargain in lieu of a new trial. The plea bargain, which was almost identical to the one Lionel originally declined, would mean that Lionel would be sentenced to three years in prison, plus one year of house arrest, and ten years of probation. Lionel had already served much of the three-year sentence and would likely be released soon after the plea agreement.

1. As a prosecutor, would you petition for a new trial or offer a plea bargain? Why or why not?

2. If you chose a new trial, what are some arguments you would expect from those who would offer a plea bargain? If you chose to offer a plea bargain, what are some arguments you would expect from those who would pursue a new trial?

3. In your opinion, is the current plea bargain (three years in prison, one year of house arrest, and ten years of probation) fair? What might be a more appropriate sentence, if any?

4. What factors would be most important in your decision to pursue a new trial versus offering a plea bargain?

It is important to note that in each form of waiver described previously, if the youth is not waived, he or she may still face an adjudication hearing in juvenile court. The "You Are a . . . Prosecutor" box includes an exercise asking you to decide a course of action and make an argument about a case that was originally waived to adult court. (Table 6.3 summarizes the characteristics of the many transfer mechanisms discussed in this section.)

Choosing the Transfer Method

Many states have multiple methods by which they may transfer a youth to the adult system for trial. Such a mixed bag of transfer options raises the issue of which one to choose. Once the juvenile has met the statutory requirements of age and/or offense that attach to most transfers among the states, the choice may be based on whether a due process hearing is required. For example, in states with both direct file and discretionary judicial waivers (such as Arizona, Arkansas, Florida, and Louisiana), prosecutors may choose

TABLE 6.3

Transfer Characteristics

Type of Transfer	Procedure	Who Decides Transfer?	Number of States with This Option
Discretionary judicial waiver	■ Prosecutor files a waiver petition to juvenile court. ■ Due process hearing is required.	■ Juvenile court judge *may* transfer after evaluating factors according to *Kent v. United States*. ■ Prosecutor must prove factors by preponderance of evidence or, in some states, clear and convincing evidence.	46
Mandatory judicial waiver	■ Juvenile must typically meet age and offense minimums to qualify.	■ Juvenile court judge *must* transfer a youth if probable cause exists that the youth committed an offense under mandatory waiver law.	14
Presumptive judicial waiver	■ Juvenile must typically meet age and offense minimums to qualify. ■ Hearing is required wherein juvenile proves by clear and convincing evidence why he or she should not be transferred.	■ Juvenile court judge *must* waive unless the youth proves why he or she should not be transferred.	15
Prosecutorial waiver (direct file)	■ Juvenile must typically meet age, offense, and prior record minimums to qualify.	■ Prosecutor after filing charges and provided that the charged offense is covered under waiver law.	15
Statutory exclusion	■ Juvenile must meet age, offense, and/or prior record minimums to qualify.	■ Legislatures by deeming certain offenses excluded from juvenile court jurisdiction.	28
Reverse waiver	■ An already transferred juvenile petitions to have case transferred back to juvenile court.	■ Adult court judge *may* transfer case back to juvenile court.	23
Once an adult, always an adult	■ Juveniles may be prosecuted as an adult for all or certain future offenses once they have been transferred once. ■ Must usually have been convicted during first transfer offense to qualify.	■ Legislatures determine through law who qualifies for future offenses.	31

to use direct file because there is no requirement for a due process hearing, nor is juvenile court judge discretion involved. In direct file, prosecutors do not have to go to a waiver hearing and prove by a preponderance of the evidence or clear and convincing evidence the eight indicators according to *Kent*. Thus, direct file may have a practical advantage in that a hearing is bypassed and prosecutors avoid having to deal with the discretionary power of judges.

The final choice of which waiver is pursued may be initially determined by state legislatures. For example, every form of waiver has offense requirements that must be met even before a waiver is attempted, and these are determined by the legislature. Moreover, many states also have minimum age requirements that must be met before waiver becomes an option. The age threshold is also determined by the legislature. (Some analysts argue that most waivers, in essence, are legislative waivers at some level.) Table 6.4 shows these minimum requirements by state. However, once these criteria are met, the available choices may depend solely on whether a hearing is required.

TABLE 6.4

Minimum Age and Offense Transfer Provisions by State, 1997

State	Minimum Transfer Age	Any Criminal Offense	Certain Felonies	Capital Crimes	Murder	Certain Offenses Person Offenses	Property Offenses	Drug Offenses	Weapon Offenses
Alabama	14	14	16	16				16	
Alaska	NS	NS				NS	16		
Arizona	NS		NS		15	15			
Arkansas	14		14	14	14	14			14
California	14	16	16		14	14	14	14	
Colorado	12		12		12	12	14		14
Connecticut	14		14	14	14				
Delaware	NS	NS/14	15		NS	NS	16	16	
District of Columbia	NS	16	15		15	15	15		NS
Florida	NS	NS		NS	14	NS	14		14
Georgia	NS	15		NS	13	13	15		
Hawaii	NS		14		NS				
Idaho	NS	14	NS		NS	NS	NS	NS	
Illinois	13	13	15		13	15		15	15
Indiana	NS	14	NS		10	16		16	16
Iowa	14	14	16					16	16
Kansas	10	10	14			14		14	14
Kentucky	14		14	14					
Louisiana	14				14	14	15	15	
Maine	NS		NS		NS				
Maryland	NS	15		NS	16	16			16
Massachusetts	14		14		14	14			14
Michigan	14	14	14		14	14	14	14	
Minnesota	14		14		16				
Mississippi	13	13	13	13					
Missouri	12		12						
Montana	12				12	12	16	16	16
Nebraska	NS	16	NS						
Nevada	NS	NS	14		NS	14			14
New Hampshire	13		15		13	13		15	

(continued)

TABLE 6.4

Minimum Age and Offense Transfer Provisions by State, 1997 (continued)

State	Minimum Transfer Age	Any Criminal Offense	Certain Felonies	Capital Crimes	Murder	Certain Offenses			
						Person Offenses	Property Offenses	Drug Offenses	Weapon Offenses
New Jersey	14	14			14	14	14	14	14
New Mexico	15				15				
New York	13				13	14	14		
North Carolina	13		13	13					
North Dakota	14	16	14		14	14		14	
Ohio	14	14	14		14	16	16		
Oklahoma	NS		NS		13	15	15	16	15
Oregon	NS		15		NS	NS	15		
Pennsylvania	NS		14		NS	15			
Rhode Island	NS		16	NS	17	17			
South Carolina	NS	16	14		NS	NS		14	14
South Dakota	NS		NS						
Tennessee	NS	16			NS	NS			
Texas	14			14				14	
Utah	14		14		16	16	16		16
Vermont	10	16			10	10	10		
Virginia	14		14		14	14			
Washington	NS	NS			16	16	16		
West Virginia	NS		NS		NS	NS	NS	NS	
Wisconsin	NS	15	14		10	NS	14	14	
Wyoming	13	13	14						

Note: "NS" indicates "none specified."

Source: Patrick Griffin, Patricia Torbet, and Linda Szymanski, *Trying Juveniles as Adults in Criminal Court: An Analysis of State Transfer Provisions* (Washington, DC: Office of Juvenile Justice and Delinquency Prevention, 1998), 14–15.

The Impact of Juvenile Transfer

In general, waiver is used sparingly because it is usually reserved for the most problematic youths facing the juvenile court. Among all cases formally processed in juvenile court, roughly 1 percent or less involved waiver in each year after 1997, or approximately 7,000–9,000 delinquency cases where waiver was attempted in each year from 1997 to 1999 (refer to Exhibit 6.2, on page 195).[31]

One purpose of transfer is to deal with chronic offenders. Another purpose is to remove offenders from the juvenile justice system who would not benefit from rehabilitation. The final purpose is to allow courts to sentence serious and violent juveniles to longer and harsher sentences than could be imposed by the juvenile court. Most of the controversy with transfer revolves around the last purpose.[32] Evaluating this last purpose of waiver requires an examination of which offenders get transferred to adult court each year and whether they receive longer and harsher sentences in the adult system than they would have in juvenile court.

Removing Serious Offenders

Data on juvenile transfers collected since 1989 suggest that the profile of youths who are waived to the adult court has changed. In 1989, 28 percent of waived youths were person offenders, 49 percent were property offenders, 16 percent were drug-related offenders, and 7 percent were public order offenders. The early years of waivers (for which data are available) suggest that those getting transferred to the adult court were rarely violent person offenders; instead, 72 percent of all waivers were for property, drug, or public order offenses. If it is assumed that a person offense is more serious than a property, drug, or public order offense, transfer did not accomplish the goal of sending serious and violent juveniles to the adult system.

This demographic has changed slightly with time. In 1999, for example, 34 percent of judicial waivers involved person offenders, 40 percent involved property offenders, 16 percent involved drug-related offenders, and approximately 11 percent involved public order offenses. Thus, from 1989 to 1999, waivers appeared to become slightly more focused on person offenders. However, the majority of waived juvenile offenders, roughly 67 percent, still remained in the category of property, drug, and public order offenses.[33] Moreover, many of these were considered "chronic" instead of serious or violent offenders. Overall, the evidence does not support the idea that waiver is successful in ridding the juvenile justice system of the most serious and violent offenders.[34]

Longer Sentences and Harsher Penalties?

Another issue is whether juveniles who are transferred to the adult court get harsher and longer sentences than they would have received in juvenile court. A related perspective is whether juveniles transferred to adult court receive longer and harsher sentences compared to adults charged with similar crimes. Early evidence showed that waived juveniles were handled more leniently in adult court than they would have been in juvenile court. For example, one researcher found that 60 percent of waived offenders were sentenced to probation by the adult court. These were offenders who would have likely been incarcerated by the juvenile justice system.[35] Another study found that the majority of juveniles transferred to the adult system received probation, fines, or other nonincarceration sentences.[36] This disconnect between waiver and the harshness of sentences is referred to by Barry C. Feld as the **punishment gap,**[37] which demonstrates the principle that juveniles may go from "hero to zero" in their transition to the adult justice system. For example, waived offenders may be considered the worst offenders in the juvenile system (hero) but, once transferred to the adult system, tend to be viewed as less serious than many adults even with similar crimes (zero). The reasoning is that waived juveniles are younger than adult offenders, are in adult court for the first time, and usually have less extensive criminal records than adults. As such, they are often treated as first offenders deserving leniency when compared to adult offenders even though they may be charged with the same crime.[38] This trend tends to be reflected in the types of sentences they receive, which may be less harsh than what they could have expected from the juvenile court.*

Although juveniles may not receive harsher sentences when waived, there is some evidence that juveniles who are transferred to adult court receive *longer* sentences (whether community or institutional sentences) when compared to youths who are not transferred or to adults charged with similar crimes. In examining two groups of violent juvenile offenders (some who were transferred and some whose transfer was denied), Rudman and colleagues found that transferred juveniles received longer sentences than those whose transfer was denied.[39] Others have reported different results, finding that waived juveniles received shorter sentences compared to juveniles not waived but tried for similar crimes.[40] However, one recent study found that juvenile offenders in adult court received longer sentences than adults who were tried and convicted of similar crimes.[41] Overall, there is inconsistent evidence on sentence length. Some studies show that transferred juveniles receive longer sentences; others do not. In some cases, it depends on whether sentence lengths are being compared to juveniles or to adults. However, the most recent evidence suggests that the punishment gap and leniency toward juveniles may be changing.

The bottom line is that waiver does not appear to be meeting all of its goals. The overall picture is that waiver may be effective in transferring only *some* of the juvenile justice system's most troublesome juveniles to adult court. Even then, these youths do not appear to be consistently receiving longer and harsher sentences than similarly situated juveniles not transferred, although the most recent evidence suggests they may be treated more severely than adults. If anything, adult court waiver for some juveniles appears to "burden" them with an adult record that may lead to tougher and longer sentences if they continue to offend in the future. This may be the case: Some studies suggest that transferred juveniles do fare worse in terms of recidivism when compared to their juvenile court counterparts.[42]

SUMMARY

❑ Juvenile detention is used to ensure court appearance, prevent pretrial crime, and protect the juvenile from harm. Detention can occur at many points, but it usually occurs immediately after arrest and while waiting for an adjudication hearing or adult trial.

*However, recent evidence has demonstrated that juvenile offenders in adult court are sentenced more severely than their young adult counterparts. See Megan C. Kurlycheck and Brian D. Johnson, "The Juvenile Penalty: A Comparison of Juvenile and Young Adult Sentencing Outcomes in Criminal Court." *Criminology* 42(2) (2004): 485–517.

❏ Approximately 20 percent of juveniles are detained until the final disposition of their case.

❏ Juveniles do not have a constitutional right to bail, but states may provide them this right.

❏ Juveniles routinely receive rights in a detention hearing such as a notice of charges, an opportunity to consult with parents, and advisement from a lawyer.

❏ The majority of states have laws that prohibit placing a juvenile in an adult jail for detention purposes. If a juvenile is placed in an adult jail, he or she must always be separated by sight and sound from adults.

❏ There are several ways to transfer a juvenile's case to adult court. The purpose of transfer is threefold: to remove serious, violent, and chronic juveniles from the juvenile justice system; to allow another option for dealing with chronic offenders; and to send offenders who would not benefit from juvenile justice system rehabilitation to the adult system, which is based on punishment.

❏ Juveniles must usually be of a certain age or have committed a certain offense before they are waived.

❏ In some states, a juvenile may be "waived back" to the juvenile court after having been already transferred.

REVIEW QUESTIONS

1. What are two factors that juvenile court judges evaluate in a detention hearing before a juvenile may be detained in a juvenile detention center?

2. What is the rationale for denying juveniles a constitutional right to bail?

3. Do you believe that juveniles who are detained while they await their adjudication hearing are more likely to be adjudicated and receive a harsher sentence than those not detained before their adjudication hearing? Why?

4. What forms of evidence may a juvenile court judge consider in a detention hearing? Why are some forms of evidence allowed in a detention hearing but typically not in an adjudication hearing?

5. List the three purposes or goals of juvenile transfer to adult court.

6. If you were a juvenile prosecutor, which transfer mechanism would you be likely to use? Why?

7. What is the main difference between a mandatory judicial waiver and statutory exclusion?

8. According to *Kent v. United States,* which type of waiver requires a due process hearing? What rights do juveniles receive in this hearing?

9. Based on the information in this chapter, does juvenile transfer accomplish its goals? Why or why not?

10. Describe the concept of the punishment gap in your own words.

KEY TERMS AND DEFINITIONS

detention hearing: A hearing conducted by a juvenile court judge, who determines whether there is probable cause and a need to justify the continued detention of the juvenile accused of a crime.

detention intake: The process immediately after arrest wherein juvenile detention officers decide whether to detain or release a juvenile before a meeting with intake officers, who decide how to deal with the case.

direct file: Also called concurrent jurisdiction, direct file waivers occur when the prosecutor has the option of filing the case in either juvenile court or adult court.

discretionary waiver: A form of judicial waiver that is the oldest and most common type in the United States. Discretionary waivers are governed by *Kent v. United States* guidelines. In a discretionary waiver, the prosecutor files a waiver petition asking the juvenile court judge to waive the youth to adult court. The judge must consider several factors to justify a discretionary waiver.

judicial waiver: One of three types: discretionary, mandatory, and presumptive. Judicial waivers differ from prosecutorial or legislative waivers because transfer decisions in judicial waivers are left to juvenile court judges.

legislative waiver: A collection of several waiver methods whereby a youth is automatically transferred to adult court because of criteria determined by state legislatures. There are three forms of legislative waiver: statutory exclusion, reverse waiver, and "once an adult, always an adult" waiver.

mandatory waiver: A form of judicial waiver whereby the juvenile court judge must find probable cause that a juvenile meets certain age, offense, or other requirements. If the judge finds probable cause for these factors, the judge must automatically transfer the juvenile to adult court.

once an adult, always an adult waiver: A form of legislative waiver that requires juveniles who have already been transferred and prosecuted in adult court to be tried in adult court for all future offenses that they may commit as a juvenile.

presumptive waiver: A form of judicial waiver in which a juvenile must prove why he or she should not be waived to adult court. Failure to prove this means that the juvenile court judge must send the case to adult court for trial.

prosecutorial waiver: A method of transferring a juvenile's case to adult court in which the decision rests with the prosecutor and not with the judge. There is only one form of prosecutorial waiver: direct file.

punishment gap: A term coined by Barry C. Feld which refers to the fact that waived juveniles actually receive lighter sentences than those youths who are not waived to adult court or adults charged with similar crimes in adult court.

reverse waiver: A form of legislative waiver in which a juvenile who is being prosecuted as an adult (has already been transferred to adult court) may petition to have his or her case "waived back" to the juvenile court for an adjudication hearing and for the juvenile court to decide the disposition or sentence.

statutory exclusion: A form of legislative waiver wherein certain offenders are automatically transferred to adult court when they meet certain age, offense, or age/offense/prior record combinations.

transfer of jurisdiction (or **waiver of jurisdiction**): A broad definition consisting of a variety of methods in which a juvenile may have his or her case sent to adult court for trial. Whether a juvenile is transferred depends on determinations by state legislatures and the decision making of judges and prosecutors.

FOR FURTHER RESEARCH

- ❑ **Delinquency Cases Waived to Criminal Court**
  http://www.ncjrs.org/txtfiles1/ojjdp/fs200135.txt

- ❑ **Providing Effective Representation for Youth Prosecuted as Adults**
  http://www.ncjrs.org/txtfiles1/bja/182502.txt

- ❑ **Rights of Passage: An Analysis of Waiver of Juvenile Court Jurisdiction**
  http://campus.westlaw.com/Welcome/WestlawCampus/default.
  wl?RS=imp1.0&VR=2.0&SP=samhous-2000&FN=_top&MT=
  Westlaw&SV=Full

- ❑ **The Waiver of Juveniles to Criminal Court: Policy Goals, Empirical Realities, and Suggestions for Change**
  http://campus.westlaw.com/Welcome/WestlawCampus/default.wl?RS=
  imp1.0&VR=2.0&SP=samhous2000&FN=_top&MT=Westlaw&SV=Full

- ❑ **Juvenile Transfers to Criminal Court in the 1990s: Lessons Learned from Four Studies**
  http://www.ncjrs.org/html/ojjdp/summary/08_2000/index.html

For an up-to-date list of web links, go to the Juvenile Justice Companion Website at **http://cj.wadsworth.com/del_carmen_trulson_jj**

The National Court System and the Juvenile Courts

CHAPTER SEVEN OUTLINE

The Court System and Its Process / 210

The Federal Court System / 210
The State Court System / 211
The Appeals Process / 213
The Geographical Boundaries of Court Decisions / 214
Judicial Precedent (*Stare Decisis*) / 214
Federal Versus State Jurisdiction / 216
Juveniles in Federal Court / 217
A Cautionary Note / 219

The Origin and Formation of the First Juvenile Court / 219

What Led Up to Juvenile Courts / 219
The First Juvenile Court / 221

The Juvenile Court Structure / 224

The Organization of Juvenile Courts / 224
Do Juvenile Courts Have Jurisdiction in All Matters Involving Juveniles? / 224
Should There Be a Unified or Coordinated Juvenile Court? / 225
The Administration of Juvenile Courts / 226
Specialized Juvenile Courts / 229

Juvenile Teen Courts / 229
Juvenile Drug Courts / 232

Juvenile Court Personnel / 233

Is a Separate Juvenile Court Needed? / 237

IN THIS CHAPTER YOU WILL LEARN

- About the court system in the United States.

- That most court decisions, with the exception of U.S. Supreme Court decisions, are limited by geographical boundaries.

- About the history and formation of the world's first juvenile court.

- About the organization of juvenile courts and critical issues in their administration.

- That the actors in the juvenile court function as an informal work group, making the juvenile court different from the adult court.

- About arguments for and against abolishing the juvenile court.

INTRODUCTION

Court decisions, both federal and state, influence the juvenile justice process in numerous ways. Court decisions clarify the purpose and structure of juvenile courts, establish who is subject to the court's jurisdiction, and determine how the juvenile court operates. However, these decisions are often limited in effect. For example, a court decision in California or Iowa is limited to the boundaries of those states. Alternatively, a decision by the U.S. Supreme Court applies to all states. Knowing the jurisdictional limit of courts in the United States is vital to understanding the way that court decisions influence the juvenile justice process.

The first section of this chapter addresses the U.S. court system. It then covers the history and formation of juvenile courts. Although a separate juvenile court and the juvenile court system are relatively new (just over a century old), a rich history characterizes their development. This chapter next examines the structure of juvenile courts today. The fourth section evaluates the need for a separate juvenile court and justice system.

The Court System and Its Process*

The United States has a **dual court system,** meaning that there is one system for federal cases and another for state cases. However, the term *dual court system* is misleading. The United States has fifty-two separate judicial systems: one court system in each of the fifty states, the federal court system, and the courts of Washington, D.C. Because these systems have much in common, they justify general grouping into two categories: federal and state.

The Federal Court System

The highest court in the federal court system is the U.S. Supreme Court. (Note that whenever the word *Court* is used with a capital *C* in this text, the reference is to the U.S. Supreme Court. The word *court* in lowercase refers to all other courts at the federal and state levels.) The Court is composed of a chief justice and eight associate justices. All U.S. Supreme Court justices are nominated and appointed by the president of the United States, with the advice and consent of the Senate. Justices hold their position for life (called life tenure) and may be removed only by impeachment, which rarely occurs. Members of the U.S. Supreme Court are called justices, but all others, from the federal courts of appeals down to the lower courts, are called judges.

The Court is located in Washington, D.C., and always decides cases **en banc** (as one body) and never in small groups or panels (in division). The Court meets to hear arguments and decide cases beginning on the first Monday in October and continues sessions usually through the end of June the following year. Court cases are argued and decisions are announced during this time, but the Court holds office throughout the year. Normally, the votes of five justices are needed to win a case because there are nine justices. In 1869, federal law set the number of U.S. Supreme Court justices at nine, but this number may be changed by law.

The Court has *original jurisdiction* (meaning that it hears a case first as opposed to hearing the case on appeal) over certain cases as specified in the Constitution. However, most cases reach the Court either on appeal or a writ of certiorari. The Court can avoid hearing a case on appeal by saying that the case "lacks substantial federal question" to deserve full consideration by the Court. Most cases get to the Court on a writ of certiorari, which is an order by the appellate court (in this case the U.S. Supreme Court) directing the lower court to provide a record of the case for review. In writ of certiorari cases, the **rule of four** applies. This means that at least four of the nine justices must agree for the Court to hear a case. If the case fails to obtain four votes for inclusion on the Court docket, the decision of the court where the case was last heard (usually a federal court of appeals or a state high court) is deemed upheld.

Between eight thousand and nine thousand cases reach the Supreme Court each year from various federal and state courts, but the Court hears only a limited number on their merit (eighty-five cases in 2001–2002, eighty-four cases

---

*This section is adapted from Rolando V. del Carmen, *Criminal Procedure: Law and Practice,* 6th ed. (Belmont, CA: Thomson/Wadsworth, 2004), 1–25.

in 2002–2003, and eighty cases in 2003–2004). The rest are dismissed. This means that the decision of the immediate lower court in which the case originated (whether it be a state high court or a federal court of appeals) is left undisturbed. This action does not imply that the Supreme Court agrees with the decision of the lower court. It simply means that the case could not get the votes of at least four justices to deserve further attention and be considered on its merits. The perception that only the "most important" cases are accepted and decided by the Supreme Court is not necessarily true. Cases usually get on the Supreme Court docket because at least four justices have voted to include the case as among those worthy to be considered. The standard used for inclusion is left to individual justices to decide.

Below the Supreme Court in the federal system are the U.S. courts of appeals, officially referred to as the United States Court of Appeals for a particular circuit. A total of 179 judges are dispersed among thirteen judicial "circuits" located in different regions of the country. Each circuit covers three or more states, except the District of Columbia, which has a circuit unto itself. Each court has six or more judges, depending upon the caseload of the circuit. For example, the First Circuit has six judges, whereas the Ninth Circuit has twenty-eight. Judges of the courts of appeals are nominated and appointed by the president of the United States, with the advice and consent of the Senate. They are appointed for life tenure and may be removed only by impeachment. Unlike the Supreme Court, courts of appeals may hear cases as one body (en banc) or in groups (in division) of three or five justices.

Occupying the lowest level in the hierarchy of federal courts are the district courts, the trial courts for federal cases. The federal government has 646 federal judgeships located in 94 judicial districts in the United States, Guam, Northern Mariana Islands, Puerto Rico, and the Virgin Islands. Each state has at least one judicial district, but some states have as many as four. For example, Iowa has two federal district courts: one for the Northern District and one for the Southern District. Federal district court judges are nominated and appointed by the president of the United States for life, with the advice and consent of the Senate, and can be removed only by impeachment.

Also under the federal system are the U.S. magistrate courts. These courts were established primarily to relieve the heavy caseloads of federal district court judges. They are presided over by U.S. magistrates and have limited authority, such as trying minor federal offenses and misdemeanor cases in which the possible penalty is incarceration of one year or less. Magistrates are appointed by federal court judges in that district and are not guaranteed life tenure. Exhibit 7.1 shows the basic federal and state court organization in the United States.

The State Court System

The structure of state court systems varies from state to state. In general, state courts follow the same pattern as the federal judicial system, meaning that states have one high court (usually, but not always, named the supreme court) that makes final decisions on cases involving state laws and provisions of the state constitution. However, Texas and Oklahoma have two highest courts—one for civil cases and the other for criminal. For example, the Texas Supreme Court

EXHIBIT 7.1   *Flowchart of the State and Federal Court Systems*

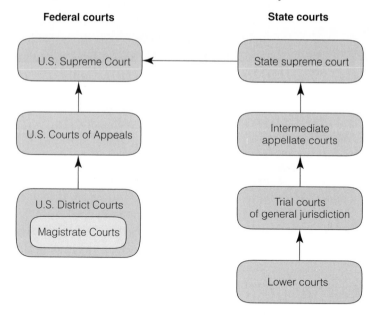

Source: Rolando V. del Carmen, *Criminal Procedure: Law and Practice,* 5th ed. (Belmont, CA: Wadsworth, 2001), 4.

handles civil cases on appeal, and the Texas Court of Criminal Appeals handles criminal cases on appeal, but both are considered the highest courts in the state. Although the Texas Court of Criminal Appeals handles appealed criminal cases in Texas, delinquency cases that are appealed are handled by the Texas Supreme Court. It does so because delinquency cases in Texas, as in most states, are considered civil proceedings.

Below the state's high court are the intermediate appellate courts. Only thirty-five of the fifty states have intermediate appellate courts. In states without intermediate appellate courts, cases appealed from trial courts go directly to the state's high court. Each state also has several trial courts with general jurisdiction, meaning that they try both civil and criminal cases. These courts go by various names, such as circuit court, district court, or court of common pleas. In New York, the general jurisdiction trial court is called the supreme court. Although these courts are of general jurisdiction, some states divide them according to specialty areas, such as probate, family, juvenile, and domestic relations. Such divisions will be discussed later in the section on the juvenile court structure.

At the base of the state judicial hierarchy are lower courts such as county courts, justice of the peace courts, and municipal courts. They have limited jurisdiction in both civil and criminal cases and also deal with laws passed by county or city governments. Juvenile courts may fall under this category in some jurisdictions.

The Appeals Process

With rare exceptions, cases enter the federal and state judicial systems at the trial court level. At that level, a jury or a judge determines the facts of the case based on the evidence presented. By applying principles of law to the facts of the case, the judge or jury determines its outcome. In criminal cases, the outcome is usually conviction or acquittal. In juvenile cases, which are usually decided by a juvenile court judge (juveniles do not have a constitutional right to a jury trial, although some states allow jury trials for juveniles), there are terminological differences for outcomes. A juvenile is processed in an adjudication hearing (the equivalent of a trial in adult cases). If the allegations are found to be "true," the juvenile is "found to have engaged in delinquent conduct" and adjudicated (the equivalent of being found guilty in adult cases). The juvenile is then dispositioned (the equivalent of sentencing for an adult).

By law, cases from trial courts can usually be appealed at the next higher level of court. If convicted, the defendant may appeal. Acquittals may not be appealed by the government unless the acquittal is based on a question of law, not of guilt or innocence. Additionally, courts of appeals do not hear further evidence and generally do not reevaluate the facts of the case presented at the trial court. Instead, appellate courts consider whether errors of law occurred during the trial that might have affected the outcome of the trial.

A trial court judge makes numerous important decisions in the course of a trial, such as what evidence should be admitted, what motions should be granted or denied, and the choice of a jury. Not every error made by a trial judge results in the reversal of a conviction. Appellate courts often use the "harmless error" standard to determine whether a conviction should be reversed because of error at trial. If the appellate court determines that the error during trial is harmless to the outcome, the conviction is upheld. However, some errors violate fundamental rights and automatically result in reversal of conviction. These errors include the denial of the right to counsel, denial of the right to trial by jury, and a judge's failure to instruct the jury properly on the reasonable doubt standard.[1] The appeals court may affirm, reverse, or reverse and remand the decision of the lower court. *Affirmation* means that the decision from the lower court is upheld or left alone. *Reversal* means that the decision from the lower court is thrown out, vacated, or set aside by the appellate court. In a *reverse-and-remand decision,* the appellate court reverses the lower court's decision but gives that court an opportunity to hear further arguments and rule on the case again.[2]

If a defendant wins a reversal on an appeal, the case may be tried again by the government prosecutor without violating the constitutional prohibition against **double jeopardy,** which means being punished more than once for the same offense. The right to protection from double jeopardy is considered to have been waived by the defendant if he or she appeals. In appealed convictions, the defendant is essentially saying, "Give me a new trial; there was something wrong with my conviction." This constitutes a waiver of the right to protection against double jeopardy. This same rule applies equally to adults and juveniles.

The Geographical Boundaries of Court Decisions

Except for the U.S. Supreme Court, the jurisdiction of every U.S. court is limited in some way. One type of limitation is territorial or geographic, meaning that court decisions are binding only in certain geographical areas over which the court legally has control or jurisdiction. For example, decisions of the Fifth Circuit Court of Appeals apply only to states covered by that circuit (Texas, Louisiana, and Mississippi). Decisions of the Fifth Circuit Court of Appeals are not binding to the Ninth Circuit states or the First Circuit states. Exhibit 7.2 details the circuit and district court geographical boundaries in the United States. Importantly, U.S. Supreme Court decisions are binding on all U.S. courts because the whole country is under its jurisdiction. This fact helps explain why U.S. Supreme Court cases are so important: They establish the rule of law for the entire country. When the U.S. Supreme Court has not ruled on an issue, one must look to lower federal courts for the rule of law.

As mentioned above, decisions of federal courts of appeals apply only to a specific circuit if there is no Supreme Court action. The federal district courts work on the same principle. When a federal district court encompasses an entire state, as is the case in Maine, its decision on a federal law (provided that the federal court of appeals or the U.S. Supreme Court has not decided the issue) produces a uniform rule within the state. If a state has more than one judicial district, such as in Texas or Wisconsin, divergent and even conflicting decisions can be issued from the different districts within the state. These conflicts may be resolved only by the U.S. Supreme Court or by a U.S. court of appeals decision within a particular circuit.

The same process operates in the state court systems, but with one exception: State supreme court decisions are recognized as extending beyond state borders. Because the Constitution declares the sovereignty of the states from the federal government, the high court in each state has the final say on issues of state and local law. For example, a ruling by the California Supreme Court on a state law or a local ordinance will be respected even by the U.S. Supreme Court, unless the ruling goes against (or offends) the Constitution, in which case the U.S. Supreme Court may make the final decision on the issue.

The existence of a dual court system and the limited jurisdictional authority of the vast majority of courts make it highly probable that courts will render conflicting decisions on a given legal issue. An important function of the appellate process described above is to resolve these conflicts if the cases are appealed. If no appeal is made, the conflict remains. For example, the federal district court for the Southern District of Ohio may rule that juveniles are entitled to contact visits in juvenile institutions, whereas the federal district court in the Northern District of that state, deciding a similar but different case, may rule otherwise. The inconsistency will be resolved only if the federal appellate court for Ohio (the Seventh Circuit Court of Appeals) decides the issue in an appealed case.

Judicial Precedent (*Stare Decisis*)

Stare decisis is a Latin term that literally means "to abide by, or adhere to, decided cases." In practice, this means that when a court has laid down a principle of law as applicable to a certain set of facts, it will follow that principle in

EXHIBIT 7.2

Geographical Boundaries of U.S. Courts of Appeals and U.S. District Courts

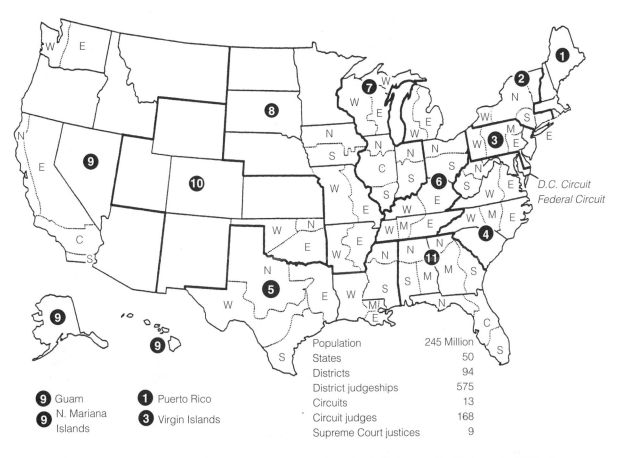

Population	245 Million
States	50
Districts	94
District judgeships	575
Circuits	13
Circuit judges	168
Supreme Court justices	9

9 Guam
9 N. Mariana Islands
1 Puerto Rico
3 Virgin Islands

Source: Rolando V. del Carmen, *Criminal Procedure: Law and Practice,* 5th ed. (Belmont, CA: Wadsworth, 2001), 7.

all future cases with similar facts and circumstances. Abiding by decided cases with similar facts *(stare decisis)* sets **judicial precedent,** meaning that past court decisions have value as precedent for future cases with similar facts and/or circumstances. It is a way to avoid reinventing the wheel. The rationale in the court system is "why invent a new ruling for a particular set of facts and circumstances when one has already been applied?"

Any court decision may set a precedent; however, a decision provides precedent only for cases that come within that court's jurisdiction. For example, the decisions of the Fifth Circuit Court of Appeals are valued as precedent only in the states within the Fifth Circuit (Texas, Louisiana, and Mississippi). U.S. Supreme Court decisions are precedent for cases anywhere in the United States. As such, the most binding kind of precedent is that set by cases decided by the Court.

Sometimes, lower courts do not follow a precedent set by a higher court. In these cases, the lower court may be reversed on appeal. For example, if the

Supreme Court of Mississippi were to hold that juveniles may be put to death for crimes committed before age eighteen, this decision would go against precedent: The U.S. Supreme Court has decided that only juveniles age eighteen and older can be tried for capital murder and be sentenced to death (see Chapter 12, on the death penalty for juveniles, for a discussion of *Roper v. Simmons,* an important case decided by the U.S. Supreme Court on capital murder trials for persons under the age of eighteen). This situation would also hold true if the Mississippi Legislature passed a law that authorized the death penalty for anyone at least thirteen years of age. The decision by the U.S. Supreme Court prevails over such a law.

Note that U.S. Supreme Court decisions are authoritative for the entire country and serve as precedent for future cases of all courts. These rulings provide the guidelines for the entire nation. For example, no state can try a juvenile for capital murder and sentence him or her to death if the crime was committed before age eighteen because the U.S. Supreme Court has held this to be unconstitutional. This does not mean that every state must have the death penalty, nor does it mean that any state choosing to have the death penalty must impose it on everyone who is at least eighteen who commits a capital crime. In the latter example, what it means is that states may choose to structure their laws, and state courts may decide cases, in ways that raise this minimum age. For example, a state may establish a law that only persons nineteen and older may be eligible for the death penalty, even though the U.S. Supreme Court has determined the death penalty is constitutional for those eighteen years of age at the time of the crime. The highest court in that state may also rule that it is cruel and unusual to sentence a juvenile to death if he or she was not at least nineteen at the time of the offense. The minimum age is only a minimum. It can be raised but not lowered.

Federal Versus State Jurisdiction

The basic rule that determines whether a case should be tried in federal or state court is whether it involves a violation of state or federal law. If an act is a violation of federal law, the trial will be held in federal court; if the act is a violation of state law, the trial will be held in a state court. This rule generally applies to both adults and juveniles (see "Juveniles in Federal Court," below).

An act that violates both federal and state laws (such as kidnapping, transportation of narcotics, robbery of a federally insured bank, or certain firearms offenses) may be tried in *both* federal and state courts if prosecutors so desire. Such prosecutions can be for the same act and will not be considered double jeopardy. There is no double jeopardy involved because of the concept of **dual sovereignty:** Federal and individual state governments are considered different sovereigns, each with its own unique authority over acts that have been criminalized in its jurisdiction.

The case of the two snipers who terrorized the Maryland–Washington, D.C.–Virginia areas in October 2002 provides an example. John Allen Muhammad (an adult) and Lee Boyd Malvo (a juvenile), accused of shooting nineteen people and killing thirteen, can be tried and punished in federal court as well as in the state courts of Maryland and Virginia because their actions violated both federal law and the laws of those two states. In the event that Malvo and/or Muhammad is tried in both federal and state court for the same act, and regardless of whether the outcome of the trial is acquittal or conviction, no double jeopardy is involved because of the concept of dual sovereignty. The cases of these two snipers also illustrate the principle that two different states (not just a combination of one state and the federal government) can prosecute the same act if elements of the act occurred in each state and if the act has been made criminal by state law in each of the states.[3]

The sovereignty that first obtains custody of the suspect is usually allowed to try him or her first. In most cases, this is the state. Although the federal government can try the defendant for the same offense, it usually refrains from doing so if the defendant has been convicted and sufficiently punished under state law. Although rare, in high-profile cases, federal prosecutors may want to try the defendant regardless of the verdict and punishment in other state jurisdictions. In theory, each sovereign could try the offender, who could receive multiple punishments without this being considered double jeopardy.

Juveniles in Federal Court

For a variety of reasons, juveniles are rarely tried in federal court: (1) there is no federal juvenile court *per se;* (2) the federal government does not operate juvenile correctional facilities; (3) juvenile violations of federal law usually indicate a simultaneous violation of an identical or similar state law, so federal prosecutors usually defer prosecution to the state; and (4) juvenile delinquency prosecutions are limited by federal law.[4] The last two reasons are perhaps the most important ones explaining why it is rare for juveniles to be prosecuted in federal court even if they have violated federal law.

Despite the rarity of federal juvenile prosecutions, the federal government has defined what constitutes delinquency at the federal level. Delinquency in the federal system is any violation of federal law committed by a person under age eighteen that would have been a crime if committed by an adult.[5] This is similar to the definition of *delinquency* in Chapter 1, except that the act is a violation of federal law instead of state law, and the maximum age to be tried for delinquency as a juvenile in the federal system is seventeen, instead of sixteen or fifteen as it is in a few states (although it is seventeen in the majority of states). Therefore, delinquency at both the state and federal levels includes acts that would be considered crimes if committed by an adult.*

As mentioned, perhaps the main reason why federal juvenile delinquency proceedings in the United States are rare is because such prosecutions are limited by federal law. Federal law requires that prosecutors prove that there is a "substantial federal interest" before they try a juvenile in federal court. In doing so, prosecutors must show that[6]

---

*According to federal law, a person may be processed as a juvenile in federal court as long as he or she is under age twenty-one and is accused of an act of juvenile delinquency. See Scalia, *Juvenile Delinquents in the Federal Criminal Justice System,* and also 18 U.S.C. Section 5031.

- The state does not have jurisdiction or refuses to assume jurisdiction.

- The state with jurisdiction does not have adequate programs or services for juvenile offenders.

- The offense charged is a violent felony, a drug trafficking or importation offense, or a firearms offense.[7]

Because of these provisions, the federal government usually refrains from trying juveniles in federal court if the state has jurisdiction, the state tries the case, and the juvenile is sufficiently punished. In some juvenile cases, however, such as with Lee Boyd Malvo, federal prosecutors may opt to prosecute the case because the case was high profile, especially heinous, and involved the use of firearms.

If a juvenile is charged with a federal law violation and is tried in federal court, the trial will take place in front of a U.S. district court judge or a federal magistrate, as opposed to a juvenile court judge. As is the case in most states, juveniles tried in federal court do not have a constitutional right to a jury trial or open hearing. If a juvenile is adjudicated, there will be a separate disposition hearing, and the juvenile may face many of the same sanctions that would apply at the state level, including probation and institutionalization.[8] If the juvenile is institutionalized, it is likely that he or she would be placed in a state juvenile facility through a contract with the Federal Bureau of Prisons (FBP) because the FBP does not operate juvenile facilities. That option would likely occur unless the juvenile is certified as an adult before trial. In this case, the juvenile will be prosecuted as an adult and may receive an adult disposition, including placement in a federal adult penal facility.

A juvenile prosecuted in federal court may be transferred, certified, or waived to adult status and be considered an adult for prosecution purposes. If a juvenile is prosecuted as an adult in federal court, he or she receives the same rights as adults receive, including a jury trial. According to federal law, a person who violates a federal law before age eighteen may be adjudicated as an adult if

- The offense charged was a violent felony, drug trafficking, or importation offense and the offense occurred after the person's fifteenth birthday.

- The person possessed a firearm during a violent offense and the offense was committed after the person's thirteenth birthday.

- The person had been previously adjudicated delinquent of a violent felony or drug offense.[9]

The most recent evidence available reveals that in one year approximately five hundred juveniles were referred for prosecution in federal court, about one-half of these cases were dismissed, and just over one hundred cases were actually adjudicated.[10] However, many of the juveniles handled in federal court are Native Americans. Although minor crimes committed by Native American juveniles on reservations are dealt with by reservation tribal courts, serious crimes may be tried in federal court according to U.S. law. Crimes that occur off reservation are handled in state juvenile courts.[11] Thus, if Native American juveniles were removed from the number of juveniles dealt with in federal court, the total number would be much lower.

The bottom line is that very few juveniles violate federal law compared to state law, even fewer are prosecuted in federal court when they do, and even fewer are adjudicated. The federal system is not set up for juvenile processing, and perhaps more important is the fact that the state is usually given the opportunity to try the juvenile. If the juvenile is adjudicated, the punishment is usually sufficient to preclude a federal trial for additional punishment.

A Cautionary Note

The foregoing discussion shows that the court system in the United States is complex. Understanding the basic structure of the court system, including the scope and authority of judicial decisions, is crucial for an examination of juvenile justice. Because the overwhelming majority of cases involving juvenile justice issues are not decided by the U.S. Supreme Court, the binding effect of most judicial decisions involving juveniles is geographically limited. As a result, many of the cases and statutes presented in this text serve as examples of how some states and jurisdictions deal with a particular issue. They are not meant to be national law. National applicability of a court decision happens only when the case has been decided by the U.S. Supreme Court. In the U.S. system of government, the differences among the various states in juvenile justice structure, process, and law are accepted and, in many cases, considered beneficial.

The Origin and Formation of the First Juvenile Court
What Led Up to Juvenile Courts

The juvenile court is just over a century old. The idea that children are different from adults, and need to be treated as such, reached an apex with the formation of the first juvenile court, in 1899. However, the development of this juvenile court was not the first sign that children were less responsible than adults and deserved to be treated differently. Rather, it represented the culmination of many changes involving youths in U.S. society.

Prior to the early nineteenth century, it was common for children to be viewed and treated as adults in all aspects of public life. At the turn of the nineteenth century, however, well before the introduction of the first juvenile court, children were being treated in ways that differed from adult practice. One indicator of this shift was the development of institutions that were strictly youth based. Orphanages represent one institution in the move toward separate child-caring institutions and a separate forum for dealing with child matters. However, orphanages are not considered the first "juvenile institutions" in the United States; orphanages were few, mainly operated by private authorities, and held mostly orphaned and abandoned children instead of juvenile lawbreakers. Because of the nature of orphanages, *houses of refuge* are regarded as the first U.S. juvenile institutions. Houses of refuge were first established in New York in 1825 but were found in most major U.S. cities by 1850.[12] Most of these institutions shared basic principles that ushered in a new era for the treatment of youths: (1) juveniles would be separated from adults; (2) rehabilitation, not punishment, was the goal of confinement; and (3) institutions would be restricted to children who demonstrated an ability to be rehabilitated—whether they were delinquent, dependent, or neglected.[13]

Houses of refuge embodied the guiding concept that juvenile courts later adopted—*parens patriae*. The historical roots of *parens patriae* can be traced to England, where chancery courts (early equity or property courts) could take temporary custody of property left to orphaned children of wealthy families. By the time the concept was adopted in America, however, it was used to justify state intervention into the lives of children when they violated the law or when their parents were deemed unfit or unable to care for them properly.[14] Such intervention usually meant placement in a house of refuge. Prior to 1838 in America, however, *parens patriae* was not legally established and was only loosely based on English common law. An early challenge to the house of refuge, and its foundation of *parens patriae*, provided the legal justification for the state to intervene in the lives of troubled and lawbreaking youths.

This first challenge to *parens patriae* came in the form of an 1838 Pennsylvania Supreme Court case titled *Ex parte Crouse* (1838).[15] Mary Ann Crouse was sent to the Philadelphia House of Refuge by a local magistrate after complaints by her mother that she was beyond control "by reason of vicious conduct." Mary Ann's father contested her confinement, arguing that she was being punished for conduct that was not criminal and that such confinement was unconstitutional. On a writ of certiorari, the Pennsylvania Supreme Court denied the father's claim and held that Mary Ann "has been snatched from a course which must have ended in confirmed depravity . . . not only is the restraint of her person lawful, but it would be an act of extreme cruelty to release her from it."[16] The court determined that confinement in a house of refuge was for reformation, not punishment—it was in Mary Ann's best interests regardless of whether she had committed a crime. This ruling is important because the Pennsylvania Supreme Court gave legitimacy to *parens patriae* and provided the legal foundation of the coming juvenile court, which would draw on this doctrine for its authority. This ruling stressed that *parens patriae* allowed, indeed mandated, the state to intervene into the lives of children whose parents could not control them or would not provide proper supervision for them.

Ex parte Crouse applied just in Pennsylvania but was not the only case that dealt with the issue of juvenile confinement and *parens patriae*. For example, the Illinois Supreme Court decided in *O'Connell v. Turner* (1870) that placement in the Chicago House of Refuge for a noncriminal offense constituted punishment, not reformation.[17] Despite this and other conflicting rulings, *Ex parte Crouse* was significant because it was the first time that *parens patriae* withstood legal challenge. As a result, *Crouse* "became the precedent for twentieth-century cases holding that the juvenile court could . . . commit children without the traditional legal formalities afforded to adults."[18] The court could do so under the premise that such commitment was in the best interests of the child.

Houses of refuge and other child-caring institutions represented a significant beginning toward a separate legal arena for dealing with youths and their problems. But houses of refuge did not completely do away with the practice of dealing with children in adult ways. Although houses of refuge operated on the promise of rehabilitation, their activities sometimes resembled punishment. Administrators of houses of refuge believed that the best way to achieve the reformation of juveniles was through harsh discipline and habit training. Moreover, houses of refuge were restricted to children who were deemed to be amenable to rehabilitation or "good prospects" for change. The practice of using adult institutions and practices as a sentencing option for the "unamenables" remained in place.[19] In sum, houses of refuge provided a separate path for only some juveniles, not all. It seemed that U.S. society was not completely ready to accept a new system with a different philosophy to deal strictly with juveniles.

The development of houses of refuge, and other child-specific institutions, provided some evidence that the status of children in U.S. society was changing. The changing status of children could also be found outside of the justice system.* By the mid- to late nineteenth century, state and federal legislation demonstrated that children were being considered as more than simply miniature versions of adults. In many ways, this legislation was linked to gains in fields such as psychiatry and social work, which pressed the notion that children did not go from toddlers to adults overnight. Rather, a developmental period, which is called adolescence today, was used to urge the idea that children needed ample opportunity for physical, mental, and moral development. Such development could not come from treating juveniles as if they were adults.[20]

Efforts by reformers to restrict child labor and mandate education were two important steps extending the division between adults and children. Although actual laws restricting child labor did not become implemented until the early twentieth century, efforts to do so championed the idea that children were inherently different from adults. The same can be said for compulsory education laws.[21] Prior to the 1850s, no state in the United States had laws that required the compulsory attendance of youths in schools. In 1852, however, Massachusetts became the first state to require compulsory education and attendance. Although it would be fifteen more years before other states followed the lead of Massachusetts, by 1890 a number of states had passed compulsory education laws, and by 1918 all the states had compulsory education laws. Compulsory education laws, like efforts to restrict child labor and the development of specific institutions for youths, indicated significant changes in the way U.S. youths were viewed and treated.[22] Ultimately, these changes contributed to the first legal arena for juveniles in the world—the juvenile court.

The First Juvenile Court

The juvenile court represented the culmination of nearly a century of change in the way that children were perceived. The first juvenile court in the world was established in Cook County (Chicago), Illinois, by the Illinois Legislature. By way of the **Illinois Juvenile Court Act of 1899**, it provided a distinct legal arena for children, an idea tied closely to the growing sentiment that children were different from adults. Children were not little people in big people's clothing. Driven by this philosophy, the goal of the act was to "regulate the

*For an excellent historical review of the precursors to a formal juvenile court in 1899, see Ellen Ryerson, *The Best-Laid Plans: America's Juvenile Court Experience* (New York: Hill and Wang, 1978).

treatment and control of dependent, neglected, and delinquent children."[23] Children were to receive greater scrutiny for their behavior, but such scrutiny was not to be used for punishment. Rather, when the state and the juvenile court intervened, it was to protect and reform. To accomplish this goal, the juvenile court's power was broad. The juvenile court judge was to act as a wise parent for and on behalf of the child.[24]

The passage of the Illinois Juvenile Court Act of 1899 resulted from the efforts of a group who have been labeled by history as the **child-savers.** At the time, women such as Jane Addams, Julia Lathrop, Ellen Henrotin, and Louise Bowen were prominent child advocates. They were responsible for a variety of social reforms involving children, from child labor practices to the care of orphaned and abandoned youths; however, their biggest accomplishment may have been the juvenile court.[25] It was women who took the role as activists for children because it was thought that their maternal nature made them "natural caretakers" and advocates for such an issue. Women were regarded as better teachers than men and more influential in child training and discipline.[26] This combination made them a perfect fit, according to the views of their era.

Scholars have questioned whether the intentions of the child-savers were purely philanthropic, however. Anthony Platt contends that the child-savers were motivated by ideals of justice and equality for the downtrodden but not by these interests alone. The child-saving movement came at a time when middle-class and upper-class women, including the child-savers, were experiencing a change in their traditional function as housewives. Women's domestic roles were being weakened, and child-saving was a way for women to fill the void created by the "decline of traditional religion, increased leisure and boredom, the rise of public education [instead of home education], and the breakdown of communal life in impersonal, crowded cities."[27] Child-saving became a "reputable task for any woman who wanted to extend her 'housekeeping' functions into the community" without aggravating societal stereotypes of a woman's nature and place in the home.[28]

The child-saving movement also came at a time of increasing economic and social changes in U.S. society. Increasing immigration and economic changes meant threats to the existing class system. Because the child-savers generally consisted of women married to wealthy husbands with power and influence, some contend that the movement was really intended to maintain wealth stability and order in growing cities such as Chicago. Child-saving was a way to capture and train new immigrant workers in a growing industrial society—to make sure they knew their proper place in the social order and remained in it. Accordingly, the "child saving movement tried to do for the criminal justice system what the industrialists and corporate leaders were trying to do for the economy . . . achieve order, stability and control while preserving the existing class system and distribution of wealth."[29]

Whatever the motivation, the Juvenile Court Act was influenced heavily by the work of the child-savers, and their efforts resulted in a separate legal arena for children. Much different from the adult system of justice, the juvenile court was structured in a way that could identify, treat, and cure the problems leading to youth misbehavior. The court was not so much concerned with the "specific charge facing the delinquent, but with his character and lifestyle, his psychological strengths and weaknesses, the advantages and disadvantages of his home environment."[30] As juvenile court judge Julian Mack explained, the court's purpose was to discover "what he is, physically, mentally, morally, and then, if he is treading the path that leads to criminality," to intervene "not so much to punish as to reform, not to degrade but to uplift, not to crush but to develop, to make him not a criminal but a worthy citizen."[31]

In practice, this new philosophy meant that dealing with children in court became substantially different from dealing with adults. The act gave the juvenile court exclusive and broad power to deal with youths under the age of sixteen that it determined to be neglected, dependent, and/or delinquent.* It established a separate courtroom for juvenile matters, a special judge, and separate record-keeping procedures for juvenile cases so they could be kept confidential and separate from criminal records to minimize stigma to the child. The act also maintained that the juvenile court would not be considered a criminal court, would employ heavily the use of probation officers, and would have the right to supervise the progress of youths well after they had been adjudicated and placed.[32] The court also did away with formal rules of procedure like those found in the adult system. Because the juvenile court avoided punishment and favored rehabilitation, proof of guilt was not even necessary for the juvenile court judge to intervene into the life of the child. It was up to the juvenile court judge acting as a wise parent: If the wise judge determined there was a need for intervention, there was little need for evidence of guilt.[33] As one scholar maintains:

> Once in court, the child's procedural due process rights evaporated under the parental glare of *parens patriae*. Under the *parens patriae* ideology, both the probation officer and the juvenile judge would assume the mantle of the surrogate parent–counselor–confessor to the child. . . . Constitutional protections heretofore employed on behalf of juveniles . . . were routinely dismissed as an impediment to rehabilitation.[34]

The idea of a separate court to deal with child matters spread quickly throughout the United States. By 1910, thirty-two states had passed legislation establishing a juvenile court, and by 1925, all but two states had done so. By 1950, every state had a separate juvenile court.[35] For more than a century, the juvenile court has undergone substantial changes, many of which are detailed in Chapter 1, the most significant being the constitutionalization of the juvenile court process. Today, the juvenile court has moved from complete informality and the absence of procedural protections to being a smaller version of the adult court system. However, the juvenile justice system has not been completely "adultified," and though there are similarities in process, it is still distinct from the adult justice system in a number of ways.

---

*See David L. Parry, *Essential Readings in Juvenile Justice* (Upper Saddle River, NJ: Prentice Hall, 2005), 57–60, for a reprinting of the original Juvenile Court Act, which is actually titled "An Act to Regulate the Treatment and Control of Dependent, Neglected, and Delinquent Children" and was approved on April 21, 1899.

The Juvenile Court Structure

The Organization of Juvenile Courts

All states have at least one court that deals with juveniles who break the law or are considered dependent and neglected. This court is usually referred to as the juvenile court, but this is not the term used in all states. Some states refer to these courts as family or probate courts, to name a few variations.[36] Juvenile courtrooms may be located in a central courthouse where all the other courts in a county are located, or the juvenile court may be a part of a larger central juvenile justice center. Central juvenile justice centers are usually found in more populous areas and are often situated close to other juvenile-based services, such as probation offices and the county juvenile detention center.[37]

Juvenile courts are created by statute, except for a few states in which juvenile courts are specified in the state constitution. State law usually determines the jurisdiction of the juvenile court: the types of cases that the court can hear, the age limits for juvenile court, court procedures, and the scope of authority of judges.[38] State and federal case law has had arguably the greatest effect on shaping juvenile court structure and operation. However, the type of case involved is important. State and federal judicial decisions are most important for juvenile courts that deal with delinquents, but federal statutes (such as the JJDPA of 1974) have been more influential when juvenile courts deal with dependent and neglected youths or status offenders.[39]

Juvenile courts are found in different places in the judicial structure, depending on the state. Generally, however, juvenile courts may be found within a larger general-jurisdiction court or as a specialized court handling only delinquency or related matters as described below. According to H. Ted Rubin, juvenile courts come in three general ways:

- *General jurisdiction trial courts.* These courts are courts that have jurisdiction over both criminal and civil cases. In some states, general jurisdiction trial courts have jurisdiction over juvenile cases.

- *Special jurisdiction trial courts.* These courts are granted decision-making power over certain or specialized cases. Examples of these courts include juvenile, probate, family, and domestic relations courts.

- *Limited jurisdiction trial courts.* These courts hear cases typically involving misdemeanors, local ordinance violations, and limited-dollar civil suits. In some states, this is where juvenile court jurisdiction is located.[40]

Do Juvenile Courts Have Jurisdiction in All Matters Involving Juveniles?

A characteristic of most juvenile courts is that they do not have jurisdiction in *all* matters involving juveniles. States in which juvenile courts are considered courts of specialized or limited jurisdiction may have one court for serious delinquency cases (the juvenile court), another court for minor delinquency (limited jurisdiction juvenile court), another court for related family matters such as divorce or child custody disputes (domestic relations court), and yet another court for cases involving status offending, dependency, and neglect (probate court). Family members with multiple legal problems may, under some state structures, find their cases being heard by different judges, at different times, and in different places. Even in states where general jurisdiction trial courts handle juvenile matters, other familial issues are rarely combined with the juvenile case because the same problem of different judges and times remains.[41] This lack of unification can present many issues. As family court judge Leonard P. Edwards says:

> A domestic relations court may award custody to one parent only to have a juvenile court remove the child from that parent and make a different custodial order. A family may have to go to one judge for paternity determination or child support enforcement, to another to determine the child's delinquency status, to another for a restraining order in a domestic violence case, and still another to receive a custody order. Such a system requires families to return to the courthouse many times, strains both court and litigant resources, and maximizes the possibility that court orders will be in conflict with one another.[42]

Should There Be a Unified or Coordinated Juvenile Court?

A unified court structure is one proposed alternative: All juvenile-related issues in families with multiple obstacles could be addressed in one juvenile court by one judge. Such a court would bring together the administration of all juvenile issues, domestic relations (such as custody and child support), dependency and neglect, and other issues involving the family, such as youth emancipation, adoption, divorce, and the termination of parental rights.[43] Unification could also be extended to include any criminal or civil cases involving family members. In states with a unified court structure, such as Hawaii and Rhode Island, a family could theoretically have all of its legal issues resolved by one judge. Such a structure would prevent conflicting rulings among judges (such as the situation described in the passage above) while making the court process more efficient and convenient for all parties involved.[44]

Unifying a specialized court structure would be a formidable task for many judicial structures, and progress toward a unified court system has been slow across the United States. Another option that some state judicial systems have attempted is coordination of courts. A coordinated court system allows many of the same benefits of unification but does not require a complete restructuring of existing judicial structures. Under a coordinated system, courts with overlapping issues concerning a single family may be joined so that the resolution of issues can be streamlined. Such coordination can be accomplished in many ways. First, different judges or court personnel (from domestic and juvenile courts, for example) can come together and devise a method to deal with each case in one setting. Second, some court systems have made it possible for different cases involving families to be heard before one judge. Third, some court structures enable personnel from various juvenile agencies to get together to share information on families for a coordinated court response.[45] For example, the juvenile probation department and a state's child protective services agency may share information on a youth who is both delinquent and neglected, and both agencies may be responsible for reporting to the same court instead of in two different proceedings.

Juvenile courts come in a variety of forms both between and within states. In many cases, juvenile courts may handle only delinquency issues, whereas other issues such as status offending or dependency and neglect may be handled by a different and specialized court. As such, juvenile court structure is not a clear-cut issue, and specific information about a particular state or jurisdiction is best obtained by consulting that state's laws and/or constitution.

The Administration of Juvenile Courts

The "administration" of juvenile courts is a broad subject that includes many areas, such as staffing, record keeping, budget preparation, and information storage. However, major issues in the administration of juvenile courts are the workload of the court, case processing time, and case disposition. **Court workload** refers to the number of cases that come in front of the juvenile court each year. **Case processing** is the time it takes to hear and resolve a case once it reaches the court. **Case disposition** is the time it takes for a case to reach the court in the first place after a delinquency petition or other action has been accepted.

- *Court workload.* The most recent data indicate that approximately 1.7 million cases are handled each year by juvenile courts in the United States. The number of cases heard by juvenile courts peaked in 1996–1997 at approximately 1.8 million but has remained relatively stable or declined over the last several years to its current level. However, these figures include only delinquency and status offense cases, which constitute approximately 70–80 percent of cases heard by juvenile courts. Other cases, such as dependency and neglect, make up the remaining 20–30 percent of cases heard each year.[46] Thus, juvenile courts process roughly two million cases each year.[47] Exhibit 7.3 shows the number of estimated delinquency cases from 1960 to 2000, and Table 7.1 displays the numbers and types of cases processed by the nation's juvenile courts in 1999.

- *Case processing.* Originally, a major reason for a separate juvenile court was so the judge could preside over an "unhurried" hearing that would contribute to the individualized consideration of each case.[48] Such an unhurried hearing would promote intervention that was in the best interests of the child. In reality, however, having sufficient time to devote to each case was only an ideal and may never have been truly realized. For example, in 1963 the National Council on Crime and Delinquency (NCCD) conducted an assessment of 1961 case processing in Cook County, Illinois. This assessment assumed that each case would take an average of 1.5 hours. If each judge sat approximately 220 days per year at 6.5 hours per day (the formula used), a judge could hear and decide approximately 1,000 cases per year. In 1961 the juvenile court in Cook County handled 10,164 cases dispersed among five judges (thus, each case received approximately 45 minutes).[49]

EXHIBIT 7.3

Juvenile Court Delinquency Caseload, 1960–2000

Estimated delinquency cases

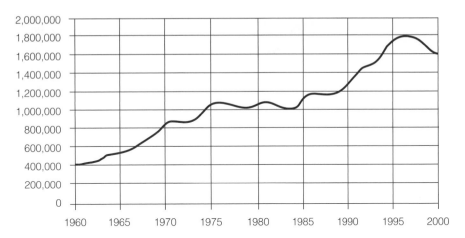

Note: On any given day in 2000, juvenile courts handled 4,500 delinquency cases. In comparison, in 1960 approximately 1,100 delinquency cases were processed daily.

Source: Charles Puzzanchera, Anne L. Stahl, Terrence A. Finnegan, Nancy Tierney, and Howard N. Snyder, *Juvenile Court Statistics 2000* (Pittsburgh: National Center for Juvenile Justice, forthcoming). See also *OJJDP Statistical Briefing Book* (http:ojjdp.ncjrs.org/ojstatbb/html/qa182html), Aug. 17, 2004.

Calculating case processing times is difficult. Because cases involving juveniles vary in complexity, the time it takes to hear and decide such cases varies as well. For example, depending on the state, juveniles may receive a jury trial, although this is not a constitutional right. A jury trial can take considerably longer than a case with similar facts and circumstances in a state that does not provide juveniles a right to a jury. Moreover, cases involving serious crimes can take much longer than cases involving less serious crimes. Although case processing is an inexact science, researchers have developed various ways to examine it. For example, in 1993, Steelman, Rubin, and Arnold assigned weights to different cases being heard by Chicago's juvenile courts to address the amount of time needed for a typical case. The researchers determined that the "typical" time needed to hear dependency cases ranged from 300 minutes (5 hours) when a child was taken into custody to 353 minutes (almost 6 hours) when the child remained in the home; the typical time for delinquency cases was 112 minutes (almost 2 hours) when the child was not detained and 141 minutes (2 hours and twenty-one minutes) when the child was detained.[50] These findings may be a substantial overestimate of the actual amount of time that juvenile court judges take; these judges become more hurried each year in their efforts to hear the large number of cases entering the court.

TABLE 7.1

Delinquency Cases Handled by Juvenile Courts in 1999

Most Serious Offense	Number of Cases
Total delinquency	**1,673,000**
Person offenses	**387,100**
Criminal homicide	1,800
Forcible rape	4,200
Robbery	25,100
Aggravated assault	55,800
Simple assault	255,900
Other violent sex offenses	11,600
Other person offenses	32,700
Property offenses	**706,200**
Burglary	113,900
Larceny-theft	322,100
Motor vehicle theft	38,500
Arson	8,600
Vandalism	111,400
Trespassing	58,700
Stolen property offenses	26,300
Other property offenses	26,800
Drug law violations	**191,200**
Public order offenses	**388,600**
Obstruction of justice	171,800
Disorderly conduct	90,600
Weapons offenses	39,800
Liquor law violations	19,900
Nonviolent sex offenses	13,700
Other public order offenses	52,700
Violent Crime Index*	**86,900**
Property Crime Index**	**483,100**

*Includes criminal homicide, forcible rape, robbery, and aggravated assault.

**Includes burglary, larceny-theft, motor vehicle theft, and arson.

Note: Detail may not add to totals because of rounding. Percent change calculations are based on unrounded numbers.

Source: Charles Puzzanchera, Anne L. Stahl, Terrence A. Finnegan, Nancy Tierney, and Howard N. Snyder, *Juvenile Court Statistics 1999* (Pittsburgh: National Center for Juvenile Justice, 2003), 7.

- *Case disposition.* Coupled with the time it takes to hear and decide a case is the time it takes for the case to get to court in the first place. Professional association standards (such as the American Bar Association) suggest that juvenile cases should reach the court no more than 30 to 90 days after the delinquency petition is accepted by the court. A study of seventeen states and almost three million juvenile cases found that almost one-half of delinquency cases processed by juvenile courts exceeded 90 days in jurisdictions with over 400,000 individuals in the population. Cases got to court more quickly in jurisdictions with smaller populations, but approximately 24 percent of jurisdictions with fewer than 100,000 people did exceed the 90-day suggested time limit.[51] In sum, a large number of jurisdictions exceed the maximum suggested time for a juvenile's case to reach the court.

Case disposition time is an important issue. For example, delays in getting cases to court may mean that the juvenile system may "lose its bite," especially when the juvenile is not detained prior to the adjudication hearing. Arguably, the further away the sanction is from the act, the less its deterrent value if that is a goal of a juvenile justice system. Additionally, significant delays may mean even more severe consequences for juveniles outside the justice system. For example, if a juvenile is detained until his or her case is heard (and is found not guilty of delinquency allegations), he or she may miss an entire semester or half-year of school. These types of consequences, as a result of delays in cases reaching the court, may contribute to a cumulative effect on youths who may already be facing multiple obstacles.[52]

Legally, juveniles do not have much redress when their cases exceed suggested time limits for processing. National standards on suggested case processing times are not legally binding and are meant only to be recommendations. Moreover, federal constitutional protections for a speedy trial have not been granted to juveniles, and only six states (Arkansas, Florida, Minnesota, New Hampshire, New York, and Washington) provide remedy for juveniles whose cases have not been heard by juvenile courts within a time frame set by those states' laws.[53]

Specialized Juvenile Courts

Since the 1990s, the structure of the juvenile court has changed because of the development of specialized juvenile courts. As the name suggests, specialized juvenile courts deal with specialized cases involving juveniles. Two variations are juvenile teen courts and juvenile drug courts.

Juvenile Teen Courts

A popular variation of a regular juvenile court is the juvenile teen court (also called a youth or peer court). Teen courts were developed in earnest in the early 1990s as a diversion from formal juvenile justice processing whereby a juvenile would be sanctioned by his or her peers. The justification for teen court programs is that youths respond better to sanctioning from their peers than from adult authority figures. Advocates of teen courts argue that youths who go through teen court will change their delinquent ways out of a desire for approval and acceptance from their peers.[54]

Teen courts generally handle first-time offenders charged with misdemeanor offenses such as theft, simple assault, disorderly conduct, possession of alcohol, and vandalism. The majority of teen courts do not accept youths with prior arrest records, particularly youths with prior felony arrests. Approximately 66 percent of the cases handled by teen courts nationwide involve youths who are under age sixteen.[55] As a diversionary alternative to formal juvenile justice processing, youths may be diverted to teen court at numerous points both before and during the formal juvenile justice process. Youths may be referred to teen court from schools, from law enforcement officers, during intake, and even at the beginning of the formal court process through plea bargaining. Exhibit 7.4 examines the offenses handled in teen court.

EXHIBIT 7.4   *Offenses Handled in Teen Courts*

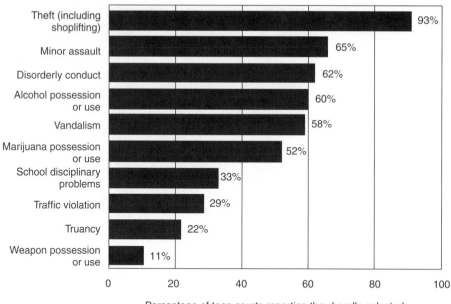

Percentage of teen courts reporting they handle selected
offenses "often" or "very often"

Source: Jeffrey Butts and Janeen Buck, *Teen Courts: A Focus on Research* (Washington, DC:
Office of Juvenile Justice and Delinquency Prevention, 2000), 5.

A notable difference between teen courts and regular juvenile courts is that
most teen courts are dispositional, meaning that they do not decide guilt or innocence but instead determine the sanctions for the youth defendant. Most
teen courts require youths to admit to the charges against them in regular
juvenile court before they may qualify for teen court. Youths who choose not
to admit to the charges will usually be processed in regular juvenile court. This
situation indicates that a major difference between teen courts and regular
juvenile courts is that teen courts are predominantly viewed as a diversion
from the formal juvenile justice system. Despite their diversionary nature, and
the fact that teen courts are not "regular" adjudicatory juvenile courts, teen
courts are important in this discussion because they provide an alternative for
a number of cases that might have been processed in the formal juvenile justice system.

Sanctions imposed by teen courts usually include community service, victim apology letters, restitution, and teen court jury duty. Teen courts may
also impose such dispositions as drug and alcohol counseling or victim
awareness.[56] The use of teen courts is sometimes controversial; therefore, the
"Controversial Issue" box examines arguments for and against their
existence.

CONTROVERSIAL ISSUE: WHICH SIDE DO YOU FAVOR?

Should teens be responsible for sanctioning other teens?

Teen or youth courts are considered by some as a cure-all for minor delinquency. To qualify for teen court, a youth must generally admit to a delinquency charge in a regular juvenile court. In exchange for this guilty plea, the youth may then be sanctioned by his or her peers in teen court while avoiding an official record with the court if the youth completes the teen court terms successfully. Sanctions come in many forms but generally include community service, jury terms, apology letters, and restitution.

This raises a question: *Is using teens to determine sanctions for offending teens an effective way to deal with minor delinquents?*

Proponents argue that teen courts take advantage of one of the most powerful motivators in a young person's life—peer approval and acceptance. When youths are sanctioned by their peers, they are much more likely to internalize the harmful impact of their behavior and change than when sanctioned by adults. Youths who have been sentenced in teen court are also allowed to participate as jury members in the future. Both the juvenile justice system and juveniles benefit from teen court. Juveniles benefit because they are held accountable and are given future responsibility. They also avoid an official record with the court. The juvenile justice system benefits because teen courts divert a number of youths from regular juvenile court, freeing up time for more serious delinquency.

Opponents of teen courts argue that they widen the net of the juvenile justice system for youths who would have been unlikely to be processed in regular juvenile court in the first place. Without teen courts, most of these youths would have been left alone by the juvenile justice system because their offenses are minor. Teen courts typify the "build it and they will come" phenomenon. Because these courts are usually locally based and often subsidized by federal or state grant money, they must be supplied with youths to justify future funds. Teen courts do not provide an important diversionary alternative to regular court because very few juveniles are handled in teen courts each year. Rather, they act as a supplement to regular court. They do not divert offenders from the juvenile justice system; they add offenders. Furthermore, the sanctions that youths receive in teen court are often more harsh than what they would have received in regular court if they were prosecuted in the first place. Teen courts tend to "pile on the sanctions" for youths such that they are set up to fail and are then labeled and stigmatized as delinquents. What good could come from a system in which "delinquents" are in charge of sanctioning other "delinquents"?

U.S. teen courts have multiple forms. Generally, four variations of the teen court model account for more than five hundred teen court programs in this country:

- *Adult judge model.* An adult serves as the judge, and youths serve as attorneys, jurors, bailiffs, and other court personnel. The adult judge rules on evidence and courtroom procedure; the youth juries are responsible for determining a disposition for the youth defendant. This is the most common type of teen court and is used in 47 percent of teen courts.

- *Peer jury model.* This model does not use youth attorneys or judges. Rather, an adult or a youth presents the case to a youth jury for disposition. The jury may also question the defendant directly. This model is the second most common type of teen court and is used in 12 percent of teen courts.

- *Youth tribunal model.* In this model, youth attorneys present the case to three youth judges. No jury is involved, and the panel of three judges recommends a disposition for the youth defendant. This is the third most common type of teen court and is used in 10 percent of teen courts.

- *Youth judge model.* This model has teens occupying all roles, including that of judge. A jury recommends a disposition. This is the least common type of teen court and is used in 9 percent of teen courts.[57]

Adults are involved in teen courts in a variety of ways: administering the program, supervising court activity, and coordinating community resources such as when drug and alcohol counseling is included in a disposition. Adults are also responsible for budgeting and personnel decisions. However, teen courts are structured so that youths have maximum participation in the court and in the sanctioning process. Adults handle "behind the scenes" activities.

Juvenile Drug Courts

An alternative that is closer to a regular juvenile court is the juvenile drug court, which is focused on juveniles who are drug users (as opposed to sellers, manufacturers, possessors, etc.). Because substance-abusing juveniles need to be treated for their substance-abuse problem as well as be held accountable for their delinquent behavior, traditional juvenile courts face a variety of problems not encountered when dealing with "regular" delinquents. For example, traditional juvenile courts can usually handle delinquency problems; however, they often find it difficult to get a youth timely and appropriate treatment for a substance-abuse problem because of lengthy treatment lists and disjointed service delivery. To deal with these special-problem juveniles, in the mid-1990s a number of juvenile courts started dockets specifically for drug users—better known as juvenile drug courts.[58]

It is a common misperception that juvenile drug courts are similar to teen courts. In reality, juvenile drug courts are much different in that these courts do not use a youth's peers in the process. Moreover, juvenile drug courts can operate as either a diversionary alternative or a formal process, and can handle both adjudication and disposition functions, whereas teen courts are almost solely diversionary and dispositional. In this way, juvenile drug courts are more similar to traditional or regular juvenile courts than to teen courts.

However, juvenile drug courts do differ from traditional juvenile courts in important ways. In jurisdictions with juvenile drug courts, youths identified as having substance-abuse problems are placed on a special "drug docket." The drug court judge then works closely with representatives from the juvenile justice system (such as probation officers, prosecutors, and defense attorneys), from social services (such as drug and alcohol counseling agencies), and from other community organizations. Together with the drug court judge, these representatives determine how best to intervene to address a youth's substance-abuse and delinquency problems. Unlike most regular juvenile court judges, the juvenile drug court judge conducts frequent hearings (sometimes weekly) with the defendant, his or her parents, and his or her attorney to examine the youth's progress.[59] Used in this way, juvenile drug courts are much more intensive than regular juvenile court. Other ways in which drug courts differ from regular juvenile courts include the following:

- Juvenile drug courts intervene much earlier and conduct more comprehensive intake assessments.
- Juvenile drug courts place additional emphasis on family functioning and the integration of the family into the treatment process.
- Juvenile drug courts place greater emphasis on coordination with treatment agencies, schools, and other community organizations in addressing the needs of the youth.
- Juvenile drug courts use much more active judicial supervision of the juvenile and his or her treatment progress.
- Juvenile drug courts have increased sanctions for noncompliance and incentives for youth and family progress.[60]

Participation in juvenile drug court programs is usually voluntary. Juvenile drug courts may offer incentives for youths to participate, such as deferred prosecution and avoiding an official record with the court upon successful participation in treatment. When operated in this way, juvenile drug courts are sometimes considered a diversionary alternative to the formal juvenile justice process. Moreover, juvenile drug courts can also be viewed as a regular juvenile court alternative for a specialized type of juvenile. Whereas teen courts are used for relatively minor offenders, drug courts are used for youths with both substance-abuse and delinquency problems. Although drug courts are not as common as teen courts, between 1995 and 2001 the drug court movement began to grow, and today there are more than 140 juvenile drug courts with an additional 125 being planned throughout the nation.[61]

Juvenile Court Personnel

The juvenile court is composed of many individuals who make important determinations for youths and their families. Juvenile court personnel have a key role in the organization and administration of juvenile courts across the country. This role often exceeds the myth of what is typically considered their "official duty" (for example, juvenile court judges do not merely "decide cases"; instead, they make many other decisions affecting the operation of the court and the future of the juvenile). The most important juvenile court actors include the juvenile court judge, the juvenile court administrator, juvenile court masters or referees, juvenile prosecutors, juvenile defense attorneys, youth advocates, and probation officers:

- *Juvenile court judge.* The most important figure in the juvenile court is the juvenile court judge. He or she ultimately decides the fate of a juvenile who enters the juvenile court. Judges are more than decision makers about how to dispose of a certain case. In many jurisdictions, they are responsible for the entire administration of the court. They may be responsible for hiring and firing court personnel, monitoring the court's budget, establishing court rules, belonging to juvenile justice boards, and ensuring the timely processing of cases. Because of the multiple responsibilities of juvenile court judges, they often depend on additional personnel for a variety of tasks.*

- *Juvenile court administrator.* At the direction of the juvenile court judge, the **juvenile court administrator** takes on such tasks as staffing, budgeting, and case scheduling. Juvenile court administrators may also have an active role in the juvenile court process and be charged with coordinating programs that link to the goals of the juvenile court. For example, a juvenile court administrator may have the responsibility of arranging substance-abuse counseling for a youth who has been ordered by the judge to undergo treatment. Such a diverse range of duties means that juvenile court administrators must be well versed in a number of areas, from accounting to community liaison.[62]

- *Juvenile court master.* Because of the large number of cases that many juvenile courts have, especially in populous areas, juvenile court masters (sometimes called referees, magistrates, or commissioners) may be used by the juvenile court judge. **Juvenile court masters** are usually lawyers and may preside over many hearings that take valuable court time, such as minor delinquency cases and detention hearings. However, juvenile court masters usually have limited power to hear certain cases, such as waiver hearings and felony trials. In the organization of the juvenile court, they are invaluable officers who can take pressure off the juvenile court judge.[63]

- *Juvenile prosecutors.* Juvenile prosecutors (called district attorneys or DAs) are usually responsible for bringing cases to the court's attention. In this way, they are very powerful figures in the juvenile justice system because their decisions determine the court's caseload to a great extent. Because of this responsibility, juvenile prosecutors must be judicious with delinquency petitions and ensure that only the most deserving cases are petitioned for an adjudication hearing.[64] Other cases can be disposed of without a formal adjudication hearing through plea bargaining or diversion. Such decisions are often relegated to the juvenile prosecutor.

- *Juvenile defense attorneys.* Juvenile defense attorneys represent juveniles at many points in time, starting as early as interrogation. There are generally

*For an excellent and comprehensive review of juvenile court personnel and their functions, see Preston Elrod and R. Scott Ryder, *Juvenile Justice: A Social, Historical, and Legal Perspective* (Gaithersburg, MD: Aspen, 1999), 238–250.

two ways that juveniles may receive an attorney: by court appointment or by private retention. Juveniles are appointed a court attorney when they are determined to be indigent, meaning they cannot afford an attorney. If not appointed a court attorney, a juvenile may always hire or retain his or her own private attorney, provided that he or she (or his or her family) has the resources to do so. Defense attorneys are a premium in the juvenile justice system because juveniles who are facing an adjudication hearing that could result in institutionalization have a constitutional right to the services of a lawyer. Juveniles not facing institutionalization are usually granted this right by the various states that provide for a defense lawyer "in all delinquency proceedings."

Juvenile defense attorneys are important to court administration because they often have a heavy hand in deciding whether their client will exercise the right to a full adjudication hearing.[65] Defense attorneys may be categorized in two ways concerning their involvement with juveniles: social worker or client-advocate. In a social worker role, the defense attorney may act as a negotiator with the prosecutor in determining the best and most helpful disposition for his or her client—not necessarily as the client's advocate fighting to free him or her from the charges. In contrast, the client-advocate attorney fights for his or her client's rights at all stages of the juvenile justice process, with the ultimate goal of getting the charges dropped or proving the client innocent of the charges. The dual role of defense attorneys sometimes makes their position in the juvenile court controversial, as discussed in the "Controversial Issue" box.

- *Youth advocates.* A youth advocate's duty is to represent the youth's interests in juvenile court (as opposed to what the court sees as in the best interests of the youth). A youth advocate goes by different names but is usually referred to as a **guardian ad litem** or **court-appointed special advocate (CASA).** Youth advocates are almost solely involved in cases of child abuse and neglect, rather than delinquency proceedings. However, guardian ad litem or CASA workers may be involved to advocate the child's best interests in delinquency cases when a youth does not have a parent or other suitable guardian available (as is the case with Lee Boyd Malvo, the Maryland sniper, who was appointed a guardian ad litem because his parents are from out of the country). States have different requirements for youth advocates. For example, some are required to be lawyers. More frequently, however, youth advocates are citizen volunteers.[66]

- *Probation officers.* The final key members of the juvenile court are probation officers, who perform a variety of functions for the juvenile court. They may be intake officers who decide whether a case gets petitioned for an adjudication hearing or is diverted. They are frequently charged with conducting predisposition investigations and making recommendations to the juvenile court judge. Such recommendations can be held in high regard and accepted by the juvenile court judge. Probation officers also supervise juveniles sentenced to probation and monitor their progress. Finally, they are usually the ones to initiate motions that lead to probation revocation and to the juvenile being institutionalized.

Should juvenile defense lawyers act as social workers or as client-advocates?

Under a pure *parens patriae* doctrine, the juvenile defense attorney acts as a social worker who aims for a disposition that is "in the best interests of the child." Social worker defense attorneys do not aim at getting the charges against the juvenile dropped or winning an acquittal. Instead, they work closely with others in the juvenile court (such as the judge and prosecutor) to solve the youth's problems. By contrast, the client-advocate juvenile defense attorney operates much like a defense attorney in the adult system. For client-advocates, the objective is to zealously defend the rights of their juvenile client and to gain an acquittal. Working with the court "in the best interests of the child" is not necessarily their goal.

This raises a question: *What should be the role of defense attorneys in the juvenile justice system—social workers or client-advocates?*

Those who argue that defense attorneys should act as social workers say that defense attorneys are in the best position to persuade their client to get the help they need. Many juveniles need intervention in their lives, and the role of a defense attorney is to promote the juvenile's best interests—even if that means that the juvenile does not agree that he or she must face consequences. A defense attorney who fails to act in the best interest of the child is working against a client who will surely be in the court again in the future. Social worker defense attorneys are in a unique position to assist in the rehabilitation of a child even if the child sees it as punishment.

Those who argue that juvenile defense attorneys should be client-advocates say that juveniles need a rigorous defense in a juvenile justice system that has become more adult-like in procedure and punishment. Today, juvenile proceedings often focus on punishment, and juveniles need to be protected by a defense attorney who will make sure that they receive their full rights. Juveniles are not mature enough to understand the proceedings against them. Without a zealous advocate, they may be manipulated by the court system and punished in the name of "the best interests of the child." Without rigorous representation, the juvenile court becomes a kangaroo court where fairness is replaced with arbitrariness. It becomes a place where a juvenile gets neither the rehabilitation promised from the juvenile justice system nor the procedural protections afforded adults.

The previous discussion is limited to the basic functions of key juvenile court personnel, but these positions have a variety of functions that will be presented in the various chapters that deal with the juvenile justice process in detail. The relationship among these various professionals is impartial. Unlike the adult court, which tends to place an emphasis on adversarial relationships between actors, the juvenile court is more often characterized as an informal work group whose personnel are considered to be focused on the same outcome— the best interests of the child. Although such informal relationships tend to be weakened with more serious charges against the juvenile, the fact that the overwhelming majority of cases entering juvenile courts are minor offenses suggests that this characterization holds in most juvenile cases.

Is a Separate Juvenile Court Needed?

Today's juvenile courts bear only a small resemblance to their original formulation in 1899. The most significant change occurred after the U.S. Supreme Court's decision in *In re Gault* (1967), which granted juveniles most due process protections that were formerly guaranteed only to adults.[67] Since *Gault*, the juvenile court has become even more "adultified." According to some scholars, these changes argue against the need for a separate system to deal with juvenile offenders.[68] According to others, such changes do not mean that the juvenile court and justice system should be discarded.[69]

For abolition. Abolitionists cite several reasons why the juvenile court should be abandoned. Among these are that juveniles are more responsible today than when the first court was formed, juveniles are not treated equally in the juvenile system, the adult court can handle serious and violent juveniles more effectively, and the adult system could adapt to juveniles so that there would be no need for a separate and duplicative system, especially one that abolitionists contend has made rehabilitation a nongoal.*

One of the main arguments of abolitionists is that the juvenile court has simply become a smaller version of the criminal court where juveniles face the same punishments (or worse) as adults but do not enjoy an equal level of procedural protection (for example, bail, speedy/public trial, and jury trial).[70] They propose that an alternative way to deal with juveniles would be to abolish the juvenile court altogether and integrate juvenile cases into adult court, where juveniles would receive full due process protections. Integrating juvenile cases into the adult system could still recognize the differences between children and adults, according to advocates, and a juvenile's young age could serve as a mitigating factor in sentencing. For example, adult courts could give juveniles a **youth discount:** A juvenile's age would serve as a coupon of sorts for a reduction in sentence.[71] In this type of framework, for example, a sixteen-year-old who is "convicted" in adult court might receive a sentence equivalent to 66 percent of what an adult would receive. Thus, a juvenile's age would provide justification for a lesser sentence. An eighteen-year-old might then receive 100 percent of the sanction that an adult would receive. Because abolitionists contend that juveniles are facing the same or worse sanctions than adults when they are tried in juvenile court for similar crimes, they view the integration of juvenile cases into adult court as a benefit to juveniles, for they would receive more procedural protection than they currently receive in the "adultified" juvenile court.

---

*For a presentation of both sides of the issue, see Tory Caeti and Eric Fritsch, "Abolishing the Juvenile Justice System." In Barbara Sims and Pamela Preston (eds.), *Handbook of Juvenile Justice: Theory and Practice* (New York: Marcel Dekker, forthcoming).

Against abolition: Those who advocate keeping the juvenile court argue that it provides numerous helpful services that are foreign to the adult justice system. They contend that the juvenile system, unlike the adult system, provides helpful interventions both before and after adjudication and sentencing. In this line, they also disagree that rehabilitation has been lost in the juvenile court for most offenders. To those who would keep the juvenile court, adopting the adult system would preclude individualization in sentencing, which is the hallmark of juvenile rehabilitation. To them, individualization is necessary because not all juveniles are the same and the fact that some juveniles get treated differently simply reflects their different needs—not that the juvenile system is biased or unfairly applied.[72]

Advocates for keeping the juvenile court also downplay arguments that the juvenile court cannot handle serious and violent offenders. Their response is that only a very small percentage of delinquents are serious, chronic, and/or violent in their offending. Advocates note that the juvenile court can adapt to these offenders by transferring or waiving them to the adult system—the remaining majority of youths can remain in the juvenile court and benefit from its youth-appropriate activities. Further, because most juveniles do not re-offend once they have been processed by the juvenile court, proponents of the juvenile court argue that throwing away the entire juvenile system for a small number of serious, violent, and/or chronic juveniles who cannot be rehabilitated is not logical. Rather, they contend that the juvenile justice system

YOU ARE A... **State Juvenile Justice Legislator**

In recent months, several highly publicized incidents of juvenile crime have spurred much debate around your state about the continuing need for a separate juvenile court and justice system. As a state juvenile justice legislator, you have been placed in charge of a special committee on the juvenile court and juvenile justice system. Specifically, the committee that you head is to evaluate a proposed bill that, if made into law, would abolish all juvenile courts and separate juvenile justice systems in your state and transfer jurisdiction of all cases involving persons under age eighteen to the adult justice system. You are in charge of addressing the following questions as head of this special committee:

1. What would be the potential benefits of juvenile court and justice system abolition? What would be the potential drawbacks if such a law was passed?

2. If the juvenile court and juvenile justice system were abolished, would any special provisions be made for juveniles under adult court jurisdiction? If no, explain why not. If so, what would be the special provisions, who would qualify for such special provisions, and at what stages of the justice system would they apply?

3. If the juvenile court were abolished, how would status offenders and dependent and neglected youths be handled?

4. What would be your final recommendation to legislators? Explain and justify your response.

5. At the end of this course, revisit these questions to see if your responses and justifications have changed. If your responses have changed, what factors or evidence influenced you the most?

is the most successful component in the entire justice system for the majority of offenders.[73]

In addition to this, there are many other considerations in the debate to keep or abolish the juvenile court and separate juvenile justice system. The "You Are a . . . State Juvenile Justice Legislator" box includes an exercise in which you are a state legislator charged with balancing these issues and making an informed recommendation.

In practice, the juvenile court may be procedurally similar to the adult court, but when viewed in relation to the entire adult justice process, it is distinctly different. The informal and rehabilitative interventions of the juvenile justice system still remain for the majority of offenders who face the court despite a process that is more adult-like. In short, the juvenile court offers to families and youths a wide array of beneficial services that are not offered in the adult process. As a result, it is unlikely that the juvenile court and juvenile justice system will be abolished, for most juveniles need to be treated in a way that is different from how adults are treated: Most juveniles are in fact different from adults in a number of important ways.[74] However, uncertainty is the rule for the future.

SUMMARY

- ❏ All court decisions, with the exception of cases decided by the U.S. Supreme Court, are geographically limited. This means that a court's decisions are binding only on a certain area in which it has jurisdiction.

- ❏ The U.S. Supreme Court sets judicial precedent for the entire country. Thus, when it decides a case, all other courts that decide future cases with similar facts and circumstances must follow its decision. If they do not, these lower courts may be reversed on appeal.

- ❏ Most cases on juvenile justice are not decided by the U.S. Supreme Court. This fact helps explain why different states and jurisdictions have different rules for dealing with juvenile offenders.

- ❏ If a juvenile violates federal law, it is rare for his or her case to be tried in federal court. Violations of federal law usually imply a violation of state law, and federal prosecutors will defer to the state to try the case. There are also federal limitations on prosecuting a juvenile.

- ❏ The juvenile court in Cook County, Illinois, was not the first sign that children deserved to be treated differently from adults. Rather, it was the culmination of several events in U.S. social history.

- ❏ Juvenile courts are found either within larger general jurisdiction trial courts that hear many types of cases or as specialized or limited jurisdiction courts that may hear only juvenile cases.

- ❏ The juvenile court workload has decreased slightly in recent years, but case processing and disposition times are still a concern. Juvenile court judges do not appear to have enough time to devote to each case, and many juvenile courts exceed the recommended times for disposition of a case.

❑ The juvenile court today is very similar in terms of process to the adult court. However, the philosophy of the juvenile court and youth-specific interventions in the juvenile justice system make it distinctly different from the adult system.

❑ The juvenile court work group operates more informally than the adult court system.

❑ A central argument for abolishing the juvenile court is that juveniles are facing adult-type sanctions but do not receive equal constitutional protections. Proponents of keeping the juvenile court claim that the juvenile justice system provides many important services that the adult court never could.

REVIEW QUESTIONS

1. If the Fifth Circuit Court of Appeals decided a case holding that mentally challenged juveniles cannot be institutionalized for acts committed before their fourteenth birthday, what states would be bound by this decision?

2. The U.S. Supreme Court has ruled that juveniles do not have a constitutional right to a jury trial. Why is it that in some states, juveniles do have this right?

3. Was the formation of the juvenile court in Cook County the first sign that children were being viewed and treated differently from adults? Explain.

4. Who were the child-savers? Why do you believe women took the role of child advocates in the early twentieth century?

5. Why did the early juvenile court consider constitutional protections for juveniles as unnecessary and as an impediment to rehabilitation?

6. In terms of court organization, what are some problems with today's juvenile court? What are two proposed alternatives for addressing these problems?

7. What is the maximum time that professional associations recommend for a juvenile's case to be heard by the court? What are the potential consequences for a juvenile when case disposition times exceed the maximum time?

8. Juvenile defense attorneys are characterized as either social workers or client-advocates. Explain this distinction in detail.

9. List and discuss the potential benefits and drawbacks of integrating juvenile cases into the adult system and providing juveniles a youth discount based only on age.

10. List and discuss the various role responsibilities of a juvenile court judge.

KEY TERMS AND DEFINITIONS

case disposition: The time it takes for a case to reach the juvenile court once it has been petitioned.

case processing: The time it takes for the juvenile court to decide a case once it reaches the court.

child-savers: Child advocates in the early twentieth century who were responsible for a variety of social reforms for children. They are credited for helping to establish the world's first juvenile court.

court workload: The number of cases petitioned to the juvenile court each year.

double jeopardy: Being punished more than once for the same offense.

dual court system: The two court systems of the United States, one for federal cases and the other for state cases.

dual sovereignty: The concept that federal and state governments are sovereign in their own right.

en banc: A decision made by an appellate court as one body—that is, by all of the justices on the court or Court.

general jurisdiction trial courts: Courts that have jurisdiction over criminal and civil cases. These courts sometimes have jurisdiction over juvenile cases.

guardian ad litem (also called a **court-appointed special advocate [CASA]**): A youth advocate whose responsibility is to represent a child's best interests. A guardian ad litem is usually involved in cases of dependency or neglect when the parents are not available. Usually citizen volunteers, some guardians ad litem must be lawyers if state law requires it.

Illinois Juvenile Court Act of 1899: Act of the Illinois Legislature that established the world's first juvenile court.

judicial precedent: The concept that decisions of courts have value as precedent for future cases with similar facts and circumstances.

juvenile court administrators: Staff members who coordinate activities of the juvenile court at the direction of the juvenile court judge. Juvenile court administrators may be responsible for budgeting, hiring and firing court personnel, monitoring cases on the court's docket, and coordinating treatment services for juveniles. Their roles are diverse.

juvenile court masters (or **referees, magistrates, or commissioners**): Usually, lawyers authorized to hear certain juvenile cases involving minor delinquency and detention hearings. They do not have full hearing authority like the juvenile court judge and may not generally preside over cases involving serious delinquency or waiver hearings.

limited jurisdiction trial courts: Courts with jurisdiction over certain cases such as misdemeanors and local ordinance violations. Juvenile courts are sometimes considered to be limited jurisdiction trial courts.

rule of four: A rule providing that the Supreme Court needs the votes of at least four justices to consider a case on its merits.

special jurisdiction trial courts: Courts that have jurisdiction in special matters or cases. Juvenile courts are sometimes considered special jurisdiction courts because they hear only juvenile cases.

stare decisis: Literally, "to abide by, or adhere to, decided cases." When a court has laid down a principle of law applicable to a set of certain facts and circumstances, it will follow that principle in all future cases with similar facts and circumstances. Abiding by cases decided sets judicial precedent.

youth discount: A proposal by those who want to abolish the juvenile court. With a youth discount, all juveniles could be dealt with in adult court but receive a discount on their sentence based on their age. For example, a youth who is sixteen may receive only a portion of what an adult would receive for a similar crime (66 percent of an adult sentence, or a discount of 33 percent).

 FOR FURTHER RESEARCH

❑ **Juvenile Court Statistics 1999**
http://ncjrs.org/html/ojjdp/201241/index.html

❑ **Reentry Courts Process Evaluation (Phase 1), Final Report**
http://www.ncjrs.org/pdffiles1/nij/grants/204272.pdf

❑ **Abolish the Juvenile Court: Youthfulness, Criminal Responsibility, and Sentencing Policy**
http://campus.westlaw.com/Welcome/WestlawCampus/default.
wl?RS=imp1.0&VR=2.0&SP=samhous2000&FN=_top&MT=
Westlaw&SV=Full

❑ **Re-Imagining Childhood and Reconstructing the Legal Order: The Case for Abolishing the Juvenile Court**
http://campus.westlaw.com/Welcome/WestlawCampus/default.
wl?RS=imp1.0&VR=2.0&SP=samhous-2000&FN=_top&MT=
Westlaw&SV=Full

❑ **A *Parens Patriae* Figure or Impartial Fact Finder: Policy Questions and Conflicts for the Juvenile Court Judge**
http://md2.csa.com/htbin/ids64/procskel.cgi

For an up-to-date list of web links, go to the Juvenile Justice Companion Website at **http://cj.wadsworth.com/del_carmen_trulson_jj**

CHAPTER 8

Adjudication of Juveniles

© Joel Gordon

The Past and the Present / 245
    Adjudication of Juveniles in the Past / 245
    Adjudication of Juveniles Today / 246

Juvenile Adjudication Compared with Adult Criminal Trial / 246
    Similarities to the Adult Trial / 246
    Differences with the Adult Trial / 247

Procedures During Adjudication / 247
    The Arraignment / 247
    The Plea / 248
        Plea of Not Guilty / 248
        Plea of Guilty / 248
        Plea of *Nolo Contendere* (No Contest) / 249
    The Selection of Jurors (in Cases Tried Before a Jury) / 249
        Challenge for Cause / 249
        Peremptory Challenge / 249
    The Presentation of the Case for the Prosecution / 250
    The Presentation of the Case for the Defense / 250
    The Closing Arguments / 250
    The Judge's Instructions to the Jury / 251
    Jury Deliberation / 251
    The Verdict / 251

The Rights of Juveniles During Trial / 252
    In re Gault (1967): The Leading Case in Juvenile Adjudication / 252

The Right to a Lawyer / 253
    At What Stages Does a Juvenile Have a Right to a Lawyer? / 254
    How Is a Lawyer Obtained? / 255
    What Is the Role of a Defense Lawyer for Juveniles? / 256

The Privilege Against Self-Incrimination / 256
    The Privilege of the Alleged Offender / 256
    The Privilege of a Witness / 257
    Distinctions Between the Two Privileges / 257

The Right to Notice of the Charges / 257
The Right Against Double Jeopardy: *Breed v. Jones* (1975) / 258
The Right to Due Process / 258
The Right to Proof of Guilt Beyond a Reasonable Doubt / 259
    The *In re Winship* Case / 259
    What Is Reasonable Doubt? / 260

Waiver of Constitutional Rights / 261

Constitutional Rights During Trial Not Given to Juveniles / 262
    No Right to a Trial by Jury / 262
    No Right to a Public Trial / 264

The Exclusionary Rule and Juvenile Adjudication / 265

Case Brief: *In re Winship* / 260

IN THIS CHAPTER YOU WILL LEARN

- That there are similarities and differences between juvenile and adult proceedings.

- That juvenile delinquency cases are processed more formally than status and dependency and neglect cases.

- That juvenile proceedings can vary in practice from one state to another.

- That the procedure in juvenile delinquency cases generally consists of arraignment, plea, selection of jurors, presentation of the case for the prosecution, presentation of the case for the defense, closing arguments, judge's instructions to the jury, jury deliberation, and verdict.

- That juveniles now enjoy basic constitutional rights during trial.

- That the leading case in juvenile law is *In re Gault* (1967), which gave juveniles four constitutional rights and paved the way for other constitutional rights.

- That the right to a jury trial and the right to a public trial have not been given to juveniles.

- That the exclusionary rule applies to juvenile adjudication.

INTRODUCTION

As noted in previous chapters, juvenile courts in many states have jurisdiction over, and therefore adjudicate, three types of cases: juvenile delinquency, status offenses (conduct in need of supervision), and dependency and neglect cases. However, this chapter deals mainly with the adjudication of juvenile delinquency, referring generally to offenses that if committed by adults would constitute a violation of criminal laws. The chapter also applies to juvenile cases that have been waived to or transferred to adult court. Note that juvenile courts do not hear cases involving offenders who have been waived to adult court. Once transferred, these juvenile cases are treated just like adult criminal cases, and the penalties imposed, if the accused is found guilty, are the same as those given to adult offenders.

Adjudication of juvenile cases differs slightly from state to state. In general, status offense cases are handled informally and in a nonadversarial fashion. These are offenses that if committed by adults would not be punishable and are therefore minor offenses (see Exhibit 8.1). Dependency and neglect cases are handled even more informally because they resemble social welfare cases, with the child being a victim rather than an offender. The twin goals of the court in dependency and neglect cases are to determine if the child is dependent and neglected and, if the answer is yes, to protect the child.

The Past and the Present
Adjudication of Juveniles in the Past

As noted in previous chapters, juvenile courts in the United States were originally designed to be different from adult courts. Judges were to act as wise parents instead of neutral arbiters in an adversary proceeding. No lawyers were

EXHIBIT 8.1

Juvenile Courts and Status Offenders

Despite their laudable goals, juvenile courts were plagued with contradictions in their first 50 years. Critics saw that salvation was not always the outcome of juvenile court intervention and that institutions for children were sometimes punitive or cruel. Around 1960, new state laws began to place limits on classes of children subject to court intervention. California and New York were among the first states to differentiate between status offenders and delinquents. Other states followed with laws that redefined status offenders in various ways, either by reclassifying them as dependent/neglected children or by creating new jurisdictional categories with appellations such as MINS, CHINS, and PINS (minors/children/persons in need of supervision). These new jurisdictional statutes were at once more specific and more complex than the statutes they replaced. They established new rules of processing and disposition that were largely separate from the rules that applied to delinquents.

Source: Adapted from *The Future of Children: The Juvenile Court* (Center for the Future of Children, the David and Lucile Packard Foundation) 6(3) (Winter 1996): 90. Used by permission.

allowed, rules of evidence were waived, and the juvenile enjoyed no legal or constitutional protections except those voluntarily given by the judge or by state law. This situation led some critics to label early juvenile courts as "kangaroo courts." The early reformers were "appalled by adult procedures and penalties and by the fact that children could be given long prison sentences and mixed in jails with hardened criminals." The reformers believed that society's role was not to determine if the child was guilty or innocent but "what is he, how has he become what he is, and what had best be done in his interest and in the interest of the state to save him from a downward career."[1] The U.S. Supreme Court acknowledged the existence of this practice in the case of *In re Gault* (1967):

> The rules of criminal procedure were therefore altogether inapplicable. The apparent rigidities, technicalities, and harshness which they observed in both substantive and procedural criminal law were therefore to be discarded. The idea of crime and punishment was to be abandoned. The child was to be "treated" and "rehabilitated" and the procedures, from apprehension through institutionalization, were to be "clinical" rather than punitive.

Adjudication of Juveniles Today

This original concept that gave birth to juvenile courts in the United States has changed considerably over the years and continues to change. As Peter Greenwood says, "Originally, four basic characteristics distinguished the juvenile court system from the criminal courts: informality in procedures and decorum; a separate detention center for juveniles; contributory delinquency statutes that encouraged the judge to punish adults, primarily parents, who actively contributed to the delinquency of juveniles; and probation."[2] He then goes on to conclude the following about the present juvenile courts: "The informality is largely gone. Juveniles sit with their lawyers like adult defendants. Juvenile hearings or trials proceed along the same lines as criminal trials. The rules of evidence and rights of parties are about the same, except that juveniles still do not have the right to a jury trial or to bail."[3]

These changes have been triggered by two factors. First is the realization by the courts that the informal procedure, driven by *parens patriae*, can be unfair to juveniles because it deprives them of basic due process rights. Second, the public quickly got jaded and started to equate pure *parens patriae* with "coddling the juvenile," who, in some cases, had the same discernment and awareness as adult criminals. Therefore, juveniles deserved to be processed as harshly as adults under the adversarial adult justice system.

Juvenile Adjudication Compared with Adult Criminal Trial
Similarities to the Adult Trial

The similarities between juvenile adjudication and adult criminal trials may be summarized as follows:

- The offender has a constitutional right to due process.
- The offender has a constitutional right to counsel.
- The offender has a constitutional right against self-incrimination.
- The offender has a constitutional right to notice of charges.
- The offender has a constitutional right to confront and cross-examine witnesses.
- Evidence illegally obtained by the police is not admissible for adjudication purposes.

These similarities apply only to juvenile delinquency cases because, as noted previously, status offender and dependency and neglect cases are usually processed informally. The U.S. Supreme Court has not decided whether the same rights apply to status offender and dependency and neglect cases. However, these rights are provided in many states either by state law or by judicial practice.

Differences with the Adult Trial

Juvenile Adjudication	*Adult Criminal Trial*
1. Involves juvenile delinquency, status offending, and dependency and neglect cases.	1. Involves misdemeanors or felonies.
2. Judge acts as wise parent.	2. Judge acts as neutral person.
3. Proceeding is formal or informal.	3. Proceeding is formal.
4. No constitutional right to public trial.	4. Constitutional right to public trial.
5. No constitutional right to jury trial.	5. Constitutional right to jury trial.
6. Grand jury indictment is not used.	6. Grand jury indictment is used in some states.
7. Proceeding is usually confidential.	7. Proceeding is usually public.

As in the case of similarities, differences in juvenile adjudication and adult criminal trial are sometimes made less pronounced by state law or judicial practice. For example, a few states provide that a juvenile will receive a right to a jury trial, although this is not a constitutionally given right.

Procedures During Adjudication[4]
The Arraignment

At a scheduled time and after prior notice, the juvenile is called into court for an **arraignment,** meaning that the juvenile is informed of the charges and asked how he or she pleads. The juvenile's presence during arraignment is generally required. If the juvenile has not been arrested or is free on bail and does not appear, a **bench warrant** or *capias*—a warrant issued by the court for an officer to take a named defendant into custody—will be issued to compel his or her appearance.

The Plea

A **plea** is the response in court to the indictment or information that is read to the accused in court. There are generally three kinds of pleas: not guilty, guilty, and *nolo contendere*.

Plea of Not Guilty

If the juvenile pleads not guilty, the hearing is usually postponed to a later time. This delay is allowed to give both the prosecution and the defense time to prepare their cases. If the defendant refuses to plead, or if the court is not sure of the defendant's plea, the court will enter a not guilty plea. A variation of the not guilty plea is the plea of "not guilty by reason of insanity." This plea means that the offender in fact committed the offense, which often involves a homicide, but is not guilty because the mental state needed for that offense is lacking due to the fact that the defendant was insane at the time of the offense. However, this plea is seldom used in juvenile or adult cases, and when it is used, it rarely succeeds.

Between the not guilty plea and the start of the trial, the defense lawyer often files written motions with the court. One of the most common is a *motion to suppress* evidence that allegedly was illegally seized. This motion requires a hearing, at which time the police officer who made the search testifies to the facts surrounding the seizure of the evidence, and the court determines whether the evidence was legally obtained. If it was illegally obtained, as determined by the judge, the evidence is not admissible in court. Another often-used motion is for a change of venue, which is a request to move the trial to another location. Change of venue requests may be made when there has been massive prejudicial pretrial publicity against the accused, and such publicity might risk a fair trial.

Plea of Guilty

When a juvenile pleads guilty, the court record must show that the plea was voluntary and that the accused had a full understanding of its consequences; otherwise, the plea is not valid. By pleading guilty, the juvenile waives constitutional rights, so judges must make sure that the juvenile knows exactly what he or she is doing and is not forced or coerced into making the plea.

An important part of the guilty plea is plea bargaining. A **plea bargain** is an arrangement whereby a juvenile agrees to plead guilty to an offense in exchange for a lower charge, a lower sentence, or other considerations favorable to the accused, such as a withdrawal of waiver petition to adult court. Noted authors LaFave, Israel, and King identify three forms of plea bargaining: (1) "an arrangement whereby the defendant and prosecutor agree that the defendant should be permitted to plead guilty to a charge less serious than is supported by the evidence"; (2) "an agreement whereby the defendant pleads 'on the nose,' that is, to the original charge, in exchange for some kind of a promise from the prosecutor concerning the sentence to be imposed"; and (3) an arrangement whereby the defendant pleads guilty "to one charge in exchange for the prosecutor's promise to drop or not to file other charges."[5]

Plea of Nolo Contendere *(No Contest)*

Most juvenile cases are uncontested, meaning that the juvenile pleads guilty or *nolo contendere*. A *nolo contendere* plea literally means "no contest." Under this plea, the defendant accepts the penalty without admitting guilt. The effect of this plea is the same as that of a guilty plea, but the defendant may benefit in that the plea cannot be used as an admission in any subsequent civil proceeding arising out of the same offense. For example, Juvenile X pleads *nolo contendere* to a criminal charge of driving while intoxicated. Her guilty plea cannot be used as an admission of guilt in a subsequent civil case for damages that may be brought against her by an injured party. The injured party must independently prove liability and not simply rely on the *nolo contendere* plea. By contrast, had Juvenile X pleaded guilty to the charge of driving while intoxicated, the plea could have been used by the injured party against her in a civil case. The guilty plea automatically establishes civil liability and thus relieves the injured party of the burden of proving it by independent evidence.

The Selection of Jurors (in Cases Tried Before a Jury)

Juveniles do not have a constitutional right to a jury trial, and many states do not provide for it. In cases tried before a jury, however, the next stage of the process is the selection of jurors. A **venire** is a group of prospective jurors assembled according to procedures established by state law. Twenty-three of the fifty states use the voter registration list as the sole source of names for selecting potential jurors for jury duty. Ten states and the District of Columbia use a merged list of voters and holders of driver's licenses.[6] Most states have various statutory exemptions for jury duty, the most common of which are undue hardship, bad health, and status as an officer of the court. Many states also exempt people in certain occupations (such as doctors, dentists, members of the clergy, elected officials, police officers, firefighters, teachers, and sole proprietors of businesses) from jury duty.

There are two types of challenges to prospective jury members: challenge for cause and peremptory challenge.

Challenge for Cause

A **challenge for cause** is a dismissal of a juror for causes specified by law. Although the causes vary from state to state, typical causes are that the person is not a qualified voter in the state or county, the person is under indictment for or has been convicted of a felony, the person is insane, the person is a prospective witness for either party in the case, the person served in the grand jury that handed down the indictment, the person has already formed an opinion on the case, or the person is biased for or against the defendant.

Peremptory Challenge

A **peremptory challenge** is a dismissal of a juror for which no reason need be stated. Such challenges are made entirely at the discretion of each party. The number of peremptory challenges allowed varies from one state to another and may also depend on the seriousness of the offense. The more serious the offense, the more challenges may be allowed. For example, the prosecution and the defense might be allowed six peremptory challenges each in misdemeanor cases and twelve each in felony cases. For capital offenses, the number may go as high as sixteen or twenty. However, jurors may not be stricken from the venire through a peremptory challenge as a result of certain factors, such as race or gender. Doing so is unconstitutional.

If tried before a jury, a juvenile is entitled to a **jury of peers.** This does not mean that the jury must be composed of young people. Instead, it means that jury service must not be consciously restricted to a particular group. It also means that jurors must be drawn from a group that represents a reasonable cross-section of the community.

The Presentation of the Case for the Prosecution

The prosecutor starts by presenting evidence in support of the charge. Although physical evidence may be introduced, most evidence is in the form of testimony of witnesses. Witnesses are examined in the following order:

- Direct examination (by the prosecutor)
- Cross-examination (by the defense lawyer)
- Redirect examination (by the prosecutor)
- Recross-examination (by the defense lawyer)

Theoretically, this cycle can go on and on, but the judge usually puts a stop to the examination of witnesses at this stage. After presenting all its evidence, the prosecution rests its case.

The Presentation of the Case for the Defense

When the prosecution has rested, the defendant or the defendant's lawyer opens the defense and offers supporting evidence. Witnesses are examined in the order noted above, with the defense lawyer conducting the direct examination and the prosecutor cross-examining the witness. After presenting all the evidence, the defense rests its case.

The Closing Arguments

In most jurisdictions, the prosecution presents its closing argument first, the defense replies, and the prosecution then offers a final argument to rebut the defense. The prosecution summarizes the evidence and presents theories on how the evidence should be considered to establish the juvenile's guilt. The defense then presents its closing argument. It emphasizes the heavy burden of proof placed on the prosecution to establish all elements of the crime charged beyond a **reasonable doubt** in juvenile delinquency cases and at least a *preponderance of the evidence* in status offense cases. The defense invariably stresses that this obligation has not been met; therefore, the defendant must be set free or charges must be dismissed.

The Judge's Instructions to the Jury

In jury trials, the judge must properly instruct the jury on the law relevant to the charge and the issues raised by the evidence. In some states, judges do this after the closing arguments; other states give judges the option of doing so before or after the closing arguments. An informal conference on instructions is often held among the judge, prosecutor, and defense counsel, but the decision on what instructions to give rests with the judge. Any errors in the instructions can be challenged on appeal. (Exhibit 8.2 discusses some issues about the training and qualifications of juvenile court judges as well as some problems that may occur because of the nature of their position.)

Jury Deliberation

The foreperson of the jury is usually elected by the jury members immediately after the jury has been instructed by the judge and has retired from the courtroom to start its deliberations. Jury deliberations are conducted in secret, and jurors are not subject to subsequent legal inquiry, regardless of their decision. A **hung jury** is one that fails to reach a decision to convict or acquit. How long a jury is to be kept in deliberation before it is dismissed because of deadlock is up to the judge.

The Verdict

In juvenile delinquency cases, the equivalent of being found "guilty" is that the juvenile is "found to have engaged in delinquent conduct." In waiver cases and adult trials, a jury or judge's **verdict** is the pronouncement of guilt or innocence—"guilty" or "not guilty." In most jurisdictions, the jury vote for conviction or acquittal must be unanimous. Failure to reach a unanimous vote either way results in a hung jury. If the jury is dismissed by the judge because it cannot agree on the result, the case may be tried again before another jury. To retry

---

EXHIBIT 8.2

The Training of Juvenile Court Judges

Typically, there is no required experience or training for juvenile court judges. This situation is particularly critical given that law school education and prior practice most often do not prepare a lawyer to handle cases involving juveniles. Most judges learn while on the job, but this valuable experience is lost in many jurisdictions where judges are assigned to the juvenile division for only a short period of time— for example, six months to one year. The lack of training and experience is particularly troublesome given the unique nature of juvenile court work. Handling cases involving children requires knowledge not only of statutory and case law but also of child development and of a community system of social services and its educational and correctional institutions.

Source: Adapted from *The Future of Children: The Juvenile Court* (Center for the Future of Children, the David and Lucile Packard Foundation) 6(3) (Winter 1996): 19. Used by permission.

or not to retry the case is a decision made by the prosecutor. However, there is no constitutional limit on how many times an offender may be tried if the jury cannot agree on a verdict.

The Rights of Juveniles During Trial[7]

The U.S. Supreme Court has given juveniles basic rights during adjudication. These rights cannot be taken away by federal or state law, although they can be waived. However, many states give juveniles more rights than those given in the Constitution. Here are two examples:

- The Constitution does not guarantee a juvenile the right to appeal a criminal conviction, but the federal government and all states provide for the right to appeal, either by state law (or federal law for federal cases) or by a provision of the state constitution.

- There is no constitutional right to a jury trial in juvenile proceedings, but it may be given by state law.

Until 1967, juveniles were not deemed entitled to constitutional rights during adjudication. Juvenile courts were first established in 1899, but for sixty-eight years the U.S. Supreme Court did not decide any major case involving the constitutional rights of juveniles during trial. Those "hands-off" years resulted from the *parens patriae* doctrine. The Court believed there was no need for constitutional rights to be given because juvenile court judges were acting as wise parents, would do the juvenile no harm, and needed discretion to perform their function properly. However, this attitude changed in 1967 with the *In re Gault* case. From then on, the ground rules became different for juveniles.

In re Gault (1967): The Leading Case in Juvenile Adjudication[8]

On June 8, 1964, fifteen-year-old Gerald Gault and a friend were taken into custody as a result of a complaint that they had made lewd phone calls to a woman. Gault's parents were not informed that he was in custody. The parents were never shown the complaint that was filed against their son. The complainant did not appear at any hearing, and no written record was made at the hearings. Gault was committed to the Arizona State Industrial School as a delinquent until he reached the age of majority, a total of six years from the date of the hearing. The maximum punishment for an adult found guilty of the same offense was a fine from $5 to $50, or imprisonment for a maximum of two months.

Gault appealed his conviction, claiming it was unconstitutional because he was not given constitutional rights during the adjudication hearing. The Court agreed, saying that juveniles are entitled to constitutional due process rights in proceedings (such as an adjudication of delinquency) that might result in commitment to an institution where their freedom would be curtailed. Ruling that juveniles have a right to due process (interpreted as fundamental fairness), the Court gave them four constitutional rights during adjudication:

- The right to counsel, his or her own, or given by the state if the juvenile is indigent
- The right against self-incrimination
- The right to reasonable notice of the charges
- The right to confront and cross-examine witnesses

In re Gault is the most important case ever decided by the U.S. Supreme Court in juvenile justice because it signaled a shift from the pure *parens patriae* model in juvenile justice (where juveniles did not have any constitutional rights during adjudication) to a due process model (where juveniles are given certain constitutional rights). After almost seven decades since the founding of juvenile courts in the United States in 1899, the *Gault* case formally reshaped the legal adjudication landscape by giving juveniles constitutional rights during adjudication, if that adjudication could result in the juvenile being sent to an institution where freedom would be curtailed. Once that breakthrough was made, other constitutional rights followed.

The *Gault* case is doubtless significant, but its reach is limited because it applies only if the adjudication could result in the juvenile being sent to a "secure" institution. In most states, this applies only to juvenile delinquency proceedings, not status offense proceedings, because the most severe penalty in status offense cases is usually probation or service in the community. However, states may give juveniles these rights even in status offense proceedings, thus affording juveniles more rights than those required by the Constitution.

The Right to a Lawyer

The Sixth Amendment to the Constitution provides that "in all criminal prosecutions, the accused shall enjoy the right . . . to have the Assistance of Counsel for his defence." As noted previously, this constitutional right has been given to juveniles in juvenile delinquency proceedings. In *Gault* the Court said the following: "We conclude that the Due Process Clause of the Fourteenth Amendment requires that in respect of proceedings to determine delinquency which may result in commitment to an institution in which the juvenile's freedom is curtailed, the child and his parents must be notified of the child's right to be represented by counsel retained by them, or if they are unable to afford counsel, that counsel will be appointed to represent the child."

The right to counsel is constitutionally guaranteed, but there are indications that in juvenile cases it is not used very frequently. For example, in an analysis of data from six states, Barry Feld found that a number of jurisdictions did not appoint juveniles counsel in a majority of cases.[9] Although Feld found that more serious offenders were usually afforded counsel, and that larger urban jurisdictions did a better job appointing counsel than other jurisdictions, the implication from this study is that a large number of delinquents who face the juvenile court may not benefit from having a lawyer.[10]

Juveniles might not be represented by counsel in juvenile court for a variety of reasons. One reason is that the constitutional right to counsel given in *Gault* was meant to apply only to delinquents facing possible institutionalization. Thus, unless state law provides otherwise, juveniles not facing institutionalization do not have a constitutional right to counsel. Additionally, a number of states have laws that give the juvenile court judge power or discretion to determine the appointment of counsel. For example, Caeti, Hemmens, and Burton found that twenty-six states give the juvenile court judge discretion to determine the appointment of counsel in juvenile cases.[11] This discretion may vary because of a number of criteria, but most important may be the seriousness of the offense for which the juvenile is charged. Juveniles who commit serious offenses and are facing serious consequences (such as institutionalization) may always be appointed counsel because it is their constitutional right, whereas less serious juveniles, such as a juvenile charged with vandalism, may not. Although states could provide these less serious juveniles with a right to a lawyer, the twenty-six states mentioned above give the juvenile court judge discretion to determine appointment of counsel.

Another important reason that many juveniles go without counsel, even those facing possible institutionalization, is that they simply waive their right to counsel. A 2004 publication by the Office of Juvenile Justice and Delinquency Prevention (OJJDP) found that "in some jurisdictions, as many as 80 to 90 percent of youth waive their right to an attorney because they do not know the meaning of the word 'waive' or understand its consequences."[12] Although no comparative figures are readily available for adult offenders, a safe estimate is that the number of adult offenders who waive their right to an attorney is likely much less than the 80–90-percent figure quoted for juveniles. Moreover, the same study says that "state studies of juvenile access to counsel indicate that most juvenile cases—often as many as 90 percent—result in a plea bargain."[13] In plea-bargained cases, the role of the lawyer is not as crucial as in a trial, and may explain the lack of lawyer presence in many processed juvenile cases.

To be sure, there are many other explanations for the lack of counsel for juveniles, such as high juvenile caseloads and overburdened public defender systems.[14] But the bottom line for access to counsel for juveniles is perhaps best stated by Taylor, Fritsch, and Caeti, who maintain that "while the right to counsel exists, provision of an attorney to juveniles is conditional in many states."[15] Access to counsel is conditional upon state law, whether the youth waives his or her rights, and whether or not a plea bargain is used to resolve the case. Additionally, the right to counsel given in the *Gault* decision is conditional in that the juvenile delinquent must be facing possible institutionalization. The outcome of the conditional nature of the right to counsel is that many juveniles may never receive a lawyer when facing the juvenile court and juvenile justice system.

At What Stages Does a Juvenile Have a Right to a Lawyer?

Is a juvenile entitled to a lawyer only during adjudication or throughout the whole juvenile justice process—from arrest to an appeal of a conviction? This issue has not been specifically addressed by the Court, but an analogy to adult criminal proceedings is appropriate. An adult defendant has the right to be represented by a lawyer at "every critical stage" of the criminal proceeding. Although Court decisions on the extent of the right to a lawyer involve adult defendants, there is every reason to believe (and most courts assume) that the same rights apply to juveniles, at least in delinquency cases. Some states provide a lawyer in all types of juvenile cases and at all stages. The *Juvenile Justice Standards* of the Institute for Judicial Administration–American Bar Association includes a recommendation that "juveniles must be represented by counsel from the earliest stages of the court process."[16]

The Court has held that for purposes of triggering the *Miranda* warnings, a request by a juvenile to see his or her probation officer is not equivalent to asking for a lawyer.[17] Probation officers and lawyers perform different functions. The same case held that communications between a probation officer and a probationer are not shielded by the lawyer–client privilege, which ensures absolute confidentiality between the lawyer and the client. In other words, anything a juvenile tells a probation officer, even in confidence, can be required by the judge to be disclosed in court.

How Is a Lawyer Obtained?

As in any juvenile or adult criminal case, the services of a lawyer are obtained in two ways: retained by the defendant or appointed by the court. **Retained counsel** is an attorney chosen and paid for by the offender. The state provides a lawyer to indigent defendants. In general, a defendant is indigent if he or she is too poor to hire a lawyer. Standards used by judges to determine indigence include being unemployed, not having a car, not having posted bail, and not having a house. The judge enjoys wide discretion on this issue, and that determination is rarely reversed on appeal. Therefore, the meaning of *indigence* varies from one jurisdiction or judge to another. The method of appointing counsel for an indigent juvenile also varies. In some jurisdictions, judges use a list containing the names of available and willing attorneys, who are then assigned to cases on a rotating basis. In others, judges make assignments at random, sometimes assigning any lawyer who may be available in the courtroom at the time the appointment is made. Still other jurisdictions employ full-time public defenders to handle indigent cases.

A survey by the American Bar Association (ABA) that included responses from all 50 states and from 46 juvenile defenders has found serious problems with representation by juvenile public defenders. Problems included annual caseloads of more than 500 cases, with up to 300 being juvenile cases.[18] Heavy caseloads and lack of funding were identified as the most significant barriers to effective representation of juveniles. In the words of the ABA report:

> Because of the workload, attorneys often are unable to keep their clients appropriately informed and to adequately develop detention and dispositional alternatives. This may lead to the unnecessary secure detention of youth who are not a danger to themselves or the community. . . . Serious gaps also exist in training for juvenile defenders: 78 percent of public defender offices have no budget for lawyers to attend training programs, nor do they have a training program for all new attorneys, an ongoing training program, or a juvenile delinquency section in the office training manual. About 40 percent do not have a specialized manual for juvenile court lawyers, and one-third do not include juvenile delinquency work in their general training unit.[19]

What Is the Role of a Defense Lawyer for Juveniles?

In the U.S. system of justice, the loyalty of a defense lawyer is solely to the client, not to the public. A lawyer is not expected to act for the good of the community, but instead is obligated to give the juvenile the best possible defense, whether the client is innocent or guilty. In fact, lawyers have an obligation to defend guilty clients. Some lawyers do not want to know whether their client is innocent or guilty, believing that this knowledge should not affect the way they do their job.

The limitations on the conduct of lawyers when defending a client come from two sources: a professional code of ethics and the penal code. A defense lawyer cannot do that which is unethical or illegal, but working for the good of the public is not among the responsibilities expected of a lawyer when defending a client. However, the role of a lawyer in juvenile cases is difficult to confine within the limits of the traditional defense lawyer's role. Since juvenile proceedings are less adversarial, particularly in status offense cases, should the defense lawyer be less of a client-advocate and more of a family member or social worker who seeks to serve the juvenile's interest by promoting rehabilitation and public protection? Scholars and court observers differ in their views. Some say the lawyer's role does not change in juvenile cases; others maintain there is more room for negotiation and compromise that reconcile the interest of the juvenile and society, particularly if the long-term interest of juvenile rehabilitation is better served. The defense lawyer ultimately decides what role he or she should play.

The Privilege Against Self-Incrimination

The prohibition against compulsory self-incrimination springs from the Fifth Amendment provision that "no person . . . shall be compelled in any criminal case to be a witness against himself." This guarantee is designed to restrain the government from using force, coercion, or other such methods to obtain any statement, admission, or confession. This right was one of the four constitutional rights given to juveniles in the *Gault* case, the Court saying that "It would indeed be surprising if the privilege against self-incrimination were available to hardened criminals but not to children," then adding that the "language of the Fifth Amendment . . . is unequivocal and without exception." However, *In re Gault* was a juvenile delinquency case that involved possible loss of freedom for the juvenile. As noted earlier, the U.S. Supreme Court has not decided whether juveniles have the right against self-incrimination in status offense cases, where loss of freedom (secure institutionalization) is not a disposition option.

The privilege against compulsory self-incrimination during trial is best understood if discussed as two separate privileges: the privilege of the alleged offender and the privilege of a witness.

The Privilege of the Alleged Offender

The juvenile in a criminal case has a **privilege of the accused** not to take the witness stand and not to testify. The Court has ruled that the accused "may stand mute, clothed in the presumption of innocence."[20] Moreover, prosecutors cannot comment on a defendant's assertion of the right not to testify. No conclusion of guilt may be drawn from the failure of the accused to testify during the trial. Therefore, the prosecutor is not permitted to make any comment or argument to the jury suggesting that the defendant is guilty because he or she refused to testify. Once the juvenile takes the witness stand in his or her own defense, however, the privilege against self-incrimination ceases. The juvenile must then answer all relevant inquiries about the crime. Refusal to answer can mean contempt of court. This is one reason that many defense lawyers do not want the accused to take the witness stand, particularly if the accused is a poor witness, has a bad record, or has a background that is better kept undisclosed.

The Privilege of a Witness

Any witness, except an accused on the witness stand, has the **privilege of the witness** to refuse to disclose any information that may "tend to incriminate" him or her. The reason for this is that the witness is not on trial; he or she is in court merely to provide information about what happened. A question tends to incriminate a witness if the answer would directly or indirectly implicate that witness in the commission of a crime. The privilege does not apply if the answer merely exposes the witness to civil liability, however, but if the facts would make the witness subject to criminal liability, the privilege can be claimed. Moreover, the privilege cannot be claimed merely because the answer would hold the witness up to shame, disgrace, or embarrassment.

Distinctions Between the Two Privileges

The Offender	*The Witness*
1. The juvenile cannot be forced to testify. Refusal cannot be commented on by the prosecution.	1. A witness can be forced to testify if ordered by the court. Refusal can result in a contempt citation.
2. The juvenile who testifies cannot refuse to answer incriminating questions because the privilege is considered waived.	2. A witness who testifies can refuse to answer questions that might result in criminal prosecution.

The Right to Notice of the Charges

The right to notice of charges was the third right given to juveniles in the *Gault* case and is best understood in the context of that case. The juvenile claimed in *Gault* that the proceedings in the juvenile court were constitutionally defective because "no notice was given to Gerald's parents when he was taken into custody on Monday, July 8." The juvenile further alleged that "on that night, when Mrs. Gault went to the Detention Home, she was orally informed that there would be a hearing the next afternoon and was told the reason why Gerald was in custody." But the only written notice that Gerald's parents received at any time in connection with their son's case was a note on plain paper from the arresting officer to the effect that the judge had set a certain date for further hearing on the issue of Gerald's delinquency. The Court said that this constituted improper notification:

We cannot agree with the court's conclusion that adequate notice was given in this case. Notice, to comply with the due process requirements, must be given sufficiently in advance of scheduled court proceedings so that reasonable opportunity to prepare will be afforded, and it must "set forth the alleged misconduct with particularity."

Without proper notice in the form of a formal written charge, a juvenile will not know the charges and how to prepare a defense. The Court implied that surprise and uncertainty have no place in an adult or juvenile trial.

The Right Against Double Jeopardy: *Breed v. Jones* (1975)

The Fifth Amendment to the U.S. Constitution provides that "no person shall be . . . subject for the same Offense to be twice put in jeopardy of life or limb." In the case of *Breed v. Jones* (1975), the U.S. Supreme Court held that a juvenile who has been adjudicated in juvenile court cannot be tried again on the same charge as an adult in a criminal court because such would constitute double jeopardy.[21] The facts in *Breed v. Jones* are that on February 9, 1971, a petition was filed in Los Angeles County Juvenile Court alleging that a seventeen-year-old juvenile committed acts that, if committed by an adult, would constitute robbery with a deadly weapon. A detention hearing was held, and the accused was ordered to be detained pending a hearing on the petition. At the adjudicatory hearing, the juvenile court found the allegations to be true and ordered further detention. At the disposition hearing, the juvenile court found the offender unfit for treatment as a juvenile and therefore ordered that he be prosecuted as an adult. The juvenile was subsequently found guilty of robbery in an adult court. The juvenile appealed, claiming a violation of his constitutional right against double jeopardy because he was adjudicated in the juvenile court and then tried for the same offense in an adult criminal court. The Court agreed, saying that the right against double jeopardy applies to juveniles.

Breed v. Jones is significant for two reasons: (1) it extends the double jeopardy protection to juvenile proceedings, and (2) it implies that juvenile proceedings, although deemed civil proceedings (to which double jeopardy does not apply), do in fact have criminal consequences and are therefore considered criminal trials for the purposes of adjudication. The Court concluded that "Respondent was subject to the burden of two trials for the same offense; he was twice put to the task of marshaling his resources against those of the State, twice subjected to the 'heavy personal strain' which such an experience represents." The implication of this case is clear: If a juvenile is transferred to an adult court for prosecution, that transfer must be made before a juvenile is adjudicated in juvenile court. If the youth is waived to adult court after an adjudication hearing, double jeopardy attaches, and the juvenile cannot be retried.

The Right to Due Process

Section 1 of the Fourteenth Amendment provides that "No state shall make or enforce any law which shall abridge the privileges or immunities of citizens of the United States; nor shall any state deprive any person of life, liberty, or property, without due process of law; nor deny to any person within its jurisdiction the equal protection of the laws." The four constitutional rights given to juveniles in *In re Gault* all come under due process in its broadest sense: The right to a lawyer, the right against self-incrimination, the right to reasonable notice of charges, and the right to confront and cross-examine witnesses are all components of the broad concept of due process.

Due process generally means "fundamental fairness," but it really has no fixed meaning. What process is due varies from one proceeding to another, depending on the type of proceeding and what is at stake. For example, due process during a juvenile delinquency case is different from due process in a juvenile probation or parole revocation proceeding, in a disciplinary proceeding when a juvenile is in a secure institution, or when a juvenile is facing an expulsion hearing from school. The rights given in a particular proceeding are ultimately decided by the courts.

Due process is most highly protected during criminal trials involving either a juvenile or an adult. As part of the due process requirement, the prosecutor is duty-bound to disclose evidence favorable to a defendant. Failure to disclose "exculpatory" evidence violates a defendant's constitutional rights. For example, in the course of an investigation, a prosecutor comes across credible evidence indicating that Juvenile Z was not at the scene of the crime when it was committed. If requested by the defense, the prosecutor must disclose this exculpatory evidence to the defendant. Failure to do that means that the defendant's due process rights were violated and that the conviction must be overturned if appealed.

The Right to Proof of Guilt Beyond a Reasonable Doubt

The requirement that guilt be proved beyond a reasonable doubt derives from the due process clause of the Constitution. The Bill of Rights contains no specific provisions on the degree of certainty needed for conviction, but the assumption is that it would be fundamentally unfair to convict anyone if there was a reasonable doubt that he or she had committed the crime.

The In re Winship *Case*

The U.S. Supreme Court in the case of *In re Winship* (1970)[22] held that proof beyond reasonable doubt is required in juvenile adjudication hearings where the offense charged would have been a crime if committed by an adult (see the "Case Brief"). *Winship* does not say that all juvenile proceedings require proof beyond reasonable doubt. What it says is that all juvenile proceedings in which a juvenile is "charged with an act that would constitute a crime if committed by an adult" are subject to a higher standard of proof. This generally means juvenile delinquency cases. Any other juvenile proceeding that does not fall under this category is governed by the preponderance of the evidence standard, unless state law provides otherwise. The reason for this higher standard is the seriousness of the offense and the possible punishment. Most cases in which a juvenile is charged with a criminal act constitute juvenile delinquency, which can result in institutionalization in a state facility, thus a deprivation of freedom. By contrast, the maximum punishment for status offense cases is usually probation and therefore does not involve any loss of freedom. However, some states require by law that proof beyond reasonable doubt be established even in status offense cases.

What Is Reasonable Doubt?

Reasonable doubt is difficult to define. One court has defined it as follows:

> It is such a doubt as would cause a juror, after careful and candid and impartial consideration of all the evidence, to be so undecided that he cannot say that he has an abiding conviction of the defendant's guilt. It is such a doubt as would cause a reasonable person to hesitate or pause in the graver or more important transactions of life. However, it is not a fanciful doubt nor a whimsical doubt, nor a doubt based on conjecture.[23]

Case Brief

Leading Case on the Need for Guilt Beyond a Reasonable Doubt in Juvenile Cases

In re Winship, 397 U.S. 358 (1970)

Facts: During an adjudication hearing, a New York family court judge found that the juvenile involved, then a 12-year-old boy, had broken into a locker and stolen $112 from a woman's purse. The petition, which charged the juvenile with delinquency, alleged that his act, "if done by an adult, would constitute the crime or crimes of larceny." The judge acknowledged that guilt might not have been established beyond a reasonable doubt but that the New York Family Court Act required that the verdict need be based only on a preponderance of the evidence. At the dispositional hearing, the juvenile was ordered placed in training school for an initial period of 18 months, subject to annual extensions of his commitment until his 18th birthday.

Issue: Does the due process clause of the Fourteenth Amendment require proof beyond a reasonable doubt in a juvenile adjudication?

Court Decision: Proof beyond a reasonable doubt, not simply a preponderance of the evidence, is required during adjudication proceedings if a juvenile is charged with an act that would constitute a crime if committed by an adult.

Case Significance: Juvenile proceedings are technically civil in nature and, as such, are supposedly subject to the "preponderance of the evidence" standard required in civil cases. In this case, however, the Court said that in juvenile cases in which a juvenile is charged with an act that would constitute a crime if committed by an adult, the standard of proof for a finding of guilt is "proof beyond a reasonable doubt." The implication is that although juvenile proceedings are technically civil proceedings, they are in fact considered like criminal proceedings in some instances. This decision gives credence to the assertion by some writers that juvenile proceedings are civil only in name and that in reality they are criminal proceedings and are considered as such by the U.S. Supreme Court.

(continued)

Case Brief   *(continued)*

This case does not hold that all juvenile proceedings require proof beyond a reasonable doubt. What it says is that all juvenile proceedings where a juvenile "is charged with an act that would constitute a crime if committed by an adult" are subject to a higher standard of proof. Other juvenile proceedings that do not fall under this category are governed by the preponderance of the evidence standard, unless state law provides otherwise. The reason for this distinction is the seriousness of the offense and the possible punishment. Most cases in which a juvenile is charged with an act that would constitute a crime if committed by an adult constitute juvenile delinquency, which can result in institutionalization and therefore a deprivation of freedom. On the other hand, CINS (children in need of supervision), MINS (minors in need of supervision), or PINS (persons in need of supervision) cases result in probation or other forms of nonpunitive rehabilitative sanctions and therefore are not subject to the proof beyond a reasonable doubt standard. The exception is if that higher standard is required by state law even for minor offenses or violations.

Source: This brief originally appeared in Rolando V. del Carmen, Mary Parker, and Frances P. Reddington, *Briefs of Leading Cases in Juvenile Justice* (Cincinnati: Anderson, 1998).

This and other definitions used in various jurisdictions are unclear and do not provide a clear rule to guide jurors in their deliberation. In some states, reasonable doubt is defined by law; in other states, the term is defined by case law; and in a few states, there is no definition at all—leaving each court in the state to come up with its own definition. As well, federal courts do not prescribe a single definition.

In reality, despite instructions from the judge (couched in terms similar to those in the definition), an individual juror subjectively determines what is meant by reasonable doubt. Definitions such as the above are too legalistic and difficult to apply for most laypersons. In most cases, they merely provide a general framework for decision making. Ultimately, and because of vagueness, jurors define the term the way they want to define it. Quantifying the term (such as defining reasonable doubt as comparable to 95-percent certainty of guilt) removes some confusion, but quantification is frowned upon by the legal community and is not used in court.

Waiver of Constitutional Rights

The constitutional rights given to juveniles during trial, as is true with other constitutional rights, may be waived. In the case of juveniles, however, waiver of rights can become a problem for the prosecution for two reasons. First, any waiver of a constitutional right must be intelligent and voluntary; otherwise, the waiver is invalid. The burden of establishing a valid waiver rests with the prosecution. Proving that the waiver was intelligent and voluntary in juvenile cases can be challenging, particularly when the juvenile is very young. Judged in terms of awareness of possible consequences, waiver of a constitutional right by a sixteen-year-old is different from a waiver by a ten-year-old. Second, some state laws provide that the juvenile cannot waive a constitutional right alone. The waiver must be made in the presence of or with the consent of parents, a guardian, or a lawyer. The assumption in these cases is that waiver of rights by a juvenile, because of age, can never be intelligent or voluntary. Parents or guardians would likely want to consult a lawyer before waiver, and most lawyers would not want their clients, juvenile or adult, to waive any constitutional right unless the waiver is clearly for the benefit of the client.

Constitutional Rights During Trial Not Given to Juveniles

As this discussion shows, most rights given to adults in criminal trials have now been given to juveniles in adjudication proceedings. However, two constitutional rights given to adults during trial have not been given to juveniles: the right to trial by jury and the right to a public trial.

No Right to a Trial by Jury

The Constitution provides that "The Trial of all Crimes, except in cases of Impeachment, shall be by Jury." The Sixth Amendment also provides that "In all criminal prosecutions, the accused shall enjoy the right to a speedy and public trial, by an impartial jury of the State and district wherein the crime shall have been committed."

The U.S. Supreme Court held in *McKeiver v. Pennsylvania* (1971) that juveniles do not have a constitutional right to trial by jury even in a delinquency proceeding (see the "Controversial Issue" box).[24] In that case, sixteen-year-old Joseph McKeiver was charged with robbery, larceny, and receiving stolen goods—all delinquency offenses. Under Pennsylvania criminal law, these offenses constituted felonies. McKeiver was represented by a lawyer at his adjudication hearing. He requested but was denied trial by jury. McKeiver was convicted and placed on probation. He appealed, claiming that his trial was unconstitutional because he was not afforded the right to trial by jury. The Court disagreed, saying that juveniles have no constitutional right to trial by jury even in a juvenile adjudication hearing. In denying this right, the Court gave the following reasons:

- Requiring a jury trial might remake the proceeding into a fully adversarial process and effectively end the idealistic prospect of an intimate, informal, protective proceeding.

- Imposing a jury trial on the juvenile court system would not remedy the system's defects and would not greatly strengthen its fact-finding function.

- Jury trial would mean delay, formality, and encourage clamor for the adversary system, and possibly a public trial.

- Equating the adjudicative phase of the juvenile proceeding with a criminal trial ignores the aspects of fairness, concern, sympathy, and paternal attention inherent in the juvenile court system.

CONTROVERSIAL ISSUE: WHICH SIDE DO YOU FAVOR?

Should juveniles have the constitutional right to trial by jury?

The U.S. Supreme Court ruled in 1971 (*McKeiver v. Pennsylvania*) that juveniles do not have a constitutional right to trial by jury even in cases where they face confinement in a juvenile institution and are therefore deprived of freedom. The Court said that this would convert the juvenile justice process from *parens patriae* into a full adversarial proceeding, would hasten the time when the adversary system becomes the norm, would not strengthen the fact-finding function of the court, would cause delay, would encourage formality, and would ignore the fairness, concern, sympathy, and paternal attention that have traditionally been the hallmarks of the juvenile court process. Juveniles are different and should be treated differently. Trial by jury does not promote the ends of society. It is better to leave both the adjudication and disposition of a juvenile in the hands of the juvenile court judge, who acts as a wise parent when deciding how best to rehabilitate the youth.

However, trial by jury is given by law in many states, particularly in delinquency cases. Those who support trial by jury say that in cases where a juvenile's freedom is at risk because of the possibility of being sent to an institution, justice requires a jury trial rather than a trial before a judge who may not necessarily act in the juvenile's best interest. Members of the community know better about what is best for the juvenile and for society. The process of rehabilitation is enhanced if the juvenile knows that he or she must deal with members of the community rather than with one judge. Supporters of trial by jury go on to say that the *parens patriae* justification used by the Court in *McKeiver* has been weakened by subsequent decisions that have extended due process and other rights to juveniles. The 1971 decision is out of date because since then juveniles have become subject to more severe penalties imposed by state legislatures for serious juvenile delinquency offenses. If we trust juries to administer justice in adult cases, why do we not trust them to do at least the same in juvenile delinquency cases?

1. If you were a delinquent facing an adjudication hearing, would you rather face a trial by jury or by a juvenile court judge? Explain.

2. Think about and explain the advantages and disadvantages of a trial by a jury from a defense lawyer's perspective and from a prosecutor's perspective.

3. Think about and explain the advantages and disadvantages of a trial by judge from a defense lawyer's perspective and from a prosecutor's perspective.

As noted elsewhere, however, the right to a jury trial may be given by state law. In the *Gault* case (1967), the Court virtually encouraged jury trials: "If, in its wisdom, any state feels the jury trial is desirable in all cases, or in certain kinds, there appears to be no impediment to its installing a system embracing that feature." Some states give juveniles this right, particularly in juvenile delinquency cases. In these states, the number of jury members, their function, and the number of votes needed for conviction vary. Because juvenile proceedings are considered civil or semi-criminal proceedings, some states allow a majority vote by jurors whereas others require unanimity for a verdict.

At present, only four states (Michigan, Massachusetts, Alaska, and West Virginia) provide for a jury trial in *all* juvenile cases. By contrast, other states do not provide a jury trial at all in juvenile cases, whether the charge be for juvenile delinquency or status offending. However, under specified circumstances, some states allow juveniles to have a jury trial, particularly youths charged with serious juvenile delinquency. In all states, once a juvenile is waived or transferred to an adult court, trial by jury becomes a constitutional right because the juvenile is now tried as an adult and ceases being a juvenile.

No Right to a Public Trial

An adult defendant has a right to a **public trial,** meaning a trial that can be seen and heard by persons interested in ensuring that the proceedings are fair and just. However, the right is limited. The trial judge may exclude some or all spectators during particular parts of the proceedings for good cause, but under almost no circumstances may the friends and relatives of the accused be excluded from the trial. Spectators are frequently excluded if necessary to spare a victim extreme public embarrassment or humiliation, as in sexual assault cases. Likewise, a judge may properly exclude certain persons if it can be shown that they are likely to threaten or intimidate witnesses by their presence. Criminal defendants also have a constitutional right to have their pretrial hearings conducted in public. However, the Court has not decided whether the public and the press have a right to attend pretrial hearings when the defendant wants the pretrial hearing conducted in secret.

Juveniles have no constitutional right to a public trial, meaning that the juvenile cannot insist on a public trial even if he or she desires it. In most cases, however, the right not to have a public trial is what the juvenile desires. Many states hold closed juvenile adjudication proceedings and either limit or prohibit press access and reports. These practices are justified by *parens patriae*. However, the practice of a nonpublic trial and confidentiality in juvenile proceedings to protect the juvenile is changing in some states. In the past few years, several states have passed laws allowing victims roles, presence, and participation in juvenile proceedings. Some examples illustrate recent trends:

- A law passed in South Dakota allows a judge to open the courtroom to victims if the offense committed by the juvenile would be a crime of violence if committed by an adult. The law also requires the state's attorney to notify the victim of the time and place of hearings.

- A legislative initiative in Nevada requires the judge to consider the interests of the victim when deciding to close juvenile proceedings for youths charged with certain violent crimes.

- Indiana law mandates that a judge consider the nature of the allegation against a juvenile, together with the age and maturity of the victims, when deciding whether the hearings should be private or open to the public.

■ A provision in the Arizona Bill of Rights for Victims of Juvenile Crime allows victims to be present and heard at any pre-disposition or disposition proceedings. They are also allowed to present to probation officials an impact statement on the effect the juvenile crime had on the victim and the victim's immediate family.[25]

Related to public juvenile hearings, another troubling issue is whether juvenile court records should remain confidential. The "You Are a . . . State Legislator" box asks you to consider this issue.

The Exclusionary Rule and Juvenile Adjudication

The **exclusionary rule** provides that any evidence obtained by law enforcement officers in violation of the Fourth Amendment prohibition against unreasonable search and seizure is not admissible in a criminal prosecution to prove guilt. The U.S. Supreme Court held in *Mapp v. Ohio* (1961) that evidence obtained without probable cause and a valid search warrant is not admissible in

---

YOU ARE A... → State Legislator

Are you in favor of making juvenile records public? Juvenile delinquency records are confidential in most states, meaning that juvenile records cannot be accessed by the public unless access is authorized by legislation. Unauthorized disclosure can lead to administrative, civil, and criminal proceedings. This policy is designed to protect the juvenile from being labeled a criminal at an early age and ensures that mistakes which juveniles make in the past will not predetermine their future. The assumption is that juveniles regret what they did at an early age and should be given every chance to rehabilitate and lead a normal life without being hounded by past misdeeds. The public loses much when a juvenile is known as and branded a criminal at an early age, taking away chances for the juvenile to start afresh when reaching the age of majority. The young make mistakes; they should not have to live with those mistakes forever.

However, the strict confidentiality of juvenile records is eroding. Some states now make juvenile records available to the public, to law enforcement, to corrections personnel, and even to schools. This information may include fingerprints, pictures,

identity, place of residence, and the nature and history of their offenses. In some cases, laws authorize juveniles to be identified in public as serious offenders, particularly in sexual assault and other violent offenses. This change is partly a response to high-profile cases in which neighbors and friends became victims because they did not know a juvenile's background. Reducing confidentiality also caters to a need to monitor juveniles with past records so that future crimes are prevented and, if the juvenile is in an institution, rehabilitation is aided. Those dealing with juveniles, be they police officers, school authorities, probation and parole authorities, or those working in correctional institutions, should know a juvenile's background so they can more effectively attend to the juvenile's needs.

The confidentiality of juvenile records presents a classic confrontation between the rights of the juvenile and those of the public. As a legislator, which side will you choose? If you are not comfortable with an either-or policy of full disclosure or no disclosure at all, what exceptions will you suggest?

state criminal cases.[26] The purpose of the exclusionary rule is to deter police misconduct, the assumption being that if evidence obtained illegally is not admissible in court, police misconduct in search and seizure cases will decline or stop.

The exclusionary rule generally applies to juvenile adjudication hearings, meaning that if the evidence was obtained by the police illegally, the evidence cannot be admitted in court to prove the juvenile's guilt. For example, the police seize a gun from J., a fifteen-year-old juvenile. The gun turns out to be a murder weapon. If the stop and search that led to the seizure is illegal (as later determined by the court), the weapon cannot be admissible in court. Moreover, any evidence later obtained as a result of the illegal stop and seizure cannot be admitted into evidence either. For instance, police officers force H, a juvenile, to confess to selling cocaine. In H's confession, he says that more cocaine can be found in his parents' house. Neither the confession nor the cocaine obtained from the parents' house is admissible in court during adjudication. In sum, anything obtained by the police *after* an illegal act on their part cannot be admitted in court, whether the evidence is obtained directly (the confession) or indirectly (the cocaine).

Although the Court has not directly addressed the issue, chances are that illegally seized evidence is acceptable in nonadjudication hearings, such as probation revocation and school disciplinary hearings: The exclusionary rule prohibits the admission of illegally seized evidence only in a proceeding that establishes guilt. The evidence may be admissible in an administrative proceeding in which guilt is not the main issue.

SUMMARY

- ❏ The adjudication of delinquency cases generally resembles adult trials; the adjudication of CINS and dependency and neglect cases is more informal.
- ❏ The role of a judge in a juvenile adjudication hearing is that of a wise parent, not of a neutral arbiter.
- ❏ *In re Gault,* decided in 1967 by the U.S. Supreme Court, holds that juveniles are entitled to basic constitutional rights in proceedings that can result in a juvenile's commitment to an institution in which his or her freedom is curtailed.
- ❏ *In re Gault* is the most significant case decided by the U.S. Supreme Court in juvenile justice because for the first time juveniles were given constitutional rights during adjudication.
- ❏ The U.S. Supreme Court has held in various cases that juveniles are entitled to the following constitutional rights during adjudication: the right to a lawyer, the privilege against self-incrimination, notice of charges, right against double jeopardy, right to due process, and right to proof of guilt beyond a reasonable doubt.
- ❏ Rights not given by the Constitution may be given by state law.
- ❏ Juveniles may waive their constitutional rights, but the waiver must be intelligent and voluntary.

❑ Juveniles do not have the following constitutional rights during trial: the right to trial by jury and the right to a public trial. However, these rights are given in some states by law.

❑ The exclusionary rule applies to juvenile adjudication.

REVIEW QUESTIONS

1. How has the role of juvenile court judges changed over the years?
2. Discuss the similarities and then the differences between juvenile adjudication and adult criminal trial.
3. Prior to 1967, juveniles were not given constitutional rights during trial. Explain why.
4. Why are juveniles not entitled to the constitutional right of trial by jury?
5. What did the Court say in *In re Gault*? Why is that case significant?
6. "A juvenile is entitled to a lawyer only during adjudication." Is this statement true or false? Explain.
7. Discuss how lawyers for indigent juveniles are chosen by courts.
8. Distinguish between the right against self-incrimination of an offender and that of a witness.
9. What does the case of *Breed v. Jones* say, and why is this case important for juveniles?
10. What does the case of *McKeiver v. Pennsylvania* say? Is this case important?
11. Explain what is meant by "reasonable doubt," and then explain why this term is hard for jurors to apply.

KEY TERMS AND DEFINITIONS

arraignment: Informing the juvenile of the charges in court and asking how he or she pleads.

bench warrant (also called a *capias*): A warrant issued by the court for an officer to take a named defendant into custody.

challenge for cause: A challenge seeking the dismissal of a juror for causes specified by law.

exclusionary rule: A rule providing that any evidence obtained by law enforcement officers in violation of the Fourth Amendment prohibition against unreasonable search and seizure is not admissible in a criminal prosecution to prove guilt.

hung jury: A jury that cannot agree to convict or acquit the defendant.

jury of peers: A jury that is not consciously restricted to a particular group.

peremptory challenge: Disqualification of a juror, by the defense or the prosecution, for which no reason is given.

plea: Response by the juvenile in court to the indictment or information.

plea bargain: An arrangement whereby a juvenile agrees to plead guilty to an offense in exchange for a lower charge, a lower sentence, or other considerations favorable to the juvenile, such as a withdrawal of waiver petition to adult court.

privilege of the accused: The Fifth Amendment right of the accused not to answer incriminating questions or to take the witness stand. If the accused takes the witness stand, he or she must answer incriminating questions.

privilege of a witness: The right of a witness not to answer incriminating questions while on the witness stand.

public trial: A trial open to all persons interested in ensuring that the proceedings are fair and just.

reasonable doubt: "Such a doubt as would cause a juror, after careful and candid and impartial consideration of all the evidence, to be so undecided that he or she cannot say that he or she has an abiding conviction of the defendant's guilt."

retained counsel: A lawyer paid by the defendant, not by the state.

venire: A group of prospective jurors assembled according to procedures established by state law.

verdict: The pronouncement of guilt or innocence at the end of a trial.

 FOR FURTHER RESEARCH

❑ **Juvenile Court Placement of Adjudicated Youth**
   http://www.ncjrs.org/txtfiles1/ojjdp/fs200202.txt

❑ **Collateral Consequences of Juvenile Proceedings**
   http://www.abanet.org/crimjust/juvjus/cjmcollconseq1.html

❑ **Court Appointed Special Advocate Program**
   http://ojjdp.ncjrs.org/Programs/ProgSummary.asp?pi=14&ti=3&si=
   12&kw=&strItem=&strSingleItem=&p=topic&PreviousPage=SearchResults

❑ **Delays in Juvenile Court Processing of Delinquency Cases**
   http://www.ncjrs.org/txtfiles/fs-9760.txt

❑ **How Juveniles Get to Criminal Court**
   http://www.ncjrs.org/pdffiles/juvcr.pdf

For an up-to-date list of web links, go to the Juvenile Justice Companion Website at **http://cj.wadsworth.com/del_carmen_trulson_jj**

CHAPTER 9

Disposition and Appeal

© Joel Gordon

Disposition / 271

    The Goals of Disposition: Ideals Versus Reality / 272
    Discretion in Dispositions / 276
    When Disposition Takes Place / 276
    The Disposition Plan / 278
    Roles During Dispositions / 278

Kinds of Dispositions / 279

    Placement in an Institution / 280
    Probation / 281
    Other Sanctions That Leave the Juvenile in the
    Community / 282
        Community Service / 282
        Fines / 283
        Restitution / 283
        Electronic Monitoring / 284
        Other Disposition Alternatives / 285
    The Death Penalty / 285

Blended Sentencing / 286

Legal and Constitutional Issues in Dispositions / 289

    The Rights of Juveniles During Dispositions / 289
        The Right to Counsel / 289
        The Right of Allocution / 289

The Use of Illegally Obtained Evidence in Dispositions / 289
Juveniles and "Three Strikes and You're Out" Sentences / 292
Juveniles Confined Longer Than Adults for Similar
Offenses / 293
The Use of Juvenile Records If Later Sentenced as an
Adult / 293
Punishing Parents for What Their Children Do / 294

Juveniles and the Right to Appeal / 296

    Juveniles May Appeal a Conviction and Disposition / 296
    Juveniles May Be Released While an Appeal Is Pending / 296
    Appeal Distinguished from Habeas Corpus / 297

**Towards a More Progressive Approach to Juvenile
Disposition / 297**

Case Brief: *Haley v. Ohio* **/ 290**

IN THIS CHAPTER YOU WILL LEARN

- That disposition has various goals.

- That rehabilitation has traditionally been the main goal of disposition but that this may not be true in reality and practice.

- That judges have great discretion in dispositions but that judicial discretion is sometimes limited by state law.

- That blended sentencing blurs the line between juvenile and adult systems and why more states are using it.

- The many kinds of dispositions and the differences among them.

- The legal and constitutional issues raised in dispositions.

- The differences between appeal and habeas corpus.

INTRODUCTION

Disposition follows after a juvenile is found to have engaged in the act alleged by the prosecutor. It is the equivalent of adult sentencing but is different in that the disposition imposed is usually set by law within broad limits, leaving juvenile court judges much discretion about the type and duration of sanctions to be imposed. Juvenile court judges enjoy more discretion than adult court judges do in the punishment stage and therefore can be more creative and innovative. That discretion is given to promote rehabilitation. This approach is consistent with the traditional role played by judges in juvenile justice, which is that of a wise parent who acts for and in the best interests of the child. However, that role has changed over the years because experience shows that the original concept of *parens patriae* does not always lead to the best interests of the child being served. Moreover, judicial discretion is disfavored by the general public when a juvenile commits a serious offense. In high-profile cases, the public often wants juveniles to get their "just dessert," just like adults.

The trend in juvenile justice disposition in the last decade is toward more punitive punishment for juveniles. This movement was triggered several years ago by the rapid rise in serious crimes committed by juveniles at that time. Serious juvenile crime rates have since decreased, but more punitive disposition alternatives have become part of the laws in many states and are there to stay. The most significant shift away from rehabilitation is blended sentencing, the practice whereby youths may be sanctioned under the juvenile justice system and/or the adult justice system.

Despite the move to "adultify" juvenile dispositions, the types of dispositional alternatives available to judges remain basically the same as they have been since juvenile courts were first created in the United States more than a century ago. Juvenile dispositions generally remain less punitive than those of adults, and judges still choose from a wide variety of alternatives for most juvenile offenses. These alternatives are discussed in this chapter along with the legal rights given to juveniles and the legal issues that arise in disposition proceedings.

Disposition

Disposition is the equivalent of sentencing in adult cases. It is defined as the formal pronouncement of judgment and punishment on the juvenile following a finding that the juvenile engaged in the conduct charged. Dispositions are imposed by a judge, but a few states provide for jury recommendation. A recent publication from the Office of Juvenile Justice and Delinquency Prevention (OJJDP) summarizes the wide-ranging alternatives available to the judge:

> At the disposition hearing, the court decides the placement, sanctions, and services the juvenile offender will receive. Disposition may include (ranging from least to most restrictive) fines, community service, restitution, in-home probation, electronic monitoring, group home placement, and secure detention. Services may include psychological, psychiatric, and educational evaluation; individual and family counseling; substance abuse treatment; and medical care.[1]

As in the case of adult sentencing, juvenile disposition is an art rather than an exact science. It is difficult to predict with certainty the kind of disposition a juvenile offender will receive: Various factors converge to determine the disposition's length. In many states, the judge is given wide discretion in dispositions, subject only to broad limits set by state law and the Constitution. Some states provide for fixed sentences in adult criminal proceedings, but this does not usually happen in juvenile proceedings, where more discretion is vested in the juvenile court judge (see Table 9.1). The judge is expected to play the role of a wise parent who acts for the good of the child when determining the penalty to be imposed.

The Goals of Disposition: Ideals Versus Reality

Disposition of juveniles and sentencing of adults are both punishments for law violations. They reflect the goals that society sets when punishing offenders. These goals may be classified into five categories:

- *Retribution:* giving juveniles their "just dessert" and expressing society's disapproval of criminal behavior.

- *Incapacitation:* separating juveniles from the community and placing them in a state institution to reduce the opportunity for committing more crime.

- *Deterrence:* discouraging the juvenile (specific deterrence) or others (general deterrence) from committing crime.

TABLE 9.1

Differences Between Juvenile and Adult Sentencing

Juvenile Justice System	Common Ground	Criminal Justice System
Disposition—Sentencing		
■ Disposition decisions are based on individual and social factors, offense severity, and youth's offense history.	■ Decisions are influenced by current offense, offending history, and social factors.	■ Sentencing decisions are bound primarily by the severity of the current offense and by the offender's criminal history.
■ Dispositional philosophy includes a significant rehabilitation component.	■ Decisions hold offenders accountable.	■ Sentencing philosophy is based largely on proportionality and punishment.
■ Many dispositional alternatives are operated by the juvenile court.	■ Decisions may give consideration to victims (e.g., restitution and "no contact" orders).	■ Sentence is often determinate, based on offense.
■ Dispositions cover a wide range of community-based and residential services.	■ Decisions may not be cruel or unusual.	
■ Disposition orders may be directed to people other than the offender (e.g., parents).		
■ Disposition may be indeterminate, based on progress demonstrated by the youth.		

Source: Howard N. Snyder and Melissa Sickmund, *Juvenile Offenders and Victims: 1999 National Report* (Washington, DC: Office of Juvenile Justice and Delinquency Prevention, 1999), 96.

- *Restitution:* making the offender repay the victim or the community in money or services.
- *Rehabilitation:* providing various types of psychological, medical, and physical services to juveniles in hopes they acquire needed skills and values that help them refrain from committing crime.[2]

There is no agreement among states about these goals or how they are to be achieved. As one source comments, "Some codes emphasize prevention and treatment goals, some stress punishment, and others seek a balanced approach."[3] However, these goals usually blend together and do not exclude one another. For example, retribution and incapacitation often go together, as do deterrence and rehabilitation. But expressed goals often yield to reality, and that reality is often driven by lack of funding rather than the absence of a systemic goal.

In some states, rehabilitation is often listed as one of the major goals, if not the only goal, of juvenile disposition. As one observer notes:

> Traditionally, the focus of the juvenile justice system has been on the rehabilitation of the juvenile. The juvenile court was seen as the common guardian of the youth who came before it, and the court was charged with ensuring that the child's best interests were considered when determining the proper disposition of a juvenile case. As a result, individuals adjudicated in the juvenile justice system were not subject to the same punitive standards and stringent sentences commonly imposed in adult criminal court.[4]

However, different states have different goals for the juvenile justice system, as enumerated in Table 9.2.

Although rehabilitation is traditionally the expressed goal in juvenile justice, many states allocate limited resources to it, giving priority instead to other goals such as retribution or incapacitation. Public preference may be at odds with official policy. For example, giving juveniles substantial freedom and treatment while confined in state institutions may be rehabilitative as an official policy but might be perceived by the public as "coddling." Regardless of the official stated goal, such as rehabilitation, reality in juvenile justice often leans toward incapacitation and retribution. As one writer observes, "Historically, the rehabilitative ideal and its focus on the 'best interest' of the child provided a ready answer [to the question of disposition goals]. However, with the erosion of public and political support for penal rehabilitation, the juvenile court has become an institution in search of a rationale."[5] Rehabilitation is no longer the consensus goal in juvenile

YOU ARE A... **Juvenile Court Judge**

Rank from 1 to 5 the disposition goals if you were sentencing a juvenile. Justify your first choice based on what is good for society:

____ Retribution

____ Incapacitation

____ Deterrence

____ Restitution

____ Rehabilitation

Would your first choice be different if your main consideration was what is good for the juvenile instead of what is good for society? Defend your response.

TABLE 9.2   *The States and Their Varying Goals for Juvenile Justice*

Prevention/Diversion/Treatment	Punishment	Both Prevention/Diversion/Treatment and Punishment	
Arizona*	Arkansas	Alabama	Nevada
Dist. of Columbia	Georgia	Alaska	New Hampshire
Kentucky	Hawaii	California	New Jersey
Massachusetts	Illinois	Colorado	New Mexico
North Carolina	Iowa	Connecticut	New York
Ohio	Louisiana	Delaware	North Dakota
South Carolina	Michigan	Florida	Oklahoma
Vermont	Missouri	Idaho	Oregon
West Virginia	Rhode Island	Indiana	Pennsylvania
		Kansas	Tennessee
		Maryland	Texas
		Maine	Utah
		Minnesota	Virginia
		Mississippi	Washington
		Montana	Wisconsin
		Nebraska	Wyoming

- Most states seek to protect the interests of the child, the family, the community, or some combination of the three.
- In 17 states, the purpose clause incorporates the language of the balanced and restorative justice philosophy, emphasizing offender accountability, public safety, and competency development.
- Purpose clauses also address court issues such as fairness, speedy trials, and even coordination of services. In nearly all states, the code also includes protections of the child's constitutional and statutory rights.

*Arizona's statutes and court rules did not contain a purpose clause; however, the issue is addressed in case law.

Source: Adapted from Howard N. Snyder and Melissa Sickmund, *Juvenile Offenders and Victims: 1999 National Report* (Washington, DC: Office of Juvenile Justice and Delinquency Prevention, 1999), 87.

dispositions. (The "You Are a . . . Juvenile Court Judge" box allows you to examine and rate the choices that such a judge must make.)

Most jurisdictions impose more punitive sanctions on juvenile delinquents than on status offenders (by law and/or by practice). This approach is justified on the grounds that juvenile delinquents committed acts that are equivalent to criminal violations for adults, whereas status offenders merely committed acts that if done by adults would not have been punishable at all. In many jurisdictions, juvenile delinquency can result in being sent to a state institution, whereas status offenses can lead only to probation or a more lenient community-based punishment. Studies show that in 1999, juvenile courts ordered residential placement (which includes treatment centers, boot camps, training schools, private placement, or group homes) in 24 percent of juvenile delinquency cases. In most cases, however (62 percent), probation was the

EXHIBIT 9.1   *Case Processing Overview, 1999*

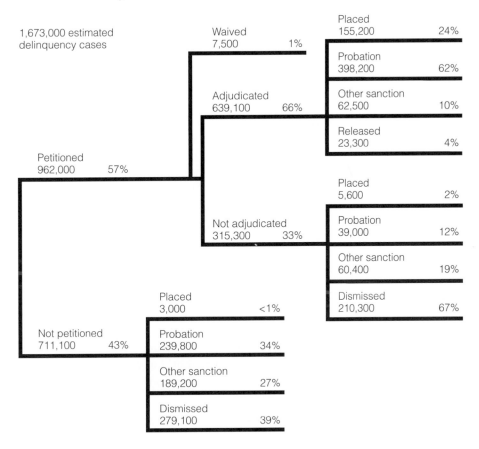

Note: Cases are categorized by their most severe or restrictive sanction. Detail may not add to totals because of rounding.

Source: Charles Puzzanchera, Anne L. Stahl, Terrence A. Finnegan, Nancy Tierney, and Howard N. Snyder, *Juvenile Court Statistics 1999* (Pittsburgh, PA: National Center for Juvenile Justice, 2003).

most severe punishment imposed—even in delinquency dispositions.[6] (See Exhibit 9.1.)

Although juvenile delinquency cases are also violations of criminal law, many states view status offenses by their common acronyms, such as CINS—children in need of supervision. As a result, these cases are often treated as needing supervision rather than warranting punitive sanction. One observer notes that from 1989 to 1998, most status offenders were given probation during disposition. Some cases were dispositioned to out-of-court placement, but others were released without punishment.[7]

In many states, juvenile courts also have jurisdiction in child abuse and neglect cases. Dispositions in these cases differ from those in juvenile delinquency and status offense cases. As one source notes, "The goal of the court in handling these cases has always been to protect the children by first determining the validity of child abuse and neglect allegations and then deciding whether the children need to be placed in foster care or can remain at home with supervision and services from public or private agencies."[8] Therefore, dispositions in dependency and neglect cases are done with the help and supervision of child welfare agencies. Dispositions are not meant as a punishment to the child.

Discretion in Dispositions

Juries in some states participate in dispositions but generally only recommend the sentence for the judge to impose. In some states, the sentence set by the jury is binding on the judge; in most states, however, the judge is free to disregard jury recommendation. In plea-bargained cases, the disposition results from an agreement between the prosecution and the defense. The role of the judge is to stamp the seal of approval if he or she finds the disposition acceptable. If the judge disagrees, the disposition is disregarded and the case goes to a hearing. The judge may also propose a different disposition to which both parties can agree.

The factors taken into account when deciding the sanction to be imposed vary from one judge to another, but the most influential factors are usually the seriousness of the offense and the juvenile's prior record.[9] Other factors that are influential include recommendations from probation officers who conduct the social history report and the judge's personal philosophy about the role of the juvenile court. A judge who believes in rehabilitation is less likely to impose a harsh sentence than one who feels the community wants retribution for the crime committed and that the wish of the community must be respected. Table 9.3 shows the national trend toward punitive sanctions in juvenile court.

When Disposition Takes Place

Disposition may occur immediately after the case is heard or within a few days or weeks. This delay enables the court to order a disposition or social history report to help the judge determine the proper sanction (see Exhibit 9.2). The

TABLE 9.3

The Movement Toward Punitive Sanctions in Juvenile Court

From 1992 through 1997, legislatures in 47 states and the District of Columbia enacted laws that made their juvenile justice systems more punitive.

State	Changes in Law or Court Rule*			State	Changes in Law or Court Rule*		
Alabama	T		C	Montana	T	S	C
Alaska	T		C	Nebraska			
Arizona	T	S	C	Nevada	T		C
Arkansas	T	S	C	New Hampshire	T	S	C
California	T		C	New Jersey		S	C
Colorado	T	S	C	New Mexico	T	S	C
Connecticut	T	S	C	New York			
Delaware	T	S	C	North Carolina	T		C

TABLE 9.3   *(continued)*

State	Changes in Law or Court Rule*			State	Changes in Law or Court Rule*		
Dist. of Columbia	T	S		North Dakota	T		C
Florida	T	S	C	Ohio	T	S	C
Georgia	T	S	C	Oklahoma	T	S	C
Hawaii	T		C	Oregon	T	S	C
Idaho	T	S	C	Pennsylvania	T		C
Illinois	T	S	C	Rhode Island	T	S	C
Indiana	T	S	C	South Carolina	T		C
Iowa	T	S	C	South Dakota	T		
Kansas	T	S	C	Tennessee	T		C
Kentucky	T	S	C	Texas	T	S	C
Louisiana	T	S	C	Utah	T		C
Maine			C	Vermont			
Maryland	T		C	Virginia	T	S	C
Massachusetts	T	S	C	Washington	T		C
Michigan		S	C	West Virginia	T		C
Minnesota	T	S	C	Wisconsin	T	S	C
Mississippi	T			Wyoming	T		C
Missouri	T	S	C				

*T = Transfer provision, S = Sentencing authority, C = Confidentiality

Source: Adapted from Howard N. Snyder and Melissa Sickmund, *Juvenile Offenders and Victims: 1999 National Report* (Washington, DC: Office of Juvenile Justice and Delinquency Prevention, 1999), 89.

EXHIBIT 9.2   *The Disposition Hearing*

In preparation for the disposition hearing, the probation department conducts a formal investigation of the juvenile and his or her background (sometimes called a "social history" or "pre-disposition report") and submits a written report and recommendation for the court's consideration. Probation officers must develop a detailed understanding of the juvenile, determine the impact of the crime on the victim, and assess available options. To assist the department in preparing recommendations, the court may order the juvenile to undergo psychological evaluations or other tests, or spend a period of confinement in a diagnostic facility.

At the disposition hearing, the probation officer presents the results of the investigation and makes a recommendation to the judge. The prosecutor, victim, defense attorney, or judge orders a disposition in the case, which may include probation supervision, community service, restitution and other sanctions, residential placement, or secure confinement.

Source: Adapted from Patrick Griffin and Patricia Torbet (eds.), *Desktop Guide to Good Juvenile Probation Practice* (Pittsburgh: National Center for Juvenile Justice, 2002), 37.

report is generally made by a juvenile probation officer, who consolidates the information needed for an informed disposition. It may include such factors as the other circumstances surrounding the juvenile's act, the home environment, previous record, psychological findings, ties to the community, educational interest or lack of it, and the overall prospect of rehabilitation. Just about anything and everything that sheds light on the proper disposition may legally be included in the report.

In states with *bifurcated trials* (the trial or adjudication hearing is divided into two stages—the guilt or innocence stage and the punishment or sentencing stage), prosecutors and lawyers for the juvenile present evidence during the sentencing stage. The prosecution seeks a heavier penalty, while the defense argues for a lighter disposition. As in adult proceedings, the rules of evidence are loosened during the disposition hearing. For example, hearsay testimony and the prior record of the juvenile may be introduced, unless specifically prohibited by state law. Other forms of evidence taken into account are probation reports, psychological reports, and/or reports from schools. At this stage, the full juvenile record becomes available to the jury (if the jury has a role in sentencing) during the hearing. The role of whoever writes the disposition report, usually a probation officer, can be crucial because many reports carry recommendations for disposition. Judges do not have to follow these recommendations but may use them for final determination.

The Disposition Plan

In adult cases, sentencing is often postponed for a few weeks while a presentence investigation report (PSIR) is prepared by a probation officer. The equivalent in a juvenile proceeding is a **disposition report** or pre-disposition report. The probation officer prepares this plan by assessing the youth, including looking into available support systems and programs for the juvenile. The plan may include psychological evaluations or diagnostic tests, if ordered by the court. As in adult cases, dispositional reports usually end with recommendations to the court for a suitable punishment. These are presented by the probation staff during the disposition hearing. The prosecutor and the defense lawyer for the juvenile may also submit their own disposition plans to the judge. The judge may then choose from the alternatives or may completely disregard them.[10] In some cases, the disposition takes place immediately after adjudication, but the more common practice is to hold a disposition hearing sometime after the juvenile is found to have engaged in the conduct charged (usually one to two weeks after adjudication).[11]

Roles During Dispositions

In a decision involving a juvenile case, then Chief Justice Neeley of the West Virginia Supreme Court outlined the roles of the various officials during juvenile adjudication:

- *Role of the court-appointed counsel:* "[I]t is the obligation of any court appointed or retained counsel to continue active and vigorous representation of the child through that stage. . . . Armed with adequate information, counsel can then present to the court with all reasonable alternative dispositions to incarceration and should have taken the initial steps to secure the tentative acceptance of the child into these facilities."

- *Role of the probation officer or welfare worker:* "The probation officer or welfare worker when requested by the judge is also responsible for discovering whether there are forces which are at work upon the child which either the Department of Welfare or other social service agencies can correct."

- *Role of the court:* "It is the obligation of the court to hear all witnesses who might shed light upon the proper disposition of a child and before incarcerating a child, to find facts upon the record which would lead a reasonable appellate court to conclude in the words of the statute, either that no less restrictive alternative would accomplish the requisite rehabilitation of the child. . . . or the welfare of the public requires incarceration."

- *Role of the child:* "There is an affirmative obligation on the part of the child to cooperate. When, however, there is a consistent pattern of noncooperation which makes alternative rehabilitative programs impossible, the court should set forth the facts upon the record so that this court will understand why the trial court concludes that there are no alternatives to placement in an institution."[12]

In reality, what happens during disposition, and during all juvenile court hearings, depends mainly on the personality and philosophy of the juvenile court judge. Some judges are liberal, and others are conservative; some act as wise parents, and others play power games. Given the discretion usually enjoyed by juvenile court judges, their control over the roles played by the various actors in the juvenile justice system during disposition exceeds that of judges in adult criminal proceedings. This has led cynical critics to label juvenile courts as "little kingdoms" that are sometimes ruled by imperial monarchs whose word is law, at least in that court.

Kinds of Dispositions

As in the case of adults, penalties for juveniles may be broadly classified into those that involve confinement and those that do not. Confinement ranges from home stay (least severe) to adult prisons (most severe). Between these two extremes are other types of confinement, such as jails, juvenile institutions, electronic monitoring while at home, and foster home care. The more common nonincarceration dispositions include a verbal warning or reprimand, payment of a fine, restitution, counseling, and community service. In most states, only those adjudged to be juvenile delinquents (generally those who committed acts punishable by the state's penal code) may be confined; status offenders are usually left in the community, except if they violate the conditions of probation, in which case they may be sent to a state institution for violating a valid court order and being in contempt of court. Exhibit 9.3 examines the widely varied skills and qualifications that a juvenile judge should have.

EXHIBIT 9.3

A Recommendation About Juvenile Court Judges

All judges and other judicial officers serving in a juvenile division of juvenile court should be required to have intensive and ongoing training not only in statutory and case law governing delinquency, status offense, and dependency matters but also in child development, cultural factors, resources for families, the court's relationship with and other duties toward social welfare agencies, and research findings regarding rehabilitative interventions.

Juvenile court judges should serve in the juvenile court division for at least two or three years.

Source: Adapted from *The Future of Children: The Juvenile Court* 6(4) (Winter 1996) (The David and Lucile Packard Foundation): 20. Used by permission.

Placement in an Institution

Institutionalization is the juvenile equivalent of adult imprisonment, but it goes by a different label. It is the most severe form of punishment imposed on a juvenile, other than death, and is usually given to delinquents rather than status offenders. One report shows that in 1997, "about 107,0000 juveniles younger than age 18 are incarcerated on a given day, and of those, about 9,100 were in local jails and 5,400 in adult prisons." The report also states that in 1999 a total of 176,700 juvenile delinquents were in some form of residential placement.[13]

Juvenile institutions such as state schools are managed by state youth authorities and are different from prisons in that they are less restrictive and usually have a wider range of rehabilitative programs. They also differ from prisons in that juveniles in state institutions may be released by juvenile authorities when they are deemed rehabilitated, unlike adult prisons, where offenders serve a set period of time, subject to parole laws. Another difference is that juveniles are usually released from a state institution upon reaching the upper age limit for juveniles. That age varies from state to state, but usually ranges from eighteen to twenty-one.[14] These differences may be summarized as follows:

Juvenile Institutions

1. Managed and financed either by the state, the local government, or a private group.

2. Less restrictive and more rehabilitative programs.

3. Juvenile may be released at any time by administrators if deemed rehabilitated.

4. Juvenile must usually be released upon reaching the upper age limit set by law.

Adult Prisons

1. Managed and financed by the state.

2. Security conscious and less rehabilitative.

3. Prisoners serve sentence in full, subject to parole laws.

4. No upper age limit is set by law.

5. Expressed goal is usually rehabilitation.

5. Expressed goals are usually a mix of retribution, incapacitation, deterrence, restitution, and rehabilitation.

Short-term juvenile offenders and detainees may also be placed in local jails. In 1997 an estimated 9,100 youths under 18 years of age were held in adult jails and constituted 2 percent of the total jail population of the United States.[15] The institutionalization of noncriminal status offenders is prohibited by the Juvenile Justice and Delinquency Prevention Act of 1974 (JJDPA); otherwise, the state faces possible loss of federal funds. Housing juveniles with adults is also prohibited by the same act, but the practice continues, particularly in places where there are no separate jails for adults and juveniles. Placing a juvenile in a juvenile jail in a different county or city can be expensive for any state or local government, but may still be cost-effective for small counties or rural areas that do not have a great number of juvenile offenders.

In many states, juveniles may be placed in institutions managed and operated by private individuals or organizations. In 1997, Massachusetts placed the largest proportion of juveniles in private in-state facilities (64 percent), while Mississippi had only 1 percent of its youths in private in-state facilities.[16] These arrangements are made on a contract basis by which private agencies are paid a specified amount per day by the state or a local government. Private facilities can be less expensive for the government and may be more specialized and innovative in their treatment programs.

Probation

Probation is defined as a type of disposition in which a convicted offender is allowed to remain free in the community, subject to court-imposed conditions and under the supervision of a probation officer. If the conditions imposed are violated, the probation may be revoked, and the probationer may be sent to an institution or prison. Probation is the most widely used form of punishment because it is inexpensive and leaves the offender in the community. Also, as one observer notes, "All things being equal, treatment programs run in community settings are likely to be more effective in reducing recidivism than similar programs provided in institutions."[17] It is usually given to first-time or less-serious nonviolent offenders.

Probation can be informal or formal. **Informal probation** is usually given prior to adjudication or disposition, meaning before the juvenile has been tried or found guilty. In some jurisdictions informal probation is simply known as a form of diversion and is not considered an official disposition. Informal probation is done in two ways. The first is through the prosecutor's office: The juvenile accepts informal probation on the condition that the charges will either be suspended or dismissed by the prosecutor if the offender successfully completes the term of probation. A second type of informal probation takes place after the charges are filed. The judge postpones hearing the case if the juvenile accepts informal probation. In either case, the charges are dismissed if there are no violations of probation conditions during the term of probation. If violations occur, the probation is revoked, and a hearing is held to determine guilt or innocence.

A legal issue in informal probation is whether it is valid in view of a presumption of innocence before trial. If raised, the issue seldom succeeds because informal probations are given only after voluntary consent by the juvenile or the family. Having consented to probation even before a finding of guilt, the juvenile or the family therefore waives the presumption of innocence and all other rights to which the juvenile would have been entitled had there been a trial.

Formal probation takes place after an adjudication hearing and a finding of guilt. A study shows that in 1999, 62 percent of adjudicated delinquency cases resulted in formal probation, making probation the most severe disposition in the majority of adjudicated juvenile cases.[18] In many jurisdictions, formal and informal probationers are supervised by the same probation authority. There are usually no differences in the conditions imposed or in supervision because in both cases the juvenile is on probation. In most jurisdictions, probation—informal or formal—is available only at the discretion of the prosecutor, judge, or jury; hence, it is a privilege and not a right. In other words, a juvenile cannot demand that the prosecutor, judge, or jury grant probation, unless such is the penalty specifically imposed by law for that offense. If probation is denied, the juvenile has no legal remedy.

Other Sanctions That Leave the Juvenile in the Community

Some sanctions leave juvenile offenders in the community without placing them on probation. These may be independent of or may be a condition of probation. For example, restitution or a fine may be imposed as a condition of probation, or the juvenile may be required to perform community service and placed on electronic monitoring as part of probation. These may be independent punishments and not a part of probation conditions. The sanctions discussed below are community service, fines, restitution, and electronic monitoring. These are just some of the many punishment options whose common theme is leaving the juvenile in the community.

Community Service

A **community service** program is a sentencing option or condition that places a juvenile in an unpaid position with a nonprofit or tax-supported agency to perform a specified number of hours of work or service within a given time limit. Community service programs operate under a variety of labels: court referral, volunteer work, service restitution, and symbolic restitution programs. There are as many types of programs as there are opportunities for service in the community. Among them are hospital work, helping the elderly, cleaning public parks, maintaining lawns, and providing manual labor in educational and public service agencies.

Whether juveniles are on probation or not, probation officers are the ones who generally supervise offenders required to perform community service, although variation exists. For example, X is guilty of vandalism and is sentenced to 200 hours of community service in the form of free hospital work. X will likely not be under the supervision of a probation officer, but supervision may be provided by other volunteers or the hospital staff. Judges may also impose some form of community service as a condition of probation. For example, as a condition for placing a person guilty of littering on probation, the judge may require that the person help clean up the streets during weekends. In one case, the Vermont Supreme Court noted the following justification for community service work for juveniles: "One of the preparations for future life is responsibility and accountability. And we see that as our responsibility as a Court. . . . And we see accountability and responsibility as a part of his rehabilitation. . . . And we feel that it is important that he be made to understand that he has to be responsible for that act, and he is accountable for having done it. . . ."[19] Some states by law limit community service to public agencies, not to private individuals or businesses, the assumption being that it is improper for the government to provide service benefits to private entities.

Fines

A **fine** is a monetary punishment imposed by the court on a person convicted of a crime. The amount imposed may be fixed by state or left to the discretion of the court. The equal protection clause of the Constitution prohibits the imposition of a greater punishment on a poor person than on a rich person. The U.S. Supreme Court has said that "there can be no equal justice where the kind of trial a man gets depends on the amount of money he has."

Most states impose fines that are proportionate to the offenses committed. A grossly disproportionate fine could be unconstitutional, amounting to cruel and unusual punishment. For instance, a fine of $10,000 for a juvenile caught shoplifting a bag of potato chips might be deemed disproportionate to the offense. Although the offender could be in a position to pay it, some courts have held that a juvenile court may impose a fine only if authorized by law because the purpose of juvenile courts is to rehabilitate, not to punish. According to a Pennsylvania case, fines are punitive and must therefore be authorized by law and not simply imposed on the juvenile by the judge without authorization.[20] The Pennsylvania legislature later changed the law to authorize the juvenile court to impose fines. In many states, the maximum fine is determined by law, but the judge is authorized to specify an amount within that maximum.

Restitution

Restitution means restoring the property or right of a person who has been unjustly deprived of it by the offender. It compensates the damage done by the offender. Restitution is a popular form of punishment because the money goes to the victim of crime instead of to the state, as is the case with a fine. Moreover, it is an act of atonement for the delinquent because the restitution helps rehabilitate the victim financially. Restitution is authorized by law in many states as a form of criminal sanction, but even in states where it is not specifically provided for by law, courts consider it a valid sanction because it is restorative and rehabilitative both for the victim and the offender.

Restitution differs from a fine in that the money paid in a fine does not go to the victim; instead, it goes to the state. It differs from victim compensation in that the money in restitution is given by the offender, whereas the money given to the victim in victim compensation programs comes from the state. Restitution may be imposed together with other forms of punishment. For example, Z is found guilty of driving while intoxicated, in the process of which he injures a pedestrian. Z may be placed on probation, ordered to perform community service, and pay restitution to the injured party. Restitution money is usually paid through the court or the probation officer. It is a punishment that goes well as a condition of probation, but it may also be imposed even if the offender is sent to an institution. As in the case of fines, a judge may ask for help from the probation officer or other court officers in determining the amount of restitution to be imposed within the limit prescribed by law. The differences among fines, restitution, and victim compensation (a variation of the concept of restitution) may be summarized as follows:

Forms of Restitution	Who Pays?	Who Gets the Money?
Fine	Offender	Government
Restitution	Offender	Victim of the crime
Victim compensation	Government/offender	Victim of the crime

In one case, a West Virginia court of appeals set reasonableness as a condition for validity of the restitution: "A trial judge may order restitution as part of a 'program of treatment or therapy' designed to aid in the rehabilitation of the child in a juvenile case when probation is granted. . . . Such order, however, must be reasonable in its terms and within the child's ability to perform. . . ." In this case, three juvenile delinquents were ordered to pay restitution in the amount of $7,947.52 for damages to a mobile home. In the absence of specifics, the court nullified the award, saying that there was no indication of any reasonable chance that the juveniles would be able to pay the amount imposed, adding that "the record does not show that the total amount of damages assessed as restitution was properly calculated."[21] In another case, a state of Washington court ordered juveniles to pay $946.78 as restitution for damages to a motor scooter. The amount was based on an estimate by the victim, which the court upheld. Said the court, "If the amount of damages is established by 'substantial credible evidence' at the restitution hearing, no abuse of discretion will be found."[22]

Some states authorize the juvenile court to order parents to pay restitution for damage or injury caused by a child. Whether restitution is to be paid by the child or the child's parents, there are limitations on the powers of the court both in setting the amount of restitution and in determining the consequences of failure to pay. According to a Maryland case, there are generally three requirements for awarding restitution: (1) criminal activity, (2) pecuniary damages, and (3) a causal relationship between the criminal conduct and the damage.[23] These requirements imply that restitution is generally awarded in juvenile delinquency cases, but not in status offense cases.

Electronic Monitoring

Electronic monitoring is a form of curfew. It may be used as a separate sanction or as a condition of probation, parole, or **house arrest** (an arrest in which the offender is allowed to stay at home instead of being kept in jail). The monitoring system is usually composed of a computer located at the controlling agency, a receiver unit located in the offender's home, and a transmitter device worn by the offender. The transmitter is worn on the ankle, on the wrist, or around the neck. It monitors the presence of an offender in a vicinity, usually the home, during times when he or she is required to be there. Although the offender can conceivably remove the device by cutting the strap or stretching it and taking it off, an electronic circuit within the device detects such tampering and sends an alarm to the receiving unit. The technology has continually improved over the years and is now accepted by the scientific community as reliable and is also difficult for the offender to tamper with or manipulate.

Other Disposition Alternatives

Other popular alternatives available to the judge in juvenile cases are reprimands, halting proceedings, suspending the imposition of sanctions, foster care (out-of-home placement), counseling, therapy, psychological treatment, boot camps, wilderness programs, special skills training, acquiring a diploma, alternative dispute resolution, and victim/offender mediation. Lawsuits have arisen over the constitutionality of some of these programs. In one California case, the challenge made by a juvenile to the rigor of a boot camp program was rejected by the court, which upheld the program as constitutional despite the severity of its regimen.[24] Courts have generally upheld the authority of the state to impose and sponsor these programs in the name of rehabilitation. Unless conditions in these programs are abusive or grossly negligent, the chances of legal success when challenging them are slim.

The Death Penalty

Death is the ultimate penalty for juveniles in the most serious cases, but it is not imposed in a juvenile proceeding or by a juvenile court. Juvenile cases involving the death penalty are heard in adult courts and never in juvenile courts. They are regular criminal trials in adult courts, the difference being that they involve young offenders who are transferred to adult court because of the seriousness of their offense. The issue in these cases is whether young offenders deserve the death penalty and whether it constitutes cruel and unusual punishment.

The death penalty for juveniles is discussed more extensively in Chapter 12. For the purposes of this chapter, however, three cases decided by the U.S. Supreme Court must be mentioned because they constitute the main history of the death penalty for juveniles. In the first case, *Thompson v. Oklahoma* (1988),[25] the U.S. Supreme Court held that a state cannot execute an offender who committed first-degree murder when he was only fifteen years old. An execution at that young age constitutes cruel and unusual punishment and is therefore unconstitutional according to the Court. However, the Court in *Thompson* failed to state the exact age when a juvenile defendant can be given the death penalty. That issue was resolved one year later when the Court ruled in *Stanford v. Kentucky* (1989) that the imposition of the death penalty for a crime committed at age sixteen and above does not constitute cruel and unusual punishment.[26] These two cases controlled the death penalty for juveniles for nearly twenty years. However, this changed in 2005. In March 2005, the U.S. Supreme Court held in *Roper v. Simmons* that executing a juvenile for a crime committed prior to his or her eighteenth birthday constitutes cruel and unusual punishment. It is clear for now that the crucial starting age for juveniles in death penalty cases is eighteen. Anyone under eighteen cannot be tried and executed for a capital crime.

The age of the juvenile at the time of arrest or trial is not important in death penalty cases. What is important is the age at the time the crime was committed. For instance, Y committed a murder when he was fourteen years old but was arrested and tried four years later, when he was eighteen. Y cannot be given the death penalty, according to the U.S. Supreme Court. Moreover, even if Y committed the crime when he was seventeen years and 364 days old, Y still could not be tried for capital murder. The "bright line" established by the Court is age eighteen.

Blended Sentencing

Blended sentences are defined as sentences that combine juvenile court sanctions with adult sanctions. Juveniles tried in juvenile courts are usually sent to juvenile institutions if found to have committed delinquent acts. This practice has changed, however, with the more recent use of "blended sentences" in several states. They usually provide for a juvenile's sentence to be served in sequence, first in a juvenile institution and then in an adult correctional institution—if further detention is warranted. If no further offenses are committed or if the juvenile is deemed sufficiently rehabilitated, the adult sanction may be waived/suspended and the punishment shortened or mitigated. For example, X, a fifteen-year-old juvenile, commits rape and attempted murder. X is tried and convicted in a juvenile court. He is sent to a juvenile institution until age eighteen. A hearing is then held to determine if X should be sent to an adult prison because X is now an adult. The procedures whereby the consecutive punishments are carried out vary from state to state, but all fall under the general title of blended sentencing. Exhibit 9.4 displays the various types of blended sentences in states that have blended sentencing statutes.

As of 2003, laws in twenty-two states authorized blended sentencing.[27] These laws expand the authority of the judge and go beyond the traditional concept of juvenile disposition. One observer notes that "blended sentencing policies were devised primarily to provide longer terms of incarceration for juveniles, but they also helped to blur the distinction between juvenile justice and adult justice."[28] Another writer adds that as "many States have shifted the purpose of juvenile court away from rehabilitation and toward punishment, accountability and publicity, the emerging trend is toward dispositions based more on the offense than the offender."[29]

Blended sentences have many variations, but what most forms have in common is the use of both juvenile and adult sanctions, one after the other. Some states impose a maximum age when a juvenile can be kept in the juvenile or adult institution; other states do not set any maximum age, meaning that the sentence can be served in full regardless of the offender's age when it ends. For

EXHIBIT 9.4

Blended Sentencing Options

Blended sentencing options create a "middle ground" between traditional juvenile sanctions and adult sanctions.

Blended sentencing option	State
Juvenile-exclusive blend: The juvenile court may impose a sanction involving either the juvenile or adult correctional systems.	New Mexico

Juvenile-inclusive blend: The juvenile court may impose both juvenile and adult correctional sanctions. The adult sanction is suspended pending a violation and revocation.	Connecticut Kansas Minnesota Montana

Juvenile-contiguous blend: The juvenile court may impose a juvenile correctional sanction that may remain in force after the offender is beyond the age of the court's extended jurisdiction, at which point the offender may be transferred to the adult correctional system.	Colorado[1] Massachusetts Rhode Island South Carolina Texas

Juvenile court ———— Juvenile ———— Adult

Criminal-exclusive blend: The criminal court may impose a sanction involving either the juvenile or adult correctional systems.	California Colorado[2] Florida Idaho Michigan Oklahoma Virginia West Virginia

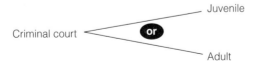

Criminal-inclusive blend: The criminal court may impose both juvenile and adult correctional sanctions. The adult sanction is suspended, but is reinstated if the terms of the juvenile sanction are violated and revoked.	Arkansas Iowa Missouri Virginia[3]

Note: Blends apply to a subset of juveniles specified by state statute.

[1]Applies to those designated as "aggravated juvenile offenders."
[2]Applies to those designated as "youthful offenders."
[3]Applies to those designated as "violent juvenile felony offenders."

Source: Adapted from Howard N. Snyder and Melissa Sickmund, *Juvenile Offenders and Victims: 1999 National Report* (Washington, DC: Office of Juvenile Justice and Delinquency Prevention, 1999), 108.

example, Texas law allows the commitment of a juvenile to adult prison for a maximum of forty years for such offenses as capital murder, murder, manslaughter, aggravated kidnapping, sexual assault, and aggravated robbery.[30] Upon conviction, a juvenile is first sent to a juvenile institution. A month before he or she reaches the age of eighteen, a hearing is held in juvenile court to determine if the juvenile is to be released, placed on parole, or sent to adult prison. If sent to an adult prison, the juvenile in Texas can be kept there for up to forty years.

A legal issue in blended sentencing is whether such sentences are constitutional; by definition, a juvenile hearing is civil in nature. Can a juvenile be sent to an adult prison after going through a civil proceeding? The answer is yes, for two reasons. First, states that use blended sentencing are careful to provide the same rights to juveniles during juvenile court hearings that are given to adults in criminal cases. For example, statutes that authorize judges to impose blended sentences also provide that juveniles must be indicted by a grand jury (in states where a grand jury is used), afforded a trial before a jury of twelve people, be given the right to counsel during trial, found guilty beyond a reasonable doubt, and then given a lawyer during sentencing. Juveniles subject to blended sentences are tried the same way as are adults and are given the same rights as adult defendants, although the trial may be held in juvenile court in some cases.

Second, although juvenile hearings are still considered civil in nature, U.S. Supreme Court decisions have in effect "criminalized" those hearings by extending constitutional rights to juveniles, particularly in delinquency cases. For example, juveniles enjoy the right to counsel, cross-examination, presentation of evidence, and a fair trial when their freedom may be at stake, as it usually is in juvenile delinquency cases. Thus, basic constitutional rights have already been incorporated in juvenile delinquency proceedings, although not in status offense cases—unless given by state law. A Texas appellate court has held that a trial court does not exceed its authority in transferring a juvenile to prison on his or her eighteenth birthday, as allowed by state law.[31] This decision upheld the constitutionality of state transfer laws that allow juveniles to be transferred to adult court after a stay in a juvenile institution.

Are blended sentences the more effective dispositional approach in serious juvenile cases? There is no definitive answer because no studies have yet shown that they are more effective or less effective in dealing with juvenile crime. However, what is certain is that blended sentencing helps quench the public's thirst for more punitive punishment involving serious juvenile crimes and affords better public protection. Nevertheless, a recent study reveals that blended sentences may "cause more confusion than good." The study found that "Blended sentencing creates confusing options for all system actors, including offenders, judges, prosecutors, and corrections administrators," adding that "contact with juvenile and criminal justice personnel across the country revealed that confusion exists about these statutes and the rules and regulations governing them, especially with respect to the juvenile's status during case processing and subsequent placement."[32] Blended sentences may not be the ideal sanction that society expected.

Legal and Constitutional Issues in Dispositions

The Rights of Juveniles During Dispositions

Juveniles have few rights during dispositions because guilt has been established, so their constitutional rights are diminished. Even the rules of evidence are loosened so the judge may consider evidence not admissible during the regular adjudication or trial. Almost any kind of record or documentation that helps determine the proper sanction to be imposed may be admitted by the judge during the disposition stage. Hearsay evidence, which is generally excluded during trial, is also admitted.

In adult criminal cases, the defendant has the following rights during sentencing:

The Right to Counsel

The accused has a right to counsel because sentencing is considered a "critical stage" of the criminal proceeding. If the accused is indigent, a lawyer must be appointed for him or her by the state. The issue of the constitutional right to counsel for juveniles during the disposition proceeding has not been specifically addressed by the U.S. Supreme Court. However, several state courts have held that this right extends to juveniles. In one case, a Nebraska state appellate court held that a juvenile has a right to counsel at a disposition hearing and that a juvenile court's failure to provide a juvenile with a lawyer at a hearing that revoked his probation was "plain error."[33] In another case, an Indiana state court ruled it improper for the juvenile court to conduct a disposition hearing without providing a lawyer or obtaining a waiver of the right to counsel.[34]

The Right of Allocution

Most courts provide that the defendant has the **right of allocution:** to make a statement on his or her own behalf about why the sentence should not be imposed. This is not a constitutional right, but it is usually given by state law. This issue has not been addressed by courts in dispositions, although court judges usually allow juveniles, their guardians, or their parents to speak out during the disposition stage.

As in adult cases, a juvenile has no constitutional right to be present in court during adjudication. However, most states give such right by law, subject to two exceptions: if the defendant escaped before or during the trial and can no longer be found, or if the offense is minor, in which case the juvenile may be sentenced in his or her absence or be represented by a lawyer.

The Use of Illegally Obtained Evidence in Dispositions

The *exclusionary rule* provides that evidence obtained by the police in violation of the Fourth Amendment prohibition against unreasonable searches and seizures is not admissible in a court of law to prove a defendant's guilt. For instance, the police seize drugs from an apartment based on suspicion (instead of probable cause) and without a warrant. The seizure is clearly unconstitutional; the seized drugs are not admissible in court. The main purpose of the exclusionary rule is to deter police misconduct, the assumption being that if evidence illegally obtained cannot be used in court, the police will behave legally and not violate a defendant's right against unreasonable searches and seizures. This assumption is debatable, but it continues to be the basis for applying the exclusionary rule.

However, the exclusionary rule applies during trial only when the sole issue is whether the defendant is guilty or innocent. Whether or not it also applies to proceedings before and after trial (such as during sentencing or disposition) has not been addressed by the U.S. Supreme Court. Illegal evidence is admitted in some proceedings (such as school disciplinary hearings, parole revocation, and grand jury proceedings) and not in others. However, a California court has ruled that in some cases illegally obtained evidence may be admitted during dispositions. In that case, a California appellate court concluded that "In the case the minor cannot hide behind the illegality of his former arrest to prevent the juvenile court from obtaining a full picture of his character and need for rehabilitative treatment."[35] It may be concluded that although the issue has not been addressed directly by the U.S. Supreme Court, illegally obtained evidence will likely be admissible to establish certain facts during juvenile disposition proceedings, where the rules of evidence are not as strict. A related issue is the admissibility of coerced confessions. See the "Case Brief."

Case Brief   *Leading Case on the Admissibility of Coerced Confessions in Juvenile Proceedings*

Haley v. Ohio, 332 U.S. 596 (1948)

Facts: On October 14, 1945, a confectionery store was robbed, and the owner of the store was shot and killed. Five days later, a 15-year-old black juvenile named Haley was arrested for his alleged involvement in the crime. Beginning sometime after midnight, Haley was questioned for five hours by the police. He was questioned in relays by various police officers or teams of police officers. At no time during this questioning was anyone present on Haley's behalf. At no time was Haley informed of his right to counsel. A statement appeared at the top of the written confession informing Haley that the document could be used against him and that he was giving his statement voluntarily. He was then held incommunicado for three days before being taken before a magistrate and formally charged. No attorney attempted to see him until five days after his arrest. At Haley's trial, the defense objected to the admission of the confession on the grounds that it violated Haley's rights under the Fourteenth Amendment. The judge admitted the confession into evidence and instructed the jury to disregard the confession if it believed that the confession was not given voluntarily and of free will. Haley was convicted of murder in the first degree and sentenced to life imprisonment.

(continued)

Case Brief *(continued)*

Issue:

Does the Fourteenth Amendment prohibit the use of coerced confessions in juvenile proceedings?

Supreme Court Decision:

The due process clause of the Fourteenth Amendment prohibits the police from extracting involuntary or coerced confessions from adults and juveniles; any evidence obtained involuntarily cannot be used in court.

Case Significance:

In this case, the Supreme Court for the first time suggested that, despite *parens patriae*, there are constitutional requirements that protect all accused persons, whether they are adults or juveniles. The Court was not willing to go so far as to say that juveniles have recognized constitutional rights, but juveniles have a lesser chance of protecting themselves against police tactics; hence, it is only reasonable that juveniles be given the same, if not greater, protection against coercion than adults.

This decision is easy to accept today, but was not as easily reached in 1948 under the pure *parens patriae* philosophy. At present, the concept that juveniles deserve better protection than adults against possible police abuses is accepted. This was not the case in 1948, when *parens patriae* insulated police and courts from judicial scrutiny on the ground that these agencies were entitled to greater authority when dealing with juveniles.

Excerpts from the Decision:

"We do not think the methods used in obtaining this confession can be squared with that due process of law which the Fourteenth Amendment commands.

"What transpired would make us pause for careful inquiry if a mature man was involved. And when, as here, a mere child—an easy victim of the law—is before us, special care in scrutinizing the record must be used. Age 15 is a tender and difficult age for a boy of any race. He cannot be judged by more exacting standards of maturity.

"No friend stood at the side of this 15-year-old boy as the police, working in relays, questioned him hour after hour, from midnight until dawn. No lawyer stood guard to make sure that the police went so far and no farther, to see that they stopped short of the point where he became the victim of coercion.

"The age of the petitioner, the hours when he was grilled, the duration of his quizzing, the fact that he had no friend or counsel to advise him, the callous attitude of the police towards his rights combine to convince us that this was a confession wrung from a child by means which the law should not sanction. Neither man nor child can be allowed to stand condemned by methods which flout constitutional requirements of due process of law."

Source: This brief originally appeared in Rolando V. del Carmen, Mary Parker, and Frances P. Reddington, *Briefs of Leading Cases in Juvenile Justice* (Cincinnati, OH: Anderson Publishing Co., 1998).

Juveniles and "Three Strikes and You're Out" Sentences

Three strikes and you're out laws are a form of mandatory sentencing that increases sentences for offenders who commit serious crimes. These laws are society's answer to concerns that many serious and chronic offenders are released from juvenile institutions or prisons too soon. The purpose of three-strikes laws is clear: People who repeatedly commit serious offenses are removed from society and placed in prison for long periods of time, in many cases for life. The first three-strikes laws were passed in California and Washington in the early 1990s, but this approach is now used in twenty-four states and by the federal government.[36] These laws differ in specifics and scope, but what they have in common is a "get-tough" approach to crime and punishment.

Three-strikes laws raise constitutional questions because of their severity and disproportionality to the offenses committed. The U.S. Supreme Court recently decided two cases on three-strikes sentences: *Ewing v. California* (2003) and *Lockyer v. California* (2003).[37] In the *Ewing* case, an offender shoplifted three golf clubs whose total price was $1,200. This amounted to grand theft, a felony under California law. He also had prior a criminal record of four burglaries and one robbery. The California three-strikes law provides for an indeterminate term of life imprisonment for a felon who has had two or more prior convictions for serious or violent felonies. The defendant was sentenced to twenty-five years to life. On appeal, he alleged that his sentence constituted cruel and unusual punishment, but in a 5–4 vote, the U.S. Supreme Court upheld the sentence, saying it was not grossly disproportionate to the offense.[38]

In the *Lockyer* case, decided the same day, a defendant stole videotapes on two occasions. The tapes were worth a total of $150. The defendant had a long record of offenses, among them petty theft, transportation of marijuana, escape, and residential burglary. He was charged with a felony and sentenced to two consecutive terms of twenty-five years to life. Again, on a 5–4 vote, the U.S. Supreme Court held that this sentence did not constitute cruel and unusual punishment and therefore upheld it.

Although these two decisions involved adult cases, they will likely apply to juvenile cases if a similar issue is raised. Three-strikes questions arise in transfer of jurisdiction cases where a juvenile has a prior record of offenses that may qualify for three strikes under state law if and when tried and sentenced as an adult. Although provisions of three-strikes laws differ among states, these two decisions make it clear that disproportionality for repeat offenders of the magnitude involved in the *Ewing* and *Lockyer* cases is valid.

A related issue is whether it is constitutional to use a prior juvenile adjudication to increase a sentence. Two recent cases from appellate courts in California have said yes. In a 2003 case, a California appellate court affirmed convictions for firearms possession despite claims that the defendant's prior juvenile adjudication could not be used as a "strike" because he did not have the right to a jury trial during the prior juvenile proceeding.[39] In another 2003 case, involving conviction for the sale of cocaine to two undercover narcotics officers, another California appellate court also approved of the use of juvenile adjudication as a strike under California's three-strikes law despite the juvenile not having been given the right to a jury trial in the delinquency proceeding.[40]

Juveniles Confined Longer Than Adults for Similar Offenses

In some states, a juvenile may be sent to a state institution until he or she reaches the age of majority, which is usually from ages eighteen to twenty-one. This indeterminate disposition can result in confinement that would be longer than if an adult committed a similar crime. For example, X, a juvenile, burglarizes a store at age twelve. X can be institutionalized until reaching age eighteen or twenty-one, whichever is the age of majority in the state. In contrast, if X were an adult, the State Penal Code might provide that burglaries are punishable with confinement in prison for a maximum of four years. In the *Gault* (1967) case, by far the most significant juvenile case decided by the U.S. Supreme Court, Gerald Gault, a juvenile, was charged with making lewd telephone calls.[41] He was committed to an Arizona state institution as a delinquent until he reached the age of majority, a total of six years from the date of the hearing. The maximum punishment for an adult found guilty of the same offense in Arizona was a fine from $5 to $50, or imprisonment for a maximum of two months. Is this longer confinement for juveniles constitutional?

Although the U.S. Supreme Court did not address this issue in the *Gault* case, lower courts have said yes. In one case, a minor was sentenced to a six-year term under the provisions of federal law for interstate transportation of a stolen motor vehicle. Upon conviction, he appealed, saying that if he were an adult he would have received a maximum of five years in prison. The federal court of appeals for the Fifth Circuit rejected his complaint, saying that juveniles are in institutions for a different reason and that confinement for a longer time was justified as consistent with his needs for rehabilitative treatment.[42] State courts have arrived at the same conclusion, saying that giving juveniles more time than adults for similar offenses is constitutional based on three grounds: (1) the juvenile court system protects instead of punishes; (2) a juvenile is committed to an institution for rehabilitation, not punishment; and (3) a longer commitment may be required to achieve rehabilitation.[43]

The Use of Juvenile Records If Later Sentenced as an Adult

Juvenile records are traditionally confidential. But can they be used in court later if the juvenile is sentenced as an adult? This issue arises because some studies show that many adult criminals start their criminal careers as juvenile delinquents. Courts have held that despite confidentiality restrictions, juvenile records can be used to increase adult sentences. The logic is that the confidentiality of juvenile records is given by state law; therefore, it is not a constitutional right. Consequently, confidentially may be taken away by state law which provides that juvenile records can be used for enhancement purposes, as in three-strikes laws. As one observer notes, "The state's interest in a complete picture of the criminal defendant is deemed superior to the state's interest in preserving the privacy of youthful offenders."[44] Juvenile court records may be used to increase or enhance criminal court punishments in at least three ways: (1) as criminal history points in sentencing guideline systems, (2) as aggravating factors considered during sentencing, (3) or as "strikes" in jurisdictions with "three-strikes" legislation.[45]

One study reveals that prosecutors routinely use juvenile records not just for sentencing but also in various aspects of criminal prosecution. A 1994 survey of national prosecutors conducted by the Bureau of Justice Statistics (BJS) showed that "82% of prosecutor offices in the U.S. reported using juvenile delinquency or court history records in felony prosecutions." The survey also revealed that among these prosecutors, "90% had used disposition records, 76% had used arrest records, and 69% had used probation reports." In sum, confidentiality does not shield juvenile records from use during subsequent criminal trial.[46]

Punishing Parents for What Their Children Do

Most states have laws holding parents responsible for what their children do. The latest figures show that at least thirty-seven states have such laws, with seventeen states holding parents criminally liable for offenses committed by their children.[47] Laws in many states authorize sending adults to jail for buying beer and liquor for minors who are later involved in drunken accidents. Some states also punish parents who allow underage friends of their children to drink beer or liquor in their home. Many counties and local governments have ordinances punishing parents if their children do not attend school. These sanctions are justified by assumptions that parents are responsible for their children's behavior and that children become wayward or delinquent because of poor parenting. It is further assumed that parents become more responsible if faced with possible punishment for not performing their duties. As one report says, "Parents across the country have spent a night or two in jail for failing to get their children to school. Some have had to pay the costs of their children's detentions. And in states such as Louisiana and California, parents can wind up in jail if their children associate with gangs or drug dealers."[48]

The U.S. Supreme Court has not addressed this issue, nor have there been leading decisions from the highest courts in various states. However, lower-court decisions generally hold that reasonable civil sanctions are valid but that severe criminal punishments are suspect. In general, requiring parents to pay fines, court costs, and restitution is valid because this is deemed a reasonable sanction for parental neglect and because children are not in a position to pay. But placing parents in jail or prison for what their children do is a more difficult legal issue. Most courts allow short penal sanctions, such as a few nights in jail, but long-term confinement of parents because of their children's behavior may violate parents' due process rights. Fundamental fairness is the essence of due process. It may be fundamentally unfair to severely punish parents for something over which they may not have any control even if they tried. It is different, however, if parents are personally involved in the criminal acts their children commit. In these cases, parents may be criminally punished as participants, not as parents. (See the "Controversial Issue" box.)

CONTROVERSIAL ISSUE: WHICH SIDE DO YOU FAVOR?

Should parents be held legally liable for what their children do?

According to a newspaper report from Philadelphia, "In a case that ups the ante for parents who turn a blind eye to underage drinking, a woman could get up to 15 years in prison for a deadly auto accident caused by a teen-ager who was drunk when he left a party at her house. Judith McCloskey, 42, will be sentenced next month for involuntary manslaughter. She was convicted in September, 17 months after a 19-year-old man leaving the rowdy gathering crashed his sport utility vehicle, killing himself and two passengers."

Many state and local laws impose sanctions on parents for the acts or nonacts of their children. These sanctions are civil, criminal, or both. Civil sanctions consist of restitution or indemnification by parents of damages caused by children. Criminal sanctions include a fine, confinement in jail, or time in prison.

Those who favor sanctions maintain that under civil law, parents are responsible for taking care of their children and therefore should be held legally liable for their behavior. CINS and juvenile delinquency are often traceable to bad parenting. In many cases, parents simply do not take good care of their children or are too weak to set rules and limits. Some parents encourage children to commit criminal acts or serve as poor models for behavior. Parents get drunk, use drugs, and commit criminal acts in the presence of their children. In the case of school truancy, there is no excuse for parents not requiring or encouraging children to attend school. Children raised by parents in a bad home environment are more likely to commit delinquent acts and later become adult criminals and further prey on society. Holding parents accountable for what their children do forces them to pay more attention to parenthood; it is irresponsible for them to do otherwise, and they deserve punishment.

Those who oppose imposing sanctions say it is unrealistic and unfair to burden parents with legal punishment for the acts or nonacts of their children. It is unrealistic because it is difficult to force individuals to become responsible parents and also because such a goal is outside the function of the government in a democratic society. It is unfair because some parents impose proper controls and draw limits that, despite all good-faith efforts, children disregard. What do parents do then? Peer pressure is sometimes more influential than parental control. Are friends to be punished too? It is grief enough for parents if children disobey them; it is totally unfair if parents, despite efforts, are also held responsible for behaviors that are sometimes outside their control. Some parents cannot control their children because they lack the mental capacity or are themselves afflicted. For example, how is a parent who is a drug addict supposed to control his or her addiction and not to be a bad model for children? Moreover, the behavior of some children is sometimes psychologically rooted. Rich parents can afford to get psychiatric counseling for their children; poor parents cannot. Should they then be punished for not being able to provide to proper treatment for their children?

Source: Adapted from *The Huntsville Item* (6 Oct. 2002): 2E.

Juveniles and the Right to Appeal
Juveniles May Appeal a Conviction and Disposition

Like adults, juveniles may appeal a conviction and disposition because the right to appeal is an integral part of the criminal justice process. It is not a constitutional right, but it is a right given to defendants by law in all states, in both juvenile and adult cases. Some appeals are automatic rather than being initiated by the defendant. For instance, in most states death penalty sentences are automatically brought to the next higher court for review (in some cases directly to the state's highest court, bypassing the state's next appellate court), unless the convicted offender refuses to appeal the case. However, appeals in non-death penalty cases must always be initiated by the defendant.

Theoretically, conviction for any offense can be appealed to that state's highest court and then all the way to the U.S. Supreme Court. In reality, the chances of an appeal being accepted by the U.S. Supreme Court are slim. Procedural rules limit how high the appeal can go, except when a constitutional issue (as opposed to an issue based on state law or the state's constitution) is involved. Even if a constitutional issue is involved, the *rule of four* governs access to the U.S. Supreme Court. This means that four of the nine Court justices must agree to hear and decide the case; otherwise, the case is rejected by the Court, and the decision of the immediate lower court prevails.[49]

Juveniles May Be Released While an Appeal Is Pending

The right to bail is found in the Constitution, but it is not an absolute right even in adult criminal cases, meaning that there are some offenses where the offender cannot be bailed out. For example, a suspect is not entitled to bail if the charge is for a serious offense and evidence of guilt is strong. After conviction, the right to bail is even weaker. Unless mandated otherwise by state law, the release of a defendant on bail pending appeal for conviction of a serious offense is usually up to the discretion of the trial judge. The rule is that a defendant is not constitutionally entitled to bail after conviction and pending appeal. However, most states allow bail pending appeal if the conviction is for a minor offense, but bail after conviction for serious offenses rests with the judge. For instance, X is charged with burglary and is sentenced to three years in prison. Pending appeal, state law will usually allow X to remain free in the community. But if X is charged with murder and convicted, bail becomes discretionary. Chances are that the judge will not allow bail if the defendant is a flight risk or may pose a continuing threat to the public if free pending trial.

Unlike adults, juveniles do not have a constitutional right to bail before, during, or after trial. This right has not been given by the courts to juveniles. No U.S. Supreme Court case has addressed the issue of whether juveniles may be released by the court pending appeal. Release of a juvenile while an appeal is pending is therefore governed by state law, and state court decisions and practices vary from state to state.

Appeal Distinguished from Habeas Corpus

Assume that X, a juvenile, is found guilty of assault and rape. X appealed his case all the way to the U.S. Supreme Court, but his conviction was affirmed. X is now serving time in a state institution, but his conviction is unconstitutional because a DNA test, which was not done during his trial, disproves his guilt. Does X have a remedy? The answer is yes, but it is not an appeal, because that process has been exhausted. Instead, his remedy is a writ of habeas corpus. **Habeas corpus** (a Latin term that literally means "you have the body") is a writ directed to any person detaining another, commanding that person to produce the body of the prisoner and to explain why detention is justified and should be continued. Unlike an appeal that is subject to time limitation, habeas corpus never expires as long as the person is still confined. A juvenile can be in an institution for years and still have the right to file a writ of habeas corpus. The differences between an appeal and a writ of habeas corpus may be summarized as follows:[50]

Appeal

1. A direct attack on the conviction.

2. Part of the criminal proceeding.

3. Purpose is to reverse the conviction.

4. Filed only after conviction.

5. Juvenile has been convicted but may be free on bail.

6. Must be filed within a certain time period.

7. All issues raised must be from the trial record, with no new evidence allowed.

Writ of Habeas Corpus

1. A collateral attack, meaning a separate case.

2. A separate civil proceeding after the criminal case.

3. Purpose is to secure release from prison.

4. May be filed at any time the juvenile is deprived of freedom illegally by a public official.

5. Juvenile must be in an institution or in detention.

6. May be filed any time as long as the juvenile is detained.

7. New evidence may be presented.

Towards a More Progressive Approach to Juvenile Disposition

The Office of Juvenile Justice and Delinquency Prevention suggests that juvenile probation and juvenile disposition need to adopt a new *paradigm*, meaning a new way of looking at juvenile justice that goes beyond the traditional approaches of treatment and just desserts. The current search focuses on the **balanced and restorative justice model.** The balanced approach "espouses the potential value of any case applying, to some degree, an entire set of principles along with individualized assessment." These are the principles of community protection, accountability, and competence of development and treatment.

Restorative justice "promotes maximum involvement of the victim, offender, and the community in the justice process." A combination of these two concepts results in the new balanced and restorative justice model, which sees that "justice is best served when the community, victim, and youth receive balanced attention, and all gain tangible benefits from their interactions with the juvenile justice system."[51] This new paradigm may be illustrated as follows: "Programs that require young offenders to engage in meaningful, productive work and service in their communities (competency development) during free time under structured adult supervision (community protection) can also provide a source of funding for repayments of victims as well as opportunities for community service (accountability).[52]

One publication identifies some of the assumptions of restorative justice:

- Crime control lies primarily in the community.

- Accountability is defined as assuming responsibility and taking action to repair harm.

- Punishment alone is not effective in changing behavior and is disruptive to community harmony and good relationships.

- Victims are central to the process of resolving a crime.

- The offender is defined by capacity to make reparation.

- Restitution is a means of restoring both parties.

- The community is a facilitator in the restorative process.[53]

Whether this new paradigm succeeds in setting a new and effective path for juvenile justice has yet to be determined. Its proponents say it holds great promise now and even more for the future. Its visibility over the last several years suggests this may be a major paradigm shift in juvenile justice. Its opponents say it is simply another example of those passing fads and fashions that have characterized the U.S. juvenile justice process during its more than a century of history.

SUMMARY

❏ Disposition is the formal pronouncement of judgment and punishment on a juvenile following a finding that the juvenile engaged in the conduct charged.

❏ There are five general goals of disposition: retribution, incapacitation, deterrence, restitution, and rehabilitation. In juvenile justice, rehabilitation has been the traditional goal, but such is not always the case in practice.

❏ Juvenile court judges have more discretion in dispositions than adult court judges have in sentencing.

❏ Blended sentences, a recent development in juvenile dispositions, combine juvenile court sanctions with adult punishment.

❏ Various dispositions are available to juvenile court judges. Among them are placement in an institution, probation, and other sanctions that leave the juvenile in the community (community service, fines, restitution, electronic monitoring, and other sanctions).

❏ The death penalty may be imposed on juveniles as long as the offender was at least eighteen years old when the crime was committed.

❏ Illegally seized evidence may be admissible in court to establish certain facts during juvenile disposition.

❏ "Three strikes and you're out" sentences apply to juveniles, and juvenile records may be used if the juvenile is later sentenced as an adult.

❏ As in adult cases, juveniles may appeal their conviction and disposition; they may also be released while the appeal is pending.

❏ Balance and restorative justice is the current "new paradigm" as society continues to look for a more effective and equitable disposition process.

REVIEW QUESTIONS

1. What are the five general goals of disposition? Describe each of them.

2. Why do juvenile court judges have more discretion in dispositions than adult judges have in sentencing?

3. What is blended sentencing? Give an example.

4. What are the various kinds of dispositions? Describe each of them.

5. Discuss the distinctions between informal and formal probation.

6. Distinguish between fines and restitution.

7. "It is unconstitutional to give a juvenile the death penalty." Is that statement true or false? Explain your answer.

8. Discuss whether parents can be held legally responsible for what their children do.

9. List four distinctions between an appeal and a writ of habeas corpus.

10. What is the essence of balanced and restorative justice? Give some of its assumptions.

KEY TERMS AND DEFINITIONS

balanced and restorative justice model: An approach suggesting that "justice is best served when the community, victim, and youth receive balanced attention, and all gain tangible benefits from their interactions with the juvenile justice system."

blended sentences: Sentences that combine juvenile court sanctions with adult sanctions.

community service: A type of adjudication that places a juvenile in an unpaid position with a nonprofit or tax-supported agency to perform a specified number of hours of work or service within a given time limit.

deterrence: Discouraging the juvenile (specific deterrence) or others (general deterrence) from committing crime.

disposition report: A report, usually prepared by the probation officer, that contains details about the juvenile's background, prior record, family circumstances, and other facts that may affect the disposition to be imposed by the judge.

electronic monitoring: An electronically monitored curfew imposed on the juvenile.

fine: A monetary punishment imposed on a person convicted of a crime; the money goes to the government.

formal probation: Probation that takes place after a finding of guilt.

habeas corpus: A writ directed to any person detaining another, commanding that person to produce the body of the prisoner and to explain why detention is justified and should be continued.

house arrest: A form of arrest in which the offender is allowed to stay at home instead of being kept in jail.

incapacitation: A goal of disposition that separates juveniles from the community and places them in a state institution to reduce the opportunity for committing more crimes.

informal probation: Probation that is usually given prior to adjudication or disposition.

rehabilitation: A goal of disposition that provides various types of psychological, medical, and physical services to juveniles in the hopes that they acquire needed skills and values to help them refrain from committing crime.

restitution: The restoring of property or a right to a person who has been unjustly deprived of it.

retribution: A goal of disposition that gives juveniles their "just dessert."

right of allocution: The right allowing a defendant to make a statement on his or her own behalf as to why the sentence should not be imposed.

three strikes and you're out: A sentencing law used in some states that increases sentences for offenders who commit subsequent crimes.

FOR FURTHER RESEARCH

❑ **Effective Intervention for Serious Juvenile Offenders**
http://www.ncjrs.org/html/ojjdp/jjbul2000_04_6/contents.html

❑ **Juvenile Admissions to State Custody, 1993**
http://www.ncjrs.org/txtfiles/fs-9527.txt

❑ **Judges in the Classroom Lesson Plan: Juvenile Justice—Disposition**
http://www.businesslessonplans.org/Disposition.htm

❑ **Juvenile Justice: Juveniles Processed in Criminal Court and Case Dispositions**
http://www.druglibrary.org/schaffer/GovPubs/gao/gao25.htm

❑ **Juvenile Court Process**
http://www.maricopacountyattorney.com/CCProcess/juvecourt.asp

For an up-to-date list of web links, go to the Juvenile Justice Companion Website at **http://cj.wadsworth.com/del_carmen_trulson_jj**

Juvenile Probation and Parole

CHAPTER TEN OUTLINE

Probation and Parole / 303
    Similarities / 303
    Differences / 303

The Origin and History of Juvenile Probation / 304

The Organization and Administration of Probation and Parole / 305

Conditions of Probation and Parole / 306
    General Conditions / 306
    Kinds of Conditions / 308
    Modification of Conditions / 309

Supervision / 309
    Standards and Goals / 309
    The Juvenile Probation Officer / 310
    Fare v. Michael C. (1979): An Important Case in Juvenile Supervision / 312

Other Community-Based Programs / 314
    Intensive Supervision Probation (ISP) / 315
    Shock Probation / 315

School-Based Probation / 316
Family Counseling / 317
Juvenile Boot Camps / 318

Legal Issues in Probation and Parole Practices / 319
    Searches and Seizures of Probationers and Parolees / 319
    Miranda Warnings and Interrogation by Probation Officers / 320
    Problems in Partnerships Between Probation Officers and Police Officers / 321
    Testing Juveniles for Drugs / 323
    Curfews / 324
    The Probation Records of Juveniles / 325

Revocation of Probation / 326
    The Initiation of Revocation / 327
    The Lack of Legal Standards for Revocation / 327
    Juveniles' Rights Prior to Revocation / 327
    The Results of Revocation / 328

Case Brief: *Gagnon v. Scarpelli* / 329

IN THIS CHAPTER YOU WILL LEARN

■ That probation and parole for juveniles have similar features but also differences.

■ That juvenile probation and parole agencies differ in structure and organization.

■ That judges and parole boards have much discretion when imposing conditions of probation or parole.

■ That supervision is the essence of probation and parole.

■ That special programs in probation and parole are aimed at effective behavior control and rehabilitation.

■ About the many legal issues in probation and parole, not all of which have been resolved by the courts.

INTRODUCTION[1]

Probation is the disposition most often used by judges when formally adjudicating juvenile delinquency cases, the second most popular disposition being residential placement. Probation is the oldest and most widely used community-based corrections disposition for first-time, low-risk delinquency offenders and for status offenders. But it is also extensively used for more serious juvenile offenders. For example, in 1999, formal probation was imposed by juvenile court judges as the most severe form of disposition in 62 percent of juvenile delinquency cases.[2] Probation has its critics, who allege that it is a slap on the wrist and does not deter the commission of future crimes. On balance, however, probation and parole are considered ideal alternatives for two reasons: They save taxpayers money and leave the juvenile in the community where rehabilitation is more likely than living in an environment, such as a state school, that may be criminogenic.

Probation and Parole

Probation is defined as a type of sentence where a convicted offender is allowed to remain free in the community, subject to court-imposed conditions and under the supervision of a probation officer. **Parole** (also known as aftercare in many states) is defined as the supervised release of an offender to the community *after* he or she has served time in a juvenile institution. To avoid confusion, however, parole is used in this chapter because it is more descriptive of the practice and is the term used in juvenile justice in many states.

The similarities and differences between probation and parole are summarized as follows:

Similarities

- Both are community-based corrections programs, meaning that the offender is out in the community instead of in jail, prison, or an institution.
- The offender has usually been convicted.
- Both are privileges, not a constitutional right. They are acts of grace, meaning that an offender can be denied probation or parole at the option of the judge or parole board in lieu of incarceration or continued incarceration.
- The offender is supervised.
- The conditions imposed are usually similar, the most common being no further commission of a criminal act and adherence to conditions imposed.
- If conditions are violated, the offender is sent to jail, prison, or an institution to serve out the sentence if on probation or the unserved term if on parole.

Differences

Probation
1. Offender has not been to jail or prison for the offense ("halfway in").
2. Granted by a judge or jury and is therefore an act of the judicial department.
3. Usually supervised by probation officers, who are state or local employees.

Parole
1. Offender has been to prison for the offense ("halfway out").
2. Granted by parole board or detention authorities and is therefore an act of the executive department.
3. Usually supervised by parole officers, who are state employees.

Most of the discussion in this chapter focuses on juvenile probation because more juveniles are on probation than are on parole or aftercare. Moreover, most of the literature and research in community-based corrections and court cases address probation rather than parole issues. However, remember that the same conditions, concerns, roles, programs, and legal issues arise in both juvenile probation and parole. Therefore, the discussions apply to both topics.

The Origin and History of Juvenile Probation

John Augustus, a Boston shoemaker, is known as the "father of juvenile probation." In 1847 he persuaded judges in Massachusetts to place wayward youths under his care. As one source notes, he "came up with a less high-handed, and ultimately much more influential method of keeping children out of jail."[3] John Augustus "simply bailed them out, though he did not know them personally, and asked the court to continue their cases on the strength of their promise to behave and his own undertaking to help them." Augustus's efforts have been described in these words:

> It was all very unofficial—Augustus never had a title or drew a salary from the court. . . . Nevertheless, he developed a kind of system. He chose suitable candidates on the basis of "the previous character of the person, his age and the influences by which he would in the future be likely to be surrounded." He assured the judge that, if those he had chosen were released, he "would note their general conduct, see that they were sent to school or supplied with some honest employment." From time to time, he would "make an impartial report to the court, whenever they should desire it." And if their good behavior continued long enough—"I wished ample time to test the promises of these youth to behave well in the future," Augustus later explained—they would be let off with small fines. Which Augustus himself sometimes paid.[4]

John Augustus later extended his care and attention to adult offenders. When he died in 1859, he had bailed out more than 1,800 people and had a liability totaling $243,234. He first used and popularized the term *probation* (a Latin term for "a period of proving or trial") and was poor when he died. His legacy is lasting and has made a major difference in how the juvenile justice system deals with wayward youths.[5]

Thanks to John Augustus, probation had long been an accepted practice by the time the first juvenile court was established in Chicago, in 1899. It was natural for juvenile courts to integrate probation into its system because the objectives of both the juvenile court and probation were similar—promoting the welfare and rehabilitation of children who were in trouble. Probation has since been an integral part of the juvenile justice system and is here to stay. As one source notes, "Despite all that has changed in a century and a half, juvenile probation still means close supervision, firm expectations, and tangible help—just the way it did in Augustus's time."[6] (See Exhibit 10.1)

EXHIBIT 10.1   *John Augustus*

"In 1847, I bailed nineteen boys, from seven to fifteen years of age, and in bailing them it was understood, and agreed by the court, that their cases should be continued from term to term for several months, as a season of probation; thus each month at the calling of the docket, I would appear in court, make my report, and thus the cases would pass on for five or six months. At the expiration of this term, twelve of the boys were brought into court at one time, and the scene formed a striking and highly pleasing contrast with their appearance when first arraigned. The judge expressed much pleasure as well as surprise, at their appearance, and remarked, that the object of law had been accomplished ... The sequel thus far shows, that not one of this number has proved false to the promises of reform they made while on probation."

Source: Patrick Griffin and Patricia Torbet (eds.), *Desktop Guide to Good Juvenile Probation Practice* (Pittsburgh: National Center for Juvenile Justice, 2002), 6, quoting from John Augustus, *A Report of the Labors of John Augustus, for the Last Ten Years, in Aid of the Unfortunate* (1852).

The Organization and Administration of Probation and Parole

The organizational structures of juvenile probation and parole (aftercare) vary greatly and can be confusing. The variations consist of the following:

- The department may be administered by the local government or by the state.

- The department may be financed by the local government or by the state.

- The department may be under the control of the judicial department or the executive department through the government offices.

- Juvenile probation may be combined with adult probation, or they may be separate.

- Juvenile probation and adult parole caseloads may be combined, or they may be separate.

As of 2004, the administrative structures for juvenile probation can be summarized as follows:

Combination	14 states
State–executive (under state control and managed by the governor's office)	12 states
Local–judicial (under local control and managed by judges)	8 states
State–judicial (under state control and managed by judges)	9 states

| Local–executive (under local control and managed by the executive department) | 3 states |

Other structural configurations:
    Decentralized (state of Illinois)
    District–judicial (Washington, D.C.).
    Local–combination (state of Washington)

The administrative structures for juvenile parole are as follows:

Combination	5 states
State–executive (under state control and managed by the governor's office)	12 states
Local–judicial (under local control and managed by judges)	2 states
State–executive	All other states

Other structural configurations:
    Local–executive (state of Indiana)
    Decentralized (state of Illinois)
    District–judicial (Washington, D.C.)
    State–judicial (state of Iowa)

This list shows that administrative structures for juvenile probation and parole vary greatly from state to state, but they may also vary even within a state. Juvenile probation and parole, more than their counterpart programs in the adult justice system, are configured to reflect what works best in a local community or within a state. Therefore, the structural patchwork is more a product of design than a lack of agreement on how juvenile probation or parole can work best.

Conditions of Probation and Parole
General Conditions

Conditions of probation and parole are designed to achieve two goals: control and rehabilitation.[7] They constitute the framework of behavior for the juvenile and guide the supervision by the probation or parole officer. Some conditions are passive ("you will not . . .") while others are active ("you will . . ."). An example of a **passive condition** is one that requires a juvenile probationer to refrain from using drugs or from committing further criminal acts. An example of an **active condition** is one requiring the juvenile to finish a high school degree or perform community service. Modern probation supervision emphasizes "active" rather than "passive" conditions because active conditions are easier to enforce and are deemed more rehabilitative because they are based on a commitment rather than fear.

Juvenile court judges have considerable discretion when imposing probation conditions. As one source notes, "Probation can range from simple periodic supervision of a juvenile permitted to live in his or her own home, through intensive (sometimes daily) supervision and even electronic monitoring of a juvenile permitted to live in his or her own home, through placement in a non-secure public or private residential facility as a probation condition, to confinement in a secure facility, such as a detention center or boot camp, as a probation condition."[8]

Most states do not specify the conditions to be imposed by law. They are instead left to the discretion of the juvenile court, usually upon recommendation of the probation officer. The practice is different in adult probation, wherein many states specify or suggest probation conditions to be imposed by the judge. The reason for the difference is that in juvenile probation the judge is supposed to act as a wise parent, a role neither expected of nor played by judges in adult probation cases. Parole conditions are also left to the discretion of juvenile institutional officers or parole board members, who are authorized to release the juvenile.

Probation conditions vary greatly depending upon the general objectives set by law (usually rehabilitation) and the creativity of the judge. Appellate courts routinely uphold conditions of juvenile probation. Despite this discretion, the imposition of conditions by judges has limits. These are best summarized by a California state court of appeals decision which stated that a probation condition is valid if (1) it has some relationship to the crime of which the offender was convicted, (2) is related to conduct which is not in itself criminal, and (3) requires or forbids conduct which is reasonably related to future criminality.[9] These three limitations are broad, vague, and leave the judge much discretion. Moreover, the overall goal of juvenile probation is rehabilitation, a broad concept that justifies just about any condition that leads to behavior improvement. For example, a condition that prohibits the youth from using drugs may be imposed for almost any type of juvenile offense because the effects of drug use are so pervasive that it is difficult to see that the offense cannot somehow be linked to possible drug use. Similarly, a condition that requires a juvenile to render community service without pay is rehabilitative, and so is a condition that requires a juvenile to observe curfew. In short, just about any condition the judge imposes can be justified under the guise of protecting society and rehabilitating the juvenile.

The following conditions of juvenile probation have been held constitutional by state courts:

- The Arizona Court of Appeals held in 1998 that although there is no specific authority given by the legislature to the court to order the juvenile to submit fingerprints as a condition, such condition imposed is valid because it does not violate basic fundamental rights and bears a relationship to the rehabilitative purpose of probation.[10]

- Another Arizona court ruled in 1990 that ordering a juvenile to perform community service as a condition of probation is valid.[11]

- A Pennsylvania state court in 1999 said that ordering payment by a juvenile of reasonable amounts of money as fines, costs, or restitution is valid as part of the plan of rehabilitation, considering the nature of the acts committed and the earning capacity of the juvenile.[12]

By contrast, the following conditions have been held invalid by state courts:

- The South Carolina Supreme Court in 1994 held that an order by the judge "emancipating" a juvenile from the obligation to attend school was invalid, saying that denying a juvenile an education has a negative impact on the child and is therefore anti-rehabilitative.[13]

- An Arizona court of appeals in 1995 ruled that an order by the judge as a condition of probation that the juvenile submit a DNA sample to the state DNA database in a child molestation case was invalid, saying that establishing the DNA database is restricted to persons who were convicted of certain crimes and therefore did not include juveniles.[14]

- A West Virginia court in 1997 held that an order imposing conditions of probation that are unreasonable or beyond the ability of the child to perform is not an order of probation at all but rather a disguised order of commitment. The frustration that would arise from the child's inherent inability to comply with an unreasonable condition of probation would negate the purpose of the statutory scheme of rehabilitation.[15]

Kinds of Conditions

Juvenile and adult probation usually have two kinds of conditions: standard and special. The same is true with parole. *Standard conditions* are those imposed on all offenders in a jurisdiction regardless of the nature of the offense committed. They are either prescribed by law (in adult probation) or set by court or agency practice (in juvenile probation). Standard conditions usually require the juvenile probationer to do the following:

- Commit no criminal offense
- Submit to drug testing
- Report regularly to the probation officer as directed
- Not leave the jurisdiction without permission from the probation officer
- Allow the probation officer to visit the juvenile's home at any time
- Not associate with persons with criminal records

Special conditions are tailored to fit the needs of an offender and are imposed only on certain offenders because of the offense committed and their particular rehabilitative needs. In many jurisdictions, special conditions are in addition to standard conditions. The purpose is to individualize the conditions to enhance the chances of successful rehabilitation. Judges impose conditions based on their assessment of an offender's needs, usually after recommendations are made by a probation officer. Special conditions may require the juvenile to do the following:

- Attend counseling sessions for substance abusers, if convicted of a DUI or drug possession
- Obtain a high school diploma or the educational equivalent, if the offender is a high school dropout
- Attend school or GED program, or obtain gainful employment if schooling has been obtained
- Attend literacy classes, if the offender does not know how to read or write
- Attend boot camp, if the offender needs strict discipline

- Pay restitution, if the offense involved property damage
- Attend anger-management sessions, if the offense results from anger fits
- Undergo family counseling, if the family is deemed dysfunctional

Modification of Conditions

Conditions imposed may be modified as needed and at the discretion of the judge. In practice, the modification is recommended by the probation officer but must be made by the judge. Probation officers do not have the authority to modify conditions on their own because modification represents an alteration of the disposition order and is a judicial function. Although conditions may be modified to make supervision more strict or less strict, most modifications are made to ensure better surveillance and control of the juvenile. The usual practice is for a warning to be given if the conditions imposed are violated. If warnings are unheeded or if the juvenile's conduct does not improve, a formal modification of the conditions is made to further limit the juvenile's behavior or ensure better compliance. For example, if a juvenile is frequently away from home during evenings and uses that time to associate with "friends of disreputable character," the court might impose a curfew so as to discourage such conduct. Courts have authority to modify conditions of probation at just about any time as long as the new conditions are valid and constitutional. However, there must be some justification for the modification, and the juvenile must be properly informed.

Supervision

Supervision is important in community-based corrections and has been accurately characterized as the "essence of juvenile probation."[16] *The Desktop Guide to Juvenile Probation*, published by the National Center for Juvenile Justice (NCJJ), states that "the common thread that runs through all approaches to supervision is utility; that is, that juvenile justice intervention must be designed to guide and correct the naturally changing behavior patterns of youth."[17] It adds that "unlike adult probation, juvenile supervision views a young offender as a developing person, as one who has not yet achieved a firm commitment to a particular set of values, goals, behavior patterns, or lifestyle. As such, juvenile justice supervision is in the hopeful position of influencing that development and thereby reducing criminal behavior."[18]

Standards and Goals

As in all corrections agencies (such as jails and prisons), standards have been established by the American Correctional Association (ACA) and other organizations for juvenile probation and parole. However, none of these standards have been enacted into law by any state or imposed upon any juvenile probation department by court order. They aim merely to persuade and remain as guidelines for "best practices." *The Desktop Guide* notes that the reason for nonadoption is that "there are no universally accepted probation standards because there is more than one way to provide probation services that observe the legal rights of minors and meet the needs for rehabilitation and safety."[19] Differences abound in the treatment of juveniles; these differences are often well-intentioned and attempt to individualize treatment to see what works best for a particular offender.

The Desktop Guide recommends that probation departments "consider the converging interests of the juvenile offender, the victim, and the community at large in developing individualized case plans for probation supervision."[20] To reconcile sometimes conflicting goals (such as rehabilitation versus punishment or treatment versus control), the same publication states that probation "must endeavor to not only protect the public and hold the juvenile offender accountable, it must also attempt to meet his needs."[21] Thus, the ideal form of juvenile probation supervision aims more at rehabilitation than merely meting out punishment.

Standards proposed by several organizations recommend that before a juvenile is placed on probation, a needs assessment should be conducted and a service plan developed.[22] These standards further suggest that the probation officer, in cooperation with the juvenile and his or her family, assess needs in the following areas: medical problems, proximity of the program to the youth, the capacity of the youth to benefit from the program, and the availability of placements.[23] In addition, the standards place strong emphasis on the "availability of supplemental services to facilitate the youth's participation in a community-based program."

The Juvenile Probation Officer

Probation officers are crucial players in juvenile probation. Theirs is an unenviable job that is made more challenging by changing punishment philosophies, chronic underfunding, experimental programs, large caseloads, and an increasingly high-risk clientele (see Exhibit 10.2). One publication reports the following data and demographics about juvenile probation officers:

There are an estimated 18,000 juvenile probation professionals impacting the lives of juveniles in the United States. Eighty-five percent of these professionals are involved in the delivery of basic intake, investigation, and supervision services at the line officer level; the remaining 15 percent are involved in the administration of probation offices or the management of probation staff.[24]

The same publication states that juvenile probation officers are generally college-educated white males, 30–49 years of age, with 5 to 10 years of field experience. In 1993 they typically earned $20,000–$39,000 per year and had an average caseload of 41 juveniles. Most had arrest powers, but they normally did not carry weapons.[25] Although states now require continuing education programs, variations abound in the number of hours required and the type of training supervision. National standards recommend 40–80 hours of pre-service or orientation training, followed by the same number of hours for ongoing training each year.[26]

EXHIBIT 10.2

Juvenile Probation Officers Need to Know the Law

Juvenile probation officers don't need to be lawyers. But they do need to be familiar with the legal framework within which they do their work, if they want to do it properly. At a minimum, they need to know something about the laws that govern the operation of their state's juvenile justice system and those that define their own powers and duties within it. They need to be aware of the legal rights of juvenile offenders and—at least in some places—those of their victims as well. And for their own protection, they should have some understanding of the scope of their potential liability to lawsuits, and how best to minimize it.

Source: Adapted from Patrick Griffin and Patricia Torbet (eds.), *Desktop Guide to Good Juvenile Probation Practice* (Pittsburgh: National Center for Juvenile Justice, 2002), 11.

In most states, juvenile probation officers are appointed and also terminated by the juvenile court judge. The following provision from the state of Indiana typifies the legal provisions in most jurisdictions:

> The judge of the juvenile court shall appoint a chief probation officer, and may appoint other probation officers, and an appropriate number of other employees to assist the probation department. The salaries of the probation officers and other juvenile court employees shall be fixed by the judge and paid by the county, subject to the approval of the county council. In addition to their annual salary, probation officers shall be reimbursed for any necessary travel expenses incurred in the performance of their duties in accord with the law governing state officers and employees.[27]

The following basic legal knowledge is needed by a juvenile probation officer:

- Basic knowledge of pertinent law
- Skill in oral and written communication
- Ability to plan and implement investigative or supervision services
- Ability to analyze social, psychological, and criminological information objectively and accurately
- Basic knowledge of criminological, psychological, and economic theories of human behavior
- Ability to use authority effectively and constructively[28]

Juvenile probation officers play many roles, and their work is often more demanding than that performed by adult probation officers. As the *Desktop Guide* observes, "The probation officer is expected to fulfill many different roles, often 'taking up the slack' after judges, attorneys, social agencies, parents, and so have met what they see as their own clearly defined responsibilities in the case and have expressed an unwillingness to extend themselves beyond these limits."[29] In many cases, the juvenile probation officer is the last hope of rehabilitation for the juvenile. The *Desktop Guide* states that a juvenile probation officer is expected, among other things, to be a cop, a prosecutor, a confessor, a rat, a teacher, a friend, a problem solver, a crisis manager, a hand-holder, and a community resource specialist.[30] To paraphrase a popular statement, no other criminal justice officials are asked to do so much for so many with so little. (The "You Are a . . . Probation Officer" box examines a controversial probation issue.)

Fare v. Michael C. (1979): An Important Case in Juvenile Supervision

The only case ever decided by the U.S. Supreme Court on juvenile probation supervision is *Fare v. Michael C.* (1979).[31] This important California case helps define the relationship between a probation officer and a probationer during probation supervision. The facts are these:

Michael C., a juvenile, was taken into police custody because he was suspected of having committed a murder. He was advised of his *Miranda v. Arizona* rights (anything he said could be used against him, and he could have a lawyer). When asked if he wanted to waive his right to have an attorney present during questioning, he responded by asking for his probation officer. He

---

YOU ARE A... **Juvenile Probation Officer**

A controversial issue in some juvenile probation and parole departments is whether officers should be allowed to carry firearms. Some departments allow officers to carry a firearm while in the office or when visiting probationers or parolees. The firearm is issued by the department, and officers are properly trained on how and when to use it. In most departments, however, the carrying of firearms while on duty is prohibited.

Those who favor officers' carrying a firearm say that it protects officers from job-related harm. Most probationers and parolees are not violent, but some pose a risk to personal safety. Times have changed. Firearms are needed for protection when the officer confers with an offender in the office, visits an offender at home, or goes into a high-risk neighborhood. Officers have been injured, some killed, while performing their duties. Without personal protection, officers become reluctant to visit risky neighborhoods or clients, thus impeding supervision. Because of prison congestion, the criminal justice system has released more violent offenders on probation or parole who might be a threat to the safety of supervising officers. Personal

protection of officers is a must and requires departmental support. If officers are not officially allowed to carry department-issued firearms, they should be allowed to do so on their own.

Those who are against officers carrying a firearm argue that doing so is unnecessary and can be dangerous. True, there are incidents of harm from probationers and parolees, but they are isolated and do not warrant extreme measures. It changes the nature of supervision for juvenile offenders, tilting it toward surveillance. Allowing officers to carry firearms changes the image of juvenile probation officers. Instead of being perceived as a big sister or big brother, officers will be viewed by juveniles as law enforcers, thus impeding rehabilitation. Departments also risk legal liabilities if an officer uses a firearm and the result is a fatality or injury. If personal safety is a concern, the department can adopt a policy requiring officers to accompany each other on such visits, or mandate that the officer be accompanied by a law enforcement officer.

As a probation officer, what is your decision? Justify it.

was informed by the police that the probation officer would be contacted later but that he could talk to the police if he wanted.

Michael C. agreed to talk and during questioning made statements and drew sketches that incriminated himself. When charged with murder in juvenile court, Michael C. moved to exclude the incriminating evidence, alleging it was obtained in violation of his *Miranda* rights. He said that his request to see his probation officer was equivalent to asking for a lawyer. However, the evidence was admitted at trial, and Michael C. was convicted.

On appeal, the U.S. Supreme Court affirmed the conviction, holding that the request by a juvenile probationer during police questioning to see his or her probation officer, after having received the *Miranda* warnings, is not equivalent to asking for a lawyer and is not considered an assertion of the right to remain silent. Evidence voluntarily given by the juvenile probationer after asking to see his probation officer is therefore admissible in court in a subsequent criminal trial.

The *Fare v. Michael C.* case is significant because the Supreme Court laid out two principles that help define the supervisory role of a juvenile probation officer. First, the Court stated that communications of the accused with the probation officer are not shielded by the lawyer–client privilege. This means that information given by a probationer to the probation officer may be disclosed in court, unlike the information given to a lawyer by a client, which cannot be revealed to anyone unless the right to confidentiality is waived by both the client and the lawyer:

> A probation officer is not in the same posture [as a lawyer] with regard to either the accused or the system of justice as a whole. Often he is not trained in the law, and so is not in a position to advise the accused as to his legal rights. Neither is he a trained advocate, skilled in the representation of the interests of his client before police and courts. He does not assume the power to act on behalf of his client by virtue of his status as advisor, nor are the communications of the accused to the probation officer shielded by the lawyer–client privilege.

Fare v. Michael C. shows that despite *parens patriae*—a doctrine based on a parent–child relationship—confidentiality of communication between the probation officer and a probationer does not exist. Confidentiality of juvenile records exists in most jurisdictions, but it stems from state law or agency policy prohibiting disclosure. Second, the Court made it clear in *Fare v. Michael C.* that a probation officer's loyalty and obligation are to the state, despite any loyalty or obligation owed to the probationer:

> Moreover, the probation officer is the employee of the State which seeks to prosecute the alleged offender. He is a peace officer, and as such is allied, to a greater or lesser extent, with his fellow peace officers. He owes an obligation to the State notwithstanding the obligation he may also owe the juvenile under his supervision. In most cases, the probation officer is duty bound to report wrongdoing by the juvenile when it comes to his attention, even if by communication from the juvenile himself.

The above statement is clear about where a probation officer's loyalty should be. Despite an officer's desire to help a juvenile with whom the officer may have established strong emotional ties, professionalism requires that the officer's loyalty be with the state and not with the probationer. Failure to realize this leads to role confusion and ineffective probation supervision. (Exhibit 10.3 takes a look at the balancing act that juvenile probation officers have to attempt to keep themselves effective and mentally healthy.)

Other Community-Based Programs

Other community-based programs have been developed by juvenile probation departments to meet the needs of juveniles. They aim to improve behavior, develop vocational skills, provide educational opportunities, and treat the mentally impaired. As is true of adult probation, juvenile programs vary among

---

EXHIBIT 10.3

Ten Survival Strategies for Juvenile Probation Officers

Beyond just staying alive, how do you really survive—and prosper through—a lifelong career in juvenile probation? After nearly four decades as a juvenile probation officer, Dave Steenson of the Hennepin County Department of Community Corrections in Minneapolis, Minnesota, offers the following ten tips:

- **"Have fun—maintain a life balance."** A probation officer's long-term health—and usefulness—depend on keeping body, mind, and spirit refreshed.

- **"Keep an open mind."** Recognize and acknowledge other perspectives than your own.

- **"Focus on the fundamentals."** Keep "bread and butter" skills—communication, writing, assessment, supervision—sharp.

- **"Be smart, be safe."** Use common sense and communication to avoid the misunderstandings that lead to conflict.

- **"Know your role."** Help clients understand what your job is (and is not) from the beginning of your relationship, to avoid being "all things to all people."

- **"Attend to best knowledge."** Stay curious about ongoing research on what works in juvenile probation, and be willing to change your approach to reflect what you learn.

- **"Acknowledge your mistakes."** If to nobody else, acknowledge your mistakes to yourself.

- **"Celebrate your success."** The feeling of accomplishment should be shared with others, too.

- **"Demonstrate personal responsibility."** Put ethical questions to the "mirror test."

- **"Take care of yourself."** Make time for activities that matter to you.

Source: Adapted from Patrick Griffin and Patricia Torbet (eds.), *Desktop Guide to Good Juvenile Probation Practice* (Pittsburgh: National Center for Juvenile Justice, 2002), 105.

states and within a state—limited only by what local communities are willing to undertake. Variations are caused by funding levels and community receptiveness to different treatment programs. Some of these **special programs** are discussed below, but the enumeration and discussions are far from comprehensive. They are discussed here simply for purposes of illustration. Although the labels may be the same, these programs differ in specifics from one jurisdiction to another.

Intensive Supervision Probation (ISP)

Intensive supervision probation (ISP) is a type of supervision used in both juvenile and adult probation. It is a program of intensive surveillance and contact with an offender and aimed at reducing criminal conduct by limiting opportunities through closer supervision. Unlike "regular probation," the goals of ISP are more closely aligned with protecting the public and risk management. As one observer notes:

> The concept of intensive supervision probation (ISP) was one of a new generation of strategies to emerge from the intermediate sanctions movement. First developed for adult offenders, ISP programs were intended to both provide an alternative to incarceration for appropriate offenders as well as to enhance the impact of supervision on high-risk probationers.[32]

One observer identifies four common features in intensive supervision for juveniles:

1. A greater reliance is placed on unannounced spot checks. These may occur in a variety of settings including home, school, known hangouts, and job sites.
2. Considerable attention is directed at increasing the number and kinds of collateral contacts made by staff, including family members, friends, staff from other agencies, and concerned residents in the community.
3. Greater use is made of curfew, including both more rigid enforcement and lowering the hour at which curfew goes into effect.
4. Surveillance is expanded to ensure 7-day-a-week, 24-hour-a-day coverage.[33]

Contrary to popular belief, intensive probation is usually not designed to deal with violent juvenile offenders. The majority of juveniles placed on intensive supervision are "serious and/or chronic offenders who would otherwise be committed to a correctional facility but who, through an objective system of diagnosis and classification, have been identified as amenable to community placement."[34]

Shock Probation

Shock probation is a form of probation whereby an offender is sentenced to incarceration but is released after a short period of confinement (the first pleasant shock) and then resentenced to probation (the second pleasant shock). In most states, only the judge who imposed the sentence can grant shock probation. In theory, the juvenile is not supposed to know that he or she will be placed on probation after serving a brief time in a juvenile institution. In practice, however, the juvenile likely knows he or she will soon be released on probation and that the period of institutionalization is designed to expose the juvenile to the harsh reality of being detained in hopes that the experience will deter future unlawful conduct.

Some states use shock probation for both juvenile and adult probationers. Shock probation may be a terminological anomaly because the offender on shock probation will have served time in an institution before being released. Serving time in jail or prison before release is a characteristic of parole, not of probation. The reason that most states classify the release as probation instead of parole is that the release is ordered by the juvenile judge instead of by juvenile institutional authorities, as in the case of parole. Moreover, the judge wants to retain control and supervision over the juvenile because if the juvenile is released on parole, the juvenile is then under the supervision and control of the parole board rather than by the judge, who wants to monitor behavioral progress.

School-Based Probation

School-based probation is new but is gaining popularity. Innovative and focused on juvenile students, it enlists the help of school authorities in monitoring a juvenile student's conduct. It is akin to regular juvenile probation except that supervision is moved "out of traditional district offices, into middle, junior high and high school buildings—and probation officers are supervising their caseloads right in the schools."[35] It makes sense that probation officers be located in places where supervised juveniles are found during weekdays and where they spend most of the day. On-the-spot supervision ensures three benefits: more contact, better monitoring, and a focus on school success.[36]

Pennsylvania currently has the most extensive school-based probation program. A study of these programs shows that "probation officers, school administrators, and students on school-based probation strongly believed that the program was effective in boosting attendance and academic performance and reducing misbehavior in school."[37] The essential components of this type of probation include the following:

- Clear goals, objectives, and outcomes
- A formal written agreement with the school laying out the philosophy, goals, objectives, and outcomes and outlining the roles and responsibilities of the probation department and the school district
- Assignment practices that restrict each probation officer to a single school building, and with an optimal caseload of no more than 30–35 students
- An information sharing agreement and protocol
- Mechanisms for using the probation officer's in-school presence as a preventive resource for the general school population[38]

Exhibit 10.4 shows some "best practices" for developing and implementing school-based probation agreements. What might be the advantages and disadvantages of school-based probation?

EXHIBIT 10.4 *School-Based Probation Agreements*

School-based probation program arrangements and procedures should be formalized via a written agreement between the juvenile court/probation department and the participating school district. At a minimum, such an agreement should contain the following:

- A statement of the philosophy, goals, and objectives of school-based probation
- A clear definition of the role of the probation officer within the school environment
- A clear definition of the role of the school district administration and staff in supporting the probation officer
- A list of probation officer responsibilities, including participation in any student assistance or pupil services team involving a probationer
- If probation officers are permitted to carry firearms, the procedure for carrying and storing that firearm while on school property
- A list of the school district's responsibilities, including the provision of a telephone line and office space affording privacy within the school for the probation officer
- Procedures assuring probation officers' access to probationers' student records, including attendance, discipline, grading, and progress reports
- Provisions for meetings between probation department administrators and school administrators to discuss ongoing program issues

Source: Patrick Griffin and Patricia Torbet (eds.), *Desktop Guide to Good Juvenile Probation Practice* (Pittsburgh: National Center for Juvenile Justice, 2002), 93, quoting from Pennsylvania Juvenile Court Judges' Commission, *Standards Governing School-Based Probation Services.*

Family Counseling

A state survey reveals that the most common program offered to juvenile probationers is family counseling.[39] This type of counseling is important because juvenile delinquency is often the result of bad parenting and a criminogenic home environment. Juvenile offenders disproportionately come from dysfunctional families where there is little awareness of the causes of delinquency. Consequently, family members might expect the courts to provide a "cure" and "fix" the child, not realizing that family relationships and negative home conditions caused the problem. In many cases, no amount of judicial threat or advice can make a difference; only total family commitment can. To encourage this, states authorize juvenile courts to require the family to undergo counseling and require other family members to participate in the rehabilitation process. This approach reflects the growing awareness that rehabilitation efforts are significantly more difficult unless the family environment is changed for the better.

A problem with family counseling is that it involves persons other than the juvenile. Consent to participate must be attained before the program can even be imposed. Without family cooperation, the program is bound to fail. The family must work together to achieve success, a hard thing to do for dysfunctional or noncaring families. If family counseling is successful, however, it achieves the twin benefit of rehabilitating the juvenile and helping the family.

Juvenile Boot Camps

One observer defines **boot camps** as "facilities that emphasize military drill, physical training, and hard labor."[40] Boot camps elude authoritative definition because structures and goals vary from one jurisdiction to another. One publication identifies the following characteristics of boot camps:

- Participation by nonviolent offenders only (to free up space in traditional facilities for violent felony offenders, meaning those who have used dangerous weapons against another person, caused death or serious bodily injury, or committed serious sex offenses)
- A residential phase of six months or less
- A regimented schedule stressing discipline, physical training, and work
- Participation by inmates in appropriate education opportunities, job training, and substance abuse counseling or treatment
- Provision of aftercare services that are coordinated with the program provided during the period of confinement[41]

In 1999, 52 boot camps housing 4,500 juveniles were located across the country.[42] Boot camps are popular because they are perceived to be more effective and less expensive than incarceration. They might be less costly than incarceration (although some maintain that boot camps are more expensive to run than juvenile institutions), but their rehabilitative effectiveness is suspect. A 1999 Koch Crime Institute study revealed that the recidivism rates for juveniles from boot camps ranged from 64 percent to 75 percent; for juveniles coming from detention, the rate ranged from 63 to 71 percent.[43] An earlier study by the U.S. Justice Department's Office of Juvenile Justice and Delinquency Prevention (OJJDP) of three boot camps had the following findings:

- Most participants completed the program.
- Academic skills were significantly improved.
- A significant number of participants found jobs during aftercare.
- No reduction in recidivism was found compared to a control group of youths who were institutionalized or placed on probation.[44]

Boot camps have become controversial because of some highly publicized abuses. One critic summarizes the negatives as follows: "The boot camp is a model that lends itself to abuses. . . . There is no evidence that the camps do any good."[45] Despite their critics, boot camps continue to thrive and enjoy public support for the time being, doubtless because a program of strict discipline and physical rigor strikes the public as effective, rehabilitative, and "just what juveniles need." Boot camps and their issues are covered in more detail in Chapter 11.

Legal Issues in Probation and Parole Practices
Searches and Seizures of Probationers and Parolees

The Fourth Amendment to the Constitution provides that "The right of the people to be secure in their persons, houses, papers, and effects, against unreasonable searches and seizures shall not be violated and no Warrants shall issue, but upon probable cause, supported by Oath or affirmation, and particularly describing the place to be search, and the person or things to be seized."

What is the extent of Fourth Amendment rights of probationers and parolees? The U.S. Supreme Court has decided several Fourth Amendment cases over the years, but many issues are still unresolved. The Court in *Griffin v. Wisconsin* (1987)[46] held that the search of a probationer's home by probation officers based on reasonable grounds is constitutional and that no search warrant or probable cause is needed. However, that search was conducted by probation officers, not by the police, and was authorized by agency policy. Would the same rule apply to searches conducted by the police on their own? What if the police were requested by probation officers to conduct the search? Would that be valid? *Griffin* did not resolve these issues.

The Court held in *United States v. Knights* (2001)[47] that warrantless searches of probationers are allowed for probation-related purposes. The Court went further, saying that police searches of probationers for investigative purposes are also valid without a warrant or probable cause. In this case, a police detective found incriminating evidence in the probationer's residence. The Court held that the warrantless search, which was authorized by a general search condition of probation and supported by reasonable suspicion, was valid. Interpreted together, these two Supreme Court decisions say that the requirements of a search warrant and probable cause are not needed in cases involving probationers as long as conditions of probation authorize such a search and it is based on at least reasonable suspicion.

These decisions have led to mixed results in state courts. For example, in 1994 the California Supreme Court held that a probationer's consent is not needed in any search conducted by a law enforcement officer.[48] The same court years earlier held that a probationer need not be notified that a search is imminent for officers to conduct a valid search.[49] In a 2003 case, however, the Illinois Supreme Court stated that "a search of a probationer's residence pursuant to a mandatory probation condition requiring submission to warrantless, suspicionless searches violates the Fourth Amendment if the searching officers lack individualized suspicion of a probation violation."[50] The Illinois Supreme Court said that the *Knights* decision did not address the issue of whether a probationer's acceptance of a search condition of probation constitutes future consent that then waives Fourth Amendment rights. The state court in Illinois looked at the language of the twenty probation conditions ordered by the judge in this case and found that compliance by the probationer was dependent on her conduct. It then held that because the language of the probation conditions required the probation officer to ask the probationer to consent to a search, the probationer's agreement to the probation order did not constitute future consent to all searches. However, this technical interpretation of the wording of the probation condition did not address the issue of whether the search without warrant or consent would have been valid had the condition of probation specifically authorized it instead of, by implication, requiring consent.

Two federal courts of appeals decisions have also placed in doubt the constitutionality of suspicionless and no-consent searches by probation officers. In one case, the First Circuit Court of Appeals held that reasonable suspicion of criminal activity is needed before an officer can search a probationer's home even if consent to search is specified as a condition of probation.[51] A year later, the Ninth Circuit Court of Appeals also held that reasonable suspicion is required for searches of probationers despite a probation condition authorizing a suspicionless and warrantless search.[52]

In sum, the issue of the extent to which probation and law enforcement officers can search probationers (and parolees) remains unresolved. It is clear that neither a warrant nor probable cause is needed for such searches. It is also clear that searches based on reasonable grounds (which has less certainty than probable cause) are also valid if authorized by agency policy. What is not clear is whether searches without any suspicion whatsoever are valid if authorized as a condition of probation. It is also unclear whether probation officers and the police have the same authority to search probationers, with or without judicial authorization in the conditions of probation. These issues will likely have to be addressed by the U.S. Supreme Court in the future.

The cases discussed previously on probationer searches and seizures involve adult probationers. The same holdings would apply to juvenile probations as well, because juveniles have the same rights as adults under the Fourth Amendment.

Miranda Warnings and Interrogation by Probation Officers

In the case of *Miranda v. Arizona* (1966)[53] the U.S. Supreme Court held that a suspect must be given the *Miranda* warnings if interrogated by the police while in custody. The ***Miranda* warnings** require that the suspect in a criminal offense must be given the following information by the police prior to custodial interrogation:

- You have the right to remain silent.
- Anything you say can be used against you in a court of law.
- You have the right to the presence of an attorney.
- If you cannot afford an attorney, one will be appointed for you prior to questioning.
- You have the right to terminate this interview at any time.

It is clear that a juvenile must be given the *Miranda* warnings if asked questions by the police while in custody. But if the interrogation is done by a probation or parole officer (who is also a public official), should the *Miranda* warnings be given? For example, a juvenile probation officer has information that a probationer committed rape. The probation officer calls the juvenile to the probation office for an interview about this alleged violation of the conditions of probation not to commit a criminal act. Must the juvenile be given the *Miranda* warnings prior to interrogation by the probation officer?

The U.S. Supreme Court decision in *Minnesota v. Murphy* (1984) provides the legal framework for analyzing this question.[54] In this case, the court held that statements made by a probationer to a probation officer during interrogation while *not* in custody are admissible in a subsequent criminal trial. The exception is if the probationer specifically asks for a lawyer during the interrogation and a lawyer is not provided. Taking into consideration all the facts in *Minnesota v. Murphy,* whether the *Miranda* warnings should be given by the probation officer when asking questions of a probationer is best answered in Table 10.1.

As Table 10.1 shows, it is important to know (1) whether the evidence obtained is to be used in a revocation proceeding or in a criminal trial and (2) whether the probationer is in custody. Evidence obtained by probation officers is usually used in probation revocation hearings, which are administrative proceedings. However, in some instances the evidence obtained by the probation officer might also be needed by the prosecutor in a subsequent criminal trial of that offender. In these cases, the *Miranda* warnings must be given if the evidence is to be used in a criminal trial and if the probationer is in custody.

From Table 10.1, an important issue arises: When is a probationer in custody? Jurisdictions differ, but the general rule is that if the probation officer will allow the probationer to leave after the interrogation, the probationer is not in custody. Conversely, if the probation officer knows that he or she will not allow the probationer to leave after the interrogation, the probationer is in custody. Under this test, asking routine questions during a routine visit with a probationer is considered noncustodial; however, asking the probationer to come to the office after the officer received information from the police and the officer asked the police to take the probationer into custody after the interrogation implies that the probationer is in custody.

Although *Minnesota v. Murphy* involves an adult, there is every reason to believe that the same rules outlined previously apply to juvenile probationers as well.

Problems in Partnerships Between Probation Officers and Police Officers

In the last few years, some states have initiated a system of collaboration between the police and probation officers in the supervision of juvenile probationers and parolees. This joint effort started with Operation Night Light in Boston and has spread to other cities. Under this arrangement, police officers are given information about juveniles on probation and their probation conditions so that

TABLE 10.1

When Should Probation Officers Give Miranda *Warnings?*

	Evidence to Be Used in a Revocation Proceeding	Evidence to Be Used in a Criminal Trial
If probationer is not in custody	No	No, unless the probationer asserts his or her right (this situation is a *Murphy* case)
If probationer is in custody	Some states say no; others say yes. It depends on statutory or case law	Yes

they can help supervise offenders. This collaboration has resulted in the removal from the streets of gang members who were probationers, based on technical violations of their probation conditions rather than the filing of new criminal charges.[55] This joint effort comes in many forms, including enhanced supervision partnerships, fugitive apprehension units, information sharing partnerships, specialized enforcement partnerships, and interagency problem-solving partnerships.

Legal issues arise from these arrangements because probation and police officers are governed by different rules when dealing with probationers. In general, police officers must deal with probationers just as they do with other individuals entitled to basic constitutional rights. Probation officers, on the other hand, have more power over probationers because they can enforce probation conditions set by the judge. One publication lists the legal issues involved in these collaborative efforts between probation officers and the police:

- What are the legal limits of the powers of the police when dealing with probationers and parolees?

- Can the police do what probation and parole officers do when dealing with offenders?

- Can judges (in the case of probationers) and parole boards (in the case of parolees) delegate to the police the same authority they usually delegate to probation and parole officers?

- Are consent searches obtained by probation officers in the presence of the police valid, or are they presumably coerced?[56]

Legal issues on probation officer–police collaboration are still developing, but existing case law gives us some idea of the direction in which court decisions are moving. One observer summarizes these decisions as follows:

> In general, courts have held that police officers are subject to the same legal constraints when dealing with probationers and parolees as when they deal with the general public. In these collaborations, the courts have stated that police officers serve merely as agents of decision-makers, but do not assume all of the powers of correctional (probation) officers. The options normally available to the police, such as seizing evidence that is in plain view during a valid search, remain constitutionally permissible. Police authority generally does not expand when the police collaborate with corrections officers, hence the greater supervisory authority corrections officers enjoy does not vest in the police by virtue of joint action. In general, collaboration with probation or parole officers does not give police officers greater authority than what they possess when dealing with other citizens.[57]

In sum, police officers are generally bound by the same rules when dealing with probationers and parolees as they are when dealing with the public, even if there is an official partnership between police and probation departments. The guiding principle is that probation officers may use the police for help because this is a part of the police function. Any citizen, probation officers included, can ask for help from the police.

For example, a juvenile probation officer who is about to visit a particularly violent juvenile probationer in his or her home can always ask the police officer to act as a security escort. Assume that in the process of escorting the probation officer, the police see drugs in the probationer's home. The police officer can legally seize these drugs under the plain view doctrine (meaning that what is seen by the police in plain view may be seized immediately as long as the item is immediately recognizable as seizable and the police's presence is legal). By contrast, assume that a police officer asks a probation officer to take her to the probationer's house because she suspects the probationer is selling drugs, but she has no probable cause to prove it. The probation officer complies and makes the visit so that the officer can ascertain if drugs are actually in the house. While there, the police officer sees drugs and seizes them. Such a seizure is illegal because the police officer used the probation officer's authority as an excuse to seize drugs in plain view. In short, the legal principle in these relationships is that probation and parole officers can use the police to help them perform their tasks; by contrast, police officers cannot use probation and parole officers to help them perform their jobs. (See the "Controversial Issue" box, which raises another question about the roles of probation and parole officers.)

Testing Juveniles for Drugs

Drug testing is a condition of probation in cases where the offense committed may have been caused by or linked to the use or sale of drugs. Legal issues arise from drug tests because of potential violation of the following rights: the right to privacy, the right against unreasonable search and seizure, the privilege against self-incrimination, and the right to due process.

In a 1995 case, the U.S. Supreme Court held that a random drug testing program for high school athletes is constitutional because the district had been experiencing widespread student drug use.[58] A 2003 decision holds that requiring students who participate in extracurricular activities to submit to random and suspicionless drug testing is constitutional. The Court said that the drug test was a reasonable means whereby the interest of the school district in preventing and deterring drug use among students could be achieved.[59] These two U.S. Supreme Court cases involved public schools, but they strengthen the authority of the judge or parole board to order tests for juveniles on the rationale that if drug tests could be required of high school students participating in certain activities (athletics or other extracurricular activities), they can also be required of juveniles who are on probation or parole and therefore have diminished constitutional rights.

Legal challenges from juvenile drug testing based on the right to privacy have been rejected because probationers have a diminished expectation of privacy as a result of their conviction. Challenges based on unreasonable searches and seizures have not succeeded because the tests are imposed as a condition of probation by the judge; therefore, obtaining urine or a hair sample is authorized by judicial order. The alleged violation of the right against self-incrimination is rejected by the courts because the Fifth Amendment of the Constitution prohibits testimonial self-incrimination but allows physical self-incrimination. Drug testing is a form of physical self-incrimination and therefore does not violate the Fifth Amendment. The claim of due process violation also fails because it is not considered unfair for the judge or board to require that a juvenile be tested for

---

?

Should juvenile probation and parole officers act as social workers or police officers?

As *The Desktop Guide to Good Juvenile Probation Practice* (2002) notes:

> Early probation officers tended to be volunteers. Massachusetts passed the first law providing for a salaried probation officer—to serve both juveniles and adults—in 1878. It was a policeman, Lieutenant Henry C. Hemnenway, working under the supervision of the Chief of Police of Boston, who drew the first probation paycheck.

This raises a question: *What is the proper role of juvenile probation and parole officers?*

Those who argue they should be social workers say this approach adheres to the mission and origin of juvenile probation. John Augustus, its founder, intended for probation officers to play that caring role. It is consistent with the *parens patriae* approach, which considers the juvenile a ward of the state who needs help, support, and understanding. Rehabilitation is enhanced if the juvenile is treated as a child who needs guidance rather than as a hard-core offender. In most cases, the juvenile is not fully aware of what he or she is doing; therefore, culpability or blame is diminished. *Parens patriae* works, except for a few juveniles who are "superpredators." Treating a juvenile like a member of a big family promotes respect for society and enhances rehabilitation. Juveniles need rehabilitation, not punishment. Society loses if juveniles are not rehabilitated and instead become future criminals.

Those who argue that juvenile probation officers should be like police officers point to the failure of the *parens patriae* approach when dealing with some juveniles. What all juveniles need, even at a young age, is a realization that they must take responsibility for their actions. The *parens patriae* approach retards maturity and postpones the time when offenders grow up and are held fully accountable for their actions. The concept of diminished responsibility for juveniles is bogus because juveniles these days, at least those above a certain age, are more mature than in decades past and know what they are doing. Many come from families in which discipline and accountability do not exist. It is society's task to instill those values in them. That will not happen unless "tough love" is used. They are to be viewed as members of our human family, but they also deserve full punishment, particularly after committing serious offenses. Society is best served and protected if probation officers play the role of police officers.

---

drugs due to the fact that many offenses are linked to drug use or drug trafficking. In sum, drug testing is constitutional as a condition of juvenile probation or parole.

Curfews

Curfews are imposed by city or county ordinance in many jurisdictions to control juvenile crime. A curfew requires juveniles to stay in their residence for specified hours, during which they are not to be found or seen in some public places. For example, a curfew might state that juveniles are not to be found outside their home between 9:00 P.M. and 6:00 A.M. Curfews are usually imposed by local ordinances passed by city or county officials, but they can also be imposed by a judge as a condition of probation for a particular juvenile offender.

Curfews have spawned numerous lawsuits about their constitutionality because they limit a juvenile's freedom to travel and be in a public place during certain hours. Several lower court cases have defined what courts or city councils can or cannot do when imposing curfews. For example, the courts have found the following curfew ordinances constitutional:

- A federal court in Pennsylvania ruled that curfew ordinances that provide a wide range of exceptions are constitutional despite allegations that they are too vague and too broad.[60]

- A Colorado state court held that curfew ordinances for juveniles enacted for order maintenance are constitutional as long as they do not unduly infringe on liberty interests.[61]

- The Federal Court of Appeals for the Fifth Circuit ruled that carefully worded juvenile curfew ordinances do not violate the equal protection clause of the Constitution, nor do they unconstitutionally infringe on the rights of parents to privacy.[62]

In contrast, courts have found the following to be unconstitutional:

- A Maryland appellate court has ruled that curfew ordinances that do not match their specified intent in law are unconstitutional on their face and that officials who enforce previously unchallenged curfew ordinances may be civilly sued in court for damages.[63]

- The Iowa Supreme Court has said that curfew ordinances that restrict all movements of juveniles, with no exceptions, are too broad and are unconstitutional.[64]

- The Federal Court of Appeals for the Fifth Circuit has concluded that curfew ordinances that restrict all movement of juveniles during the specified hours are unconstitutional.[65]

The above cases indicate that curfew ordinances passed by cities or municipalities are generally valid. They may be unconstitutional, however, if they are too restrictive, too broad, or too vague, or if they include conduct that falls solely within the control of parents.

The Probation Records of Juveniles

Juvenile records, including probation records, are confidential and therefore cannot be accessed by the public. However, a distinction must be made between being on probation and probation records. The fact that a juvenile is on probation is a public record in most states, so the record is available to anybody. But what is in the juvenile's record is confidential unless otherwise made accessible by state law. For example, in response to an inquiry from a member of the public, a probation officer may disclose that a juvenile is on probation. But what the juvenile is on probation for, the conditions of probation, the length of probation, and other matters in the juvenile's record cannot usually be revealed.

Even the fact that a juvenile is on probation may be prohibited from disclosure by state law or agency policy. Conversely, the contents of a juvenile's probation record may be made accessible to the public by state law. Confidentiality is governed by state law because juveniles do not have any constitutional right to confidentiality.

Nevertheless, the secrecy over juvenile records is eroding. In many states, the background of a juvenile, including probation record, may be disclosed to specific persons, such as the police, school officials, or corrections personnel. As one publication notes, "Juvenile Codes in 42 states allow names (and sometimes even pictures and court records) of juveniles involved in delinquency proceedings to be released to the media."[66] In sixteen states, juvenile court records or proceedings are public, and in twenty-seven states, the identity of the juvenile in delinquency cases may be released, but only in cases involving certain crimes and/or repeat offenders. In eleven states, media access to records is allowed only with a court order.[67] Confidentiality is not a constitutional right and therefore subject to state law or agency policy.

The U.S. Supreme Court has decided one case involving juvenile records and the right of the accused. In *Davis v. Alaska* (1974), the Court held that despite state confidentiality laws, the probation status of a juvenile witness may be brought out by the opposing lawyer on cross-examination.[68] In that case, Davis was convicted of grand larceny and burglary in an Alaska court. A key prosecution witness during the trial was Richard Green, a juvenile. The trial court issued a protective order prohibiting the defendant's attorney from questioning Green about his having been adjudicated as a juvenile delinquent and about his probation status at the time of the events about which he was to testify. The court's protective order prohibiting such disclosure was based on Alaska law.

On appeal, the U.S. Supreme Court held that an accused in a criminal trial is entitled to confront and cross-examine witnesses and that this right prevails over a state policy protecting the record of juvenile offenders. The Court said that an accused person's right to a fair trial prevails over a juvenile's right to confidentiality even if confidentiality is mandated by state law. The Court said that "whatever temporary embarrassment might result to Green or his family by disclosure of his juvenile record . . . is outweighed by petitioner's right to probe into the influence of possible bias in the testimony of a crucial identification witness." In sum, the right of an accused to a fair trial prevails over the right of a juvenile to confidentiality.

Revocation of Probation

Violation of probation conditions leads to revocation. As in adult probation, revocation for a conditions violation is left to the discretion of the juvenile court judge. Revocation is required only if mandated by law for certain serious violations, but this seldom happens.

For example, X, a juvenile, is on probation for robbery. X misses a scheduled weekly conference with her probation officer, and her probation is revoked by the judge. X appeals the revocation, claiming that Y, her friend who is also on probation for the same offense, was allowed to remain on probation even though neither of them conferred with the probation officer that week. The appeal will not succeed because revocation is discretionary, meaning that the decision will not be reversed on appeal unless gross abuse of discretion is shown. However, if state law provides that juveniles on probation for felonies must be revoked for failure to report to a probation officer, that provision is binding on the court, and judicial discretion is negated.

The Initiation of Revocation

Revocation of juvenile probation is usually initiated by the juvenile probation officer or the agency. In many jurisdictions, the motion to revoke is filed in court by the prosecutor. A warrant is then issued for the juvenile's arrest. In most states, the warrant is served by law enforcement officers. However, some states authorize juvenile probation officers to make an arrest and conduct searches and seizures. Once arrested, the juvenile is held in custody in a juvenile facility pending a revocation hearing.

The Lack of Legal Standards for Revocation

As noted previously, the judge has considerable discretion to revoke or not to revoke probation. These decisions are usually final and not appealable, the justification being that the judge knows what is best for the juvenile and therefore should not be second-guessed by an appellate court. The judge has options ranging from no revocation and no change of conditions all the way up to sending the juvenile to an institution. Judges usually rely on the recommendations of the probation officer to determine proper action. The *Desktop Guide* says that the probation officer's recommendation "should not, and need not, be all or nothing," urging instead that the officer "should recommend just what is needed to produce the juvenile's compliance with his probation and no more."[69] The implication is that revocation should be used as a last resort and not as a first option. The same source adds that ordering the juvenile to perform community work or adding a curfew restriction as a condition may suffice to convince the juvenile that the effects of violation are serious. Restraint, not quick revocation, is recommended.

Juveniles' Rights Prior to Revocation

The U.S. Supreme Court has not decided the question of whether juveniles have any constitutional rights during probation or parole revocation proceedings, but two allied cases involving adult probationers and parolees are instructive and should apply to juvenile proceedings.

The first case is *Morrissey v. Brewer* (1972),[70] in which a prisoner who was convicted of false drawing or uttering of checks was paroled from the Iowa State Penitentiary. Seven months later, his parole was revoked because he violated its conditions by buying a car under an assumed name, operating a motor vehicle without permission, and other related offenses. The parole officer's report showed that Morrissey was interviewed and had admitted to the violations. His parole was revoked. The issue raised on appeal was whether or not a parolee is entitled to constitutional rights prior to parole revocation. The U.S. Supreme Court said yes and specified that a parolee is entitled to the following rights prior to revocation:

- Preliminary and final revocation hearings
- Written notice of the claimed violations of parole and disclosures to the parolee of evidence against him or her
- The opportunity to be heard in person and to present witnesses and documentary evidence
- The right to confront and cross-examine adverse witnesses, unless the hearing officer specifically finds good cause for not allowing confrontation
- A neutral and detached hearing body, such as a traditional parole board, members of which need not be judicial officers or lawyers
- A written statement by the fact finders of the evidence relied on and reason for revoking parole

The due process protections granted in *Morrissey v. Brewer* (1972) were applied to probation revocation one year later in *Gagnon v. Scarpelli* (see the "Case Brief").[71] The Court in *Gagnon* said that probationers, just like parolees, are entitled to constitutional rights during probation revocation hearings and that these rights are exactly the same as those given to parolees. This ruling applies in both adult and juvenile cases.

Although probationers and parolees have rights prior to revocation, the U.S. Supreme Court held in *Pennsylvania Board of Probation and Parole v. Scott* (1998)[72] that illegally obtained evidence may be admitted in parole revocation hearings. The case is significant because it affirms that parolees have diminished constitutional rights in revocation hearings. In this case, the Pennsylvania Board of Probation and Parole admitted into evidence firearms and a bow and arrows that were confiscated from Scott's residence without a warrant or probable cause. Scott's parole was revoked, and he was sent back to prison to serve 36 months' back time. He appealed, saying that the *exclusionary rule* (which provides that evidence illegally seized is inadmissible in court) should have applied and that the evidence used against him in the revocation proceeding, collected without a warrant or probable cause, should have been thrown out. The Court disagreed, saying that the Fourth Amendment prohibition against unreasonable searches and seizures does not require the application of the exclusionary rule in parole revocation hearings because doing so "would both hinder the functioning of state parole systems and alter the traditionally flexible, administrative nature of parole revocation proceedings." Although this case involved a parolee, it likely also applies to juvenile and adult probation revocation proceedings.

The Results of Revocation

Revocation of probation may send the probationer to an institution for juveniles or, more commonly, result in a modification of conditions (such an increase in community service or more frequent reporting). In the case of parole, the juvenile may go back to a state institution or, similar to probation, may have

Case Brief   *Leading Case on the Rights of Probationers in Revocation Proceedings*

Gagnon v. Scarpelli, 411 U.S. 778 (1973)

Facts: Scarpelli, a felony probationer, was arrested after committing a burglary. At first he admitted involvement in the crime, but later he claimed that his admission was made under duress and thus was invalid. His probation was revoked without a hearing and without a lawyer present. After serving three years of his sentence, Scarpelli filed for a writ of habeas corpus, claiming denial of due process because his probation was revoked without hearing or counsel.

Issues: 1. Is a probationer entitled to due process rights in a revocation proceeding?

2. Is a probationer constitutionally entitled to be represented by counsel in a probation revocation hearing?

Court Decision: 1. Probationers, like parolees, are entitled to the same due process rights that parolees have prior to probation revocation proceedings, as given in *Morrissey v. Brewer,* 408 U.S. 471 (1972).

2. The right to counsel during probation revocation should be decided on a case-by-case basis. Although the state is not constitutionally obliged to provide counsel in all cases, it should do so when the indigent probationer or parolee may have difficulty presenting his or her version of disputed facts without the examination or cross-examination of witnesses or the presentation of complicated documentary evidence. The grounds for refusal to provide counsel must be stated in the record.

Case Significance: This is the most significant case ever decided by the Court thus far in probation law. *Gagnon* was decided one year after *Morrissey v. Brewer* (1972), a parole revocation case in which the U.S. Supreme Court held that parolees were entitled to due process rights prior to parole revocation. The Court in *Gagnon* extended the due process rights given to parolees in *Morrissey v. Brewer* to probationers, reasoning that both parole and probation revocation resulted in the loss of liberty, which is a "grievous loss." Therefore, the common element in *Gagnon* and *Morrissey* is that both probation revocation and parole revocation represent a "grievous loss" and require due process.

In both *Morrissey* (parole revocation) and *Gagnon* (probation revocation), the Court prescribed a two-step procedure for revocation: (1) the preliminary hearing and (2) the final hearing. In subsequent cases, however, the Supreme Court and lower courts relaxed these requirements, holding instead that there need not be two separate proceedings as long as some type of hearing is given. In a number of jurisdictions, only one hearing is given to a parolee or probationer prior to revocation. However, this hearing should feature all the rights given to probationers and parolees in the *Gagnon* and *Morrissey* cases.

Source: This brief originally appeared in Rolando V. del Carmen, Mary Parker, and Frances P. Reddington, *Briefs of Leading Cases in Juvenile Justice* (Cincinnati: Anderson, 1998).

his or her conditions modified. In some states, the effect of revocation is similar to a finding of juvenile delinquency in that the juvenile (even if on probation for a status offense) may now be given the same sanctions as a juvenile delinquent who has committed a more serious offense. Unlike adult probationers, who must serve the jail or prison term originally imposed (subject to parole law), juveniles may be kept in state institutions only until they reach the age of majority (adulthood). In some states, a juvenile may be paroled again even after the first parole is revoked.

After revocation, the release of an institutionalized juvenile before reaching the age of majority is again determined by the juvenile authorities who administer the state institution, not by the judge. In some cases, certain types of juveniles are kept beyond the age of majority by special laws that mandate harsher sanctions. For example, in some states, juveniles are released at age eighteen but may be kept until they reach the age of twenty-one if they are violent offenders, are parole violators, or have poor confinement records. Most youths in state juvenile correctional custody are released to parole or aftercare. In 1992, 69 percent of juveniles were released to parole or aftercare and therefore remained under the jurisdiction of the juvenile department. Only 15 percent were discharged without further supervision.[73]

SUMMARY

- ❑ Probation and parole are both community-based corrections programs, but probation means the juvenile is halfway in an institution, and a juvenile on parole is halfway out.
- ❑ The organization and structure of juvenile probation and parole agencies vary from state to state.
- ❑ Judges and parole boards have immense discretion when imposing conditions of probation and parole.
- ❑ Probation and parole officers perform many tasks, made more difficult by changing philosophies, underfunding, and an increasingly high-risk clientele.
- ❑ When supervising probationers and parolees, officers do not perform the task of lawyers; their loyalty is to the state, not to the offender.
- ❑ Special programs for probationers and parolees include intensive probation supervision, shock probation, school-based probation, family counseling, and juvenile boot camps.
- ❑ Legal issues arise in probation and parole practices in such areas as searches and seizures, the giving of *Miranda* warnings during interrogation, partnerships between probation officers and the police, drug testing, curfews, and confidentiality of probation and parole records.
- ❑ Juveniles have constitutional rights prior to revocation. These rights are enumerated in *Morrissey v. Brewer* for parolees and in *Gagnon v. Scarpelli* for probationers.

REVIEW QUESTIONS

1. Define *probation,* then define *parole.* Give similarities and then differences between the two.

2. Where, how, and by whom did juvenile probation originate?

3. "The power of a judge to impose conditions of probation is absolute and unlimited." Is that statement true or false? Defend your answer.

4. What are the two general kinds of probation conditions, and how do they differ?

5. Explain some of the roles expected of juvenile probation and parole officers.

6. What did the U.S. Supreme Court say in the case of *Fare v. Michael C.?* Why is that case important?

7. Distinguish between intensive probation supervision and school-based probation. What are the main features of each?

8. Why are juvenile boot camps popular with the public? Are they truly rehabilitative? Explain your responses.

9. Summarize what probation and parole officers can and cannot do when searching the home or residence of a juvenile who is on probation or parole.

10. Answer this question fully: Should a probation officer give a juvenile the *Miranda* warnings when asking questions?

KEY TERMS AND DEFINITIONS

active conditions of probation and parole: Conditions that tell the juvenile, "You will . . ."

boot camp: A program for juveniles that emphasizes military drill, physical training, and hard labor.

intensive supervision probation (ISP): A program of intensive surveillance of an offender, aimed at reducing criminal conduct by using supervision to limit opportunities to engage in it.

Miranda **warnings:** A rule that police officers must give suspects under custodial interrogation the following warnings: You have the right to remain silent; anything you say can be used against you in a court of law; you have the right to the presence of an attorney; if you cannot afford an attorney, one will be appointed for you prior to questioning; you have the right to terminate this interview at any time.

parole: The supervised release of an offender to the community *after* having served time in jail or a juvenile institution.

passive conditions of probation and parole: Conditions that tell the juvenile, "You will not . . ."

school-based probation: A type of probation wherein supervision is based in schools and enlists the help of school authorities in monitoring the juvenile.

shock probation: A form of probation whereby an offender is sentenced to incarceration but is released after a short period of confinement and then re-sentenced to probation.

special programs: Probation and parole programs designed to meet the needs of certain types of juveniles.

 FOR FURTHER RESEARCH

- ❏ **Juvenile Delinquency Probation Caseload, 1990–1999**
  http://www.ncjrs.org/txtfiles1/ojjdp/fs200306.txt

- ❏ **Aftercare Services**
  http://www.ncjrs.org/html/ojjdp/201800/contents.html

- ❏ **From the Courthouse to the Schoolhouse: Making Successful Transitions**
  http://ojjdp.ncjrs.org/search/SearchResults.asp

- ❏ **Effective Programs for Serious, Violent and Chronic Juvenile Offenders: An Examination of Three Model Interventions and Intensive Aftercare Initiatives**
  http://www.juvenilenet.org/jjtap/index.html

- ❏ **Implementation of the Intensive Community-Based Aftercare Program**
  http://www.ncjrs.org/html/ojjdp/2000_7_1/contents.html

For an up-to-date list of web links, go to the Juvenile Justice Companion Website at **http://cj.wadsworth.com/del_carmen_trulson_jj**

Juvenile Correctional Institutions

The Development and Evolution of Juvenile Institutions / 335

The Early Seeds of Juvenile Institutions: Almshouses and Orphanages (1600s–1820s) / 335

The First Juvenile Institutions: Houses of Refuge (1825–1850s) / 337

Reformatories, Training Schools, and the Cottage System (1846–1980s) / 338

Training Schools as a Laboratory / 340

Survival of an Institution / 341

The Juvenile Correctional Facility (1980s–Present) / 341

Types of Juvenile Placements / 342

Pre-adjudication Placements for Delinquents / 342

Adult Jails / 342

Youth Shelters / 345

Detention Centers / 346

Post-adjudication Placements for Delinquents / 347

Diagnostic Facilities / 347

Transfer Facilities / 348

Stabilization Facilities / 348

State Schools and Juvenile Correctional Facilities / 349

Juvenile Boot Camps / 355

Ranches and Forestry Camps / 357

Transition Facilities / 359

Adult Prisons / 359

Placements for Nondelinquents / 362

Parham v. J. R. (1979): Civil Commitment of Nondelinquents / 363

Conditions of Confinement and the Rights of Institutionalized Juveniles / 364

Conditions of Confinement in Juvenile Institutions / 364

Overcrowding / 365

Suicide Prevention / 366

The Rights of Institutionalized Juveniles / 367

The Right to Treatment / 367

The Right to Be Free from Cruel and Unusual Punishment / 368

Access to the Courts / 376

Case Brief: *Morales v. Turman* / 370

IN THIS CHAPTER YOU WILL LEARN

■ About the history and development of juvenile institutions.

■ That the first juvenile institution was called a house of refuge and was developed in 1825 in New York.

■ That institutions for juveniles often change names but procedures remain the same.

■ That there are a variety of different types of institutional placements for juveniles in the juvenile justice system.

■ That juvenile placements may be categorized as short and long term, secure and nonsecure, and pre- and post-adjudication.

■ That two major issues facing juvenile correctional authorities are overcrowding and suicide prevention.

■ That juveniles have a right to treatment and to be free from cruel and unusual punishment in juvenile institutions.

INTRODUCTION

Most juveniles are not institutionalized following adjudication. Institutionalization is the most formal sanction in the juvenile justice system. Delinquents committed to juvenile institutions are considered the "worst" juvenile offenders—dangerous, chronic, and disruptive, such that only separation from society is appropriate. Although institutionalized delinquents may be considered the worst juveniles, nondelinquents subject to juvenile court jurisdiction might then be considered the most dependent, neglected, or unstable youths in U.S. society. The juvenile justice system has institutions for nondelinquents, but they are never placed in institutions for security reasons or for punishment. Rather, they are sent to institutions for protection, treatment, and supervision. This chapter focuses on institutions for adjudicated delinquents, and a brief section discusses the institutionalization of nondelinquents.

Each juvenile institution has a distinct function in the juvenile correctional system. The function of a juvenile detention center is different from that of a juvenile state school, which in turn is different from the function of a youth shelter. Goals, like the functions of juvenile correctional institutions, also vary. Juvenile correctional institutions have traditionally focused on rehabilitation, yet some juvenile systems adopt a more punitive focus, and others are somewhere in between.[1] Where an institution falls in this continuum depends on many factors, such as the type of youths it serves, whether the institution is used before or after adjudication, and whether it is short or long term. Arguably, however, juvenile institutions are geared toward the best interests of the child. This chapter examines the historical development of juvenile institutions and how they have evolved over the years—all in the "best interests of the child."

The Development and Evolution of Juvenile Institutions

The development of separate institutions for juveniles began in the mid-1700s.* Since then, juvenile institutions have been called by different names: orphanages, houses of refuge, reformatories, industrial schools, training schools, state schools, and juvenile correctional facilities. Institutions for juveniles have had a rich history. Understanding the early development of juvenile institutions is critical to understanding the scope and operation of these facilities today.

The Early Seeds of Juvenile Institutions: Almshouses and Orphanages (1600s–1820s)

Prior to the early 1800s in America, separate institutions for juveniles did not exist. When a child was delinquent, it was the responsibility of parents to take care of the problem. In the most extreme cases, juvenile lawbreakers were dealt

---

*The period dates are approximations and tend to overlap. The beginning dates generally reflect the year when a new institution was developed. This does not suggest that other institutions ceased to exist with the development of a new one.

with in the same fashion as adults—whipped, beaten, flogged, jailed, and even executed. When parents were not available, and using the adult system was not suitable, the delinquent, poor, abandoned, and vagrant were taken in and cared for by neighbors and other townspeople. Life was close-knit in early colonial America, and helping the poor or needy was the responsibility of a good Christian family. Communities did not reject the underprivileged; rather, society believed that the presence of the poor and disadvantaged, including the delinquent, was a God-given opportunity for the privileged to serve the community.[2]

This philosophy changed with time. In the mid-1700s, approximately 1.5 million individuals were dispersed throughout the American colonies. By the mid-1800s, the population of the United States had grown to twenty-five million. The simpler rural life in the former colonies soon became more diverse and complex. Methods of informal social control eroded, and social disorder emerged as a major national problem. In the face of massive social changes spurred by population growth, an alternative to the informal community control of **wayward** youths came in the form of apprenticeships. **Apprenticeships** entailed sending delinquent or other "needy" youths out of the community to learn a skill. Many youths were sent to farmers, and others were sent to shoemakers, carpenters, journeymen, or in some cases ship captains to learn a useful skill. In the eyes of early Americans, removal through apprenticeships substituted for parenthood or when the community could not find the time or resources to deal with the problem.[3]

Not every needy child was sent to the high seas or to a farm. There were also "quasi-institutions" in the mid- to late eighteenth century. The most prevalent was the **almshouse,** or poorhouse. These institutions were intended for inept, impoverished, and debtor adults, but they were soon busy with the growing population of delinquent and abandoned youths. Almshouses were not a cure-all for wayward youths. With resources exhausted and the limited number of almshouses filled with adults, a growing number of youths were sent to a newly developed child-care institution known as the **orphanage.**[4]

One of the first orphanages was organized in Savannah, Georgia, in 1740, but large-scale development of these institutions did not begin until the 1830s. By then, orphanages began to take a prominent role in dealing with children. Orphaned children were admitted, but eventually a range of youths from the vagrant to the delinquent also came in. The popularity of orphanages grew so much that in the 1830s, there were twenty-three orphanages and by the 1840s, thirty more.[5]

Although not technically considered the first juvenile institutions, almshouses and orphanages were the seeds that led to the growth of separate child-caring institutions. They were designed to address the shortcomings of overburdened informal social control systems, and they offered a place for children in need or for those who had fallen prey to the sinful influence of their criminal parents and the temptations of society. As Rothman notes:

> The founders of orphan asylums . . . shared fully with the proponents of other caretaker institutions a fear that anyone not carefully and diligently trained to cope with the open, free-wheeling, and disordered life of the community would fall victim to vice and crime. The orphan, robbed of his

natural guardians, desperately needed protection against these dangers. Many children of the poor were in no better positions, since their parents—at best too busy to eke out a living and at worst intemperate—provided no defense against corruption. The vagrant, by definition lacking in supervision, would certainly come under the sway of taverns, gambling halls, and theaters, the crowd of drunks, gamblers, thieves, and prostitutes. The nightmare come true, of course, was the juvenile delinquent, his behavior ample testimony to the speed and predictability of moral decline.[6]

The First Juvenile Institutions: Houses of Refuge (1825–1850s)

Houses of refuge gained popularity in the early to mid-1800s. Although intended for juvenile lawbreakers, they eventually admitted a range of youths—from the disobedient child to the homeless vagrant. Established in 1825, the New York House of Refuge is considered the first refuge home in the United States. By 1828, two more cities had followed the lead of New York, with refuge homes being established in Boston and Philadelphia. By the 1850s, houses of refuge were found in most major cities in the United States: Rochester, New Orleans, Cincinnati, Chicago, St. Louis, and in Massachusetts. Houses of refuge held anywhere from 1,000 juveniles in New York to ninety juveniles in Massachusetts, usually for a period ranging from one to two years.[7]

The guiding principle of the houses of refuge was rooted in the problems associated with a growing society. Advocates argued that wayward children must be shielded from a society of vice and ills, especially from the sins of their weak and immoral parents, who had already been converted by vice. Not only must vulnerable juveniles be shielded from society, but they must also be trained to adopt a life of moral behavior. Discipline and habit training helped juvenile offenders learn the skills necessary to resist the temptations of life once they were released.

The daily routine for houses of refuge is best likened to the military. Each hour of the day was carefully planned, with little time for idleness. Under the belief that "idle hands are the devil's workshop," youths were summoned at sunrise and marched in a single-file line to the washroom. They would then be marched into the open grounds for close inspection of uniform and body for cleanliness. Following inspection, youths prayed in the chapel. Breakfast was at 7:00 A.M., and youths were then required to work until 5:00 P.M., with a one-hour lunch break at noon. At 5:00 P.M., the youths were given two hours to wash and eat, followed by one and one-half hours of evening classes. The day ended with evening prayers. Youths were assigned "apartments" or "cells" and were required to remain silent through the night; silence was strictly enforced.[8]

The promise of the houses of refuge to isolate and train juveniles was embraced throughout the United States, especially in the Northeast. Despite the promise of houses of refuge, critics questioned their effectiveness. Some felt they did more harm than good. Although they featured strict rules, enforced discipline, and habit training, houses of refuge eventually deteriorated into overcrowded and filthy institutions, almost unmanageable in size, where discipline, order, and care digressed into chaos, disorder, and recidivism. Critics also noted that they were schools of crime and that the mix of delinquent and non-delinquent youths had the unintended consequence of turning nondelinquents into delinquents, and delinquents into hardened criminals. More than one hundred years after their opening, the passage below typifies the feelings of critics of the houses of refuge:

> My criminal career began at the Maryland Training School for Boys, where I was committed for the heinous crime of truancy. . . . At the training school, I soon learned to steal a car . . . how to mug someone so they could not make an outcry, how to use celluloid to open a house door, how to make checks to see whether people were at home before a burglary, how to make up and use a burglar's kit and various other little things necessary to a successful criminal career.[9]

Eventually, the houses of refuge were replaced, but their era represented an important shift in U.S. society. First was the realization that parental and informal community control methods were not the only way to deal with problematic youths.[10] Second, the advent of the houses of refuge signaled that population growth, to some extent, was correlated with breakdowns in society. More people led to more problems, and, predictably, the community could not adapt. Houses of refuge supplemented the overrun informal control systems in society and assumed the role of a careful and responsible parent. They offered the perfect society by simulating the ideal puritan family—engaged in hard work, discipline, religion, and self-denial.[11] But the promise of the houses of refuge was short-lived, and their demise ushered in a new method for dealing with delinquents and other disadvantaged youths.

Reformatories, Training Schools, and the Cottage System (1846–1980s)

Houses of refuge did not disappear overnight. By the 1880s, they were being called reformatories or reform schools.[12] In a distinction more terminological than real, reformatories were houses of refuge with a different name. However, they differed in that the focus of reformatories was on educating youths, yet education was often superseded by a preoccupation with juvenile work to support the institution. Work was justified by the belief that it instilled good habits and values.[13]

The first reform school in the United States was established in Westboro, Massachusetts, in 1847. Originally called the Massachusetts State Reform School in Westboro, its name was changed in the 1860s to the Lyman School for Boys. In 1848 Massachusetts also opened the Massachusetts School for the "idiotic and feebleminded." This was followed by the State Industrial School for Girls at Lancaster in 1856.[14] Several states followed the lead of Massachusetts, and by 1900 most of the United States had reform schools.* By the turn of the

---

*This includes all except for the southern United States. Little research exists on the absence of juvenile institutions during the mid-1800s in the South. The most plausible reason is the agricultural foundation of these states, where juveniles, especially African American and Hispanic juveniles, would be sent to face hard labor on plantations. These facilities would be the backdrop of the southern plantation prison in the mid-1800s, where juveniles were typically sent along with adults.

twentieth century, however, there were still fewer than one hundred reform schools across the nation, mostly housing boys. Contrary to popular assumptions, the types of youths held in these institutions were petty offenders and, according to Schlossman, "belonged to the wayward, incorrigible, or vagrant class."[15]

The first juvenile court was created in Cook County, Illinois, in 1899, and by 1925 almost every state had instituted a separate juvenile court. The adoption of juvenile courts meant increases in the number of youths sent to reform schools and, eventually, criticism of their operation. The full force of these arguments, usually coming from a group that history has labeled the **progressives,** did not peak until the early 1900s. Criticisms by the progressives centered on the use of reform schools for noncriminal youths—youths who would later be labeled status offenders or children in need of supervision. Critics also reinvigorated the argument that reformatories were schools of crime, where offenders worked without purpose and received little education and skills training that would benefit them upon release.

What had been labeled houses of refuge in the 1830s and **reformatories** by the 1850s were regarded as **training schools,** *industrial schools,* or *boys' homes* by the early 1900s.[16] As Hart notes:

> Juvenile reformatories were known first as houses of refuge; when that term became opprobrious, they were called reform schools; when that term in turn became obnoxious, the name industrial school was used; when that name became offensive, they were called training schools.[17]

More than just a symbolic name changing, training schools were meant to be different from reformatories and houses of refuge. Rothman notes that the "reformatory suggested a military model: marching, uniforms, rigid rules of conduct, a barracks-like quality. Training school suggested a campus-like atmosphere, an organization no different from others in the community."[18] The reformatory was "old-fashioned"; the training school was modern and sophisticated. The training school would train, not discipline, the juvenile into becoming a productive member of society. Most importantly, training schools made the reform of the juvenile normal rather than stigmatizing. In other words, training schools provided juveniles with aspects of life they would experience upon their release. The justification for "normalizing" the institutional experience was based on the belief that juveniles would better adapt and experience less "shock" upon entering the outside world, making them less likely to re-offend.

The normalized method of the training school made it different from the reformatory in several ways. First, complete structure was replaced with certain freedoms. Amenities such as freedom of the "yard," recreation time, sports, and the commissary (the institution store) were implemented. Second, administrators instituted classification and grading systems. Classification systems served as a way to sort different types of youths and their problems, and grading systems provided a benchmark of progress for youths during their stay. Administrators also expanded educational and **vocational programs** so that juveniles could earn a living upon release. Training schools placed a premium on education and vocation. Advocates and administrators agreed that education and training should not be for the purpose of supporting the institution, but rather to give youths a marketable skill upon release.[19]

But what really made the training school different from the reformatory was the living arrangements. During the second half of the nineteenth century, one of the most contentious debates concerning juvenile institutionalization centered on whether "congregate" living, as found in houses of refuge and reformatories, was the best method to deal with delinquents. Houses of refuge and reformatories caged youths in prison-like cells or "apartments," where silence was enforced and each youth was treated as part of a whole or congregate. Proponents of the training school implemented what is known as the **cottage system.** Situated in a "free layout," or campus-style plan, each training school had a number of cottages spread throughout the common grounds so that the overall effect was of an open college campus. In the cottage system, the training school was placed far from the busy city—reformation would take place in the simpler and unhurried countryside.[20] The cottage plan had other important components. First, each youth was to be supervised by a cottage "mother" or "father." In this way, the cottage system avoided institutional living via the **school model** but instead became the functional equivalent of a home away from home under the **family model**—it provided love, care, and nurturing rather than strict discipline, standardization, and routine. Second, the cottage system promoted individualization, meaning that each child would be treated as an individual based on his or her unique situation. Children would have their own rooms and possessions, uniforms were no longer required, and specific classification and programming were tailored to the juveniles so they could develop their own personality.

Although not all training schools featured such ideal conditions, the cottage scheme and other changes spread rapidly in early-twentieth-century juvenile institutions. With these innovations came others, positioning the training school as a laboratory to identify, treat, and cure the individual of delinquency.

Training Schools as a Laboratory

The focus on normal and individualized treatment led to further developments in the treatment of institutionalized youths during the first decades of the twentieth century, one of which was the scientific study of delinquents in training schools. This trend was the result of a few factors. First, the fields of psychology, psychiatry, social work, and sociology were developing rapidly in the early 1900s, and the training school provided a perfect laboratory for the study of a captive audience. Second, advances in these fields led to changes in the assumptions about the causes of crime and prescriptions on how to cure it.

In early colonial America, crime was seen as synonymous with sin, and this belief lasted into roughly the early 1800s. As synonymous with sin, crime was viewed as the product of free will and the rational choices of those who allowed themselves to fall to the wicked ways of the "devil." This idea was simplistic, however, and did not account for the variety of circumstances that may push someone to delinquency. In the late 1800s, positivism developed in the study of criminals and delinquents. Unlike the proponents of rational choice, positivists (and positivism) assumed that delinquency was the result of something inherent in the child's biological makeup or the conditions of the environment in which he or she was raised—but delinquency was not necessarily the child's fault or choosing.[21] It was the acceptance of this thinking that led to the study of delinquents in training schools across the United States. This thinking also led to the practice of "treating" the juvenile delinquent, for it would be improper to "punish" juveniles for acts that were not entirely their fault. Rather, they could be reformed.

Survival of an Institution

The training school seemed to have the best of all worlds. On the one hand, it moved away from the strict rules and complete routine of the reformatory. It allowed more amenities and freedom, including an emphasis on individualization rather than congregate treatment. It was a complete and total institution: school, family, community, and even laboratory. It was a microcosm of the larger society but had none of its problems and all of its advantages.

Not every training or industrial school was perfect. In some cases, training schools were not much different from their close cousins: reformatories or—worse—adult penitentiaries. Some institutions substituted vocational training for work to support the institution and even generate a profit. Others could not recruit enough properly trained teachers for schooling. Moreover, in some institutions, not every youth was meaningfully involved in education or vocation—thus, idleness was the rule of the day. The cottage system for training schools also suffered from problems. Originally meant to hold a nominal number of youths, usually fewer than forty, some held upwards of sixty to eighty youths each.[22] Overcrowding replaced an intimate, family-like environment. Staff turnover also became a concern. Abuse and other forms of corporal punishment were commonplace in some institutions, especially in the face of relatively minor infractions (writing letters or talking). Inmates also abused one another, and recidivism increased for some youths following their release from training schools.[23]

However, training schools stood the test of time for years and in many ways resemble what are called state schools today in some areas. As history has shown, juvenile institutions do not die quickly. In the 1960s and 1970s, however, state schools came under a new round of criticism. Critics pointed out that state schools became overcrowded and violent institutions, where inmates were victimized by both staff and other juveniles. Like those who criticized past juvenile institutions, critics maintained that state schools taught juveniles to be better criminals, especially youths housed in them who were considered status offenders or dependent and neglected.

Criticisms of training schools and state schools resemble those levied against the houses of refuge a century earlier, which led to the development of reformatories. Ultimately, reformatories were replaced by the training school or state school. The future of the state school is unknown, but changes are occurring, and these changes are being realized with the newly named **juvenile correctional facility.**

The Juvenile Correctional Facility (1980s–Present)

The most important difference between the state school and the juvenile correctional facility (if states distinguish between the two) is the emphasis on controlling the serious, violent, and chronic juvenile offender. Today, some juvenile correctional facilities deal only with the most serious, violent, and chronic among all juveniles institutionalized within a particular state. Used in this way, they serve as "concentration points" for the most troublesome juveniles with whom the juvenile system has to deal. All other juveniles are held in state schools.

Juvenile correctional facilities resemble junior prisons, where delinquents live in a strict environment with few to no amenities and less of an emphasis on rehabilitation. These facilities are usually reserved for juveniles who will be transferred to the adult prison system or have longer sentences, so rehabilitation has become a second- or third-tier goal. "Inmates" will find that participation in rehabilitative programs, such as counseling or education, is secondary to the main goal of providing a strict, supervision-intense environment. This is not to suggest that all juvenile correctional facilities warehouse youths waiting for admission into adult prison, for there is variation across the United States. The "You Are a . . . Juvenile Correctional Officer" box focuses on the N. A. Chaderjian Youth Correctional Facility operated by the California Youth Authority (CYA). Decide if this may be a forum where you would like to work with troubled juveniles.

Time will further delineate the difference between the state school and the juvenile correctional facility. For now, the primary difference lies in the types of offenders they house. Juvenile correctional facilities, which they will be increasingly called, are reserved for the worst of the worst juveniles—meaning those for whom separation from society and other institutionalized juveniles and staff is the paramount concern. Training, industrial, or other named state schools will continue for the garden-variety institutionalized youth.

Types of Juvenile Placements

Although state schools are the most recognized juvenile institution, juveniles falling under the jurisdiction of the juvenile court may be sent to a variety of "residential placements." State schools normally hold only adjudicated delinquents, but juveniles are held in institutions both before and after adjudication. These institutions may be either secure or nonsecure and may be operated as long-term or short-term facilities. These are just a few of the ways that juvenile placements can be characterized. This section classifies juvenile placements as pre-adjudication or post-adjudication—in other words, whether they are used before or after the youth has been adjudicated. It also discusses whether juvenile placements are considered short or long term and secure or nonsecure. This section also discusses the institutionalization of nondelinquents in placements such as foster homes, group homes, and mental institutions.

Pre-adjudication Placements for Delinquents

Pre-adjudication juvenile placements consist of adult jails, youth shelters, and detention centers.

Adult Jails

Jails perform a variety of functions in the criminal justice system. They are short-term, secure lockups for adult offenders who are awaiting trial or for convicted offenders typically serving sentences of less than one year. Jails also hold adult probation and parole violators until their final disposition is decided.

YOU ARE A... **Juvenile Correctional Officer**

N. A. Chaderjian Youth Correctional Facility or "Chad" is one of eleven institutions for youth in the California Youth Authority (CYA). One look at Chad might make one mistake it as a small college campus. There is a football field, a new running track, well-kept grounds, and several large dormitories. Do not mistake this institution for a college campus, however. If the imposing fence topped with rolls of Constantine wire doesn't tip you off, Chad holds 600 of California's most violent 18- to 25-year-olds convicted of offenses ranging from murder to aggravated rape. Many of Chad's residents are what some refer to as "state-raised youth." They have literally been raised in state facilities and by correctional staff. Many youth have spent more time in institutions than in the free world, and their development has suffered. Some have characterized youth committed to Chad as crack babies in young men's bodies with the emotional maturity of a 4-year-old.

Like most juvenile institutions, youth committed to Chad are afforded the opportunity to improve themselves through educational programs and other activities. The most violent students at Chad even get their own special cage during instruction, or what CYA officials call "learning kiosks," which are equipped with a metal desk and seat that are anchored to the floor. Teachers instruct youths in "flak-jackets" and are ever cognizant to stay clear of openings in the learning kiosks in fear of being "gassed down" (a slang term for having a combination of urine and feces thrown in one's face).

Visitors to Chad are afforded the same precautions as staff. They are given an alarm-equipped security belt with a pin that can be pulled in the event of danger. Once the pin is pulled, guards at Chad are alerted to trouble and come running with metal batons in hand. These precautions are a necessary evil because of the violent concoction of youth it holds. Each of the six dormitories at Chad is divided into two separate halls, all named after California rivers. Most halls house specialized populations. American Hall is gang-free while Tuolumne Hall is dedicated to substance abusers. Merced Hall is for youth with severe mental problems. Another hall is for sex offenders. Sacramento Hall, also known as the "Special Management Program," is the area for gang-related juveniles. At Chad, it is policy to mix rival gang members as much as possible because sooner or later these youth will have to live among one another in the free world.

1. What would you say to these juveniles to help them change their ways? Do you believe juveniles like this can change?

2. A position in a juvenile correctional institution is one of the most readily available jobs in the juvenile justice system. Would you ever work in an institution like Chaderjian as a juvenile counselor or correctional officer? Why or why not?

3. Committed delinquents can be held only so long in juvenile institutions. In California, this means that juveniles must normally be released by age 25. How should states deal with youths released from this type of environment—many of whom are still violent, gang related, and mentally ill?

Source: Adapted from Jimmy Jellinek, "Caged!" *FHM* magazine (August 2003): 86–92.

Although jails are intended for adults, some juveniles are held in adult jails each year. This occurs despite the mandate of the federal Juvenile Justice and Delinquency Prevention Act of 1974 (JJDPA), which called for the "sight and sound" separation of juveniles from adults in jails and other lockups. As with many other juvenile justice policies and laws, compliance does not happen overnight. This is especially the case with juvenile offenders in adult jail lockup.

In 1974 the JJDPA required the sight and sound separation of juveniles from adults. In 1980 Congress mandated that the JJDPA sight and sound separation requirement be fully complied with by 1985 if states were to receive federal monies. This deadline was later extended through 1989 and again dealt with in 1999. Despite evidence that the practice is waning, by 2004 juveniles were still being held in adult jails. A number of causes are to blame. First, in many states, youths under eighteen may be considered adults by state law but are typically counted as juveniles (by researchers) when found in adult jails. Second, many states do not have the necessary room to house all juveniles needing secure detention. In these cases, states and their counties rely, to some degree, on adult jail lockup for juveniles accused of serious crimes. Many times their placement is limited, so one-day counts of juveniles in adult jails (by researchers) may count some of these temporarily held juveniles. Third, although juveniles are held in adult jails, it is likely that they are segregated by age; thus, many juvenile justice personnel feel that they are at least separated from adults. Finally, some juveniles in adult jails may have been waived to adult court, and despite the fact that their age indicates that they are juveniles, they may be held in adult jails because they will face adult trial.[24]

The best sources of information on the number of juveniles in adult jails come from two publications. One is a Bureau of Justice Assistance report titled *Juveniles in Adult Prisons and Jails: A National Assessment.* According to this report, released in October 2000, approximately 8,100 youths under eighteen were held in adult jail facilities across the United States.[25] The second publication is from the Office of Juvenile Justice and Delinquency Prevention and is titled *Juveniles in Corrections.* According to this national report, released in June 2004, 7,600 youths under eighteen were held in adult jails. Use caution in interpreting these figures, because in both reports, exactly 80 percent of the youths were considered adults according to particular state law—mostly because they were sixteen or seventeen and considered as adults in their respective states or, less frequently, because they were waived to adult court for trial and considered as adults for prosecution purposes. If one considers state law variations or waiver situations, only about 20 percent of juveniles in adult jails are being held in violation of the JJDPA requirement (for example, in some states being sixteen or seventeen is considered an adult and would not violate the JJDPA guidelines but would cause the juvenile prisoner to be counted as a "juvenile" in both national reports, for they counted anyone under eighteen).[26] Indeed, the Office of Juvenile Justice and Delinquency Prevention (OJJDP) recently reported that in 2003 seven states and the District of Columbia had completely removed juveniles from adult jails, forty states were in full compliance with only a few exceptions, and only one state (Ohio) was not in compliance but did "sight and sound" separate juveniles from the adult population.* In sum, the majority of youths under eighteen held in adult jails are considered adults by state law or

---

*J. Robert Flores, *OJJDP Annual Report, 2001* (Washington, DC: Office of Juvenile Justice and Delinquency Prevention, 2003): 24–28. Compliance with separation and adult jail removal of juvenile offenders was also examined in the five U.S. territories (American Samoa, Guam, Northern Mariana Islands, Puerto Rico, and the Virgin Islands). These territories were in full compliance with both separation and adult jail removal. South Dakota and Wyoming were the only two states that did not participate, according to this study.

have been waived to adult court for trial. Approximately 20 percent of youths held in adult jails are considered juveniles by state law, have not been waived, and are held in violation of the JJDPA mandate.

Youth Shelters

Youth shelters are short-term, nonsecure facilities typically used for status offenders or for the temporary care and custody of dependent and neglected children. Delinquent youths are sometimes held in shelter facilities, but only if another placement cannot be found or if a delinquent youth is transitioning to parole/aftercare from a secure placement (such as state school) back to the community. Because status offenders and dependent and neglected youths cannot be institutionalized in a secure facility, youth shelters serve an important function in the juvenile justice system, so they are included in the pre-adjudication classification.

Before the 1970s, there were relatively few shelter care facilities in the United States. However, following the requirements of the JJDPA of 1974, which mandated the **deinstitutionalization** of status offenders and other noncriminal youths from secure facilities, the popularity and use of these facilities increased. Getting an accurate count of youth shelters is difficult, but some have estimated their prevalence to range from 700 to more than 1,300.[27] These figures probably underestimate the number of youth care facilities in the nation because a number of private youth shelter facilities get overlooked.

Shelter care facilities are best considered a "bus stop" for nondelinquent youths waiting further placement or release. Although no reliable national estimate exists, the length of stay in a youth shelter can vary from overnight to several weeks but is perhaps close to the average stay in juvenile detention, which is around fifteen days nationally.[28] For status offenders, shelter care is often used until the youth's parents can be located to take him or her home. For example, a youth is taken into custody for breaking a juvenile curfew law, and police officers cannot locate the parents. For dependent and neglected children, shelter care facilities serve as a short-term placement until foster care can be found, adoption occurs, or the child is placed back with his or her biological parents or other guardian. Dependent and neglected children often have longer stays than status offenders because it is usually more difficult to find alternative placements for such youths. However, these practices vary considerably by state and jurisdiction.

Shelter care facilities are unlocked, a tradition that reflects the philosophy of the JJDPA of 1974 that noncriminal youths are not delinquents thus should not, and cannot, be locked up like delinquents. Youths are generally not allowed off the premises, but in rare exceptions they may be allowed weekend furloughs with parents or guardians. "Residents," in some cases, may be permitted to leave the premises for schooling. Predictably, the unlocked nature of the youth shelter combined with movement restrictions off the premises presents problems. For example, some youths feel that they are being "locked down" for a minor offense or for what their parents failed to do for them. For many youths, this generates anxiety and motivates problematic behavior such as efforts to escape from the facility.

Although intended for noncriminal youths, youth shelters occasionally accept delinquents. However, this situation is rare, occurring only when there are no other placements available or, more typically, when a delinquent is transitioning from a secure to a nonsecure environment such as aftercare. When used this way, a shelter facility might also be seen as a "halfway out" placement for delinquents who are not "street" ready but will be in a short time. Overwhelmingly, however, youth shelters serve as a bus stop for status offenders and dependent and neglected youths on their way to their final destination—home or a foster home.

Detention Centers

Juvenile detention centers are short-term, secure facilities operated primarily at the county level. They hold juveniles in four situations. First, detention centers hold juveniles awaiting their adjudication hearing. When used this way, they can be considered pre-adjudication facilities. Second, in some instances juvenile detention centers also house juvenile offenders for a short time after they have been adjudicated and are awaiting transfer to a state-run institution. When used this way, detention centers can be considered post-adjudication transfer facilities. Third, juvenile detention centers are more recently becoming popular as a separate disposition for adjudicated youths.* When used in this way, detention centers can be considered as secure post-adjudication facilities. Finally, juvenile detention centers also function as a placement for youths on parole or aftercare with the state juvenile justice agency. In the fourth instance, detention centers temporarily hold paroled youths who have committed a new delinquent offense or have violated the conditions of parole. When used in these ways, juvenile facilities parallel the functions of a jail in the criminal justice system.

There are more than 600,000 *admissions* to detention centers in the United States each year.[29] However, this does not mean that there are 600,000 youths in detention centers across the country. In reality, of the approximately 1.7 million juveniles processed by the juvenile justice system, about 20 percent of formally petitioned juveniles are held in a detention center until the final disposition of their case: A large number of youths will be released at detention intake or after a few days. This practice explains why the average length of stay in detention is just fifteen days.[30] The average population of detention facilities is approximately forty-three juveniles, and the overwhelming majority of youths held in detention are delinquent offenders, most of whom had engaged in violent or serious property crimes.[31] Because of the short lengths of stay in juvenile detention centers, programming is minimal. However, the juvenile's day is not idle. Youths in detention centers, like those in a youth shelter, participate in a variety of short-term activities such as facility maintenance, recreation, and group projects.

---

*See the National Juvenile Detention Association (http://www.njda.com/learn-guiding-ps2.html) for more information on the perspectives and purposes of juvenile detention today. Detention centers are also becoming popular as separate dispositions or punishments—for example, using detention as a disposition in lieu of probation or in combination with probation. The latter example might be referred to as shock probation in some jurisdictions.

Juvenile detention centers perform an important function in the juvenile justice system, but there is some indication that their use is becoming too popular.[32] By 2000, almost one-half of all public detention centers in the United States were filled above capacity.[33] One obvious consequence of overcrowding is its impact on staff and their ability to deal effectively with youths. Another by-product of overcrowding is the victimization of youths by other delinquents. Large facility populations have also begun to dictate the reliance on control mechanisms for disruptive youths—for example, observation rooms, longer-term room lockdowns (24–72 hours), and physical restraints such as straitjackets, four-point ties, handcuffs, and ankle cuffs.[34]

The reliance on these measures is in response to growing detention populations. These methods have been criticized, and some jurisdictions have begun to emphasize the diversion of youths from detention to supervision in the community—even for serious offenders. This is a double-edged sword. On the one hand, reducing overcrowding and its associated problems is a beneficial goal, yet on the other, the need to protect the community puts judges and detention administrators at odds with the interests of society and public opinion. Because of this conflict, several innovative programs have been developed to address both the needs of the community and overcrowding in detention centers— these are called detention diversion programs. One example of a detention diversion program is the Key Program, Inc., in Boston. In this program, youths are monitored on a 24-hour basis and are required to conform to strict requirements of school, work, counseling, and victim restitution.[35] Currently, the Key Program supervises approximately 500 offenders in Massachusetts who would have otherwise been placed in detention. There are similar detention diversion programs in New York (Spofford Detention Center Project), in Washington, D.C. (Oak Hill Youth Center Depopulation Project), and in Florida (Associated Marine Institutes).[36] These programs have demonstrated some success in supervising serious offenders in the community without incident. Despite their promise, however, the success of these programs in preventing pretrial offending has yet to be fully explored.

Post-adjudication Placements for Delinquents

Post-adjudication (after trial) **juvenile placements** are secure (locked) facilities. They hold adjudicated delinquent offenders and are typically operated at the state level. The main post-adjudication placements for delinquent offenders include diagnostic and transfer facilities, stabilization facilities, training schools, juvenile boot camps, youth ranches and forestry camps, and transition facilities. Adult prisons also serve as post-adjudication facilities for some delinquent offenders, primarily for those delinquents who have been waived and convicted in adult court or those who have been sentenced under blended sentencing statutes.

Diagnostic Facilities

Diagnostic facilities (also known as reception, orientation, or assessment centers) are usually the first stop for an adjudicated and institutionalized delinquent. The purpose of a diagnostic facility is to assess and classify delinquents, then assign them to the most suitable placement in the state juvenile correctional system. To accomplish this, diagnostic facilities employ a diverse staff comprising psychologists, psychiatrists, social workers, and medical doctors. These individuals conduct a battery of tests on delinquents, including psychological testing, intelligence testing, physical testing, and dental exams. Social workers or sociologists are also included as diagnostic staff and complete what is commonly referred to as a social history report, which details the youth's background with the juvenile justice system, family life, prior drug/alcohol use, school progress, and any other relevant factor that may assist in the development of a rehabilitation plan. In short, diagnostic facilities aim to place the juvenile in the right facility/program based on his or her needs.

Most states do not have a separate diagnostic facility solely for the assessment of youths, and diagnostic procedures are commonly done at a designated state school. However, larger states usually have a separate diagnostic facility. For example, the Texas Youth Commission (TYC) operates the Marlin Orientation and Assessment Unit, which is a "gateway" unit for all male and female delinquents committed to the TYC.[37] Youths stay at the Marlin Unit for an average of fifty-two days, just a few weeks longer than the national average of thirty-four days.[38] During their stay, youths are evaluated by clinicians, educators, correctional staff, social workers, and licensed counselors. A major part of the assessment includes observed interaction with other residents. After assessment, youths are then placed in one of several secure public and private residential facilities operated by the TYC. Other states have similar diagnostic facilities—for example, the Logansport Juvenile Diagnostic/Intake Facility in Indiana receives all male delinquents ages twelve to eighteen who have been committed to the Indiana Department of Correction Juvenile Division.[39] Similarly, the C. R. Minor Reception Center in Chesterfield County, Virginia, serves as a central intake and diagnostic center for all delinquents committed to the Virginia Department of Juvenile Justice before they are placed in a permanent facility.[40]

The bottom line is that diagnostic facilities seek to assess a youth's needs and place him or her in the appropriate program to address those needs. Some states have central diagnostic facilities, and others use state schools. However they are structured, diagnostic facilities are usually the first stop for the adjudicated delinquent sentenced to institutionalization.

Transfer Facilities

Transfer facilities are similar to diagnostic facilities in that they receive youths immediately after adjudication. Transfer facilities are typically short term and secure. Their purpose is to hold an adjudicated delinquent until a "bed" opens up in state school. Most states do not have separate, state-operated transfer facilities and typically hold adjudicated delinquents in a county detention center until there is room at state school.

Stabilization Facilities

Stabilization facilities hold mentally ill or emotionally disturbed youths. These facilities are secure and typically short term. Adjudicated delinquents come to stabilization facilities usually by referral from other secure institutions, such as a diagnostic facility or state school, if there is evidence that the youth suffers from a serious mental disorder. Once these youths arrive at a stabilization facility, they are given a mental health evaluation to determine if they meet the criteria for placement. Because most state juvenile institutions do not have specialized staff to deal with seriously mentally ill juveniles, many states have a central location, with specially trained staff, to handle these special-needs offenders. In states without a separate stabilization facility, inpatient psychiatric hospitals operated at the county level typically fill the gap.

The types of youths admitted to a stabilization facility include those who are determined to be a danger to themselves or to others, or those found to have serious deficiencies in day-to-day functioning due to psychiatric disorders. These often include suicidal behavior, self-mutilation (cutting), and other emotional disorders such as depression or schizophrenia. Youths demonstrating these behaviors and symptoms are held until they become stabilized. Once stabilized, they are transitioned back to state school to complete the remainder of their sentence. Youths who do not stabilize upon expiration of their sentence may be sent to an inpatient psychiatric hospital until their situation improves. Once (and if) they become stabilized, these youths are typically transitioned into the community through halfway houses. Rarely are juveniles released outright into the community without at least some services, such as outpatient treatment or other forms of counseling. These youths will also typically be required to complete a period of time in aftercare under the supervision of a juvenile parole officer and may be required, as a condition of aftercare, to take prescribed medication to manage their illness.

Estimates are that 20 percent of all youths in the juvenile justice system have serious emotional disorders.[41] This estimate goes up if it includes youths with less serious mental-health-related problems such as substance abuse, situational depression, and low self-esteem. A 2001 study by Linda A. Teplin estimated that almost 700,000 youths processed by the juvenile justice system demonstrated symptoms that would meet the criteria for one or more alcohol, drug, or mental disorders that require treatment.[42] This is a huge total, involving around half of all juveniles processed by the juvenile justice system—a number of whom will be institutionalized without proper treatment. The "Controversial Issue" box examines both sides of the issue on the proper role of juvenile institutions when dealing with youths who are mentally ill.

State Schools and Juvenile Correctional Facilities

However they are labeled, state schools, training schools, industrial schools, and juvenile correctional facilities are, in short, prisons for juveniles. Juvenile correctional facilities (both public and private) are considered the most secure placement in the juvenile justice system. They are locked, secure, and long term.

Prior to 1997, there were few systematic national-level data on the number and characteristics of juveniles housed in state schools or juvenile correctional facilities. In 1997 the U.S. Bureau of the Census administered an institutional census for the Office of Juvenile Justice and Delinquency Prevention and began counting the number of juveniles in residential placement. This information is compiled in the Census of Juveniles in Residential Placement (CJRP).[43]

CONTROVERSIAL ISSUE: WHICH SIDE DO YOU FAVOR?

Should juvenile institutions serve double duty as mental hospitals?

One journalist noted that in the 1950s and 1960s, the picture of a typical juvenile offender was driven by images of the Jets and Sharks of *West Side Story,* which portrayed decent kids trapped by their own circumstances. In the 1990s, the image was of a violent gang member in *Boyz in the Hood.* Today, the poster child for juvenile crime is the victim of mental illness. It is these youths who constitute a large share of institutional populations today.

This raises a question: *What is the proper role of the juvenile correctional system when dealing with mentally ill youths*?

Those who argue that juvenile institutions should serve double duty as mental health centers say the juvenile correctional system may be the last hope for juveniles to receive a proper diagnosis and treatment for their illness. If not in a juvenile institution, many juveniles could neither afford mental health treatment nor would bother finding free treatment once released because of strapped public mental health systems and long waits for an appointment. This is what their history before commitment has shown. Many mentally ill youths would likely not have committed their crimes had it not been for their illness; however, their delinquency must still be dealt with. Sending them to a mental hospital or mitigating their sentence because of their illness would not address the delinquency issue. Juvenile institutions are a good place to deal with treatment and delinquency issues.

Those who argue that juveniles should not be treated for their mental illness in juvenile institutions say they should be committed instead to mental hospitals. Their delinquency should come second to their mental illness because many would not have committed their crimes if they were not mentally ill. Treating juveniles in correctional institutions is a noble idea, but it has shortcomings. Although some state juvenile correctional agencies have stabilization facilities to treat mental illness, most can handle only a small number of juveniles who are in the worst stages of mental illness. Moreover, states can hold juveniles only so long. Juveniles cannot be held until their mental illness can be properly managed because their delinquency, not their mental illness, dictates their length of stay in the juvenile correctional system. As a result, mentally ill juveniles are still plagued with the same problems that led to their crimes and commitment upon their release. Nothing has really changed; thus, changes in their behavior cannot be expected. A better place for them is a mental institution where they can remain until their illness is treated or managed.

Source: Adapted from Skip Hollandsworth, "Their Last Good Chance to Get Better." *Texas Monthly* (November 2003): 136.

The CJRP provides a "one-day" population count of juveniles in residential placement. It does not provide data on annual admissions and releases but rather, on one given day, the number of juveniles in secure residential facilities. Despite some problems with this method of collection, it is the best-known count of juveniles in state schools and other types of residential facilities.

As of October 27, 1999, approximately 134,000 juveniles were being held in more than 3,700 public, private, and tribal facilities.[44] Of these 134,000 juveniles, almost 109,000 met the CJRP criteria:

■ Under age 21; *and*

■ Assigned a bed in a residential facility at the end of the day on October 27, 1999; *and*

■ Charged with an offense or court-adjudicated for an offense; *and*

■ In residential placement because of that offense.[45]

From 1997 until 1999, the number of juveniles in residential placement increased approximately 3 percent, or about 3,000. More than one-third of all juveniles were held for person-related offenses such as homicide, sexual assault, and aggravated assault. Another 48 percent were held for a property, drug, or public order offense (see Table 11.1). Four percent of youths held in residential placements were status offenders.[46] The picture obtained from these figures is that most juveniles held in residential placement are there for serious person or property offenses.

The average population of juvenile state schools is around 125 to 175. The average length of stay ranges from 225 to 365 days, or approximately eight to twelve months.[47] However, there is considerable variation with these figures that can be attributed to different state laws. The gap is most evident in states with legislation that have a more punitive focus for juveniles, especially serious and chronic offenders.

Of particular importance to juvenile institutionalization have been federal efforts to explore the disproportionate confinement of minority juveniles. As an additional amendment to the JJDPA of 1974, starting in 1996 states were required to determine whether the proportion of minority juveniles confined exceeds their proportion in the general population.[48] Nearly every state has a disproportionate number of minorities in residential placement based upon their proportion of the juvenile population in their state. Nationally, minority juveniles make up approximately 34 percent of the entire population of juveniles but constitute 62 percent of all juveniles in residential placement.[49] Whether this is due to discrimination in the juvenile justice system or that minorities tend to commit crimes or have additional background characteristics that are more likely to result in arrest, adjudication, and institutionalization is subject to intense debate. Table 11.2 examines the proportion of juveniles in each state that are considered minorities compared to the proportion of minorities institutionalized under CJRP criteria. What factors might help explain the disproportionate number of minority juvenile offenders in residential placement?

Institutional Programming   State schools attempt to rehabilitate delinquents through a diverse range of programs and services, including counseling, basic mental health treatment, and accredited educational and vocational programming. Residential placements for juveniles also have recreation programs, health and wellness activities, and religious services. Moreover, some state schools have specialized counseling, such as sex offender treatment, gang renunciation programs, and capital offender treatment.

TABLE 11.1   *Juvenile Offenders in Residential Placement*

More than one-third of juvenile offenders in residential placement were held for person offenses.

Most Serious Offense	Juvenile Offenders in Residential Placement		Percent Change 1997–99
	Number	Percent	
Total juvenile offenders	**108,931**	**100**	**3**
Delinquency	104,237	96	5
Person	38,005	35	7
Criminal homicide	1,514	1	−21
Sexual assault	7,511	7	34
Robbery	8,212	8	−13
Aggravated assault	9,984	9	5
Simple assault	7,448	7	12
Other person	3,336	3	50
Property	31,817	29	−1
Burglary	12,222	11	−3
Theft	6,944	6	−5
Auto theft	6,225	6	−5
Arson	1,126	1	23
Other property	5,300	5	13
Drug	9,882	9	6
Drug trafficking	3,106	3	2
Other drug	6,776	6	9
Public order	10,487	10	8
Weapons	4,023	4	−4
Other public order	6,464	6	17
Technical violation*	14,046	13	12
Violent Crime Index*	27,221	25	3
Property Crime Index*	26,517	24	−3
Status offense	4,694	4	−32

*Technical violations include violations of probation, parole, and valid court orders. Violent Crime Index offenses include criminal homicide, sexual assault, robbery, and aggravated assault. Property Crime Index offenses include burglary, theft, auto theft, and arson.

Source: Melissa Sickmund, *Juvenile Offenders in Residential Placement: 1997–1999* (Washington, DC: Office of Juvenile Justice and Delinquency Prevention, 2002), 1.

Of all services, educational programs represent the cornerstones of juvenile rehabilitation. Traditional academic or vocational instruction constitutes the bulk of a juvenile's day in training school. Educational programs in juvenile institutions are usually accredited by the state so that delinquents, once released, can transfer their credit hours into any public high school to count toward their diploma. State schools typically offer instruction in the basic courses that high school students are required to take: consumer math, English, typing, and biology. Some state schools also offer college preparatory classes for juveniles who want to attend college upon release.

Education is stressed in state schools; however, its quality is often limited by a number of realities. First, state juvenile facilities often lack substantial funding for education; therefore, delinquents may have access only to outdated materials and the most rudimentary teaching methods. Second, teachers in state

TABLE 11.2

Minority Proportion of Juvenile Offenders in Residential Placement

In 1999, minority youth accounted for 34% of the U.S. juvenile population and 62% of juveniles in custody.

| State of Offense | Minority Proportion | | | Committed | | State of Offense | Minority Proportion | | | Committed | |
	Juvenile Population	Total CJRP	Detained	Public	Private		Juvenile Population	Total CJRP	Detained	Public	Private
U.S. total	**34%**	**62%**	**62%**	**66%**	**55%**	Missouri	18%	41%	56%	37%	*
Alabama	35	59	63	60	55	Montana	13	41	*	37	*
Alaska	34	56	*	52	*	Nebraska	14	45	41	45	50
Arizona	43	60	58	63	52	Nevada	37	49	49	50	*
Arkansas	26	56	*	59	58	New Hampshire	4	13	*	22	*
California	59	79	72	84	70	New Jersey	37	84	81	87	60
Colorado	27	54	51	60	51	New Mexico	62	78	76	79	*
Connecticut	25	77	78	82	63	New York	41	70	81	76	58
Delaware	32	68	66	*	*	North Carolina	34	63	68	69	36
Dist. of Columbia	86	97	100	*	*	North Dakota	11	39	*	*	34
Florida	41	58	63	58	55	Ohio	17	47	51	46	42
Georgia	41	66	65	67	66	Oklahoma	26	48	42	54	44
Hawaii	75	91	*	*	*	Oregon	16	27	16	29	22
Idaho	12	19	*	22	*	Pennsylvania	17	64	57	71	66
Illinois	35	69	75	70	53	Rhode Island	18	55	*	68	38
Indiana	15	38	42	41	29	South Carolina	40	67	78	67	65
Iowa	7	25	23	27	26	South Dakota	16	42	*	43	*
Kansas	17	48	52	49	38	Tennessee	24	50	39	53	42
Kentucky	11	37	53	39	25	Texas	52	74	74	74	74
Louisiana	44	78	74	82	74	Utah	12	27	30	28	25
Maine	3	4	*	4	*	Vermont	3	*	*	*	*
Maryland	40	70	61	73	75	Virginia	32	63	63	63	67
Massachusetts	20	62	58	75	54	Washington	22	41	42	40	*
Michigan	23	55	54	47	60	West Virginia	5	22	18	*	25
Minnesota	12	45	52	46	41	Wisconsin	15	59	58	65	47
Mississippi	47	73	74	73	*	Wyoming	12	28	*	29	28

- Minorities accounted for 66% of juveniles committed to public facilities nationwide—a proportion nearly twice their proportion of the juvenile population (34%).

- In most states, minority proportions tended to be lower for youth committed to private rather than public facilities.

- In six states and the District of Columbia, the minority proportion of the total population of juvenile offenders in residential placement was greater than 75%.

*Too few juveniles in category to calculate a reliable percentage.
Note: The juvenile population is the number of juveniles age 10 through the upper age of original juvenile court jurisdiction in each state. U.S. total includes 2,645 juvenile offenders in private facilities for whom state of offense was not reported and 174 juvenile offenders in tribal facilities. Minorities include blacks, Hispanics, American Indians, Asians/Pacific Islanders, and those identified as "other race."

Minority Proportion of Juveniles in Residential Placement

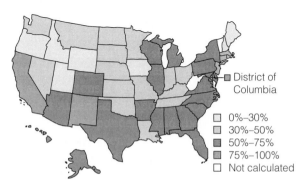

- District of Columbia
- □ 0%–30%
- □ 30%–50%
- ■ 50%–75%
- ■ 75%–100%
- □ Not calculated

Source: Melissa Sickmund, *Juveniles in Corrections* (Washington, DC: Office of Juvenile Justice and Delinquency Prevention, 2004), 10.

training schools deal with youths who have already had significant academic problems in the "free world" school setting and are usually behind their age-appropriate grade. The fact that these juveniles represent some of the state's most troublesome youths does not help the problem. Instructors have a disproportionate number of youths with learning disabilities, and teachers often instruct students of varying ages, grade levels, and competencies, often in the same classroom. Third, state schools have a difficult time finding instructors willing to teach there because many teachers are simply not prepared to deal with the challenges of teaching in a secure environment.

State schools also have vocational programs that focus on providing youths with a marketable skill upon release. The most common types of vocational training are carpentry or building trades, engine repair, computer training, forestry/agriculture, and electrical trades.[50] Learning a skill does not mean that institutionalized delinquents will always find gainful employment once released from training school. Many youths are still hindered by the behavior that got them committed in the first place. Even the best welder or carpenter will not be able to obtain and hold down a job if he or she does not have the self-discipline to arrive at work on time, follow rules, do quality work, and avoid further delinquent behavior. Moreover, although juveniles released from state school do not technically have a "conviction" on their record, their past can come back to haunt them in terms of employability, particularly because more and more states and jurisdictions are making it easier for employers to obtain information about a juvenile's past record. This is especially the case for serious offenders, a label that characterizes most institutionalized juveniles.

Because academic training and vocational training are considered the cornerstones of rehabilitation in state training schools, every youth is required to participate in these activities. However, some youths will be subject to specialized programming not required of all institutionalized delinquents. These programs focus on delinquents with special issues, including chemically dependent youths, sex offenders, mentally ill offenders, and violent or capital offenders. For example, the Giddings State School in Texas operates the Texas Youth Commission's (TYC's) Capital and Serious Violent Offender Treatment Program for youths committed for murder, capital murder, or offenses involving weapons. This program is designed to help violent TYC juveniles recognize feelings associated with their crime and identify "trigger" situations that may relate to re-offending. Delinquents in this program are also required to reenact their crimes with other youths in role-playing schemes.[51]

The programs and activities for institutionalized youths are aimed at the most efficient and effective ways to rehabilitate institutionalized delinquents. These were the goals of the original training schools and still remain in contemporary state schools and juvenile correctional facilities.

Future Trends in State Schools Rehabilitation has always been the main goal of state schools, yet there is some evidence that this may be changing. In a 2003 study, Caeti and colleagues completed a national survey of juvenile facility directors concerning the goals of their juvenile correctional system. Juvenile facility directors ranked rehabilitation as the number-one goal; however, many ranked deterrence, incapacitation, and retribution as goals as well. The survey also revealed that facility directors believed that fewer than one-half of their juveniles could be rehabilitated.[52] The facility directors might not have been too far off the mark, for emerging evidence suggests that recidivism rates for "state delinquents" is high. For example, Trulson and colleagues examined the recidivism outcomes for nearly 2,500 youths released to parole from a large southwestern juvenile correctional system in 1997 and 1998. They followed these youths five years from their release, through 2003, and found that 77 percent were rearrested for a felony. Approximately 60 percent were re-incarcerated during the five-year follow-up as a result of the felony rearrest.[53] Thus, for some facility directors the move away from rehabilitation may be reflecting these and similar findings from other important studies on the recidivism of state delinquents.

The finding that rehabilitation remains the main focus of most juvenile correctional agencies is not surprising. What is surprising is that a number of facility directors believe that one-half of juveniles are not amenable to rehabilitation through treatment programs. States are opting for increasingly tough responses to serious and violent juveniles. The move from "state schools" to "juvenile correctional facilities" may be one indicator of the trend that the first-tier goal of juvenile correctional departments is to incapacitate and protect rather than to treat and rehabilitate.

Juvenile Boot Camps

Juvenile boot camps dominated the 1990s as the panacea for juvenile delinquency. Enjoying much public and political support, boot camps were popular because they claimed to punish and rehabilitate juvenile delinquents simultaneously. Boot camps appealed to various groups. The public and media were quick to approve of drill instructors screaming at disrespectful offenders. Politicians embraced the concept of the "get-tough" atmosphere. Correctional officials accepted the boot camp as a cost-effective alternative to confinement; it was a program with more "bang for the buck."[54]

Although boot camps for juveniles are a relatively recent phenomenon, boot camps to correct (or punish) criminal behavior are not new. The roots of today's boot camps can be traced to the nineteenth century, when early penitentiary administrators used lockstep marches, silence, and military-type discipline in the handling of prisoners. However, the first contemporary boot camp program began in Georgia in 1983. This was a boot camp for adult offenders. The first juvenile boot camp was established in 1985 in Orleans Parish, Louisiana. Boot camps developed in earnest for juvenile offenders across the nation in the 1990s.

Boot camps are guided by the philosophy that hard work and disciplined training are effective ways to accomplish rehabilitation. This same philosophy justified the existence of houses of refuge, reformatories, and, to a lesser extent, training schools. Juvenile boot camps were influenced by and modeled after adult boot camps, but the core components of juvenile boot camps are found in juvenile justice programs initiated in the 1960s such as Outward Bound and Vision Quest. These programs were characterized by a mixture of physical, exciting, and adventurous challenges often based in a wilderness setting.[55] Similar juvenile-based programs that influenced the development of boot camps included "shock probation" and "Scared Straight." These were characterized by "shocking" the delinquent into compliance with the law through short periods of unexpected incarceration or frightening visits to the local penitentiary.[56] Juvenile boot camps also include components of work or community service, general and specialized counseling (substance abuse), and a lengthy component of aftercare or parole supervision.[57] Taken together, boot camps appear to have the best of all worlds.

Determining the number of juvenile boot camps and the populations served is difficult; they are dispersed among numerous local, county, and state jurisdictions. MacKenzie and Rosay conservatively estimate that more than 10,000 juveniles are in boot camps across the country.[58] Typically, boot camps are designed for mid-range offenders who have failed at less restrictive sentences such as probation or house arrest.[59] Most boot camp programs typically exclude serious or violent offenders, special offenders (sex offenders), and those who cannot pass physical health requirements and/or have a preexisting physical condition. The length of stay in boot camps varies considerably but generally ranges from 75 to 120 days. The ages of admission to boot camps vary as well, being as young as ten in Mississippi and as old as twenty in California.[60] Although boot camp delinquents spend a significant portion of their day outdoors, boot camp participants are locked down at night in cells or, more typically, in barracks-style dormitories.

The ultimate measure of success for boot camp programs is whether they reduce recidivism. However, evaluations of this subject are few. In 1991 three pilot juvenile boot camps (in Cleveland, Denver, and Mobile) were funded by the Office of Juvenile Justice and Delinquency Prevention. The objective was to evaluate the effectiveness of juvenile boot camps in areas such as education, substance-abuse counseling, job training, and recidivism reduction.[61] The secondary goals of the evaluation were to examine program implementation.

Studies from these programs indicate that youths increased their academic performance and that the boot camp was cost effective compared to secure institutionalization. However, boot camp youths did no better than a comparison group of delinquents in terms of recidivism, and in one site (Cleveland) they did worse. Boot camp participants also re-offended quicker than a comparison group of delinquents.[62] Staff turnover also kept the boot camps from fully instituting their programs. However, these problems were not peculiar to Cleveland, Denver, and Mobile. Other boot camp evaluations have led to similar findings. Evaluators of the Leadership, Esteem, Ability, and Discipline (LEAD) boot camp operated by the California Youth Authority (CYA) found that participants in this state-level boot camp did no better in terms of recidivism than a group of similar delinquents not assigned to the camp.[63] Similarly, evaluators of the Bay County Sheriff's Juvenile Boot Camp in Panama City, Florida, that state's fifth juvenile boot camp, found that 64 percent of boot camp graduates were rearrested within one year of graduation, 49 percent of graduates had been re-adjudicated for new crimes, and only 52 percent of the graduates even completed parole aftercare. Despite some positive achievements in academic performance, boot camp participants did not do significantly better than a comparison group of delinquents who were not assigned to the camp.[64] These findings seem to reflect the general findings from other juvenile boot camp evaluations.[65]

By the end of the 1990s, the lack of promising results was not the most serious obstacle that faced juvenile boot camp programs. Instances of corporal punishment, deprivation, and even death led to calls for boot camp abolition. A poster picture of abuse occurred in Buckeye, Arizona, in a private boot camp operated by the America's Buffalo Soldiers Re-Enactors Association (ABSRA). Fourteen-year-old Anthony Haynes died in a motel bathtub after camp drill instructors attempted to revive him with cold water after he collapsed from dehydration and physical exertion. This same boot camp allegedly forced "recruits" to eat mud during "mud treatments" and to lie on their backs in a "dead cockroach" position while having muddy water poured into their mouths. Other abuses included tying a noose around one recruit's neck, dousing recruits with water to attract bees, and threatening corporal punishment for reporting the abuse.[66] Such abuses have not gone unpunished, however, and in February 2005 the director of the Buffalo Soldiers boot camp was convicted of manslaughter for the death of Anthony Haynes.

Since 1980, thirty-one children have died in juvenile boot camps, and numerous others have been abused or excessively punished. In March 1998, Nicholaus Contreraz died at the privately run Arizona Boys Ranch Boot Camp after being told by the camp nurse that his vomiting and diarrhea were "in his head." Nicholaus died while doing forced push-ups over a bucket of his soiled clothes. An autopsy later revealed seventy-one cuts and bruises on his body and nearly three quarts of pus in his left lung and pneumonia in his right lung.[67] Similarly, Gina Score, age fourteen, died in the custody of a state training school in Plankinton, South Dakota, with a temperature of 108 degrees after participating in a forced run. Camp authorities allegedly ridiculed the girl and made jokes about her limp body despite her purple lips and frothing mouth. Deaths are not the only abuses that have focused increasing attention on boot camps. For example, in 1997 in Georgia a boot camp drill sergeant was accused of breaking a juvenile's arm because the child was unable to do push-ups, and in March 2001 a twelve-year-old Conroe, Texas, girl filed a complaint against Montgomery County juvenile justice officials after she was allegedly kicked in the face and slammed against a wall in that county's boot camp program.[68]

Such horror stories have dampened the public's enthusiasm for boot camps, but they are still popular in certain circles. Boot camps will likely be around in one form or another for the foreseeable future.

Ranches and Forestry Camps

Some delinquents never experience the steel doors and spartan cells of a juvenile correctional facility. A relatively recent advance in the juvenile justice system has been the "noninstitutional institution," a program increasingly used for a special type of offender. These types of programs, rather than institutions *per se*, are the functional equivalent of a traditional correctional facility without its steel doors and cells. These programs are called ranches and forestry camps.

Ranches and forestry camps are designed to hold medium-security juveniles. Although they are not new, dating from the 1950s, ranches and forestry camps are an increasingly popular way to deal with delinquent youths. Today, there are more than 150 ranch and forestry camp placements in the United States.[69] On average, ranches and forestry camps hold 50 juveniles who stay an average of 194 days.[70] They are second only to state training schools in their average length of stay for juvenile offenders. Ranches and forestry camps are distinguished from two closely related programs, adventure and wilderness camps. Ranches and forestry camps are post-adjudication placements. Wilderness and adventure camps are diversionary programs that occur prior to a youth being petitioned to juvenile court. Wilderness and adventure camps are not considered a form of institutionalization.

Youth ranches and forestry camps are situated in rural or tree-laden areas. These juvenile placements assume that youths can benefit from a challenging structure while at the same time learn survival skills, work as a team, and accomplish a goal. In addition to skills training and team building, delinquents in these programs are involved in daily activities consisting of conservation work or landscaping, as well as a treatment component such as group counseling, peer groups, or problem-solving activities.

Sometimes, youth ranches and forestry camps are designed to address juvenile offenders with specific problems. For example, McFadden Ranch in Roanoke, Texas (operated by the Texas Youth Commission), is a community-based residential program for juveniles with substance-abuse problems. Staff members at McFadden Ranch combine substance-abuse-resistance programming with a wide array of activities to help youths develop skills to succeed after their sentence is completed. For example, one activity that McFadden youths participate in is teen court in Denton, Texas. In this teen court, McFadden juveniles serve as jury members and are responsible for deciding sentences for youths referred to the court. McFadden also promotes the integration of family members, parole officers, counselors, and volunteers in a comprehensive drug treatment program.[71] Similarly, the Youth Forestry Camp at Trough Creek State Park in State College, Pennsylvania, offers a multi-program approach in the open wilderness. This camp combines substance-abuse treatment, physical exercise, and rigorous outdoor activities in a secure yet open environment. It also offers various forms of counseling, such as victims' awareness, anger management, and behavioral counseling.[72]

As mentioned, ranches and forestry camps typically handle mid-range or specific-needs offenders (such as chemically dependent youths). This is not the case for all ranches and forestry camps. The Florida Environmental Institute (FEI) operates "The Last Chance Ranch," which targets Florida's most serious and violent juvenile offenders. It is located in a remote area of the Everglades, and delinquents in this program have been adjudicated for serious and/or frequent offending. The most recent information reveals that referrals to FEI averaged eighteen prior offenses, almost twelve of which were felonies. Two-thirds of the offenders were adjudicated for crimes against persons, with the remainder referred for chronic property or drug offenses. The average length of stay in the FEI Last Chance Ranch was eighteen months, and youths also served a lengthy aftercare (parole) term in the free community. The Last Chance Ranch serves those juveniles who would have otherwise been waived to the adult court and given an adult sentence.[73]

Currently, ranches and forestry camps receive roughly 10–15 percent of institutionalized juveniles. They generally function as an alternative to overcrowded juvenile institutions where "best-risk" adjudicated juveniles will be sent. Best-risk juveniles represent those offenders for whom institutionalization might be too harsh but diversion to a nonsecure community program would be too lenient. However, some programs, such as the FEI's Last Chance Ranch, serve both serious and frequent offenders. One of the main problems with ranches and forestry camps is the real potential for escapes. Although considered secure, these placements do not have locked doors, and juveniles are typically not placed in a locked facility at night (especially forestry camps). Another problem is that in the remote location, juveniles sometimes turn on staff members and hurt them. Although this situation is rare, it has occurred and is a source of concern.

Transition Facilities

Nearly all juveniles are released from state school within nine to twelve months from the date they were committed. Few are released outright without a period of aftercare or parole. Some released juveniles will also be required to gradually move back into the community by way of a transition facility (also called a halfway house, a residence home, or a group home). Transition facilities may be used at many points in time in the juvenile justice process. For example, some transition facilities operate as a diversionary alternative and can be considered pre-adjudication facilities. Many transition facilities operate at the back end of the juvenile justice process once a youth is to be released from state school.

A transition facility is a "halfway out" placement for youths who have completed their sentence at state school but are determined by institutional staff and caseworkers to need additional structure before entry into the free community on parole. Transition facilities are just short of the complete structure of state school but more structured than community release on aftercare, and their justification is that some youths are not completely ready to face an unstructured home life; thus, a slow transition may be in the best interests of the long-term rehabilitation of the youth and/or the protection of the community.

Youths sent to transition facilities typically include those who have a particular need or meet some certain criteria. For example, special-needs youths such as sex offenders, violent offenders, and high-needs chemically dependent youths are the ones most often sent to transition facilities. For these youths, the transition facility is a "test run" for slow integration back into the free society. On the other hand, youths who have demonstrated particular motivation or promise in certain areas may also be assigned to more specialized transition facilities that emphasize continued job skills, job training, or college entrance preparation. Placement for these youths is not meant to ensure extra supervision for punishment or to monitor them to make sure they are ready to face the community; instead, it is seen as a benefit for youths in terms of their future potential. When used in these ways, transition facilities are reserved for youths who are not typical as they exit from state school. This situation varies considerably by state and a number of jurisdictional criteria.

Adult Prisons

Approximately 7,000–9,000 juveniles are waived to the adult court each year,[74] a figure representing about 1 percent of all juveniles petitioned to the juvenile court. Of these waived juveniles, some will be convicted in adult court and sent to adult prisons.

According to a 2000 report by the Bureau of Justice Assistance titled *Juveniles in Adult Prisons and Jails: A National Assessment,* approximately 5,000 juveniles are in adult prisons.* Of the juveniles held in state prisons, 75 percent were sentenced as adults (meaning they were under eighteen but considered adults in the state they were sentenced), and 23 percent were held as adjudicated juveniles.[75] Almost 60 percent of youths held in adult prisons were sentenced for a person offense, 21 percent for a property offense, and 10 percent for a drug-related offense. Blacks were the most represented racial category, constituting 55 percent of juveniles in state prisons.[76] The age of juveniles sent to adult prisons ranged from thirteen (one reported juvenile of this age) to seventeen, with 80 percent of juveniles being at least age seventeen. The average maximum sentence for juveniles sent to adult prisons was approximately eight years.[77] Males made up roughly 96 percent of all juveniles in adult prisons. In sum, the typical juvenile sent to an adult prison was a black male, age seventeen or eighteen, who had committed a person offense.[78]

Sending juveniles to adult prisons represents the culmination of the "get-tough" trend for serious and violent juveniles. Adult prisons are the last stop for the youthful offender, arguably the most secure, long-term form of post-adjudication confinement available. Although confinement is confinement, state prisons differ from juvenile state schools. The most important difference is that the first-tier goal of adult prisons is retribution or punishment, whereas in most state schools, rehabilitation is the primary goal.[79]

Despite the emphasis on retribution in adult prisons, juveniles are not necessarily dumped and warehoused in adult prisons without treatment or hope for rehabilitation. Although they are considered the "worst of the worst" juveniles, there is still some hope that they may be changed. As a result, many state prison systems have programs that are meant to benefit youthful offenders. For example, almost all state prison systems offer formal education, special education, vocational education, and GED preparation specifically for youthful offenders. The majority of state prisons also include programs such as psychological/psychiatric counseling, family counseling, employment counseling, health and nutrition, and HIV/AIDS counseling. Other states offer drug and alcohol treatment, sex offender treatment, and violent offender treatment.[80] Because most youths will be released within five to eight years of adult confinement (at approximately age twenty-two to twenty-five), it is in the best interests of state prison authorities to afford juveniles placed in adult prisons the advantage of counseling and other forms of rehabilitation, that which is not necessarily provided to or forced upon adult offenders. The "Controversial Issue" box asks you to think about juveniles sent to adult prisons and the debate over rehabilitation and incapacitation.

Certain states also have special housing policies for juveniles sentenced to adult prisons. Some states house convicted juveniles in a juvenile facility until they come of age. Some segregate all juveniles within a particular adult prison,

*James Austin, Kelly Dedel Johnson, and Maria Gregoriou, *Juveniles in Adult Prisons and Jails: A National Assessment* (Washington, DC: Bureau of Justice Assistance, 2000). See also Melissa Sickmund, *Juveniles in Corrections* (Washington, DC: Office of Juvenile Justice and Delinquency Prevention, 2004), on the numbers of juveniles under eighteen admitted to prisons from 1985 to 1999.

CONTROVERSIAL ISSUE: WHICH SIDE DO YOU FAVOR?

Should juveniles receive special treatment in adult prisons or simply be incapacitated?

Juveniles who have been sent to adult prison arguably represent the most serious, violent, and chronic juveniles with whom the juvenile justice system has had to deal. In fact, such juveniles are so problematic that they have been deemed unsuitable for the juvenile justice system altogether, despite their age. Yet most states, upon sending juveniles to adult prison, still provide special provisions for them, including special housing and special rehabilitative programs that are not offered to adult prisoners. This is despite the fact that the histories of these youths are riddled with multiple referrals and multiple interventions, none of which have been successful in changing the behavioral path of these serious juvenile delinquents.

This raises a question: *At what point should incapacitation, rather than rehabilitation, be the focus of the justice system when juvenile offenders are incarcerated in adult prisons*?

Those who would argue against rehabilitation for juveniles sent to adult prisons suggest that juveniles with so much consistency in their delinquent behavior are unlikely to change. For the most part, juveniles who have made it to the adult system have a long history of delinquency beginning in early adolescence and have failed to change their ways despite the most intensive efforts of the juvenile justice system. The best predictor of what someone is going to do tomorrow is what the person did yesterday. As a result, these juveniles have demonstrated that rehabilitation does not work for them and will not work for them in the future. Trying to rehabilitate such "deep-end" delinquents is an exercise in diminishing returns and a waste of time. They are simply too far gone; thus, they must be incapacitated to protect the public, other inmates, and correctional staff. Rehabilitation is unlikely to make much difference because these serious juveniles have shown resistance to change. Even if a few change, this is not enough because most will not. The point at which a juvenile is sent to adult prison is the point where incapacitation must take precedence over rehabilitation.

Those who would argue for rehabilitation for juveniles sent to adult prison suggest that youths can change their delinquent ways. If not for the juvenile's sake, rehabilitation should be used for the public's future benefit. Since most juveniles sent to adult prison will get out sooner than later, it is in the public's interest to at least attempt rehabilitation. If juveniles are simply caged up for their entire sentence, they will exit the adult prison angrier, more frustrated, and more determined than ever to be criminals. Because warehousing juveniles in adult prisons cuts off all opportunities for improvement, doing something is always preferable to doing nothing. Without rehabilitation, juveniles will return to the same dysfunctional environment, but this time it will be as young adults with an adult record and even less opportunity to do well. Although not all juveniles may change their ways because of treatment, an important number do, suggesting that rehabilitation is still important for juveniles sent to adult prison.

whereas others mix juveniles and adults from day one. **Straight adult incarceration** refers to the practice of housing juveniles with adults with no effort to differentiate between the two in programming and housing.[81] **Graduated incarceration** refers to the practice of housing juvenile offenders convicted as adults in a juvenile institution (such as N. A. Chaderjian of the California Youth Authority) until they reach a certain age, at which time they are transferred to an adult prison.[82] Finally, **segregated incarceration** refers to assigning youthful offenders to specific age-segregated adult facilities (for offenders eighteen to twenty-four years old).[83] For example, in Florida, juveniles convicted in adult court are sentenced to a youthful offender program that separates fourteen- to eighteen-year-olds from nineteen- through twenty-four-year-olds.[84]

Placing juveniles in adult prisons has many potentially harmful consequences, so some states try to separate youthful offenders from older adult inmates. Juveniles may be more prone to physical and sexual assault in prison by older inmates once intermixed. The consequence is that juveniles, lacking the means to protect themselves from physical or sexual attacks, are an increasingly attractive target for gang recruitment for protection. Gang membership in prison has several negative consequences, the most serious being that juveniles can often be forced, out of fear and/or need for protection, to prove themselves to the gang, in some cases by committing a murder or a serious assault on inmates and/or staff. This means more prison time. Other consequences of gang membership include being labeled a member of a security threat group, members of which are often placed in single segregated cells for the duration of their sentence. These young inmates will miss out on the opportunity to use in-prison programs that may assist them upon release.

State statutes allowing for the more efficient transfer of juveniles to adult court or placement in the adult punishment process through blended sentencing may make the adult prison an increasingly used option for juveniles, especially for those who are serious, chronic, or violent in their offending. At present, there is not enough evidence to accurately document this trend, but data over the last five years suggest that there is a slight reduction in the trend of placing juveniles in adult prisons.[85] Whether this is a long-term trend or simply a short-term anomaly has yet to be determined. In any case, the reality is that most juveniles, once adjudicated, will reside in juvenile institutions, not adult institutions, if they are confined at all. Table 11.3 reviews the types of juvenile placements just discussed.

Placements for Nondelinquents

Before the 1970s, nondelinquents such as status offenders, dependent and neglected youths, the mentally ill, and substance-addicted juveniles could be locked inside the same institutions as delinquents. Following the JJDPA in 1974, states removed these youths from secure residential placements. Today, few nondelinquents are held in secure residential placements because state laws typically prohibit such practices. This does not mean that these youths cannot be institutionalized; rather, it means that they cannot be institutionalized in certain facilities, mainly state schools. However, each year a number are placed in unlocked facilities or nonsecure programs. These youths are institutionalized

TABLE 11.3

Types of Placements for Delinquent Offenders

Type of Placement	Adjudication Placement*	Security Level	Length
Adult jails	pre-adjudication	secure	short term
Youth shelters	pre-adjudication	nonsecure	short term
Detention centers	pre-adjudication	secure	short term
Diagnostic facilities	post-adjudication	secure	short term
Transfer facilities	post-adjudication	secure	short term
Stabilization facilities	post-adjudication	secure	short term limited long term
Training schools and juvenile correctional facilities	post-adjudication	secure	long term
Juvenile boot camps	post-adjudication	secure	mid to long term
Ranches and forestry camps	post-adjudication	secure	long term
Transition facilities	post-adjudication	secure	short term
Adult prisons	post-adjudication	secure	long term

*Some facilities may actually be used as both pre- and post-adjudication facilities. This table denotes the typical use.

under the justification that they are being supervised or treated instead of punished. As a result, they are often referred to as "hidden delinquents."

The types of placements for nondelinquent youths are numerous and are operated by both public and private agencies. Some of the more common types of placements for nondelinquents include youth shelters, foster homes, and group homes. The greatest controversy surrounds the institutionalization of nondelinquents in mental asylums and hospitals for mental health therapy, including inpatient substance-abuse treatment.

Parham v. J. R. (1979): Civil Commitment of Nondelinquents

The U.S. Supreme Court held in *Parham v. J. R.* (1979) that parents may voluntarily commit their child to a state mental hospital (even when the child does not want to go) upon diagnosis of mental illness by a neutral fact finder.[86] This finding means that nondelinquent youths, such as those who are mentally ill or those with a drug problem, may be institutionalized with less due process protection than delinquents receive.

After *Gault*, juveniles who are charged with a crime and face institutionalization are provided with a notice of charges, counsel, the right to confront and cross-examine witnesses, the right to remain silent, and the privilege against self-incrimination.[87] Moreover, youths must be found to have engaged in delinquent conduct under the standard of beyond a reasonable doubt instead of preponderance of the evidence.[88] In *Parham*, the Court held that in a parent-initiated civil commitment hearing for mental health care, nondelinquent juveniles do not have a constitutional right to a formal hearing, to counsel, or to have their case heard by a judge. Instead, for due process to be satisfied, the juvenile must only be evaluated by a neutral fact finder (such as a psychiatrist) to determine whether the child has "evidence of a mental illness." Upon evidence of a mental illness, a juvenile can be institutionalized until the parents request that the child be released or upon evidence that the child no longer suffers from the mental illness or has substantially improved. Although a state may provide more due process protection, doing so is not required by the Constitution according to the U.S. Supreme Court.

Critics have attacked the *Parham* decision because it allows hundreds of children who have not broken the law to be "dumped" into mental-health-related institutions each year by parents who are frustrated by their child's behavior. They also say that mental hospitals, including inpatient substance-abuse facilities, are ready to accept any and all patients because of insurance payments or third-party reimbursements and will thus find "evidence of mental illness" in many cases. As Feld notes, such policies "have coalesced to provide an economical and efficient alternative to the juvenile justice system to confine troubled and troublesome youths."[89]

Conditions of Confinement and the Rights of Institutionalized Juveniles

Juvenile institutions came under heavy criticism in the 1960s and 1970s as violent, crowded, and frenzied places where victimization by both juveniles and staff was a frequent occurrence. Juvenile institutions were increasingly being labeled as schools of crime that turned status offenders into criminals and made delinquent offenders recidivists.

Criticism about the operation of juvenile institutions is not new, as this chapter has documented. Indeed, every major juvenile institution since the houses of refuge has been criticized. Recent years have revived another cycle of emphasis on the conditions of confinement in juvenile institutions. Among contemporary issues, researchers have examined institutional abuse, medical services, overcrowding, security, suicide prevention, and mental health services. Discussions about the conditions of juvenile confinement have also centered on the rights of institutionalized juveniles, most specifically the right to treatment, the right to be free from cruel and unusual punishment, and the right of access to the courts.

Conditions of Confinement in Juvenile Institutions

In 1988 Congress asked the Office of Juvenile Justice and Delinquency Prevention (OJJDP) to study the conditions of confinement for institutionalized juveniles and to assess whether these conditions conformed to national standards. The resulting report, *Conditions of Confinement: Juvenile Detention and Correctional Facilities* (hereafter "the conditions report"), was released in 1994 and is the most comprehensive study of conditions in juvenile facilities to date. This report detailed a number of conditions in juvenile institutions across the country. Among others, juvenile facilities were found to be overcrowded and lacking suicide prevention.[90]

Overcrowding

The conditions report indicated that nearly 35 percent of state training schools around the nation were overcrowded. About 29 percent of all institutionalized juveniles were housed in these overcrowded facilities. Overcrowded facilities were typically filled to 20 percent beyond their designed capacity. For example, a state school with room for 150 juveniles typically contained approximately 180 juveniles on any given day. In sum, although the majority of institutions were not overcrowded, overcrowded facilities did hold a significant portion of all juveniles in state training schools.[91]

Overcrowding is a problem in juvenile institutions because of its results: heightened stress, increased victimization and injury, more rapid spread of sickness and disease, and decreased security.[92] However, overcrowding in juvenile facilities is not necessarily unconstitutional. The U.S. Supreme Court held in *Rhodes v. Chapman* (1981) that an Ohio adult prison operating at 38 percent above designed capacity was not unconstitutional.[93] In this case, the Court said that overcrowding *per se* is not unconstitutional because it did not lead to the deprivation of food or medical care, nor did it compromise sanitation or cause a rise in inmate-on-inmate violence. This same finding likely applies to overcrowded juvenile institutions. In sum, if overcrowding interferes with the delivery of food, medical care, or sanitary conditions, or leads to increased violence and victimization, it may be unconstitutional. Although this ruling concerned conditions within adult institutions and likely applies to juvenile institutions, if overcrowded conditions are thought to be more damaging to juveniles than to adults—that is, adults are more immune or able to withstand the effects of crowding than juveniles—juvenile institutions may be held to a higher standard by the courts.[94]

Here are some measures that can be used to relieve overcrowding in juvenile correctional facilities:

- Restricting the number of incoming juveniles
- Granting the early release of juveniles
- Refusing to take new admissions
- Building new facilities to make more room for committed juveniles
- Diverting offenders to community programs
- Changing revocation policies

However, many of the solutions listed here are not available to state juvenile correctional administrators. For example, state juvenile administrators have no discretion as to whom they will and will not accept once a youth is adjudicated and sentenced to a state juvenile facility by the court. Juvenile correctional administrators also do not control the construction of new facilities or the diversion of offenders to community programs. Construction decisions are generally made by legislators, and diversion decisions are generally made by judges and prosecutors (intake officers). Granting early release may be one way to reduce the institutionalized juvenile population; however, most committed juveniles have minimum lengths of stay dictated by state law.[95] State juvenile correctional systems can control, to some degree, their intake of parole violators. For example, the director of the state juvenile justice agency may direct juvenile parole officers to avoid locking up technical parole violators and instead to focus on juveniles who commit new and serious delinquent offenses. This step may reduce acute overcrowding problems but is not a long-term solution.

Suicide Prevention

Youth suicide has long been recognized as a serious public health problem, but suicide among institutionalized juveniles has received little attention until just recently.[96] There are numerous cases of suicide attempts each year in juvenile correctional facilities, a smaller number of which are actually successful. Suicides shed a negative light on juvenile confinement, and some well-publicized incidents have awakened the public to the problem of juvenile suicide in institutions.

There are few systematic, national-level data on the number of attempted and completed youth suicides that occur each year in juvenile facilities.[97] The available data indicate that suicide is four times more likely among institutionalized youths than among youths in the general population.[98] According to the conditions report, residents in secure juvenile facilities engage in more than 17,000 instances of suicidal behavior each year.[99] These numbers are even more disturbing when considering attempts not discovered or reported.[100] For example, one author of this book was conducting suicide checks in a county juvenile detention facility and found a youth hanging from an air vent with a bedsheet wrapped around his neck. This youth attempted suicide because he was upset after being committed to a state juvenile facility. Ultimately, the juvenile lived. Although a report was written, it was not likely reflected in national statistics. Although completed suicides are usually well documented, suicide attempts are probably grossly underestimated.

Suicide is particularly problematic among institutionalized juveniles because they are generally less stable than youths in the general population.[101] Institutionalized juveniles have a greater incidence of substance abuse, impulsiveness, and poor family support, and many have long histories of physical and emotional abuse—factors that are all risk correlates for suicidal behavior.[102] Moreover, juvenile correctional staff are usually ill-equipped to detect and protect juveniles from suicide, which compounds the problem. Although institutions usually have a "suicide watch" or "close observation" policy, such an approach is typically not enough to significantly reduce suicidal behavior.[103]

Efforts to prevent suicide in juvenile facilities will become increasingly important in the future as more juveniles are placed in secure institutions. More attention to intake screening and assessment, and better staff training, appear to be most important in the prevention of youth suicide. Some argue that closer attention should be paid to youth risk factors and classification, with additional efforts made to place "risky" youths in facilities with highly trained staff. Furthermore, some observers believe that staff practices such as isolation should be rethought, as evidence suggests that isolation in punishment cells or "observations rooms" may further depress youths, making their problem behavior worse.[104] Separation from others is a reality in juvenile institutions, and researchers suggest that when separation must be used, rooms or cells should be made suicide-resistant: inaccessible vents, attached sheets, and padded walls.[105]

The Rights of Institutionalized Juveniles

Prior to *In re Gault* in 1967 and the JJDPA of 1974, juvenile institutions held a variety of youths, ranging from the dependent and neglected to the hardened delinquent. Youths were sentenced to juvenile institutions with little or no due process. A typical scenario involved parents agreeing with a judge to have their "disobedient" child institutionalized or the hasty sentencing of a delinquent (without the aid of a lawyer) to an indeterminate stay in state school. U.S. Supreme Court cases in the 1960s and 1970s gave juveniles due process rights in adjudication proceedings. These cases provided juveniles with such protections as a right to a lawyer, a right to remain silent, and the privilege against self-incrimination when they faced possible institutionalization. Attention paid to the "sending" process in the 1960s and 1970s also fostered an emphasis on the "treating" process once juveniles were institutionalized. Among the many issues examined by the courts, the more important are the right to treatment, the right to be free from cruel and unusual punishment, and the right to court access. These three issues changed the nature of juvenile institutionalization.

The Right to Treatment

An important legal issue is whether juveniles are entitled to treatment once committed to a juvenile institution. Proponents argue that juveniles have the right to programs and activities that aim to accomplish rehabilitation because that is the foundation of the juvenile justice system under *parens patriae.* However, there is considerable debate about the best way to rehabilitate juveniles, if they are to be treated at all. Courts from various levels have decided a number of cases on juveniles' right to treatment.

The U.S. Supreme Court has not directly addressed the constitutional right to treatment for institutionalized juveniles, but several lower courts have. Courts have held that a juvenile may challenge his or her confinement as unconstitutional if not provided treatment.[106] For example, in *White v. Reid* (1954), the Federal District Court for the District of Columbia prohibited the confinement of juveniles in facilities that did not provide for their treatment and rehabilitation.[107] In *Inmates of the Boys' Training School v. Affleck* (1972), the Federal District Court for Rhode Island held in 1972 that a juvenile's rights might be violated if he or she is not offered activities that are intended to rehabilitate: The rationale for juvenile confinement is rehabilitation.[108] And in *Nelson v. Heyne* (1974), the Seventh Circuit Court of Appeals ruled that juveniles sentenced to the Indiana Boys' School have a right to treatment under the due process clause of the Fourteenth Amendment.[109]

Some courts hesitate to spell out exactly what treatment should entail in juvenile facilities. However, courts have spoken on what treatment is not. Treatment is not the use of solitary confinement; the unregulated use of antipsychotic medications; the withholding of food, shelter, or clothing; or the use of corporal punishment.[110] Some courts have been more specific. In one of the most sweeping right to treatment cases ever decided, Judge William Wayne Justice held in *Morales v. Turman* (1973) that the Texas Youth Commission (TYC) must institute procedures for the assessment of confined youths, provide medical and psychiatric care, and meet or exceed minimum national standards for such assessment and care (see the discussion following on *Morales v. Turman*).[111] Judge Justice also held that juveniles must not be denied adequate living conditions—for example, they must be provided proper lighting, bedding, clothes, daily showers, and access to medical facilities.[112] In a more recent case, the Federal District Court for South Carolina held in *Alexander S. v. Boyd* (1995) that juveniles have a constitutional right to a minimally adequate level of programming designed to teach them the necessary principles to correct their behavior.[113]

As these cases indicate, courts have generally held that juveniles have a right to treatment if they are institutionalized. Despite the more "adultified" juvenile court process, including evidence that juvenile facility administrators believe that a substantial percentage of juveniles are not amenable to rehabilitation, treatment still remains a focus in juvenile institutions across the country.[114] However, some courts have rejected the idea that "all" juveniles are entitled to a right to treatment once confined. For example, in *Santana v. Collazo* (1983), the First Circuit Court of Appeals ruled that certain juveniles can be confined solely for the protection of society and that doing so did not violate their rights.[115] Similarly, the U.S. Supreme Court held in *Ralston v. Robinson* (1981) that a juvenile who has received an adult sentence does not have an absolute right to individualized treatment.[116] In this case, the Court denied an absolute right to treatment for juveniles if it can be proven that they would not benefit from it. In the *Ralston* case, Robinson was in a juvenile institution when he assaulted a federal officer. For this assault, a federal district court imposed an adult sentence on Robinson while he was still a juvenile. While still incarcerated, Robinson assaulted another federal officer. The court imposed an additional adult sentence, and Robinson was placed in the general prison population with adult offenders. After the case reached the U.S. Supreme Court, the Court upheld the lower federal court ruling denying a claim by Robinson that he was entitled to treatment because he was a juvenile. Instead, the Court ruled that the seriousness and frequency of his conduct outweighed any prospect for rehabilitation and negated his right to treatment.[117]

In sum, courts generally prescribe that juveniles are entitled to be treated if institutionalized. This may not be the case for all juveniles, however, especially for juveniles who commit violent acts in institutions and have been given an adult sentence. In these instances, the U.S. Supreme Court has ruled that simply being a juvenile does not automatically entitle one to an absolute right to treatment. If a juvenile's conduct indicates that he or she would not benefit from treatment, it can be denied without violating his or her rights.

The Right to Be Free from Cruel and Unusual Punishment

Cruel and unusual punishment is defined as "punishment that is torturous, degrading, inhuman, and grossly disproportionate to the crime in question or otherwise shocking to the moral sense."[118] A great deal of literature and case law documents instances of cruel and unusual punishment in juvenile institutions.

Most of the worst incidents occurred in the 1970s, but episodes of cruel and unusual punishment against juveniles still occur today. Unlike any other time, however, the abuse of juveniles in the 1970s served as the change agent to ensure that the most egregious abuses were eliminated from juvenile institutions.

In the 1970s, abuses uncovered in Arkansas's juvenile facilities were some of the worst ever documented in the United States. Juveniles confined to Arkansas's facilities were forced to eat feces, vomit, and kneel down and oink like a pig.[119] One boy was chased by a car upon entering an institution's gates and shot at, while many boys were subject to a punishment called "Texas TV," which entailed having the youths lean their foreheads and nose on a wall while guards kicked their feet out from underneath them.[120] Other types of abuses pervaded in juvenile institutions across the country: using a child's head to mop up urine on a floor; "forced inaction," such as standing against a wall; being forced to kill a dog with a stick; being forced to wear a dead dog's tail around the neck; and lying in pools of "water and excrement" while being forced to throw it at other boys.[121] In an Ohio state school, Clemmens Bartollas and colleagues found evidence of staff members failing to protect juveniles from a variety of inmate attacks.[122] They uncovered a staff-supported juvenile hierarchy in which predatory juveniles would prey on weaker youths, in some cases uncovering evidence of severe beatings, sodomy, and degrading sexual acts such as forced masturbation.

One of the most pervasive instances of the cruel and unusual treatment of juveniles was experienced in Texas's juvenile facilities. Episodes within Texas Youth Commission (TYC) facilities culminated in one of the most extensive orders ever issued against a juvenile correctional department. In 1973 Judge William Wayne Justice declared in *Morales v. Turman* that two TYC facilities were in violation of the Eighth Amendment ban on cruel and unusual punishment.[123]

Morales v. Turman *(1973): The Leading Case on Cruel and Unusual Punishment in Juvenile Correctional Institutions* *Morales v. Turman* is considered one of the most extensive cases concerning juvenile confinement ever decided. Federal Judge William Wayne Justice addressed three areas in this case: the right to treatment for juveniles (discussed previously), Eighth Amendment violations of the prohibition against cruel and unusual punishment, and the procedures by which juveniles were committed to the TYC. The last area was the impetus for *Morales v. Turman,* but the Eighth Amendment violation made this case well documented.

Morales v. Turman began on February 12, 1971, when two attorneys were denied access to their clients by TYC authorities at Gatesville (at the time, a Texas juvenile state school). The attorneys had gone to interview their clients to determine whether they had been afforded due process rights during their adjudication proceedings in accordance with *Gault. Gault* required that juveniles be afforded an attorney, a right to a reasonable notice of the charges, the right to confront and cross-examine witnesses, the privilege against self-incrimination, and the right to remain silent in adjudication hearings that could result in institutionalization.[124] Despite the U.S. Supreme Court's ruling in *Gault,* there was evidence that Texas's juvenile courts did not comply with the requirements of this ruling. After the attorneys were denied access to their clients, they filed suit in federal district court. The judge was William Wayne Justice. He took an avid interest in the case and initiated an investigation into the practices of Texas's juvenile courts and the Texas Youth Commission. The "Case Brief" focuses on this important court case.

Upon further investigation into the practices of Texas's juvenile courts, Judge Justice uncovered evidence that a substantial percentage of youths were

Case Brief | ## Leading Case on Conditions of Confinement in Juvenile Institutions

Morales v. Turman, 383 F. Supp. 53 (E.D. Tex. 1974)

Facts: On February 12, 1971, attorneys tried to confer in private with some children who were committed to the Texas Youth Council (TYC) facilities (currently the Texas Youth Commission). When access to their clients was denied, the attorneys filed a civil action for a "preliminary injunction seeking to stop TYC and their agents from interfering with the children's right to confer privately with counsel and from impeding in any manner their correspondence with counsel through the mail." The concern was that these children had not received the due process right during their adjudication hearings as guaranteed in *In re Gault.* Questionnaire results showed that many juveniles had not received full rights, and the suit expanded to include the question of procedural due process during their adjudication hearings.

Some of the questionnaires returned to Judge William Wayne Justice also contained descriptions of the abuse that children had suffered at the hands of TYC officials. Judge Justice then approved a number of unique investigative requests by the plaintiffs to get into TYC institutions and determine whether practices within the institutions violated the Eighth Amendment prohibition against cruel and unusual punishment. Judge Justice allowed juveniles within the institutions to be interviewed about how they were treated, and he also granted permission for participant observation teams of professionals to observe conditions of confinement in some selected institutions.

The trial took place in the summer of 1973; TYC lost. Judge Justice addressed many practices of the TYC. The issues were numerous and included corporal punishment, the use of mace and tear gas, segregation, solitary confinement, visitation, and screening of prospective staff. The court found that the practices at TYC constituted cruel and unusual punishment, and that juveniles were denied their right to treatment. Among other actions, Judge Justice ordered two juvenile institutions closed.

Issue: Did the Texas Youth Council engage in policy and practices that violated the Eighth Amendment's prohibition against cruel and unusual punishment?

Court Decision: Juveniles confined in Texas Youth Council have a right to proper treatment. Some of the practices and procedures of TYC constituted cruel and unusual punishment.

(continued)

Case Brief *(continued)*

Case Significance: *Morales v. Turman* was one of the lengthiest cases concerning conditions of confinement in juvenile institutions and is regarded as one of the most extensive orders ever issued against a juvenile correctional department. Judge Justice was concerned about the totality of conditions of confinement, the treatment, and the due process rights of juveniles. He took an active interest in the case and employed a number of legal tools to uncover and change unconstitutional conditions in Texas's juvenile facilities. For example, he authorized the distribution of questionnaires regarding due process rights in adjudication proceedings for all incarcerated juveniles, interviews of incarcerated juveniles, and finally a participant observation team living in some training schools for a short period of time. Moreover, when a settlement was finally reached, Judge Justice appointed a consultant committee to oversee implementation and compliance with the settlement for four years.

Against the backdrop of *parens patriae,* this decision was startling at the time. Since then, courts have been less reluctant to probe into allegations involving juvenile facilities. This case took almost fifteen years to settle and is an example of how conditions of confinement cases develop and how long it takes for such cases to be finally resolved.

Excerpts from the Decision: "The Court of Appeals for the Fifth Circuit has recently held that a person involuntarily committed to a state mental hospital in a civil proceeding had the constitutional right to receive such individual treatment as will give him a reasonable opportunity to be cured or to improve his mental condition. . . . In the instant case, the state is charged with a statutory duty to provide a 'program of constructive training aimed at rehabilitation and re-establishment in society of children adjudged to be delinquent.' This basis for commitment—to rehabilitate and reestablish the juvenile in society—is clearly grounded in a *parens patriae* rationale. Thus, under the *parens patriae* theory, the juvenile must be given treatment lest the involuntary commitment amount to an arbitrary exercise of governmental power proscribed by the due process clause.

"Schools under the jurisdiction of the TYC, particularly Mountain View and Gatesville, have been the scenes of widespread physical and psychological brutality. In the emergency interim relief order, several practices found to be in violation of the Eighth Amendment's proscription of cruel and unusual punishment were enjoined on the grounds that such practices were so severe as to degrade human dignity; were inflicted in a wholly arbitrary fashion; were so severe as to be unacceptable to contemporary society; and finally, were not justified in serving any necessary purpose.

"Practices found by this court to violate the Eighth Amendment were: the widespread practices of beating, slapping, kicking, and otherwise physically abusing juveniles in the absence of any exigent circumstances; the use of tear gas and other chemical crowd-control devices in situations not posing an imminent threat to human life or an imminent and substantial threat to property; the placing of juveniles in solitary confinement or other secured facilities, in the

(continued)

Case Brief Leading Case on Conditions of Confinement in Juvenile Institutions (continued)

absence of any legislative of administrative limitation on the duration and intensity of the confinement and subject only to the unfettered discretion of correctional officers; the requirement that inmates maintain silence during periods of the day merely for the purpose of punishment; and the performance of repetitive, nonfunctional, degrading and unnecessary tasks. Included as such tasks (the so-called "make work") were: requiring a juvenile to pull grass without bending his knees on a large tract of ground not intended for cultivation or any other purpose; forcing him to move dirt with a shovel from one place on the ground to another and then back again many times; and making him buff a small area of the floor for a period of time exceeding that in which any reasonable person would conclude that the floor was sufficiently buffed."

Source: This brief originally appeared in Rolando V. del Carmen, Mary Parker, and Frances P. Reddington, *Briefs of Leading Cases in Juvenile Justice* (Cincinnati, OH: Anderson Publishing Co., 1998)

---

committed to Texas's juvenile institutions without due process, and a large number of them had not committed a delinquent offense. Judge Justice found that almost 30 percent of the boys and 70 percent of the girls were committed to TYC because their parents could not control them.[125] Indeed, the commitment of the plaintiff in the case (Morales—a name picked from one of twelve TYC inmates in the original suit against TYC) was evidence of this practice. Alicia Morales was committed to the TYC for "disobedience" by her father because she had lost her job and failed to obtain another one. She had no hearing, nor was she represented by a lawyer before being committed to the TYC.[126]

Judge Justice sent a letter to all 2,500 youths committed to the TYC. This letter informed them of the lawsuit and asked each youth to complete a questionnaire to help the court better understand the circumstances of their confinement. From this survey, 2,294 responses were returned. The findings revealed that more than 1,000 juveniles had not been represented by counsel in their adjudication hearing and that 280 of them had had neither a lawyer nor a hearing prior to being committed.[127] Furthermore, a number of the questionnaires (approximately 50) contained written accounts by youths concerning abuses in the TYC. At this point, the *Morales v. Turman* case transformed from a procedural case examining how youths became confined to a conditions of confinement case that examined how the juveniles were treated once they arrived in the TYC.

Judge Justice approved of an investigation to determine whether practices within TYC institutions violated the Eighth Amendment. The results of the investigation revealed pervasive violence and abuse in the TYC. Some juveniles testified how new commitments were physically abused by staff and co-opted juveniles. Other juveniles testified that the staff at Mountain View placed youths with "homosexual tendencies" in "punk" dorms and that these dorms were segregated by race. Evidence and testimony also revealed that the use of force was encouraged by TYC staff members for minor and arbitrary rule violations. For example, youths were often beaten for speaking Spanish or "loudtalking."[128] In other instances, youths were subject to corporal punishments for wearing their pants too low or failing to clean up after themselves. These types of infractions might earn a boy a "peel," whereby a youth was forced to bend over while staff hit him on the back with an open hand or fist. Similarly, a "tight" was a punishment whereby staff would force the youth to bend down and hold his ankles, while striking him on the buttocks with a broom handle. Other punishments included a "brogueing," which entailed getting kicked in the shins, or a "racking," in which staff made inmates stand against a wall with their hands in their pockets while being punched in the stomach. Forms of psychological punishment were also documented, such as being placed "on crumb": Youths were forced to sit on a chair facing the wall all day long without acknowledging the presence of anyone.[129]

These examples represent only a sampling of the punishments TYC youths faced. They were also subjected to menial and harsh forms of labor. A variety of "make-work" tasks structured the day for juveniles committed to the TYC. A common make-work task was to have youths bend over straight legged while "mowing" the grass with their hands. Another make-work task was labeled "picking," which was characterized by the regimented striking of the ground with pickaxes all day.[130] Some youths were relegated to chores such as moving dirt from one place to another for no apparent reason or the repeated buffing of a small area of floor for a considerable period of time. Beyond these types of punishments, TYC staff regularly used tear gas and other crowd-control devices in nonthreatening situations. In addition, TYC staff used solitary confinement as a punishment for excessive periods of time.[131]

Judge Justice ruled on *Morales v. Turman* on August 31, 1973. He found the TYC in violation of the Eighth Amendment prohibition against cruel and unusual punishment. In his written opinion, Judge Justice ordered that the TYC limit the use of physical force, solitary confinement, and chemical crowd-control devices such as tear gas. Judge Justice also ruled that the Mountain View and Gatesville Schools be transferred to the Texas Department of Corrections (TDC). He remarked that "If ever confinement in an institution constituted a form of cruel and unusual punishment, Gatesville and Mountain View fully met the applicable criteria."[132] Today, Mountain View and Gatesville are adult female prisons in Texas.

The *Morales* case was appealed by the state of Texas to the Fifth Circuit Court of Appeals. The Fifth Circuit vacated Judge Justice's ruling on procedural grounds. On a writ of certiorari, the U.S. Supreme Court upheld Judge Justice's ruling. In between these times, whether the result of Judge Justice or not, the TYC literally reorganized how juveniles were treated and also addressed forms of cruel and unusual punishment.

Other Cases on Cruel and Unusual Punishment *Morales v. Turman* is regarded as the most extensive case involving the conditions within juvenile institutions. However, it was not the first case, and it will not be the last. Other cases have addressed the conditions of confinement for juveniles and their right to be free from cruel and unusual punishment.

In the case of *Inmates of Boys' Training School v. Affleck* (1972), the Federal District Court for Rhode Island ruled that the isolation of juveniles in cold and dark isolation cells containing only a mattress and a toilet constituted cruel and unusual punishment.[133] In *Nelson v. Heyne* (1974), the Seventh Circuit Court of Appeals ruled that corporal punishment (in the form of a fraternity paddle) and the use and administration of tranquilizing drugs by untrained staff violated the Eighth Amendment.[134] Similarly, in *Pena v. New York State Division of Youth* (1976), the court for the Southern District of New York held that the use of solitary confinement, mechanical restraints, and tranquilizers was a violation of the Eighth Amendment.[135] Furthermore, in *Morgan v. Sproat* (1977), the Federal District Court for the Southern District of Mississippi held that the use of padded cells without windows combined with the denial of access to services and programs was cruel and unusual.[136]

Clarifying Cruel and Unusual Punishment   Over the years, courts have further clarified what constitutes cruel and unusual punishment in juvenile institutions. The results include the use of chemical restraints such as tear gas as punishment for troublesome or uncooperative youths,[137] isolation for prolonged periods of time,[138] and the failure to protect children from violence and sexual assault.[139] Several cases have also examined the use of mechanical restraints such as four-point ties and hand restraints, and have indicated when the use of these devices may constitute a violation of rights. Generally, courts have held that mechanical restraints may be used for the protection of the juvenile, staff, or other residents, although restraints should be used for a minimum period of time to stabilize and calm the youth (under thirty minutes). Several courts have held that restraints should never be used as a form of punishment.[140]

Today, the most severe forms of cruel and unusual punishment have been remedied; however, problems persist. One of the more recent cases concerning the conditions of confinement in juvenile institutions came in *Gary H. v. Hegstrom* (1987).[141] In this case, Oregon's MacLaren facility violated the rights of juveniles through prolonged isolation (several days or weeks) in solitary confinement (called D–1). At MacLaren, more than one-half of the population at the facility had been isolated in D–1 during a one-month period. D–1 isolation was used for offenses that the court concluded did not justify isolation: mouthing off to staff, yelling and swearing, refusing to obey an order, and getting out of bed at night.[142] Furthermore, D–1 cells were dirty and unsanitary. The court noted that they were infested with insects and body lice; the walls were covered with food, spit, blood, toilet paper, and feces; the rooms smelled like urine.[143]

The court also determined several disciplinary practices to be inhumane and degrading, such as the "tagging" process. At MacLaren, staff frequently "white tagged" juvenile inmates, a process that included stripping the bedding, clothing, mattresses, reading material, and toilets from the cells. Staff also blocked natural light from entering windows. For the first twenty-four hours of being tagged, youths were not permitted to leave their cells, even for meals or exercise.[144] The court also uncovered the use of restraints for arbitrary rule violations such as refusing to quiet down or singing. The court also noted deficiencies in exercise, education, food, and medical care for youths assigned to D–1. The court found that untrained staff administered medication, that D–1 youths were denied sick calls, and that a high number of residents in D–1 were severely mentally disordered and engaged in suicidal or self-destructive behavior without appropriate treatment.[145]

The Current State of Cruel and Unusual Punishment and Juvenile Abuse   The majority of juvenile institutions in the United States conform to the Constitution regarding the treatment of juvenile offenders today. But some institutions are not compliant. These violations have been documented into the twenty-first century.

One of the most damning indictments of juvenile institutions comes from Human Rights Watch (HRW). In March and May 1995, HRW conducted investigations into the conditions of confinement in four Louisiana juvenile institutions.[146] HRW uncovered evidence of pervasive abuse, including physical abuse, isolation punishment, and the excessive use of chemical and mechanical restraints on children, such as "clear out" (a blend of CS tear gas and 1-percent OC pepper) and handcuffs. HRW conducted more than sixty interviews with youths housed in all of Louisiana's four long-term secure juvenile facilities during private sessions separated by sight and sound from staff.

During the interviews, one juvenile housed in the East Baton Rouge facility remarked on the physical abuse suffered by some residents:

> EBR [East Baton Rouge], that's a messed up place. The guards will beat you. One of them named Mr. O., he has a thing called a "house party," if you work on weekends, he wake you up at 5 A.M. He calls you in the back where we take showers and beats you for a whole house. When we go to mess hall to eat we have to count, and he tells you to come see, then he calls you into the washroom and beats you up and another sergeant comes to beat you. It has only happened two times to me.[147]

Accounts like the above were found at all four institutions studied by HRW. As a result of such revelations, in May 2004, Louisiana shut down the Tallulah juvenile facility and is turning it into an adult prison, based on evidence that few teens had been rehabilitated in addition to evidence of the aforementioned abuses. However, documented abuse is not limited to Louisiana. A year-long investigation by the *Arkansas Democrat-Gazette* uncovered similar findings in Arkansas. In this investigation, reporters found that in 1998:

> Children have been routinely degraded; verbally, physically and sexually abused; hogtied; forced to sleep outside in freezing weather; and threatened with punishment and even death by staff members if the children report the abuse. . . . Staff members have slugged children in the face and then refused to allow them to be treated by a nurse. They have locked children naked in cells overnight after turning the air conditioner on high.[148]

In 2002, California, which holds the largest population of confined juveniles in the United States, was also subject to claims of abuse. A civil rights group and a prison reform group filed suit in federal district court alleging unconstitutional conditions in the California Youth Authority (CYA). This suit contends that inhumane conditions are pervasive in CYA facilities and claims that mentally ill youths are stripped to their underwear and held in "cages" twenty-three hours a day, that prisoners are subjected to biomedical experiments and injected with mind-altering drugs, and that youths are sexually and physically abused by guards.[149] There are also claims that staff at some CYA facilities staged "gladiator"-type contests among rival gang members.

As a result of these and other documented abuses, the U.S. Department of Justice has investigated a number of facilities under CRIPA (Civil Rights of Institutionalized Persons Act). CRIPA allows the U.S. Attorney General to investigate allegations of abuse and unconstitutional conditions in state and local institutions. In the presence of unconstitutional conditions, the Department of Justice may sue state and local facilities to bring about a change in such conditions. Recent investigations in Georgia and Colorado under CRIPA have found violations similar to those in Louisiana, Arkansas, and California, including overcrowding, excessive use of punitive segregation, excessive and punitive use of mechanical and chemical restraints, and physical and sexual abuse by guards.

The most blatant and systematic abuses of the 1970s have been sharply curtailed, but the cruel and unusual punishment of juveniles in institutions continues. However, efforts by the Department of Justice and the Attorney General under CRIPA and that of organizations such as HRW have helped to make sure that abuses in juvenile institutions are uncovered and stopped. Perhaps the bottom line on the treatment of institutionalized juveniles is that the great majority of juvenile institutions are operated according to the law; however, some state facilities still operate outside the law.

Access to the Courts

The U.S. Supreme Court has never decided a case on the issue of whether adjudicated delinquents have a constitutional right to access to the courts. Although states give juveniles a right to court access, only a few court cases have addressed whether juveniles have a "constitutional" right to court access. Some of the debate concerning whether juveniles have a constitutional right to court access, which adult prisoners enjoy, focuses on the difference between the juvenile and adult court process. Under *parens patriae,* the juvenile court is protective and rehabilitative versus adversarial and punitive. Sentences are for treatment. They are tailored to the best interests of the child, so there is no need for court access: The juvenile court and agencies of the juvenile justice system aim to help rather than punish.

Thus far, three federal cases have addressed the question of juveniles' access to the courts. In *Morgan v. Sproat* (1977), the Federal District Court for the Southern District of Mississippi held that juveniles adjudicated and committed to state training schools have a constitutional right to access the courts.[150] The court did not find any difference between incarcerated adults and incarcerated juveniles, saying each was incarcerated; thus, each should enjoy access to the courts. In *Germany v. Vance* (1989), the First Circuit Court of Appeals noted that the stigma of having violated the law, being arrested, being adjudicated, and being incarcerated is similar for juveniles and adults; therefore, juveniles should have a constitutional right to court access like that enjoyed by adults.[151]

Similarly, in *John L. v. Adams* (1992), the Sixth Circuit Court of Appeals held that juveniles have a constitutional right to court access. The court reasoned, like the courts in *Morgan* and *Germany,* that there is no difference between an incarcerated juvenile and an incarcerated adult.[152]

SUMMARY

❑ Houses of refuge signaled that parents and the community were no longer effective forms of controlling children.

❑ Reformatories were houses of refuge with a different name. Treatment did not differ substantially.

❑ The first real reform to the juvenile institution came with the training or industrial school. Training schools sought to normalize the institutional experience for juveniles through the cottage system and a focus on schooling.

❑ The difference between the state school and the juvenile correctional facility is not clear and is more terminological than real. Juvenile correctional facilities may be used for the most serious juveniles within the juvenile correctional system.

❑ Most juveniles committed to a post-adjudication facility serve about one year. Few juveniles are committed to long-term institutionalization in the same way as adults.

❑ About 7,000–9,000 juveniles are waived to adult court each year. Only a small number of these juveniles will be placed in adult prisons.

❑ There are more than 100,000 juveniles housed in juvenile institutions and about 5,000 juveniles in adult prisons. There are approximately 8,000 juveniles held in adult jails.

❑ Juveniles convicted in adult court and sentenced to adult prison can be housed in three ways. Straight adult incarceration refers to the practice of housing juveniles with adults with no effort to segregate them by age. Graduated incarceration refers to the practice of housing juveniles in juvenile institutions until they reach a certain age. Segregated incarceration refers to assigning juveniles convicted in adult court to age-segregated adult facilities (for offenders between eighteen and twenty-four) until they reach a certain age. Most states do not simply place young juveniles with adults right away.

❑ The majority of juvenile institutions are not overcrowded, but overcrowded institutions do hold a large number of juveniles.

❑ Suicide is four times more likely among institutionalized juveniles than among juveniles in the general population.

❑ Institutionalized juveniles have a greater incidence of substance abuse, impulsiveness, poor family histories, and histories of physical and emotional abuse than do juveniles in the general population.

❑ The extreme abuses in juvenile institutions characteristic of the 1960s and 1970s have been addressed today. However, abuses do still continue in some juvenile institutions.

REVIEW QUESTIONS

1. Compare and contrast the reformatory with the training or industrial school.

2. List and describe two pre-adjudication juvenile placements.

3. What type of post-adjudication facility might best be called a "halfway out" house?

4. Describe the significance of the cottage system in the treatment of institutionalized juveniles.

5. What were some problems experienced with the training school? Did all training schools operate under ideal conditions?

6. Define *cruel and unusual punishment.* What are some punishments that courts have considered cruel and unusual for institutionalized juveniles?

7. What types of youths are sent to a stabilization facility? If a state does not have a separate stabilization facility, where will these youths be sent?

8. This chapter refers to ranches and forestry camps as "noninstitutional institutions." What does this term mean?

9. Which post-adjudication program is second only to state school in terms of the average length of stay?

10. What is one way that juvenile correctional administrators can reduce overcrowding in juvenile institutions?

KEY TERMS AND DEFINITIONS

almshouse: Another word for a poorhouse. Almshouses were intended for debtor adults but held wayward juveniles as well.

apprenticeship: The practice of sending a delinquent child out of the community to learn a skill such as carpentry or commercial fishing. This practice was sometimes called placing out or binding out.

cottage system: A key component of the training and industrial school. The cottage system resembled a college campus, with a number of buildings, each holding twenty to forty juveniles. Each cottage was supervised by a "mother and father."

deinstitutionalization: A product of the JJDPA of 1974, which required the removal of status offenders and other noncriminal youths from secure juvenile institutions.

family model: As applied to juvenile institutions, a model based on individualism, care, and nurturing. The family model was the basis for the training and industrial school.

graduated incarceration: The practice of housing juvenile offenders convicted as adults in a juvenile institution until they reach a certain age, at which time they are transferred to an adult prison.

juvenile correctional facility: The modern name for the training, industrial, or state school. The juvenile correctional facility is different from the state school in some states in that it houses the most serious, violent, and chronic juveniles within a particular juvenile correctional system.

orphanage: An institution for orphaned or abandoned children.

post-adjudication juvenile placements: Juvenile placements that house youths after they have been adjudicated. A state school is an example of a post-adjudication placement.

pre-adjudication juvenile placements: Juvenile facilities that house youths before they have been adjudicated. A detention center is an example of a pre-adjudication placement.

progressives: A label given to groups that sought reforms in all aspects of society, including juvenile institutionalization.

reformatory: By the 1880s, the name given to houses of refuge in the United States. Reformatories were literally identical to houses of refuge and in many cases were actually former houses of refuge.

school model: As applied to juvenile institutions, a model based on standardization, order, and predictability. The school model was the basis for the reformatory.

segregated incarceration: Refers to the practice of housing juveniles convicted in adult court to a specific age-segregated adult facility (for offenders ages eighteen to twenty-four) until they reach a certain age.

straight adult incarceration: The practice of housing juveniles convicted in adult court in an adult prison with no effort to segregate them by age.

training schools (also called *industrial schools*): Juvenile institutions introduced by the 1900s in the United States. The training and industrial school differed substantially from the reformatory, most notably with the development of the cottage system.

vocational program: A trade- or skill-learning program in juvenile institutions. An example is automobile maintenance or computer programming.

wayward: A term used to describe a child who has strayed from a law-abiding life.

FOR FURTHER RESEARCH

❑ **Juvenile Boot Camps: Lessons Learned**
http://www.ncjrs.org/txtfiles/fs-9636.txt

❑ **An Assessment of Space Needs in Juvenile Detention and Correctional Facilities**
http://www.ncjrs.org/html/ojjdp/jjbul2001_3_1/contents.html

❑ **Conditions of Confinement in Juvenile Detention and Correctional Facilities**
http://ojjdp.ncjrs.org/search/SearchResults.asp

❑ **Counting What Counts: The Census of Juveniles in Residential Placement**
http://www.ncjrs.org/txtfiles/fs-9874.txt

❑ **Innovative Information on Juvenile Residential Facilities**
http://www.ncjrs.org/txtfiles1/ojjdp/fs200011.txt

For an up-to-date list of web links, go to the Juvenile Justice Companion Website at **http://cj.wadsworth.com/del_carmen_trulson_jj**

The Death Penalty for Juveniles: *Roper v. Simmons* (2005)

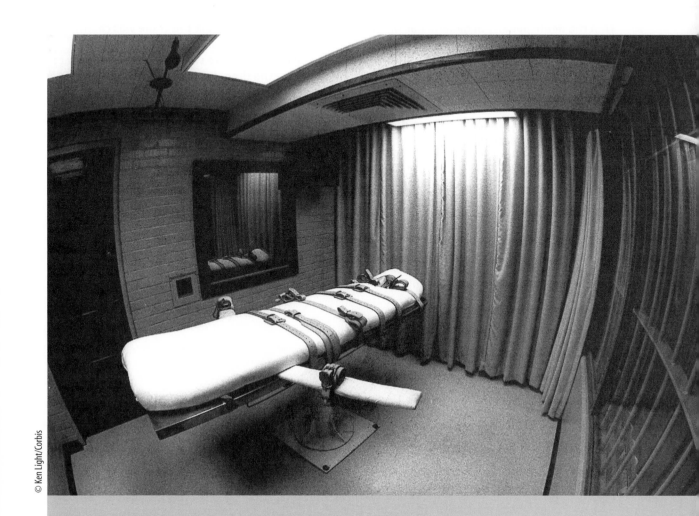

CHAPTER TWELVE OUTLINE

The Death Penalty in General / 383

Background / 383

U.S. Supreme Court Cases / 384

Furman v. Georgia (1972) / 385

Gregg v. Georgia (1976) / 385

The Death Penalty for Juveniles Before *Simmons* / 386

Background / 386

The Laws and Practices Before *Simmons* / 386

U.S. Supreme Court Cases Before *Simmons* / 388

Eddings v. Oklahoma (1982) / 388

Thompson v. Oklahoma (1988) / 389

Stanford v. Kentucky (1989) and *Wilkins v. Missouri* (1989) / 389

"Evolving Standards of Decency" as a Test for Constitutionality / 390

Developments Before *Simmons* / 392

Infrequent Executions / 392

The International Scene / 392

Atkins v. Virginia (2002): A Judicial Precedent for *Simmons* / 392

Roper v. Simmons (2005): The Death Penalty for Juveniles Is Unconstitutional / 393

The Holding and the Issue / 393

The Facts / 393

Unusual Circumstances / 394

The Majority Opinion by Five Justices / 395

The Dissenting Opinions by Four Justices / 396

What Happens After *Roper v. Simmons?* / 398

IN THIS CHAPTER YOU WILL LEARN

- That the death penalty in general has been declared constitutional by the U.S. Supreme Court.

- That death has been an acceptable form of punishment throughout U.S. history.

- That in 1972 the U.S. Supreme Court declared the death penalty unconstitutional but in 1976 reversed that decision and declared it constitutional.

- That the death penalty for juvenile offenders has always been imposed in the United States, the first juvenile execution having taken place in 1642.

- That before 2005, the Court held that executing juveniles who are fifteen years old or younger at the time the crime was committed is unconstitutional but that executing juveniles who are sixteen or seventeen years old at the time the crime was committed is constitutional.

- That on a 5–4 vote, the Court on March 1, 2005, held in *Roper v. Simmons* that executing juveniles under eighteen years old at the time the crime was committed violates the Eighth Amendment prohibition against cruel and unusual punishment and is therefore unconstitutional.

- That unless the Court changes its mind, no juveniles can now be executed in the United States regardless of the seriousness of the crime.

INTRODUCTION

Death is the ultimate punishment that a government entity can impose on any criminal. The death penalty in general is controversial; that controversy is heightened when applied to juveniles. There are serious legal, moral, social, and religious issues involved in killing a person even if the act is done by the state and follows the commission of a serious crime. Central to the controversy is this legal issue: Does the death penalty for juveniles constitute cruel and unusual punishment as prohibited by the Eighth Amendment to the U.S. Constitution? Here are some issues surrounding the death penalty and juvenile offenders for which society has no clear answers even after the *Roper v. Simmons* case:

- Are juveniles fully aware of the consequences when committing heinous crimes?

- Do juveniles deserve mercy because of their age?

- Are juveniles more susceptible to rehabilitation and deterrence than adults?

- Are juveniles the product of a bad upbringing and poor home environment such that society must share the blame for what they do?

- Are juvenile criminals and adult criminals different?

- Does it make sense to draw the line at eighteen years of age?

The controversy over the death penalty for juveniles will likely continue even after the Court's 2005 decision that executing juvenile offenders is unconstitutional. The **retentionists** (those for keeping juvenile executions) are not about to give up the fight even after the abolition of the death penalty for juveniles by the Court's narrow 5–4 vote.

This chapter starts with a look at capital punishment in general and then goes to the specifics of death as a punishment for juveniles who are age sixteen and seventeen. It discusses U.S. Supreme Court decisions on the death penalty for adults and then focuses on cases that involve juveniles. The chapter ends with an analysis of *Roper v. Simmons* (2005), in which the Court declared the death penalty for juveniles to be in violation of the Eighth Amendment prohibition against cruel and unusual punishment, and therefore unconstitutional.

The Death Penalty in General
Background

Any discussion of the death penalty for juveniles must begin with the background of the death penalty in general. Death as a punishment for serious crimes has always been part of human history. As of 2003, more than half of the countries in the world retained death as the ultimate punishment for heinous crimes. That same year, 76 countries and territories abolished the death penalty for any and all crimes. Twenty countries have retained the death penalty but have not carried out any executions in the past decade. In 2002, at least 1,526 prisoners were executed in 31 countries, and a total of 3,248 people were sentenced to death.[1]

Throughout its history, the United States has considered the death penalty an acceptable form of punishment (see Exhibit 12.1). The earliest documented execution of an adult criminal occurred in 1608, in Virginia.[2] At present, 38 out of the 50 states and the federal government allow the death penalty for the most serious crimes. Sixty-five prisoners were executed in the United States in 2003 and 59 in 2004. As of December 31, 2004, a total of 945 prisoners had

EXHIBIT 12.1   *The U.S. Death Penalty in General*

STATES WITH THE DEATH PENALTY (38†)

Alabama	Florida	Louisiana	N. Hampshire*	Oregon	Virginia
Arizona	Georgia	Maryland	New Jersey*	Pennsylvania	Washington
Arkansas	Idaho	Mississippi	New Mexico	S. Carolina	Wyoming
California	Illinois	Missouri	New York*†	S. Dakota*	
Colorado	Indiana	Montana	N. Carolina	Tennessee	U.S. government
Connecticut*	Kansas*†	Nebraska	Ohio	Texas	U.S. military
Delaware	Kentucky	Nevada	Oklahoma	Utah	

*Indicates jurisdictions with no executions since 1976.
†In 2004, the death penalty statutes in New York (June 24) and Kansas (Dec. 17) were declared unconstitutional.

STATES WITHOUT THE DEATH PENALTY (12)

Alaska	Maine	Minnesota	Vermont	Dist. of Columbia
Hawaii	Massachusetts	N. Dakota	W. Virginia	
Iowa	Michigan	Rhode Island	Wisconsin	

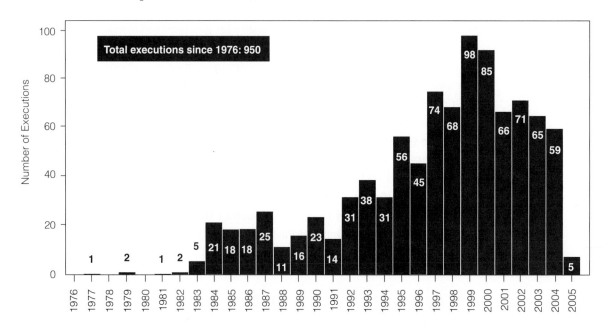

Source: Adapted from Death Penalty Information Center (http://www.deathpenaltyinfo.org) (7 Mar. 2005).

been executed in the United States since executions resumed in 1977. More than 3,455 prisoners were on death row as of January 1, 2005. Approximately 20,000 offenders have been legally executed in the United States in the 350 years of its history.[3]

U.S. Supreme Court Cases

During the past few decades, the U.S. Supreme Court has resolved many death penalty issues. However, two cases stand out among the many as framing the core controversy on the death penalty. These cases produced different results.

Furman v. Georgia *(1972)*

The first major case on the death penalty was decided in 1972 in the case of *Furman v. Georgia*.[4] The issue brought to the U.S. Supreme Court on appeal was simple: Is the death penalty constitutional? On a 5–4 vote, the Court held that the death penalty, as administered at the time, was unconstitutional. However, that vote was misleading because the Court did not decide whether the death penalty *per se* constituted cruel and unusual punishment. Only two justices (Marshall and Brennan) held that view. Three out of five justices in the majority said that the death penalty is unconstitutional not because the punishment itself is cruel and unusual, but rather because the way it had been imposed and carried out was so arbitrary and capricious that it violated the constitutional guarantee of equal protection. One of the three justices who found an equal protection problem with the imposition of the death penalty said that the Constitution was violated because the death penalty was administered in a "wanton and freakish manner" and was so arbitrarily and capriciously applied that it was comparable to being struck by lightning.

After *Furman,* thirty-five states and the federal government revised their death penalty laws to eliminate equal protection problems and to ensure fairness. The revised laws fell into two categories: those that made the death penalty mandatory for certain crimes (therefore eliminating discretion) and those that allowed the judge or jury to decide which penalty to impose, but based on specified legislative guidelines (therefore reducing discretion for those who imposed the death penalty).

Gregg v. Georgia *(1976)*

Four years after *Furman,* the Court changed its mind in *Gregg v. Georgia*[5] and declared the death penalty constitutional. While hitchhiking in Florida, Gregg and a companion were picked up by two motorists. The bodies of the two motorists were found beside a road near Atlanta, Georgia. Gregg and his companion were later arrested, and the murder weapon was found in their possession. Gregg confessed to the robberies and murders but claimed that he was acting in self-defense. He was found guilty of all charges and sentenced to death. On appeal, Gregg claimed that Georgia's death penalty law was unconstitutional because it did not contain enough safeguards against arbitrary imposition. The Court disagreed, saying that Georgia's death penalty law had sufficient safeguards against a possible violation of the equal protection provision of the Constitution, and therefore upheld the law. The vote was 7–2, with justices Marshall and Brennan reiterating their opinions from *Furman* that the death penalty in itself constitutes cruel and unusual punishment, prohibited by the Eighth Amendment.

Gregg v. Georgia is doubtless the most significant case decided thus far by the U.S. Supreme Court on the death penalty. For the first time in the nation's history, a majority of the Court said that the death penalty is not in itself unconstitutional as a form of punishment and may be imposed if sufficient safeguards against arbitrariness are set by law. This ruling did not mean that the revised statutes in the thirty-five states and the federal government at the time were automatically declared constitutional and that executions could resume.

Instead, it meant that the Court, if asked in a proper case, could now examine each state's death penalty law to determine if its provisions contained sufficient safeguards against arbitrariness and therefore could be declared constitutional.

The Death Penalty for Juveniles Before *Simmons*
Background

The first documented execution of a juvenile offender took place in 1642, when Thomas Graunger, who was charged with and found guilty of bestiality (defined as "the crime of having a sexual connection with an animal"),[6] was put to death in Plymouth Colony, Massachusetts.[7] At the time of Graunger's execution, the favorite punishment for juveniles by colonial Americans was to "beat the devil" out of their children if they committed a crime, the assumption being that the act was partially or totally caused by the devil. The state authorized—indeed, sometimes required—parents to publicly "execute, whip, or even banish their children if society found them to be criminally liable."[8] Since its founding and as of 2003, the United States had executed 355 juveniles.[9]

The Laws and Practices Before *Simmons*

Until early 2005 and prior to *Simmons*, thirty-one states and the federal government either prohibited the execution of offenders who were under the age of eighteen at the time that the offense was committed or had no death penalty law (see Table 12.1). By contrast, nineteen states allowed juveniles to be executed. Of this group of nineteen states, only twelve had juveniles on death row, and only seven of them actually used this punishment.[10]

As of February 2004, there were 73 juvenile offenders on death row in 12 states, half of them in Texas and Alabama. All were males, 64 percent were minorities, 81 percent had committed their crimes at age 17, and all had been sentenced to death for murder.[11] Juvenile offenders on death row constituted 2 percent of the total death row population, which was approximately 3,500 as of 2004.[12] Although the percentage of juveniles on death row is not high compared to the entire death row population, juveniles on death row generate intense publicity because of their heinous crimes and young age. Over the years, however, the number of juvenile offenders sentenced to death has gone down. For example, only four juvenile offenders were sentenced to death in 2002, two in 2003, and two in 2004.[13] Moreover, executing persons who committed capital crimes as juveniles is also rare, and since capital punishment resumed in the United States in 1976, only 22 of more than 900 executions have involved juveniles.[14]

Previous research conducted on the juveniles sentenced to death has revealed the following characteristics:

- Almost half of those sentenced had troubled family histories, troubled social backgrounds, and problems such as physical abuse, unstable childhood environments, and illiteracy.

- Just under one-third suffered psychological disturbances (such as profound depression, paranoia, and self-mutilation).

TABLE 12.1

Minimum Ages for the Death Penalty in the United States Before Roper v. Simmons

Most states that specify a minimum age for the death penalty set the minimum at age 16 or 18.

None Specified	Age 16 (or Less)	Age 17	Age 18
Arizona	Alabama	Georgia	California
Idaho	Arkansas (14)[b]	New Hampshire	Colorado
Louisiana	Delaware	N. Carolina[e]	Connecticut[f]
Montana	Florida	Texas	Federal system
Pennsylvania	Indiana		Illinois
S. Carolina	Kentucky		Kansas
S. Dakota[a]	Mississippi (13)[c]		Maryland
Utah	Missouri		Nebraska
	Nevada		New Jersey
	Oklahoma		New Mexico
	Virginia (14)[d]		New York
	Wyoming		Ohio
			Oregon
			Tennessee
			Washington

[a] Juveniles may be transferred to criminal court. Age can be a mitigating factor.

[b] See Arkansas Code Ann. 9–27–318(b)(2)(Repl. 1991).

[c] The minimum age defined by statute is 13, but the effective age is 16 based on interpretation of U.S. Supreme Court decisions by the State attorney general's office.

[d] The minimum age for transfer to criminal court is 14 by statute, but the effective age for a capital sentence is 16 based on interpretation of U.S. Supreme Court decisions by the State attorney general's office.

[e] The age required is 17 unless the murderer was incarcerated for murder when a subsequent murder occurred; then the age may be 14.

[f] See Conn. Gen. Stat. 53a–46a(g)(1).

Note: Minimum ages (at the time of the capital offense) reflect interpretation by State attorney general offices. States not listed do not have the death penalty.

Source: Adapted from Howard N. Snyder and Melissa Sickmund, *Juvenile Offenders and Victims: 1999 National Report* (Washington, DC: Office of Juvenile Justice and Delinquency Prevention, 1999), 211.

■ Just under one-third exhibited mental disability as evidenced by low or borderline IQ scores.

■ More than half were indigent.

■ Roughly 20 percent were involved in intensive substance abuse before the crime.[15]

This data show that juveniles on death row disproportionately come from dysfunctional families, have serious mental problems, are not blessed with a high IQ, have drug problems, and are poor. In sum, they come from a disadvantaged underclass of U.S. society (see Table 12.2).

U.S. Supreme Court Cases Before *Simmons*

Before 2005, three cases had been decided by the U.S. Supreme Court involving juveniles on death row. All were decided on split votes. These cases set the stage for *Roper v. Simmons*.

Eddings v. Oklahoma *(1982)*

Eddings was sixteen years old when he shot and killed an Oklahoma patrol officer.[16] He was certified to stand trial as an adult, convicted, and given the death sentence. On appeal, the U.S. Supreme Court, on a 6–3 split vote, reversed Eddings's conviction, saying that the trial judge failed to properly consider Eddings's age, unhappy upbringing, and emotional disturbance during the sentencing phase. However, the Eddings case did not raise and therefore did not decide the issue of whether juveniles can be given the death penalty. What it simply said was that all reasonable and relevant mitigating factors must be considered by the trial court in juvenile capital offense cases. The Court ruled that age is a relevant mitigating factor that should be considered when deciding whether death should be imposed, but it left the question of the constitutionality of the death penalty for juveniles unresolved.

TABLE 12.2

*Characteristics of Victims and Offenders in Juvenile Delinquency Cases**

Juvenile Offenders						Victims of Juvenile Offenders								
Age	Number	%	Race	Number	%	Age	Number	%	Race	Number	%	Gender	Number	%
16	14	19	Native American	1	1	0–15	13	14	Native American	1	1	Male	49	51
17	58	81	Asian	2	2	16–19	12	13	Asian	7	7	Female	48	49
			Black	29	40	20–29	15	16	Black	8	9			
			Latino	15	21	30–39	15	16	Latino	10	11			
			White	25	35	40–49	14	15	White	65	71			
						50–59	8	9	Unknown	6	6			
						60–69	4	4						
						70–79	9	10						
						80–82	1	1						
						Unknown	6	6						

*As of December 31, 2004.

Source: Adapted from Death Penalty Information Center (http://www.deathpenaltyinfo.org)(7 Mar. 2005).

Thompson v. Oklahoma *(1988)*

Thompson was fifteen years old when, along with three other persons, he was charged with the brutal murder of his former brother-in-law.[17] Certified as an adult for trial, he was convicted and given the death penalty. On appeal, he claimed that executing a juvenile is unconstitutional because it constitutes cruel and unusual punishment in violation of the Eighth Amendment. Thompson alleged that executing juveniles is out of step with "evolving standards of decency that mark the progress of maturing society." A plurality of the Court (four out of nine justices) agreed, saying that executing juveniles who are at age fifteen or younger when the crime was committed constitutes cruel and unusual punishment. The plurality considered three factors: (1) the ages that the different states set for the imposition of the death penalty, (2) the willingness of jurors to impose the death penalty in cases involving juveniles, and (3) what other countries and organizations have said about imposing the death penalty on juveniles.[18] The plurality opinion concluded by saying that "The conclusion that it would offend civilized standards of decency to execute a person who was less than sixteen-years-old at the time of his or her offense is consistent with the views that have been expressed by respected professional organizations, by other nations that share our Anglo-American heritage, and by the leading members of the Western European community." However, the Court did not decide whether executing sixteen- or seventeen-year-olds was also unconstitutional.

The fifth vote that led to the reversal of Thompson's death sentence came from Justice O'Connor. She disagreed with the conclusions of the plurality opinion on the three issues noted above, but observed that when a state legislature does not set the minimum age (as Oklahoma did not) for executing offenders, the Court could and should not conclude that such execution is allowed. Instead, she concluded that the legislature simply had not addressed that issue and therefore voted to reverse the conviction.

Stanford v. Kentucky *(1989) and* Wilkins v. Missouri *(1989)*

The third Court decision consolidated two cases that raised the same issue and were decided together by the Court. It is referred to simply as the Stanford case.[19] Defendant Stanford was charged with the capital murder of a twenty-year-old gas station attendant whom Stanford and his accomplice repeatedly raped and sodomized. They drove her to a secluded area near the gas station and then shot her point-blank in the face and in the back of her head. Stanford was seventeen years and four months old when the crime was committed. He was certified for trial in an adult court after a juvenile hearing. Stanford was convicted and sentenced to death. Defendant Wilkins was charged with and convicted of the murder of a twenty-six-year-old mother. She was stabbed several times while working behind the sales counter of a convenience store. She begged for her life but was stabbed again four more times in the neck and was left to die on the floor. Wilkins and his accomplice then helped themselves to liquor, cigarettes, rolling papers, and $450 in cash and checks. Wilkins was sixteen years and six months old when he committed the offense.

The main issue on appeal to the U.S. Supreme Court was specific: Does the imposition of the death penalty for a crime committed at age sixteen or seventeen constitute cruel and unusual punishment? In a 5–4 vote, the Court said no, holding that executing sixteen- or seventeen-year-olds is constitutional. A plurality of the Court (four out of the nine justices) concluded that several states required that juvenile offenders be either sixteen or seventeen years of age before they can be given the death sentence. A heavy burden of establishing a national consensus rested on those challenging its constitutionality, a burden that was not met. The plurality opinion did not address the other issues raised by defendants Stanford and Wilkins (the issues of deterrence and **proportionality,** the concept that the punishment must be equal to the crime), concluding instead that it is not the Court but the citizenry who have the final say on whether a form of punishment is cruel and unusual.

As in the Thompson case, Justice O'Connor provided the deciding vote in *Stanford,* saying in a concurring opinion that "it is sufficiently clear that no national consensus forbids the imposition of capital punishment on sixteen-year-old capital murderers."

Stanford v. Kentucky resolved an issue that the Court failed to address the previous year in *Thompson v. Oklahoma*—whether a defendant who was of juvenile age (either sixteen or seventeen) at the time the offense was committed could be given the death penalty. The decision in *Stanford* is clear: The imposition of capital punishment on an individual for a crime committed at sixteen or seventeen years of age does not constitute cruel and unusual punishment under the Eighth Amendment. Thus, the Court set the minimum age at sixteen if a state wanted to impose the death penalty. Juveniles who were under sixteen years of age during the commission of the offense could not be given the death penalty regardless of circumstances.*

It is important to note that the crucial event that determines death penalty eligibility for juveniles is age at the time of the commission of the offense, not the age of the offender at arrest, trial, or conviction. Moreover, state law may set a higher age for executing offenders (such as eighteen or above), but none of the states that authorize the death penalty have set the minimum at an age higher than eighteen: This age is considered the age of adulthood for many purposes in the various states.

"Evolving Standards of Decency" as a Test for Constitutionality

In both the *Thompson* and *Stanford* cases, the Court relied on "evolving standards of decency that mark the progress of a maturing society." This is an elusive and hard-to-define standard that the Court has used in previous Eighth Amendment cases. In deciding whether a certain penalty is cruel and unusual, and therefore its constitutionality, the Court examines such factors as the laws

*Postscript to the *Stanford* case: In 2003, Kevin Stanford was still on Kentucky's death row, but his death sentence was commuted to life in prison without parole by the governor. In essence, the governor stated that the death penalty for juveniles is excessive. What Stanford did not get from the judiciary he got instead from the executive department.

of various states, how often the penalty is used (for example, by examining prosecutor charging decisions and/or jury willingness to impose the penalty), public opinion, whether the penalty is proportionate to the offense committed, and whether other countries use the penalty. The standard is highly subjective, as juvenile death penalty cases demonstrate. The four justices in *Stanford* who opposed the execution of sixteen- and seventeen-year-olds believed that society had reached a stage where the execution of juveniles was no longer acceptable. By contrast, the five justices who approved of the punishment in *Stanford* claimed the opposite, saying that the stage had not in fact been reached and that it is an issue for state legislatures to decide.

To Justice O'Connor, legislative enactments (state laws) are the crucial determinant in the **evolving standards of decency** test. As she said, "The day may come when there is such general legislative rejection of the execution of sixteen or seventeen-year-old capital murderers that a clear national consensus can be said to have developed. Because I do not believe that day has arrived, I concur in the judgment." Relying heavily on state laws, the majority in *Stanford* held that there was no consensus against the execution of sixteen- and seventeen-year-olds, stating that "of the 37 states that permit capital punishment, 15 states decline to impose it on 16-year-olds and 12 states decline to impose it on 17-year-olds." The Court then concluded that "this does not establish the degree of national agreement this Court has previously thought sufficient to label a punishment cruel and unusual." (See Exhibit 12.2.)

EXHIBIT 12.2

Results of a Public Opinion Survey on the Death Penalty for Juveniles Before Roper v. Simmons

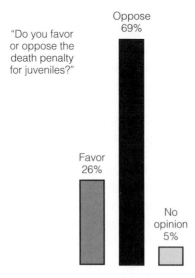

"Do you favor or oppose the death penalty for juveniles?"

Oppose 69%

Favor 26%

No opinion 5%

Source: "Overview of the Death Penalty Today." American Bar Association, Criminal Justice Section, Juvenile Justice Center (Spring 2003): 2.

Developments Before *Simmons*

Infrequent Executions

Prior to 2005, the annual death sentencing rate for juvenile offenses declined and was at its lowest point in fifteen years. The most recent execution (in 2003) was in Oklahoma, but there are no more juvenile offenders on death row in that state, and Oklahoma has not sentenced a juvenile offender to death in eight years.[20] A recent poll in Missouri found that only 34 percent of Missourians support the death penalty for juveniles.[21] In a much-publicized case involving a juvenile, a jury in Virginia refused to impose the death penalty on Lee Boyd Malvo, the Washington area sniper, who was seventeen years old when he and John Allen Muhammad, an adult, went on a shooting spree that killed ten people. Muhammad was given the death penalty, but Malvo, the juvenile, was given life imprisonment.

The American Bar Association notes that despite current laws, the execution of juveniles in the United States is in fact rare. Before *Simmons*, of the nineteen states that retained the death penalty for juvenile offenders, only Texas (which has executed thirteen) and Virginia (which has executed three) used executions with any frequency. The ABA observes that "these two states have carried out 76% of all executions of juvenile offenders in the United States in the last 125 years."[22]

The International Scene

Before *Simmons*, the United States was one of only eight countries known to have executed offenders for crimes committed while the offender was under eighteen years of age. The seven other countries are Iran, Pakistan, Saudi Arabia, Yemen, Nigeria, the Congo, and China. However, all of these countries have either abolished the death penalty for juveniles or have disavowed the practice.

International law considers the execution of juveniles to be a human rights issue that should be governed by treaties. Several international treaties have banned the execution of juveniles, but the United States has signed these treaties with the reservation that it be exempted from complying with such provisions. For example, the International Covenant on Civil and Political Rights (ICCPR) states that "the sentence of death shall not be imposed for crimes committed by persons below eighteen years of age." The United States signed the ICCPR but expressly reserved the right to impose the death penalty for crimes committed by juveniles under the age of eighteen.[23] A second international law document that bans the execution of children is the United Nations Convention on the Rights of the Child (CRC). Article 37(a) of that document provides that "neither capital punishment nor life imprisonment without possibility of release shall be imposed for offences committed by persons below eighteen years of age." Former President Clinton signed the CRD in 1995 but did not subscribe to Article 37(a); therefore, the United States is not bound by it.[24]

Atkins v. Virginia (2002): A Judicial Precedent for *Simmons*

In 2002 the U.S. Supreme Court decided a case that set the stage and greatly influenced the *Roper v. Simmons* decision. In *Atkins v. Virginia* (2002)[25] the Court held that the execution of a "mentally retarded offender" (the term used by the

Court in the decision) is unconstitutional. The Court considered the following factors in declaring such executions unconstitutional: the reluctance of juries to impose the death penalty on the mentally retarded, the infrequency of executions, the opposition of authoritative organizations, and the practice in other countries of not executing the mentally retarded. These were the same factors relied upon by the Missouri Supreme Court (from where *Simmons* was appealed) when it boldly disregarded *Stanford* and held, by a split decision, the execution of juveniles to be unconstitutional. The *Atkins* case was cited repeatedly in the Court's opinion in *Simmons* and made it easier for the Court to overrule its 1989 decision in *Stanford,* which declared the execution of sixteen- and seventeen-year-olds constitutional. Without the *Atkins* decision three years earlier, the Court would likely have found *Simmons* a more difficult case to decide. *Atkins* (regarding the mentally retarded) paved the way for *Simmons* (regarding juveniles) and set judicial precedent that the Court found easy to follow.

Roper v. Simmons (2005): The Death Penalty for Juveniles Is Unconstitutional

This chapter makes frequent mention of *Roper v. Simmons* (2005),[26] which is currently the leading and latest case on the juvenile death penalty. *Simmons* resolves, at least for now, the issue of the constitutionality of the death penalty for juvenile offenders, and it deserves extended discussion.

The Holding and the Issue

The Court held that "the Eighth and Fourteenth Amendments forbid imposition of the death penalty on offenders who were under the age of 18 when their crimes were committed." It affirmed the judgment of the Missouri Supreme Court, which had set aside the death sentence imposed on Christopher Simmons.

In reality, the issue in *Simmons* focused only on the constitutionality of executing persons sixteen and seventeen years old at the time of their capital crime. The constitutionality of executing juveniles fifteen years of age or younger when the crime was committed was settled years earlier, in *Thompson v. Oklahoma* (1988). Taken together, the *Simmons* and *Thompson* cases say that the execution of offenders who are under the age of eighteen at the time the crime was committed is unconstitutional.

The Facts

Christopher Simmons, age seventeen and a junior in high school, killed a Missouri woman, Shirley Crook, in 1993. His guilt was clear, and so was the fact that he instigated the crime. Before the crime, Simmons said he wanted "to murder someone." With two other juvenile friends (ages fifteen and sixteen), Simmons proposed that they "commit burglary and murder by breaking and entering, tying up a victim, and throwing the victim off a bridge"—which was exactly what they did. Simmons told his friends that they could "get away with it" because they were juveniles.

On the night of the murder, the three juveniles met at 2:00 A.M. and entered the home of Shirley Crook, the victim. Simmons recognized her from a previous car accident involving both of them. The three juveniles used duct tape to cover Shirley Crook's eyes and mouth and bind her hands. They placed her in a minivan and drove to a state park, tied her up further, and then threw her from a bridge. Shirley Crook drowned in the waters below. *Simmons* later bragged about the killing and told friends that he killed the woman "because the bitch seen [sic] my face."

Based on information, the police arrested Simmons at his high school; took him to the police station in Fenton, Missouri; and read him his *Miranda* rights. He waived his right to a lawyer and agreed to answer questions from the police. After two hours of interrogation, Simmons confessed to the murder and performed a videotaped reenactment of the crime at the crime scene.

Simmons was charged with burglary, kidnapping, stealing, and murder in the first degree. He was seventeen at the time of the crime and, based on Missouri law, was tried as an adult. Convicted and given the death penalty, he appealed the case to the Missouri Supreme Court, which affirmed his conviction and sentence, and later rejected his petition for post-conviction relief.

After *Atkins v. Virginia* (which held that execution of the mentally retarded is unconstitutional) was decided in 2002, Simmons again sought relief. On a split vote, the Missouri Supreme Court said that "This Court concluded that the United States Supreme Court would hold that the execution of persons for crimes committed when they were under 18 years of age violates the evolving standards of decency and is prohibited by the Eighth Amendment to the United States constitution." It found that in the fourteen years since the *Stanford* decision, "a national consensus has developed against the execution of juvenile offenders." It then held that "many of the same principles and factors that have guided the Supreme Court's determination of the constitutionality of the death penalty for the mentally retarded have also guided the Supreme Court's determination of the constitutionality of the death penalty for juveniles." The state of Missouri appealed, and the U.S. Supreme Court agreed to hear the case.

Unusual Circumstances

Even before the Court's March 1, 2005, decision, *Roper v. Simmons* was already viewed in legal circles as an unusual case. First, it provided the U.S. Supreme Court a forum to revisit the issue of juvenile executions less than two years after it refused to do so—amid strong protests from within the Court itself. Some members of the Court had long wanted to revisit the issue of the constitutionality of juvenile executions. Second, the Missouri Supreme Court was amazingly bold in predicting the reversal of and going against the Court's decision in *Stanford v. Kentucky.* It virtually goaded the nation's highest court into action, in essence saying that "It is time to change your mind." Third, and more significantly, seldom has a case reached the Court where the votes of at least seven justices (out of the nine) were known even before the case was decided. Court observers knew that unless the composition of the Court changed, justices Stevens, Souter, Ginsburg, and Breyer (known in the Court as the liberals) would hold juvenile executions unconstitutional. In October 2002, these four justices publicly called such executions "shameful" and in violation of the "evolving standards of decency in a civilized society." Conversely, justices Rehnquist, Scalia, and Thomas (acknowledged as the conservatives) would uphold the constitutionality of juvenile executions primarily on the grounds that the issue was a matter for state legislatures to decide and that nothing much had changed since *Stanford v. Kentucky.* Court observers knew the decision depended on how the two other justices would vote—Kennedy and O'Connor. It was going to be either a 5–4 or a 6–3 vote.

The Majority Opinion by Five Justices

The majority opinion in *Simmons* was written by Justice Kennedy, with a concurring opinion by Justice Stevens. Justice O'Connor, the other "swing" justice, voted with the dissent and wrote her own opinion. Justice Scalia also wrote a dissenting opinion.

The main justifications for the majority opinion are as follows (arguments are in the order presented in the opinion):

- The Court must refer to the "evolving standards of decency that mark the progress of a maturing society" to determine which punishments are so disproportionate that they constitute cruel and unusual punishment.

- "Evolving standards of decency" have now reached a point at which the execution of juveniles is considered by U.S. society as cruel and unusual punishment.

- Five of the states that allowed the death penalty for juveniles when *Stanford v. Kentucky* was decided (1989) have now abandoned it—four by law and one through judicial decision—demonstrating the "consistency of direction of change." By contrast, no state that previously prohibited capital punishment for juveniles has reinstated it. The trend is toward abolition.

- Three general differences between juveniles under eighteen and adults show that juvenile offenders are less culpable than adult criminals: (1) Lack of maturity and an underdeveloped sense of responsibility are found in youths more often than in adults and are more understandable among the young. These factors often result in impetuous and ill-considered actions and decisions. (2) "Juveniles are more vulnerable or susceptible to negative influences and outside pressures, including peer pressure." (3) "The character of a juvenile is not as well formed as that of an adult. The personality traits of juveniles are more transitory, less fixed."

- Retribution and deterrence, the penological justifications for the death penalty, apply with lesser force to juveniles than to adults.

- Eighteen years of age is the point at which society draws the line for many purposes between childhood and adulthood; therefore, it is the age at which the time for death eligibility should be drawn.

- The death penalty is a disproportionate punishment for offenders under eighteen. This is reaffirmed by the fact that the United States is the only country in the world that continues to give official sanction to the death penalty for juveniles.

The Dissenting Opinions by Four Justices

Justice O'Connor and Justice Scalia wrote dissenting opinions.

The main points in Justice O'Connor's dissent are as follows (arguments are in the order presented in her opinion):

- "Neither the objective evidence of contemporary societal values, nor the Court's moral proportionality analysis, nor the two in tandem suffice to justify this ruling."
- The majority opinion does not reflect the "evolving standards of decency." Instead, it "rests, ultimately, on its independent moral judgment that death is a disproportionately severe punishment for any 17-year old offender."
- Very little has changed since the Court's decision in *Stanford;* therefore, overruling it is unwarranted.
- Some juvenile offenders may be just as culpable as many adult offenders who are deemed bad enough to deserve the death penalty.
- Despite evidence of an international consensus, "the Eighth Amendment does not, at this time, forbid capital punishment of 17-year old murderers in all cases."
- Despite the change of laws in four states, there is no clear showing that a genuine national consensus forbids the execution of juvenile offenders.
- The Court should not substitute its own subjective judgment on how best to resolve this difficult moral question. That judgment should be left to democratically elected legislatures.

The main points in Justice Scalia's dissent are as follows (arguments are in the order presented in his opinion):

- The meaning of our Eighth Amendment should not be determined "by the subjective views of five Members of the Court and like-minded foreigners." Instead, it should be left to state legislatures.
- It is true that eighteen states—or 47 percent of states that permit capital punishment—now have legislation prohibiting the execution of offenders under eighteen and that four states have adopted such legislation since *Stanford.* But this does not mean a national consensus against executing juveniles has emerged.
- The "real force driving today's decision is not the actions of four state legislatures, but the Court's 'own judgment' that murderers younger than 18 can never be as morally culpable as older counterparts."
- The majority has not established that the scientific and sociological studies it cites are methodologically sound. Other studies contradict those findings. The studies cited by the Court offer little support for an outright prohibition of the death penalty for murderers under eighteen.
- The Court's claim that the goals of retribution and deterrence are not served by executing murderers under eighteen is false.
- The premise that U.S. law should conform to the laws of the rest of the world should be rejected. Other decisions show that the Court itself does not really believe this.

- What the United States does should not be influenced by the approval or disapproval of other nations.

Scalia lamented the fact that the Court affirmed the Missouri Supreme Court decision without even admonishing that court for its flagrant disregard of the Court's precedent in *Stanford,* saying "This is no way to run a legal system."

For a comparison of the majority and dissenting opinions, see Table 12.3.

TABLE 12.3

The Majority and Dissenting Opinions in Roper v. Simmons

Issues	Majority	Dissent
Is the execution of juvenile offenders ages 16 or 17 at the time the crime was committed constitutional?	No	Yes
Who voted?	Justice Kennedy Justice Stevens Justice Souter Justice Breyer Justice Ginsburg	Justice Scalia Justice Rehnquist Justice Thomas Justice O'Connor
Opinion written by:	Justice Kennedy	Justices O'Connor and Scalia
Is there now a national consensus against executing juveniles based on "evolving standards of decency"?	Yes	No
Are there differences between juvenile and adult offenders?	Yes	Not established
Do retribution and deterrence provide adequate justification for imposing the death penalty on juveniles?	No	Yes
Should the infrequency of juvenile executions in the United States be given significance (only 19 executions since 1990, the most recent being in 2003)?	Yes	No
Is drawing the line at 18 years old justified?	Yes	No
Is the death penalty disproportionate for offenders under 18?	Yes	No
Should state legislatures—instead of the U.S. Supreme Court—decide whether juveniles should be executed for certain crimes?	No	Yes
Should practices in other countries be considered when determining the constitutionality of the death penalty for juveniles?	Yes	No, or should not be determined
Should U.S. laws on the death penalty for juveniles conform to the laws of other countries?	Yes	No
Should scientific and sociological studies on the death penalty for juveniles be considered?	Yes	No, they are contradictory and unreliable
Should the Missouri Supreme Court be rebuked for going against the Court's decision in *Stanford v. Kentucky* (1989)?	Did not address this	Yes, it "is no way to run a legal system"

Memorable lines from the opinions: "The age of 18 is the point where society draws the line for many purposes between childhood and adulthood. It is, we conclude, the age which the line for death eligibility ought to rest."—*Justice Kennedy* (Majority)

"Because I do not believe that the meaning of our Eighth Amendment . . . should be determined by the subjective views of five members of this Court and like-minded foreigners, I dissent."—*Justice Scalia* (Dissent)

What Happens After *Roper v. Simmons?*

The *Simmons* case settles the issue of the constitutionality of the death penalty for juveniles, but not for adults. The Court has spoken, declaring juvenile executions unconstitutional. The immediate effect is that juveniles in the United States who commit crimes of any kind, regardless of seriousness or heinousness, cannot now be given the death penalty. *Simmons* has the same effect on juvenile executions that the case of *Furman v. Georgia* had on all executions in 1972. No executions took place in the United States after the *Furman* decision came out until *Furman* was reversed in 1976 by the Court in *Gregg v. Georgia*, which declared that the death penalty was not per se unconstitutional. After *Gregg*, executions in the United States resumed. This does not mean that the Court will reverse itself on the execution of juveniles at a later time. Note, however, that the vote against executions was a narrow 5–4 and could be overturned when the composition of the Court changes.

Laws in states that authorize the execution of juveniles are now unconstitutional because of *Simmons*. Some states might repeal them to conform to the Court decision; other states might leave them as they are and not bother to repeal. That is for the states to decide. However, any unrepealed state law is now unconstitutional and therefore unenforceable. Table 12.4 lists the states that will be immediately affected.

The debate over the execution of juveniles will likely continue in future years. Despite what the majority opinion says, the controversy over the effectiveness and morality of the death penalty for juveniles will not soon cease (see Exhibit 12.3). However, it is clear that unless the Court changes its mind in another future case, no juvenile executions can take place in the United States from now on. The death sentences for juveniles currently on death row will likely be commuted to life imprisonment. In most cases, these prisoners will be

TABLE 12.4

States Immediately Affected by Roper v. Simmons

State	Number on Death Row
Texas	28
Alabama	13
Mississippi	5
Arizona	4
Louisiana	4
North Carolina	4
Florida	3
South Carolina	3
Georgia	2
Pennsylvania	2
Vermont	1
Nevada	1

Source: Adapted from *USA Today* (2 Mar. 2005): 1.

EXHIBIT 12.3

A Summary of the Major Cases Decided by the U.S. Supreme Court on the Death Penalty

A. Crimes Committed by Adults:

Furman v. Georgia (1972): The death penalty is unconstitutional because it violates the provisions of the equal protection clause and the prohibition against cruel and unusual punishment in the Constitution.

Gregg v. Georgia (1976): The death penalty is constitutional as a form of punishment and may be imposed provided sufficient safeguards against arbitrariness are set by law.

B. Crimes Committed by Juveniles:

Eddings v. Oklahoma (1982): All reasonable relevant mitigating factors must be considered by the trial court when imposing sentence in juvenile capital offense cases.

Thompson v. Oklahoma (1988): Executing a juvenile who was 15 years old or younger at the time of the commission of the offense constitutes cruel and unusual punishment and is unconstitutional.

Stanford v. Kentucky (1989) and *Wilkins v. Missouri* (1989): It is constitutional to impose the death penalty for a crime committed at age 16 or 17.

Roper v. Simmons (2005): The death penalty for juveniles is unconstitutional because it violates the Eighth Amendment prohibition against cruel and unusual punishment.

eligible for parole, unless they are in a state that has a sentence of **life without parole.** For now, *Simmons* is the law of the land, but nobody knows whether or not it will stay that way in the years to come.

SUMMARY

❑ The U.S. Supreme Court decided in *Furman v. Georgia* (1972) that the death penalty for offenders was unconstitutional. Executions were suspended. The Court reversed that decision four years later in *Gregg v. Georgia* (1976) and declared the death penalty constitutional. Executions resumed.

❑ The death penalty for juveniles has been used throughout history in many states in the United States.

❑ Figures show that juveniles on death row disproportionately come from dysfunctional families, have serious mental problems, have low IQs, have drug problems, and are poor.

❑ In *Thompson v. Oklahoma* (1988), the Court held that executing juveniles fifteen years old or younger at the time the crime was committed is unconstitutional. A year later, in *Stanford v. Kentucky* (1989), the Court held that it is constitutional to execute juveniles who were sixteen or seventeen years of age at the time the crime was committed.

❑ In *Atkins v. Virginia* (2002), the Court held that executing a mentally retarded offender is unconstitutional. This ruling set a judicial precedent for a reversal of the Court holding in juvenile cases.

❑ In *Roper v. Simmons,* decided on March 1, 2005, the Court held, in a 5–4 vote, that "the Eighth and Fourteenth Amendments forbid imposition of the death penalty on offenders who were under the age of 18 when their crimes were committed."

❑ Unless the Court later changes its mind, *Simmons* has ended juvenile executions in the United States.

REVIEW QUESTIONS

1. Why did the U.S. Supreme Court say in *Furman v. Georgia* (1972) that the death penalty for offenders in general was unconstitutional?

2. "Juveniles on death row disproportionately come from the disadvantaged underclass in U.S. society." From data in this chapter, argue that the statement is true.

3. What factors did the Court take into account when it decided in *Thompson v. Oklahoma* (1988) that the death penalty for juveniles fifteen years of age or younger at the time the crime was committed is unconstitutional?

4. What does the phrase "evolving standards of decency" mean? What factors does the Court consider when determining the meaning of this phrase?

5. "Execution of juvenile offenders in the United States is popular with the public." Is this statement true or false? Support your answer.

6. Two international treaties ban the execution of juveniles. Are they binding in the United States? Explain why or why not.

7. What did the Court say in *Atkins v. Virginia* (2002)? Why is that case a good judicial precedent for *Roper v. Simmons*?

8. What did the Court hold in *Roper v. Simmons* (2005)? Give at least four justifications for the majority opinion.

9. Discuss four issues in *Roper v. Simmons* on which the dissenting opinions disagreed with the majority.

10. "The death penalty for juveniles is now banned forever in the United States because the Court has declared it unconstitutional." Is that statement true or false? Justify your answer.

KEY TERMS AND DEFINITIONS

evolving standards of decency: The standards generally used by the U.S. Supreme Court to determine whether a form of punishment, such as the death penalty, is constitutional. These standards are used together with the phrase "that mark the progress of a maturing society."

life without parole: A form of punishment in which an offender stays in prison for life and will never be released.

proportionality: The idea that the punishment given to an offender must be proportionate to the offense committed.

retentionists: Those who favor keeping laws that authorize the execution of juvenile offenders.

FOR FURTHER RESEARCH

- ❏ **Juvenile Offenders on Death Row**
  http://www.deathpenaltyinfo.org/article.php?did=204&scid=27

- ❏ **Characteristics of Offenders and Victims in Juvenile Death Penalty Cases (as of December 31, 2003)**
  http://www.deathpenaltyinfo.org/article.php?did=204&scid=27#steibstats

- ❏ **The Juvenile Death Penalty Today: Death Sentences and Executions for Juvenile Crimes, January 1, 1973–December 31, 2004**
  http://www.law.onu.edu/faculty/streib/documents/JuvDeathDec2004.pdf

- ❏ **On the Wrong Side of History: Children and the Death Penalty in the USA**
  http://www.amnestyuse.org/rightsforall/juvenile/dp/index.html

- ❏ **Juveniles and the Death Penalty**
  http://ww.ncjrs.org/html/ojjdp/coordcouncil

For an up-to-date list of web links, go to the Juvenile Justice Companion Website at **http://cj.wadsworth.com/del_carmen_trulson_jj**

CHAPTER 13

Schools, School Crime, and the Rights of Students

Juveniles, the Law, and Schools / 404

The Legal Basis of School Authority / 404

In Loco Parentis / 405

Reasonableness and School Rules / 405

The Legal Issues in Regulating Student Behavior / 405

Due Process in Schools / 405

Searches and Seizures in Schools / 408

Cruel and Unusual Punishment in Schools / 416

The Extent of School Crime / 417

Measuring School Crime / 418

School Crime in the 1990s / 418

Violent Deaths at School / 418

Nonfatal Student Victimization / 422

Nonfatal Teacher Victimization / 423

General School Environment Safety Issues / 423

The Bottom Line on School Crime / 424

Making Schools Safe—Can It Be Done? / 425

Zero Tolerance Policies / 425

The Legal Aspects of Zero Tolerance Policies / 427

The Prevalence of Zero Tolerance Policies / 428

Security Measures in Schools—Are They Effective? / 429

Closed School Campuses / 430

Metal Detectors / 431

School Partnerships with the Criminal and Juvenile Justice Systems / 431

Case Brief: *Pottawatomie County v. Earls* / 414

IN THIS CHAPTER YOU WILL LEARN

- Where schools derive their authority over students and what schools may do to maintain order and keep students safe.

- That students must receive a fair hearing before they are suspended or expelled from school.

- About the search and seizure of students in schools and that school officials may generally search without probable cause or a warrant.

- That corporal punishment is not unconstitutional in schools and that a number of states still authorize its use.

- About the extent of school crime and how school crime has meant significant changes in many schools.

- That school crime has led to collaboration between schools and the juvenile justice and criminal justice systems.

INTRODUCTION

Outside of the family, the school is the most important place for the education and socialization of children. In the last several years, however, several dramatic incidents of school crime have changed the role of schools. Although they remain the cornerstone of youth education and socialization, schools and their officials are increasingly viewed as agents of formal social control. A most notable change is the presence of criminal justice and juvenile justice system personnel within schools. Another change is the prevalence of tough, zero tolerance behavioral policies and physical security measures aimed at preventing crime and removing troublesome students from regular school settings altogether. The changes have led some to conclude that schools have become another arm of the criminal and juvenile justice system. These changes have raised several practical and legal questions in the school setting.

This chapter discusses the legal rights of juveniles in schools in controversial areas, such as suspension and expulsion, search and seizure, drug testing, and disciplinary procedures. It then discusses the extent of school crime. The extent of school crime is examined because it is a major factor that has spurred school- and criminal/juvenile-justice-based initiatives that seek to reduce crime and make schools safer. As a result, the last section of this chapter examines these specific initiatives: behavioral policies, security measures, and collaboration with the criminal justice and juvenile justice systems.

Juveniles, the Law, and Schools
The Legal Basis of School Authority

Justice Abe Fortas noted over thirty-five years ago in *Tinker v. Des Moines Independent Community School District* (1969) that the Constitution does not stop at the schoolhouse gate.[1] He maintained that students are persons under the Constitution whether they are in public or in schools. However, having rights that are protected by the Constitution does not mean that students' rights are absolute. Nor does this mean that schools have complete power over students who violate school policy. When students are found in violation of school rules, it is the duty of the school to enforce such policies, maintain order, and, when appropriate, discipline the student. However, controversy arises when forms of discipline or practices to keep schools safe and orderly are challenged by students as unfair, unreasonable, and, ultimately, unconstitutional.*

School administrators and teachers have a responsibility to educate students. With such a responsibility comes wide latitude to accomplish this mission. Teachers are educators, but they also serve as a youth's parents away from home. They have the authority to both supervise and regulate youth behavior during the school day.[2]

---

*Richard Lawrence, *School Crime and Juvenile Justice* (New York: Oxford University Press, 1998). See this excellent source for a more in-depth review of legal issues involving juveniles and schools.

In Loco Parentis

The broad authority of teachers to supervise and regulate student conduct derives from English common law. Under English common law, educators acted ***in loco parentis,*** a Latin term literally meaning "in the place of the parent." In contemporary U.S. society, teachers derive their authority primarily from federal and state laws and school policies reflecting those laws. These laws and policies are also influenced by the doctrine of *in loco parentis,* which holds that school authorities, who act in the place of parents during the school day, may establish rules of order and may discipline youths for failing to adhere to those rules. Although schools may establish rules to ensure order in schools, and discipline students for violating those rules, the rules and disciplinary procedures must be "reasonable."

Reasonableness and School Rules

To be valid, school rules, regulations, and disciplinary procedures must be reasonable. According to Richard Lawrence, they must "be related to educational objectives, and the discipline or sanctions for violation of the rules must not be unfair or excessive."[3] School rules that are not reasonably related to the mission of schools and disciplinary procedures that are unfair or excessive violate students' rights.

In practice, schools (and teachers) differ in their concept of reasonableness, and the same goes for notions of fair or excessive sanctions. Therefore, the courts have become involved. They have considered these issues against a backdrop of constitutional rights as applied to the school setting, particularly the Fourteenth Amendment (due process), the Fourth Amendment (prohibition against unreasonable searches and seizures), and the Eighth Amendment (prohibition from cruel and unusual punishment).

Legal Issues in Regulating Student Behavior

The most common challenges to student regulations and discipline for students have been through the Fourteenth, Fourth, and Eighth amendments to the U.S. Constitution. Challenges to school rules and discipline procedures under the Fourteenth Amendment are in the areas of suspension, transfer, and expulsion. Fourth Amendment issues in schools include search and seizure of students and their property, drug testing, and the use of metal detectors and drug dogs. Issues concerning the Eighth Amendment relate to corporal punishment.

Due Process in Schools

The Fourteenth Amendment to the U.S. Constitution mandates that no state shall deprive any person of life, liberty, or property without due process of law. In other words, before an individual is deprived of "life, liberty, or property," he or she must be given *at least* a notice of the rule violation, a fair hearing, and an opportunity to present his or her version of the issue.[4] There are two due process requirements that schools must meet for disciplinary practices to be constitutional under the Fourteenth Amendment: procedural and substantive.[5] **Procedural due process** requires that before someone is deprived of life, liberty, or property, the *procedure* followed must be fair. For example, an expulsion of a student without a hearing for smoking marijuana (primarily to determine if a student really did it) is fundamentally unfair and violates procedural due process.

However, just because the process is fundamentally fair does not mean that the rule or regulation is fair. **Substantive due process** requires that *laws, rules, and regulations* be related to a legitimate governmental interest to be constitutional. Suspension or expulsion policies may be presumed to be related to a legitimate interest of keeping order in schools and preserving the educational mission of schools by suspending or expelling physically violent students or students who bring drugs to school. For instance, a *rule* that provides expulsion from school for disobeying parental rules at home will likely violate substantive due process. Thus, both requirements of due process must be met for a school regulation or punishment to be constitutional.

Short-Term Removal from School In *Goss v. Lopez* (1975), the U.S. Supreme Court held that juveniles are entitled to due process procedures in short-term school suspension cases and outlined the minimum procedural due process requirements for such cases.[6]

Goss was a class-action suit filed on behalf of all students in the Columbus, Ohio, public school system (CPSS). In *Goss,* nine students were temporarily suspended from school without a hearing for disruptive conduct, including unauthorized demonstrations in a school auditorium, attacking a police officer, and damaging school property. The Supreme Court held that removal from school by way of suspension, although far milder than expulsion, carries with it deprivation and stigma that are serious events in a child's life. Even for a period of ten days or less (as in *Goss*), the suspension and charges could "seriously damage the students' standing with their fellow pupils and teachers as well as interfere with later opportunities for higher education and employment."[7] The Court noted that students facing removal from school in the form of suspension have *minimum* due process rights:

- Oral or written notice of the charges
- An explanation of evidence against the student
- An opportunity for the student to present his or her side of the story[8]

The Court refused to require additional measures for all short-term suspensions:

> We stop short of construing the Due Process Clause to require, countrywide, that hearings in connection with short suspensions must afford the student the opportunity to secure counsel, to confront and cross-examine witnesses supporting the charge, or to call his own witnesses to verify his version of the incident. Brief disciplinary suspensions are almost countless. To impose in each such case even truncated trial-type procedures might well overwhelm administrative facilities in many places and, by diverting resources, cost more than it would save in educational effectiveness. Moreover, further formalizing the suspension process and escalating its formality and adversary nature may not only make it too costly as a regular disciplinary tool but also destroy its effectiveness as part of the teaching process.[9]

Although not required, states and local jurisdictions may include more protective procedures than required by the U.S. Supreme Court for short-term suspensions, such as providing counsel or allowing students to call and cross-examine witnesses.

Long-Term Removal from School Expulsions are generally used in cases of chronic or repeated offending, serious misconduct such as attacking a student or teacher, drug use or possession, and particularly weapons possession or use.[10] Unlike short-term suspension (or transfer to an alternative school), the more severe consequences of expulsion normally require an increase in due process protections to ensure that the process is fundamentally fair.

A general rule concerning expulsions or suspensions longer than ten days is that they require more formalized procedures than those laid out in *Goss.* Thus, the more harsh the penalty, the more formalized and "protective" the due process requirements need to be to be constitutional and, hence, fundamentally fair. Due process hearings involving long-term suspension or expulsion might include the following:

- The right to be represented by counsel
- Reasonable time to prepare for the hearing
- An opportunity to review evidence
- An opportunity to cross-examine witnesses
- An opportunity to present evidence and witnesses
- A record or recording provided of the proceedings
- An impartial hearing board
- A requirement that the school board's decision be based on substantial evidence
- A right to appeal the decision[11]

For the student, these additional protections ensure that the disciplinary process is fair. For schools, providing more protections for students who are facing expulsion (these cases are much less prevalent than suspension cases) may insulate them from later liability, including money damages.*

Emergency Removal from School In some cases it is not practical to hold a hearing before a student is removed from the school setting. In "emergency situations," immediate suspensions or expulsions of a student, without a hearing, may follow conduct that seriously disrupts the academic atmosphere of the school, such as endangering other students, teachers, or school officials, or when a student has seriously damaged property.[12]

In emergency situations, a writer suggests that a two-step approach be employed. The first is the imposition of an immediate temporary suspension or expulsion. The second is the enforcement of a permanent expulsion after a proper

---

*The U.S. Supreme Court held in *Wood v. Strickland,* 420 U.S. 308 (1975), that students may sue school officials, who may be held financially liable for damages if they deliberately deprive students of their constitutional rights.

notice has been given and a hearing is conducted. The same writer suggests that notice should be sent to the student's parents within twenty-four hours of a decision to conduct a disciplinary hearing and that the hearing commence within seventy-two hours of the student's initial removal.[13] These procedures ensure both that the student body is protected and that the offending student receives his or her due process.

Searches and Seizures in Schools

The Fourth Amendment to the U.S. Constitution states that persons have a right to be free from unreasonable searches and seizures. The Fourth Amendment applies to children in ways similar to adults; however, the school setting represents a "special need" situation (See Exhibit 13.1).* Because school officials are charged with the authority to create and administer rules to ensure that the educational mission is fulfilled, students do not have the same expectation of privacy from search and seizure guaranteed by the Fourth Amendment while they are at school.

The leading case on search and seizure in schools is *New Jersey v. T. L. O.* (1985).[14] In this case, the U.S. Supreme Court held that public school officials need only **reasonable grounds** to search juveniles; they do not need a warrant or *probable cause* as typically required by the Fourth Amendment. This ruling is important for school administrators because the Court allowed searches and seizures under the standard of reasonable grounds as long as they

---

EXHIBIT 13.1   ## Schools Represent a "Special Need" Situation

For a search to be valid under the Fourth Amendment, law enforcement officers normally need probable cause. Citizens have a reasonable expectation of privacy from government intrusion into their lives. However, schools are in a special situation in relation to searches because they have the duty to protect the entire student body. As a result of this "special need" situation, school officials may search students without probable cause because students' privacy rights are diminished while they are in school. For a search to be valid, school officials need only show that reasonable grounds (a lower standard than probable cause) are present that the student has or is about to violate a school rule or the law.

1. Think of several situations in which the entire student body might be at risk if school officials had to have probable cause or a warrant before they searched a student.

2. What are the benefits of and drawbacks to allowing school officials to search students and their property under the lower standard of reasonable suspicion?

---

*This section on legal rights of juveniles in schools is a general discussion and not meant to be legal advice or indicate a national rule of law. Specific consultation of local state laws, including case law, is suggested.

were minimally intrusive and related to the educational objectives of schools. Physical violence, drug use, and weapons carrying are all occurrences in school that require immediate responses. The Court reasoned that schools and their officials should not be hampered by obtaining warrants or probable cause in these and other situations that require immediate action.*

New Jersey v. T. L. O. clarified the burden that school officials must satisfy before they perform a search and seizure of students. However, the Court did not clarify all issues concerning such searches. It did not speak directly to more extensive searches, such as strip searches, locker and desk searches, metal detector screening, searches of student automobiles, drug testing, or searches in conjunction with law enforcement officers. These are all questions under the Fourth Amendment that the Court left unanswered.

Strip Searches   Strip searches are arguably the most intrusive searches that can be performed in the school setting. Various courts have found strip searches valid based upon the "reasonable grounds" standard articulated in *New Jersey v. T. L. O.* In *Cornfield v. Consolidated High School District No. 230* (1993), the Seventh Circuit Court of Appeals held that a strip search (removal of pants) was valid after school officials had reason to believe the student was hiding drugs in the crotch of his pants.[15] In another circuit court of appeals case, a strip search (removing shirt, shoes, and socks and lowering jeans to knees) was deemed valid after school officials had reason to believe the student was using drugs.[16]

Some courts have required more than reasonable grounds to conduct student strip searches. These courts note that strip searches are of such an intrusive nature that a higher standard, such as probable cause instead of reasonable grounds, must be established by school officials. This is usually the case when the strip search involves the recovery of missing or stolen property, as opposed to weapons or drugs.[17] In *Bellnier v. Lund* (1977), for example, the District Court for the Northern District of New York held that a strip search to locate three dollars was too intrusive, considering what was involved.[18] This ruling was similar to that in *Jenkins v. Talladega City Board of Education* (1997), wherein the Eleventh Circuit Court of Appeals found excessive a strip search of several eight-year-old girls to find seven dollars.[19] Other courts have held similarly when small amounts of money or property are involved.[20]

The general rule is that school officials need reasonable grounds to justify a strip search. In situations that blur the line, such as searching for money or property as opposed to searching for weapons or drugs, probable cause may be required.[21]

Locker and Desk Searches   Several states consider lockers and desks school property in which students do not have a reasonable expectation of privacy. Therefore, these states hold that lockers and desks may be searched at any time with or without any suspicion that the student is violating school rules or the law. Courts have generally upheld schools' right to inspect lockers and desks

---

*New Jersey v. T. L. O., 469 U.S. 325 (1985). Searches in which evidence might be used in delinquency proceedings, instead of procedures relating to the educational mission of schools, may require a warrant and/or probable cause.

and to regulate their use. This also applies to *random* locker and desk searches. For example, *In the Interest of Isiah B.* (1993) was a case in which a Wisconsin state court held that the random search of a student's locker was valid in the presence of a school policy that authorized the search of a locker for any reason.[22] However, some courts have found that students have a property interest in their lockers and other storage places and thus have a reasonable expectation of privacy in them.[23]

Despite divergent court rulings, the general rule is that schools may inspect lockers and desks with or without an individualized or *reasonable suspicion* that the student is violating school rules or the law. Such policies are usually deemed legitimate in relation to the mission of schools.

It is one thing to simply open a locker or desk and inspect contents in plain view, but additional controversy surrounds searching items *inside* lockers and desks that are not the property of schools, such as book bags, coats, or other closed personal containers. In *New Jersey v. T. L. O.* (1985), the U.S. Supreme Court noted that "schoolchildren may find it necessary to carry with them a variety of legitimate, noncontraband items, and there is no reason to conclude that they have necessarily waived all rights to privacy in such items merely by bringing them onto school grounds."[24] The Pennsylvania Superior Court addressed this concern for items in locker searches in the case of *In re Dumas* (1986), where the court held that students do not lose all expectation of privacy in their personal effects simply because they place them in a school-provided locker.[25]

In general, for school officials to do more than simply open the locker or desk, courts generally require a reasonable or individual suspicion on the part of school officials that the student has or is about to violate a school rule or the law. For searches of personal items such as coats, book bags, and other non-school property, probable cause may be needed.[26]

Metal Detector Screening There are two types of metal detectors used in schools: pass through and hand held. Metal detectors are much less intrusive than strip searches or pat downs, and most courts have held that their use does not even constitute a "search" in terms of the Fourth Amendment.[27] If using metal detectors is not a search under the Fourth Amendment, schools do not need probable cause, reasonable suspicion, or individualized suspicion before they conduct metal detector searches. However, courts have differed in their views of whether the use of metal detectors constitutes a search.

In *People v. Dukes* (1992), a New York court held that the use of metal detectors was based on a legitimate governmental interest in that such a search prevented dangerous weapons from being brought to the school. This was the first case in the United States that examined the metal detector issue. The policy in this case was held as reasonable based on the reality of violence in schools and the need to detect weapons related to that violence.[28] In the case of *In re F. B.* (1995), a Pennsylvania superior court reached a similar conclusion, noting that no individualized suspicion is needed to conduct a metal detector search, for such searches are minimally intrusive and are justified because of episodes of violence in that particular school.[29] In a more recent case, an Illinois appellate court held in 1996 that metal detector screening was a reasonable practice because the search was justified and was reasonably related to the circumstances that led to it. This case involved the mass metal detector search at a Chicago public high school. Serrick Pruitt was found in possession of a loaded .38 caliber handgun after a positive reading from the metal detector. Deciding this case on appeal, the court in *People v. Pruitt* said the following:

> We long for the time when children did not have to pass through metal detectors on their way to class, when hall monitors were other children, not armed guards, when students dressed for school without worrying about gang colors. Those were the days when sharp words, crumpled balls of paper, and, at worst, the bully's fists were weapons of choice. We must consider this case and the issue of Fourth Amendment reasonableness in light of the times . . . we cannot say the screening in this case violated the Fourth Amendment.[30]

Suspicionless metal detector searches are usually valid. However, the Appellate Court of Illinois in *People v. Parker* (1996) held that turning back and leaving from a metal detector did not provide enough reasonable suspicion to justify detention by an officer. In this case, a Chicago police officer observed a sixteen-year-old boy turn around to exit the school after he was informed about a random metal detector search being conducted that day. The police officer stopped the boy, at which time he threw up his shirt and remarked that someone had put a gun in his waistband. The court held that the stop of the boy, which was initiated after he turned from the metal detector, was not based on enough reasonable suspicion to be valid.[31]

The general rule is that random metal detector searches are reasonable and legitimate for the purpose of keeping schools safe and may be conducted without probable cause or reasonable suspicion. However, if a student simply turns away from a metal detector, this does not provide enough reasonable suspicion for a stop and frisk.

Student Automobile Searches on School Grounds

As in locker or desk searches, the school owns the parking lot of a school campus and has the authority to conduct routine patrols of parking lots and inspect the exteriors of cars. But cases indicate that only when reasonable suspicion exists are school officials authorized to inspect *inside* a student's vehicle.

The law on nonclassroom searches has not been heavily litigated. Most of the controversy revolves around establishing reasonable suspicion to search a student's automobile and whether an automobile search is related to a legitimate interest of schools in their pursuit of maintaining an orderly educational environment. In one case, *State v. Slattery* (1990), a Washington appellate court held that a student tip provided enough reasonable suspicion in conducting a search of a student's vehicle. In this case, a student reported to the principal of Thomas Jefferson High School that a certain Mike Slattery was dealing marijuana in the school parking lot. After questioning Slattery and finding more than $200 and a piece of paper with pager numbers on his person, school officials searched Slattery's locker. Finding nothing, the principal informed Slattery that his vehicle would be searched. Slattery refused to comply; the principal then called Slattery's mother. Following this phone conversation, Slattery handed the keys over to school officials, who found in his vehicle a pager, names, numbers, dollar amounts, and a briefcase with over eighty grams of marijuana. Slattery moved to suppress the evidence, saying that the search was illegal. His motion was denied, and the evidence was used to convict him of possession of marijuana.[32]

School officials may generally search automobiles or other vehicles when they have a reasonable suspicion to believe that the student has violated or is about to violate a school rule or the law. Schools may conduct such searches without a warrant or probable cause as long as the evidence obtained will be used for school disciplinary purposes. However, the use of such evidence in any future delinquency proceeding may require a warrant or probable cause.

Drug Testing of Students   One of the most contentious issues surrounding schools today is drug testing. In student drug testing cases, courts have examined whether the intrusion of individual privacy (a drug test) is outweighed by the state's interest in keeping drugs from schools. The U.S. Supreme Court has answered this question affirmatively—that student drug testing is minimally intrusive considering the interest in maintaining a drug-free school environment.

The Supreme Court held in *Vernonia School District v. Acton* (1995) that the random, suspicionless, and mandatory drug testing of student-athletes was constitutional.[33] The Court stressed that there was a compelling need of such a policy and relied on evidence from the Vernonia School District of increased drug use, disciplinary problems, and the general threat to student athletes. The Court said that drug testing was a legitimate activity and a reasonable means of tackling Vernonia School District's drug problem.

In determining the constitutionality of a drug testing policy in schools, the Supreme Court in *Vernonia* used several criteria:

- Whether there is a compelling need
- Whether the drug testing policy is limited in scope and goals
- Whether less intrusive methods have been attempted (awareness programs such as D.A.R.E.)
- Whether students have diminished expectations of privacy
- Whether school officials have constraints in discretion for selecting students for drug testing
- Whether the testing is used to enforce school rules rather than to produce evidence for criminal prosecution[34]

The Supreme Court held that the Vernonia School District satisfied all of these criteria. The *Vernonia* case concerned only student-athletes, however. In June 2002, the U.S. Supreme Court expanded student drug tests. In *Pottawatomie County v. Earls,* the Supreme Court held that school districts could require drug tests of all students involved in any school-supported extracurricular activity (see the "Case Brief"). The Court held that School District No. 92 in Pottawatomie County, Oklahoma, did not violate the Fourth Amendment because its drug testing policy was a reasonable means of furthering the school district's interest in preventing and deterring drug use among its students.[35] The Court revisited the *Vernonia* criteria and determined that the school district's drug testing procedures were not overly intrusive, results were kept in confidential files, and test results were not turned over to law enforcement authorities. Furthermore, the consequences of a positive drug test consisted only of limiting the student's participation in extracurricular activities and did not result in other disciplinary procedures, such as suspension, expulsion, or a delinquency referral to the juvenile justice system. The Court also clarified whether or not schools must have evidence of a drug problem before they can justify a drug testing policy as a legitimate activity. The Court noted that evidence of a drug problem in schools is not required to justify the legitimacy of a drug testing policy. The Court said that preventing drug use is as important as dealing with a drug problem that has already surfaced.

Drug Detection with Dogs   In one of the earliest cases on the use of drug-detecting dogs, the Seventh Circuit Court of Appeals held in *Doe v. Renfrow* (1980) that the use of a drug-sniffing dog was valid, for it was intended to address a serious drug problem in school, the search was minimally intrusive, and all findings would be used only for school discipline and not referral to law enforcement authorities.[36] The court further explained that a signal by the dog created enough reasonable suspicion to search. However, such suspicion did not justify a strip search. Similarly, in *Zamora v. Pomeroy* (1981), the Tenth Circuit Court of Appeals upheld the use of drug-sniffing dogs for exploratory locker "sniffs" and determined such a practice was needed for school officials to maintain a drug-free school environment.[37] Not all courts have agreed with these rulings. In one case, the Fifth Circuit Court of Appeals held that the use of drug dogs constituted a search protected by the Fourth Amendment and that getting smelled by dogs was demeaning and of such an intrusive nature that it required more than a generalized suspicion to be reasonable.[38]

The previously mentioned cases came before *New Jersey v. T. L. O.*'s "reasonable grounds" standard. Since *New Jersey v. T. L. O.*, courts have generally concluded that the use of drug-sniffing dogs requires schools to show a substantial need for their use that is related to a legitimate school interest. Schools must also generally show that there is a reasonable suspicion before using a drug dog, and in some cases, courts have held that probable cause must be established for the search to be valid.[39] Thus, unlike most other searches in school, the use of drug dogs in schools requires more than just reasonable suspicion and may require probable cause.[40]

Searches Involving Law Enforcement Officers in Schools   Law enforcement officers are typically involved in school searches in three ways:

- School-official-initiated search with outside police assistance
- Searches initiated by school **liaison officers, school resource officers,** or **independent school district police** acting on their authority and/or in conjunction with school officials
- Searches initiated by outside police officers themselves

Case Brief   *Leading Case on Student Drug Testing in Schools*

Pottawatomie County v. Earls, 122 S.Ct. 2559 (2002)

Facts: In the fall of 1998, School District No. 92 in Tecumseh, Oklahoma, adopted the Student Activities Drug Testing Policy. This policy required all middle and high school students to consent to drug testing in order to participate in any extracurricular activity. Under the policy, students are required to take a drug test before participating in any extracurricular activity, must submit to random drug testing, and must agree to be tested at any time if school officials have a reasonable suspicion of drug use. Lindsay Earls and Daniel James brought a suit against the school, alleging that the drug testing policy violated their Fourth Amendment rights. They argued that the school district failed to demonstrate a "special need" for testing students in extracurricular activities and that the policy serves no legitimate governmental interest. Earls and James claimed that the policy neither addresses a proven drug problem in school nor brings any benefit to the school.

Issue: Is Tecumseh's drug testing policy a reasonable means of furthering the school district's interest in preventing and deterring drug use among its schoolchildren?

Supreme Court Decision: Tecumseh's drug testing policy is a reasonable means of furthering the school district's important interest in preventing and deterring drug use among its schoolchildren and does not violate the Fourth Amendment.

Case Significance: The Supreme Court extended its holding in *Vernonia School District v. Acton,* 115 S.Ct. 2386 (1995), by ruling that mandatory and suspicionless drug tests may be conducted on any student involved in any extracurricular activity, not just student-athletes. This case is significant because the Court noted that a documented drug problem in schools is not always necessary to justify the validity of a drug testing policy. In *Vernonia,* school officials provided substantial evidence of a drug problem and evidence that their drug testing policy related to a legitimate governmental interest of keeping drugs out of schools. In *Pottawatomie,* School District No. 92 offered evidence of a drug problem, but the Court said that such evidence is not a prerequisite to a drug testing policy, for preventing and deterring drug use is a legitimate governmental interest.

Excerpts from the Decision: "In *Vernonia,* this Court held that the suspicionless drug testing of athletes was constitutional. The Court, however, did not simply authorize all school drug testing, but rather conducted a fact-specific balancing of the intrusion on the children's Fourth Amendment rights against the promotion of legitimate governmental interests. Applying the principles of *Vernonia,* to the somewhat different facts of this case, we conclude that Tecumseh's policy is also constitutional.

"This Court has already articulated in detail the importance of the governmental concern in preventing drug use by school children. The drug abuse problem among our Nation's youth has hardly abated since *Vernonia* was decided in 1995. In fact, evidence suggests that is has only grown worse. . . . The health and safety risks identified in *Vernonia* apply with equal force to

(continued)

Case Brief *(continued)*

Tecumseh's children. . . . Additionally, the School District in this case has presented specific evidence of drug use at Tecumseh schools. . . .

"Teachers testified that they had seen students who appeared to be under the influence of drugs and that they had heard students speaking openly about using drugs. A drug dog found marijuana cigarettes near the school parking lot. . . . Respondents consider the proffered evidence insufficient and argue that there is no 'real and immediate interest' to justify a policy of drug testing nonathletes. We have recognized, however, that a demonstrated problem of drug abuse . . . is not in all cases necessary to the validity of a testing regime . . . *Chandler v. Miller*, 520 U.S. 305, 319 (1997). . . . Furthermore, this Court has not required a particularized or pervasive drug problem before allowing the government to conduct suspicionless drug testing . . . the need to prevent and deter the substantial harm of childhood drug use provides the necessary immediacy for a school testing policy. Indeed, it would make little sense to require a school district to wait for a substantial portion of its students to begin using drugs before it was allowed to institute a drug program designed to deter drug use.

"The Fourth Amendment does not require a finding of individualized suspicion and we decline to impose such a requirement on schools attempting to prevent and detect drug use by students . . . testing students who participate in extracurricular activities is a reasonably effective means of addressing the School District's legitimate concerns in preventing, deterring, and detecting drug use."

Provisions for law enforcement help in schools come in various ways. Some schools operate and pay for their own independent school district police agency. Other schools rely on outside police officers not immediately affiliated with the school, and still others use liaison or school resource officers (SROs).

Generally, where police officers work and are paid for by the school (independent school district police), or act as school liaison or school resource officers with substantial school duty, the standard is reasonable suspicion to search a student and his or her property. For example, in *People v. Dilworth* (1996), the Illinois Supreme Court held that a school liaison officer, acting on his or her own authority, is bound by reasonable suspicion rather than probable cause because it is the specific duty of the officer to assist the school in the furtherance of its goals.[41] In a similar ruling, the Eighth Circuit Court of Appeals held in *Cason v. Cook* (1987) that reasonable grounds instead of probable cause must be the standard used in public schools even if the search is conducted with the assistance of a police officer (who is a liaison officer).[42]

In general, when outside police officers (hired and paid for by the city, the county, or the state *without* substantial school duty) initiate a search, when outside police officers contact school authorities requesting permission to search, or when school officials act at the request of outside police officers, the standard is probable cause instead of reasonable grounds.[43]

Cruel and Unusual Punishment in Schools

The Eighth Amendment to the U.S. Constitution provides as follows: Excessive bail shall not be required, nor excessive fines, nor cruel and unusual punishment. *Cruel and unusual punishment* is defined as "punishment that is torturous, degrading, inhuman, and grossly disproportionate to the crime in question or otherwise shocking to the moral sense."[44] The issue in schools is whether corporal punishment is cruel and unusual.

The U.S. Supreme Court decided the issue in *Ingraham v. Wright* (1977).[45] In this case, James Ingraham and Roosevelt Andrews brought suit against officials at Charles R. Drew Junior High School in Florida. They alleged that corporal punishment policies and practices at Drew violated the Eighth Amendment prohibition against cruel and unusual punishment. At the time, Drew school policy authorized teachers to use a flat wooden paddle on the buttocks of students for certain forms of misbehavior. The normal punishment consisted of one to five "licks." Ingraham and Andrews were both paddled several times, and both received injuries. Ingraham suffered a hematoma, requiring medical attention that kept him out of school for several days, and Andrews lost the full use of his arm after being hit with the paddle.

The U.S. Supreme Court held that *reasonable* corporal punishment is not cruel and unusual, hence not unconstitutional. It noted that when corporal punishment is used, all of the circumstances should be taken into account to determine whether the punishment is reasonable in a particular case. Factors that should be taken into account include the seriousness of the offense, the attitude and past behavior of the child, the nature and severity of the punishment, the age and strength of the child, and the availability of less severe methods to discipline the student. A notice of charges and a hearing, no matter how informal, are not required before school officials use corporal punishment.[46]

School problems sometimes require that unconventional measures be used to maintain control of the school environment so that the student body may be adequately educated. The Supreme Court ruled that corporal punishment, when reasonable, is an acceptable method to accomplish this mandate. Currently, twenty-three states authorize the use of corporal punishment in their public schools (nine of these states and/or their school districts limit the use of corporal punishment), and the other twenty-seven states have made corporal punishment in schools illegal.[47] In states and schools that employ corporal punishment, it is likely sparingly used and not of the sort detailed by James Ingraham and Roosevelt Andrews. Moreover, many schools will first solicit parental consent in writing before administering corporal punishment. This step is because of the potential for school and teacher liability. As a result, more common than corporal punishment today is the use of suspension, expulsion, or transfer to an alternative school for disruptive students. These options lessen the liability of school officials for claims against cruel and unusual punishment, and arguably make the school environment safer by removing problematic students.

The Extent of School Crime

Well-publicized episodes of extreme violence in schools have led to the belief in some quarters that control has been lost in the nation's classrooms. There have always been sensational episodes of crime in schools, but the belief today is that school crime is worse than in the past. This belief is the result of several factors: the random nature of the attacks, the younger age of the attackers, the use of high-powered weapons, multiple victimizations per incident, and the irrational and often trivial motives behind these acts. Despite the immense media attention paid to school victimization, however, serious crimes are relatively uncommon in schools. Moreover, like most juvenile crime, school crime is disproportionately nonserious and property related.

In the last few years, several incidents further fueled the perception that schools are a place for crime and victimization, not learning. Shootings, rapes, riots, threats, and beatings claimed the headlines across the nation. Some of the noteworthy incidents include the following:

1. Approximately 1,000 students rioted at Montwood High School in El Paso, Texas, throwing objects at police officers and school officials after an organized protest to a new school policy that provided for longer class periods.[48]

2. Five students at Anderson High School in Austin, Texas, beat and kicked a special-education student and videotaped the thirty-minute assault.[49]

3. Seventeen-year-old Terry Carter of Dunbar High School in Fort Worth, Texas, ranked sixth in his 186-member class, recited an extra-credit poem in which he mentioned a student's name and then said "But I got myself a gun, ready to pull the trigger, for any gold digger."[50] He was suspended from school.

4. A fourteen-year-old boy shot and killed his high school principal and then killed himself with a second handgun. James Sheets had brought three loaded handguns to Red Lion Junior High in Red Lion, Pennsylvania, allegedly upset because his girlfriend had begun dating another boy.[51]

5. A nine-year-old boy was charged with sexually assaulting a seven-year-old girl in a school bathroom in Stamford, Connecticut.[52]

6. A fifteen-year-old boy was gunned down in a New Orleans high school gymnasium in front of 200 students. The victim was found dead carrying a loaded handgun, and the attack is alleged to have been in retaliation for an earlier shooting. The boy's body was riddled with AK-47 and 9-mm slugs.[53]

Even a brief review of "newsworthy" incidents over the last few years leads to the perception that schools are a breeding ground for violence. It is precisely these types of incidents that serve to characterize schools as dangerous and violent places, replete with scared students. Whether this fear is justified is a different story. The next section presents the reality of school crime and violence. Examining the true incidence of school crime and violence is important, for this chapter concludes with the juvenile justice system's and the schools' reactions to these incidents.

Measuring School Crime

Information on the trends of school crime is derived from *Indicators of School Crime and Safety, 2002,* a report completed through a joint effort by the Bureau of Justice Statistics (BJS) and the National Center for Education Statistics (NCES).[54] This report gives the most current and comprehensive picture of the trends in school crime in the nation.

School crime is grouped into four categories: violent deaths at school, nonfatal student victimization at school, nonfatal teacher victimization at school, and general school environment safety issues. These categories are generally defined as follows:

- *Violent deaths at school.* This category includes homicide, suicide, death by legal intervention, and unintentional firearm-related death, with the death occurring on the campus of an elementary or secondary school in the United States, while the victim was on the way to school or leaving a regular school session, or while the victim was attending or traveling to or from a school-sponsored activity or event. This indicator includes victim deaths of nonstudents, students, and staff members.

- *Nonfatal student victimization (violent and nonviolent).* Violent victimization includes rape, sexual assault, robbery, and simple and aggravated assault. Nonviolent victimization includes crimes such as theft, threatening with or without a weapon, and bullying.

- *Nonfatal teacher victimization (violent and nonviolent).* Violent victimization includes rape, sexual assault, robbery, and simple and aggravated assault. Nonviolent victimization includes theft and threats of injury by a student. Both elementary and secondary schoolteachers are counted.

- *General school environment safety issues.* This category includes reports of weapons carrying, feelings of fear and safety by students, use of hate-related words and graffiti, presence of street gangs, and reports of alcohol and drug use.[55]

Note that this section explores the general characteristics of school crime across the country. It does not focus on specific school districts or states. Thus, the general picture may not always be true in some schools; some may have more or less crime and disorder.

School Crime in the 1990s

Violent Deaths at School

There are more than 51,000,000 students and approximately 3,000,000 teachers in public and private schools in the United States.[56] From 1992 to mid-year 1999, 218 youths ages 5 to 19 were victims of homicides *at school,* and there were 37 youth suicides. The average number of homicides among school-aged youths at school is approximately 31 per year, and the average number of suicides is approximately 5 per year (see Table 13.1).

Homicide and suicides are much less likely to occur away from school than in school. Away from school, there were 22,323 homicides of youths ages 5 to 19 and 14,183 suicides between 1992 and 1999. According to these numbers, youths

TABLE 13.1

School Shootings in the United States, 1996–2003

Date	Location	Synopsis
February 2, 1996	Moses Lake, Washington	Barry Loukaitis, 14, opened fire on his algebra class, killing two students and one teacher.
February 19, 1997	Bethel, Alaska	Evan Ramsey, 16, killed his principal and one other student. Two other students were wounded.
October 1, 1997	Pearl, Mississippi	Luke Woodham killed two students and wounded seven; he was also accused of killing his mother.
December 1, 1997	West Paducah, Kentucky	Michael Carneal, 14, killed three students and wounded five more while they were in a prayer circle at Heath High School.
December 15, 1997	Stamps, Arkansas	Colt Todd, 14, wounded two students while hiding in the woods. The students were standing in the school parking lot.
March 24, 1998	Jonesboro, Arkansas	Mitchell Johnson, 13, and Andrew Golden, 11, killed one teacher and four students during a false fire alarm at Westside Middle School. Ten others were wounded in the attack.
April 24, 1998	Edinboro, Pennsylvania	Andrew Wurst, 14, killed one teacher and wounded two students at a dance at James W. Parker Middle School.
May 19, 1998	Fayetteville, Tennessee	One student was killed in the parking lot of Lincoln County High School three days before his graduation. The killer, 18-year-old Jacob Davis, murdered the victim because he was dating Davis's ex-girlfriend.
May 21, 1998	Springfield, Oregon	Kip Kinkel, 15, killed a student and wounded nineteen others in his high school cafeteria. He also killed his parents in their home.
June 15, 1998	Richmond, Virginia	Quinshawn Booker, 14, opened fire in a high school hallway.
April 20, 1999	Littleton, Colorado	Eric Harris, 18, and Dylan Klebold, 17, killed fourteen students (including themselves) and one teacher.
May 20, 1999	Conyers, Georgia	Thomas Solomon, 15, injured six students at his high school.
November 16, 1999	Pontiac, Michigan	Nathaniel Abraham, 11, shot and killed another student.
November 19, 1999	Deming, New Mexico	Victor Cordova, Jr., 12, shot and killed a fellow classmate.
December 6, 1999	Fort Gibson, Oklahoma	Seth Trickey opened fire at his middle school and wounded four students.
February 29, 2000	Mount Morris Township, Michigan	A boy, 6, fatally wounded a classmate at their elementary school.
March 10, 2000	Savannah, Georgia	Darrell Ingram, 19, killed two students as they were leaving a dance.
May 26, 2000	Lake Worth, Florida	Nate Brazill, 13, shot and killed his middle school teacher on the last day of class.
July 17, 2000	Renton, Washington	Josh Warnock, 13, shot a gun in the school cafeteria. No one was hurt in the incident.
September 26, 2000	New Orleans, Louisiana	During a fight, two students were shot by the same gun.

(continued)

TABLE 13.1

School Shootings in the United States, 1996–2003 (continued)

Date	Location	Synopsis
January 17, 2001	Baltimore, Maryland	One student was killed in front of his high school.
March 5, 2001	Santee, California	Charles Andrew Williams, 15, killed two students and wounded thirteen more after firing into the restroom at his high school.
March 7, 2001	Williamsport, Pennsylvania	Elizabeth Catherine Bush, 14, wounded a fellow student in their high school cafeteria.
March 22, 2001	Granite Hills, California	Jason Hoffman, 18, wounded one teacher and three students at his high school.
March 30, 2001	Gary, Indiana	Donald R. Burt, Jr., 17, shot and killed a student at the high school both attended.
November 12, 2001	Caro, Michigan	Chris Buschbacher, 17, killed himself after taking two hostages.
January 15, 2002	New York, New York	Two students were shot by a classmate.
April 14, 2003	New Orleans, Louisiana	One student was killed and three were injured by four shooters at a high school.
April 24, 2003	Red Lion, Pennsylvania	James Sheets, 14, killed his principal, then turned the gun on himself.

Source: Adapted from http://www.infoplease.com/ipa/A0777958.html.

are in substantially more danger away from school.[57] Schools are expected to be safe havens for children, and this is why school crime is especially disturbing—even though it is much less frequent than crime away from school, especially regarding gun crimes. More than any other form of school-related homicide, shootings have spurred initiatives to make schools safer, even though schools are one of the safest places for children. Attention has been most concentrated on profiling the "who, what, when, where, and why" of school shooters and others who carry out violent attacks on students. In 1999 the U.S. Secret Service took this challenge.

The U.S. Secret Service and Lethal School Violence In 1999 Brian L. Stafford, director of the U.S. Secret Service, met with the U.S. Secretary of Education to determine whether the Secret Service could assist in the prevention of school shootings and other violent attacks. It was agreed that the Secret Service's National Threat Assessment Center (NTAC), an organization that studies assassinators and assassination attempts, would conduct an exceptional case study project (ECSP) aimed at gathering and analyzing information about the behavior and thinking of youths who commit acts of violence in U.S. schools. In 2000 the Secret Service released interim reports and preliminary analyses from its study of thirty-seven school shootings involving forty-one attackers, including case studies and interviews with ten school shooters.[58]

The Secret Service report revealed that violent school shootings and other forms of targeted violence took place in twenty-six states. All of the attackers were male, and more than one-half of the incidents targeted faculty, staff, or school administrators. In more than 60 percent of the incidents, the perpetrators killed one or more students, faculty, or other staff. Firearms (handguns, rifles, or shotguns) were the primary weapon of choice, and more than one-half of all incidents occurred in the middle of the school day.

The Secret Service also found the following:[59]

■ *Most incidents are planned; rarely are they impulsive or "snap decisions."* According to the report, almost every incident of targeted violence involved an idea for violence well before the attack. In more than 75 percent of incidents, the perpetrator actually planned the attack, and the majority did so at least two days prior. More than one-half of the perpetrators had revenge as a reason, and more than 60 percent had multiple reasons cited for their attack (breakup with girlfriend, bullying, argument with teacher).

■ *Prior to most incidents, the perpetrator told someone about his idea or plan.* Sixteen-year-old Evan Ramsey, who shot and killed his principal and a fellow student in Bethel, Alaska, remarked that "I told everyone what I was going to do." Ramsey had a well-publicized "hit list," so public that on the day of the attack students crowded around the library balcony to observe the event. One student reportedly brought a camera, and as one female student remarked to another, "You're not supposed to be up here [on the balcony], you're on the list."[60] In more than 75 percent of the incidents, the perpetrator confided in someone prior to the attack. In some cases, peers or friends knew detailed information about the planned attack, such as how it would be carried out or when it would occur. The majority of attackers did not communicate with the victim immediately prior to the incident.

■ *Bullying seems to have a place in attacks.* Although not all bullied children will turn to extreme violence, in almost 66 percent of incidents studied by the Secret Service, the perpetrators had been bullied prior to the attack.

■ *The majority of attackers demonstrated behaviors sometime prior to the attack that caused concern or indicated a need for help from others.* In more than 75 percent of incidents, an adult (teacher, administrator, staff member) had expressed concerns about the behavior of the perpetrator sometime prior to the incident. In over 50 percent of the cases, the perpetrator had come to the attention of more than one individual because of his behavior. The types of behavior varied but included writing poems indicating notions of homicide and suicide, and talk about violence. There was no information given about the time between the behavior change and the actual attack, however. Nor is it known whether the behavior change was documented before the attack or instead made in hindsight after the attack. Attesting to the destructive and fatalistic behavior of the attackers, almost 75 percent had either threatened or tried to kill themselves in the past. More than half had a history of feeling depressed or desperate.

■ *There is no reliable stereotype or "profile" of a typical school shooter.* One of the most important findings in the Secret Service report is that school shooters are a diverse group and that *there is no "typical" school shooter.* More than 75 percent of the perpetrators were white, but ages ranged from eleven to twenty-one, and the perpetrators came from intact to broken homes and from the lower, middle, and upper classes. Some offenders were enrolled and excelling in advanced placement courses at school, whereas others had poor academic histories. Moreover, some attackers had lengthy and multiple records of problematic behavior, whereas others had no documented behavioral problems. A very small portion of the perpetrators had been diagnosed with a mental or emotional disorder. Fewer than 30 percent had documented histories of drug or alcohol abuse. Very few perpetrators demonstrated changes in their behavior in areas of academic performance, friendship status, interest in school, or having documented disciplinary cases prior to the attack. Thus, their behavior was "normal" in relation to their past behaviors immediately prior to the attack.

In sum, there were no clear demographic, behavioral, or other identifying factors to help profile the typical school shooter or any other student who carries out violent attacks in school. Unfortunately, the practical implications for schools and the justice system of these findings are that there is no reliable guideline on who may or may not pose a risk for attack, or help in the early identification of possible future perpetrators. For instance, involvement in gothic or satanic cultures, poor academic performance, having behavioral problems, wearing black trench coats, and listening to shock rocker Marilyn Manson are not consistent indicators.

The bottom line is that homicides among youths in school are very few relative to homicides outside of school. Further, although school shootings may be the most sensational of all school deaths, they are quite rare, and schools are very safe places for children. From a practical standpoint, however, there is little evidence for school officials and others to go by in determining who is likely to commit violent acts in school, and this presents problems for preventing these and other seemingly random attacks.

Nonfatal Student Victimization

Incidents of extreme violence resulting in homicide at school are rare. In the United States, school homicides represent about .5 percent of all homicides among youths ages 5 to 19.[61] A far greater incidence of school crime is reflected in victimizations that are not fatal. In 2000, students ages 12 to 18 were victims of approximately 700,000 nonfatal violent crimes at school, mostly simple assault, and more than 920,000 victimizations away from school. Between 1992 and 2000, there was a 46-percent *decrease* in the nonfatal rate of violent crime victimization at school.[62] Among nonfatal victimizations, certain offenses have declined, such as theft (which still remains one of the most frequent nonfatal victimizations in schools) and fighting on school property. Threats and injuries with a weapon remained stable from 1993 to 2001, but student reports of bullying increased from 5 percent to 8 percent from 1999 to 2001.[63]

Reports of victimizations are helpful indicators of school crime. Clearly, nonfatal victimization in the form of assaults, thefts, and threats represents the greatest portion of school crime, according to reports by students. A much smaller portion of nonfatal victimizations includes crimes such as rape or sexual assault, aggravated assault, and robbery. In sum, the overwhelming majority of school crime does not consist of violent shootouts, rampage killings, rapes, or robberies.

Rather, the majority of crime in schools is relatively nonserious, generally theft or simple assault, with a number of threats and instances of bullying.

Nonfatal Teacher Victimization

Teachers are vulnerable to victimization by juveniles. From 1996 to 2000, teachers were the victims of more than 1.6 million nonfatal crimes at school in the United States. Of these 1.6 million victimizations, more than 1 million were theft incidents, 530,000 were simple assaults, and 69,000 were rape, sexual assault, robbery, or aggravated assault.

These numbers are disproportionate to victimizations experienced by students when considering that students greatly outnumber teachers. The teacher victimization data just presented reflect nonfatal victimizations in a five-year period from 1996 through 2000, as opposed to the 700,000 nonfatal victimizations among twelve- to eighteen-year-old students in a one-year period. Thus, there are fewer teacher victimizations per year in numbers. However, considering that students greatly outnumber teachers, teachers are victimized at a much higher rate than students (at a rate of approximately 106 victimizations per 1,000 teachers versus 14 nonfatal victimizations per 1,000 students). However, the majority of teacher victimizations consist of theft and simple assault, although some teachers are seriously injured.[64]

General School Environment Safety Issues

General school environment safety issues include a variety of areas: carrying weapons, perceptions of safety and feelings of fear, hate speech and hate vandalism/graffiti, reports of gangs in school, and reports of alcohol and drug use. These issues are important indicators of school crime and safety because they represent the real or potential consequence of creating a threatening, hostile, or risky school environment. Such an environment may lead to problematic behaviors by school-age youths, such as truancy and drug use. For others, it may create an arena ill suited for learning, where students avoid school out of fear of being victimized or harassed. Such issues present practical problems for school administrators.

The *Indicators of School Crime and Safety* report revealed a number of findings concerning school environment safety issues:

Weapons Carrying on School Property
- In 2001, 6 percent of students in grades nine through twelve reported carrying a weapon such as a gun, knife, or club on school property.
- From 1993 to 2001, there was a 6-percent decline in the percentage of students who reported carrying a weapon to school (12 percent to 6 percent).

Perceptions of Safety at School
- In 1999 and 2001, students were more afraid of being attacked at school or on the way to school than away from school. In 2001, 6 percent of students reported this fear.

- Between 1995 and 2001, the percentage of students ages twelve to eighteen who reported feeling fearful some or most of the time at school declined from 12 percent to 6 percent.

Reports of Hate-Related Speech and Graffiti

- In 2001, 12 percent of students ages twelve through eighteen reported that someone at school had used hate words against them pertaining to race, religion, ethnicity, disability, gender, or sexual orientation.
- In 2001, 36 percent of students reported instances where they saw hate-related graffiti at school.

Reports of Gangs in School

- In 2001, 20 percent of students reported that street gangs were present at their schools.
- Gangs were more likely in public schools than in private schools, according to student reports.

Alcohol and Drugs at School

- In 2001, 47 percent of students in the ninth through the twelfth grade had at least one drink of alcohol anywhere, but 5 percent had at least one drink on school grounds.
- In 2001, 5 percent of students reported using marijuana on school property.
- According to 2001 reports, 24 percent of students in grades nine through twelve reported that someone had offered, sold, or given them an illegal drug on school property in the last twelve months.[65]

The Bottom Line on School Crime

The overwhelming majority of school crime is nonserious, nonfatal, and property related, such as theft—for both students and teachers. Homicides and suicides in school are extremely rare, and students are much more likely to be killed away from school than in school. In 2001, general school safety indicators improved as students were less likely to carry weapons and to fight, and were less fearful of being attacked at school. In short, schools are still safe places for students; in fact, they are one of the safest places for children, teachers, and other staff.[66]

Although children are safer in schools than outside, and victimizations are on the decline in recent years, students were more likely to be bullied in 2001 than in 1999, and a number of students were targeted with hate-related speech or saw hate-related graffiti in their school—occurrences that were linked by the U.S. Secret Service to episodes of extreme violence. Moreover, a number of students reported using alcohol or drugs on school property, and almost 25 percent of students reported that someone had offered, sold, or given them an illegal drug on school property.[67]

To make schools safer for students, school officials, community leaders, and local, state, and federal legislators have embarked on several initiatives. These include implementing intervention programs for entire student bodies in an effort to address a number of issues, such as violence prevention, bullying, understanding cultures and diversity, and healthy lifestyles. Other efforts are focused on school-based programs for the prevention of delinquency for at-risk youths. For example, in 1999 former President Clinton announced the Safe Schools/Healthy Students Initiative, which awarded grants to school districts to develop plans for a variety of prevention and intervention programs in the school environment to address factors related to school crime.[68] This support from the federal government ushered in several new programs with these goals in mind.

Concern about school crime has not stopped at prevention and early intervention programs, however. One of the most controversial areas regarding the control of school crime is the use of tough suppression measures. Unlike prevention and intervention, suppression measures are not aimed at fixing the alleged cause of school crime (poor home life, intolerance, criminal parents, frustration with studies, poor communities) but rather are focused on investigating, detecting, removing, and/or suppressing those who commit crimes in school. These efforts have meant important changes in the school environment and have led to tough behavioral guidelines by way of zero tolerance policies, heightened security measures, and, most importantly, school collaboration with agents of the criminal justice and juvenile justice systems. Such issues are important to the study of juvenile justice and have been directly affected by the extent of crime in U.S. schools.

Making Schools Safe—Can It Be Done?

As a response to school violence, in 1997 the National Center for Education Statistics (NCES) and the U.S. Department of Education (DOE) conducted a nationally representative survey of 1,234 elementary, middle, and high schools to explore school crime, security, and disorder. The findings of this survey were compiled in a report titled *Violence and Discipline Problems in U.S. Public Schools, 1996–1997.*[69] In addition to reporting on the extent of school crime and violence, this report also examined school initiatives to combat school crime.

Schools have risen to the challenge of creating and maintaining safe schools. Some do this through prevention programs for at-risk youths, others have instituted strict policies and security measures, and still others have opted for criminal justice system and juvenile justice system intervention. A number of schools do all of these things. However, controversy surrounds those schools that seek to "get tough" in order to achieve their goals.

Zero Tolerance Policies

Zero tolerance policies became popular in U.S. schools in the mid-1990s as a get-tough response to school crime and disorder. **Zero tolerance** policies are designed to apply a uniform set of punishments based on the offense rather than on the characteristics of the student (such as race, ethnicity, socioeconomic status, religion, age) or the circumstances of the incident (intentional versus unintentional). Punishments under zero tolerance include expulsion, suspension, and transfer to an alternative school. They may also include referral to the juvenile justice system.

Originally, zero tolerance policies were aimed at serious offenses in school, particularly the use or possession of a firearm. They became prevalent in the mid-1990s, after Congress passed the Gun-Free School Zones Act.* This federal act required states that receive federal money to draft and implement a law requiring the expulsion of a student for at least one year for possession or use of a weapon on school grounds.[70] Although these laws were originally meant to apply to weapons offenses, a number of states expanded the scope to include physical attacks and the distribution and use of alcohol, drugs, or tobacco. More recently, zero tolerance policies have been broadened by some states to include behaviors such as threats, gestures, gang participation, disobedience, profanity, and "disruptive behavior."[71] The "You Are a . . . School Disciplinary Officer" box gives an example of a situation that would qualify as an offense under many school districts' zero tolerance policies today. What would you do in this situation if you were a school disciplinary officer?

Zero tolerance policies were instituted to make schools safe, but negative consequences have surfaced. Critics contend that zero tolerance policies are inflexible, unfair, and biased because they leave school authorities with little discretion. Although they agree that zero tolerance policies should be used for

---

YOU ARE A... **School Disciplinary Officer**

Seventeen-year-old Terry Carter of Dunbar High School in Fort Worth, Texas, recited an extra-credit poem as an assignment for his drama class. In this "rap" poem, Terry mentioned several of his classmates by name and focused on one girl in particular as he rhymed about getting a gun "ready to pull the trigger, for any gold digger." After class, the girl told the police she felt threatened by the poem. Terry was accused of making a "terroristic threat" and sent to alternative school for fourteen weeks. This punishment was later reduced, to ten days to two weeks.

1. What punishment should Terry Carter have received—nothing, suspension, expulsion, or alternative school?

2. Would your views change if you found out that Terry was second in his class and an honor student?

3. Would your views change if you found out that this particular school had episodes of gun violence in the past?

4. Would your views change if Terry had a previous history of negative conduct toward the girl—who happened to be ranked first in their class?

5. Should schools with "zero tolerance" policies consider factors other than the current offense (such as prior behavior of the student or whether the school has had a history of gun incidents in the past) in determining the punishment to be imposed?

---

*See, however, *U.S. v. Lopez,* 514 U.S. 549 (1995), in which the U.S. Supreme Court struck down the Gun-Free Schools Zones Act by saying that the act exceeded Congress's power of regulation of interstate commerce.

serious offenses, they argue that such policies have been "trivialized" when they include minor offenses such as smoking cigarettes, swearing, and having a poor demeanor. One of the biggest complaints by critics is that zero tolerance policies draw no distinction between the first offender who has made a typical mistake and the chronic offender who consistently disrupts the educational process.[72] They maintain that many offenses do not need to be dealt with by zero tolerance and that discretion must be used for minor offenses. Alternatively, proponents of zero tolerance reply that such policies allow for an unbiased response to serious offenses and that they keep schools safe. They are neutral regarding race, gender, demeanor, class rank, family status, and socio-economic status—they react to the offense, not the offender, and this protects from bias. Advocates also maintain that zero tolerance policies send an important message to youths about the consequences of their actions.

There is widespread agreement among advocates and critics alike that bringing a firearm to school, using drugs and alcohol on school grounds, and physically attacking others are serious offenses and must be dealt with harshly. However, states that have no clear definition of what is a weapon, what is a drug, and what is a physical attack cause the greatest controversy regarding the use of zero tolerance. For example, a Michigan girl was suspended after bringing a knife to school to cut birthday brownies (weapon). In Ohio, a fourteen-year-old girl was suspended from school for giving a classmate a tablet of Midol (drugs). In Savannah, Georgia, an honor student and Eagle Scout was suspended for having in his car an axe and a pocket knife that he had used for a presentation at a Boy Scout meeting the night before (weapon). In Canada, an eight-year-old boy was suspended from school for pointing a chicken leg at a teacher and saying "bang." According to the Nova Scotia school policy, the chicken leg was considered a weapon, for it was able to cause death, injury, or intimidation. These incidents illustrate the controversy surrounding zero tolerance. As one writer notes, "Now, things you can get at Toys R Us can get you kicked out of school."[73]

The Legal Aspects of Zero Tolerance Policies

The long-term and detrimental consequences of zero tolerance policies (such as expulsion) have raised legal issues. One legal question is whether zero tolerance policies, and the way they are applied, are fundamentally unfair. Zero tolerance policies are usually automatic and leave little or no discretion for considering individual circumstances, such as determining whether the offense was intentional. When used in this way, zero tolerance policies may violate due process and the Fourteenth Amendment. These are the more common zero tolerance issues that the courts have had to decide.[74]

In the case of *Lyons v. Penn Hills School District* (1999), a Pennsylvania appellate court invalidated the one-year expulsion of a seventh-grade student under the district's zero tolerance weapons policy after the youth was found in possession of a small Swiss Army knife. The appellate court ruled against the school board's suspension, saying that the school's zero tolerance policy failed to consider the background of the youth and the circumstances behind the incident as required by state law.[75] In a similar case, the Federal District Court for the

Northern District of Mississippi held in *Colvin v. Lowndes County School District* (1999) that the expulsion of a student under the school's weapons policy violated the student's due process rights because the school did not properly consider the circumstances behind the case. In this case, Colvin was a sixth grader and was suspended for bringing a Swiss Army knife key chain to school. The knife was given to Colvin by his mother, and it was discovered by school officials when it fell out of his book bag. Colvin then gave the key chain to his teacher without further incident. These are just a few instances where zero tolerance policies were invalidated by the courts.[76] These policies were invalid because they did not allow a review of the individual circumstances behind the incidents and therefore were fundamentally unfair, according to the courts.

Not all courts feel the same, however. For example, an Indiana appellate court ruled in *Board of School Trustees v. Barnell* (1997) that the automatic expulsion of a student, without consideration of the circumstances, for possessing a knife was valid because the school clearly outlined that it was an offense and articulated the consequences for such an offense.[77] In the case of *Clinton Municipal Separate School District v. Byrd* (1985), the Mississippi Supreme Court concluded that there was nothing inherently unconstitutional about a mandatory school policy (such as zero tolerance) that did not require a review of the circumstances of the incident. In this case, the court noted that even if a policy is worded in a mandatory manner (*must* or *shall* be expelled/suspended/transferred to alternative school), it does not preclude the school board from using its discretion and giving leniency if it so desires because, as the court noted, there is no law prohibiting leniency.[78]

The legal debate over zero tolerance policies has just started. The U.S. Supreme Court has not finally decided the issue, and courts around the country continue to interpret it differently. Ultimately, zero tolerance policies may be upheld if they involve weapons, drugs, and physical attacks regardless of the reasons or circumstances that students may have when they become involved in these behaviors. For other offenses, such as having a poor demeanor or swearing, courts may rule differently and may require individual consideration of the circumstances underlying each case, especially if zero tolerance consequences for these behaviors are harsh.

The Prevalence of Zero Tolerance Policies

Nationwide, available data indicate that zero tolerance policies are becoming popular in schools across the country. Of the 1,234 schools surveyed by the NCES, more than 75 percent of them reported having a zero tolerance policy for a variety of offenses such as physical violence; possession/use of tobacco, alcohol, or drugs; and possession of weapons (see Exhibit 13.2). The preferred and most frequent punishment for these offenses has been suspension, but transferring students to alternative schools and expelling them are two other responses. This is particularly the case for firearm-related infractions, which tend to get the harshest response (see Exhibit 13.3). A general rule is that the more serious the offense, the more likely expulsion becomes and the less likely suspension or alternative school transfer becomes.[79]

EXHIBIT 13.2

The Percentage of Schools with Zero Tolerance Policies, 1996–1997

Percentage of schools having zero tolerance policy for offenses

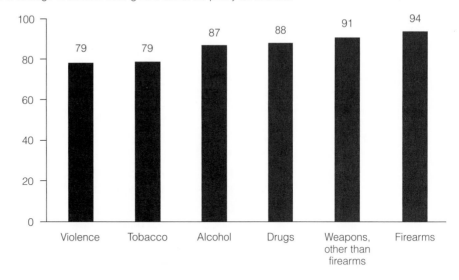

Source: Adapted from Sheila Heaviside, Cassandra Rowand, Catrina Williams, and Elizabeth Farris, *Violence and Discipline Problems in U.S. Public Schools: 1996–1997* (Washington, DC: National Center for Education Statistics and Office of Educational Research and Improvement, 1998), 18.

Security Measures in Schools—Are They Effective?

Zero tolerance policies are one initiative to make schools safe. However, no other change in the school setting may be more noticeable than the increase in physical security measures.

Security measures in schools have increased since 1994, when Congress passed the Safe Schools Act. This act authorized granting schools up to $3 million to develop security measures such as violence prevention programs and security training of school staff, including the implementation of physical security measures such as metal detectors and video cameras.[80]

School officials across the country have put various security measures into place to ensure that their schools are safe. Most common among them are the following:

- Visitor sign-in
- Controlled access to school grounds
- Controlled access to school buildings
- Closed campuses for lunch
- Metal detector pass through
- Random metal detector checks
- Drug sweeps[81]

EXHIBIT 13.3

Disciplinary Actions by Public Schools for Specific Offenses, 1996–1997

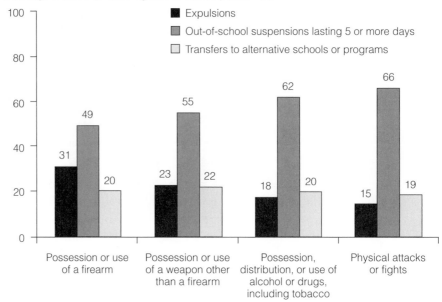

Percentage of students receiving zero tolerance punishment

Legend:
- Expulsions
- Out-of-school suspensions lasting 5 or more days
- Transfers to alternative schools or programs

Offense	Expulsions	Out-of-school suspensions	Transfers
Possession or use of a firearm	31	49	20
Possession or use of a weapon other than a firearm	23	55	22
Possession, distribution, or use of alcohol or drugs, including tobacco	18	62	20
Physical attacks or fights	15	66	19

Source: Adapted from Sheila Heaviside, Cassandra Rowand, Catrina Williams, and Elizabeth Farris, *Violence and Discipline Problems in U.S. Public Schools: 1996–1997* (Washington, DC: National Center for Education Statistics and Office of Educational Research and Improvement, 1998), 17.

According to the U.S. Department of Education, 96 percent of surveyed schools required visitor check-in, 80 percent closed the campus for lunch, 53 percent controlled access to school buildings, and 24 percent controlled access to school grounds. More stringent security measures were less prevalent; for example, only 19 percent of schools conducted one or more drug sweeps, only 4 percent conducted random metal detector searches, and only 1 percent of the 1,234 schools reported daily metal detector passes.[82]

Of all the security measures being implemented in schools, two measures appear to be particularly important: closed school campuses and metal detectors.

Closed School Campuses

Closed campuses—those not allowing students to leave the campus for the lunch hour and preventing nonschool-related individuals from entering the school—may have an important impact during the idlest time of the school day. Although *open campuses* are not common across the United States (20 percent of schools surveyed overall had open campuses), schools that have open campus policies allow a greater potential for "external" crime, meaning crime perpetrated by individuals who are not students. Such policies may also allow a greater opportunity for offenses by the enrolled population—for example, drinking, smoking, and drug use off campus.

Although most in-school crime is due to students who are enrolled in schools, open school campuses literally open the door for potential problems, such as drug and alcohol use and gang behavior (recruitment and victimization) because nonstudents are able to roam unabated in and out of school campuses.[83] Although there are no national data on the impact of closed campuses, such "closed-door" policies may help insulate schools from crime attributed to nonstudents during the school day and from crimes committed by students who leave the campus and then return. In schools with metal detectors and other security devices, closed campuses also do away with the need to scan students again for weapons and other contraband, a significant time-taking activity.

Metal Detectors

Metal detectors may be another important tool in the fight against school crime, especially weapons possession. Despite their value, the daily use of metal detectors was employed in only 1 percent of the 1,234 schools surveyed across the United States. Schools that were most likely to use metal detectors were those that had reported serious violent crimes in the past. Random metal detectors were most likely to be used by large schools. Generally, metal detectors are viewed as appropriate and justified in some schools: The individual intrusion of a pass-through metal detector, or a random metal detector check, is far outweighed by the benefit to the student population as a whole to have a school free of dangerous weapons (see the previous discussion in this chapter on metal detector searches).

Metal detectors can be an important tool in the battle to keep weapons out of school, yet determined students will still be able to circumvent them. As a result, metal detectors may help but are obviously not a panacea.

Zero tolerance policies, closed campuses, metal detectors, and other physical security measures are among current initiatives to deal with school crime. Schools are also working with officials of the criminal justice and juvenile justice systems. School–justice system collaboration is driven by the rationale that the presence of law enforcement officers or other agents of the justice system in schools may encourage students to "go to the police." Their presence is also thought to open an outlet for students to voice their concerns, a step that may preempt various forms of school crime. Having these agents in schools is also justified under the belief that their presence provides immediate responders in the event of an incident and contributes to an overall environment in which students are not afraid to go to school. School–justice system partnerships are not without controversy, however.

School Partnerships with the Criminal and Juvenile Justice Systems

There is a growing trend of partnerships between schools and agents of the criminal and juvenile justice systems in an effort to alleviate school crime.[84] Although information about school partnerships with the justice system is far from comprehensive, schools appear to be using law enforcement officers or other agents of the justice system on a more frequent basis to help with securing safe schools.

The U.S. Department of Education revealed that 97 percent of schools in their survey reported using at least some security measures in schools. Eighty-four percent of schools reported having *low security measures* (no guards/police officers, no metal detectors, but controlled access to campus), and 13 percent reported *stringent to moderate security measures* (full-time guards/police officers, metal detectors, controlled access to campus). Only 3 percent of schools reported that they had no security in their schools.[85] Thus, the majority of schools reported low levels of security, but an important number (13 percent) use police officers and other security measures on at least a part-time basis.

Much of the controversy over having law enforcement officials in schools relates to what they do there. Partnerships with schools are not new. Historically, law enforcement officers entered schools to fulfill roles as community liaisons and role models. Police officers served as educators on a variety of topics, many that were simple and not intrusive, such as good citizenship, avoiding drugs, road safety, and "stranger danger." Some of the better-known programs that developed from these police roles are Police Athletic League (P.A.L.), Drug Abuse Resistance and Education (D.A.R.E.), and Gang Resistance Education and Training (G.R.E.A.T.).

Law enforcement officers were not the only officials from the justice system to fulfill roles in partnerships with schools; agents from both the judicial system (district attorneys and probation officers) and the correctional system (parole officers and prison inmates) have participated in school–justice system partnerships.[86] For example, Allentown, Pennsylvania, was one of the first school districts in the nation to place a full-time juvenile probation officer on a school campus. One goal of the Allentown partnership was the supervision of probationers while they were in school; another goal was to coordinate services for probationers and their families to help transition the youths from the courthouse to the schoolhouse.[87]

Although partnerships focused on preventing crime and educating students such as those previously described have not been abandoned in schools, the traditional roles of agents from the criminal justice and juvenile justice systems in schools have changed. Activities now more frequently align with fighting campus crime, supervising probationers, combating victimization, and conducting drug sweeps. This situation is especially true for law enforcement officers and security officers. Originally, these types of duties (although on a much more limited basis) were performed by teachers, principals, and other staff already in the school environment. As the school population grew, school districts sought help. Schools began by hiring private *school security departments* and private security officers. Security officers were typically employed by the district itself, although they were not sworn police officers and had no power of arrest and no right to carry weapons. A disadvantage of this type of arrangement was that officers had little training, were poorly paid, and had little legal control over youths.

Private security in schools is still found in the United States, but several states, particularly in the West and South, have instituted a more formal police presence in schools by developing independent school district police. *Independent school district police* have the benefit of working for and being paid by the school district. Independent school district police officers are also vested with the authority of the law and may detain youths upon probable cause for delinquent behavior or that which indicates a need for supervision in accordance with state law. Independent school district police officers are typically trained in a regular police academy and are thus considered more professional than security officers. These officers are also authorized to carry weapons.

Schools in many areas of the country have opted for using local police services through *school resource officer (SRO)* or liaison programs.[88] School resource officers are defined as a "career law enforcement officers, with sworn authority, deployed in community-oriented policing, and assigned by the employing police department or agency to work in collaboration with school and community-based organizations."[89] SROs are *not* officers employed by the school district; they are sworn police officers who are assigned to a school district by the local police agency. SROs do not represent a new initiative in schools; the concept was originally tried in Flint, Michigan, in the 1950s. In the 1960s and 1970s, SRO programs were prominent in many school jurisdictions across the nation but waned in the 1980s, only to be revived in the mid-1990s as a result of outbreaks of school violence. SRO partnerships are so popular that in 2000 the Department of Justice (DOJ) announced that the Community Oriented Policing Services (COPS) program would award $68 million in grants to hire almost 600 school resource officers in 289 communities across the nation. This grant money is used to encourage working relationships with law enforcement officers and schools, and ultimately to improve school security and decrease the fears of students, parents, teachers, and the community at large.[90]

The increasing presence of police and other agents of the criminal justice and juvenile justice systems signals important changes in the methods of control used on children. More frequently, teachers and principals defer to in-school law enforcement officers to take care of problems that were traditionally handled within the school environment by school staff. Some have suggested that these changes have "criminalized" schools and transformed them into an extension of the criminal justice and juvenile justice systems. The "Controversial Issue" box examines the debate.

The increasing presence of the police also leads to legal questions. For example, do school police officers need probable cause to search a student's locker and/or possessions whereas school officials need only a reasonable suspicion or reasonable grounds? Does this standard vary depending on whether the officer is employed by the school district (independent school district police) or employed by the city (SRO)? What responsibility do officers have toward youths who are known to be already involved in the juvenile justice system (on probation) versus those who are not? To what extent must school violations be reported to the juvenile justice system for possible legal sanctions to apply? These and other issues face schools in their efforts to team with the justice system. Some of these questions have already been addressed in this text, but the issues are far from decided.

CONTROVERSIAL ISSUE: WHICH SIDE DO YOU FAVOR?

Should police officers be in schools?

Police officers are taking a more prominent role in schools as agents of formal control. As a result of this trend, one scholar has commented that prep schools are turning into prisons and that the school term now resembles a prison sentence.*

This raises a question: *Should schools depend on criminal justice and juvenile justice system personnel to maintain order?*

Those who argue that schools should use agents from the criminal justice and juvenile justice systems say this is the only way that students and teachers can be safe in schools. Teachers and principals are simply not equipped to deal with students who commit crimes or demonstrate severe behavioral problems. A teacher's job is to educate students. Having a formal police presence allows teachers to focus on their primary mission. A police presence also serves to keep order by deterring problem students. Students are much less likely to misbehave and commit crimes in school when they know police officers are immediately available and will arrest them for their actions. Ultimately, having police in schools allows all students to get the education they deserve without fearing for their safety.

Those who argue that criminal justice and juvenile justice system personnel should not be in schools suggest that their presence is not justified. The vast majority of schools in the nation do not have a crime problem serious enough to warrant having police officers in schools. Having a formal police presence makes it look as if schools are a crime zone when in fact they are not. Moreover, when schools collaborate with the criminal justice and juvenile justice systems, the result is the "criminalization" of the student population. Now, minor behavioral problems, once handled within schools, are resulting in criminal justice and juvenile justice system action. What has resulted is a class of students who will incur a juvenile record that will affect them for the rest of their lives.

*J. Klofas, "Prison Term: Do We Really Want Cops in the Schools?" *City* (June 1998): 17–23.

SUMMARY

- ❏ Schools and their authorities may do what is reasonable to maintain order in schools and to preserve their educational mission.
- ❏ Students may be suspended or expelled from school only after a fair hearing.
- ❏ School officials may generally search a student and his or her possessions if they have reasonable grounds to believe the student has or is about to violate a school rule or the law.
- ❏ Law enforcement officers employed by schools, or who are assigned to work in schools, need reasonable grounds and not probable cause to search students and their possessions.

- Student strip searches generally require probable cause or an individualized suspicion unless the strip search is for weapons or drugs. A strip search for weapons or drugs may generally be conducted with reasonable suspicion.

- All students who participate in extracurricular activities may be randomly drug tested in schools.

- School officials may use reasonable corporal punishment in cases of student misbehavior. Most schools refrain from corporally punishing students out of fear of liability and opt for suspension or expulsion instead.

- Most forms of school crime have declined in recent years.

- Crime among students is more prevalent away from school than in schools. Schools are one of the safest places for children.

- In an effort to combat school crime and make schools safer, schools have implemented zero tolerance policies, enhanced security measures, and collaborated with the criminal justice and juvenile justice systems.

REVIEW QUESTIONS

1. Under English common law, educators derived their authority from the concept of *in loco parentis*. What does this concept mean, and from where do teachers derive their authority today?

2. In your own words, define *due process*. What does *procedural and substantive due process* mean?

3. What must school officials generally establish before they search a student and his or her possessions?

4. Of all the Fourth Amendment search and seizure issues discussed in this chapter, which do you feel are "unreasonable"? Why?

5. When would suspending or expelling a student before a hearing be justified?

6. What is the rationale that courts have used to justify a fair hearing before a student is suspended or expelled from school, even if only for a short time?

7. The U.S. Supreme Court said that reasonable corporal punishment in public schools is constitutional. Why do you believe reasonable corporal punishment is allowed in schools but is prohibited in juvenile correctional institutions and adult prisons?

8. What are some criticisms of zero tolerance policies in schools?

9. What are the benefits to having a "closed campus"? Are there any drawbacks to having a closed campus during the school day?

10. What is the main difference between an independent school district police officer and a school resource officer (SRO) as it relates to school searches?

KEY TERMS AND DEFINITIONS

closed campuses: A school policy by which the school campus is closed to outside persons (those who do not have business in the school) during the school day.

independent school district police: Sworn officers hired and paid for by the school district and stationed in schools. School district police have the power to arrest people and to carry weapons.

in loco parentis: "In the place of parents," meaning that teachers act in the place of parents during the school day and may establish rules and reasonably discipline students for violating those rules.

liaison officer: Usually a sworn officer hired and paid for by the city and who is stationed in school. Liaison officers typically have the power to arrest people and to carry weapons.

procedural due process: According to the Fourteenth Amendment, before someone is deprived of life, liberty, or property, the procedure must be fundamentally fair. Typically, this requires that there be at least a notice and a fair hearing.

reasonable grounds: A degree of proof that is less than probable cause but more than suspicion. It represents a degree of certainty (around 30 percent) that a crime has been or will be committed and that the suspect is involved in it.

school resource officer: Career law enforcement officers, with sworn authority, typically assigned by a city police department or agency to work in collaboration with schools. School resource officers have the power to arrest people and to carry weapons.

substantive due process: Requirement of the Fourteenth Amendment that a rule, regulation, policy, or law that allows the deprivation of life, liberty, or property must be fundamentally fair and related to a legitimate governmental interest.

zero tolerance: Behavioral policies in schools with mandatory punishments for certain rule violations. Punishments consist of suspension, transfer to alternative school, expulsion, and/or referral to the juvenile justice system.

FOR FURTHER RESEARCH

❏ **Combating Fear and Restoring Safety in Schools**
http://www.ojjdp.ncjrs.org/jjbulletin/9804/contents.html

❏ **Gang-Free Schools and Communities Program**
http://www.ojjdp.ncjrs.org/Programs/ProgSummary.asp?pi=6&ti=11&si=
62&kw=&strItem=&strSingleItem=&p=topic&PreviousPage=SearchResults

❏ **Increasing School Safety Through Juvenile Accountability Programs**
http://www.ojjdp.ncjrs.org/search/SearchResults.asp

❏ **Juveniles and Legal Rights**
http://www.b418.com/JuvenilesandLegalRights.htm

❏ **Indicators of School Crime and Safety**
http://www.ojp.usdoj.gov/bjs/pub/pdf/iscs99.pdf

For an up-to-date list of web links, go to the Juvenile Justice Companion Website at **http://cj.wadsworth.com/del_carmen_trulson_jj**

Juvenile Justice: Past, Present, and Future

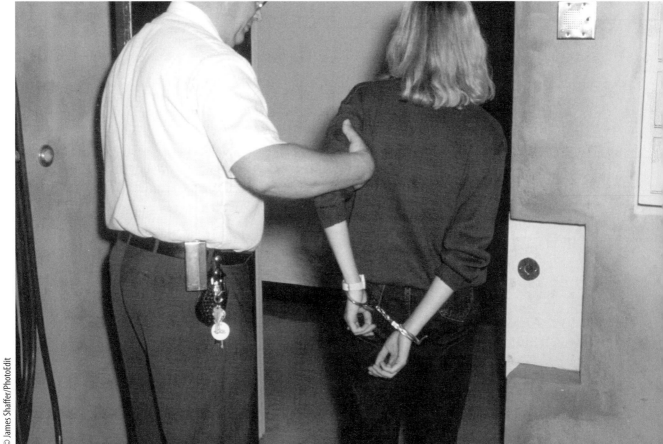

CHAPTER FOURTEEN OUTLINE

Reliving the Past / 439

The Discovery of Childhood / 439
A Separate Legal System for Youths / 440
Juvenile Justice Reform and the Erosion of *Parens Patriae* / 440
Recognizing Nondelinquents and Diversity in Juvenile Courts / 441
A Juvenile Crime Wave? / 441
The Dual Path of Juvenile Justice / 442

A Look at the Present / 442

The Current State of the Juvenile Court and the Juvenile Justice System / 442

Some Current Issues and Trends / 443

Adult Courts with "Delinquency Jurisdiction" / 443
Specialty Courts and Individualized Justice / 443
Restorative Justice / 446
Disproportionate Minority Representation in Juvenile Justice / 447

Public Opinion and Pendulum Shifts / 449

A Glimpse of the Future / 450

Females and Juvenile Justice / 450
Reinventing Juvenile Probation / 451
Five Themes and Trends in State Laws Targeting Serious Crimes Committed by Juveniles / 453
A Juvenile Justice System for This Century / 454

IN THIS CHAPTER YOU WILL LEARN

- About the significant events that have transformed juvenile justice since its formation more than a century ago.

- That one proposed change to juvenile courts is that the adult system would have jurisdiction in all matters of delinquency.

- About another proposed change to juvenile courts, which is to establish a youth justice system with a number of specialty courts to handle juveniles by their offense and individual circumstances.

- About a significant movement in juvenile justice called restorative justice.

- About efforts to reduce the disproportionate representation of minorities in the juvenile justice system.

- That juvenile justice policy is responsive to public opinion concerning the treatment of juveniles.

- That the growing presence of female offenders presents challenges to the juvenile justice system, which in the past has focused on males.

- About "reinventing probation," a movement that addresses current and future challenges facing probation—the most common juvenile disposition.

- About five themes and trends in state laws targeting serious juvenile offenders.

- That even when juveniles must be processed in the adult justice system, they are still recognized as needing more protective safeguards than adults before, during, and after trial.

INTRODUCTION

The preceding chapters in this book have presented a substantial amount of information about the juvenile justice system, process, and law. It is evident that "juvenile justice" is always changing. Even as you read this chapter, new programs are introduced, legislation is debated, and cases are decided that will change the juvenile justice system, process, and law in the immediate future.

But, as the saying goes, the more things change, the more they stay the same. This is certainly something that may be happening in juvenile justice.

This chapter examines where we have been, where we are, and where we may be going in juvenile justice. It begins by summarizing the significant events that have transformed juvenile justice for more than a century. It then looks at current issues and future trends in juvenile justice. Several areas are examined: current proposals to modify the jurisdiction and structure of juvenile courts, restorative justice, disproportionate minority representation, and public opinion about the treatment of juveniles. The chapter then examines issues and trends in juvenile justice such as the growing number of female offenders, changes in juvenile probation, and handling serious and violent juvenile offenders. These current issues and trends provide perspective about what can be expected in the future.

Reliving the Past
The Discovery of Childhood

The only major distinction between juveniles and adults prior to the 1800s was transplanted to America through English common law. That distinction saw children under the age of seven as unable to understand the consequences of their actions and thus not criminally responsible. Once children passed the age of seven, however, early Americans regarded them as miniature adults. As miniature adults, they did "adult things" and have been described by Charles Friel as little people in big people's clothing.[1] Consequently, they would be dealt with in adult ways when they violated the law.

Things started to change by the late 1800s. The United States was in the midst of massive population increases as scores of immigrants came to this country to partake of the American dream. The growing numbers of foreign born entering the country necessitated that they be "Americanized." A starting place for Americanization was children; this process would take place in the schools. By the 1900s, the states had passed compulsory education laws, and children were taken out of the work force as a result of growing child labor restrictions. This significant shift in the division between children and adults was further promoted by advances in the fields of social work, psychiatry, psychology, and sociology. Scholars in these fields began to focus on the development of children. They developed the concept of adolescence and held that children did not mature to adults overnight—there was a period in between. As a result of these twentieth-century insights, offending children were no longer considered miniature adults. Instead, they were viewed as developing persons who needed treatment in a different way.

The dividing line between children and adults was advocated by the child-savers—a group of reformers who sought to protect young children from the harshness of adult life and adult punishments. By the early 1900s, their efforts led to the establishment of hundreds of private societies for the protection of children. However, perhaps their biggest achievement was the creation of a separate legal forum for youths in the form of a juvenile court. Its establishment in 1899 "carved a boundary that put adults on one side of the line and young people on the other, a penal code and its punishments on the former side, and the juvenile code and its sanctions on the other."[2] It created a two-tier system that has been with us ever since.

A Separate Legal System for Youths

The juvenile court was based on the *parens patriae* doctrine, which holds that it is the duty of the state to intervene in a child's life when it would be in his or her best interests. However, such intervention was not for punishment. Instead, it was for the benefit of the child and sought to help rather than to push the offender further into the system.

Focusing on the child's best interests left little need for precision in determining who would be subject to juvenile court intervention. In practice, this meant many of the youths that came before the juvenile court were not delinquents; rather, they were beggars, vagrants, and orphans. This caused little concern for the juvenile court because these children, like delinquents, were also in need of help. Because their circumstances sometimes led to delinquency and adult criminality, juvenile court intervention was viewed as a benefit because a wise judge would do what was in the best interests of the child in an effort to prevent delinquency.

Therefore, the juvenile court judge became the "superparent" by exercising guardianship rights for youths who had broken the law or for those headed that way. This experiment did not generate any major criticism for nearly seven decades, but changes were to take place in juvenile courts and the juvenile justice system across the country.

Juvenile Justice Reform and the Erosion of *Parens Patriae*

By 1950, every state had established a juvenile court, and a separate legal system for juveniles had become entrenched in the U.S. system of justice. The first major change came sixty-eight years after the Illinois Legislature passed the Illinois Juvenile Court Act of 1899. In 1967 the U.S. Supreme Court noted in the now well-known case of *In re Gault* that the juvenile court had come to resemble a "kangaroo court." It said that juvenile courts had not fulfilled the promise of rehabilitation, nor did they offer juveniles the protections that adults received even though they faced the same consequences. Thus, the juvenile received the "worst of both worlds." The Court questioned the broad intervention power of juvenile courts under *parens patriae*. Through *Gault*, the Court weakened the wall between the juvenile and adult system by giving juveniles some due process rights.

The ensuing decade of decisions by the U.S. Supreme Court continued to erode the line between the juvenile and adult justice systems as the Court granted additional due process rights to juveniles in adjudication proceedings similar to adult rights at trial. By the mid-1970s, the juvenile justice process had become "adultified." By that time, juveniles received due process rights like adults except the constitutional right to bail, a jury, and a speedy and public trial. These constitutional rights are not given to juveniles even today.

Recognizing Nondelinquents and Diversity in Juvenile Courts

By the 1970s, criticism hounded all aspects of the juvenile justice system. Critics questioned whether one juvenile court fitted all circumstances. These criticisms focused mostly on the treatment of youths who had not broken the law and yet found themselves in juvenile court for minor behaviors or because of abuse at the hands of their parents. Criticism was heaviest for the practice of incarcerating these juveniles along with more hardened delinquents.

With reform in mind, Congress passed sweeping legislation in 1974: the Juvenile Justice and Delinquency Prevention Act (JJDPA). This act required that distinctions be made among youths who committed acts that would be considered crimes if committed by an adult, youths who committed acts prohibited only for minors, and youths who were abused and neglected by their parents. The last two categories of youth would be considered nondelinquents and were to receive different treatment by the juvenile justice system.

The effects of the JJDPA were felt throughout the country. States began to recognize the stigmatizing effects of juvenile court intervention for nondelinquents and therefore emphasized community placement for these youths when possible. States also decentralized the juvenile court process by transforming juvenile courts from entities with one jurisdiction in all cases involving children into several courts with limited or special jurisdiction. The "juvenile court" would now handle delinquent youths while other "courts of juvenile jurisdiction" (called family, domestic, or probate courts) would handle nondelinquents. The system erected a boundary that put delinquents on one side of the line and nondelinquents on the other. *Punishment* and *responsibility* were the buzz words for delinquents; assistance and supervision were the themes for nondelinquents.

A Juvenile Crime Wave?

By the late 1980s, a rise in certain forms of violent juvenile crime led to fears of the juvenile "superpredator." Some scholars predicted that the growing population of juveniles was a demographic crime bomb waiting to happen. They warned that U.S. citizens should "just wait"—the upsurge in juvenile crime then was nothing compared to what was coming in the future.[3]

The picture of the violent and unremorseful juvenile—murdering, raping, and high on drugs—necessitated tough legislation to protect the public. By the early to mid-1990s, almost every state had passed legislation that focused on dealing with juvenile offenders in the adult system and ensured that their threat to public safety would be diminished. This was accomplished through waiver or transfer laws that made it possible for judges to sentence serious offenders to terms that extended well beyond juvenile age. These sentences were handed out in adult court, not juvenile court. Transfer laws further weakened the boundary between the juvenile system and the adult system and implied that some juveniles are indeed adults in little people's bodies and should be treated as such when they violate laws.

By the late 1990s, it became clear that the prediction of an explosion of violent juvenile crime was incorrect. Violent juvenile crime fell after a peak in 1994 and continues to fall into 2005. The "crime bomb" failed to materialize, but juvenile justice policy makers had by then created a dual path for delinquents in juvenile justice, a path that still exists today.

The Dual Path of Juvenile Justice

The get-tough approach to juvenile justice is still in effect. In most jurisdictions, however, the guiding philosophy has been to recognize that "most" delinquents can be dealt with effectively by the juvenile justice system.

There is a road less traveled, and this is the second path of juvenile justice, which is reserved for a smaller number of serious, violent, and chronic juvenile offenders. Waiver laws were used to deal with these offenders only a few years ago; today, laws more punitive than just waivers exist. They are called blended sentencing laws, determinate sentencing laws, habitual and serious offender laws, or mandatory minimum laws. These laws remove some discretion from the juvenile court and make it easier for juveniles to be sentenced to long terms of confinement by a juvenile or adult court in the juvenile and/or adult correctional system.

A Look at the Present
The Current State of the Juvenile Court and the Juvenile Justice System

The juvenile court has gone through significant transformation since its founding more than a century ago. It bears little resemblance to what its founders had originally intended—it has been "adultified" and is sometimes referred to as a junior criminal court because of the following changes:

- Legal merit and formalized procedures have replaced informal intervention and individualized attention under *parens patriae*.

- Due process protections for juveniles parallel those that adults receive in criminal justice.

- Offense severity, instead of youth circumstances, drives dispositions.

- Defense attorneys and prosecutors have embraced the adversarial adult model.

- Terminological distinctions have been discarded in some jurisdictions.[4]

Changes have not been limited to the juvenile court. They are also reflected in the juvenile justice system. For example, these changes have taken place:

- Juveniles are "arrested" for crimes versus "taken into custody" for delinquency.

- Confidentiality restrictions have been eroded.

- Probation has been transformed from reintegration and rehabilitation to supervision and risk management.

- State schools are deemed juvenile correctional facilities, where some favor retribution and incapacitation over rehabilitation.

- Youths are released to "juvenile parole" for strict supervision and public safety management instead of to "aftercare" for reintegration and rehabilitation.[5]

It is clear that the boundary between juvenile justice and criminal justice has become less pronounced than originally envisioned by founders of the juvenile court.[6] With this erosion has come the debate between those who say that the juvenile court and the juvenile justice system are obsolete and should be abolished and those who maintain that they should be retained. Despite these divergent views, no state today has abolished the juvenile court and separate youth justice system. However, state practices have chipped away at the system's traditional boundaries. In sum, the juvenile court has not disappeared for the majority of juvenile offenders—but it is a far cry from what its founders originally intended.[7]

It is unlikely that the juvenile court will completely disappear in the near future. Abolition would mean that adult courts would take care of all delinquents. At present, however, adult courts are not equipped to provide the many services that juvenile courts offer. Adult courts can handle juvenile delinquents for trial and sentencing, but juvenile courts do more than convict and sentence. They feature numerous interventions for the benefit of the juvenile both before and after adjudication and disposition. As Butts and Harrell note, "children and adolescents will continue to be cognitively, emotionally, and socially different from adults"; thus, there remains the need for a separate legal forum for youths.[8] Despite acknowledgment of the need to keep juvenile systems and courts separate, problems remain that must be addressed.

Some Current Issues and Trends

Adult Courts with "Delinquency Jurisdiction"

Of the proposals to merge juvenile courts with adult courts, one type of suggested merger envisions adult courts having delinquency jurisdiction, meaning they would decide all delinquency cases but would use juvenile-specific programs not currently available in adult court. For example, adult judges could send juveniles to juvenile-specific probation, treatment services, and separate juvenile institutions (see Exhibit 14.1). "Juvenile courts" would be retained for status offending and dependency and neglect cases.

Observers say that the takeover of delinquency jurisdiction by adult courts may result in juveniles being placed "in a different set of crowded courtrooms that are even less capable than the juvenile court of providing close offender monitoring, intensive rehabilitation, and creative, individualized sanctions."[9]

Specialty Courts and Individualized Justice

One major criticism of the juvenile court is that it is the only forum dealing with the various types of juvenile delinquency. For example, in the current system, the juvenile court uses the same procedures for a young first offender (twelve-year-old shoplifter) as it uses for an older offender on a second or third offense (seventeen-year-old drug dealer). But having the adult court take over all delinquency cases would not fix this problem, and would likely aggravate it.[10]

EXHIBIT 14.1

The Debate over Giving Adult Courts Delinquency Jurisdiction

Policy makers must decide what type of court should have responsibility for young people who violate the law. Currently, youthful offenders are charged and tried under the juvenile court's "delinquency" jurisdiction. The debate centers on whether to continue defining law violations by young people as "delinquent" acts, or to classify them as "crimes" and refer all law violations to criminal (or adult) court.

■ Abolishing the concept of delinquency is not the same thing as abolishing the entire juvenile court. Even if lawmakers ended the juvenile court's jurisdiction over law violations, the juvenile court could continue to handle other types of cases (e.g., abused and neglected children, truants, curfew violators, runaways).

■ Some states have created "family courts" to handle all family matters, including abuse and neglect, divorce, and custody disputes. Abolition of the delinquency jurisdiction would have no impact on the viability of family courts. They would simply no longer handle criminal law violations by minors.

The debate is about choosing the best court process for adjudicating and sentencing young offenders, *not* the services and sanctions that follow the court process.

■ Abolition of the delinquency jurisdiction would not require that all young offenders be sent to adult prison. Many states already operate separate correctional facilities for young adults (under age 21, under 23, etc.). The decision to handle all young offenders in the criminal court would not prevent such correctional specialization. States would still be free to separate offenders by age when incarcerating or otherwise supervising convicted offenders, and the federal government would still be free to require such separation as a condition of financial support for state corrections agencies.

■ The relative effectiveness of the current system of juvenile probation and juvenile corrections has no inherent relevance to the debate over abolishing the juvenile court's delinquency jurisdiction. Existing youth offender programs could operate just as they do now, but a different court would be the source of their client referrals.

Source: Adapted from Jeffrey A. Butts and Adele V. Harrell, *Delinquents or Criminals: Policy Options for Young Offenders* (Washington, DC: The Urban Institute, June 1998), p. 2. Used by permission.

A solution to the current "all-or-nothing" approach to the court system may be specialty or alternative courts such as gun, drug, misdemeanor, and felony courts (see Exhibit 14.2). Specialty courts allow for remedies that are matched to specific offenders, their circumstances, and their acts—regardless of whether the juvenile or adult court has jurisdiction.[11] This structure is different from the current system, which has a single juvenile court to deal with all types of delinquency, or the proposed alternative, whereby one adult court would do the same. Under this proposed system, the twelve-year-old shoplifter mentioned pre-

EXHIBIT 14.2

The Juvenile Justice System in the Past, the Present, and the Future?

The past

The present

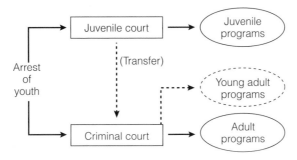

The future?

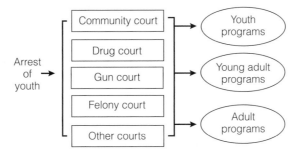

Source: Jeffrey A. Butts and Adele V. Harrell, *Delinquents or Criminals: Policy Options for Young Offenders* (Washington, DC: The Urban Institute, June 1998), p. 9. Used by permission.

viously may be tried in a "community" or "misdemeanor" court that specializes in minor offenses and has at its disposal several youth programs to deal with less serious offenders and the special needs they present. Alternatively, the seventeen-year-old drug dealer may be handled in "drug" court or "felony" court and face similar specialized court processes and outcomes. This system allows individualized attention based on the offense and the unique circumstances that offenders bring to court. Advocates of specialty courts say that this system ensures that different juveniles with different needs are dealt with in different ways.

They maintain that this type of system is necessary because of the increasing diversity of offenders in the juvenile justice system.

The specialty court approach recognizes that one court does not fit all juveniles. It gives policy makers and judges more options as they look for an appropriate way to deal with the diverse range of juvenile offenders. Such a system goes back to the original intent of the founders of the juvenile court, which involved individual attention and flexibility, and at the same time tried to ensure that juveniles are held accountable for delinquent acts.

Restorative Justice

A movement with much momentum is **restorative justice.** This approach suggests that juvenile justice must get beyond the debate about whether juveniles should be punished or rehabilitated. Instead, restorative justice is described as a "back-to-basics mission for juvenile justice that supports a community's need to sanction crime, rehabilitate offenders, and ensure public safety."[12]

Restorative justice (also known as balanced and restorative justice) advocates that the justice system must move beyond focusing solely on the offender and instead focus on victims and the community in the rehabilitation of delinquents. As Bazemore and Day note:

> Whether treatment or punishment is emphasized, the offender is the passive and solitary recipient of intervention and service. . . . The juvenile justice system excludes victims and other community members from what could be meaningful roles in sanctioning, rehabilitation, and public safety.[13]

Restorative justice involves the community, victims, and offender in the juvenile justice process because "the most significant aspect of crime is that it victimizes citizens and communities."[14] Restorative justice holds promise for juvenile justice because it ensures that the offender will be sanctioned, but at the same time victims and the community will have a role in the process and may participate in the offender's rehabilitation. The offender is reintegrated (or restored), but victims and the community are restored as well.

The restorative justice approach has three goals:

- *Accountability.* Juvenile offenders must be held accountable by making amends and restoring losses to victims and communities. Accountability is not met by obeying curfew, going to counseling, meeting with a probation officer, or avoiding drugs. Instead, accountability means repairing the harm done while at the same time having offenders take responsibility for their actions.

- *Competency.* Competency is the capacity to do something well that others value. The standard for competency is not the absence of illegal behavior (such as remaining violation free on probation), but instead is the ability of adults and the community to get offenders involved in activities that others value, such as work, service in the community, dispute resolution, and community problem solving. Such activities restore the offender, victim, and the community.

- *Public safety.* Restorative justice assumes that public safety cannot be accomplished simply by locking offenders up or incapacitating them. It can be achieved by bolstering a community's capacity to prevent and control crime by getting offenders involved in the community through developing relationships with organizations such as schools and employers and individuals such as juvenile justice professionals. Adults have a role in monitoring offenders to ensure that their activities while under supervision are focused on these areas.[15]

The essence of restorative justice is that "justice" is best served when all parties affected by crime (offenders, victims, and the community) are involved. Although a main thrust is that offenders are held accountable for their behavior, "the responsibility for restoring mutual respect, understanding, and support among those involved must be shared by the community."[16] Only the future will tell if this new approach will succeed in the current climate of juvenile justice, but it appears promising.

Disproportionate Minority Representation in Juvenile Justice

There are indications that minority youths are treated differently by the juvenile justice system. A major concern is the **disproportionate minority representation** in secure confinement facilities, such as in state-run juvenile institutions. The percentage of minority youths in secure confinement is more than two times greater than their proportion in the general population, and minority juveniles account for 70 percent of confined juveniles overall.[17] The overrepresentation of minority youths is not limited to secure confinement. Studies by the Office of Juvenile Justice and Delinquency Prevention (OJJDP) have found that minorities are overrepresented at all stages of the juvenile justice system compared to the general population—from arrest through disposition.[18] Exhibit 14.3 examines the overrepresentation of black juveniles in the juvenile justice system.

The overrepresentation of minority youths at all stages of the juvenile justice process is troubling and indicates that the juvenile justice system likely works differently for some youths than for others and that such differences are based directly or indirectly on race or other extralegal factors, such as socioeconomic status. As a result, Congress has required through the Juvenile Justice and Delinquency Prevention Act (JJDPA) that states receiving federal grant funds must "address juvenile delinquency prevention efforts and system improvement efforts designed to reduce, without establishing numerical standards or quotas, the number of juvenile members of minority groups, who come into contact with the juvenile justice system."[19] States participating in federal grant programs must implement the following phases to address disproportionate minority confinement and overrepresentation of minorities in the juvenile justice system or risk losing federal grant funds:

1. *Identification.* States must determine the extent to which disproportionate minority confinement exists.

2. *Assessment.* States must determine the reasons for disproportionate minority confinement if it exists.

EXHIBIT 14.3

The Overrepresentation of Blacks in the Juvenile Justice System

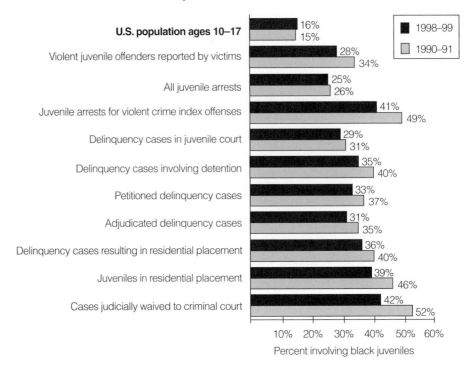

Note: Nationally, for all stages of juvenile justic system processing, the black proportion was smaller in 1998–99 than in 1990–91.

Source: Melissa Sickmund, *Juveniles in Corrections* (Washington, DC: Office of Juvenile Justice and Delinquency Prevention, 2004), 12.

3. *Intervention.* States must work to develop and implement intervention strategies to address the reasons for disproportionate minority confinement.

4. *Evaluation.* States must evaluate the effectiveness of intervention strategies.

5. *Monitoring.* States must monitor changes in disproportionate minority confinement and adjust their intervention strategies if needed.[20]

The most recent information on disproportionate minority confinement indicates that thirty-nine states have completed the identification and assessment phases and are implementing the intervention phase.[21] Most states are making significant progress in determining the extent of disproportionate minority confinement and the reasons that it exists. It is still unclear whether intervention strategies have been successful in alleviating this problem and identifying the real reasons for disparity in the juvenile justice system. This disparity could stem from outright discrimination or may be the effect of more subtle behavioral and legal factors at work in U.S. society.

Public Opinion and Pendulum Shifts

Pendulum shifts happen and are to be expected in juvenile justice. More than a century of juvenile justice has shown that the pendulum swings from punishment and responsibility to rehabilitation. These swings revolve around public opinion. In a democratic society, the public usually gets what it wants, including what it wants to do with errant juveniles.

Most polls on public attitudes concerning juveniles ask whether they should be tried in adult court and, if convicted, punished like adults. Polls in the last several years generally show that the public supports trying juveniles as adults when they are charged with certain crimes, such as a violent crime involving persons, selling illegal drugs, or being involved in a serious property crime. One survey found that nearly 87 percent of the public supported transfer to adult court for a violent crime, 70 percent for selling illegal drugs, and 63 percent for a serious property crime.[22] These results are similar to those of the National Opinion Survey on Crime and Justice (NOSCJ) conducted in 1995, which found that 87 percent of the public supported waiver for a violent crime, 69 percent for selling illegal drugs, and 62 percent for being involved in a serious property crime.[23]

A second issue addressed in opinion polls is whether the public believes that juveniles should be treated like adults if convicted. In 1992, according to a nationally representative survey, about 42 percent of Americans believed juveniles should be sent to adult prisons for committing a serious violent crime, approximately 28 percent said juveniles should be sent to adult prisons for selling drugs, and 15 percent believed that juveniles should be sent to adult prisons for serious property crimes.[24] A decade later, 55 percent of Americans said that juveniles convicted of a violent crime should be sent to adult prison. In terms of age, most Americans believed that juveniles ages fifteen and older should be eligible for adult punishment. Moreover, a substantial proportion believed that adult punishment should start at age thirteen, and 8 percent of Americans believed youths twelve and under should be punished like adults for a violent offense.[25] In short, more Americans supported adult court transfer compared to sending youths to adult prisons, but they also agreed that if juveniles are to be punished like adults, such punishment should start early, around age fifteen.[26]

Public opinion polls over the last several years show that most Americans support the transfer of violent and serious juveniles to adult court and, to a lesser extent, punishment in adult prisons if convicted. For the remaining majority of juveniles, however, most Americans support rehabilitation.[27] In a recent poll, for example, 90 percent of respondents said that intervention and rehabilitation should be the focus of the juvenile justice system.[28]

Public sentiment about juvenile offenders has shifted away from reforming or rehabilitating them toward punishment and responsibility. However, this conclusion may be misleading in that the pendulum swings for punishment, but only for the few juveniles who commit serious crimes. Even for these serious offenders, there is public support that they should be given a chance at rehabilitation even if sent to adult prison. Thus, rehabilitation remains an objective in juvenile justice as it did more than a century ago.[29] This situation is unlikely to change in the future, for juveniles will continue to be viewed as persons with less responsibility than adults and in need of supervision, assistance, and rehabilitation. For most Americans, a purely punitive approach in juvenile justice swings the pendulum too far in the opposite direction.

A Glimpse of the Future
Females and Juvenile Justice

For years, female delinquency took a backseat to male delinquency, perhaps because female adolescents made up a small percentage of the juvenile offender population and their offenses were less serious. This situation has changed. Female adolescents today commit a growing percentage of offenses among juvenile offenders. A recent report by the Office of Juvenile Justice and Delinquency Prevention found that females constituted 28 percent of all juvenile arrests in 2001.[30] Between 1988 and 1997, the number of delinquency cases involving females increased 83 percent. Moreover, delinquency cases involving females under age sixteen increased over the last several years, and female juveniles are being increasingly referred to the juvenile justice system for person offenses, as opposed to property or other offenses.[31]

However, note that percentage increases among females can be misleading because the absolute number of female arrests and referrals to juvenile court is still much lower than the number of arrests and referrals among male juveniles. Thus, examining percentage increases tends to give the false impression that female juveniles are increasing their delinquency in tremendous numbers when in fact the actual *change* in the absolute number of arrests is relatively small (for example, going from one arrest to two arrests is a 100-percent increase although the actual number increase is one arrest). Moreover, there is some debate on whether these increases are the result of female juveniles actually increasing their delinquent behavior or whether such increases in female delinquency simply reflect different reactions of the police to female juvenile offenders.[32] Regardless of whether the increasing arrest rate of female juveniles is a product of increased offending or that police are just reacting differently to them when they do so, trends do show that female juvenile crime is rising from years past and is apparently becoming more serious. As a result, the conclusion can be made that female adolescents are offending (or being arrested) more than in the past, are offending at an earlier age, and are committing more serious offenses. Although the degree and change in female juvenile arrests and reasons for these changes are debatable, female juveniles are nonetheless becoming more involved in the juvenile justice system as a result, and this situation has led some to conclude that "female involvement in the juvenile justice system, once seen as an anomaly, has evolved into a significant trend."[33]

Perhaps one of the most significant implications of the increasing presence of female delinquents in the juvenile justice system is that historically "male-based" juvenile justice systems must now pay attention to the special circumstances of female delinquents. Acoca and Dedel note that the circumstances of female delinquents are different from male delinquents in the following ways:

■ *Victimization outside the juvenile justice system.* Most girls in the juvenile justice system have a history of victimization, and many violent victimizations, before they come to the attention of the system.

■ *Victimization inside the juvenile justice system.* While in the juvenile justice system, girls are more vulnerable to physical and sexual abuse than are male delinquents.

■ *Separation of incarcerated delinquent mothers from their children.* A growing number of female delinquents are mothers who have been separated from their children.

■ *Nonviolent offenders.* A majority of female delinquents are nonviolent offenders charged with minor status, property, or drug offenses. Females charged with assault may be inappropriately labeled as violent although such assaults often arise out of family conflict situations.[34]

The differences between males and females who become involved in juvenile justice suggest that juvenile justice systems must develop programs and policies that take into consideration the characteristics of female offenders.[35] The good news is that states are already embarking on initiatives that recognize these differences and are not simply assuming that what works best for males applies to females as well.[36] Dealing with females in a historically male-focused juvenile justice system means that these and other practical implications will become increasingly important in the future juvenile justice system.[37]

Reinventing Juvenile Probation

Probation is regarded as "the most troubled and the most promising component" of the justice system.[38] It is the juvenile justice system's "workhorse" and has changed much over the years.[39] These changes have created challenges for juvenile probation.

Perhaps the biggest change for juvenile probation has been increases in the number and dangerousness of probationers over the last several years. Probation is used in more than 60 percent of adjudicated juvenile court cases. This figure has grown tremendously since 1988 and has made probation the most frequent juvenile court disposition.[40] Because probation is considered "limitless" as a correctional sanction (meaning that probation agencies cannot refuse a youth once sentenced by a juvenile court judge), it often serves as a "catch basin" for the juvenile justice system.[41] As a result, the type of juveniles under probation has also changed. A greater proportion of juveniles who would have formerly been institutionalized (such as offenders against persons) are now being placed on probation due to lack of space in juvenile institutions or other programs. This trend has led to concerns about officer safety, higher rates of recidivism, and lack of public confidence, among others.

One consequence of the increase in the number and dangerousness of juvenile probationers is the capacity of probation to provide meaningful supervision and rehabilitation. Although the median caseload nationwide is

41 juveniles, juvenile probation caseloads of 200 cases or more in some juris-dictions have necessitated that supervision become the first goal while rehabil-itation becomes a second, third, or nongoal.[42] For example, changes in the types and increases in the number of offenders on probation caseloads have led to a **normalization** of certain law and probation violations,[43] meaning that violations which would have received a strict response in the past are being tol-erated because more dangerous juveniles are being placed on probation. For example, positive drug tests are considered normal and expected for juvenile probationers because probation officers are forced to place the most emphasis on the serious behavior of more dangerous probationers. In other words, fail-ing a drug test may not be viewed as seriously as it once would have been.

One response to these and other realizations has been to **reinvent proba-tion.** Advocates of reinventing probation have suggested strategies to restruc-ture probation so that it might respond more effectively to current and future challenges:

1. *Emphasis on public safety first.* Probation agencies must focus on concerns for public safety first. Members of the public need to feel that they are safe be-fore they accept probationers in the community and before they feel confi-dent in the job that probation departments are doing.

2. *Supervision of probationers in the neighborhood, not the office.* Probation officers should be in the community where the offender resides. They should not wait for the probationer to come to the office (called the **bunker** or **fortress mentality**). The value of **field supervision** is that the officer has firsthand knowledge of where the offender lives and can get the community involved in supervision by cultivating information sources. An additional benefit is that it serves to connect probationers to local community resources that might not otherwise be used in a traditional probation format.

3. *Rationally allocate resources.* A probation officer's time should be used where the most "risky" offenders are at, in the most risky places, at the most risky times. This strategy might include the placement of evening reporting cen-ters in the neighborhoods where juvenile probationers reside or checks by probation officers working outside of normal office hours.

4. *Provide for strong enforcement of probation conditions and a quick response to viola-tions.* Probationers have become accustomed to expecting two or three vio-lations before meaningful sanctions are applied. Reinventing probation suggests that violations should be acted on swiftly and surely. This does not mean that all violations must result in institutionalization through revoca-tion because doing so would be impractical. Instead, violations can be met with increased "discomfort" for the probationer in the form of more report-ing requirements, curfew, house arrest, electronic monitoring, and/or in-creased fines.

5. *Develop partners in the community.* High caseloads, declining budgets, and staff shortages have dictated that probation officers must rely on the community to help supervise offenders. This does not necessarily mean that citizens must organize community watch groups but rather that the community can

play an important role in offender supervision by providing information or positive avenues for probationers. To do this, probation must develop partnerships with community members and community organizations.[44]

The value of reinventing probation has yet to be proved, but this idea is gaining momentum across the country. It will take time before old ways of doing things are replaced with new approaches. To achieve more effective supervision and to be able to provide strong enforcement of probation conditions, more officers must be hired. Bigger budgets to hire more officers must be approved by state, county, and local policy makers. Accomplishing these and other structural changes are at the core of reinventing probation.

Five Themes and Trends in State Laws Targeting Serious Crimes Committed by Juveniles

At the end of the twentieth century, the National Center for Juvenile Justice identified five themes and trends in state laws targeting violent and other serious crimes committed by juveniles. The focus is on these specialized delinquents because serious, violent, and chronic juveniles, while representing the minority of juvenile offenders overall, present a disproportionate number of problems to policy makers, to practitioners, and to the general public. As a result, dealing with these offenders represents a priority trend in juvenile justice. Here are the five themes and trends for these offenders:

1. *Diminution of jurisdictional authority of juvenile courts.* More serious and violent juvenile offenders are being removed from the juvenile justice system in favor of criminal court prosecution.

2. *Expansion of judicial disposition and sentencing authority.* More state legislatures are experimenting with new disposition and sentencing options—for example, blended sentencing schemes that allow the juvenile or adult court to sentence serious, violent, and chronic juveniles to juvenile and/or adult sanctions without having to go through a waiver process.

3. *New correctional programming.* Correctional administrators are under pressure to develop programs as a result of new transfer and blended sentencing laws in which serious, violent, and chronic juveniles may be placed in adult prisons or on other adult sanctions.

4. *Less confidentiality of juvenile court records and proceedings for serious, violent, and chronic juveniles.* Traditional confidentiality provisions are being revised in favor of more open proceedings and records.

5. *Participation of victims of juvenile crime.* Victims of juvenile crime are being included as active participants in the juvenile justice process.[45]

As a result of the trend to deal with serious, violent, and chronic juveniles in the adult system, the American Bar Association's Criminal Justice Section Standards and Juvenile Justice Committee authorized the creation of a task force to examine the implications of the increasing adult justice system treatment for juvenile offenders. In a report titled *Youth in the Criminal Justice System:*

Guidelines for Policymakers and Practitioners, the ABA task force developed several general principles for the transfer of juveniles to the criminal justice system. These principles include the following:

1. That youths are developmentally different from adults and that such differences need to be considered at all stages and in all aspects of the criminal justice system when juveniles are transferred to adult court and punished in the adult system.

2. Decisions about whether to detain or release juveniles awaiting trial in adult court should be determined by each youth's special characteristics.

3. The right to counsel for juveniles in the adult justice system should not be waived by youths unless they have consulted with a lawyer and a full inquiry is made into whether the youth understands the right to waive counsel and has the capacity to make the choice intelligently, voluntarily, and knowingly. If, after these safeguards, the right to counsel is voluntarily waived, stand-by counsel should be appointed.

4. Judges in the adult system should consider the individual characteristics and circumstances of the juvenile during sentencing instead of relying on standard sentencing guidelines in spite of individual characteristics.

5. If convicted in adult court and incarcerated, youths should be housed in institutions or facilities separate from adult facilities until at least their eighteenth birthday.

6. Juveniles incarcerated in the adult criminal justice system should be provided rehabilitation programs addressing educational, treatment, health, mental health, and vocational needs.[46]

The ABA report suggests that it is appropriate for most juveniles to stay in the juvenile justice system because the fact remains that most juveniles are far from serious, violent, and chronic. For some juveniles, however, adult court intervention may be the only suitable choice. In these cases, observers still believe that juveniles should be processed with great care because they are vulnerable and need more protection than adults who commit similar offenses.

A Juvenile Justice System for This Century

In a monograph titled *A Juvenile Justice System for the 21st Century,* the Office of Juvenile Justice and Delinquency Prevention concludes that "an effective juvenile justice system must meet three objectives: (1) hold the juvenile offender accountable; (2) enable the juvenile to become a capable, productive, and responsible citizen; and (3) ensure the safety of the community."[47] The monograph adds that "these objectives are best met when a community's key leaders, including representatives from the juvenile justice system, health and mental health systems, schools, law enforcement, social services, and other systems are jointly engaged in the planning, development and operation of the juvenile justice system." The monograph's author concludes that "a carefully conceived, properly implemented, and adequately funded juvenile justice system in the 21st century can be expected to bring about the following: (1) increased juvenile justice system responsiveness; (2) increased accountability; (3) increased

---

YOU ARE A... **Juvenile Justice Policy Maker**

The juvenile justice system in your county has been subject to criticism as being old, outdated, and unable to deal with the unique issues that today's youths bring into the system. As a result, some worry that the existing juvenile justice system will be unable to respond effectively to youths and their issues in the new millennium. As the head juvenile justice policy maker in your county, you are charged with a proposal to develop a juvenile justice system for the twenty-first century.

1. As a juvenile justice policy maker, what would your "ideal" juvenile justice system for the twenty-first century look like? Make sure to think about the various stages of the juvenile justice process and the many agencies and different types of youths and behaviors involved.

2. Identify four main features of your ideal system, and explain how these features are an improvement over the existing system.

3. In your opinion, are the features of your ideal system feasible?

---

community involvement; (4) decreased costs of juvenile corrections; and (5) increased program effectiveness." The "You Are a . . . Juvenile Justice Policy Maker" box gives you an opportunity to devise your ideal juvenile justice system in light of these and other perspectives about juvenile justice structure, process, and law to which you have been exposed.

Most scholars and field practitioners would likely agree that "the most effective long-term response to the problem of juvenile delinquency and violence lies in improving the juvenile justice system and working to prevent delinquency before it occurs."[48] These are twin goals that must be addressed, but primarily by different sectors. Improving the juvenile justice system calls for strong government leadership at the federal, state, and local levels, and preventing delinquency primarily begins at home with good parenting. Both of these sectors must mesh and cooperate. However, achieving these goals may be easier said than done in a democratic society that values privacy and rejects excessive governmental intrusion into family life. Yet despite obstacles, there is the strong belief that a properly structured juvenile justice system and process may be the best way to deal with juveniles involved in the legal system in a manner that is in their best interests. This was the mandate of the original juvenile court and justice system, and more than a century later, the juvenile justice system still operates by this goal.

SUMMARY

❑ The juvenile court and juvenile justice system are substantially different than what their founders had originally intended. Despite changes, most juveniles are treated differently from adults when they come to the attention of juvenile justice.

❑ Having the adult court absorb juvenile cases would not fix the criticisms of the juvenile court. Giving adult courts jurisdiction in delinquency matters would place juveniles in a different set of courtrooms that might be even less effective at dealing with juvenile issues than the current juvenile court.

❑ A promising approach to restructuring juvenile courts is devising specialty courts that can handle offenders based on their specific needs and circumstances.

❑ Restorative justice as a view for juvenile justice suggests that victims and communities get involved in the rehabilitation of the juvenile offender.

❑ Minority youths are overrepresented at all stages of the juvenile justice process, including disproportionate numbers in secure confinement. States are currently assessing the extent of the problem and developing ways to reduce minority overrepresentation.

❑ In a democratic society, the public usually gets what it wants. Public opinion polls show that Americans favor transfer of violent and serious juveniles to adult court and, for some, adult prison sentences. For the majority of juvenile offenders, the public supports rehabilitation.

❑ The juvenile justice system must change from a focus on males to include females as they become more serious and frequent in their offending. Evidence shows that female offenders come to the juvenile justice system with different needs and circumstances than male offenders.

❑ The increasing number and dangerousness of juvenile probationers have led to a focus on "reinventing probation." Advocates of reinventing probation offer a back-to-basics mission for probation characterized by a renewed emphasis on supervision and rehabilitation while protecting the community.

❑ Themes and trends in state laws for serious and violent offenders include declining jurisdictional authority of juvenile courts, more and different sentencing options, new correctional programming, reduced confidentiality, and victim participation in the juvenile justice process.

❑ The juvenile justice system for this century will be characterized by multiple partnerships among individuals and agencies who deal with juvenile offenders in one form or another.

REVIEW QUESTIONS

1. Identify at least four significant events that have transformed the juvenile court.

2. List several criticisms of the current juvenile court. Would giving adult courts jurisdiction in delinquency matters solve these problems? Would developing specialized juvenile courts fix these problems?

3. If you were a juvenile justice administrator, how would you go about implementing a juvenile justice system based on restorative justice? Do you believe that the goals of restorative justice are feasible?

4. Sum up U.S. attitudes on the treatment of juveniles. What role should public opinion play in this issue?

5. Search the Internet for general public opinions, attitudes, and beliefs regarding juveniles and juvenile justice. Based on your research, is the public well informed about the reality of juvenile crime?

6. What are some special issues that female offenders may bring to juvenile justice that are different from the issues of male offenders? What are some practical steps that juvenile justice systems across the country might have to take as more female juveniles become involved in the system?

7. Identify two challenges to juvenile probation. Does reinventing probation have the ability to address those problems?

8. What is the "fortress" or "bunker" mentality concerning probation? What practical implications does this mentality have for juvenile probation in the future?

9. What do probation authorities mean when they say that "normalization" has occurred due to larger and more dangerous caseloads?

10. What are some factors that can explain disproportionate minority representation at all stages of the juvenile justice system? Which factors do you think are most important in explaining disproportionate minority representation? Are these factors legitimate reasons for this problem?

KEY TERMS AND DEFINITIONS

bunker or fortress mentality: The practice of having probation officers wait in their offices for probationers to check in with them. Advocates of reinventing probation say that probation agencies must get out on the streets where probationers reside and not "bunker" themselves in offices.

disproportionate minority representation: The finding that members of minority groups are overrepresented in all stages of the juvenile justice system compared to their proportion of the total juvenile population in the United States.

field supervision: Supervising probationers in their communities, at work, or in school. It is the opposite of office supervision.

normalization: The practice by probation officers of overlooking minor offenses as a result of larger and more dangerous caseloads. In the past, these violations would have received attention but now have become normal and expected.

reinventing probation: A back-to-basics mission for probation that emphasizes public safety, field supervision, directing resources toward the most problematic probationers, strict supervision, and community partnerships in the supervision of probationers.

restorative justice: A new paradigm to involve the community, victim, and offender in the juvenile justice process instead of focusing solely on the offender.

❏ **American Bar Association Report on Youth in the Criminal Justice System**
www.aba/crimjust/pubs/reports/index.html

❏ **American Bar Association: Juvenile Justice and Girls**
http://www.abanet.org/crimjust/juvjus/justicebygenderweb.pdf

❏ **Disproportionate Minority Confinement in Juvenile Justice**
http://www.ncjrs.org/94612.pdf

❏ **Reinventing Juvenile Probation**
http://www2.courtinfo.ca.gov/probation/documents/part3.pdf

❏ **Restorative Justice**
http://www.restorativejustice.org

For an up-to-date list of web links, go to the Juvenile Justice Companion Website at **http://cj.wadsworth.com/del_carmen_trulson_jj**

U.S. Supreme Court Decisions in Juvenile Justice

Cases Giving Constitutional Rights to Juveniles

- *Haley v. Ohio* (68 S.Ct. 302 [1948]): Coerced confessions are not admissible as evidence in criminal proceedings in adult court against juveniles.

- *Kent v. United States* (383 U.S. 541 [1966]): Juveniles must be given due process rights when transferred from juvenile to adult court. These rights are a hearing, representation by counsel at such hearing, access to records considered by the juvenile court, and a statement of the reasons in support of the waiver order.

- *In re Gault* (387 U.S. 1 [1967]): Juveniles must be given four due process rights in adjudication proceedings that can result in confinement in an institution where their freedom would be curtailed. These rights are reasonable notice of the charges; counsel, appointed by the state if the juvenile is indigent; the ability to confront and cross-examine witnesses; and the privilege against self-incrimination.

- *In re Winship* (397 U.S. 358 [1970]): Proof beyond a reasonable doubt, not simply a preponderance of the evidence, is required in juvenile adjudication hearings in cases where the act would have been a crime if committed by an adult.

- *Ivan v. City of New York* (407 U.S. 203 [1972]): The decision in *In re Winship*—that juveniles are entitled to proof beyond a reasonable doubt in adjudication hearings—should be applied retroactively to all cases in the appellate process.

- *Goss v. Lopez* (419 U.S. 565 [1975]): Due process must be given to juveniles even in short-term school suspension cases.

- *Breed v. Jones* (421 U.S. 517 [1975]): Juveniles are entitled to the constitutional right against double jeopardy in juvenile proceedings.

Cases Not Giving Constitutional Rights to Juveniles

- *McKeiver v. Pennsylvania* (403 U.S. 528 [1971]): Juveniles have no constitutional right to trial by jury even in delinquency cases where the juvenile faces possible incarceration.

- *Davis v. Alaska* (415 U.S. 308 [1974]): Despite confidentiality laws, the fact that a juvenile is on probation may be brought out by the opposing lawyer in the cross-examination of a juvenile witness.

- *Swisher v. Brady* (438 U.S. 204 [1978])]): Double jeopardy does not attach in juvenile cases when after a hearing before a master, a juvenile court judge goes ahead anyway and holds a new hearing or makes supplemental findings on the same case.

- *Smith v. Daily Mail Publishing Co.* (443 U.S. 97 [1979]): A state law making it a crime to publish the name of a juvenile charged with a crime is unconstitutional because it violates the First Amendment right to freedom of the press.

- *Schall v. Martin* (467 U.S. 253 [1984]): Preventive detention of juveniles is constitutional.

- *Fare v. Michael C.* (442 U.S. 707 [1985]): A request by a juvenile to see his probation officer is not equivalent to asking for a lawyer. Moreover, there is no probation officer–client privilege, meaning that any information a juvenile gives to a probation officer may be divulged in court even if the information was given by the juvenile in confidence.

- *New Jersey v. T. L. O.* (469 U.S. 325 [1985]): Public school officials need reasonable grounds to search students; they do not need a warrant or probable cause.

Death Penalty Cases

- *Eddings v. Oklahoma* (455 U.S. 104 [1982]): Mitigating circumstances, including age and social history, must be considered in juvenile capital cases.

- *Thompson v. Oklahoma* (487 U.S. 815 [1988]): It is unconstitutional to sentence a juvenile to death if he or she was fifteen years of age or younger at the time of the commission of the offense.

- *Stanford v. Kentucky* (492 U.S. 361 [1989]): It is constitutional for a state to impose the death penalty on a juvenile who was sixteen years old or older at the time the crime was committed.

- *Roper v. Simmons* (No. 03–0633 U.S. Supreme Court [2005]): It is unconstitutional to impose the death penalty on a person who is younger than eighteen years of age at the time the crime was committed.

Where State Juvenile Laws Are Found*

Alabama: Alabama's Juvenile Code resides in Alabama Statutes, Title 12, Chapter 15.

Alaska: Alaska's Juvenile Code resides in sections 47.12.010 to 47.12.990 of Title 47 (Welfare, Social Services and Institutions).

Arizona: Arizona's Juvenile Code can be found in sections 8–201 to 8–420 of Title 8.

Arkansas: Arkansas Family Code, Title 9, Subtitle 3 contains the core of the statutes governing delinquency court proceedings and is available online on the Arkansas General Assembly Website by selecting Research Resources, then Arkansas Code.

California: California's Juvenile Code resides in the Welfare and Institutions Code (numerous sections).

Colorado: Colorado's Children's Code resides in sections 19–2–101 to 19–2–1105 of Title 19.

Connecticut: Juvenile Justice Act, Title 46b (Family Law), Chapter 815t (Juvenile Matters).

Delaware: Delaware Code, Title 10 (court and Judicial Procedure), Chapter 9 (The Family Court of the State of Delaware).

District of Columbia: District of Columbia Bar.

Florida: The core of the statutes governing court proceedings in delinquency proceedings is contained in Title XLVII, Criminal Procedure and Corrections, Chapter 985, Delinquency; Interstate Compact on Juveniles. The statutes are available online at www.leg.state.fl.us/Welcome/index.cfm.

Georgia: Georgia's Juvenile Code resides in Georgia Statutes, Title 15, Chapter 11.

Hawaii: Hawaii's Juvenile Code resides in sections 571–1 to 571–88 of Title 31, Family.

*Source: State Profiles, National Center for Juvenile Justice (http://www.nccjj.org/stateprofiles).

Idaho: Idaho Juvenile Rules. Idaho Statutes, Title 20 (State Prison and County Jails), Chapter 5 (Juvenile Corrections Act).

Illinois: Juvenile Court Act of 1987 resides in Chapter 705, section 405 of the Illinois Compiled Statutes.

Indiana: Indiana's Juvenile Code (31–10–1 to 31–40–4 of Title 31, Family Law and Juvenile Law).

Iowa: Iowa Administrative Code and Iowa Code, Title VI (Human Services), Subtitle 5 (Juveniles), Chapter 232 (Juvenile Justice).

Kansas: Kansas Juvenile Justice Code, Chapters 38, 75 and 76 of the Kansas Revised Statutes. Visit the JJA Website and select "documents."

Kentucky: Kentucky's Juvenile Code is found in sections 600.010 to 640.120 of Title LI—Unified Juvenile Code.

Louisiana: The Louisiana Children's Code, Title VIII, Delinquency, contains the core of the statutes governing delinquency court proceedings and is available on the Louisiana Legislature Website by selecting Louisiana Laws.

Maine: Maine Juvenile Code resides in Title 15 (Court Procedure—Criminal), Part 6 (Maine Juvenile Code).

Maryland: Maryland Juvenile Code (Maryland Statutes/Maryland Code Online/Maryland Rules/MARYLAND RULES/Title 11. Juvenile Causes).

Massachusetts: General Laws of Massachusetts, Part I (Administration of the Government), Title XVII (Public Welfare), Chapter 119 (Protection and Care of Children, and Proceedings Against Them).

Michigan: State Bar of Michigan.

Minnesota: Minnesota's Juvenile Code resides in sections 260B.001 to 260B.446 of Chapter 260, Juveniles.

Mississippi: Title 43. Public Welfare, Chapter 21, Youth Court contains the core of the statutes governing delinquency court proceedings. Although local youth court rules may provide additional structure for case processing, state court rules for youth courts do not currently exist. For more information, visit the Mississippi Code Website.

Missouri: Revised Statutes—Juvenile Courts.

Montana: Montana Youth Court Act (Title 41 Minors, Chapter 5 Youth Court Act).

Nebraska: Nebraska's juvenile code resides in Chapters 28 (Crime and Punishment), 29 (Criminal Procedure), 43 (Infants), and 83 (State Institutions).

Nevada: Title 5—Procedure in Juvenile Cases, Chapter 62—Juvenile Courts.

New Hampshire: Various provisions of New Hampshire statutes regarding delinquent juveniles are found in RSA 169–B; some sections of RSA 170–G; RSA 621; RSA 621–A; and some sections of RSA 651:61–A through 651:67.

New Jersey: Rules Governing Practice in the Chancery Division, Family Part, Part 5:19, General Provisions.

New Mexico: Juvenile Code is found at New Mexico Statutes, Title 32A, Articles 1 and 2.

New York: New York Statutes and Court Rules.

North Carolina: Chapter 7B North Carolina Juvenile Code.

North Dakota: 2001 North Dakota Century Code.

Ohio: With several exceptions, the Ohio Rules of Juvenile Procedure prescribe the procedure to be followed in all juvenile court proceedings in Ohio within the jurisdiction of the respective courts.

Oklahoma: Oklahoma Juvenile Code.

Oregon: Oregon State Juvenile Code.

Pennsylvania: Pennsylvania Bar Association.

Rhode Island: Rhode Island State Bar Association.

South Carolina: South Carolina Children's Code, Code of Laws, Title 20 Domestic Relations Juvenile Justice Code (20–7–6600).

South Dakota: South Dakota Codified Laws, Title 26, Minors.

Tennessee: Tennessee Code Annotated Title 37, Juveniles.

Texas: The Juvenile Justice Code is found in Chapters 51–60 of Title 3 of the Texas Family Code.

Utah: The core of the statutes governing court proceedings in delinquency proceedings is contained in Title 78, Judicial Code, Part 1 Courts, Chapter 3a Juvenile Courts. The Utah Rules of Juvenile Court Procedure support the statutes' requirements with additional structure for delinquency and dependency cases. Both the juvenile court statute sections and the court rules are available online on the Utah State Legislature Website.

Vermont: Vermont Statutes, Title 33 (Human Services), Chapter 55 (Judicial Proceedings).

Virginia: Virginia State Bar.

Washington: Washington's juvenile code is found in Sections 13.04 to 13.80 of Title 13 of the Revised Code of Washington (Juvenile Courts and Juvenile Offenders).

West Virginia: West Virginia State Code, Chapter 49 (Child Welfare), Article 5 (Juvenile Proceedings).

Wisconsin: The Wisconsin Juvenile Justice Code, Chapter 938 in the Wisconsin Revised Statutes, contains the core of the statutes governing delinquency proceedings. Local court rules may support the statutes' requirements with additional structure for delinquency and dependency cases in certain counties. Both the Juvenile Justice Code and local court rules are available online on the Wisconsin Revisor of Statutes Bureau Website.

Wyoming: Wyoming's Juvenile Code resides in sections 14–6–201 to 14–6–252 (Juvenile Justice Act) and 14–6–301 to 14–6–308 (Juvenile Probation).

Finding and Interpreting Court Cases*

This appendix discusses the mechanics of and access to court cases. The following brief discussion should help demystify the aura that surrounds court cases and enable the reader to understand what basic case citations mean. Any academic field has its own language and symbols; the field of law is no exception. Knowing these symbols leads to better understanding and, hopefully, to further research.

Court cases, particularly those decided by the U.S. Supreme Court, are important because they constitute case law and set precedent for cases decided by lower courts throughout the country. Where does one go to read court decisions in full? To various law publications, either in the library or on the Internet. To use these sources, one must know the basics of case citations, which provide the road map for the location of court cases.

Case Citations

Case citations indicate where a case may be found in the vast firmament of legal publications. For example, a reader wants to read the U.S. Supreme Court decision in the case of *In re Gault*, whose official case citation is 387 U.S. 1 (1967). This means that *In re Gault* is found in volume 387 of the *United States Reports*, starting on page 1, and was decided in 1967 (volume/publisher/page/year).

Court cases may be published by official government sources or by private publishers. The better practice is to use the official government source for citation purposes, although private publications may also be used when the official government source is unavailable or if there is no official government publication. For example, the case of *In re Gault*, above, is also found in 87 S.Ct. 1428 (the *Supreme Court Reporter* is not a government publication) and 18 L.Ed.2d 527 (the *Lawyer's Edition* is not a government publication). The better practice is to use 387 U.S. 1 (1967) because it is the official case citation.

*This section is adapted in part from Rolando V. del Carmen, *Criminal Procedure: Law and Practice*, 6th ed. (Belmont, CA: Thomson/Wadsworth, 2004), 1–25.

Here are examples of case citations, some government and others private, and what they mean:

- U.S. *United States Reports:* The official source of the U.S. Supreme Court decisions. Published by the U.S. government, it reports only U.S. Supreme Court cases. Example citation: *In re Gault,* 387 U.S. 1 (1967).

- S.Ct. *Supreme Court Reporter:* Reports U.S. Supreme Court decisions. Published by West Publishing Company, a private publisher. Example citation: *In re Gault,* 87 S.Ct. 1428 (1967).

- CrL *Criminal Law Reporter:* Reports U.S. Supreme Court decisions. Published by the Bureau of National Affairs, Inc., a private publisher. Example citation: *Powell v. Nevada,* 54 CrL 2238 (1992).

- L.W. *United States Law Week:* Reports U.S. Supreme Court decisions. Published by the Bureau of National Affairs, Inc. Example citation: *Alabama v. White,* 58 L.W. 4747 (1990).

- F.2d *Federal Reports, Second Series:* Reports decisions of the federal courts of appeals (thirteen circuits). Published by West Publishing Company. Example citation: *Doe v. Renfrow,* 631 F.2d 91 (7th Cir. 1980).

- F. Supp. *Federal Supplement:* Reports decisions of federal district courts throughout the United States. Published by West Publishing Company. However, only a small percentage of cases decided by federal district courts are published in the *Federal Supplement;* most federal district court cases are not published at all. Example citation: *United States v. Doe,* 801 F. Supp. 1562 (E.D. Tex. 1992).

- P.2d *Pacific Reporter, Second Series:* Reports state court decisions in the Pacific states. The *Pacific Reporter* is one of seven regional reporters that publish state court cases. The other six reporters are *Atlantic Reporter* (A), *Northeastern Reporter* (N.E.), *North Western Reporter* (N.W.), *Southeastern Reporter* (S.E.), *Southern Reporter* (S), and *South Western Reporter* (S.W.). These reporters are published by West Publishing Company. Example citation: *Doe v. State,* 487 P.2d 47 (Alaska 1971).

- Cal. Rptr *California Reporter:* Publishes California state court appellate-level cases. The various states have a state reporter series like the *California Reporter.* Example citation: *In re Gerald B.,* 164 Cal. Rptr. 193 (Cal. App. 1 Dist. 1980).

Internet Sources

In addition to printed sources, law cases are now also available on the Internet. Here are some of the free Internet sources:

For U.S. Supreme Court decisions, go to www.findlaw.com. Under "Laws, Cases & Codes," click on "U.S. Sup Ct." Under "U.S. Supreme Court Decisions," click "by year." Then click the year the case was decided. The cases are alphabetically arranged. The U.S. Supreme Court also has its own Website: http://www.supremecourtus.gov/opinions/opinions.html.

For United States Courts of Appeals decisions:

Decisions of the First Circuit	www.ca1.uscourts.gov
Decisions of the Second Circuit	www.law.touro.edu/2ndcircuit
Decisions of the Third Circuit	www.ca3.uscourts.gov
Decisions of the Fourth Circuit	www.ca4.uscourts.gov
Decisions of the Fifth Circuit	www.ca5.uscourts.gov
Decisions of the Sixth Circuit	www.ca6.uscourts.gov
Decisions of the Seventh Circuit	www.ca7.uscourts.gov
Decisions of the Eighth Circuit	www.ca8.uscourts.gov
Decisions of the Ninth Circuit	www.ca9.uscourts.gov
Decisions of the Tenth Circuit	www.kscourts.org/ca10
Decisions of the Eleventh Circuit:	ww.ca11.uscourts.gov/opinions.htm
Decisions of the D.C. Circuit	www.cadc.uscourts.gov
Decisions of the Federal Circuit	www.fedcir.gov

For decisions of federal district courts, note that some federal district courts have their own Web sites. If you do not have a federal district court's Website, you can to go http://www.lawcornell.edu (Cornell Legal Information Institute) or to http://www.uscourts.gov/links.html (Federal Judiciary).

If you are a student, your institution may have access to Academic Universe, an excellent source of federal and state cases on all levels. Instructions for accessing Academic Universe vary from one institution to another.

Other legal sources are available on the Internet for a fee. The most popular are VersusLaw, Westlaw, and Lexis. VersusLaw is recommended for nonlawyers as the best legal site for a fee because it is simple and inexpensive to use. It costs less than $10 a month and has no specific minimum period of time. It contains federal and state court opinions on various levels. At some universities, Westlaw Campus is available to students and is a great and convenient source of materials for legal research.

active conditions of probation and parole: Conditions that tell the juvenile, "you will . . ."

adjudication hearing: The equivalent of an adult trial.

adjustment (sometimes called **informal adjustment**): The process of dealing with a delinquency referral informally. The case is "adjusted," which means that the youth is offered diversion in lieu of facing an adjudication hearing.

aftercare (sometimes called **juvenile parole**): A period of supervised time after release from a state juvenile facility.

almshouse: Another word for a poorhouse. Almshouses were intended for debtor adults but held wayward juveniles as well.

apprenticeship: The practice of sending a delinquent child out of the community to learn a skill such as carpentry or commercial fishing. This practice was sometimes called placing out or binding out.

arraignment: Informing the juvenile of the charges in court and asking how he or she pleads.

atavist: A term used by Cesare Lombroso to describe people he thought were born criminals because they were throwbacks to earlier stages of evolution. Atavists, or born criminals, could be distinguished by physical features or stigmata that only criminals were thought to possess.

balanced and restorative justice model: An approach suggesting that "justice is best served when the community, victim, and youth receive balanced attention, and all gain tangible benefits from their interactions with the juvenile justice system."

bench warrant (also called a *capias*): A warrant issued by the court for an officer to take a named defendant into custody.

bifurcated: Refers to the two-part juvenile court process for petitioned juvenile offenders. The adjudica-

tion hearing is the first part, and disposition or sentencing is the second part.

blended sentences: Sentences that combine juvenile court sanctions with adult sanctions.

boot camp: A program for juveniles that emphasizes military drill, physical training, and hard labor.

bootstrapping: The practice of elevating a status offender to a delinquent offender for the same status offense that brought the youth to juvenile court the first time. The status offense becomes a delinquent offense because the youth violated a valid court order.

bunker or fortress mentality: The practice of having probation officers wait in their offices for probationers to check in with them. Advocates of reinventing probation say that probation agencies must get out on the streets where probationers reside and not "bunker" themselves in offices.

case disposition: The time it takes for a case to reach the juvenile court once it has been petitioned.

case processing: The time it takes for the juvenile court to decide a case once it reaches the court.

challenge for cause: A challenge seeking the dismissal of a juror for causes specified by law.

Child Abuse Prevention and Treatment Act (CAPTA): A 1974 federal act that made states eligible for federal grant money if they created child protection agencies, passed mandatory reporting laws, and appointed youth child advocates in court proceedings. The act covered many other areas, including funding for states to establish data-collection procedures to track the incidence and prevalence of dependency and neglect situations.

Child Protective Services (CPS): The state agency responsible for investigating and resolving cases of dependency and neglect. Child protective services are services provided by an agency authorized to act on behalf of the child when the parents are unable or unwilling to do so.

child-savers: Child advocates in the early twentieth century who were responsible for a variety of social reforms for children. They are credited for helping to establish the world's first juvenile court.

chivalry factor: The idea that female adolescents are treated more leniently by police officers when they commit crimes that male adolescents typically commit.

CINS: An acronym for children in need of supervision that is typically given to status offenders. Other popular acronyms include PINS (persons in need of supervision) or MINS (minors in need of supervision).

classical school: A school of thought, most heavily influenced by Cesare Beccaria, that suggested people are rational beings who engage in acts (such as crime and delinquency) after they calculate the pleasure or benefits versus the costs or pain expected. According to Beccaria, to prevent crime a punishment must be swift, severe, proportionate to the act, and, most importantly, certain.

clear and convincing evidence: The burden of proof in dependency and neglect cases when termination of parental rights is sought. It represents a degree of certainty around 80 percent that the allegations are true. States may raise this standard.

closed campuses: A school policy by which the school campus is closed to outside persons (those who do not have business in the school) during the school day.

community service: A type of adjudication that places a juvenile in an unpaid position with a nonprofit or tax-supported agency to perform a specified number of hours of work or service within a given time limit.

controversy of culpability: Refers to the controversy concerning the age at which a child can be held responsible for his or her actions because of the ability to possess *mens rea*, or a guilty mind. The controversy centers on different ideas about the age of responsibility, as evidenced by the differing minimum ages of jurisdiction in states.

cottage system: A key component of the training and industrial school. The cottage system resembled a college campus, with a number of buildings, each holding twenty to forty juveniles. Each cottage was supervised by a "mother and father."

court workload: The number of cases petitioned to the juvenile court each year.

crime control era: Generally, the point in time starting in the 1980s that was known for a concern about the rise in drug use, gun possession, and drug sales (particularly crack cocaine) among juveniles. Public scrutiny of the rise in these types of juvenile crime caused a get-tough policy for juvenile offenders.

critical stage: A stage in which incriminating evidence may be obtained from a suspect. Defendants have a right to a lawyer and are protected from self-incrimination at all critical stages.

deferred prosecution: Similar to deferred probation and is an agreement not to prosecute or petition the youth as long as he or she completes a period of time without further delinquent involvement.

deferred/informal probation: An agreement with the court intake officer (either a probation officer or a prosecutor) whereby a juvenile is not petitioned to the juvenile court in lieu of the successful completion of a period of time without further delinquency offenses. The period of time is typically six months.

deinstitutionalization: A product of the JJDPA of 1974, which required the removal of status offenders and other noncriminal youths from secure juvenile institutions.

delinquency: Any act committed by a juvenile that would be considered a criminal offense if committed by an adult.

delinquency petition: A formal complaint or request, typically from a prosecutor, asking the juvenile court judge to adjudicate a youth delinquent. A delinquency petition may contain information about the alleged crime and other information, such as the juvenile's prior record.

delinquency referral: A notice to an intake officer that a juvenile has engaged in delinquent conduct. Delinquency referrals typically come from law enforcement officers, but some states allow school officials, parents, and general citizens to make referrals directly to an intake officer.

dependency: A situation in which parents are not able to adequately take care of their children, typically because of death or disability.

dependency and neglect: A broad category that refers to situations in which parents are unable (dependency) or unwilling (neglect) to care for their child, resulting in some form of abuse. Other common terms include child abuse, child neglect, and child maltreatment.

desist: The stopping of an activity, such as status offending.

detention facility: A short-term locked facility that holds juveniles at three points in time: after arrest, before the adjudication hearing, and after disposition while the youth awaits transfer to a state-operated juvenile justice facility. Detention facilities also hold probation and parole violators.

detention hearing: A hearing conducted by a juvenile court judge, who determines whether there is probable cause and a need to justify the continued detention of the juvenile accused of a crime.

detention intake: The process immediately after arrest wherein juvenile detention officers decide whether to detain or release a juvenile before a meeting with intake officers, who decide how to deal with the case.

determinism: A theory which suggests that the causes of crime are predetermined or out of the control of the individual. For example, biological determinism refers to the cause of crime as something inherent or inborn in a person's biological makeup that may manifest in his or her physical features.

deterrence: Discouraging the juvenile (specific deterrence) or others (general deterrence) from committing crime.

direct file: Also called concurrent jurisdiction, direct file waivers occur when the prosecutor has the option of filing the case in either juvenile court or adult court.

discharge: The release from aftercare and state supervision.

discretion: The choice between two or more options that involves personal decision making.

discretionary waiver: A form of judicial waiver that is the oldest and most common type in the United States. Discretionary waivers are governed by *Kent v. United States* guidelines. In a discretionary waiver, the prosecutor files a waiver petition asking the juvenile court judge to waive the youth to adult court. The judge must consider several factors to justify a discretionary waiver.

disposition: The sentencing stage of the juvenile justice process. Disposition in the juvenile justice system is the equivalent to sentencing in the criminal justice system.

disposition report: A report, usually prepared by the probation officer, that contains details about the juvenile's background, prior record, family circumstances, and other facts that may affect the disposition to be imposed by the judge.

disproportionate minority representation: The finding that members of minority groups are overrepresented in all stages of the juvenile justice system compared to their proportion of the total juvenile population in the United States.

diversion: Another name for informal adjustment or informal processing. Diversion refers to the process of "diverting" youths from the formal juvenile justice system by offering them an informal way to resolve their delinquency referral.

double jeopardy: Being punished more than once for the same offense.

dual court system: The two court systems of the United States, one for federal cases and the other for state cases.

dual sovereignty: The concept that federal and state governments are sovereign in their own right.

electronic monitoring: An electronically monitored curfew imposed on the juvenile.

en banc: A decision made by an appellate court as one body—that is, by all of the justices on the court or Court.

evolving standards of decency: The standards generally used by the U.S. Supreme Court to determine whether a form of punishment, such as the death penalty, is constitutional. These standards are used together with the phrase "that mark the progress of a maturing society."

exclusionary rule: A rule providing that any evidence obtained by law enforcement officers in violation of the Fourth Amendment prohibition against unreasonable search and seizure is not admissible in a criminal prosecution to prove guilt.

extralegal factors concerning arrest: A factor or factors that are not theoretically relevant to whether a suspect should get arrested versus warned. Examples are race, gender, and SES.

family model: As applied to juvenile institutions, a model based on individualism, care, and nurturing. The family model was the basis for the training and industrial school.

field supervision: Supervising probationers in their communities, at work, or in school. It is the opposite of office supervision.

fine: A monetary punishment imposed on a person convicted of a crime; the money goes to the government.

formal diversion: A type of diversion in which youths are required to do more than remain violation free during a specified adjustment period. Formal diversion typically includes community service, restitution, and/or attendance in a counseling program.

formal probation: Probation that takes place after a finding of guilt.

general jurisdiction trial courts: Courts that have jurisdiction over criminal and civil cases. These courts sometimes have jurisdiction over juvenile cases.

graduated incarceration: The practice of housing juvenile offenders convicted as adults in a juvenile institution until they reach a certain age, at which time they are transferred to an adult prison.

guardian ad litem (also called a **court-appointed special advocate [CASA]**): A youth advocate whose responsibility is to represent a child's best interests. A guardian ad litem is usually involved in cases of dependency or neglect when the parents are not available. Usually citizen volunteers, some guardians ad litem must be lawyers if state law requires it.

habeas corpus: A writ directed to any person detaining another, commanding that person to produce the body of the prisoner and to explain why detention is justified and should be continued.

hierarchy rule: The UCR procedure in which only the most serious crime is recorded in the event that multiple crimes occur in one incident.

house arrest: A form of arrest in which the offender is allowed to stay at home instead of being kept in jail.

houses of refuge: An institution of the early 1800s for delinquent and other wayward children. Houses of refuge are considered the first juvenile institutions.

hung jury: A jury that cannot agree to convict or acquit the defendant.

Illinois Juvenile Court Act of 1899: Act of the Illinois Legislature that established the world's first juvenile court.

in loco parentis: "In the place of parents," meaning that teachers act in the place of parents during the school day and may establish rules and reasonably discipline students for violating those rules.

incapacitation: A goal of disposition that separates juveniles from the community and places them in a state institution to reduce the opportunity for committing more crimes.

independent school district police: Sworn officers hired and paid for by the school district and stationed in schools. School district police have the power to arrest people and to carry weapons.

indeterminate: A sentence without a fixed amount of time. The juvenile will be held until rehabilitated.

indicated: A term used by child protective agencies that means there is reason to believe a situation of dependency and neglect is occurring but there is not enough evidence to support a claim.

informal diversion: A type of diversion in which youths are required only to remain violation free during a specified period of time. Youths are not required to attend to other stipulations, such as community service, as they are with formal diversion.

informal probation: Probation that is usually given prior to adjudication or disposition.

institutionalization: Being placed in a state-operated juvenile justice facility.

intake: The screening process of all delinquency referrals after arrest. Procedures at intake determine which cases will be informally adjusted and which cases will be petitioned to the juvenile court.

intake conference: An informal meeting, typically including intake officers, the juvenile, and his or her parents. Intake conferences are intended to be informal, information-gathering sessions so that the intake officer can make an informed decision on whether to adjust the

youth's case or file a delinquency petition. Intake conferences around the country vary in style, and some of them resemble mini-interrogations with the goal of eliciting incriminating information.

intake officer: Usually a probation officer or prosecutor, who screens all delinquency referrals for their legal merit. Intake officers make decisions on which cases will be dealt with informally and which cases will be petitioned to the juvenile court.

intelligent waiver: A waiver of rights by a suspect who knows what he or she is doing and is competent to waive those rights.

intensive supervision probation (ISP): A program of intensive surveillance of an offender, aimed at reducing criminal conduct by using supervision to limit opportunities to engage in it.

judicial precedent: The concept that decisions of courts have value as precedent for future cases with similar facts and circumstances.

judicial waiver: One of three types: discretionary, mandatory, and presumptive. Judicial waivers differ from prosecutorial or legislative waivers because transfer decisions in judicial waivers are left to juvenile court judges.

jury of peers: A jury that is not consciously restricted to a particular group.

juvenile correctional facility: The modern name for the training, industrial, or state school. The juvenile correctional facility is different from the state school in some states in that it houses the most serious, violent, and chronic juveniles within a particular juvenile correctional system.

juvenile court administrators: Staff members who coordinate activities of the juvenile court at the direction of the juvenile court judge. Juvenile court administrators may be responsible for budgeting, hiring and firing court personnel, monitoring cases on the court's docket, and coordinating treatment services for juveniles. Their roles are diverse.

juvenile court era: The period of time from 1899, when the first separate juvenile court was established in Cook County, Illinois, until 1966.

juvenile court masters (or **referees, magistrates,** or **commissioners**): Usually, lawyers authorized to hear certain juvenile cases involving minor delinquency and detention hearings. They do not have full hearing authority like the juvenile court judge and may not generally preside over cases involving serious delinquency or waiver hearings.

Juvenile Justice and Delinquency Prevention Act (JJDPA): A 1974 act that required states to deinstitutionalize status offenders and other nondelinquents from secure facilities and to provide for the sight and sound separation of juveniles from adults in any facility if the states were to receive federal money. Amendments to this act included the adult jail and lockup removal clause of 1980 and the disproportionate minority confinement amendment of 1992.

juvenile rights era: The period of time from 1967 until 1979—it saw the juvenile justice system become more like the adult system in the processing of juvenile delinquents.

legal factors concerning arrest: A factor or factors that are based on current or past legal criteria and are considered legitimate in arrest decisions. For example, prior record and seriousness of the crime are legal factors.

legalistic style: A police department operational style that is characterized by approaching all situations "by the book," with little to no officer discretion.

legislative waiver: A collection of several waiver methods whereby a youth is automatically transferred to adult court because of criteria determined by state legislatures. There are three forms of legislative waiver: statutory exclusion, reverse waiver, and "once an adult, always an adult" waiver.

liaison officer: Usually a sworn officer hired and paid for by the city and who is stationed in school. Liaison officers typically have the power to arrest people and to carry weapons.

life without parole: A form of punishment in which an offender stays in prison for life and will never be released.

limited jurisdiction trial courts: Courts with jurisdiction over certain cases such as misdemeanors and local ordinance violations. Juvenile courts are sometimes considered to be limited jurisdiction trial courts.

mandatory waiver: A form of judicial waiver whereby the juvenile court judge must find probable cause that a juvenile meets certain age, offense, or other requirements. If the judge finds probable cause for these factors, the judge must automatically transfer the juvenile to adult court.

mediation: A pretrial proceeding in dependency and neglect cases in which the perpetrator, the child protective services agency, the victim, and lawyers consult to determine if the case can be settled out of court.

mens rea: A guilty mind.

middle-class measuring rod: Proposed by Albert Cohen in 1955, a concept which refers to the idea that lower-class children gain status and acceptance based on the values of the middle class. That is the standard or "measuring rod" with which they must compete in schools.

minimum age of responsibility: The earliest age at which juveniles can be held responsible for their acts.

Miranda **warnings:** A rule that police officers must give suspects under custodial interrogation the following warnings: You have the right to remain silent; anything you say can be used against you in a court of law; you have the right to the presence of an attorney; if you cannot afford an attorney, one will be appointed for you prior to questioning; you have the right to terminate this interview at any time.

National Crime Victimization Survey (NCVS): An annual survey that asks household participants age twelve and older about any victimizations they have experienced in the past six months.

National Incident-Based Reporting System (NIBRS): A reporting system developed in the late 1980s as a supplement to the UCR. It provides much more detailed information about criminal incidents, including information about perpetrators, victims, and the location of the crime. Currently, it is not operated nationally, and only twenty states are authorized to use NIBRS when reporting crimes to the FBI.

neglect: A situation in which parents do not take care of their children but have the ability to do so. Abandonment and abuse generally fall under neglect.

net widening: Occurs when juveniles who would not have been petitioned to juvenile court are placed on diversion. The increasing use of diversion programs brings more youths under the eyes of police and other monitors, making it more likely that juveniles will have further contacts with the juvenile justice system.

nonpetitioned: Youths who will not face a juvenile court hearing but have been diverted in another way or had their cases dismissed.

nontypical delinquent: Serious and violent juveniles. Most delinquents are not serious offenders.

normalization: The practice by probation officers of overlooking minor offenses as a result of larger and more dangerous caseloads. In the past, these violations would have received attention but now have become normal and expected.

once an adult, always an adult waiver: A form of legislative waiver that requires juveniles who have already been transferred and prosecuted in adult court to be tried in adult court for all future offenses that they may commit as a juvenile.

original jurisdiction: The court that will hear a delinquency case originally or for the first time.

orphanage: An institution for orphaned or abandoned children.

parens patriae: "Parent of a country": the doctrine that states that the state has the authority to intervene in the life of a child.

parole: The supervised release of an offender to the community *after* having served time in jail or a juvenile institution.

Part I offenses: The eight most serious person or property offenses that are most likely to be reported to the police: murder and nonnegligent manslaughter, forcible rape, robbery, aggravated assault, burglary, larceny-theft, motor vehicle theft, and arson. UCR counts of these crimes include both crimes reported and arrests made.

Part II offenses: A category that includes all offenses in the United States, with the exception of traffic violations, that are not Part I offenses. UCR counts include only arrests made for these crimes.

passive conditions of probation and parole: Conditions that tell the juvenile, "you will not . . ."

peremptory challenge: Disqualification of a juror, by the defense or the prosecution, for which no reason is given.

petition: A formal complaint to the juvenile court by an intake officer requesting an adjudication hearing.

plea: Response by the juvenile in court to the indictment or information.

plea bargain: An arrangement whereby a juvenile agrees to plead guilty to an offense in exchange for a lower charge, a lower sentence, or other considerations favorable to the juvenile, such as a withdrawal of waiver petition to adult court.

positive school: A school of thought that attributed the causes of crime to factors not necessarily in the control of the individual. This school focused on the individual and not the act committed, and it explained delinquency as the result of factors such as the environment. Early positive school theorists, such as Cesare Lombroso, attributed delinquency to a lack of biological development or evolution, which could be demonstrated by physical "stigmata."

positivism: A term that refers to the ability to measure and study a certain phenomenon that is presumed to cause something. For example, positivists would reject demonological explanations of crime (the devil made me do it) because the devil cannot be measured or observed. Thus, positivism is the application of scientific principles, specifically the ability to measure a phenomenon as in the study of crime and delinquency.

post-adjudication juvenile placements: Juvenile placements that house youths after they have been adjudicated. A state school is an example of a post-adjudication placement.

pre-adjudication juvenile placements: Juvenile facilities that house youths before they have been adjudicated. A detention center is an example of a pre-adjudication placement.

pre-disposition report: A report conducted by a juvenile probation officer that details a juvenile's history, such as substance abuse, home life, abuse, prior juvenile record, and/or evidence of psychological evaluations. This report is used by the juvenile court judge prior to making a ruling on the juvenile's disposition.

pre-juvenile court era: The time period from 1600 to 1898, characterized by juveniles being dealt with the same way as adults. There was no separate juvenile court during this era.

preponderance of the evidence: The burden of proof in dependency and neglect cases when a disposition other than the termination of parental rights is sought. It represents a degree of certainty around 51 percent that the allegations are true. States may raise this standard.

presumptive waiver: A form of judicial waiver in which a juvenile must prove why he or she should not be waived to adult court. Failure to prove this means that the juvenile court judge must send the case to adult court for trial.

privilege of a witness: The right of a witness not to answer incriminating questions while on the witness stand.

privilege of the accused: The Fifth Amendment right of the accused not to answer incriminating questions or to take the witness stand. If the accused takes the witness stand, he or she must answer incriminating questions.

probable cause: More than bare suspicion. It exists when an officer has a reasonable belief that an offense took place and that the suspect is the individual who committed or was in the process of committing the offense.

probation: A sentence whereby a youth is released to the custody of his or her parents but is subject to conditions of behavior stipulated by the juvenile court.

probation revocation: The process of taking away a youth's probation status because of noncompliance with the law or with the stipulations of probation. A youth who has had his or her probation revoked can face institutionalization in a state-operated juvenile justice facility.

procedural due process: According to the Fourteenth Amendment, before someone is deprived of life, liberty, or property, the procedure must be fundamentally fair. Typically, this requires that there be at least a notice and a fair hearing.

progressives: A label given to groups that sought reforms in all aspects of society, including juvenile institutionalization.

proportionality: The idea that the punishment given to an offender must be proportionate to the offense committed.

prosecutorial waiver: A method of transferring a juvenile's case to adult court in which the decision rests with the prosecutor and not with the judge. There is only one form of prosecutorial waiver: direct file.

protective factor: The idea that female adolescents are taken into custody more frequently for offenses that are morality based or sexualized than are their male counterparts.

public trial: A trial open to all persons interested in ensuring that the proceedings are fair and just.

punishment gap: A term coined by Barry C. Feld which refers to the fact that waived juveniles actually receive lighter sentences than those youths who are not waived to adult court or adults charged with similar crimes in adult court.

reasonable doubt: "Such a doubt as would cause a juror, after careful and candid and impartial consideration of all the evidence, to be so undecided that he or she cannot say that he or she has an abiding conviction of the defendant's guilt."

reasonable grounds: A degree of proof that is less than probable cause but more than suspicion. It represents a degree of certainty (around 30 percent) that a crime has been or will be committed and that the suspect is involved in it.

reasonable suspicion: A degree of proof that is less than probable cause but more than suspicion. It represents a degree of certainty (around 30 percent) that a crime has been or will be committed and that the suspect is involved in it.

reformatory: By the 1880s, the name given to houses of refuge in the United States. Reformatories were literally identical to houses of refuge and in many cases were actually former houses of refuge.

rehabilitation: A goal of disposition that provides various types of psychological, medical, and physical services to juveniles in the hopes that they acquire needed skills and values to help them refrain from committing crime.

reinventing probation: A back-to-basics mission for probation that emphasizes public safety, field supervision, directing resources toward the most problematic probationers, strict supervision, and community partnerships in the supervision of probationers.

restitution: The restoring of property or a right to a person who has been unjustly deprived of it.

restorative justice: A new paradigm to involve the community, victim, and offender in the juvenile justice process instead of focusing solely on the offender.

retained counsel: A lawyer paid by the defendant, not by the state.

retentionists: Those who favor keeping laws that authorize the execution of juvenile offenders.

retribution: A goal of disposition that gives juveniles their "just dessert."

reverse waiver: A form of legislative waiver in which a juvenile who is being prosecuted as an adult (has already been transferred to adult court) may petition to have his or her case "waived back" to the juvenile court for an adjudication hearing and for the juvenile court to decide the disposition or sentence.

right of allocution: The right allowing a defendant to make a statement on his or her own behalf as to why the sentence should not be imposed.

rule of four: A rule providing that the Supreme Court needs the votes of at least four justices to consider a case on its merits.

school model: As applied to juvenile institutions, a model based on standardization, order, and predictability. The school model was the basis for the reformatory.

school resource officer: Career law enforcement officers, with sworn authority, typically assigned by a city police department or agency to work in collaboration with schools. School resource officers have the power to arrest people and to carry weapons.

school-based probation: A type of probation wherein supervision is based in schools and enlists the help of school authorities in monitoring the juvenile.

segregated incarceration: Refers to the practice of housing juveniles convicted in adult court to a specific age-segregated adult facility (for offenders ages eighteen to twenty-four) until they reach a certain age.

self-report surveys: Surveys that inquire about behavior. Regarding juvenile delinquency, self-report surveys are usually anonymous or confidential, conducted over the phone or in person, and attempt to measure how much delinquency a juvenile is involved in and whether the juvenile was caught. Self-report surveys are routinely done on incarcerated juveniles but may be used on schoolchildren and others. The bottom line of self-report surveys is if you want to know something, just ask.

service style: A police department operational style that is characterized by the use of referral and diversionary alternatives to arrest.

shock probation: A form of probation whereby an offender is sentenced to incarceration but is released after a short period of confinement and then resentenced to probation.

slippery slope phenomenon: The belief that status offending behavior is a gateway or "slippery slope" to delinquent behavior.

social capital: A concept discussed by Robert Sampson and John Laub that refers to the product of certain events or transitions in life that provide a reason for someone to get off of a delinquent path. For example, getting married and having a child can result in "social capital" whereby the individual has a reason not to continue to be delinquent. In simpler terms, social capital is gaining something valuable that can be lost.

socioeconomic status: A rank based on an individual's education, occupation, and income. Socioeconomic status (SES) is used to determine classes within society, such as lower, middle, and upper class. A juvenile's SES is determined by his or her parents' SES. SES is usually viewed in the aggregate based on residential areas.

special conditions: Conditions of probation/aftercare to which only some offenders will be subjected. For example, sex offenders may be subject to a special condition of sex offender counseling.

special jurisdiction trial courts: Courts that have jurisdiction in special matters or cases. Juvenile courts are sometimes considered special jurisdiction courts because they hear only juvenile cases.

special programs: Probation and parole programs designed to meet the needs of certain types of juveniles.

standard conditions (sometimes called **general conditions**): Conditions of probation or parole that every youth will face. Common examples include reporting and community service.

stare decisis: Literally, "to abide by, or adhere to, decided cases." When a court has laid down a principle of law applicable to a set of certain facts and circumstances, it will follow that principle in all future cases with similar facts and circumstances. Abiding by cases decided sets judicial precedent.

status offenders (CINS, PINS, MINS, CINA): A label given to youths who violate laws prohibiting behavior only for juveniles. Status offenders are commonly referred to as children in need of supervision (CINS), persons in need of supervision (PINS), minors in need of supervision (MINS), or children in need of assistance (CINA).

status offense: An act prohibited only for juveniles.

statutory exclusion: A form of legislative waiver wherein certain offenders are automatically transferred to adult court when they meet certain age, offense, or age/offense/prior record combinations.

stop and frisk: A police practice that allows an officer to make a brief investigatory stop to ask questions if the officer has reason to believe that the individual has or is about to commit a crime and to conduct a protective frisk of the individual for weapons if the officer has a reasonable concern for his or her personal safety.

straight adult incarceration: The practice of housing juveniles convicted in adult court in an adult prison with no effort to segregate them by age.

substantiated: A term used by child protective agencies meaning that according to state law, there is enough evidence to support a claim of dependency and neglect.

substantive due process: Requirement of the Fourteenth Amendment that a rule, regulation, policy, or law that allows the deprivation of life, liberty, or property must be fundamentally fair and related to a legitimate governmental interest.

supremacy of parental rights: The principle which maintains that parents who are "able and willing" to care for their child have the ultimate custody rights to him or her. In practice, parents should have the opportunity to resolve conditions of dependency and neglect before they must go to court and/or face losing custody of their child.

three strikes and you're out: A sentencing law used in some states that increases sentences for offenders who commit subsequent crimes.

totality of circumstances test: The test that determines whether a juvenile has made a valid waiver of his or her rights or has given consent to search. The test involves evaluating the juvenile's age, experience, education, background, and intelligence and whether the juvenile has the capacity to sufficiently understand his or her rights and the consequences of waiving those rights or of giving consent to search.

training schools (also called *industrial schools*): Juvenile institutions introduced by the 1900s in the United States. The training and industrial school differed substantially from the reformatory, most notably with the development of the cottage system.

transfer (or **waiver of jurisdiction**): A broad definition consisting of a variety of methods in which a juvenile may have his or her case sent to adult court for trial. Whether a juvenile is transferred depends on determinations by state legislatures and the decision making of judges and prosecutors.

typical delinquent: A juvenile guilty of nonserious offenses.

uncontested: A situation in which a juvenile does not contest, or dispute, the petition or charges against him or her. An uncontested plea is often the result of a plea bargain between the prosecution and the juvenile.

Uniform Crime Reports (UCR): A national program begun in 1930 by the International Association of Chiefs of Police to provide a statistical count of crime, specifically arrests and crimes known to and reported to the police. The UCR is published annually by the FBI in a report titled *Crime in the United States*.

unsubstantiated: A term used by child protective agencies which means that according to state law, there is not enough evidence to support a claim of dependency and neglect.

upper age of jurisdiction: The maximum age in which the juvenile court has decision-making power over a youth. The most common upper age of jurisdiction is seventeen in the United States. In states that use this standard, youths who have reached the age of eighteen are considered adults and must usually be tried in adult court.

venire: A group of prospective jurors assembled according to procedures established by state law.

verdict: The pronouncement of guilt or innocence at the end of a trial.

vocational program: A trade- or skill-learning program in juvenile institutions. An example is automobile maintenance or computer programming.

voluntary waiver: A waiver that is not the result of threat, force, or coercion and is of free will.

waiver: An intentional relinquishment of a known right or remedy. A waiver of rights is valid only if it is intelligent and voluntary.

waiver petition: A petition or request by an intake officer or prosecutor asking the juvenile court judge to consider that the case be heard in adult court, not juvenile court. Juvenile court judges typically make final decisions on petitions to waive a juvenile. Waiver petitions are usually based on the seriousness of the offense.

warrant: A written order from a court based on a determination of probable cause that authorizes a law enforcement officer to conduct a search or to arrest a person.

watchman style: A police department operational style that is characterized by the informal resolution of incidents, with arrest as a last resort. Watchman-style departments operate with high discretion.

wayward: A term used to describe a child who has strayed from a law-abiding life.

youth discount: A proposal by those who want to abolish the juvenile court. With a youth discount, all juveniles could be dealt with in adult court but receive a discount on their sentence based on their age. For example, a youth who is sixteen may receive only a portion of what an adult would receive for a similar crime (66 percent of an adult sentence, or a discount of 33 percent).

zero tolerance: Behavioral policies in schools with mandatory punishments for certain rule violations. Punishments consist of suspension, transfer to alternative school, expulsion, and/or referral to the juvenile justice system.

CHAPTER 1

1. William J. Bennet, John J. Dilulio, Jr., and John P. Walters, *Body Count* (New York: Simon and Schuster, 1996), 21.

2. *Black's Law Dictionary,* 7th ed. (St. Paul, MN: West, 1999), 999.

3. Jeffrey A. Butts and Ojmarrh Mitchell, "Brick by Brick: Dismantling the Border Between Juvenile and Adult Justice." In C. Friel (ed.), *Boundary Changes in Criminal Justice Organizations,* Vol. 2 (Washington, DC: U.S. Department of Justice, 2000), 167–213.

4. Charles M. Friel, "A Century of Changing Boundaries." In C. Friel (ed.), *Boundary Changes in Criminal Justice Organizations,* Vol. 2 (Washington, DC: U.S. Department of Justice, 2000), 1–18.

5. Friel, "A Century of Changing Boundaries."

6. David J. Rothman, *Conscience and Convenience: The Asylum and Its Alternatives in Progressive America* (Boston: Little, Brown, 1980).

7. Rothman, *Conscience and Convenience.*

8. Anthony M. Platt, *The Child Savers: The Invention of Delinquency* (Chicago: University of Chicago Press, 1977).

9. David J. Rothman, *The Discovery of the Asylum* (Boston: Little, Brown, 1971).

10. Robert M. Mennel, "Attitudes and Policies Toward Juvenile Delinquency in the United States: A Historiographical Review." In P. Sharp and B. Hancock (eds.), *Juvenile Delinquency: Historical, Theoretical, and Societal Reactions to Youth* (Englewood Cliffs, NJ: Prentice Hall, 1995), 29–51.

11. Howard N. Snyder and Melissa Sickmund, *Juvenile Offenders and Victims: 1999 National Report* (Washington, DC: Office of Juvenile Justice and Delinquency Prevention, 1999).

12. Butts and Mitchell, "Brick by Brick," 167–213.

13. Platt, *The Child Savers.*

14. Butts and Mitchell, "Brick by Brick."

15. *In re Gault,* 387 U.S. 1 (1967).

16. Rolando V. del Carmen, Mary Parker, and Frances P. Reddington, *Briefs of Leading Cases in Juvenile Justice* (Cincinnati: Anderson, 1998).

17. *Kent v. United States,* 383 U.S. 541, 555–556 (1966).

18. Kathleen Kositzky Crank, *The JJDP Act Mandates: Rationale and Summary.* OJJDP Fact Sheet #22 (January 1995).

19. Howard Snyder, *Juvenile Arrests 2001* (Washington, DC: Office of Juvenile Justice and Delinquency Prevention, 2003).

20. Snyder and Sickmund, *Juvenile Offenders and Victims.*

21. Melissa Sickmund, Howard N. Snyder, and Eileen Poe-Yamagata, *Juvenile Offenders and Victims: 1997 Update on Violence* (Washington, DC: Office of Juvenile Justice and Delinquency Prevention, 1997).

22. Sickmund, Snyder, and Poe-Yamagata, *Juvenile Offenders and Victims.*

23. Sickmund, Snyder, and Poe-Yamagata, *Juvenile Offenders and Victims.*

24. Sickmund, Snyder, and Poe-Yamagata, *Juvenile Offenders and Victims.*

25. Sickmund, Snyder, and Poe-Yamagata, *Juvenile Offenders and Victims.*

26. Carol DeFrances, *Juveniles Prosecuted in State Criminal Courts* (Washington, DC: Office of Juvenile Justice and Delinquency Prevention, 1997), 1.

27. Shay Bilchik, *Offenders in Juvenile Court, 1996* (Washington, DC: Office of Juvenile Justice and Delinquency Prevention, 1999), 3.

28. DeFrances, *Juveniles Prosecuted in State Criminal Courts,* 1.

29. *Crime in the United States 2002* (Washington, DC: U.S. Department of Justice, 2002), 244.

30. *Crime in the United States 2002,* 244.

31. Snyder, *Juvenile Arrests 2001.*

32. Snyder and Sickmund, *Juvenile Offenders and Victims.*

33. Snyder and Sickmund, *Juvenile Offenders and Victims.*

34. Snyder and Sickmund, *Juvenile Offenders and Victims.*

35. Joseph Sanborn, "Philosophical, Legal, and Systematic Aspects of Juvenile Court Plea Bargaining." *Crime and Delinquency* 39 (1993): 509–527.

36. *Black's Law Dictionary,* 7th ed. (St. Paul, MN: West, 1999), 1273.

37. Charles Puzzanchera, Anne L. Stahl, Terrence A. Finnegan, Howard N. Snyder, Rowen S. Poole, and Nancy Tierney, *Juvenile Court Statistics 1997* (Pittsburgh: National Center for Juvenile Justice, 2000).

38. Snyder and Sickmund, *Juvenile Offenders and Victims.*

39. Snyder and Sickmund, *Juvenile Offenders and Victims.*

40. Snyder and Sickmund, *Juvenile Offenders and Victims.*

CHAPTER 2

1. Werner Einstadter and Stuart Henry, *Criminological Theory: An Analysis of Its Underlying Assumptions* (New York: Harcourt Brace, 1995).

2. See Geoffrey Abbott, *The Book of Execution* (London: Headline, 1994), for an overview of execution methods, including trial by ordeal punishments.

3. George Vold, Thomas Bernard, and Jeffrey Snipes, *Theoretical Criminology,* 4th ed. (New York: Oxford University Press, 1998).

4. Vold, Bernard, and Snipes, *Theoretical Criminology.*

5. Cesare Beccaria, *An Essay on Crimes and Punishments,* 4th ed. (Boston: International Pocket Library, 1983).

6. Randy Martin, Robert Mutchnick, and W. Timothy Austin, *Criminological Thought: Pioneers Past and Present* (New York: Macmillan, 1990), 8.

7. Robert Regoli and John Hewitt, *Delinquency in Society,* 5th ed. (New York: McGraw-Hill, 2003).

8. Vold, Bernard, and Snipes, *Theoretical Criminology.*

9. Einstadter and Henry, *Criminological Theory,* 73.

10. Einstadter and Henry, *Criminological Theory.*

11. Vold, Bernard, and Snipes, *Theoretical Criminology,* 32. Lombroso is the most commonly recognized, but evidence suggests that there were many others doing the same or similar work. See, for example, David M. Horton, *Pioneering Perspectives in Criminology: The Literature of 19th Century Positivism* (Incline Village, NV: Copperhouse, 2000).

12. See Gina Lombroso-Ferrero, *Lombroso's Criminal Man* (Montclair, NJ: Patterson Smith, 1972), for an excellent extended focus on Lombroso's work, including illustrations and a broad range of "defects" of criminals.

13. Martin, Mutchnick, and Austin, *Criminological Thought.*

14. Ysabel Rennie, *The Search for Criminal Man: A Conceptual History of the Dangerous Offender* (Lexington, MA: Lexington, 1978), 70.

15. Horton, *Pioneering Perspectives in Criminology,* 24.

16. Vold, Bernard, and Snipes, *Theoretical Criminology.*

17. Mark Lanier and Stuart Henry, *Essential Criminology* (Boulder, CO: Westview, 1998).

18. Lanier and Henry, *Essential Criminology.*

19. Lanier and Henry, *Essential Criminology.*

20. Rennie, *The Search for Criminal Man,* 82.

21. Vold, Bernard, and Snipes, *Theoretical Criminology.*

22. Vold, Bernard, and Snipes, *Theoretical Criminology.*

23. Diana Fishbein, "Biological Perspectives in Criminology." *Criminology* 28(2) (1990): 27–72.

24. Lanier and Henry, *Essential Criminology.*

25. See Ysabel Rennie, *The Search for Criminal Man: A Conceptual History of the Dangerous Offender* (Lexington, MA: Lexington, 1978). This important book provides perspective on early positivists such as Lombroso, Sheldon, and the Gluecks, tracing their professional training to their claims about crime and delinquency.

26. LaMar T. Empey and Mark Stafford, *American Delinquency,* 3rd ed. (Belmont, CA: Wadsworth, 1991), 165.

27. Rennie, *The Search for Criminal Man.*

28. Empey and Stafford, *American Delinquency.*

29. Ronald Akers, *Criminological Theories,* 3rd ed. (Los Angeles: Roxbury, 2000).

30. Empey and Stafford, *American Delinquency,* 183.

31. Empey and Stafford, *American Delinquency,* 182.

32. Einstadter and Henry, *Criminological Theory,* 132.

33. Empey and Stafford, *American Delinquency.*

34. Vold, Bernard, and Snipes, *Theoretical Criminology.*

35. Vold, Bernard, and Snipes, *Theoretical Criminology,* 162–163.

36. Empey and Stafford, *American Delinquency.*

37. Quoted in Akers, *Criminological Theories,* 145.

38. Albert Cohen, *Delinquent Boys: The Culture of the Gang* (New York: Free Press, 1955), 99.

39. Akers, *Criminological Theories.*

40. Cohen, *Delinquent Boys,* 132.

41. Akers, *Criminological Theories.*

42. Quoted in Empey and Stafford, *American Delinquency,* 230.

43. Quoted in Empey and Stafford, *American Delinquency,* 230.

44. Akers, *Criminological Theories.*

45. Robert Agnew, "Foundation for a General Strain Theory of Crime and Delinquency." *Criminology* 30(1) (1992): 50–58.

46. Agnew, "Foundation for a General Strain Theory of Crime and Delinquency," 57.

47. Agnew, "Foundation for a General Strain Theory of Crime and Delinquency."

48. Akers, *Criminological Theories.*

49. Edwin Sutherland and Donald Cressey, *Principles of Criminology,* 6th ed. (New York: Lippincott, 1960), 77–80.

50. Akers, *Criminological Theories.*

51. J. Robert Lilly, Francis Cullen, and Richard Ball, *Criminological Theory: Context and Consequences,* 2nd ed. (Thousand Oaks, CA: Sage, 1995), 47.

52. Sutherland and Cressey, *Principles of Criminology,* 79.

53. Lilly, Cullen, and Ball, *Criminological Theory.*

54. Robert Burgess and Ronald Akers, "A Differential Association–Reinforcement Theory of Criminal Behavior." *Social Problems* 14 (1966): 128–147. See also Ronald Akers, *Deviant Behavior: A Social Learning Approach,* 3rd ed. (Belmont, CA: Wadsworth, 1985).

55. Akers, *Deviant Behavior,* 50–51.

56. Akers, *Criminological Theories,* 78.

57. Travis Hirschi, *Causes of Delinquency* (Berkeley, CA: University of California Press, 1969).

58. Hirschi, *Causes of Delinquency,* 20.

59. Akers, *Criminological Theories.*

60. Akers, *Criminological Theories,* 106.

61. Edwin Lemert, *Social Pathology* (New York: McGraw-Hill, 1951).

62. Rennie, *The Search for Criminal Man.*

63. See Erving Goffman, *Stigma: Notes on the Management of Spoiled Identity* (New York: Simon and Schuster, 1963), on the concept of "master status."

64. Lemert, *Social Pathology.*

65. Goffman, *Stigma.*

66. Edwin Lemert, *Human Deviance, Social Problems, and Social Control* (Englewood Cliffs, NJ: Prentice Hall, 1967), 17.

67. Akers, *Criminological Theories,* 126.

68. Akers, *Criminological Theories,* 181.

69. Vold, Bernard, and Snipes, *Theoretical Criminology,* 237.

70. Vold, Bernard, and Snipes, *Theoretical Criminology.*

71. Michael Gottfredson and Travis Hirschi, *A General Theory of Crime* (Stanford, CA: Stanford University Press, 1990), 87–89.

72. Gottfredson and Hirschi, *A General Theory of Crime,* 95.

73. Gottfredson and Hirschi, *A General Theory of Crime,* 97.

74. Francis Cullen and Robert Agnew, *Criminological Theory: Past to Present* (Los Angeles: Roxbury, 1999), 75.

75. Terrie Moffitt, "Adolescence-Limited and Life-Course-Persistent Antisocial Behavior: A Developmental Taxonomy." *Psychological Review* 100(4) (1993): 674.

76. Moffitt, "Adolescence-Limited and Life-Course-Persistent Antisocial Behavior," 679.

77. Avshalom Caspi and Daryl Bem, "Personality Continuity and Change Across the Life Course." In L. Pervin (ed.), *Handbook of Personality Theory and Research* (New York: Guilford, 1990), 549–575.

78. Moffitt, "Adolescence-Limited and Life-Course-Persistent Antisocial Behavior."

79. Moffitt, "Adolescence-Limited and Life-Course-Persistent Antisocial Behavior," 685.

80. Moffitt, "Adolescence-Limited and Life-Course-Persistent Antisocial Behavior," 688.

81. Moffitt, "Adolescence-Limited and Life-Course-Persistent Antisocial Behavior," 690.

82. Robert Sampson and John Laub, *Crime in the Making: Pathways and Turning Points Through Life* (Cambridge, MA: Harvard University Press, 1993), 18.

83. Sampson and Laub, *Crime in the Making,* 14.

84. Sampson and Laub, *Crime in the Making,* 8.

85. Sampson and Laub, *Crime in the Making,* 8–9.

86. *Crime in the United States 2002* (Washington, DC: U.S. Department of Justice, 2002).

87. Howard Snyder, *Juvenile Arrests 2001* (Washington, DC: Office of Juvenile Justice and Delinquency Prevention, 2003).

88. *Crime in the United States 2002.*

89. Ramona Rantala, *Effects of NIBRS on Crime Statistics* (Washington, DC: Bureau of Justice Statistics, 2000).

90. See the University of Michigan's Monitoring of the Future Website: http://www.monitoringthefuture.org.

91. For an overview of the Causes and Correlates of Delinquency Program, see http://ojjdp.ncjrs.org/ccd.

92. George Knight, Michelle Little, Sandra Losoya, and Edward Mulvey, "The Self-Report of Offending Among Serious Juvenile Offenders." *Youth Violence and Juvenile Justice* 2(3) (2004): 273–295. See also Terrence Thornberry and Marvin Krohn, "The Self-Report Method of Measuring Delinquency and Crime." In D. Duffee (ed.), *Measurement and Analysis of Crime and Justice,* Vol. 4 (Washington, DC: U.S. Department of Justice, 2000), 33–84.

93. *Crime in the United States 2002,* 459–461.

94. *Crime in the United States 2002.*

CHAPTER 3

1. Frank W. Miller, Robert O. Dawson, George E. Dix, and Raymond I. Parnas, *The Juvenile Justice Process: Cases and Materials,* 4th ed. (New York: Foundation, 2000).

2. *Bringar v. United States,* 338 U.S. 160 (1949).

3. *Lanes v. State,* 7678 S.W.3d 789 (Tex. Crim. App. 1989).

4. Rolando V. del Carmen, *Criminal Procedure: Law and Practice,* 5th ed. (Belmont, CA: Wadsworth, 2001).

5. Del Carmen, *Criminal Procedure.*

6. Del Carmen, *Criminal Procedure,* 63.

7. National Conference of Commissioners on Uniform State Laws, *Uniform Juvenile Court Act* (Chicago: National Conference on Uniform State Laws, 1968), Sect. 13.

8. *United States v. Watson,* 423 U.S. 411 (1976).

9. *Vasquez v. State,* 739 S.W.2d 37 (Tex. Crim. App. 1987).

10. Miller, Dawson, Dix, and Parnas, *The Juvenile Justice Process.*

11. *In the Matter of Mark Anthony G.,* 739 S.W.2d 37 (SCNY 1987).

12. *Matthews v. State,* 677 S.W.2d 809 (1984).

13. *Alabama v. White,* 496 U.S. 325 (1990).

14. Irving Piliavin and Scott Briar, "Police Encounters with Juveniles." *American Journal of Sociology* 70 (1964): 206–214.

15. See, for example, Christopher Cooper, *Unlawful Motives and Race Based Arrest for Minor Offenses* (San Francisco: Center on Juvenile and Criminal Justice, 2001).

16. Howard Snyder, *Juvenile Offenders and Victims: Law Enforcement and Crime* (Washington, DC: Office of Juvenile Justice and Delinquency Prevention, 2001).

17. Darnell F. Hawkins, John H. Laub, Janet L. Lauritsen, and Lynn Cothern, *Race, Ethnicity, and Serious and Violent Juvenile Offending* (Washington, DC: Office of Juvenile Justice and Delinquency Prevention, 2000).

18. Howard Snyder, *Juvenile Arrests 2001* (Washington, DC: Office of Juvenile Justice and Delinquency Prevention, 2003), 9.

19. Hawkins, Laub, Lauritsen, and Cothern, *Race, Ethnicity, and Serious and Violent Juvenile Offending.*

20. Carl Pope and Howard Snyder, *Race as a Factor in Juvenile Arrests* (Washington, DC: U.S. Department of Justice, Office of Juvenile Justice and Delinquency Prevention, 2003).

21. Snyder, *Juvenile Arrests 2001.*

22. Meda Chesney-Lind, "Judicial Enforcement of the Female Sex Role: The Family Court and the Female Delinquent." *Issues in Criminology* 8 (1973): 51–60.

23. Snyder, *Juvenile Arrests 2001.*

24. Otto Pollak, *The Criminality of Women* (Philadelphia: University of Pennsylvania Press, 1950).

25. Merry Morash, "Establishment of a Juvenile Police Record: The Influence of Individual and Peer Group Characteristics." *Criminology* 22 (1984): 97–111.

26. Snyder, *Juvenile Arrests 2001.*

27. Office of Juvenile Justice and Delinquency Prevention, *Juvenile Female Offenders: A Status of the States* (Washington, DC: U.S. Department of Justice, 1998).

28. Office of Juvenile Justice and Delinquency Prevention, *Guiding Principles for Promising Female Programming: An Inventory of Best Practices*

(Washington, DC: U.S. Government Printing Office, 1998).

29. Robert J. Sampson, "Effects of Socioeconomic Context on Official Reaction to Juvenile Delinquency." *American Sociological Review* 51 (1986): 876–885.

30. Delbert S. Elliott and David Huizinga, "Social Class and Delinquent Behavior in a National Youth Panel." *Criminology* 21 (1983): 149–177.

31. David A. Klinger, "Demeanor or Crime? Why Hostile Citizens Are More Likely to Be Arrested." *Criminology* 32 (1994): 475–493. Also see "More on Demeanor and Arrest in Dade County." *Criminology* 34 (1996): 61–82.

32. Piliavin and Briar, "Police Encounters with Juveniles."

33. James Q. Wilson, *Varieties of Police Behavior* (Cambridge, MA: Harvard University Press, 1968).

34. Douglas A. Smith, "The Organizational Context of Legal Control." *Criminology* 22 (1984): 19–38.

35. Snyder, *Juvenile Offenders and Victims.*

36. Snyder, *Juvenile Arrests 2001.*

37. Snyder, *Juvenile Arrests 2001.*

38. Snyder, *Juvenile Arrests 2001.*

39. Snyder, *Juvenile Arrests 2001.*

40. Snyder, *Juvenile Arrests 2001.*

41. *Black's Law Dictionary,* 7th ed. (St. Paul, MN: West, 1999), 1710.

42. *Terry v. Ohio,* 392 U.S. 1 (1968).

43. Del Carmen, *Criminal Procedure,* 481.

44. *Minnesota v. Dickerson,* 113 S.Ct. 2130 (1993).

45. *In the Interests of J. L., A Child,* 623 So.2d 860 (Fla. App. 1993).

46. *Dunaway v. New York,* 442 U.S. 200 (1979).

47. Del Carmen, *Criminal Procedure,* 480.

48. *United States v. Robinson,* 414 U.S. 218 (1973).

49. *Chimel v. California,* 395 U.S. 752 (1969).

50. *In re Terrence G.,* 109 A.D.2d 440 (N.Y.A.D. 1985).

51. *In re Jermaine,* 582 A.2d 1058 (Pa. Sup. 1990). See also Barry Feld, *Juvenile Justice Administration in a Nutshell* (St. Paul, MN: West, 2003), 69–74.

52. *Schneckloth v. Bustamonte,* 412 U.S. 218 (1973).

53. *United States v. Matlock,* 415 U.S. 164 (1974).

54. *In re Robert H.,* 144 Cal. Rptr. 565 (Cal. Ct. App. [1978]).

55. Del Carmen, *Criminal Procedure.*

56. *New Jersey v. T. L. O.,* 469 U.S. 325 (1985).

57. *New Jersey v. T. L. O.*

58. Feld, *Juvenile Justice Administration in a Nutshell.*

59. *Cason v. Cook,* 810 F.2d 188 (8th Cir. 1987).

60. *Griffin v. Wisconsin,* 438 U.S. 868 (1987).

61. *United States v. Knights,* 534 U.S. 112 (2001).

62. *In re Tyrell J.,* 876 P.2d 519 (Cal. 1994).

63. Feld, *Juvenile Justice Administration in a Nutshell.*

64. Feld, *Juvenile Justice Administration in a Nutshell,* 67.

65. *In re Marcellus L.,* 278 Cal. Rptr. 901 (Cal. App. 1991).

66. *In re Tyrell J.*

67. Del Carmen, *Criminal Procedure.*

68. *Miranda v. Arizona,* 384 U.S. 436 (1966).

69. Thomas Grisso, "Juveniles' Competence to Stand Trial: What We Need to Know." *Quinnipiac Law Review* 18 (1999): 371–382.

70. See also Thomas Grisso, "Juveniles' Capacities to Waive Miranda Rights: An Empirical Analysis." *California Law Review* 68 (1980): 1134–1142.

71. Bruce Ferguson and Alan Douglas, "A Study of Juvenile Waiver." *San Diego Law Review* 7 (1970): 39.

72. *State v. Nicholas S.,* 444 A.2d 373 (Me. 1982).

73. Del Carmen, *Criminal Procedure.*

74. *Yarborough v. Alvarado,* 124 S.Ct. 2140 (2004).

75. *Yarborough v. Alvarado.*

76. *Alvarado v. Hickman,* 316 F.3d 841 (9th Cir. 2002).

77. *Yarborough v. Alvarado.*

78. *Yarborough v. Alvarado.*

79. Del Carmen, *Criminal Procedure,* 329.

80. Del Carmen, *Criminal Procedure.*

81. *Fare v. Michael C.,* 442 U.S. 707, 724 (1979).

82. Feld, *Juvenile Justice Administration in a Nutshell.*

83. Linda Szymanski, *Juvenile Waiver of Miranda Rights: Interested Adult Test* (Pittsburgh: National Center for Juvenile Justice, *NCJJ Snapshot* 7[3], 2002).

84. Thomas Von Wald, "No Questions Asked! *State v. Horse:* A Proposition for a Per Se Rule When Interrogating Juveniles." *South Dakota Law Review* 48 (2003): 143–171.

85. *People v. J. D.,* 989 P.2d 762 (Colo. 1999).

86. Feld, *Juvenile Justice Administration in a Nutshell.*

87. *Lewis v. State,* 288 N.E. 2d 138 (Ind. 1972), and see also Feld, *Juvenile Justice Administration in a Nutshell,* and Szymanski, *Juvenile Waiver of Miranda Rights: Interested Adult Test.*

88. *In re Robert M.,* 576 A.2d 549 (Conn. App. 1990), and see also Feld, *Juvenile Justice Administration in a Nutshell,* and Szymanski, *Juvenile Waiver of Miranda Rights: Interested Adult Test.*

89. *Commonwealth v. Williams,* 475 A.2d 1283 (S. Ct. Pa. 1984), and see also Feld, *Juvenile Justice Administration in a Nutshell,* and Szymanski, *Juvenile Waiver of Miranda Rights: Interested Adult Test.*

90. Linda Szymanski, *Juvenile Waiver of Miranda Rights: Per Se Age Test* (Pittsburgh: National Center for Juvenile Justice, *NCJJ Snapshot* 7[3], 2002). See also Feld, *Juvenile Justice Administration in a Nutshell.*

91. Feld, *Juvenile Justice Administration in a Nutshell.*

92. *Miranda v. Arizona.*

93. Feld, *Juvenile Justice Administration in a Nutshell.*

94. Feld, *Juvenile Justice Administration in a Nutshell.*

95. Kimberly Larson, "Improving the Kangaroo Courts: A Proposal for Reform in Evaluating Juveniles' Waiver of *Miranda.*" *Villanova Law Review* 48 (2003): 629–667.

96. *Davis v. United States,* 512 U.S. 452 (1994).

97. Linda Szymanski, *Confidentiality of Juvenile Delinquency Hearings: 2002 Update* (Pittsburgh: National Center for Juvenile Justice, *NCJJ Snapshot* 7[12], 2002).

98. Linda Szymanski, *Public Juvenile Court Records* (Pittsburgh: National Center for Juvenile Justice, *NCJJ Snapshot* 5[10], 2000).

99. Linda Szymanski, *Sealing/Expungement/Destruction of Juvenile Court Records: When Is Sealing Not Sealing?* (Pittsburgh: National Center for Juvenile Justice, *NCJJ Snapshot* 4[10], 1999).

100. Linda Szymanski, *Law Enforcement, Court Notice to School of Student's Delinquent Act* (Pittsburgh: National Center for Juvenile Justice, *NCJJ Snapshot* 6 [11], 2001).

101. Danielle R. Oddo, "Removing Confidentiality Protections and the Get Tough Rhetoric: What Has Gone Wrong with the Juvenile Justice System." *Boston College Third World Law Journal* 18, 105 (1998): 105–140.

102. Patricia Torbet, Richard Gable, Hunter Hurst, Imogene Montgomery, Linda Szymanski, and Douglas Thomas, *State Responses to Serious and Violent Juvenile Crime* (Washington, DC: Office of Juvenile Justice and Delinquency Prevention, 1996).

103. Clemmens Bartollas, *Juvenile Delinquency,* 6th ed. (Boston: Allyn and Bacon, 2002).

104. Patricia Torbet and Linda Szymanski, *State Legislative Responses to Serious and Violent Juvenile Crime: 1996–1997 Update* (Washington, DC: Office of Juvenile Justice and Delinquency Prevention, 1998).

105. Florida Statute 985.2122: Fingerprinting and Photographing of Juveniles.

106. Torbet and Szymanski, *State Legislative Responses to Serious and Violent Juvenile Crime: 1996–1997 Update.*

107. Richard Willing, "FBI May Collect Juveniles' DNA" (http://usatoday.com/news/washington/2003-11-16-fbi-juvenile-dna_x.htm).

108. Jennifer Graddy, "The Ethical Protocol for Collecting DNA Samples in the Criminal Justice System" (http://www.mobar.org/journal/2003/sepoct/graddy.htm).

109. Graddy, "The Ethical Protocol for Collecting DNA Samples in the Criminal Justice System."

110. Torbet and Szymanski, *State Legislative Responses to Serious and Violent Juvenile Crime: 1996–1997 Update.*

111. *Kirby v. Illinois,* 406 U.S. 682 (1972).

112. *United States v. Wade,* 388 U.S. 218 (1967).

113. *United States v. Ash,* 413 U.S. 300 (1973).

114. *Neil v. Biggers,* 409 U.S. 188 (1973).

115. *Oklahoma Publishing Company v. District Court in and for Oklahoma City,* 480 U.S. 308 (1977).

116. *Smith v. Daily Mail Publishing Company,* 443 U.S. 97 (1979).

117. Torbet and Szymanski, *State Legislative Responses to Serious and Violent Juvenile Crime: 1996–1997 Update.*

118. Torbet and Szymanski, *State Legislative Responses to Serious and Violent Juvenile Crime: 1996–1997 Update.*

CHAPTER 4

1. Melissa Sickmund, *Juveniles in Court* (Washington, DC: Office of Juvenile Justice and Delinquency Prevention, 2003).

2. Carrie Petrucci and H. Ted Rubin, "Juvenile Court." In A. Roberts (ed.), *Juvenile Justice Sourcebook: Past, Present, and Future* (New York: Oxford University Press, 2004), 247–288.

3. Frank Miller, Robert Dawson, George Dix, and Raymond Parnas, *The Juvenile Justice Process: Cases and Materials,* 4th ed. (New York: Foundation, 2000).

4. Barry Feld, *Juvenile Justice Administration in a Nutshell* (St. Paul, MN: Thomson/West, 2003).

5. Anne L. Stahl, *Delinquency Cases in Juvenile Courts, 1999* (Washington, DC: Office of Juvenile Justice and Delinquency Prevention, 2003).

6. Stahl, *Delinquency Cases in Juvenile Courts,* 1999.

7. Stahl, *Delinquency Cases in Juvenile Courts,* 1999.

8. Feld, *Juvenile Justice Administration in a Nutshell.*

9. *Miranda v. Arizona,* 384 U.S. 436 (1966).

10. *White v. Maryland,* 373 U.S. 59 (1963).

11. *United States v. Wade,* 388 U.S. 218 (1967).

12. *Massiah v. United States,* 377 U.S. 201 (1964).

13. *Hamilton v. Alabama,* 368 U.S. 52 (1961).

14. *In re Frank H.,* 337 N.Y.S.2d 118 (1972).

15. *In re Wayne H.,* 596 P.2d 1 (Cal. 1979).

16. Rolando V. del Carmen, Mary Parker, and Frances P. Reddington, *Briefs of Leading Cases in Juvenile Justice* (Cincinnati: Anderson, 1998), 114.

17. *Minnesota v. Murphy,* 465 U.S. 420 (1984).

18. Feld, *Juvenile Justice Administration in a Nutshell.*

19. *State v. McDowell,* 685 P.2d 595 (Wash. 1984).

20. *Blackledge v. Perry,* 417 U.S. 21 (1974).

21. *Bordenkircher v. Hayes,* 434 U.S. 357 (1978).

22. *Washington v. Chatham,* 624 P.2d 1180 (Wash. App. 1981).

23. Del Carmen, Parker, and Reddington, *Briefs of Leading Cases in Juvenile Justice.*

24. *State v. Tracy M.,* 720 P.2d 841 (Wash. Ct. App. 1986).

25. Feld, *Juvenile Justice Administration in a Nutshell.*

26. *State v. Tracy M.*

27. See *State v. W. S.,* 700 P.2d 1192 (Wash. Ct. App. [1985]), and *State v. Chatham,* 624 P.2d 1180 (Wash. Ct. App. [1981]). Refer to Barry C. Feld, *Cases and Materials of Juvenile Justice Administration* (St. Paul, MN: West Group, 2000).

28. Go to http://www.ncjj.org/stateprofiles/profiles and click on the state of Alabama under the NCJJ state profiles.

29. *Gagnon v. Scarpelli,* 411 U.S. 778 (1973).

30. *Morrissey v. Brewer,* 408 U.S. 471 (1972).

31. *In the Matter of Edwin L.,* 671 N.E.2d 1247 (1996).

32. See Miller, Dawson, Dix, and Parnas, *The Juvenile Justice Process,* 316–324.

33. See Miller, Dawson, Dix, and Parnas, *The Juvenile Justice Process,* 316–324.

34. 421 U.S. 517 (1975).

35. Rolando V. del Carmen, *Criminal Procedure: Law and Practice,* 5th ed. (Belmont, CA: Wadsworth, 2001).

36. *State v. Quiroz,* 733 P.2d 963 (Wash. 1987), and see Feld, *Juvenile Justice Administration in a Nutshell.*

37. *In re D. S. S.,* 506 N.W.2d 650 (Mn. Ct. Ap. 1993), and see Feld, *Juvenile Justice Administration in a Nutshell.*

38. Charles Puzzanchera, Anne L. Stahl, Terrence A. Finnegan, Nancy Tierney, and Howard N. Snyder, *Juvenile Court Statistics 1999* (Pittsburgh: National Center for Juvenile Justice, 2003).

39. Ruth Triplett and Laura Myers, "Evaluating Contextual Patters of Delinquency: Gender-Based Differences." *Justice Quarterly* 12 (1995): 59–84.

40. Puzzanchera, Stahl, Finnegan, Tierney, and Snyder, *Juvenile Court Statistics 1999.*

41. Donna Bishop and Charles Frazier, "Race Effects in Juvenile Justice Decision Making: Findings of a Statewide Analysis." *Journal of Criminal Law and Criminology* 86 (1996): 392–414.

42. Puzzanchera, Stahl, Finnegan, Tierney, and Snyder, *Juvenile Court Statistics 1999.*

43. Kenneth Polk, "Juvenile Diversion: A Look at the Record." *Crime and Delinquency* 30 (1984): 648–660.

44. Polk, "Juvenile Diversion: A Look at the Record."

45. Gensheimer and associates, "Diverting Youth from the Juvenile Justice System: A Meta-Analysis of Intervention Efficacy." In S. J. Apter and A. Goldstein (eds.), *Youth Violence: Programs and Prospects* (Elmsford, NY: Pergamon, 1986), 39–57.

46. Polk, "Juvenile Diversion: A Look at the Record." See also A. Binder and G. Geis, "Ad Populum Argumentation in Criminology: Juvenile Diversion as Rhetoric." *Crime and Delinquency* 30 (1984): 624–627.

47. Polk, "Juvenile Diversion: A Look at the Record."

48. Polk, "Juvenile Diversion: A Look at the Record."

CHAPTER 5

1. Edwin Sutherland and Donald R. Cressey, *Principles of Criminology* (Chicago: Lippincott, 1960), 400.

2. Kenneth Wooden, *Weeping in the Playtime of Others: America's Incarcerated Children* (Columbus: Ohio State University Press, 2000).

3. Wooden, *Weeping in the Playtime of Others.*

4. Wooden, *Weeping in the Playtime of Others.*

5. Howard Snyder and Melissa Sickmund, *Juvenile Offenders and Victims: 1999 National Report* (Washington, DC: Office of Juvenile Justice and Delinquency Prevention, 1999).

6. Snyder and Sickmund, *Juvenile Offenders and Victims,* 88.

7. Snyder and Sickmund, *Juvenile Offenders and Victims,* 88.

8. David Rothman, *The Discovery of the Asylum* (Boston: Little, Brown, 1971).

9. Howard Snyder, *Court Careers of Juvenile Offenders* (Washington, DC: Office of Juvenile Justice and Delinquency Prevention, 1988).

10. Thomas Kelly, "Status Offenders Can Be Different: A Comparative Study of Delinquent Careers." *Crime and Delinquency* 29 (1983): 365–380.

11. Solomon Kobrin, Frank Hellum, and John Peterson, "Offense Patterns of Status Offenders." In David Shichor and Delos Kelley (eds.), *Critical*

Issues in Juvenile Delinquency (Lexington, MA: Heath, 1980).

12. Snyder and Sickmund, *Juvenile Offenders and Victims.*

13. *In re Gault,* 387 U.S. 1 (1967).

14. *In re Winship,* 397 U.S. 358 (1970).

15. Robert Coates, Alden Miller, and Lloyd Ohlin, *Diversity in a Youth Correctional System: Handling Delinquents in Massachusetts.* (Cambridge, MA: Ballinger, 1978), 173.

16. Barry Feld, *Juvenile Justice Administration in a Nutshell* (St. Paul, MN: West, 2003).

17. Harry J. Rothgerber Jr., "The Bootstrapping of Status Offenders: A Vicious Practice." *University of Louisville Children Rights Journal* 1 (1991): 1–3.

18. Rothgerber, "The Bootstrapping of Status Offenders."

19. Gwen A. Holden and Robert A. Kapler, "Deinstitutionalizing Status Offenders: A Record of Progress." *Juvenile Justice* 2(2) (Fall/Winter 1995): 3–10.

20. Barry C. Feld, *Cases and Materials on Juvenile Justice Administration* (St. Paul, MN: West Group, 2000), 890.

21. *Parham v. J. R.,* 442 U.S. 584 (1979).

22. Snyder and Sickmund, *Juvenile Offenders and Victims.*

23. Howard Snyder, *Juvenile Arrests 2001* (Washington, DC: Office of Juvenile Justice and Delinquency Prevention, 2003).

24. Charles Puzzanchera, Anne Stahl, Terrence Finnegan, Nancy Tierney, and Howard Snyder, *Juvenile Court Statistics 1999* (Pittsburgh: National Center for Juvenile Justice, 2003).

25. Puzzanchera, Stahl, Finnegan, Tierney, and Snyder, *Juvenile Court Statistics 1999.*

26. Puzzanchera, Stahl, Finnegan, Tierney, and Snyder, *Juvenile Court Statistics 1999.*

27. Puzzanchera, Stahl, Finnegan, Tierney, and Snyder, *Juvenile Court Statistics 1999.*

28. LaMar T. Empey and Mark C. Stafford, *American Delinquency: Its Meaning and Construction,* 3rd ed. (Belmont, CA: Wadsworth, 1991), 62.

29. Richard Wiebush, Raelene Freitag, and Christopher Baird, *Preventing Delinquency Through Improved Child Protection Services* (Washington, DC: Office of Juvenile Justice and Delinquency Prevention, 2001).

30. Barbara Tatem Kelley, Terence P. Thornberry, and Carolyn A. Smith, "In the Wake of Childhood Maltreatment." *Juvenile Justice Bulletin* (Washing-

ton, DC: Office of Juvenile Justice and Delinquency Prevention, 1997), 4.

31. Snyder and Sickmund, *Juvenile Offenders and Victims,* 40.

32. Richard P. Barth, "The Juvenile Court and Dependency Cases." *The Future of Children* 6(3) (1996): 100–110.

33. Snyder and Sickmund, *Juvenile Offenders and Victims.*

34. "Children as Victims." *Juvenile Justice Bulletin* (Washington, DC: Office of Juvenile Justice and Delinquency Prevention, May 2000), 17.

35. "Children as Victims," 17.

36. Barth, "The Juvenile Court and Dependency Cases."

37. David Finkelhor and Richard Ormrod, *Child Abuse Reported to the Police* (Washington, DC: Office of Juvenile Justice and Delinquency Prevention, 2001).

38. Brian J. Ostrom, Neal B. Kauder, and Robert C. LaFountain, *Examining the Work of State Courts, 2001* (Washington, DC: Conference of State Court Administrators, State Justice Institute, Bureau of Justice Statistics, National Center for State Courts' Court Statistics Project, 2002).

39. U.S. Department of Health and Human Services, Administration on Children, Youth and Families, *Child Maltreatment 2001* (Washington, DC: U.S. Government Printing Office, 2003).

40. U.S. Department of Health and Human Services, Administration on Children, Youth and Families, *Child Maltreatment 2001,* 3.

41. U.S. Department of Health and Human Services, Administration on Children, Youth and Families, *Child Maltreatment 2001,* 69.

42. *Santosky v. Kramer,* 455 U.S. 745 (1982).

43. "Children as Victims," 18.

44. David Finkelhor and Richard Ormrod, *Characteristics of Crimes Against Juveniles* (Washington, DC: Office of Juvenile Justice and Delinquency Prevention, 2000).

45. Finkelhor and Ormrod, *Characteristics of Crimes Against Juveniles.*

46. Finkelhor and Ormrod, *Characteristics of Crimes Against Juveniles.*

47. David Finkelhor and David Ormrod, *Reporting Crimes Against Juveniles* (Washington, DC: Office of Juvenile Justice and Delinquency Prevention, 1999).

48. Finkelhor and Ormrod, *Characteristics of Crimes Against Juveniles.*

49. Finkelhor and Ormrod, *Characteristics of Crimes Against Juveniles*.

50. Finkelhor and Ormrod, *Characteristics of Crimes Against Juveniles*.

51. David Finkelhor, Kimberly Mitchell, and Janis Wolak, *Highlights of the Youth Internet Safety Survey* (Washington, DC: Office of Juvenile Justice and Delinquency Prevention, 2001).

CHAPTER 6

1. *Schall v. Martin,* 104 S.Ct. 2403 (1984).

2. Anne Stahl, *Delinquency Cases in Juvenile Courts, 1999* (Washington, DC: Office of Juvenile Justice and Delinquency Prevention, 2003).

3. Charles Puzzanchera, Anne L. Stahl, Terrence A. Finnegan, Nancy Tierney, and Howard N. Snyder, *Juvenile Court Statistics 1999* (Pittsburgh: National Center for Juvenile Justice, 2003), 22–26.

4. *Gerstein v. Pugh,* 420 U.S. 103 (1975).

5. Preston Elrod and R. Scott Ryder, *Juvenile Justice: A Social, Historical, and Legal Perspective* (Gaithersburg, MD: Aspen, 1999).

6. IJA–ABA Juvenile Justice Standards Project, "Standards Relating to Interim Status: The Release, Control and Detention of Accused Juvenile Offenders Between Arrest and Disposition." Institute of Judicial Administration and the American Bar Association (Cambridge, MA: Ballinger, 1980).

7. *Alfredo A. v. Superior Court of Los Angeles County,* 865 P.2d 56 (Cal. 1994), and see also Barry C. Feld, *Juvenile Justice Administration in a Nutshell* (St. Paul, MN: Thomson/West, 2003).

8. *In Re McCall,* 438 N.E.2d 1269 (1982), and see also Feld, *Juvenile Justice Administration in a Nutshell*.

9. See *Schall v. Martin*.

10. See *L.O.W. v. The District Court,* 623 P.2d 1253 (Colo. 1981), and see also Feld, *Juvenile Justice Administration in a Nutshell*.

11. Kathleen Baldi, "The Denial of a State Constitutional Right to Bail in Juvenile Proceedings: The Need for Reassessment in Washington State." *Seattle University Law Review* 19 (1996): 19–60.

12. *Schall v. Martin*.

13. *L. O. W. v. The District Court,* and see also Feld, *Juvenile Justice Administration in a Nutshell*.

14. Elrod and Ryder, *Juvenile Justice*.

15. Howard Snyder and Melissa Sickmund, *Juveniles Offenders and Victims 1999: A National Report* (Washington, DC: Office of Juvenile Justice and Delinquency Prevention, 1999).

16. Robert Taylor, Eric Fritsch, and Tory Caeti, *Juvenile Justice: Policies, Programs, and Practices* (New York: Glencoe–McGraw-Hill, 2002).

17. Stahl, *Delinquency Cases in Juvenile Courts, 1999*.

18. Patrick Griffin, Patricia Torbet, and Linda Szymanski, *Trying Juveniles as Adults in Criminal Court: An Analysis of State Transfer Provisions* (Washington, DC: Office of Juvenile Justice and Delinquency Prevention, 1998), 3.

19. *Kent v. United States,* 383 U.S. 541 (1966).

20. Howard Snyder, Melissa Sickmund, and Eileen Poe-Yamagata, *Juvenile Transfers to Criminal Court in the 1990s: Lessons Learned from Four Studies* (Washington, DC: Office of Juvenile Justice and Delinquency Prevention, 2000), 3–6.

21. Feld, *Juvenile Justice Administration in a Nutshell*.

22. Stahl, *Delinquency Cases in Juvenile Courts, 1999*.

23. See also Patrick Griffin, *Trying and Sentencing Juveniles as Adults: An Analysis of State Transfer and Blended Sentencing Laws* (Pittsburgh: National Center for Juvenile Justice, 2003).

24. Griffin, Torbet, and Szymanski, *Trying Juveniles as Adults in Criminal Court*.

25. Griffin, Torbet, and Szymanski, *Trying Juveniles as Adults in Criminal Court*.

26. Snyder, Sickmund, and Poe-Yamagata, *Juvenile Transfers to Criminal Court in the 1990s*.

27. Snyder, Sickmund, and Poe-Yamagata, *Juvenile Transfers to Criminal Court in the 1990s*.

28. Griffin, Torbet, and Szymanski, *Trying Juveniles as Adults in Criminal Court,* 10.

29. Griffin, Torbet, and Szymanski, *Trying Juveniles as Adults in Criminal Court,* 10.

30. Griffin, Torbet, and Szymanski, *Trying Juveniles as Adults in Criminal Court*. See also Griffin, *Trying and Sentencing Juveniles as Adults*.

31. Charles M. Puzzanchera, *Delinquency Cases Waived to Criminal Court, 1990–1999* (Washington, DC: Office of Juvenile Justice and Delinquency Prevention, 2003).

32. See also Taylor, Fritsch, and Caeti, *Juvenile Justice: Policies, Programs, and Practices,* for an excellent synopsis of these and additional issues with waiver outcomes.

33. Melissa Sickmund, *Juveniles in Court* (Washington, DC: Office of Juvenile Justice and Delinquency Prevention, 2003). See also Puzzanchera, *Delinquency Cases Waived to Criminal Court, 1990–1999*.

34. J. Howell, "Juvenile Transfers to the Criminal Justice System: State of the Art." *Law & Policy* 18 (1996): 17–60.

35. M. Bortner, "Traditional Rhetoric, Organizational Realities: Remand of Juveniles to Adult Court." *Crime and Delinquency* 32 (1986): 53–73.

36. D. Hamparian, L. Estep, S. Muntean, R. Priestino, R. Swisher, P. Wallace, and J. White, *Major Issues in Juvenile Justice Information and Training Youth in Adult Courts—Between Two Worlds* (Washington, DC: Office of Juvenile Justice and Delinquency Prevention, 1982).

37. B. Feld, "The Juvenile Court Meets the Principle of the Offense: Legislative Changes in Juvenile Waiver Statutes." *Journal of Criminal Law and Criminology* 78 (1987): 471–533.

38. Compare with Melissa Sickmund, *Juveniles in Court*, 28.

39. C. Rudman, E. Hartstone, J. Fagan, and M. Moore, "Violent Youth in Adult Court: Process and Punishment." *Crime and Delinquency* 32 (1986): 75–96.

40. J. Fagan, *The Comparative Impacts of Juvenile and Criminal Court Sanctions on Adolescent Offenders* (Washington, DC: U.S. Department of Justice, Office of Justice Programs, National Institute of Justice, 1991).

41. Megan C. Kurlycheck and Brian D. Johnson, "The Juvenile Penalty: A Comparison of Juvenile and Young Adult Sentencing Outcomes in Criminal Court." *Criminology* 42(2) (2004): 485–517.

42. See, for example, Donna Bishop and Charles Frazier, "Consequences of Transfer." In J. Fagan and F. Zimring (eds.), *The Changing Borders of Juvenile Justice: Transfer of Adolescents to the Criminal Court* (Chicago: University of Chicago Press, 2000), 207–276.

CHAPTER 7

1. J. W. Peltason and Sue Davis, *Understanding the Constitution* (Orlando: Harcourt, 2000), 215–216.

2. H. J. Spaeth, *An Introduction to Supreme Court Decision Making* (San Francisco: Chandler, 1972), 71.

3. John Scalia, *Juvenile Delinquents in the Federal Criminal Justice System* (Washington, DC: U.S. Department of Justice, 1997).

4. Scalia, *Juvenile Delinquents in the Federal Criminal Justice System.*

5. Scalia, *Juvenile Delinquents in the Federal Criminal Justice System*, 1.

6. Scalia, *Juvenile Delinquents in the Federal Criminal Justice System*, 1.

7. 18 U.S.C. Section 5032.

8. Scalia, *Juvenile Delinquents in the Federal Criminal Justice System.*

9. Scalia, *Juvenile Delinquents in the Federal Criminal Justice System*, 2.

10. Scalia, *Juvenile Delinquents in the Federal Criminal Justice System.*

11. Carrie Petrucci and H. Ted Rubin, "Juvenile Court." In A. Roberts (ed.), *Juvenile Justice Sourcebook: Past, Present, and Future* (New York: Oxford University Press, 2004), 247–288.

12. David Rothman, *The Discovery of the Asylum* (Boston: Little, Brown, 1971).

13. Sanford J. Fox, "The Early History of the Court." *The Future of Children* 6(3) (1996): 30.

14. Jeffrey A. Butts and Ojmarrh Mitchell, "Brick by Brick: Dismantling the Border Between Juvenile and Adult Justice." In C. Friel (ed.), *Boundary Changes in Criminal Justice Organizations*, Vol. 2 (Washington, DC: U.S. Department of Justice, 2000), 167–213.

15. *Ex parte Crouse*, 4 Whart. 9 (Pa. 1838).

16. *Ex parte Crouse*, 4 Whart. 9, 11 (Pa. 1838).

17. *O'Connell v. Turner*, 55 Ill. 280 (1870).

18. Fox, "The Early History of the Court," 32.

19. Fox, "The Early History of the Court."

20. David Rothman, *Conscience and Convenience: The Asylum and Its Alternatives in Progressive America* (Boston: Little, Brown, 1980).

21. Theodore Ferdinand, "History Overtakes the Juvenile Justice System." *Crime and Delinquency* 37(2) (1991): 204–224.

22. Rothman, *Conscience and Convenience.*

23. Fox, "The Early History of the Court," 33.

24. Ellen Ryerson, *The Best-Laid Plans: America's Juvenile Court Experience* (New York: Hill and Wang, 1978).

25. Anthony M. Platt, *The Child-Savers: The Invention of Delinquency* (Chicago: University of Chicago Press, 1977), 75.

26. Anthony M. Platt, "The Child-Saving Movement and the Origins of the Juvenile Justice System." In Paul Sharp and Barry Hancock (eds.), *Juvenile Delinquency: Historical, Theoretical and Societal Reactions to Youth* (Englewood Cliffs, NJ: Prentice Hall, 1995), 13–27.

27. Platt, *The Child-Savers*, 77.

28. Platt, "The Child-Saving Movement," 17.

29. Platt, "The Child-Saving Movement," 15.

30. Rothman, *Conscience and Convenience*, 215.

31. Rothman, *Conscience and Convenience*, 215.

32. "The Juvenile Court: One Hundred Years in the Making" (www.buildingblocksforyouth.org/juvenile_court.htm).

33. Preston Elrod and R. Scott Ryder, *Juvenile Justice: A Social, Historical, and Legal Perspective* (Gaithersburg, MD: Aspect, 1999).

34. John C. Watkins, Jr., *The Juvenile Justice Century* (Durham, NC: Carolina Academic Press, 1998), 47.

35. Butts and Mitchell, "Brick by Brick," 167–213.

36. Elrod and Ryder, *Juvenile Justice.*

37. H. Ted Rubin, "The Nature of the Court Today." *The Future of Children* 6(3) (1996), 43.

38. Rubin, "The Nature of the Court Today."

39. Rubin, "The Nature of the Court Today."

40. Rubin, "The Nature of the Court Today," 42.

41. Leonard P. Edwards, "The Future of the Juvenile Court: Promising New Directions." *The Future of Children* 6(3) (1996): 143.

42. Edwards, "The Future of the Juvenile Court," 143.

43. Edwards, "The Future of the Juvenile Court."

44. Edwards, "The Future of the Juvenile Court."

45. Edwards, "The Future of the Juvenile Court."

46. B. Ostrom, N. Kauder, and R. LaFountain, *Examining the Work of State Courts* (Williamsburg, VA: National Center for State Courts, 2001).

47. Anne L. Stahl, *Delinquency Cases in Juvenile Courts, 1999* (Washington, DC: Office of Juvenile Justice and Delinquency Prevention, 2003).

48. Rubin, "The Nature of the Court Today."

49. National Council on Crime and Delinquency, *The Cook County Family (Juvenile) Court and Arthur J. Andy Home* (San Francisco: National Council on Crime and Delinquency, 1963).

50. D. Steelman, T. H. Rubin, and J. M. Arnold, *Circuit Court of Cook County, Illinois: Juvenile Division Judge Workloads and Judgeship Needs: From the Cook County Circuit Court Improvement Project* (Cook County, IL: National Council for State Courts, 1993).

51. Jeffrey A. Butts, *Delays in Juvenile Court Processing of Delinquency Cases* (Washington, DC: Office of Juvenile Justice and Delinquency Prevention, 1997).

52. Butts, *Delays in Juvenile Court Processing of Delinquency Cases.*

53. Butts, *Delays in Juvenile Court Processing of Delinquency Cases.*

54. Jeffrey Butts and Janeen Buck, *Teen Courts: A Focus on Research* (Washington, DC: Office of Juvenile Justice and Delinquency Prevention, 2000).

55. Jeffrey Butts, Dean Hoffman, and Janeen Buck, *Teen Courts in the United States: A Profile of Current Programs* (Washington, DC: Office of Juvenile Justice and Delinquency Prevention, 1999).

56. Butts, Hoffman, and Buck, *Teen Courts in the United States.*

57. Butts, Hoffman, and Buck, *Teen Courts in the United States,* 1.

58. National Drug Court Institute and National Council of Juvenile and Family Court Judges, *Juvenile Drug Courts: Strategies in Practice* (Washington, DC: Bureau of Justice Assistance, 2003).

59. National Drug Court Institute and National Council of Juvenile and Family Court Judges, *Juvenile Drug Courts.*

60. Marilyn Robbers, Jennifer Brophy, and Caroline Cooper, *The Juvenile Drug Court Movement* (Washington, DC: Office of Juvenile Justice and Delinquency Prevention, 1997), 1.

61. Robbers, Brophy, and Cooper, *The Juvenile Drug Court Movement,* 1.

62. Elrod and Ryder, *Juvenile Justice.*

63. Elrod and Ryder, *Juvenile Justice.*

64. Elrod and Ryder, *Juvenile Justice.*

65. Elrod and Ryder, *Juvenile Justice.*

66. Rubin, "The Nature of the Court Today."

67. *In re Gault,* 387 U.S. 1 (1967).

68. Barry C. Feld, "Criminalizing the American Juvenile Court." In Michael Tonry (ed.), *Crime and Justice: Annual Review of Research* (Chicago: University of Chicago Press, 1993), 197–280.

69. Tory Caeti and Eric Fritsch, "Abolishing the Juvenile Justice System." In Barbara Sims and Pamela Preston (eds.), *Handbook of Juvenile Justice: Theory and Practice* (New York: Marcel Dekker, forthcoming).

70. Barry C. Feld, "Juvenile (in) Justice and the Criminal Court Alternative." *Crime and Delinquency* 39(3) (1993): 403–424.

71. Feld, "Criminalizing the American Juvenile Court," 264.

72. Caeti and Fritsch, "Abolishing the Juvenile Justice System."

73. Caeti and Fritsch, "Abolishing the Juvenile Justice System."

74. Caeti and Fritsch, "Abolishing the Juvenile Justice System."

CHAPTER 8

1. As quoted in Robert E. Shepherd, Jr., "The Juvenile Court at 100 Years: A Look Back." In *Juvenile Justice: An Evolving Juvenile Court, 100th*

Anniversary of the Juvenile Court, 1899–1999 (Washington, DC: National Center for Juvenile Justice, Office of Juvenile Justice and Delinquency Prevention), 16.

2. As quoted in Shepherd, Jr., "The Juvenile Court at 100 Years."

3. As quoted in Shepherd, Jr., "The Juvenile Court at 100 Years."

4. Parts of this section are adapted from Chapter 2 of Rolando V. del Carmen, *Criminal Procedure: Law and Practice,* 5th ed. (Belmont, CA: Wadsworth, 2001).

5. Wayne R. LaFave, Jerold H. Israel, and Nancy J. King, *Criminal Procedure,* 3rd ed. (St. Paul, MN: West Group, 2000), 956.

6. Del Carmen, *Criminal Procedure,* 67.

7. Parts of this section are adapted from Chapter 12 of Rolando V. del Carmen, *Criminal Procedure,* 5th ed. (Belmont, CA: Wadsworth, 2001).

8. *In re Gault,* 387 U.S. 1 (1967).

9. Barry Feld, "*In re Gault* Revisited: A Cross-State Comparison of the Right to Counsel in Juvenile Court." *Crime and Delinquency* 34 (1998).

10. Barry Feld, "The Right to Counsel in Juvenile Court: An Empirical Study of When Lawyers Appear and the Difference They Make." *Journal of Criminal Law and Criminology* 79 (1989).

11. Tory Caeti, Craig Hemmens, and Velmer Burton, "Juvenile Right to Counsel: A National Comparison of State Legal Codes." *American Journal of Criminal Law* 23 (1996).

12. Judith B. Jones, "Access to Counsel." *Juvenile Justice Bulletin* (OJJDP) (June 2004): 2.

13. Jones, "Access to Counsel," 5.

14. See, for example, Barry Feld, "The Right to Counsel in Juvenile Court."

15. Robert Taylor, Eric Fritsch, and Tory Caeti, *Juvenile Justice: Policies, Programs, and Practices* (New York: Glencoe–McGraw-Hill, 2002), 234.

16. Jones, "Access to Counsel," 2.

17. *Fare v. Michael C.,* 442 U.S. 707 (1979).

18. *American Bar Association Standards,* "Providing Defense Services," Sec. 6.

19. *American Bar Association Standards,* "Providing Defense Services," Sec. 6.

20. *Griffin v. California,* 380 U.S. 609 (1965).

21. *Breed v. Jones,* 421 U.S. 517 (1975).

22. *In re Winship,* 397 U.S. 358 (1970).

23. *Moore v. United States,* 345 F.2d 97 DC Cir. (1965).

24. *McKeiver v. Pennsylvania,* 403 U.S. 528 (1971).

25. *Juvenile Justice Reform Initiatives in the States: 1994–1996.* OJJDP: http://pjjdp.ncjrs.org/pubs/reform/ch2_i.html.

26. *Mapp v. Ohio,* 367 U.S. 643 (1967).

CHAPTER 9

1. Judith B. Jones, "Access to Counsel." *Juvenile Justice Bulletin* (OJJDP) (June 2004): 5.

2. Bureau of Justice Statistics, *Report to the Nation on Crime and Justice,* 2nd ed. (Washington, DC: U.S. Government Printing Office, 1988), 90.

3. Howard N. Snyder and Melissa Sickmund, *Juvenile Offenders and Victims: 1999 National Report* (Washington, DC: Office of Juvenile Justice and Delinquency Prevention, 1999), 3.

4. *Sentencing Authority: Juvenile Justice Reform Initiatives in the States, 1994–1996* (http://ojjdp.ncjrs.org/pubs/reform/ch2_html).

5. Barry C. Feld, *Cases and Materials on Juvenile Justice Administration* (St. Paul, MN: West Group, 2000), 774.

6. Charles Puzzanchera, Anne L. Stahl, Terrence A. Finnegan, Nancy Tierney, and Howard N. Snyder, *Juvenile Court Statistics 1999* (Pittsburgh, PA: National Center for Juvenile Justice, 2003).

7. Melissa Sickmund, "Juveniles in Court." *National Report Series Bulletin* (OJJDP) (June 2003): 30.

8. *The Future of Children* 6(3) (Winter 1996) (The David and Lucile Packard Foundation): 15.

9. Paul Bergman and Sara J. Berman-Barrett, *The Criminal Law Handbook,* 4th ed. (Berkeley, CA: Nolo, 2002), 25–32.

10. Feld, *Cases and Materials on Juvenile Justice Administration,* 3–4.

11. Patrick Griffin and Patricia Torbet (eds.), *Deskbook Guide to Good Juvenile Probation Practice* (Pittsburgh: National Center for Juvenile Justice, 2002), 37.

12. *State Ex Rel. D. D. H. v. Dostert* (165 W.Va. 1980), as cited in Feld, *Cases and Materials on Juvenile Justice Administration,* 730.

13. Melissa Sickmund, "Juvenile Offenders and Victims." *National Report Series* (2003) (http://www.ncjrs.org/htm/ojjdp/195420/contents/html).

14. Bureau of Justice Statistics, *Report to the Nation on Crime and Justice,* 187.

15. Bureau of Justice Statistics, *Report to the Nation on Crime and Justice,* 208.

16. Bureau of Justice Statistics, *Report to the Nation on Crime and Justice,* 191.

17. Feld, *Cases and Materials on Juvenile Justice Administration,* 83.

18. Puzzanchera, Stahl, Finnegan, Tierney, and Snyder, *Juvenile Court Statistics 1999.*

19. Feld, *Cases and Materials on Juvenile Justice Administration,* 771.

20. *In re Gardini,* 243 Pa. Super. 338 (1976).

21. *State v. Kristopher G.,* 201 W.Va. 703 (W.Va. Ct. App. 1997).

22. *State v. Farmbrough,* 66 Wash. App. 223 (Wa. Ct. App. 1992).

23. *In Re Jason W.,* 94 Md. App. 731 (1993).

24. *People v. Lee,* 4 Cal. Rptr. 3d 642 (Cal. App. 6 Dist. 2003).

25. *Thompson v. Oklahoma,* 487 U.S. 815 (1988).

26. *Stanford v. Kentucky,* 492 U.S. 361 (1989).

27. Feld, *Cases and Materials on Juvenile Justice Administration,* 7.

28. Jeffrey A. Butts and Ojmarrh Mitchell, "Brick by Brick: Dismantling the Border Between Juvenile and Adult Justice." *Criminal Justice* 2 (2000): 187.

29. Bureau of Justice Statistics, *Report to the Nation on Crime and Justice,* 108.

30. Samuel M. Davis, *Rights of Juveniles: The Juvenile Justice System,* 2nd ed. (St. Paul, MN: West Group, 1980), 7.

31. *J. R. W. v. State,* 879 S.W.2d 254 (Tex. App. 1994).

32. *Juvenile Justice Sentencing Alternatives in the States: 1994–1996* (http://ojjdp.ncjrs.org/pubs/reform/ch2_k.html).

33. *In Re Interest of Torrey B.,* 6 Neb. App. 658 (Neb. Ct. App. 1998).

34. *D. H. v. State of Indiana,* 688 N.E.2d 221 (Ind. Ct. App. 1997).

35. *In the Matter of Peter B.,* 84 Cal. App. 3d 583 (1978).

36. "Three Strikes and You're Out: A Review of State Legislation." *Research in Brief* (National Institute of Corrections) (September 1997): 1.

37. *Ewing and Lockyers,* 71 U.S.L.W. 4161 (2003).

38. *Ewing v. California,* 71 U.S.L.W. 4167 (2003).

39. *People v. Lee,* 4 Cal. Rptr. 3rd 642 (2003).

40. *People v. Smith,* Slip copy, Cal App. 3rd Dist. (2003).

41. *In re Gault,* 387 U.S. 1 (1967).

42. *Abernathy v. United States,* F.2d 288 (5th Cir. 1969).

43. Bureau of Justice Statistics, *Report to the Nation on Crime and Justice,* 7–36.

44. James J. Gobert and Neil P. Cohen, *The Law of Probation and Parole* (New York: Clark Boardman Callaghan, 1983), 55.

45. Bureau of Justice Statistics, *Report to the Nation on Crime and Justice,* 192.

46. Bureau of Justice Statistics, *Report to the Nation on Crime and Justice,* 143.

47. Paul F. Cromwell, Rolando V. del Carmen, and Leanne F. Alarid, *Community-Based Corrections,* 5th ed. (Belmont, CA: Wadsworth, 2002), 226.

48. Cromwell, del Carmen, and Alarid, *Community-Based Corrections.*

49. Rolando V. del Carmen, *Criminal Procedure: Law and Practice,* 6th ed. (Belmont, CA: Wadsworth, 2004), 55.

50. Del Carmen, *Criminal Procedure,* 55.

51. *Juvenile Probation: The Workhorse of the Juvenile Justice System* (Washington, DC: National Center for Juvenile Justice, OJJDP, 1996), 8–9.

52. *Balanced and Restorative Justice Program Summary* (Washington, DC: National Center for Juvenile Justice, OJJDP), 7.

53. Adapted from H. Zehr, *Changing Lenses: A New Focus for Crime and Justice* (Scottsdale, PA: Herald, 1990), as featured in *Balanced and Restorative Justice Program Summary,* 7.

CHAPTER 10

1. Some of the materials in this chapter are adapted from Chapter 14 of Paul F. Cromwell, Rolando V. del Carmen, and Leanne F. Alarid, *Community-Based Corrections,* 5th ed. (Belmont, CA: West/Wadsworth, 2001).

2. Charles Puzzanchera, Anne L. Stahl, Terrence A. Finnegan, Nancy Tierney, and Howard N. Snyder, *Juvenile Court Statistics 1999* (Pittsburgh: National Center for Juvenile Justice, 2003).

3. Patrick Griffin and Patricia Torbet (eds.), *Desktop Guide to Good Juvenile Probation Practice* (Pittsburgh: National Center for Juvenile Justice, 2002), 6 (hereinafter referred to as *Desktop Guide* 2002).

4. *Desktop Guide* 2002, 6.

5. *Desktop Guide* 2002, 7.

6. *Desktop Guide* 2002, 9.

7. Melissa Sickmund, "Juveniles in Court." *Juvenile Offenders and Victims: National Report Series Bulletin* (June 2003): 23.

8. Frank W. Miller, Robert O. Dawson, George E. Dix, and Raymond I. Parnas, *The Juvenile Justice Process: Cases and Materials* (New York: Foundation, 2000), 741.

9. *In Re Frank V.,* 233 Cal. App. 3d 1232 (Cal. Ct. App. 1991).

10. *In Re John G.,* 191 Ariz. 205 (Ariz. Ct. App. 1998)

11. *Commonwealth v. Rames,* 573 A.2d 1027 (Ariz. Super Ct. 1990).

12. *In the Interest of M. W.,* Supreme Court of Pennsylvania, 1999 W.L. 111370 (1999).

13. *In the Interest of Johnnie F.,* 313 S.C. 5331 (1994).

14. *In the Matter of Appeal in Maricopa County, Juvenile Action No. JV–508801,* 183 Ariz. 175 (Ariz. App. 1995).

15. *State v. Kristopher G.,* 201 W.Va. 703 (1997).

16. Juvenile Probation Officer Initiative Working Group, *Desktop Guide to Good Juvenile Probation Practice* (Washington, DC: National Center for Juvenile Justice, Office of Juvenile Justice and Delinquency Prevention, 1993), 32 (hereinafter referred to as *Desktop Guide* 1993).

17. *Desktop Guide* 1993, 70.

18. Cindy S. Lederman, "The Juvenile Court: Putting Research to Work for Prevention." In *Juvenile Justice: An Evolving Juvenile Court, 100th Anniversary of the Juvenile Court 1899–1999* (Washington, DC: National Center for Juvenile Justice, Office of Juvenile Justice and Delinquency Prevention), 24.

19. *Desktop Guide* 2002, 32.

20. *Desktop Guide* 2002, 32.

21. *Desktop Guide* 1993, 79.

22. *Desktop Guide* 1993, 44.

23. *Desktop Guide* 1993, 44.

24. *Juvenile Probation: The Workhorse of the Juvenile Justice System* (Washington, DC: National Center for Juvenile Justice, Office of Juvenile Justice and Delinquency Prevention, 1996), 4.

25. *Juvenile Probation: The Workhorse of the Juvenile Justice System,* 2–3.

26. *Desktop Guide* 2002, 137.

27. Indiana Juvenile Code, Title 31, Family Law and Juvenile Law.

28. *Desktop Guide* 1993, 120.

29. *Desktop Guide* 1993, 119–120.

30. *Desktop Guide* 1993, 119–120.

31. *Fare v. Michael C.,* 442 U.S. 707 (1979).

32. Ronald P. Corbett, Jr., "Juvenile Probation on the Eve of the Next Millennium." *Annual Editions, Criminal Justice 2002–2003* (New York: McGraw-Hill–Dushkin, 2002), 156.

33. *Desktop Guide* 1993, 87.

34. *Desktop Guide* 1993, 87.

35. *Desktop Guide* 2002, 92.

36. *Desktop Guide* 2002, 92.

37. *Desktop Guide* 2002, 92.

38. *Desktop Guide* 2002, 92.

39. Rolando V. del Carmen, Wendy Hume, Elmer Polk, Frances Reddington, and Betsy Witt, *Texas Juvenile Law and Practice* (Sam Houston State University, Criminal Justice Center, 1991), 180.

40. Clare A. Cripe, *Legal Aspects of Corrections Management* (Gaithersburg, MD: Aspen, 1997), 371.

41. *Boot Camps for Juvenile Offenders: A Program Summary* (Washington, DC: Office of Juvenile Justice and Delinquency Prevention, 1997), 3.

42. *New York Times* (19 Dec. 1999): 42.

43. *New York Times* (19 Dec. 1999): 42.

44. *New York Times* (19 Dec. 1999): 42.

45. *New York Times* (19 Dec. 1999): 42.

46. *Griffin v. Wisconsin,* 483 U.S. 868 (1987).

47. *United States v. Knights,* 534 U.S. 112 (2001).

48. *In Re Tyrell J.,* 876 P.2d 519 (Cal. 1994).

49. *People v. Lilientha,* 22 Cal. 3d 89 (1978).

50. *People v. Lampitok, III.* No. 93699 (9/18/03).

51. *United States v. Giannetta,* 909 F.2d 571 (1st Cir. 1990).

52. *United States v. David,* 932 F.2d 752 (9th Cir. 1991).

53. *Miranda v. Arizona,* 384 U.S. 436 (1966).

54. *Minnesota v. Murphy,* 465 U.S. 420 (1984).

55. Derek Paulsen and Rolando V. del Carmen, "Legal Issues in Police–Corrections Partnerships: Can the Police and Corrections Officers Work Together Without Violating Offenders' Constitutional Rights." *Criminal Law Bulletin,* (November–December 2000): 493–494.

56. Paulsen and del Carmen, "Legal Issues in Police–Corrections Partnerships," 493–494.

57. Paulsen and del Carmen, "Legal Issues in Police–Corrections Partnerships," 507.

58. *Vernonia School District 47J v. Action,* 515 U.S. 646 (1995).

59. *Board of Education of Independent School District v. Earls,* 536 U.S. 822 (2003).

60. *Bykosky v. Borough of Middleton,* 410 F. Supp. 1242 (M.D. Pa. 1975).

61. *People in Interest of J. M.,* 768 P.2d 219 (Colo. 1989).

62. *Quib v. Strauss,* 11 F.3d 488 (5th Cir. 1993).

63. *Brown v. Ashton,* 611 A.2d 599 (Md. App. 1992).

64. *City of Maquoketa v. Russell,* 484 N.W.2d 179 (Iowa 1992).

65. *Johnson v. City of Apelousas,* 658 F.2d 1065 (5th Cir. 1981).

66. Howard N. Snyder and Melissa Sickmund, *Juvenile Offenders and Victims: 1999 National Report* (Wash-

ington, DC: Office of Juvenile Justice and Delinquency Prevention, 1999), 101.

67. Snyder and Sickmund, *Juvenile Offenders and Victims,* 101.

68. *Davis v. Alaska,* 415 U.S. 308 (1974).

69. *Desktop Guide* 1993, 19.

70. *Morrissey v. Brewer,* 408 U.S. 471 (1972).

71. *Gagnon v. Scarpelli,* 411 U.S. 778 (1973).

72. *Pennsylvania Board of Probation and Parole v. Scott,* 524 U.S. 357 (1998).

73. *Desktop Guide* 1993, 177.

CHAPTER 11

1. Tory Caeti, Craig Hemmens, Francis T. Cullen, and Velmer S. Burton, "Management of Juvenile Correctional Facilities." *Prison Journal* 4 (2003).

2. David Rothman, *The Discovery of the Asylum* (Boston: Little, Brown, 1971).

3. Rothman, *The Discovery of the Asylum.*

4. Rothman, *The Discovery of the Asylum.*

5. Rothman, *The Discovery of the Asylum.*

6. Rothman, *The Discovery of the Asylum,* 210.

7. Rothman, *The Discovery of the Asylum.*

8. Rothman, *The Discovery of the Asylum.*

9. Kenneth Wooden, *Weeping in the Playtime of Others: America's Incarcerated Children,* 2nd ed. (Columbus: Ohio State University Press, 2000), 39.

10. Clemens Bartollas, *Juvenile Delinquency,* 6th ed. (Boston: Allyn and Bacon, 2003).

11. Rothman, *The Discovery of the Asylum.*

12. David Rothman, *Conscience and Convenience* (Boston: Little, Brown, 1980).

13. Steven Schlossman, "Delinquent Children: The Juvenile Reform School." In Norval Morris and David Rothman (eds.), *The Oxford History of the Prison* (New York: Oxford University Press, 1995).

14. Massachusetts Department of Youth Services (http://www.state.ma.us/dys/history.html).

15. Schlossman, "Delinquent Children," 373.

16. Rothman, *Conscience and Convenience,* 262–263.

17. Hastings Hart, *Preventative Treatment of Neglected Children* (New York: Russell Sage, 1910).

18. Rothman, *Conscience and Convenience,* 263.

19. Schlossman, "Delinquent Children."

20. Rothman, *Conscience and Convenience.*

21. LaMar T. Empey and Mark C. Stafford, *American Delinquency: Its Meaning and Construction,* 3rd ed. (Belmont, CA: Wadsworth, 1991).

22. Rothman, *Conscience and Convenience.*

23. Rothman, *Conscience and Convenience.*

24. Melissa Sickmund, *Juveniles in Corrections* (Washington, DC: Office of Juvenile Justice and Delinquency Prevention, 2004).

25. James Austin, Kelly Johnson, and Maria Gregoriou, *Juveniles in Adult Prisons and Jails: A National Assessment.* Institute on Crime, Justice, and Corrections at the George Washington University and National Council on Crime and Delinquency (Washington, DC: U.S. Department of Justice, 2000).

26. Howard Snyder and Melissa Sickmund, *Juvenile Offenders and Victims: 1999 National Report* (Washington, DC: Office of Juvenile Justice and Delinquency Prevention, 1999).

27. "Inventory of Mental Health Services in Juvenile Justice Facilities," 1998 (http://www.mentalhealth.org/publications/allpubs/SMA01-3537/TableC1. asp).

28. Melissa Sickmund, *Census of Juveniles in Residential Placement 1997* (Pittsburgh: National Center for Juvenile Justice, 2000). For national lengths of stay in detention, see also Melissa Sickmund, Howard Snyder, and Eileen Poe-Yamagata, *Juvenile Offenders and Victims: 1997 Update on Violations* (Washington, DC: Office of Juvenile Justice and Delinquency Prevention, 1999).

29. Dale G. Parent, Valerie Leiter, Stephen Kennedy, Lisa Livens, Daniel Wentworth, and Sarah Wilcox, *Conditions of Confinement: Juvenile Detention and Corrections Facilities* (Washington, DC: U.S. Department of Justice, Office of Juvenile Justice and Delinquency Prevention, 1994).

30. Sickmund, *Census of Juveniles in Residential Placement 1997.* For national lengths of stay in detention, see also Sickmund, Snyder, and Poe-Yamagata, *Juvenile Offenders and Victims.*

31. Parent et al., *Conditions of Confinement.*

32. Randall G. Shelden, *Detention Diversion Advocacy: An Evaluation* (Washington, DC: U.S. Department of Justice, Office of Juvenile Justice and Delinquency Prevention, 1999).

33. Shelden, *Detention Diversion Advocacy.*

34. Parent et al., *Conditions of Confinement.*

35. Shelden, *Detention Diversion Advocacy.*

36. Shelden, *Detention Diversion Advocacy.*

37. www.tyc.state.tx.us/programs/marlin/index.html.

38. Parent et al., *Conditions of Confinement.*

39. http://www.in.gov/indcorrection/facilities.html#juvenile.

40. http://www.djj.state.va.us/programs_and_facilities/rdc-in_depth.htm.

41. Linda A. Teplin, *Assessing Alcohol, Drug, and Mental Disorders in Juvenile Detainees* (Washington, DC: Office of Juvenile Justice and Delinquency Prevention, 2001).

42. Teplin, *Assessing Alcohol, Drug, and Mental Disorders in Juvenile Detainees.*

43. Snyder and Sickmund, *Juvenile Offenders and Victims.*

44. Melissa Sickmund, *Juvenile Offenders in Residential Placement: 1997–1999* (Washington, DC: Office of Juvenile Justice and Delinquency Prevention, 2002).

45. Melissa Sickmund, *Juveniles in Corrections* (Washington, DC: Office of Juvenile Justice and Delinquency Prevention, 2004).

46. Sickmund, *Juvenile Offenders in Residential Placement.*

47. Parent et al., *Conditions of Confinement.*

48. Snyder and Sickmund, *Juvenile Offenders and Victims.*

49. *OJJDP Statistical Briefing Book,* October 30, 2002 (http://www.ojjdp.ncjrs.org/ojstatbb/qa334.html).

50. Parent et al., *Conditions of Confinement.*

51. http://www.tyc.state.tx.us/programs/special_treat.html.

52. Caeti, Hemmens, Cullen, and Burton, "Management of Juvenile Correctional Facilities."

53. Chad Trulson, James Marquart, Janet Mullings, and Tory Caeti, "Escape from the Deep End: Towards an Understanding of State Delinquents, Persistence, and the Transition to Young Adulthood." Unpublished manuscript, 2004.

54. Chad Trulson and Ruth Triplett, "School-Based Juvenile Boot Camps: Evaluating Specialized Treatment and Rehabilitation (STAR)." *Journal for Juvenile Justice and Detention Services* 14(1) (1999): 19–45.

55. Dale Parent, *Shock Incarceration: An Overview of Existing Programs* (Washington, DC: U.S. Department of Justice, 1989).

56. Parent, *Shock Incarceration.*

57. Parent, *Shock Incarceration.*

58. Doris MacKenzie and Andre Rosay, "Correctional Boot Camps for Juveniles." In *Juvenile and Adult Boot Camps* (Laurel, MD: American Correctional Association, 1996), 93–119.

59. Roberta Cronin, *Boot Camps for Adult and Juvenile Offenders: Overview and Update* (Washington, DC: U.S. Department of Justice, 1994).

60. Cronin, *Boot Camps for Adult and Juvenile Offenders.*

61. Blair Borque, Roberta Cronin, Frank Pearson, Daniel Felker, Mei Han, and Sarah Hill, *Boot Camps for Juvenile Offenders: An Implementation Evaluation of Three Demonstration Programs* (Washington, DC: U.S. Department of Justice, 1996).

62. Michael Peters, David Thomas, and Christopher Zamberlan, *Boot Camps for Juvenile Offenders* (Washington, DC: Office of Juvenile Justice and Delinquency Prevention, 1997).

63. California Department of the Youth Authority, *LEAD: A Boot Camp and Intensive Parole Program: An Impact Evaluation: Second Year Findings* (Sacramento, CA: California Department of the Youth Authority, 1996).

64. Florida Department of Juvenile Justice, *Bay County Sheriff's Office Juvenile Boot Camp: A Follow-Up Study of the First Seven Platoons.* Bureau of Data and Research (Tallahassee, FL: Florida Department of Juvenile Justice, 1997).

65. Borque et al., *Boot Camps for Juvenile Offenders.*

66. Kent Black, "Camp Fear." *Maxim* (November 2001): 162–172.

67. See also ABC News (http://abcnews.go.com/section/us/DailyNews/bootcamps010702.html).

68. Harvey Rice, "12-Year-Old Alleges Boot Camp Beating." *Houston Chronicle* (15 Mar. 2001): 27A.

69. Parent et al., *Conditions of Confinement.*

70. Parent et al., *Conditions of Confinement.*

71. www.tyc.state.tx.us: link to "institutions" and "McFadden Ranch."

72. www.dpw.state.pa.us/ocyf/ocyfYfc2.asp.

73. http://www.nal.usda.gov/pavnet/yf/yfflorid.htm.

74. Snyder and Sickmund, *Juvenile Offenders and Victims.*

75. James Austin, Kelly Dedel Johnson, and Maria Gregoriou, *Juveniles in Adult Prisons and Jails: A National Assessment* (Washington, DC: Bureau of Justice Assistance, 2000), 37.

76. Austin, Dedel Johnson, and Gregoriou, *Juveniles in Adult Prisons and Jails,* 38.

77. Kevin Strom, *Profile of State Prisoners Under Age 18, 1985–1997* (Washington, DC: U.S. Department of Justice, 2000).

78. See also Sickmund, *Juveniles in Corrections.*

79. Caeti, Hemmens, Cullen, and Burton, "Management of Juvenile Correctional Facilities."

80. Austin, Dedel Johnson, and Gregoriou, *Juveniles in Adult Prisons and Jails,* 42.

81. Strom, *Profile of State Prisoners Under Age 18, 1985–1997.*

82. Strom, *Profile of State Prisoners Under Age 18, 1985–1997.*

83. Strom, *Profile of State Prisoners Under Age 18, 1985–1997.*

84. Strom, *Profile of State Prisoners Under Age 18, 1985–1997,* 10.

85. Sickmund, *Juveniles in Corrections.*

86. *Parham v. J. R.,* 442 U.S. 584 (1979).

87. *In re Gault,* 387 U.S. 1 (1967).

88. *In re Winship,* 397 U.S. 358 (1970).

89. Barry C. Feld, *Juvenile Justice Administration* (St. Paul, MN: Thomson/West, 2003), 366.

90. Parent et al., *Conditions of Confinement.*

91. Parent et al., *Conditions of Confinement.*

92. Parent et al., *Conditions of Confinement.*

93. *Rhodes v. Chapman,* 452 U.S. 337 (1981).

94. Parent et al., *Conditions of Confinement.*

95. Parent et al., *Conditions of Confinement.*

96. Lindsay M. Hayes, *Suicide Prevention in Juvenile Facilities* (Washington, DC: U.S. Department of Justice, Office of Juvenile Justice and Delinquency Prevention, 2000).

97. For general information about juvenile suicide outside of institutions, see Howard Snyder and Melissa Sickmund, *Juvenile Suicides 1981–1998* (Washington, DC: Office of Juvenile Justice and Delinquency Prevention, 2004).

98. John Memory, "Juvenile Suicides in Secure Detention Facilities: Correction of Published Rates." *Death Studies* 13 (1989): 455–463.

99. Parent et al., *Conditions of Confinement.*

100. Parent et al., *Conditions of Confinement.*

101. N. Alessi, M. McManus, A. Brickman, and L. Grapentine, "Suicidal Behavior Among Serious Juvenile Offenders." *American Journal of Psychiatry* 141(2) (1984): 286–287.

102. P. Rohde, J. Seeley, and D. Mace, "Correlates of Suicidal Behavior in a Juvenile Detention Population." *Suicide and Life-Threatening Behavior* 27(2) (1997): 164–175.

103. Parent et al., *Conditions of Confinement.*

104. Hayes, *Suicide Prevention in Juvenile Facilities.*

105. Hayes, *Suicide Prevention in Juvenile Facilities.*

106. See *Kautter v. Reid,* 183 F. Supp. 352 (D.C. D.C. 1960); *White v. Reid,* 125 F. Supp. 647 (D.C. D.C. 1954); and *Elmore v. Stone,* 122 U.S. App. D.C. 416, 355 F.2d 841 (1966).

107. *White v. Reid.*

108. *Inmates of the Boys' Training School v. Affleck,* 346 F. Supp. 1354 (D.R.I. 1972).

109. *Nelson v. Heyne,* 491 F.2d 352 (7th Cir. 1974).

110. *White v. Reid.*

111. *Morales v. Turman,* 364 F. Supp 166 (E.D. Texas 1973).

112. *Morales v. Turman.*

113. *Alexander S. v. Boyd,* 876 F. Supp. 773 (D.S.C. 1995).

114. Caeti, Hemmens, Cullen, and Burton, "Management of Juvenile Correctional Facilities."

115. *Santana v. Collazo,* 714 F.2d 1172 (1st Cir. 1983).

116. *Ralston v. Robinson,* 454 U.S. 201 (1981).

117. *Ralston v. Robinson.*

118. *Black's Law Dictionary,* 7th ed. (St. Paul, MN: West, 1999), 1247.

119. Wooden, *Weeping in the Playtime of Others,* 106–117.

120. Wooden, *Weeping in the Playtime of Others,* 114–115.

121. Wooden, *Weeping in the Playtime of Others,* 107–116.

122. Clemmens Bartollas, Stuart Miller, and Simon Dinitz, *Juvenile Victimization: The Institutional Paradox* (New York: Wiley, 1976).

123. *Morales v. Turman.*

124. *In re Gault.*

125. Frank R. Kemerer, *William Wayne Justice: A Judicial Biography* (Austin: University of Texas Press, 1991).

126. Kemerer, *William Wayne Justice,* 147.

127. Kemerer, *William Wayne Justice,* 149.

128. Kemerer, *William Wayne Justice,* 153.

129. Kemerer, *William Wayne Justice,* 153.

130. Kemerer, *William Wayne Justice,* 153.

131. *Morales v. Turman.*

132. *Morales v. Turman.*

133. *Inmates of Boys' Training School v. Affleck.*

134. *Nelson v. Heyne.*

135. *Pena v. New York State Division of Youth,* 419 F. Supp. 203 (S.D. N.Y. 1976).

136. *Morgan v. Sproat,* 423 F. Supp. 1130 (S.D. Miss. 1977). See also *State v. Werner,* 242 S.E.2d 907 (W.Va. 1978); *Lillis v. New York State Department of Social Services,* 322 F. Supp. 473 (S.D.N.Y. 1970); and *Alexander v. South Carolina Department of Juvenile Justice,* 876 F. Supp. 773 (D.S.C. 1995).

137. See *Morales v. Turman; State of West Virginia v. Werner,* 242 S.E.2d 907 (W. Va. 1978); and *Alexander v. Boyd.*

138. *Lillis v. New York State Department of Social Services,* 322 F. Supp. 473 (S.D.N.Y. 1970), 328 F. Supp. 1115 (S.D.N.Y. 1971).

139. See, for example, *Guidry v. Rapides Parish School Board,* 560 So.2d 125 (La. Ct. App. 1990), and *C. J. W. by and through L. W. v. State,* 853 P.2d 4 (Kan. 1993).

140. See, for example, *Pena v. New York State Division for Youth* and *H. C. v. Hewett by Jarrard,* 786 F.2d 1080 (11th Cir. 1986).

141. *Gary H. v. Hegstrom,* 831 F.2d 1430 (9th Cir. 1987).

142. *Gary H. v. Hegstrom.*

143. *Gary H. v. Hegstrom.*

144. *Gary H. v. Hegstrom.*

145. *Gary H. v. Hegstrom.*

146. Human Rights Watch, *Children in Confinement in Louisiana.* Human Rights Watch Children's Rights Project (http://www.hrw.org/reports/1995/Us3.htm).

147. Human Rights Watch, *Children in Confinement in Louisiana,* 18.

148. Mary Hargrove, "Abused by Juvenile 'Justice' in Little Rock." *Arkansas Democrat-Gazette* (http://www.join-hands.com/juvenile_justice/arkansas_david_g.html), 1–6.

149. Evelyn Nieves, "Youth Prisons in California Stay Abusive, Suit Contends." *New York Times* (26 Jan. 2002): A8.

150. *Morgan v. Sproat.*

151. *Germany v. Vance,* 868 F.2d 9 (1st Cir. 1989).

152. *John L. v. Adams,* 969 F.2d 228 (6th Cir. 1992).

CHAPTER 12

1. Amnesty International, "Facts and Figures on the Death Penalty" (http://web.amnesty.org/pages/deathpenalty-facts-eng).

2. Mirah A. Horowitz, "Kids Who Kill: A Critique of How the American Legal System Deals with Juveniles Who Commit Homicide." *Law and Contemporary Problems* (63): 2.

3. Death Penalty Information Center (http://www.deathpenaltyinfo.org) (7 Mar. 2005), and Amnesty International, "Facts and Figures on the Death Penalty."

4. *Furman v. Georgia.* 408 U.S. 238 (1972).

5. *Gregg v. Georgia,* 428 U.S. 153 (1976).

6. *Black's Law Dictionary,* 5th ed. (St. Paul, MN: West, 1979), 146.

7. Lynn Cothern, "Juveniles and the Death Penalty." *Coordinating Council on Juvenile Justice and Delinquency Prevention* (November 2000): 5.

8. Horowitz, "Kids Who Kill," 4.

9. Richard C. Dieter, "International Perspectives on the Death Penalty: A Costly Isolation for the U.S." Death Penalty Information Center (http://www.deathpenaltyinfo.org/article), 9.

10. Death Penalty Information Center (http://www.deathpenaltyinfo.org) (7 Mar. 2005), and Amnesty International, "Facts and Figures on the Death Penalty."

11. Death Penalty Information Center.

12. "Juvenile Offenders on Death Row." Death Penalty Information Center (http://www.deathpenaltyinfo.org/article).

13. Victor L. Streib, "Executing Juvenile Offenders: The Ultimate Denial of Juvenile Justice." *Stanford Law and Policy Review* 121 (2003): 1. See also Victor L. Streib, "The Juvenile Death Penalty Today: Death Sentences and Executions for Juvenile Crimes, January 1, 1973–December 31, 2004" (http://www.law.onu.edu/faculty/streib/documents/JuvDeathDec2004.pdf).

14. *Roper v. Simmons* (case number SC84454 [2003]).

15. Cothern, "Juveniles and the Death Penalty," 9.

16. *Eddings v. Oklahoma,* 455 U.S. 104 (1982).

17. *Thompson v. Oklahoma,* 487 U.S. 815 (1988).

18. Horowitz, "Kids Who Kill," 6.

19. *Stanford v. Kentucky,* 492 U.S. 361 (1989), and *Wilkins v. Missouri,* 109 S.Ct. 2969 (1989).

20. Cothern, "Juveniles and the Death Penalty," 2–3.

21. *Roper v. Simmons* (case number SC84454 [2003]).

22. "Juvenile Offenders on Death Row," 1.

23. Horowitz, "Kids Who Kill," 12.

24. Horowitz, "Kids Who Kill," 12–13.

25. *Atkins v. Virginia,* 536 U.S. 3074 (2002).

26. *Roper v. Simmons* (http://laws.findlaw.com/us/00/03_633.html).

CHAPTER 13

1. *Tinker v. Des Moines Independent Community School District,* 309 U.S. 506 (1969).

2. Richard Lawrence, *School Crime and Juvenile Justice* (New York: Oxford University Press, 1998).

3. Lawrence, *School Crime and Juvenile Justice,* 145.

4. Lawrence, *School Crime and Juvenile Justice.*

5. Lawrence, *School Crime and Juvenile Justice.*

6. *Goss v. Lopez,* 419 U.S. 565 (1975).

7. *Goss v. Lopez,* 419 U.S. 565, 567 (1975).

8. *Goss v. Lopez,* 419 U.S. 565 (1975).

9. *Goss v. Lopez,* 419 U.S. 565, 583 (1975).

10. Kirk A. Bailey, *School Policies and Legal Issues Supporting Safe Schools* (Portland, OR: Northwest Regional Educational Laboratory, 2002).

11. See Bailey, *School Policies and Legal Issues Supporting Safe Schools.* See also *Givens v. Poe,* 346 F. Supp. 202 (1972), and *Dixon v. Alabama State Board of Education,* 294 F.2d 150 (5th Cir. 1961).

12. Bailey, *School Policies and Legal Issues Supporting Safe Schools.*

13. Bailey, *School Policies and Legal Issues Supporting Safe Schools,* 13.

14. *New Jersey v. T. L. O.,* 469 U.S. 325 (1985).

15. *Cornfield v. Consolidated High School District No. 230,* 991 F.2d 1316 (7th Cir. 1993).

16. *Williams v. Ellington,* 936 F.2d 881 (6th Cir. 1991). See also Barry Feld, *Juvenile Justice Administration in a Nutshell* (St. Paul, MN: Thomson/West, 2003).

17. Feld, *Juvenile Justice Administration in a Nutshell.*

18. *Bellnier v. Lund,* 438 F. Supp. 47 (N.D.N.Y. 1977).

19. *Jenkins v. Talladega City Board of Education,* 115 F.3d 821 (11th Cir. 1997).

20. See *Konop v. Northwestern School District,* 26 F. Supp. 2d 1189 (D.S.D. 1998); *M. M. v. Anker,* 607 F.2d 588 (2nd Cir. 1979); *Oliver v. McClung,* 919 F. Supp. 1206 (N.D. Ind. 1995).

21. *Konop v. Northwestern School District.*

22. *In the Interest of Isiah B.,* 176 Wis. 2d 639 (1993).

23. *In re Dumas,* 515 A.2d 984 (Pa. Super. 1986).

24. *New Jersey v. T. L. O.*

25. *In re Dumas.*

26. Feld, *Justice Administration in a Nutshell.*

27. Feld, *Justice Administration in a Nutshell.*

28. *People v. Dukes,* 580 N.Y.S.2d 850 (1992).

29. *In re F. B.,* 658 A.2d 1378 (Pa. Super. 1995).

30. *People v. Pruitt,* 662 N.E.2d 540, 544–546 (Ill. App. 1996).

31. *People v. Parker,* 672 N.E.2d 813 (Ill. App. 1996).

32. *State v. Slattery,* 791 P.2d 534 (1990).

33. *Vernonia School District v. Acton,* 115 S.Ct. 2386 (1995).

34. Lawrence, *School Crime and Juvenile Justice,* 165–166.

35. *Pottawatomie County v. Earls,* 122 S.Ct. 2559 (2002).

36. *Doe v. Renfrow,* 631 F.2d 91 (7th Cir. 1980).

37. *Zamora v. Pomeroy,* 639 F.2d 662 (10th Cir. 1981).

38. *Horton v. Goose Creek Independent School District,* 690 F.2d 470 (5th Cir. 1982).

39. See, for example, *Commonwealth v. Martin,* 626 A.2d 556 (Pa. 1993), and *B. C. v. Plumas Unified School District,* 192 F.3d 1260 (9th Cir. 1999).

40. Lawrence, *School Crime and Juvenile Justice.* See also Feld, *Justice Administration in a Nutshell.*

41. *People v. Dilworth,* 661 N.E.2d 310 (Ill. 1996).

42. *Cason v. Cook,* 810 F.2d 88 (8th Cir. 1987).

43. Jacqueline A. Stefkovich and Judith A. Miller, "Law Enforcement Officers in Public Schools: Student Citizens in Safe Havens?" *BYU Education and Law Journal* 25 (1999).

44. *Black's Law Dictionary,* 7th ed. (St. Paul, MN: West, 1999), 1247.

45. 430 U.S. 651 (1977).

46. *Ingraham v. Wright,* 430 U.S. 651 (1977).

47. http://www.stophitting.com.

48. http://resist.ca/story/2003/1/30/184038/920.

49. *Dallas Morning News* (17 Jan. 2003): 29A.

50. *Dallas Morning News* (13 Feb. 2003): 27A–28A.

51. *Dallas Morning News* (15 Apr. 2003): 4A; (24 Apr. 2003): 14A; (25 Apr. 2003): 8A.

52. *New York Times* (17 Apr. 2003) (http://www.nytimes.come/2003/04/17/nyregion/17KIDS.html).

53. *Dallas Morning News* (15 Apr. 2003): 4A.

54. Jill F. DeVoe, Katharin Peter, Phillip Kaufman, Sally A. Ruddy, Amanda K. Miller, Mike Planty, Thomas D. Snyder, Detis T. Duhart, and Michael R. Rand, *Indicators of School Crime and Safety: 2002* (Washington, DC: U.S. Departments of Education and Justice, 2002).

55. DeVoe et al., *Indicators of School Crime and Safety: 2002.*

56. Phillip Kaufman, Xianglei Chen, Susan Choy, Kathryn Chandler, C. D. Chapman, Michael R. Rand, and C. Ringel, *Indicators of School Crime and Safety: 1999* (Washington, DC: U.S. Departments of Education and Justice, 1999).

57. DeVoe et al., *Indicators of School Crime and Safety: 2002,* 3–4.

58. Bryan Vossekuil, Marisa Reddy, Robert Fein, Randy Borum, and William Modzeleski, *U.S.S.S. Safe School Initiative: An Interim Report on the Prevention of Targeted Violence in Schools* (Washington, DC: U.S. Secret Service National Threat Assessment Center, U.S. Department of Education, and the National Institute of Justice, 2000).

59. Vossekuil et al., *U.S.S.S. Safe School Initiative,* 3–9. This section summarizes the *U.S.S.S. Interim Report.*

60. *Chicago Sun Times* (16 Oct. 2000) (http://www.secretservice.gov/ntac/chicago_sun_2001016).

61. DeVoe et al., *Indicators of School Crime and Safety: 2002.*

62. DeVoe et al., *Indicators of School Crime and Safety: 2002,* 5–18.

63. DeVoe et al., *Indicators of School Crime and Safety: 2002,* 5–18.

64. DeVoe et al., *Indicators of School Crime and Safety: 2002,* 24–27.

65. DeVoe et al., *Indicators of School Crime and Safety: 2002,* 30–45.

66. DeVoe et al., *Indicators of School Crime and Safety: 2002.*

67. DeVoe et al., *Indicators of School Crime and Safety: 2002.*

68. Kaufman et al., *Indicators of School Crime and Safety: 1999.*

69. Sheila Heaviside, Cassandra Rowand, Catrina Williams, and Elizabeth Farris, *Violence and Discipline Problems in U.S. Public Schools: 1996–1997* (Washington, DC: U.S. Department of Education, 1998). The following findings are derived from this report.

70. *Opportunities Suspended: The Devastating Consequences of Zero Tolerance and School Discipline.* The Civil Rights Project, Harvard University, June 2000.

71. *Opportunities Suspended.*

72. *USA Today* (www.usatoday.com/educate/ednews3. htm).

73. *Lansing State Journal* (www.lsjxtra.com/news/ 010722ZERO2.2.html): 1.

74. *Opportunities Suspended.* See also Scott F. Uhler and David J. Fish, "Zero-Tolerance Discipline in Illinois Public Schools" (www.isba.org/Member/may011j/ p256.htm).

75. *Lyons v. Penn Hills School District,* 723 A.2d 1073 (Pa. Commonwealth 1999).

76. *Colvin v. Lowndes County School District,* 114 F. Supp. 504 (ND Miss. 1999).

77. *Board of School Trustees v. Barnell,* 678 N.E.2d 799 (Ind. App. 1997).

78. *Clinton Municipal Separate School District v. Byrd,* 477 So.2d 237 (Miss. 1985).

79. Heaviside et al., *Violence and Discipline Problems in U.S. Public Schools: 1996–1997.* The following findings are derived from this report.

80. Title 20 U.S.C., Section 5961–5968.

81. Heaviside et al., *Violence and Discipline Problems in U.S. Public Schools: 1996-1997,* 19–21.

82. Heaviside et al., *Violence and Discipline Problems in U.S. Public Schools: 1996-1997,* 19–21.

83. Lawrence, *School Crime and Juvenile Justice.*

84. Chad Trulson, Ruth Triplett, and Clete Snell, "Social Control in a School Setting: Evaluating a School-Based Boot Camp." *Crime and Delinquency* 47(4): (2001): 573–609.

85. Heaviside et al., *Violence and Discipline Problems in U.S. Public Schools: 1996–1997.*

86. Trulson, Triplett, and Snell, "Social Control in a School Setting."

87. Ronald D. Stephens and June Lane Arnette, *From the Courthouse to the Schoolhouse: Making Successful Transitions* (Washington, DC: Office of Juvenile Justice and Delinquency Prevention, 2000).

88. Kenneth S. Trump, "Keeping the Peace." *American School Board Journal* (March 1998) (http://www. asbj.com/security/contents/0398trump.html).

89. Cathy Girouard, *School Resource Officer Training Program* (Washington, DC: U.S. Department of Justice, 2001), 1.

90. Girouard, *School Resource Officer Training Program,* 1.

CHAPTER 14

1. Charles M. Friel, "A Century of Changing Boundaries." In C. Friel (ed.), *Boundary Changes in Criminal Justice Organizations,* Vol. 2 (Washington, DC: U.S. Department of Justice, 2000), 1–18.

2. Friel, "A Century of Changing Boundaries," 11.

3. William Bennett, John Dilulio, and John Walters, *Body Count* (New York: Simon and Schuster, 1996).

4. Jeffrey A. Butts and Ojmarrh Mitchell, "Brick by Brick: Dismantling the Border Between Juvenile and Adult Justice." In C. Friel (ed.), *Boundary Changes in Criminal Justice Organizations,* Vol. 2 (Washington, DC: U.S. Department of Justice, 2000), 202.

5. Butts and Mitchell, "Brick by Brick," 202.

6. Butts and Mitchell, "Brick by Brick," 202.

7. Melissa Sickmund, *Juveniles in Court* (Washington, DC: Office of Juvenile Justice and Delinquency Prevention, 2003).

8. Jeffrey A. Butts and Adele V. Harrell, *Delinquents or Criminals: Policy Options for Young Offenders* (Washington, DC: The Urban Institute, 1998), summary.

9. Butts and Harrell, *Delinquents or Criminals,* 8.

10. Butts and Harrell, *Delinquents or Criminals.*

11. Butts and Harrell, *Delinquents or Criminals,* 9.

12. Gordon Bazemore and Susan Day, "Restoring the Balance: Juvenile and Community Justice." *Juvenile Justice* 3(1) (1996): 7.

13. Bazemore and Day, "Restoring the Balance," 4.

14. Bazemore and Day, "Restoring the Balance," 6.

15. Bazemore and Day, "Restoring the Balance," 7. This section is authors' interpretation.

16. Bazemore and Day, "Restoring the Balance," 9.

17. Howard Snyder and Melissa Sickmund, *Juvenile Offenders and Victims: 1999 National Report* (Washington, DC: Office of Juvenile Justice and Delinquency Prevention, 1999).

18. Snyder and Sickmund, *Juvenile Offenders and Victims.*

19. Section 223 (a) (22), 2002.

20. Heidi Hsia and Donna Hamparian, *Disproportionate Minority Confinement: 1997 Update* (Washington, DC: Office of Juvenile Justice and Delinquency Prevention, 1998).

21. Hsia and Hamparian, *Disproportionate Minority Confinement.*

22. Kathleen Maguire and Ann Pastore (eds.), *Sourcebook of Criminal Justice Statistics 1995* (Washington, DC: Bureau of Justice Statistics, 1996).

23. Ruth Triplett, "The Growing Threat: Gangs and Juvenile Offenders." In Timothy Flanagan and Dennis Longmire (eds.), *Americans View Crime and Justice: A National Public Opinion Survey* (Thousand Oaks, CA: Sage, 1996), 142.

24. *Sourcebook of Criminal Justice Statistics 1992* (Washington, DC: Bureau of Justice Statistics, 1993).

25. http://abcnews.go.com/sections/us/DailyNews/ poll_violence0100508.html.

26. J. V. Roberts and L. J. Stalans, "Crime, Criminal Justice, and Public Opinion." In Michael Tonry (ed.), *The Handbook of Crime and Punishment* (New York: Oxford University Press, 1998), 31–57.

27. Roberts and Stalans, "Crime, Criminal Justice, and Public Opinion."

28. Mark Soler, *Public Opinion on Youth, Crime, and Race: A Guide for Advocates* (Building Blocks for Youth, October 2001), at www.buildingblocksforyouth. org.

29. Roberts and Stalans, "Crime, Criminal Justice, and Public Opinion."

30. Howard Snyder, *Juvenile Arrests 2001* (Washington, DC: Office of Juvenile Justice and Delinquency Prevention, 2003).

31. Meghan C. Scahill, *Female Delinquency Cases, 1997* (Washington, DC: Office of Juvenile Justice and Delinquency Prevention, 2000).

32. Meda Chesney-Lind and Randall G. Sheldon, *Girls, Delinquency, and Juvenile Justice,* 3rd ed. (Belmont, CA: Wadsworth, 2004).

33. Kimberly Budnick and Ellen Shields-Fletcher, *What About Girls?* (Washington, DC: Office of Juvenile Justice and Delinquency Prevention, 1998), 1.

34. Leslie Acoca and Kelly Dedel, *No Place to Hide: Understanding and Meeting the Needs of Girls in the California Juvenile Justice System* (San Francisco: National Council on Crime and Delinquency, 1998).

35. Budnick and Shields-Fletcher, *What About Girls?*

36. Office of Juvenile Justice and Delinquency Prevention, *Guiding Principles for Promising Female Programming: An Inventory of Best Practices* (Washington, DC: U.S. Government Printing Office, 1998).

37. Budnick and Shields-Fletcher, *What About Girls?*

38. *Transforming Probation Through Leadership: The "Broken Windows" Model* (Reinventing Probation Council, published by the Center for Civic Innovation at the Manhattan Institute, no date), 49.

39. Patricia Torbet, *Juvenile Probation: The Workhorse of the Juvenile Justice System* (Washington, DC: Office of Juvenile Justice and Delinquency Prevention, 1996).

40. Meghan C. Scahill, *Juvenile Delinquency Probation Caseload, 1988–1997* (Washington, DC: Office of Juvenile Justice and Delinquency Prevention, 2000). See also Charles Puzzanchera, Anne L. Stahl, Terrence A. Finnegan, Nancy Tierney, and Howard N. Snyder, *Juvenile Court Statistics 1999* (Pittsburgh: National Center for Juvenile Justice, 2003).

41. Torbet, *Juvenile Probation,* 4.

42. Torbet, *Juvenile Probation.*

43. *Transforming Probation Through Leadership: The "Broken Windows" Model,* 4.

44. *Transforming Probation Through Leadership: The "Broken Windows" Model,* 19–33.

45. Patricia Torbet et al., *Executive Summary of State Responses to Serious and Violent Juvenile Crime: Research Report* (Washington, DC: National Center for Juvenile Justice), xi. This section as revised originally appeared in Paul Cromwell, Rolando V. del Carmen, and Leanne Alarid, *Community-Based Corrections,* 5th ed. (Belmont, CA: Wadsworth, 2002), 330–331.

46. Adapted from the American Bar Association Criminal Justice Section Standards and Juvenile Justice Committee Task Force, *Youth in the Criminal Justice System: Guidelines for Policymakers and Practitioners,* no date. The report in its entirety can be viewed at http://www.aba/crimjust/pubs/reports/ pdf.html.

47. Shay Bilchik, "A Juvenile Justice System for the 21st Century." *OJJDP Juvenile Justice Bulletin* (May 1998), 1. This paragraph originally appeared in Paul Cromwell, Rolando V. del Carmen, and Leanne Alarid, *Community-Based Corrections,* 5th ed. (Belmont, CA: Wadsworth, 2002), 330–331.

48. Bilchik, "A Juvenile Justice System for the 21st Century," 1. This section as revised originally appeared in Paul Cromwell, Rolando V. del Carmen, and Leanne Alarid, *Community-Based Corrections,* 5th ed. (Belmont, CA: Wadsworth, 2002), 330–331.

Abuse of children
   disposition, 275–278
   forms of, 158–159
   history of juvenile justice, 6,
      155, 157
   juveniles in institutions,
      337–338, 347, 357, 362,
      369–376
   physical, 164
   See also Dependent and
      neglected children
Access to courts, right to, 376–377
Accountability. *See* Responsibility
Acquittal. *See* Conviction and
   acquittal
Activists
   Augustus, John, 304, 305*e*
   Bergh, Henry, 157
   child-savers, 222, 439
   Wheeler, Etta, 155, 157
Adjudication. *See* Procedures,
   juvenile justice system
Adjudication hearings
   adult vs. juvenile system, 10
   evidence rules, 184
   intake process, 21, 22, 113,
      119–120, 122–126, 126*t*,
      128
   reverse waivers, 198
   status offenders, 149, 154, 155
Adjustment, informal, 118
Admissibility of evidence
   exclusionary rule, 265–266,
      289–290, 328
   intake procedures, 121–126,
      126*t*
   interrogations, 290–291
Adolescence-limited delinquents,
   52–53, 54

Adoption studies, 38–39
Adult justice system, 210–219
   death penalty, 285–286
   double jeopardy case, 258
   jails, 342
   vs. juvenile system, 9–13,
      11–12*t*, 74, 99, 237–239,
      246–247, 293, 376, 443–444,
      444*e*, 445*e*
   juveniles in federal court, 218
   juveniles transferred to, 9, 120,
      179, 187–204, 190–191*t*,
      195*e*, 200*t*, 201–202*t*,
      442–443, 449, 453–454
   original jurisdiction, 14
   partnership with schools,
      431–433
   probation and parole, 132, 307
   sentencing, 272*t*
   separation from juveniles, 146
   three strikes laws, 292
   See also Jails and prisons
Adults, reformed juvenile
   delinquents, 55
Adventure and wilderness camps,
   358
Aftercare. *See* Parole and aftercare
Age
   age of jurisdiction, 13–15, 13*t*
   blended sentencing, 286–288
   death penalty, 285–286, 387*t*,
      389–390, 391, 393
   delinquent characteristics, 388*t*
   detention, 180
   diversion, 135
   juvenile victims, 172
   juveniles in jails and prisons,
      344, 360
   of majority, 330

   minimum age of responsibility,
      3, 4*t*, 439
   status offenders, 154
   waived legal rights, 261–262
   waiver to adult courts, 187,
      187*t*, 197, 201–202*t*
Agnew, Robert, 45–47
Akers, Ronald, 48–49
Alabama, diversion procedures,
   131–132
Alaska, juvenile records
   confidentiality, 326
Alexander S. v. Boyd (1995), 368
Allocution, 289
Almshouses, 336–337
Alvarado, Michael, 97
Amendments, legislation, 147
American Bar Association (ABA),
   392, 453–454
American Dream, 43
America's Buffalo Soldiers Re-
   Enactors Association, 357
Andrews, Roosevelt, 416
Animal abuse, 131, 157
Anonymity, 102
Appeals, legal
   federal courts, 210–211, 214
   right to, 252, 296–297
   state courts, 212–213
Appointments, defense attorneys,
   235, 254, 278–279
Apprenticeships, 336
Arbitrariness, death penalty,
   385–386
Arizona
   Arizona Boys Ranch Boot
      Camp, 357
   probation conditions, 307, 308
   public trials, right to, 265

Arkansas, juvenile correction facilities, 369, 375
Arraignment, 247
Arrest and custody, 73–85, 84–85*t*
  crime rates, 1980s, 8–9
  females, 450
  interrogations, 95–102, 321, 321*t*
  National Incident Based Reporting System, 60–61
  procedures, 72, 179–187
  race issues, 79*e*
  revocation of probation, 327
  status offenders, 148
  typical delinquents, 18
  Uniform Crime Reports, 59
  Uniform Juvenile Court Act, 75*e*
Arrest warrants. *See under* Warrants
Assault, 129, 171, 297, 362, 368, 417
Atavism, 36–37
Athletes, high school, 323, 412–413
Atkins v. Virginia (2002), 392–393
Augustus, John, 304, 305*e*
Automobile searches, 411–412

Bail, 185–186, 296
Balanced and restorative justice, 297–298, 446–447
Beccaria, Cesare, 35
Behavior
  rehabilitation efforts, 354, 361
  student attackers, 421–422
  supervision goals, 309
  theories of delinquency, 47–49, 50–51, 52–55
Bellnier v. Lund (1977), 409
Bergh, Henry, 157
Bias. *See* Discrimination
Bifurcated trials, 278
Biology (theories of delinquency), 36–40
Black juveniles
  in adult prisons, 360
  arrest and custody, 78
  diversion, 134–135
  in juvenile justice system, 448*e*
  status offenders, 154
  See also Minorities
Blended sentencing, 286–288, 287*e*
Board of School Trustees v. Barnell (1997), 428
Body-type theories, 38
Bonding theory, 49–50, 55
Boot camp programs, 285, 318, 355–357

Bootstrapping, 150–151, 151*n*
Boyfriends and girlfriends, 46
Breed v. Jones (1975), 132–133, 258
Breyer, Stephen, 98
Bringar v. United States (1949), 73
Bullying, 46, 50, 421
Bureau of Justice Assistance, 344
Bureau of Justice Statistics, 418
Bureau of the Census, 349–351
Burgess, Robert, 48–49

California
  boot camp program, 356
  evidence used in disposition, 290
  juvenile correction facilities, 343, 375
  Michael G. v. Superior Court (1988), 151*n*
  probationer search case, 319
  three strikes law, 292
  Yarborough v. Alvarado (2004), 97–98
Capital and Serious Violent Offender Treatment Program (TX), 354
Capital punishment. *See* Death penalty
Carjacking, 97
Carter, Terry, 426
Case disposition, 228–229
Case processing, 226–227, 275*e*
Caseloads
  juvenile court, 228*t*
  probation officers, 451–452
  public defenders, 255
Cason v. Cook (1987), 93, 415
Causes and Correlates of Delinquency Program, 62
Causes of Delinquency (Hirschi), 49–50
Causes of delinquency theories, 33, 40, 56
Census of Juveniles in Residential Placement (CJRP), 349–351
Challenges, jury, 249–250
Charges
  bootstrapping, 150
  criminal, 168
  increasing, 129
  right to notice of, 257–258
Chicago, IL
  Cook County juvenile court, 6, 221–222
  People v. Pruitt (1996), 411
  social disorganization theory, 41–42

Child Abuse Prevention and Treatment Act (CAPTA, 1974), 159, 162*e*
Child custody, 168, 169–170
Child labor, 221
Child protective services (CPS), 159, 161–170
Child-savers (activists), 222, 439
Chivalry factor, 80
Churches. *See* Religion
Circuit Court of Appeals, 211, 215*e*
Cities. *See* Urban areas
Citizen complaints, 81
Civil commitment, 363–364
Civil Rights of Institutionalized Persons Act (CRIPA), 376
Classical theory of delinquency, 34–36
Clear and convincing evidence, 169
Client-advocate attorneys, 235, 236
Clinton Municipal Separate School District v. Byrd (1985), 428
Closed school campuses, 430–431
Closing arguments, 250
CODIS (Combined DNA Index System), 105–106
Cohen, Albert, 44, 45*e*
Colleges and universities, 45
Colorado
  curfew case, 325
  In the Interest of J. E. S. (1991), 151*n*
Colvin v. Lowndes County School District (1999), 428
Commitment. *See* Institutionalization
Communities and neighborhoods
  goals of disposition, 298
  police patrols, 78, 80–81
  probation and parole, 314–316, 452–453
  restorative justice, 446–447
  theories of delinquency, 41–42
Community Oriented Policing Services (COPS), 433
Community service, 282–283
Competency, restorative justice, 446
Complaints. *See* Petitions
Compulsory education, 221
Conditions
  institutionalization, 364–376, 369–373
  probation and parole, 26, 306–309, 319–320
Conditions of Confinement: Juvenile Detention and Correctional Facilities (report), 364–365

Confessions. *See* Statements,
  incriminating
Confidentiality
  juvenile records, 265, 293–294,
    313, 325–326, 453
  juveniles and police interaction,
    102–103, 103–104t, 105,
    106–107
  lawyer-client privilege, 255, 313
  stigmatizing, 51
Confinement
  conditions of, 364–367
  disposition options, 279–281
  parents, 294
  See also Institutionalization
Conflict theory, 51–52
Conformists (strain theory), 43
Consent decrees, 118, 136
Consent to searches, 88–90,
  319–320
Contempt of court charges, 150
Contesting charges, 22
Contraband in schools, 91, 92
Contreraz, Nicholaus, 357
Controversy of culpability, 14
Conviction and acquittal
  appeal process, 213
  juvenile vs. adult system, 12t
  Once an adult, always an adult,
    198
Cook County (IL) juvenile court, 6,
  221–222
Coping mechanisms, 46–47
Corner boys (strain theory), 44–45
*Cornfield v. Consolidated High School
  District No. 230* (1993), 409
Corporal punishment, 416
Correctional facilities. *See* Jails and
  prisons; Juvenile correctional
  institutions
Cottage system (training schools),
  340
Counsel (legal). *See* Right to
  counsel
Counseling
  common dispositions, 23t
  families, 317–318
Court administration
  juvenile courts, 226–229,
    233–237
  probation officers, 311
  public defenders, 255
Court-appointed special advocates
  (CASA), 235
Court cases
  Alexander S. v. Boyd (1995),
    368

Atkins v. Virginia (2002),
  392–393
Bellnier v. Lund (1977), 409
Board of School Trustees v. Barnell
  (1997), 428
Breed v. Jones (1975), 132–133,
  258
Bringar v. United States (1949), 73
Cason v. Cook (1987), 93, 415
*Clinton Municipal Separate School
  District v. Byrd* (1985), 428
*Colvin v. Lowndes County School
  District* (1999), 428
*Cornfield v. Consolidated High
  School District No. 230* (1993),
  409
curfew laws, 153
Davis v. Alaska (1974), 326
Doe v. Renfrow (1980), 413
Eddings v. Oklahoma (1982), 388
Ewing v. California (2003), 292
Ex parte Crouse (1838), 220
Fare v. Michael C. (1979), 99,
  312–314
Furman v. Georgia (1972), 385,
  398
Gagnon v. Scarpelli (1973), 132,
  328, 329
Gary H. v. Hegstrom (1987), 374
Germany v. Vance (1989), 376
Goss v. Lopez (1975), 406
Gregg v. Georgia (1976),
  385–386
Griffin v. Wisconsin (1987), 94,
  319
Haley v. Ohio (1948), 290–291
Hamilton v. Alabama (1961), 121
Ingraham v. Wright (1977), 416
In re D. S. S. (1993), 134
In re Dumas (1986), 410
In re F. B. (1995), 410
In re Frank H. (1972), 121–122
In re Tyrell J. (1994), 94–95
In re Wayne H. (1979), 122,
  123–124
In re Winship (1970), 145, 149,
  259–261
In the Interest of Isiah B. (1993),
  410
In the Interest of J. E. S. (1991),
  151n
In the Interest of J. L., A Child
  (1993), 86
In the Matter of Edwin L. (1996),
  132
In the Matter of Mark Anthony G.
  (1987), 75–76

*Inmates of the Boys' Training
  School v. Affleck* (1972), 367,
  374
*Jenkins v. Talladega City Board of
  Education* (1997), 409
John L. v. Adams (1992), 377
Kent v. United States (1966), 145,
  192–193
Kirby v. Illinois (1972), 106
Lockyer v. California (2003), 292
Lyons v. Penn Hills School District
  (1991), 427–428
Massiah v. United States (1964),
  121
Matthews v. State (1984), 76
McKeiver v. Pennsylvania (1971),
  262, 263
Michael G. v. Superior Court
  (1988), 151n
Minnesota v. Dickerson (1993), 86
Minnesota v. Murphy (1984), 122,
  124
Miranda v. Arizona (1966), 95,
  120
Morales v. Turman (1973), 368,
  369–373
Morgan v. Sproat (1977), 374,
  376
Morrissey v. Brewer (1972), 132,
  327–328, 329
Nelson v. Heyne (1974), 367, 374
New Jersey v. T. L. O. (1985),
  90–92, 408–409, 410, 413
O'Connell v. Turner (1870), 220
*Oklahoma Publishing Company
  v. District Court in and for
  Oklahoma City* (1977),
  106–107
Parham v. J.R. (1979), 151,
  363–364
*Pena v. New York State Division of
  Youth* (1976), 374
*Pennsylvania Board of Probation
  and Parole v. Scott* (1998), 328
People v. Dilworth (1996), 415
People v. Dukes (1992), 410
People v. Parker (1996), 411
People v. Pruitt (1996), 411
Pottawatomie County v. Earls
  (2002), 412–413, 414–415
Prince v. Massachusetts (1944),
  160–161
Ralston v. Robinson (1981), 368
Rhodes v. Chapman (1981), 365
Roper v. Simmons (2005), 286,
  383, 393–399, 397t
Santana v. Collazo (1983), 368

Court cases (*continued*)
   Santosky v. Kramer (1982), 169
   Schall v. Martin (1984), 180
   Smith v. Daily Mail Publishing
      Company (1979), 107
   Stanford v. Kentucky (1989),
      285–286, 389–390
   State v. Quiroz (1987), 133–134
   State v. Slattery (1990), 411
   State v. Tracy M. (1986), 130
   State v. McDowell (1984), 128
   Terry v. Ohio (1968), 86
   Thompson v. Oklahoma (1988),
      285, 389
   Tinker v. Des Moines Independent
      Community School District
      (1969), 404
   United States v. Knights (2001),
      94
   United States v. Matlock (1974),
      89
   United States v. Wade (1967), 106,
      121
   United States v. Watson (1976),
      74–75
   Vernonia School District v. Acton
      (1995), 412–413, 414
   Washington v. Chatham (1981),
      129–130
   White v. Maryland (1963),
      120–121
   White v. Reid (1954), 367
   Wilkins v. Missouri (1989),
      389–390
   Yarborough v. Alvarado (2004),
      97–99
   Zamora v. Pomeroy (1981), 413
   See also In re Gault (1967)
Court orders, 150
Court proceedings
   adjudication hearings, 249–252
   dependent and neglected
      juveniles, 168–170
   detention hearings, 182–185
   disposition hearings, 277*e*, 278,
      290
   due process rights, 7–8
   federal courts, 218
   intake, 21
   juvenile vs. adult system,
      11–12*t*, 288
   public, 264
   revocation hearings, 328, 329
   waiver to adult court, 191, 192,
      195, 199–200
   See also Adjudication hearings
Court workloads, 226

Courts, federal and state, 210–219,
   212*e*
   See also Supreme Court, U.S.
CPS (Child protective services),
   159, 161–170
Craniology, 37
Crime in the Making: Pathways and
   Turning Points Through Life
   (Sampson and Laub), 54–55
Crime rates
   arrests, 83–85, 84–85*t*
   black juveniles, 78, 448*e*
   dependent and neglected
      juveniles, 164–166
   detention, 180
   female offenders, 80, 450
   juvenile courts, 226, 227*e*, 228*t*
   juvenile statistics, 171*e*, 172*e*
   juvenile victims, 170–172
   juveniles in residential
      placement, 352*t*
   measuring, 56–64, 65*t*
   1980s, 8–9
   school crime, 417–424
   status offenders, 152
   typical delinquents, 18
   violent crimes, 441–442
   waiver to adult courts, 194, 195*e*
The Criminal Man (Lombroso), 36
Critical stages, 121
Crook, Shirley, 394
Crouse, Mary Ann, 220
Cruel and unusual punishment
   death penalty, 285–286,
      385–386, 389–399
   rights in institutionalization,
      368–376
   schools, 416
   three strikes laws, 292
Cultural issues in delinquency, 42,
   43
Curfews, 153, 284–285, 324–325
Custodial interrogations. *See*
   Interrogations

Damages, court-ordered, 284
Danger. *See* Safety and protection
Data and information
   arrests, 83–85
   dependent and neglected
      juveniles, 164–166
   institutionalization figures,
      350–351
   juvenile victims, 170–172
   measuring delinquency, 56–64
   status offenders, 152
   suicide, 366

Database, DNA, 105–106
Davis v. Alaska (1974), 326
Day treatment, 24*t*
Death penalty, 382–399
   appeals, 296
   minimum age, 387*t*
   public opinion, 391*t*
   sentencing options, 285–286
   states, 384*e*, 398*t*
   Supreme Court rulings, 219,
      399*e*
Death row, 386–387, 398*t*
Decency. *See* Evolving standards of
   decency
Defense, legal, 250, 258
Defense attorneys, 234–235, 236,
   255–256, 278–279
Deferred prosecution, 21
Definitions
   custodial interrogations, 96–97
   delinquency, 15–18, 16–17*t*,
      144, 145, 217
   intake, 113
   juveniles, 13–15
   probation and parole, 303
   reasonable doubt, 260–261
   social learning theories, 47–48
   status offenders, 152
Delinquency
   bootstrapping, 150–151
   definition, 15–17, 17–18
   delinquent characteristics, 388*t*
   detention, 180, 181*e*
   disposition, 23–24*t*, 274–275,
      275*e*
   federal courts, 217
   future of juvenile justice, 455
   gender differences, 80, 450
   history of juvenile justice, 6,
      144–145, 146, 338, 441
   institutionalization, 353*t*
   jurisdiction in adult courts, 443,
      444*e*
   juvenile correction facilities,
      342–362, 352*t*, 363*t*
   juvenile courts, 227*e*, 228*t*, 245*e*,
      441
   juvenile justice procedures,
      19–27, 20*e*
   juvenile records, 326
   legal rights in adjudication, 247,
      259, 261, 262, 288
   petitions, 119, 119*e*, 121, 128,
      131–132
   police involvement, 72
   referrals, 116–117
   revocation of probation, 330

status offenders escalating to,
148
teen courts, 231
theories of, 33–56, 56e, 57t
Demeanor, in police interactions,
81
Department of Education, 425
Department of Justice, 376, 433
Dependent and neglected children,
143
definition, 158–159
deinstitutionalization, 146
disposition, 275–276
history, 144
juvenile system jurisdiction,
18–19, 441
police involvement, 72
procedures, 155, 157–170, 163e
residential placement, 362
youth shelters, 345
See also Abuse of children
*The Desktop Guide to Juvenile
Probation* (NCJJ), 309–310
Detention
common dispositions, 24t
juvenile detention centers,
346–347
juvenile vs. adult system, 12t
procedures, 179–187, 181e
Determinism, 36, 38
Developmental theories, 52–55
Devil (theories of delinquency), 34
Diagnostic facilities, 347–348
Differential association, 47–48
Direct file waiver, 196–197, 200
Discharge procedures, 26–27
Discipline and rules, school,
405–408, 416, 425–431, 430e
Discretion
detention, 182
disposition, 271–272, 276
diversion, 130–131, 135
juvenile prosecutors, 234
police in arrests, 77–82
probation and parole, 306–307,
309, 326–327
specialty courts, 446
waivers to adult court,
190–191t, 191–193, 194,
196–197, 200t
zero tolerance policies, 426–427
Discrimination
diversion, 134–136
minorities in juvenile justice,
147, 447–448
similarly situated cases, 131
Dismissal, 117–118, 131, 137–138

Disposition, 270–295
case processing, 228–229, 275e
dependent and neglected
juvenile cases, 169–170
goals of, 276–277t, 297–298
history of juvenile justice, 144
informal adjustments, 118
juvenile vs. adult system, 12t,
237, 272t
juveniles in adult system, 188,
362, 453
prior diversions, 133–134
procedures, 22–25, 23–24t
In re Gault (1967), 7–8, 252
status offenders, 149–151,
154–155
waiver to adult court, 203–204
District attorneys, 234
District of Columbia
Washington, D.C. sniper case
(2002), 216–217
White v. Reid (1954), 367
Diversion, 121, 126–138, 137e,
154, 230, 347
DNA samples, 105–106, 308
Doe v. Renfrow (1980), 413
Dogs, drug-sniffing, 413
Double jeopardy, 132–133, 213,
216, 258
Driving while intoxicated, 249, 295
Drugs and drug abuse
delinquency defined, 17t
detection with dogs, 413
detention, 181e
drug courts, 232–233
drug testing, 323–324, 412–413,
414–415
juvenile court caseloads, 228t
juveniles in residential
placement, 352t
marijuana, 74
probation, 307, 452
ranches and forestry camps, 358
searches, 323, 409, 411–412
students, 424
waiver to adult court, 203
Dual sovereignty, 216–217
Due process rights
adjudication, 258–259
adult court, 237
civil commitment, 363–364
coerced confessions, 291
detention hearings, 185
diversion, 132
institutionalized juveniles, 370,
372
intake, 120–121

parents, 294
In re Gault (1967), 7–8, 252, 440
revocation hearings, 328, 329
status offenders, 149
students in schools, 405–406,
407, 428
waiver to adult court, 192–193,
199–200

Earls, Lindsay, 414
Eddings v. Oklahoma (1982), 388
Education and training
judges, 251, 280e
juvenile rehabilitation, 352
juveniles in adult prisons, 360
probation officers, 311e
reform movements, 221
See also Schools; Vocational
training
Ego (psychoanalytic theory), 40–41
Eighth Amendment. *See* Bail; Cruel
and unusual punishment
Electronic monitoring, 23t,
284–285
Emergency suspension from
school, 407–408
Employment. *See* Vocational
training
English common law, 220, 405
Environmental influences theories,
38–40
Equal Protection Clause
death penalty cases, 385
diversion, 130
fines, 283
Errors, court, 213
Escape petitions, 150
Escapes, from ranch camps, 359
Evidence
closing arguments, 250
dependent and neglected
juvenile cases, 169
detention hearings, 184
disposition hearings, 278,
289–291
diversion vs. adjudication
hearings, 128
exclusionary rule, 265–266
fingerprints, 103
juvenile and police interaction,
87t
motions to suppress, 248
probable cause in arrests, 74
proof beyond reasonable doubt,
259–261
school searches, 92
status offender cases, 149

Evidence (*continued*)
   See also Statements,
     incriminating
Evolving standards of decency, 389,
   390–391, 394, 395, 396
Ewing v. California (2003), 292
Ex parte Crouse (1838), 220
Exclusionary rule, 265–266,
   289–290, 328
Executions, 384*e*, 386, 392
Expulsion. *See* Suspension or
   expulsion, schools
Extralegal factors
   arrest and custody, 77, 78–82
   dismissal, 118
   diversion, 134–138

Families
   arrest factors, 80–81
   counseling, 317–318
   dependent and neglected
     juveniles, 162–163, 166–167
   history of juvenile justice, 5
   juvenile court jurisdiction, 19,
     225, 444*e*
   reporting crime, 64
   theories of delinquency, 38
   See also Parents
Fare v. Michael C. (1979), 99,
   312–314
Fatalities. *See* Murder or fatalities
Fault. *See* Responsibility
Federal Bureau of Investigation
   (FBI), 105–106
Federal district courts, 211, 212*e*,
   215*e*
Federal school safety programs,
   425
Females. *See* Girls and women
Fifth Amendment, 256
Fighting, 50
Fines, 23*t*, 283, 284
Fingerprinting, 103–104*t*, 307
Firearms. *See* Weapons
First Amendment, 107, 160
Florida
   boot camp program, 356
   Florida Environmental Institute,
     358
   Ingraham v. Wright (1977), 416
Forestry camps, 357–359
Foster care, 170
Fourteenth Amendment. *See* Due
   process rights
Fourth Amendment. *See* Search
   and seizure
Free will, 35–36

Freedom of religion, 160–161
Freedom of the press, 107
Freud, Sigmund, 40–41
Friends and peers
   arrest decisions, 82
   jury of, 250
   social learning theories, 47–48
   student attackers, 421
   teen courts, 229–232
Funding
   child protective services, 159
   Community Oriented Policing
     Services, 433
Furman v. Georgia (1972), 385, 398

Gagnon v. Scarpelli (1973), 132, 328,
   329
Gangs, 343, 362, 424
Gary H. v. Hegstrom (1987), 374
Gatesville School (TX), 373
Gault, Gerald, 7, 252, 257
Gender issues
   arrest and custody, 79–80, 85
   delinquent characteristics, 388*t*
   detention, 180
   diversion, 134
   juvenile victims, 172
   status offenders, 154
   See also Girls and women
General search condition of
   probation, 94–95
General Theory of Crime (Gottfredson
   and Hirschi), 52
Genetics, theories of delinquency,
   38–40
Georgia, *Gregg v. Georgia* (1976),
   385
Germany v. Vance (1989), 376
Girlfriends and boyfriends, 46
Girls and women
   arrest rates and gender, 79–80,
     85
   child-savers (activists), 222
   detention case, 183
   diversion, 134
   in juvenile justice system,
     450–451
Glueck, Sheldon and Eleanor, 38,
   54
Goals, personal, 46, 55
Goss v. Lopez (1975), 406
Gottfredson, Michael, 52
Graduated incarceration, 362
Graffiti, 424
Gregg v. Georgia (1976), 385–386
Griffin v. Wisconsin (1987), 94, 319
Grisso, Thomas, 96

Group crime, 60
Guardian ad litem, 235
Guilt or innocence
   defense lawyers, 256
   pleas, 248–249
   probation, 282
   reasonable doubt, 260
Gun-Free School Zones Act, 426

Habeas corpus, writ of, 297
Haley v. Ohio (1948), 290–291
Hamilton v. Alabama (1961), 121
Hate-related speech, 424
Haynes, Anthony, 357
Hearings. *See* Court proceedings
Hidden delinquents, 150
Hierarchy rule (crime reporting),
   60
High school students. *See* Schools
Hirschi, Travis, 49–50, 52
History
   adjudication, 245–246
   arrest reports, 83
   boot camp programs, 355
   death penalty, 383–384, 386
   dependent and neglected
     juveniles, 155, 157
   juvenile correctional
     institutions, 335–342, 367
   juvenile justice system, 3–9,
     219–223, 439–442
   nondelinquents, 143–145
   probation, 304, 324
   theories of delinquency, 34–38
Home environment
   responsibility for diversion, 136
   theories of delinquency, 34*e*, 39
House arrest, 23*t*
Houses of refuge, 6, 219–220, 221,
   337–338
Housing issues, 340
Human Rights Watch, 375
Hung jury, 251

Id (psychoanalytic theory), 40–41
Identity, bullies, 50–51
Illinois
   Cook County juvenile court, 6,
     221–222
   Illinois Juvenile Court Act
     (1899), 221–222, 221–223
   jurisdiction of juvenile courts,
     144
   O'Connell v. Turner (1870), 220
   People v. Dilworth (1996), 415
   People v. Parker (1996), 411
   People v. Pruitt (1996), 411

probationer search case, 319
social disorganization theory
    (Chicago), 41–42
Immigrants, 42
Immunity, legal, 162*e*
In loco parentis, 405
In re D. S. S. (1993), 134
In re Dumas (1986), 410
In re F. B. (1995), 410
In re Frank H. (1972), 121–122
In re Gault (1967)
    due process rights, 149, 237,
        252–253, 369–370, 440
    history of juvenile justice, 7–8,
        145, 246
    jury trials, 263–264
    loss of freedom distinction, 256
    notice of charges, 257
    proportionality, 293
In re Tyrell J. (1994), 94–95
In re Wayne H. (1979), 122,
    123–124
In re Winship (1970), 145, 149,
    259–261
In the Interest of Isiah B. (1993), 410
In the Interest of J. E. S. (1991), 151*n*
In the Interest of J. L., a Child (1993),
    86
In the Matter of Edwin L. (1996), 132
In the Matter of Mark Anthony G.
    (1987), 75–76
Incapacitation, 361
Incarceration (adult prisons)
    common dispositions, 24*t*
    history of juvenile justice, 144,
        145
    juveniles in adult prisons,
        359–362, 368, 449, 454
    See also Institutionalization; Jails
        and prisons
Independent school district police,
    433
Indeterminate sentences, 6–7, 293
Indiana
    Board of School Trustees v. Barnell
        (1997), 428
    diagnostic facilities, 348
    Nelson v. Heyne (1974), 367, 374
    probation officers, 311
    public trials, right to, 264
*Indicators of School Crime and Safety,
    2002* (report), 418, 423–424
Indigent defendants, 255
Individualized justice, 443–444
Informal resolutions, 20–21, 118
    dependent and neglected
        juveniles, 167

probation, 281–282
stigmatizing, 51
See also Diversion
Ingraham, James, 416
Ingraham v. Wright (1977), 416
Injury cases
    corporal punishment, 416
    no contest plea, 249
*Inmates of the Boys' Training School
    v. Affleck* (1972), 367, 374
Innocence. *See* Guilt or innocence
Innovators (strain theory), 43
Insanity defense, 248
Institutionalization
    blended sentencing, 286–288,
        287*e*
    common dispositions, 23*t*, 25,
        280–281
    deinstitutionalization, 146, 150,
        151
    delinquency jurisdiction, 444*e*
    history of juvenile justice, 220
    juvenile correction facilities,
        342, 364–377
    legal rights, 367–377
    nondelinquents, 144–145,
        362–363
    parole and probation, 303
    In re Gault (1967), 253
    revocation sentences, 26,
        328–330
    shock probation, 315–316
    statistics, 351, 352*t*, 353*t*
    status offenders, 149–151
Intake (juvenile justice system)
    dependent and neglected
        juveniles, 161–162
    vs. detention intake, 181–182
    procedures, 21, 112–126,
        115–116*t*
    right to counsel, 135
    status offenders, 148–149, 154
Intensive supervision probation
    (ISP), 24*t*, 315
Intent, *mens rea*, 3
International Covenant on Civil
    and Political Rights, 392
Internet victimizations, 173
Interrogations, 95–102, 290–291,
    312–313, 320–321, 394
Investigations
    dependent and neglected
        juveniles, 161–162, 166
    juvenile institution conditions,
        370–373, 375, 376
    minorities institutionalized,
        447–448

pre-disposition reports, 277*e*,
    278, 310
school searches, 93
social history reports, 348
Iowa, curfew case, 325

Jails and prisons
    blended sentencing, 286–288,
        287*e*
    Juvenile Justice and
        Delinquency Prevention Act
        (1974), 147
    juvenile vs. adult system, 12*t*,
        280–281, 342
    juveniles in, 186–187, 342–345,
        359–362, 368, 449, 454
    parents, 294
James, Daniel, 414
*Jenkins v. Talladega City Board of
    Education* (1997), 409
JJDPA. *See* Juvenile Justice and
    Delinquency Prevention
    Act
John L. v. Adams (1992), 377
Judges
    appeal process, 213
    Breyer, Stephen, 98
    dependent and neglected
        juvenile cases, 169–170
    detention hearings, 183
    disposition, 23, 271–272, 276,
        279
    drug courts, 233
    federal courts, 210–211
    jury instructions, 213
    Justice, William Wayne, 368,
        369–373
    juvenile court personnel, 234,
        311
    Kennedy, Anthony, 395
    multiple jurisdictions, 225
    O'Connor, Sandra Day, 389,
        390, 391, 396–397
    probation and parole, 307, 309,
        315–316, 326–327
    Scalia, Antonin, 396–397
    Stevens, John Paul, 395
    teen courts, 232
    training of, 251*e*, 280*e*
    waiver to adult court, 120,
        191–193, 195, 454
Jurisdiction
    court system overview, 209,
        214, 216–218, 224–226
    transfer, 238, 443, 444*e*
    transfer of, 187, 188*t*
Jurors, 249–250, 260–261

Jury trials, 227, 249–250, 251, 262–264
Justice, William Wayne, 368, 369–373
Juvenile correctional institutions, 335–377, 363*t*
  common dispositions, 25
  minorities, 447
  pre-adjudication, 179, 182
  statistics, 352*t*, 353*t*
Juvenile court masters, 234
Juvenile courts
  adjudication, 246–252
  dependent and neglected juveniles, 155, 157–158, 166–170
  history, 6–7, 144, 145, 219–223, 440
  jurisdiction, 217, 218, 227*e*, 228*t*, 230*e*, 445*e*
  jury trials, 262, 263
  legal protections, 4
  status offenders, 148, 245*e*
  structure of, 224–239
  terminology, 158*e*, 442–443
Juvenile detention centers, 179, 182, 280, 346–347
Juvenile Justice and Delinquency Prevention Act (JJDPA, 1974), 8, 145–147, 150, 186, 343, 441
A Juvenile Justice System for the 21st Century (OJJDP), 454–455
Juvenile records
  confidentiality, 102, 103–104*t*, 265, 453
  probation records, 325–326
  used in adult sentencing, 293–294
Juveniles in Adult Prisons and Jails: A National Assessment (report), 344
Juveniles in Corrections (report), 344

Kennedy, Anthony, 395
Kent, Morris, 192
Kent v. United States (1966), 145, 192–193
Key Program, Inc., 347
Kirby v. Illinois (1972), 106

Labeling theory, 50–51
Last Chance Ranch (FL), 358
Laub, John, 54–55
Law enforcement
  detention, 181

exclusionary rule, 266, 289–290
initial contact in juvenile system, 19–20, 152
intake procedures, 112–113, 116–117
interrogations, 290–291
juvenile justice procedures, 72–107, 75*e*, 88*e*
juvenile vs. adult system, 11*t*
measuring crime rates, 59–61, 63
and probation officers, 321–323, 324
in schools, 431–434
searches by, 319, 413, 415–416
status offenders, 148
Lawyer-client privilege, 255, 313
Lawyers
  access to clients, 369
  defense attorneys, 236, 255–256, 278–279
  dependent and neglected juvenile cases, 168
  juvenile court personnel, 234–235
  lineups, 106
  public defenders, 255
  socioeconomic status of offenders, 135–136
  waiving *Miranda* rights, 101
  See also Right to counsel
Learning theories, 47–49
Legal rights and protection
  adjudication, 247, 252–265
  adult court, 237
  civil commitment case, 363–364
  court cases establishing, 7–8, 145
  dependent and neglected juveniles, 157
  detention, 181–187
  disposition, 289–295
  diversion, 129–134
  intake, 120–126
  interrogations, 95–102
  juvenile correction facilities, 365, 367–377
  juvenile court, 4, 223, 236, 288
  police interactions with juveniles, 85–95
  probation and parole, 319–329
  status offenders, 149
  students in school, 404–416, 427–428
Legalistic style (police departments), 82

Legislation
  Child Abuse Prevention and Treatment Act (1974), 159, 162*e*
  Civil Rights of Institutionalized Persons Act, 376
  curfew laws, 153
  death penalty, 391
  Gun-Free School Zones Act, 426
  Illinois Juvenile Court Act (1899), 221–222, 221–223
  juvenile court records, 265
  juvenile courts, 238
  Juvenile Justice and Delinquency Prevention Act (1974), 8, 145–147, 150, 186, 343, 441
  Safe Schools Act (1994), 429–430
  state law trends, 453–454
  three strikes laws, 292
  Uniform Juvenile Court Act, 75*e*
  waiver to adult court, 197–199, 200–201, 442
Life-course theories, 52–55
Lineups, 106
Liquor laws
  delinquency defined, 17*t*
  status offenders, 156*e*
Local jails, 281
Locker and desk searches, schools, 409–410
Lockyer v. California (2003), 292
Lombroso, Cesare, 36–37, 37*e*
Louisiana, juvenile correction facilities, 375
Lower class
  arrest and custody, 80–81
  diversion, 135
  theories of delinquency, 44, 45*e*
Lyons v. Penn Hills School District (1991), 427–428

MacLaren juvenile facility (OR), 374
Magistrate courts, 211
Malvo, Lee Boyd, 133, 216–217, 392
Mandatory reporting, 161, 162*e*
Mandatory sentencing, 292
Mandatory waivers, 194–195, 196, 200*t*
Maps
  juveniles in residential placement, 353*t*
  U.S. court system, 215*e*
Marijuana, 74, 411–412

Marlin Orientation and Assessment Unit (TX), 348
Maryland
  curfew case, 325
  Lee Boyd Malvo case, 133, 216–217
Massachusetts
  Key Program, Inc., 347
  reformatories, 338
  theories of delinquency research, 38, 54
Massiah v. United States (1964), 121
Matthews v. State (1984), 76
McFadden Ranch (TX), 358
McKay, Henry, 41–42
McKeiver v. Pennsylvania (1971), 262, 263
Measuring levels of delinquency, 33, 56–64, 65*t*, 83–85, 418
Mediation
  dependent and neglected juvenile cases, 168
  victims and offenders, 127
Medical care, 160–161
Mens rea, 3
Mental age and maturity, 15, 54, 97, 395
Mental illness or defect
  death penalty, 392–393
  institutionalization, 23*t*, 350, 363–364
  mental hospitals, 151, 371
  stabilization facilities, 348–349
  waiver to adult court, 199
Merton, Robert, 42–43
Mesomorphs (body type), 38
Metal detectors, 410–411, 431
Methodology
  arrest rates, 83
  measuring delinquency, 33
  measuring neglected juveniles, 165
  self-report surveys, 61–62
Michael G. v. Superior Court (1988), 151*n*
Michigan, University of, 62
Middle class
  arrest and custody, 80–81
  theories of delinquency, 44, 45*e*
Minimum age of responsibility, 3, 4*t*, 14–15
Minnesota
  In re D. S. S. (1993), 134
  Minnesota v. Dickerson (1993), 86
  Minnesota v. Murphy (1984), 122, 124, 321

Minorities
  institutionalization data, 351
  Juvenile Justice and Delinquency Prevention Act (1974), 147
  juvenile victims, 172
  representation in juvenile justice, 447–448
  See also Black juveniles; Race issues
Miranda v. Arizona (1966), 95, 120, 320
Miranda warnings, 95–102, 126, 126*t*, 312–313, 320–321, 321*t*
Misinformation, in self-report data, 62–63
Mississippi
  Clinton Municipal Separate School District v. Byrd (1985), 428
  Colvin v. Lowndes County School District (1999), 428
  Morgan v. Sproat (1977), 374, 376
Missouri, *Roper v. Simmons* (2003), 393–394
Moffitt, Terrie, 52–53
Monitoring of the Future (MTF) study, 62
Morales v. Turman (1973), 368, 369–373
Morgan v. Sproat (1977), 374, 376
Morrissey v. Brewer (1972), 132, 327–328, 329
Motions to suppress evidence, 248
Motivation, delinquency theories, 50
Mountain View School (TX), 373
Mug shots, 106
Muhammad, John Allen, 216–217
Murder or fatalities
  boot camp programs, 357
  confessions, 290, 312–313
  crime rates, 1980s, 8–9
  death penalty, 216, 286, 385, 388, 389, 393–394
  Lee Boyd Malvo case, 133, 216–217, 392
  school crime, 417, 418–419, 419–420*t*
  waiver to adult courts, 187, 199

N. A. Chaderjian Youth Correctional Facility (CA), 343
National Center for Education Statistics (NCES), 418, 425

National Center for Juvenile Justice (NCJJ), 309, 453
National Child Abuse and Neglect Data System (NCANDS), 165
National Crime Victimization Survey (NCVS), 58, 63, 65*t*, 165, 170
National Incident-Based Reporting System (NIBRS), 58, 60–61, 65*t*, 165, 170
National Threat Assessment Center (NTAC), 420
Native Americans, 218
Needs assessments (probation), 310
Neglect, child. *See* Dependent and neglected children
Neighborhoods. *See* Communities and neighborhoods
Nelson v. Heyne (1974), 367, 374
Net widening, 137–138, 137*e*, 231
Neuropsychological deficits, 53
Nevada, right to public trials, 264
New Jersey v. T. L. O. (1985), 90–92, 408–409, 410, 413
New York
  Bellnier v. Lund (1977), 409
  child abuse case (1873), 155, 157
  House of Refuge, 337
  In re Frank H. (1972), 121–122
  In the Matter of Edwin L. (1996), 132
  In the Matter of Mark Anthony G. (1987), 75–76
  Pena v. New York State Division of Youth (1976), 374
  People v. Dukes (1992), 410
No contest plea, 249
Nolo contendere plea, 249
Non-petitioned youths, 21
Non-typical delinquents, 18, 56*e*
Nondelinquents. *See* Dependent and neglected children; Status offenses
Normalization, probation, 452

O'Connell v. Turner (1870), 220
O'Connor, Sandra Day, 389, 390, 391, 396–397
Office of Juvenile Justice and Delinquency Prevention, 344, 356, 364, 454–455
Oklahoma
  Oklahoma Publishing Company v. District Court in and for Oklahoma City (1977), 106–107

Oklahoma (*continued*)
  Pottawatomie County v. Earls
    (2002), 414–415
Once an adult, always an adult,
    198–199, 200*t*
Opinions, Supreme Court,
    395–397, 397*t*
Opportunities and access, 43
Oregon, *Gary H. v. Hegstrom* (1987),
    374
Original jurisdiction, 14
Orphanages, 219, 336–337
Overcrowding, juvenile
    institutions, 347, 365–366

Parens patriae
  access to the courts, right to,
    371
  history of juvenile justice, 3–4,
    144, 220, 223, 246, 440
  juvenile detetion, 179
  juvenile institution case, 371
  role of probation officers, 324
  Supreme Court rulings, 252,
    291
  waiver to adult court case, 192
Parents
  civil commitment, 363–364
  consent to bail, 186
  consent to searches, 89–90
  curfews, 153
  dependent and neglected
    juveniles, 19, 157, 160–161,
    166–170
  female delinquents, 451
  historic perspective, 220,
    335–336
  In re Gault (1967), 257–258
  juveniles released to, 117, 182,
    183, 345
  notification of juvenile arrest, 75
  Per se requirement, 100–101
  reporting crime, 64
  responsibility for diversion, 136
  restitution, 284
  theories of delinquency, 39, 44,
    52
  See also Families
Parham v. J.R. (1979), 151, 363–364
Parole and aftercare, 25–26,
    303–309
  juvenile vs. adult system, 12*t*
  legal rights, 319–326
  overcrowding, 366
  revocation, 26
  shock probation, 316
  similarity to diversion, 132

transition facilities, 359
Part I and II offenses, 59, 83
Partnerships
  community and probation
    officers, 452–453
  police and probation officers,
    321–323
  schools and justice systems,
    431–434
Peers. *See* Friends and peers
*Pena v. New York State Division of
    Youth* (1976), 374
Pennsylvania
  curfew case, 325
  Ex parte Crouse (1838), 220
  fines case, 283
  In re Dumas (1986), 410
  In re F. B. (1995), 410
  Lyons v. Penn Hills School District
    (1991), 427–428
  probation conditions, 307
  school-based probation, 316,
    432
  Trough Creek State Park, 358
*Pennsylvania Board of Probation and
    Parole v. Scott* (1998), 328
People v. Dilworth (1996), 415
People v. Dukes (1992), 410
People v. Parker (1996), 411
People v. Pruitt (1996), 411
Per se requirement, 100–101
Peremptory challenges, 249–250
Personnel, juvenile court, 233–237
Petitions
  delinquency, 119, 119*e*, 121,
    128, 131–132
  dependent and neglected
    juveniles, 167
  escape, 150
  status offenders, 154
Photographs
  confidentiality, 103–104*t*
  lineups and mug shots, 106
Phrenology, 37
Physical characteristics, 36, 37, 37*e*,
    38, 40, 52
Plea bargains
  juvenile justice procedures, 22,
    248, 254
  waiver to adult court, 199
Pleas, 248–249
Poetry, 426
Policies
  closed school campuses,
    430–431
  police departments, 82
  zero tolerance policies, 425–428

Pope, Carl, 78–79, 79*e*
Population, U.S., 351
Positive reinforcement, 49
Positivism, 36, 40, 340–341
Pottawatomie County v. Earls (2002),
    412–413, 414–415
Poverty and the poor
  historic perspectives, 336–337
  theories of delinquency, 42, 43,
    44
Power issues, control theory, 51–52
Pre-disposition reports, 22,
    276–277, 277*e*, 278
Precedent, judicial, 214–216
Predictors of delinquency, 36, 37*e*
Preponderance of the evidence,
    149, 169, 260
Press and media, 106–107
Presumptive waivers, 195–196,
    200*t*
Prevention
  future of juvenile justice, 455
  juvenile vs. adult system, 11*t*
  school crime, 425–431, 429–430
Primary deviance, 50
Prince v. Massachusetts (1944),
    160–161
Privacy rights, 90, 94, 408*e*, 410
Private companies
  boot camp programs, 357
  juvenile institutions, 281, 347
  school security, 432–433
Probabilistic theories, 34*e*
Probable cause
  arrest requirements, 73, 74, 87,
    87*t*, 88*e*
  detention requirements,
    182–184
  search requirements, 93–94, 319
  waiver to adult court, 195
Probation, 302–330, 305*e*
  dispositions, 24–25, 24*t*,
    281–282
  juvenile court personnel, 235
  reform, 451–453
  searches of probationers, 94–95
  similarity to diversion, 132
Probation officers
  admissibility of statements to,
    122, 123
  community service, 282–283,
    453
  coping skills, 314*e*
  disposition reports, 277*e*, 279
  intake procedures, 114–116,
    115–116*t*, 118, 312–313
  interrogations by, 320–321, 321*t*

job description, 310–312, 311*e*, 324

modifying conditions, 309

partnership with police, 321–323

privileged communications, 255

revocation of probation, 327

school-based, 316, 317*e*, 432

searches by, 319

Procedures, juvenile justice system, 19–27, 20*e*

adjudication overview, 246–252, 259

arrest and custody, 72, 73–77

criminal, 246

dependent and neglected juveniles, 159–170, 163*e*

detention, 178–187

disposition, 276–279

diversion, 128–129, 131–132

federal courts, 210, 218

intake, 113–126

interrogations, 100–101

juvenile and police interaction, 87*t*

juvenile courts, 226–237, 246–252

right to counsel, 254–255

status offenders, 147–155, 156*e*

waiver to adult court, 189–201

Profiles, student attackers, 421–422

Proof. *See* Evidence

Property crimes

crime rates, 84*t*

delinquency defined, 16*t*

detention, 181*e*

juvenile court caseloads, 228*t*

juveniles in residential placement, 352*t*

restitution, 284

waiver to adult court, 203

Proportionality

fines, 283

In re Gault (1967), 7

juvenile vs. adult sentences, 293

theories of delinquency, 35

three strikes laws, 292

Prosecution

dependent and neglected juveniles, 167

diversion, 128–129

federal courts, 217–218

immunity, 162

intake procedures, 114–116, 115–116*t*, 118

juvenile courts, 21–22, 234, 248, 250

juvenile vs. adult system, 11*t*

use of juvenile records, 294

waived legal rights, 261–262

waiver to adult courts, 194, 196–197, 199, 200, 200*t*, 218

Psychoanalytic theory, 40–41

Psychological aspects

cottage system (training schools), 340

neuropsychological deficits, 53

probation officers, 314*e*

theories of delinquency, 40–41

Psychology services, 349

Public defenders, 255

Public opinion

death penalty, 391*t*

disposition goals, 273

juvenile justice goals, 449–450

school crime, 417

sensationalism, 2

Public order, crimes against

delinquency defined, 17*t*

detention, 181*e*

juvenile court caseloads, 228*t*

juveniles in residential placement, 352*t*

waiver to adult court, 203

Public records, 325–326

Public schools. *See* Schools

Public trials, right to, 264–265

Publications

Causes of Delinquency (Hirschi), 49–50

Census of Juveniles in Residential Placement, 349–351

Conditions of Confinement: Juvenile Detention and Correctional Facilities (report), 364–365

The Criminal Man (Lombroso), 36

The Desktop Guide to Juvenile Probation (NCJJ), 309–310

General Theory of Crime (Gottfredson and Hirschi), 52

Indicators of School Crime and Safety, 2002 (report), 418, 423–424

A Juvenile Justice System for the 21st Century (OJJDP), 454–455

Juveniles in Adult Prisons and Jails: A National Assessment (report), 344

Juveniles in Corrections (report), 344

Violence and Discipline Problems in

U.S. Public Schools, 1996–1997 (report), 425

Youth in the Criminal Justice System: Guidelines for Policymakers and Practitioners (ABA report), 453–454

Publicity and public relations, 81

Punishment

history of juvenile justice, 5, 220–221

juvenile correction facilities, 372, 373, 374

juvenile justice goals, 3, 272, 274*t*, 276–277*t*, 292, 449

juveniles in adult system, 203, 360

parents for juvenile behavior, 294–295

social learning theories, 49

theories of delinquency, 35

zero tolerance policies, 425–426

Race issues

arrest and custody, 78–79, 79*e*

delinquent characteristics, 388*t*

detention, 180

diversion, 134–135

juvenile victims, 172

status offenders, 154

See also Black juveniles; Minorities

Ralston v. Robinson (1981), 368

Ranches and forestry camps, 357–359

Rape

crime rates, 1980s, 8–9

habeas corpus, 297

Kent v. United States (1966), 192

Rationality, 35

Reasonable doubt, 259–261

Reasonable suspicion

arrest and custody, 76

probationer searches, 319–320

school searches, 91, 408–409, 410, 411, 413, 415

stop and frisk, 86, 87, 87*t*, 88*e*

Reasonableness, 405, 416

Rebelliousness, 54

Records. *See* Juvenile records

Reform

child labor and education, 221

child-savers (activists), 222, 439

juvenile justice system, 6, 7, 225–226, 246, 297–298, 440

probation, 451–453

Reformatories, 338–339

Registration and notification, past offenses, 102, 103–104*t*

Regulations, school. *See* Discipline and rules, school

Rehabilitation and treatment
boot camp programs, 355–356
drug courts, 232–233
institutional programming, 351–352
juvenile courts, 238–239
juvenile justice goals, 2–3, 6–7, 189, 219–220, 271, 274*t*, 283, 337, 339, 342, 371, 449–450
juveniles in adult prisons, 360, 361
mental illness, 350
probation and parole, 306–307, 308–309, 310, 317, 318, 324
ranches and forestry camps, 358
restorative justice, 446–447
right to, 367–368
state schools, 354–355
substance abuse treatment centers, 151

Reinforcement, positive, 49

Religion
history of juvenile justice, 5
religious freedom, 160–161
theories of delinquency, 34

Repeat offenders
arrest and custody, 77–78
boot camp programs, 318, 356
diversion, 133–134, 136–137
juvenile correction facilities, 341–342, 355
juvenile records, 293–294
juveniles in adult system, 9, 189
probation, 25
three strikes laws, 292
waiver to adult courts, 187, 197

Reporting, crime, 58–64, 65*t*
dependent and neglected juveniles, 161, 162*e*, 163*e*, 164–166
status offenders, 152
suicide, 366
Uniform Crime Reports, 83
by victims, 79*e*

Representation. *See* Lawyers; Legal rights and protection; Right to counsel

Research and reports
arrest patterns and race, 78–79, 79*e*
blended sentencing, 288
boot camp programs, 318, 356

case management, 226, 228
death penalty, 386–387
discrimination in diversion, 136
institutionalization conditions, 364–365
juveniles in adult jails, 344
Miranda warnings, 96
right to counsel, 253–254
school crime, 418, 420–422, 423–424, 425
status offenders, 148
success of diversion, 136–137
theories of delinquency, 36, 38–39, 41–42, 54–55
training schools, 340–341
waiver to adult court, 203–204
See also Surveys

Researchers and theorists
Agnew, Robert, 45–47
Akers, Ronald, 48–49
Beccaria, Cesare, 35
Burgess, Robert, 48–49
Cohen, Albert, 44, 45*e*
Freud, Sigmund, 40–41
Glueck, Sheldon and Eleanor, 38, 54
Gottfredson, Michael, 52
Grisso, Thomas, 96
Hirschi, Travis, 49–50, 52
Laub, John, 54–55
Lombroso, Cesare, 36–37
McKay, Henry, 41–42
Merton, Robert, 42–43
Moffitt, Terrie, 52–53
Pope, Carl, 78–79, 79*e*
Sampson, Robert, 54–55
Shaw, Clifford, 41–42
Sheldon, William, 38
Snyder, Howard, 78–79, 79*e*
Sutherland, Edward, 47

Reservations, Native American, 218

Responsibility
community service, 283
controversy of culpability, 14
for diversion conditions, 136
goals of disposition, 298
juvenile justice history, 3, 6
juvenile vs. adult system, 9
parents for juvenile behavior, 89–90, 294–295
probation officers, 317, 324
restorative justice, 446
theories of delinquency, 41

Restitution, 23*t*, 283–284

Restorative justice, 127, 297–298, 446–447

Restraints, mechanical, 374

Retreatists (strain theory), 43

Reverse waivers, 198, 200*t*

Revocation, aftercare or parole, 26, 326–330

Rhode Island, *Inmates of the Boys' Training School v. Affleck* (1972), 367, 374

Rhodes v. Chapman (1981), 365

Right to confront witnesses, 326

Right to counsel
ABA principles, 454
adjudication, 253
defense attorneys, 235, 236
disposition, 289
intake, 121–122, 125, 134, 312
lineups, 106
revocation hearings, 329
status offenders, 149
waiving *Miranda* rights, 101
See also Lawyers

Right to court hearing, 128–129

Ritualists (strain theory), 43

Robbery and burglary, 123, 192, 258, 260, 262, 326

Roles, social, 50–51

Roper v. Simmons (2005), 286, 383, 393–399, 397*t*

Runaways, 150, 156*e*

Rural areas
cottage system (training schools), 340
juveniles detained in adult jails, 186, 281
ranches and forestry camps, 358

Safe Schools Act (1994), 429–430

Safe Schools/Healthy Students Initiative, 425

Safety and protection
dependent and neglected juveniles, 161–162, 167
juvenile arrests, 76, 80
probation officers, 312
public safety, 447, 452
restorative justice, 446
schools, 418, 423–434

Sampson, Robert, 54–55

Santana v. Collazo (1983), 368

Santosky v. Kramer (1982), 169

Scalia, Antonin, 396–397

Schall v. Martin (1984), 180

School resource officers, 433

Schools, 404–434
drug testing, 323–324
notice of delinquency, 102
probation, 307–308, 316, 317*e*

reform and training schools, 338–341

searches, 90–94

shootings, 419–420*t*

student surveys, 62, 64

theories of delinquency, 44, 45*e*

truancy, 76, 150, 156*e*

zero tolerance policies, 429*e*, 430*e*

See also Education

Score, Gina, 357

Sealed records, 102, 103–104*t*

Search and seizure

exclusionary rule, 265–266, 289–290, 328

legal protection for juveniles, 85–95

motion to suppress evidence, 248

police escorting probation officer, 323

probation and parole, 319–320

schools, 408–416

Search warrants. *See under* Warrants

Secondary deviance, 51

Secret Service, U.S., 420–422

Security policies, school, 429–434

Segregated incarceration, 362

Self-control, 52

Self-incrimination, privilege against, 125, 256–257

Self-report surveys, 58, 61–64, 65*t*, 165

Sensationalism, 2, 417, 419–420*t*

Sentencing. *See* Disposition

Seriousness of offense

arrest, 77

bail, 296

disposition, 169–170

race issues, 134–135

right to counsel, 254

right to treatment, 368

waiver to adult court, 120, 187

Service style (police departments), 82

Sexual offenses

arrest rates and gender, 79

child abuse, 158

death penalty, 386

juvenile victims, 171

Shaw, Clifford, 41–42

Sheldon, William, 38

Shock probation, 315–316

Shootings, school, 417, 419–420*t*, 420–422

Sight and sound separation, 146, 186, 343–344

Similarly situated cases, 130–131

Simmons, Christopher, 393–394

Sins (theories of delinquency), 34, 340–341

Sixth Amendment, 253, 262

Skulls (phrenology), 37

Slattery, Mike, 411–412

Smith v. Daily Mail Publishing Company (1979), 107

Smoking, 91

Snyder, Howard, 78–79, 79*e*

Social bonding/control theory, 49–50

Social capital, 55

Social disorganization theory, 41–42

Social history reports, 348

Social issues

history of juvenile institutions, 222, 336, 337, 340–341

standards of decency, 389, 390–391

theories of delinquency, 41–55

views of children, 439

Social learning theories, 47–49

Social situations

life-course-persistent behavior, 53

social learning theories, 48

Social workers, 72, 235, 236, 324

Socioeconomic status

arrest and custody, 80–81

child-savers, 222

diversion, 135–136

theories of delinquency, 44, 45*e*

Solitary confinement, 374–375

South Carolina

Alexander S. v. Boyd (1995), 368

probation conditions, 307–308

South Dakota, right to public trials, 264

Special conditions, aftercare, 26, 308–309

Specialty courts, 443–444, 445*e*

Speedy trial, right to, 229

Spiritual healing, 160

Stabilization facilities, 348–349

Standard conditions, aftercare, 26, 308

Standards

acceptable behavior, 44, 45*e*

juveniles in adult system, 454

probation and parole, 309–310

State of Texas Progressive Sanctioning Guidelines, 118*n*

Stanford v. Kentucky (1989), 285–286, 389–390

Stare decisis, 214–215

State courts, 211–219, 212*e*, 215*e*

State of Texas Progressive Sanctioning Guidelines, 118*n*

State schools, 342, 349–355

State v. Quiroz (1987), 133–134

State v. Slattery (1990), 411

State v. Tracy M. (1986), 130

State v. McDowell (1984), 128

Statements, incriminating, 95–101, 122–126, 126*t*, 256–257, 290–291, 321

States

admissibility of statements, 124–125

age of jurisdiction, 13–15, 13*t*

appeal, right to, 296

arrest warrants, 74–75

compulsory education, 221

confidentiality for juveniles, 102, 103–104*t*, 107, 326

corporal punishment, 416

death penalty, 216, 384*e*, 386, 387*t*, 391, 395, 396, 398, 398*t*

delinquency definitions, 15–17

delinquency referrals, 117

dependent and neglected juveniles, 159, 162, 168

detention, 183–184, 185, 186–187

disposition, 273, 274*t*, 276–277*t*, 283, 286, 287*e*

diversion, 127–128, 130, 131

DNA samples, 106

informal adjustments, 118

intake procedures, 114, 115–116*t*

jury pools, 249

jury trials for juveniles, 263–264

juvenile courts, 6, 223, 224

Juvenile Justice and Delinquency Prevention Act (1974), 146, 147, 441

juvenile justice legislation, 453–454

juveniles in jails and prisons, 281, 344–345, 360–362

juveniles in residential placement, 353*t*

minimum age of responsibility, 3, 4*t*

minorities institutionalized, 351, 447–448

States (*continued*)
  National Incident Based
    Reporting System (NIBRS),
    60–61
  parent consent for searches,
    89–90
  parent responsibilities, 294–295
  probation and parole, 305–306
  public trials, right to, 264–265
  right to counsel, 254, 289
  status offenders, 149, 154–155
  three strikes laws, 292
  totality of the circumstances
    test, 99–100
  waiver to adult courts, 187*t*,
    190–191*t*, 193–201, 201–202*t*
  waiving *Miranda* rights, 101
Statistics
  arrest rates, 78, 79, 80, 83–85,
    84–85*t*
  crime rates, 8–9, 18, 64
  death penalty, 383–384,
    386–387
  delinquency petitions, 119*e*
  delinquent characteristics, 388*t*
  dependent and neglected
    juveniles, 165–166
  detention, 180, 181*e*
  disposition, 274–275, 275*e*
  female offenders, 450
  institutionalization, 280
  juvenile courts, 226, 227*e*, 228,
    228*t*
  juvenile detention centers, 346,
    355, 365
  juvenile victims, 170–172, 171*e*,
    172*e*
  juveniles in jails and prisons,
    344, 360
  juveniles in residential
    placement, 349–351, 352*t*
  mental disorders, 349
  minorities, 448*e*
  National Incident Based
    Reporting System, 61
  probation officers, 310
  prosecution, 294
  school crime, 418, 421, 422,
    423–424, 430, 432
  status offenders, 152, 154,
    156*e*
  suicide, 366
  Uniform Crime Reports, 59
  waiver to adult courts, 194,
    195*e*, 203
Status and acceptance, strain
  theory, 43, 44, 45*e*

Status offenses
  arrest and custody, 59, 72
  definitions, 16–17*t*, 18, 143,
    144, 145
  deinstitutionalization, 146
  disposition, 274–275
  juvenile courts, 245*e*, 441
  legal rights, 253
  procedures, 147–155, 156*e*
  residential placement, 362
  youth shelters, 345
Statutory exclusion, 197–198, 200*t*
Stevens, John Paul, 395
Stigmata, 37*e*
Stigmatizing
  detention, 179–180
  juvenile court records, 265
  labeling theory, 50–51
  school suspension, 406
Stop and frisk, 86–87
Strain theories, 42–47
Strict scrutiny test, 153
Strip searches, 409
Students. *See* Schools
Substance abuse
  ranches and forestry camps, 358
  treatment centers, 151
  See also Drugs and drug abuse
Suburbs, 41–42
Suicide, 366–367, 418–419
Superego (psychoanalytic theory),
  40–41
Supervision of delinquents
  aftercare, 25–26, 309–314
  Augustus, John, 304
  intensive supervision probation,
    315
  probation, 452
Support services
  aftercare, 26
  child protective services, 159,
    166
  diagnostic facilities, 348
  juvenile correction facilities, 25,
    351–352
  juvenile courts, 238–239
  juveniles in adult prisons, 360
  ranches and forestry camps, 358
  stabilization facilities, 349
Supremacy of parental rights,
  166–167
Supreme Court, U.S.
  appeals process, 210–211, 296
  Breed v. Jones (1975), 132–133,
    258
  Bringar v. United States (1949), 73
  Cason v. Cook (1987), 93

Davis v. Alaska (1974), 326
death penalty cases, 383,
  384–386, 388–399, 399*e*
detention requirements, 182
drug testing case, 323
Ewing v. California (2003), 292
Fare v. Michael C. (1979), 99,
  312–314
Gagnon v. Scarpelli (1973), 132,
  328, 329
Goss v. Lopez (1975), 406
Griffin v. Wisconsin (1987), 94,
  319
Haley v. Ohio (1948), 290–291
Hamilton v. Alabama (1961), 121
In re Winship (1970), 145, 149
jurisdiction, 214, 216
Kent v. United States (1966), 145,
  192–193
Kirby v. Illinois (1972), 106
Lockyer v. California (2003), 292
Massiah v. United States (1964),
  121
McKeiver v. Pennsylvania (1971),
  262, 263
Minnesota v. Dickerson (1993), 86
Minnesota v. Murphy (1984), 122,
  124, 321
Miranda v. Arizona (1966), 95,
  120, 320
Morrissey v. Brewer (1972), 132,
  327–328, 329
New Jersey v. T. L. O. (1985),
  90–92, 408–409, 410, 413
*Oklahoma Publishing Company v.
  District Court in and for
  Oklahoma City* (1977),
  106–107
parens patriae, 252
Parham v. J.R. (1979), 151,
  363–364
*Pennsylvania Board of Probation
  and Parole v. Scott* (1998), 328
Pottawatomie County v. Earls
  (2002), 412–413, 414–415
Prince v. Massachusetts (1944),
  160–161
Ralston v. Robinson (1981), 368
In re Winship (1970), 259–261
Rhodes v. Chapman (1981), 365
Santosky v. Kramer (1982), 169
Schall v. Martin (1984), 179–180
*Smith v. Daily Mail Publishing
  Company* (1979), 107
Stanford v. Kentucky (1989),
  285–286
Terry v. Ohio (1968), 86

Thompson v. Oklahoma (1988), 285

Tinker v. Des Moines Independent Community School District (1969), 404

United States v. Knights (2001), 94

United States v. Matlock (1974), 89

United States v. Wade (1967), 106, 121

United States v. Watson (1976), 74–75

Vernonia School District v. Acton (1995), 412–413, 414

White v. Maryland (1963), 120–121

Yarborough v. Alvarado (2004), 97–99

See also In re Gault (1967)

Surveys
  death penalty, 391*t*
  juvenile facility directors, 354–355
  measuring crime rates, 58, 61–64, 65*t*, 165
  prosecutors, 294
  public opinion of juvenile justice, 449–450
  schools, 425
  Texas juvenile institutions, 372–373
  See also Research and reports

Suspension or expulsion, schools, 406–408, 427–428, 430*e*

Sutherland, Edward, 47

Tate, Lionel, 199

Teachers, 352, 354, 418, 423

Teen courts, 229–232, 230*e*

Temporary situations, 54

Terminology
  appeal process, 213
  juvenile courts, 158*e*
  juvenile vs. adult system, 9–10, 442–443
  Miranda warnings, 96
  status offenders, 18, 148

Terry v. Ohio (1968), 86

Testing
  diagnostic facilities, 348
  drug testing, 323–324, 412–413, 414–415

Texas
  blended sentencing, 288
  Capital and Serious Violent Offender Treatment Program, 354
  court system, 211–212

Marlin Orientation and Assessment Unit, 348

Matthews v. State (1984), 76

McFadden Ranch, 358

Morales v. Turman (1973), 368, 369–373

State of Texas Progressive Sanctioning Guidelines, 118*n*

Theories of delinquency, 33–56, 37*e*, 45*e*, 57*t*

Theorists. *See* Researchers and theorists

Thompson v. Oklahoma (1988), 285, 389

Three strikes laws, 292

Tinker v. Des Moines Independent Community School District (1969), 404

Totality of the circumstances, 88–89, 99–100

Training. *See* Education and training

Training schools (historic), 339–341

Transfer facilities, 348

Transition facilities, 359

Treatment. *See* Rehabilitation and treatment

Treaty, death penalty, 392

Trials. *See* Court proceedings

Trough Creek State Park (PA), 358

Truancy, 76, 150, 156*e*

Truthfulness, 62–63

Twins, 38–39

Typical delinquents, 18, 56*e*

Underreporting
  crimes, 60, 62–64, 165
  suicide, 366

Uniform Crime Reports (UCR), 58–60, 65*t*, 83, 164–165, 170

Uniform Juvenile Court Act, 75*e*

United Nations Convention on the Rights of the Child, 392

United States v. Knights (2001), 94

United States v. Matlock (1974), 89

United States v. Wade (1967), 106, 121

United States v. Watson (1976), 74–75

University of Michigan, 62

Upper age of jurisdiction, 13–14, 13*t*

Upper class
  arrest and custody, 80–81
  child-savers, 222

Urban areas
  houses of refuge, 337

self-report data, 62

theories of delinquency, 41–42

Values, social, 43, 44

Venue, change of, motion, 248

Verdicts, 251

Vermont, community service programs, 283

Vernonia School District v. Acton (1995), 412–413, 414

Victims and victimizations
  arrests and race, 79*e*
  complaints, 81
  dependent and neglected juveniles, 165
  females, 451
  juvenile statistics, 170–173, 171*e*, 172*e*
  juveniles in institutions, 144–145, 337–338, 347, 357, 362, 369–376
  measuring crime rates, 56–58, 63–64
  in public trials, 265
  restitution, 283–284
  restorative justice, 446–447
  school, 418, 422–423
  victim-offender mediation, 127
  Wilson, Mary Ellen, 155, 157

Videotaped interrogations, 101

Violence and Discipline Problems in U.S. Public Schools, 1996–1997 (report), 425

Violent vs. non-violent crimes
  blended sentencing, 288
  crime rates, 83–85, 84*t*
  detention, 181*e*
  institutionalization data, 351
  juvenile correction facilities, 341–342, 343
  juvenile court caseloads, 228*t*
  Last Chance Ranch (FL), 358
  non-typical delinquents, 18
  school crime, 418, 419–420*t*, 420, 422–423
  waiver to adult courts, 187, 203, 218, 238, 442

Virginia
  diagnostic facilities, 348
  sniper case (2002), 216–217, 392

Vocational training
  abuses, 373
  history, 336, 339–341
  rehabilitation efforts, 352, 354

Waivers
  double jeopardy protection, 213
  juveniles to adult court, 120,
      121, 187–204, 190–191*t*,
      195*e*, 200*t*, 201–202*t*, 218,
      258, 359, 441
  legal rights, 261–262
  Miranda rights, 99–102
  right to counsel, 254, 454
Warrants
  arrest, 73, 74–75
  search, 88, 89, 94, 319
Washington
  restitution case, 284
  State v. Quiroz (1987), 133–134
  State v. Slattery (1990), 411
  State v. Tracy M. (1986), 130
  Washington v. Chatham (1981),
      129–130
Washington, D.C. sniper case
    (2002), 216–217

Watchman style (police
    departments), 82
Weapons
  parole revocation, 328
  probation officers, 312
  in schools, 410–411, 423, 426,
      427–428, 431
Welfare workers, 279
West Virginia
  disposition case, 278–279
  probation conditions, 308
  restitution case, 284
Wheeler, Etta, 155, 157
White v. Maryland (1963),
    120–121
White v. Reid (1954), 367
Wilkins v. Missouri (1989),
    389–390
Wilson, Mary Ellen, 155, 157
Wisconsin, *In the Interest of Isiah B.*
    (1993), 410

Witnesses
  juvenile records confidentiality,
      326
  self-incrimination, 257
Worldwide, death penalty, 383,
    392
Writ of certiorari, 210
Writ of habeas corpus, 297

Yarborough v. Alvarado (2004),
    97–99
Youth advocates, 235
*Youth in the Criminal Justice System:
    Guidelines for Policymakers and
    Practitioners* (ABA report),
    453–454
Youth shelters, 345–346

Zamora v. Pomeroy (1981), 413
Zero tolerance policies, 425–428,
    429*e*, 430*e*

Comparison of Juvenile and Criminal Justice Systems

	Operating Assumptions	Prevention	Law Enforcement	Intake—Prosecution
Juvenile Justice System	■ Youth behavior is malleable. ■ Rehabilitation is usually a viable goal. ■ Youth are in families and not independent.	■ Many specific delinquency prevention activities (e.g., school, church, recreation) are used. ■ Prevention is intended to change individual behavior and is often focused on reducing risk factors and increasing protective factors in the individual, family, and community.	■ Specialized "juvenile" units are used. ■ Some additional behaviors are prohibited (truancy, running away, curfew violations). ■ Some limitations are placed on public access to information. ■ A significant number of youth are diverted away from the juvenile justice system, often into alternative programs.	■ In many instances, juvenile court intake, not the prosecutor, decides what cases to file. ■ The decision to file a petition for court action is based on both social and legal factors. ■ A significant portion of cases are diverted from formal case processing. ■ Intake or the prosecutor divert cases from formal processing to services operated by the juvenile court, prosecutor's office, or outside agencies.
Common Ground	■ Community protection is a primary goal. ■ Law violators must be held accountable. ■ Constitutional rights apply.	■ Educational approaches are taken to specific behaviors (drunk driving, drug use).	■ Jurisdiction involves the full range of criminal behavior. ■ Constitutional and procedural safeguards exist. ■ Both reactive and proactive approaches (targeted at offense types, neighborhoods, etc.) are used. ■ Community policing strategies are employed.	■ Probable cause must be established. ■ The prosecutor acts on behalf of the State.
Criminal Justice System	■ Sanctions should be proportional to the offense. ■ General deterrence works. ■ Rehabilitation is not a primary goal.	■ Prevention activities are generalized and are aimed at deterrence (e.g., Crime Watch).	■ Open public access to all information is required. ■ Law enforcement exercises discretion to divert offenders out of the criminal justice system.	■ Plea bargaining is common. ■ The prosecution decision is based largely on legal facts. ■ Prosecution is valuable in building history for subsequent offenses. ■ Prosecution exercises discretion to withhold charges or divert offenders out of the criminal justice system.